ORDNUNGSPOLIZEI

Massimo Arico

ORDNUNGSPOLIZEI

Ideological war and Genocide on the East front 1941–1942

Translation: Pierpaolo Russo

Editor: Chris Meadows

Leandoer & Ekholm Publishing, Stockholm
2012

Massimo Arico:

I was born in 1965 in Genoa, Italy, where I reside. My family is from Istria (now Croatia) and was a mixed Italian-Croatian family. My great-grandfather was a NCO in the KuK (Imperial Austria) Army and disappeared in Galicia (Russian front) in 1914 or 15. My grandfather worked for the Italian civil administration of the city of Pola (Istria) until 1943, then immigrated to Italy in 1946. My father served with the Italian Armed Forces for some years. I have also served in the Italian Army. I have a degree in accountancy and now work as a trader. History and military matters are my hobbies. I began the study of the German police about 20 years ago, when nothing existed about this subject, apart from a couple of books. I'm interested in the so-called "human sciences", especially human behavior related to the role played by the German police battalions in the Jewish Genocide. With an apparent paradox (if compared with the above mentioned "human interests"), I define myself as a "lone wolf" and I consider the various tragedies that afflict humanity, nothing more than the unavoidable (and obvious) product of the human tendencies, in spite of cultural, moral and social education.

Massimo Arico is now working on several new titles on the subject of the German Police and the German occupation of European countries: "Ordnungspolizei vol 2, 1942 – 1945" and "Serbia/Banat 1941 – 1945 vol 1". Both will be published by Leandoer & Ekholm Publishing in 2013-14.

Author: Massimo Arico
Translation: Pierpaolo Russo
Editor: Chris Meadows
Maps: Laurent Lecocq
Graphic Design: Daniel Åberg/Åbergs stilus et forma
Cover: Daniel Åberg/Åbergs stilus et forma

First edition
Print: Prepress Ltd, Riga, Latvia
ISBN: 978-91-85657-20-9

Coverphoto: Main photo: Warsaw: German police escorting a group of Polish civilians.

All photocredits are the writers except where noted otherwise.

CONTENTS

LATVIA
Jelgava
1/Polizei-Bataillon 9
SD-Kommando Becu
Latvian Auxiliaries
LITHUANIA
USSR
UNION OF SOVIET SOCIALIST REPUBLICS
Kaunas
3/Polizei-Bataillon 11
Lithuanian Battalion PPT-1
Lithuanian-Batalion PPT-3
Gestapo-Kommando
EAST
PRUSSIA
Minsk
Polizei-Bataillon 322
Mogilev
2/Polizei-Bataillon 9
Polizei-Bataillon 316
Polizei-Bataillon 322
Polizei-Kommando Waldendurg
Einsatzkommando 8
5/NSKK-Kompanie
Ukrainian-Auxiliaries
Bialystok
Polizei-Bataillon 309
Nesvizh
2 & 4/Polizei-Bataillon 11
Litauisch-Schuma-Btn 2
Belorussian Auxiliaries
POLAND
Brest Litovsk
Polizei-Bataillon 307
SD-Kommando
Lachwa
4/Polizei-Bataillon 69
Polizei-Bataillon 306
SD-Aussenstelle Pinsk
Ukrainian Auxiliaries
Polnische Auxiliaries
Radom
Polizei-Kompanie Muenchen
SS-Sonderkommando Feucht
Wachtkompanie SSPF/Radom
SS-Veterinar-E-Kompanie Radom
Polnische-Blaupolizei
Curzon line (1940)
Kharkov
Polizei-Bataillon 314
Sonderkmmando 4a
Schutzpolizei-Boryslav
SSPF Lemberg
KdS-Stelle Drohobycz
Ukrainian Police
Boryslav
LOVAKIA
Kamenec Podolsky
Polizei-Bataillon 320
Stabskompanie Jeckeln
Ukrainian auxiliaries
RUMANIA
HUNGARY
Simferopol
3/Polizei-Bataillon 3
4/Polizei-Bataillon 9
Sonderkommando 10a
Sonderkommando 11a
Sonderkommando 11b
Feldgendarmerie-Abt. 683
Geheime-Feldpolizei-Grp. 647
Belgrade
Polizei-Bataillon 64
Gestapo Belgrade
SLAVIA
:1000

January 24, 1943: the deportation of the Jews of Marseille by SS-Polizei-Regiment "Griese", supported by men from the French gendarmerie.

Regimental commander SS-Sturmbannführer-und Oberst der Schutzpolizei, Bernhard Griese is in the center. To his right, General Hans-Gustav Felber, commander of Army Group "Felber" in France. To his left, dressed in civilian clothes, HSSPF Carl-Albrecht Oberg. Near the right edge of the picture, between two policemen, a railway official of the Deutsche-Reichsbahn can be recognized.

January 24, 1943. SS-Sturmbannführer-und Oberst der Schutzpolizei receives the salute from his officers in front of the deployed troops. This followed the end of the mopping up operations and the Jews of Marseille being loaded onto trains.

Jews are offloaded from the prison van to be loaded on rail cars at the Gare d'Arenc, with destination the concentration camps in the northern area. Notice, near the middle of the picture a French gendarme wearing the typical Adrian helmet.

Source: Bundesarchiv.

December 1940, German police officers of an unidentified department breaking into a building in the Jewish ghetto in Lublin.

INTRODUCTION

PANDORA

To destroy a man is difficult, almost as difficult as to create one: it has not been easy, or quick, but you Germans have succeeded. Here we are, docile under your gaze; from our side you have nothing more to fear; no acts of violence, no words of defiance, not even a look of judgement.

Primo Levi, If This is a Man

In mid-March 1942, approximately 75-80 % of all future victims of the Holocaust were still alive, while 20-25 % had died. Eleven months later, in mid-February 1943, the percentage was exactly reversed[1].

So begins Ordinary Men by Christopher R. Browning, a book that since its appearance in the now distant 1992 has widely been considered of fundamental importance in the vast literature on the Jewish genocide.

Very few works can claim to represent such a turning point as this one, and there are even fewer that since their first publication decades ago have continued to prove irreplaceable and still relevant. One such book, however, is the impressive study by Raul Hilberg on *The Destruction of the European Jews* of 1985, which has been repeatedly revised and expanded and still today represents, aside from all controversy, a major contribution to our understanding of the Jewish genocide, although almost half a century has passed since it first appeared (1961). One point in particular links these two studies by Hilberg and Browning, and that is the focus they both place on the perspective of the perpetrators rather than the victims. Hilberg paints an extraordinary picture of the destructive machine, concentrating on the organizational, technical, administrative and also social dynamics that oiled the gears of extermination, thus giving a vital impetus to the functionalist current of thought. Browning, on the other hand, moves from the immensely great to the immensely small, offering new research routes across virtually unexplored territory, and turning the spotlight for the first time on aspects of the genocide that had been undervalued until that time. So, if, thanks to the theses put forward by Hilberg and the research that followed in subsequent years – still part of a traditional school of historiography – the more orthodox view of intentionalism was rendered effectively obsolete, Browning's work and the repercussions of his debate with Goldhagen[3] opened up a vast new perspective on a dual front of research: on the one hand, research that looked more specifically at the role played by a particular category of perpetrators – the Ordnungspolizei – which had for decades been hidden from view, and on the other hand, research that more generally propelled a modern reading of the Jewish Genocide and used innovative and multidisciplinary tools, outside the strictly historical context and directly connected to the sphere of the human sciences. This basically brought to the fore, sociology and social psychology, which until then had only had a marginal connection with the subject[4].

With regard to the role played by the Ordnungspolizei, right from the very first lines of *Ordinary Men* Browning focuses the readers' attention on the cornerstone around which he structures his study: he refers to the ratio between the 20-25 % of victims of the genocide who died before March 1942 – that is, until the coming into operation of the extermination camps of the General Government on an industrial scale – and the further 50-60 % added within the space of twelve months, by February 1943. In this sense, although primarily centered on the second period – during which the events described in the narrative occur and whose sordid protagonist was Polizei-Bataillon 101 – Browning's study offers innovative theses that also help depict the first period: namely, the period that saw the massive intervention on the field of large numbers of police battalions which provided direct support to the mobile extermination groups engaged in mass executions. This reinforcement, with its many thousands of men, was what made it possible for the weak kommandos of the security police inside the four Einsatzgruppen to achieve the above-mentioned percentage of 20-25 % by March 1942 with relative ease. Basically, this proportion, which in real terms meant at least one million victims, was *produced* in the period of time from 22 June 1941 – the date when *Operation Barbarossa* began – and March 1942: a period of about nine months, during which a whole series of Jewish communities were drastically *reduced* in number and sometimes completely destroyed, and which broadly corresponds to the *first wave of genocide* as identified by Hilberg[5]. Indeed, as further studies have subsequently shown, there was never a precise differentiation between the various phases of the genocide, which in fact continued as an indistinct movement, with its tactical pauses and sudden bursts, in some regions more than in others. In this sense, independently of the timeframe Hilberg suggested at the time (first and second wave of genocide, with the implementation, between the two, of the first concentration camps in the General Government), what divided the Jewish genocide into periods were essentially the technical methods with which it was perpetrated, with a first itinerant phase (the *selective* variant until August 1941, and the *systemic* phase until autumn 1942), based mainly on executions in mass graves. The second, a *stable* phase, in part overlapped with the first and mainly saw deportations to the extermination camps starting from the spring of 1942. Also, geographical distinctions can be made for the itinerant phase, with massacres distributed more along the advanced axes throughout 1941 and then concentrated later around more specific regional areas. After that, independently of the periods, local differences and operating procedures that characterized the mechanics of genocide, a common denominator was the presence of units of the Ordnungspolizei. In the Soviet territory and Poland, about 965,000 Jews fell victim, directly or indirectly, to the Ordnungspolizei in its various structures (battalions, gendarmerie units and detachments of Schutzpolizei), while there were a further 567,000 deportees, the majority going to the extermination camps of the General Government[6]; these were impressive numbers, which testify to the essential role in the genocide played by the Ordnungspolizei. They were not only a second-level structure, but an efficient destruction complex, certainly not set up institutionally for this purpose but which easily – very easily – adapted itself to it.

With regard to the approach to the study of the Jewish genocide using tools other than the strictly historical, Browning's work offers some new contributions and insights which up to then had been given little consideration, if not rejected with horror. In fact, into the rapid, disorderly and consistently crimanl extermination situation, which Hans Mommsen calls "*cumulative radicalization*"[7], Browning introduces with *Ordinary Men* and later develops with *The Origins of the Final Solution*, his essentially situational view of the genocide, that is, connected not so much to a centralized source – precise, lucid and disruptive – but rather to the interplay of semi-autonomous dynamics, set off in equal measure from above and below. Within this polycentric view, placing the focus mainly on impulses coming from below appears an innovative step rich in significant new developments: the *conscious* and rationalized involvement of large numbers of ordinary executors – which is precisely what the officials of the Ordnungspolizei were – who did not belong to significantly ideologically affected categories, uncovers disturbing scenarios in the context of research on human behavior, both in the individual sense and in terms of social relations.

The opening of the gates of Auschwitz in January 1945 had, perhaps for the first time ever, placed the most advanced part of mankind face to face with a real psychodrama which was to plunge into crisis the traditional reassuring framework which up to then had codified relations between human beings, and between human beings and society as a whole. The *post-traumatic* effects of the genocide on reason, ethics and morals, and on behavioral, social and historical dynamics were devastating, not so much and not only, as was obvious, for those directly involved in this event as victims, but also especially because of the impact they had on the body of a human society. This was a society annihilated by the conflict but precisely for this reason forced to embark on a path of self-awareness/break/reconstruction/evolution on the basis of entirely new paradigms. In this sense, knowledge, interpretation and especially awareness of the Jewish genocide was one of these paradigms, summarized by Adorno's provocative dictum to the effect that "to write poetry after Auschwitz is barbaric". However, while the other models around which the societies that emerged from the conflict had structured their political, economic, social and cultural resurgence appeared generally accepted – aside from natural oppositions of identity – in that they were seen as tending towards the desired post-war neo-modernity, the paradigm of genocide came to provoke even a counter-reaction, in which self-absolving ideological factors were only the most obvious and superficial manifestation. In fact, the dynamics on which the genocide was likely to impact with most devastating force were relational, essentially because of the disturbing questions which the interpretation of the genocide raised, particularly in the sphere of behavior and emotions, both of the victims and the perpetrators. Obviously the genocide itself was not called into question – it had indeed begun to be studied and analyzed in every aspect – but rather the result of some studies and reflections, the acceptance of which risked disrupting an entire reassuring system of values: the system, namely, based on the most immediate and Manichean opposition between good and evil, where evil was expressed in the presumed pathology of the Nazi regime and its underlying ideology, seen by many as the unexpected degeneration of mankind's process of evolution, certainly complex, fraught with obstacles and at times contradictory, but always tending towards the good. Thanks to authoritative opinions, including that of Adorno[8], Nazism was initially – with self-consoling relief – counted among the examples of behavioral deviance, and as such seen as exclusive to a minority of cruel, fanatical and/or psychologically disturbed individuals, "Inclined to obey the strong and to be ruthlessly brutal, often cruel, towards the the weak". In other words *they* were immoral, as opposed to *us* who are rich in values and morality[9]. This reassuring explanatory schema, however, soon suffered a crisis in the face of progress in research, especially in the field of the human sciences. Psychological experiments, dramatic in terms of their meaning, such as those carried out by Stanley Milgram at the University of Yale in 1961 and by Philip G. Zimbardo in the prison at Stanford in 1971, Ron Jones's experimental history lessons at Cubberly High School in 1967 (only recently rediscovered), studies by the American psychiatrist Robert J. Lifton and his insights into so-called "atrocity-producing situations", the works of Herbert C. Kelman on overcoming moral inhibitions, the conclusions of Henry V. Dicks on the possibility of separating one's own personality by erecting emotional barriers on the basis of the context in which one finds oneself, as well as Hannah Arendt's reflections on the *banality of evil* [10]– all these made it clear that the existence of oppressive and destructive behavior patterns did not have a simplistically pathological origin, but was rather due to a complex set of environmental and socio-psychological factors. In this way the Jewish genocide stopped being interpreted as the result of a generally limited social malfunction, a sudden black hole in the evolution of mankind, essentially accidental, if not unique, identifiable at its outbreak and therefore preventable / treatable by administering the appropriate antibodies, and was instead placed inside lucidly ferocious and therefore replicable behavior models, explicable using the tools of rational logic and not deviance. This view, so disturbing as to be almost inadmissible, had long held a place within the parameters of specialized research and only after the interest generated by the debate between Browning and Goldhagen did it spread to a wider audience, accompanied by new studies and investigations, including the recent book by Harald

Welzer, which applies the methods of psychosocial analysis to the historical events connected to the role played by Polizei-Bataillon 45 in Ukraine. Welzer brings us back to where we started 15 years earlier with Browning and his Polizei-Bataillon 101: the genocidal acts of a police battalion which has become the demonstration of a paradigm, with Browning's *Ordinary Men* no longer merely in the role of anonymous protagonists of relatively limited events, but truly emblematic figures transcending the riverbed of their times and able to suggest previously unthought-of interpretations of events, just like Arendt's *banal bureaucrats* had been years earlier. That includes the possibility that, regardless of the more closely historical and socio-cultural context and its particular perniciousness, the Jewish genocide was not an alien or unique phenomenon, but rather a monstrous alchemy produced by a (fortunately) rare combination of typically human dynamics, which include the power relations between individuals and between individuals and the state, instinctive anthropological and / or group diffrences, and also, paradoxically, the Enlightenment tendency towards "an objectively better human world: more efficient, more moral, more beautiful[11]. Faced with the complexity of the dynamics that acted at such a deep level in the Jewish genocide and that influenced the criminal behavior of hundreds of thousands of individuals – referred to variously as *banal, ordinary or willing* – neither the traditional historical method nor the reassuring and obsolete schemes based on ideological and pathological causation appear sufficient. What is needed is rather a multi-disciplinary approach open to psychological, social, philosophical and religious contributions. In essence, a complex that is as inclusive as possible, independent of traditional, comfortable but sectorial categorizations, which can help us think about at least four major groups of concurrent events that were synergetic in perpetrating the genocide:

1) Historical and political microcauses
2) Situational dynamics relative to individual genocide events
3) Inter-group dynamics between specific groups of perpetrators and the external context
4) Intra-group microcauses within specific groups of perpetrators.

This then is the route that has been taken in the following chapters, each of which focuses on a single massacre so as to suggest, each time, a different interpretive approach along a timeline that takes into account historical and political causes, the evolution of the situational context, the progressive involvement of motivational input from the perpetrators, as well as several interrelated factors that, depending on the situation, helped create the conditions for carrying out the massacre. All this, of course, seen in specific relationship to the role played by the Ordnungspolizei: This did not take the form of a sudden conflagration, but was rather a relatively gradual albeit systematic approach started in Poland in September 1939 and completed in the Soviet Union over the next three years. It was a role that was originally a relatively limited experiment, which Klaus-Michael Mallmann refers to in the effective expression "genesis of genocide", followed by an executive phase in turn divided into periods, during which the previous experiences of the period 1939/40 were applied on a far larger scale and with procedures that were gradually brought up to scratch by a growing number of executors. It is on this execution phase, in particular, that the attention of the next chapters will focus, starting from the only seemingly *accidental* massacre of June 27, 1941 in Bialystok (Chapter 1), going on through the massacres in Brest Litovsk and Kamenec Podolski, typically situational and paradigmatic of the relations between periphery and centre (Chapters 2 and 4), then dwelling on the *special* cases of Simferopol and Belgrade (Chapters 9 and 11), on the at first sight selective cases of Minsk and Kaunas (Chapters 5 and 7), on the cleanups of Nesvizh and Lachwa (Chapters 8 and 14), on the actions performed with the effective collaboration of local auxiliaries such as those of Jelgava and Mogilev (Chapters 3 and 6), and those implemented with the complicity of the Wehrmacht, as in Kharkov in December 1941 (Chapter 10).

There is a common denominator that links all these, aside from the most obvious aspects such as the type of victims, the routine implementation of killing procedures and the situational motivations variously present in the background – and it is the willingness on the part of the perpetrators to take on such an overwhelming task despite each of the countermeasures interposed by morality, or by usual civil conduct or even only by human compassion: a genocidal willingness put into action with judicious care and with a disconcerting simplicity. In the following chapters we will thus try to understand the various mechanisms that facilitated this willingness, which gave impetus to situations or which on occasions sometimes stood in its way. We will try to describe many points of view, both those of the victims and those of the perpetrators, in order to interpret the meaning of events. We will try to recreate the atmosphere of the time in order to understand events and reactions. We will try to do all this in a search for contingent causes. And yet, beyond logic, beyond more or less satisfactory theorems and explanations, what finally remains is a sense of inadequacy, as in the face of a metaphysical event. One can turn to God or reason to explain the event, deny the former or re-think the latter; one may reflect on the "concept of God after Auschwitz", or be horrified at the relationship between Auschwitz and Man, between the *drowned* and the *saved*. One can use all the available schemas, from classic to theological, from human to philosophical. One can call it Pandora's box, one can call it the gaze into the abyss, the heart of darkness, and give it a label in line with one's inclinations: the inevitability of fate unnecessarily held back, or the loss of the divine light, or as an unholy descent into hell, the primitivism of human nature finally free from conditioning and frills ... You can talk about the *event* in many ways, without ever being able to understand it completely. But one thing is certain, beyond all metaphor: it was the action of man against Mankind, and as a human product, imputable to man alone, to his criminal imagination, to the prevalence, once again, of his destructive tendencies.

ENDNOTES

1 Christopher Browning: Ordinary Men. German Police and the Final Solution in Poland, Turin, 1992, p. XI.

2 Raul Hilberg: The Destruction Of The European Jews. New York, 1985, ed.it., Turin, 1995

3 Daniel Jonah Goldhagen: Hitler's Willing Executioners, Milan, 1997.

4 To give only two examples: the work of the sociologist Zygmut Bauman: Modernity and Holocaust - ed.it. Bologna, 1992, and the study by the social psychologist Harald Welzer: Täter. Wie aus ganz normalen Menschen Massenmörder werden, Frankfurt am Main, 2005.

5 Hilberg, *ibid,*. p. 311.

6 Curilla Wolfgang: Die Deutsche Ordnungspolizei und der Holocaust im Baltikum und in Weißrussland, 1941-1944, Paderborn, 2006, pp. 828-833.

7 Hans Mommsen: Die Realisierung des Utopischen: Die "Endlösung der Judenfrage" im "Dritten Reich", Göttingen, 1983.

8 Theodor Adorno / Else Frenkel-Brunswich / Daniel J. Levison / Robert Newitt Sanford: The Authoritarian Personality, New York, 1959.

9 On this topic, see Bauman, *ibid.,* pp. 213-214.

10 Stanley Milgram: Obedience to the Authority, New York, 1974. Philip G.Zimbardo: The Lucifer Effect. Understanding How Good People Turn Evil, New York, 2008. Robert J. Lifton. The Nazi Doctors. Medical Killing and the Psychology of Genocide. Ed.it., Milan, 2003. Herbert C. Kelman: Violence Without Moral Restraint: Reflections on the Dehumanization of Victims and Victimizers. In Journal of Social Issues, 29 (4). Henry V. Dicks. Licensed Mass Murder: a Socio-Psychological Study of some SS Killers, New York, 1972.

11 Bauman, *ibid.,* p. 136.

PROLOGUE
JUNE DAYS

In recorded history we find many such portraits. Invariably they are floating effusively like clouds through the centuries and over the centuries. Whatever their origins or destinations, the function of these stereotypes is always the same. They are used as justification for destructive thinking; they are employed as excuses for destructive action.

Raul Hilberg[1]

1 WESTBANHOF WARSCHAU[2]

Warsaw West Station. 06:55 hours, June 10, 1941

Still very much alive in his memory were the notes of the Viennese violins he had heard that sunny afternoon in early June on the *Graben*, a few hours before leaving for Warsaw; and he still remembered the taste of the *Ersatzkaffee* he had drunk immediately afterwards sitting outside *Café Landtmann*.

The truth is that on that occasion he and his colleagues had hoped to be served real coffee, just like before the war, but they were out of luck and so they had to settle for the usual malted barley mixture, although it came with lots of thick and tasty whipped cream, known as *Schlagobers*. That day, to celebrate his imminent departure, he had also treated himself to a piece of their excellent apple strudel, and he felt he could still smell its aroma, in spite of the rough metallic aftertaste mixed with coal dust from the long train journey.

They had set out with the rest of the battalion early in the morning the previous day, immediately after listening to a speech by their commander, Major Gottlieb Nagel. It had been a brief proclamation on the Führer and Germany's inevitable imminent victory in the war, and had been greeted at the end with an enthusiastic *Sieg Heil!* by the ranks of the three companies. Then, at about 06:30 hours on June 9, 1941, to the accompaniment of the *Horst Wessel Lied* and some other military tunes, they had marched in platoon column formation from their barracks in Kagran to the *Stadlauer Bahnhof*, where the long train that would take them to Warsaw was already waiting with its steam up. They were made to line up along the platform as they gradually arrived, with their individual piles of equipment on the ground behind them. At intervals, between the carriages of the company, flat cars had already been loaded with the varied and numerous battalion vehicles: trucks, cars and field kitchens, along with vehicles from the workshop and signals departments. His company, the third, brought up the rear of the convoy whose front end could really only be imagined several hundred yards ahead in the half light of early morning. It was an impressive sight: in long rows, against an aural backdrop of repeated shouted commands, with piles of equipment stacked here and there and railway staff busy carrying out their duties, the battalion looked almost imposing, much larger than its 550 or so men actually represented, almost all new recruits just out of training. Some of them had not even made it on to the train, like the sergeant in his company, Wachtmeister Matzoll, who had been pronounced ill and had been sent back to the barracks just before boarding.

At any rate, by 07:55 hours the battalion had crammed themselves onto the wooden benches of the compartments and had set off; happy and proud. They looked out of the windows, their departure accompanied by the lively notes of *Muss i 'denn, muss i' denn zum Städtele hinaus,* played by a military band lined up along the platform. By the time they entered the old Morovian town of Prerau, it was already late afternoon. From there on, after Heidebreck in Silesia and Czestochowa in the General Government, began *Slavia*, the lands of the east. This was the monotonous and dirty Polish plain, so different from the gentle vineyards of Grinzing they were accustomed to. It was also very different to Bergstrasse in Darmstadt, where he was born twenty-six years before. None of them, however, had noticed this during the long night as they journeyed without stopping, coming ever closer to the northeast through the black countryside. They had eaten black pudding, rye bread and jam, and had dozed to the hypnotic rolling motion of the train until just before dawn, when the beet fields had finally given way to the outskirts of Warsaw.

Their convoy had obviously been allowed to overtake passenger trains; however, it had no priority over the many other troop trains making their way to Warsaw from the west, so it had to slow down gradually to let pass a long convoy of flat wagons loaded with Panzer III, probably belonging to an armored division on its way east. At that speed it took nearly two hours to reach *Warszawa Zachodnia*, Warsaw's West Station, where with a last puff of steam, their train finally came to a halt at 06:55 hours on June 10, 1941, about one hour ahead of schedule.

Although still sore from the journey and half asleep, Oltn. Gerhard Riebel, commander of the third company of Polizei-Bataillon 322 moved along the corridors of the carriages where his unit was. Certainly his lieutenants and platoon leaders were already busy reordering the ranks and soon, he was sure, sergeants and squad leaders would start shouting and hurling insults at the slowcoaches. The fact was that there was much to do that day and it was important not to waste time unnecessarily. He himself, the youngest company commander and with the lowest rank among those of the battalion, was determined not to make a bad impression on what was to be his first operational assignment. Up until then, in Vienna they had divided their time between training and garrison life, and mistakes were almost impossible when carrying out such tasks. But now, the waiting was over and this would be a completely different kettle of fish: for him, "This was the day he had looked forward to for years, the beginning of his real life. He thought of the drab days at the military academy, remembered the bitter evenings spent at his books when he could hear people passing in the streets – people who were free and presumably happy, remembered winter reveilles in the icy barrack rooms heavy with the threat of punishment. He recalled the torture of counting one by one the days to which there seemed to be no end"[3]

Passing through the carriages, Riebel noticed with satisfaction that all his men were now up and about, with many teams already lined up with their backpacks on, ready to get off the train.

He decided to do the same, and to go up to the battalion command at the head of the convoy. There were orders to receive. The *Vorkommando*, which had come to Warsaw a few days earlier to prepare the logistics and which now would take them to pre-arranged lodgings somewhere in the city, was expected at the station at 09:00 hours that morning, and by that time the entire battalion had to be ready to move. *Papa* Nagel was a good commander, well liked by his men, but he demanded efficiency and absolute compliance with his orders, which was why he wanted to avoid being caught unprepared. On his way to reach the battalion command, Riebel mentally rehearsed the subjects he would have to discuss with the major, who would perhaps explain – to him and to the other officials – further details about their mission. Nobody seemed to know anything, at least not officially, although, of course, there had been many rumors and even some clues. Radio infantry broadcast news full blast and although much of it was gossip, some items were less far-fetched than others. Before leaving on June 7, they had been inspected by the "Wien" IdO, General-Major Retzlaff, who, accompanied by the Vienna police commander, Oberst Pohlmeyer, had urged them to "do their duty, especially in enemy territory." But no one really knew what the term enemy territory meant then: some spoke of England, but it seemed unlikely; others of an impending transfer to Yugoslavia or even farther south, to Greece, perhaps Crete, where there had been a battle royal, which meant that there was now a need for fresh troops to defend the area. At that time, however, many had begun to look towards the east, where a great deal of troop and material movements seemed to be going on. The problem was that to the east of Poland there was nothing. Or rather, there was Russia so, perhaps, Russia could be their problem – a damn *big* problem. In any case, whatever the mission, there were orders to receive and to carry out scrupulously and firmly; and the fact was that this was the

Before the wall, June 1942. A view from inside the Warsaw Ghetto and a section of the wall that surrounded the perimeter. Source: Bundesarchiv.

life he had chosen for himself some years earlier. This was the job that he knew he wanted to do. All the rest was idle talk.

2 AT THE WALL

Jewish Ghetto, Warsaw, sometime in mid-June, 1941.

No one had yet figured out what the initials "zbV" meant exactly. Or rather, the literal meaning of "*zur besonderen Verwendung*" – for special use – was obvious to anyone who had any idea about military terminology. That, of course, included them, although they were policemen and not soldiers. Getting at the hidden meaning behind the words, however, was a different matter: it was like entering a no-man's land, where everyone had the right to see things his own way – and to use liberal doses of imagination. That name had been attached to the battalion a few days earlier but no one had paid any attention to it: it was just a bureaucratic label. But then the sharper minds among them had begun to ask questions. Those in uniform knew very well that nothing happened by chance and if someone up there in high places had decided to give them that name, then it followed that there *had* to be a reason. To tell the truth – and this they gradually realized with each passing day – it was more than just a mere formalism. They had in fact begun to receive a growing stream of orders coming directly from a new command structure above the regiment and not from the "Warschau" KdO which seemed to be interested in them solely in terms of paperwork. This new structure, which apparently did not yet have a title or a precise role, had been placed in the hands of someone who was said to be a bigwig, apparently appointed by *Reichsführer* Himmler himself a certain Jeckeln, who hardly anyone had ever heard of before and who seemed to have made his career through several different political offices in the territories of the west. Why then this Jeckeln had now been transferred from Düsseldorf to Warsaw, no one could tell.

In any event, apart from a number of orders mainly regarding new procedures at the level of command and control, as well as some unexpected visits to the unit by sleek SS officers (apparently sent by Jeckeln), for Polizei-Bataillon 304 almost nothing had changed in terms of operational roles. Essentially what they had to do came down to keeping a close watch over the Warsaw ghetto. Manfred Pöhlig, the platoon deputy commander, had some experience of this. By now he couldn't even remember how many times he had commanded the guard outside the ghetto wall. This had been going on since January, when the battalion had been moved to Warsaw from Chemnitz, Saxony, for its first operational engagement outside the Reich. From then on, in precisely defined shifts, a training company of some ninety men had done regular service around the ghetto wall, guarding the entrance gates, patrolling the perimeter and keeping a discreet eye on the Polish police to stop them from becoming too familiar with the Jews enclosed inside (as they spoke the same language), if only to extort money or to demand bribes in exchange for the freedom to smuggle. After all, they were Jews. Until then the Jews had been their main problem. Devious and cunning Levantines, they tried in every possible way to circumvent the rules imposed on them with the aim of keeping them in check and neutralizing them. Not a day passed that some of them did not end up under arrest for attempting to enter or leave the ghetto illegally, or for introducing or taking out different kinds of smuggled goods. In certain severe cases some of them had had to be shot on capture, while many others had been brought to *Pawiak*, the central prison, pending a decision about their fate. Obviously the rules had to be respected and in that sense the inflicted punishment, which was widely announced on posters hung up all around the ghetto wall, was completely justified, if they wanted to maintain a minimum of order. On the other hand, and Pöhlig was convinced of this, in those conditions life was not easy even for policemen like him. The frequent executions provoked a great deal of discontent among his colleagues, some of whom had also asked to be exempted from carrying them out. In itself the situation had not created any particular technical problems, given that there were always relatively few shootings and there were always a fair number willing to carry them out. Nonetheless, those who refused did not set a good example, but were rather spreading discontent among all the other comrades. So at some point, on orders from KDO "Warsaw", a *kommando* of 17 volunteers drawn from the various companies of the battalion had been sent to Krakow for a "special training" course that was meant to solve the problem. The course was held between January and February 1941 in the courtyard of the central prison in Krakow. The volunteers, including many belonging to other battalions, had to learn to carry out the executions in a professional manner, avoiding any unpleasant situations or inappropriate emotions. Technically, the course was defined *Genickshussausbildung*, in other words "training course in shooting in the neck", but it was generally agreed to give it the more somber title *Sonderlehrgang*, or simply "special training". Whatever the label, the Krakow course had ended with 75 Jews shot and an adequate number of sufficiently trained police officers who could do their duty as firing squads once they were back in their respective units. It was thought that having a specialized squad would put an end to the discontent. This is more or less what happened – except that in June 1941, when the unusual abbreviation "zbV" (*besonderen*) was added, the memory of that particular specialization obtained in Krakow cruelly returned to the surface, to the point where some police officers, more suspicious and astute than the others, felt there was a possible connection between the two things. The hypothesis, like so many other rumors that were rife in the sleeping quarters in those days, appeared farfetched to most people, although the simultaneous reorganization of the battalion into motorcycle units – that is, a second line unit, intended for tasks other than fighting, had helped to stir up suspicions and rumors. These suspicions and rumors were of very little interest to him personally. Unlike the others, he had no desire to get caught up in discussions or to cast judgment about things he did not know. He had his own ideas about the Jews and that was enough for him. There were the reason he found himself in that situation rather than at home with his wife and children. All the more reason, then, to avoid further complicating his life by discussing orders or even thinking about them: it was not part of his nature, it was not one of his duties, and what's more he lacked the intellectual tools to be able to do so with good judgement.Then there was also the fact that probably no one would have been interested in his comments anyway. He was only a deputy platoon leader, who in the small area he was responsible for knew how to obey orders and to command respect. That was it, simple and straightforward. Objectively there was no point in wondering why things were the way they were and it could only lead to trouble. And Manfred Pöhlig did not want any trouble; all he wanted was to be a good policeman.

3 ACROSS THE RIVER AND INTO THE TREES[4]

Near Tilsit, June 21, 1941

Tilsit had appeared to him almost as if suspended in mid-air in those late June days, evoking the uncertainty of a traveler at a crossroads, still waiting to decide on the path to take. Usually, the market laid out around the statue of von Schenkendorf in front of the *Rathaus*, was well-stocked and lively, but now it looked all too quiet, with just a few stalls and some hurried passers-by. Even the civilians seemed almost to have disappeared, although this may only have been an impression caused by the prevalence of military uniforms over civilian clothes. There were all kinds of uniforms, especially Luftwaffe and Wehrmacht. There were also uniforms of the *Wasserschutzpolizei*, the river police in service along the Memel. In fact, unlike everything else, the traffic of boats along the river and in particular between the two banks of the river appeared extremely chaotic, in both directions.

From his position on the southern ramp of the *Königin-Luise-Brücke*, on the northern edge of Tilsit, Hans Hespe watched the river boat Grenzland overloaded with troops ply the murky waters of Memel. In those days, since they had arrived in East Prussia from Bremen, via Gdansk, Dirschau and Marienburg, they had wondered several times about the reason for this movement in the direction of the Russian border, to the north and to the east. There was nothing clearly visible or put on show; it was rather an underground movement, a karst river whose flow you could only sense if you knew of its existence. On several occasions they had observed Luftwaffe squadrons flying over them headed for Lindental airport, southwest of Tilsit, and on the roads they had seen long columns of logistical means that someone had been able to identify (on the basis of their tactical symbols) as belonging to at least a couple of armored divisions. Many movements took place at night. He had realized this while on guard duty at the battalion garrison at Hohenbruck, when in the distance to the east he had seen the constant passage of motor vehicles along the road to Tilsit, which during the day gave way to a continuous trickle of staff, mostly belonging to ancillary services. At first they had interpreted this as an exchange of units from the border areas, but then with every passing day the inflow had far exceeded the outflow, so that now some had begun to talk openly about the massing of troops. Then in the late morning of June 21, he finally found out the reason for all the upheaval. It was his commander, Westphal, who informed him and the rest of the company – the second company of Polizei-Bataillon 105 – about what was about to happen. He had gathered them together a couple of hours earlier, and at the moment of giving the orders of the day he declared, without much ado, that they were about to go to "war against Russia!". He went on to add some details about their future tasks, which would involve the security of the rear, anti-partisan operations and surveilling objectives – such as the bridge on which he, Hespe, stood at that moment. Everything seemed very simple, objectively almost a foregone conclusion. Westphal's words had been greeted by a tense silence, broken only by a series of orders issued by officers of the platoon and squad leaders. The departure of the battalion, however, would not be immediate but subject to movements on the other side of the river by the units deployed in front of them, especially armored troops hidden among the trees, towards Tilsit and Ragnit. The tanks, the officers had said, would open the way for the infantry and only then would their turn come, behind the Hamburg and Münster *Ländser*, the 269th and 290th Infantry Divisions. Until then they would remain in close contact with the 207th Sicherungs-Division, which they had joined on May 28. Polizei-Bataillon 105 was something of a hybrid. Tactically it functioned as a division of the Wehrmacht, while remaining in all other respects a police unit. All the men, himself included, had had their blood group tattooed under their left arm, as happened with the SS, and almost all officers of the battalion were members of the SS. This had proved a problem for him, with all the associated consequences. Hespe was a reservist, a merchant who ran a coffee roasting company in Bremen. He had never joined the SS, or the party, or any of its organizations. He considered himself a democrat and had been disgusted by the fanatical violence of the *Kristallnacht* and the crazy theories about the "master race" which his officers openly shared. In truth, after he was recalled to service in the autumn of 1939, he had also tried to understand, to get into the mindset of these arrogant men who campaigned for their ethos during the ideological training sessions. He had made an honest effort, but failed, and soon he began to speak to his comrades, reservists like him, to express opinions, to whisper comments; and these words, opinions and comments were quickly passed on to his officers, the company commanders Petersen and Dittmar, who undoubtedly sent reports to the SD. Hans Hespe knew he was in their sights, even though up to that time nothing untoward had happened to him. He realized that it would be better for him to learn to take a lower profile, to conform to the general trend, like most of his colleagues, yet he also knew that he was not so malleable as to always make the best out of a bad situation; sometimes, perhaps, but certainly not always. That's how things had been going. Now, of course, he would have to go into action for the first time. For the first time they would have to cross over to the other side the river, where they would find themselves face to face with people willing to kill them if they didn't kill them first. Clearly this lack of alternatives, *mors tua vita mea*, would somehow simplify things and would force him to act accordingly, as was inevitable if he had to decide about his own life. Hespe was aware of this, and at least he was prepared for such situations. But the real problem was different.

The real problem would come up every time *his* life was not at stake, every time he was called upon to make moral choices independent of the question of survival, every time he was ordered to kill in the name of someone or something. There, that was *his* problem. And he, Hespe, knew that soon he would be at a fork in the road where he would have to choose which path to take. At that point, he would let his soul live, regardless of the order and despite the consequences. Hans Hespe did not know when all this would happen, or what faces would appear before him, which of the victims and which of the executioners, nor where his choices would lead him. He could not know these things or read the future, but he was quite certain about one thing: "he would never turn his heart into a den of thieves"[5].

4. HEART OF DARKNESS[6]

Eastern Poland, somewhere along the course of the Bug. 03:15 hours, June 22, 1941.

The journey was to begin at the edge of the plain. That was where the dividing line was: fields of sunflowers and long rivers marking the border with the east, holding it back from spreading westwards. There were scattered signs of human presence, close to the horizon, where the warmth of the soil blended with the shimmering sultry June air: a small group of farmers busy working in the fields, the buildings that made up the border guard garrison, some distant warehouses belonging to collectivized farms. There was silence and emptiness, and space beyond the line: the living space that was lacking in the crowded territories of the west, long subjugated but unable to satisfy ambition or to mark destiny. That's the word, destiny.

Destiny was somewhere beyond. Beyond the expanses of sunflowers in Belarus' and Ukraine's wheat fields, past the big slow muddy rivers of Russia, which marked the watershed between a millenary civilization yet to be constructed and a thousand years of barbarism waiting patiently to gain the upper hand. Destiny was faith – faith in the right to history. Destiny was will: the will to recognize the moment when it arrived, and to grasp it and guide it.

And destiny had at last come, and faith would make history. There was no longer time to wait for the arrival of the hordes from the east; it was time to beat them to it, to stop the small riderless Tartar horses, to push on to the edge of the desert, to frighten the garrison of the Bastiani fortress. Now the fortress was finally about to take action, to open its gates to the east, giving on to the Tartar desert where the journey would begin and where finally everything would be accomplished.

For some it was a question of glory, for many it was the solution, and for all of them it was the unknown. They had received precise instructions, commands and orders had been issued and the Führer's proclamation had reached all the soldiers on the eastern front. Now they waited silently for their hour to arrive. They would cross the plain following the caterpillar tracks of the tanks, trample on the black earth of Ukraine, and finally they would bring light to the barbarians, using the sword when necessary. They were surrounded by darkness, the darkness of the hours before dawn and the darkness of the people hidden in the unknown, such as Arminius' Cherusci in the Teutoburg Forest. Here, paradoxically, however, the roles were now reversed: it was they, the German warriors, who were to play the part of Varus' legions on the banks of the Rhine, still waiting to pass through the gates of darkness, suspicious and cautious, but conscious of their power. But unlike the legionaries who were defeated by shadows, the traps and maneuvres of the devious and evasive enemy would not be enough; here the will to forge their destiny once and for all would prevail. They would go up the Congo to its source, without fear of what they might find once they reached the heart of darkness. Like it or not, the hordes would be subjugated, and if there was not enough light, they would use flames, and screams would replace words.

It would be an epic battle and there was no room for doubts or second thoughts. From the secret rooms of the Chancellery in Berlin down to the last division waiting in place, they all knew that this would be the final battle. This was the moment to write History. This was the time to build and destroy. From airports to the west, fighter squadrons took off into the air, ready to speed eastwards. At the edge of the plain, in the early morning mist, the flames of the artillery batteries prefigured the approaching light of dawn.

5 HECKENSCHÜTZEN![7]

Near Gargzdai, Lithuania, 13:00 hours, June 24, 1941

So now it was underway. Two days earlier, at dawn on June 22, German troops had crossed the border and begun pushing deep into Soviet territory. Any uncertainty – all the speculation and the palpable anxiety that in the previous days had covered everything like a heavy shroud – had been swept away by the drumming of artillery fire on known targets beyond the border fences, the echoes of which had reached as far as Memel. Then, with air cover from fighter aircraft and taking full advantage of the element of surprise, it had fallen to the units to move to the east, like a tidal wave washing over the shoreline. In the dim light of early morning the glow of gunfire had marked the progress of the fault line to the limits of perception, until even the muffled roar of distant explosions had faded away completely, now more like a thunderstorm on the horizon. Within 24 hours silence had returned, broken only by the frequent flyovers of Luftwaffe squadrons and the constant passing of convoys of trucks heading north along the coast road towards Liepaja. Later, had it not been for the occasional air raid and the unusually large numbers of military personnel in the city, all apparently engaged in some absolutely essential task, at first sight nothing would have suggested that the great storm, more feared than expected, had already begun. The fact was that just below the surface of the rippling waters, many currents were already in motion, icy currents which left them only two choices: either get swept away like the low-lying banks of a river or let yourself float on the surface like a bobbing cork. At the time there were no other options and he, Werner Schmidt-Hammer, a reservist lieutenant in military life, but in civilian life an optician by profession, did not think he was in a position to be choosy. He walked quickly through the hall of the *Hochhaus am Dangeufer*, the dreary building at no.12 Fischerstr. on the south bank of the River Dange, and emerged into the square at the front, which was crowded with vehicles. The late nineteenth-century building of the Meyhöfers, once the head office of an important Baltic shipping and dispatch company was seven storeys high and now housed the Memel police garrison as well as the headquarters of the Schutzpolizei under Maj. Günther, his immediate superior. Despite the prosaic grandeur of the building that housed its offices, the role of the Schutzpolizei in public life in Memel was of relatively minor importance: much more important was the *Wasserschutzpolizei*, the river police, whose offices were on the nearby *Norderück* on the opposite side of the Dange near the mouth of the *Kurische Haff*, the inner lagoon that flowed directly into the Baltic. Then there were also the shipyards and the flotilla of submarines that had recently arrived from Gdansk – all of these played significant roles in the sleepy provincial town. The little esteemed local police officers, on the other hand, had been divided up into three districts, working short staffed at the thousand tasks they been assigned. And now a further heavy task had just been added to the thousand they already had. On the orders of Günther, some twenty policemen who normally worked in the *Reviere* had been formed into an alarm unit, an *Alarmzug*, to intervene in case of emergency or special needs, principally against any groups of enemy paratroopers, saboteurs or partisans. The platoon was not on permanent duty, but could be mobilized at the simple request of the authorities. He, Werner Schmidt-Hammer, had been appointed commander of the platoon by Günther, who now found himself in battle dress in front of a truck. Schmidt-Hammer approached the unit and ordered Sergeant Kersten to let the men on board. Then he took up position next to the driver and gestured to him to set off. What awaited him was a dirty job. Just the day before, in the afternoon, he had been summoned to Günther's office, where the major had explained without beating about the bush what he and his men would be required do in a Lithuanian town called Gargždai, just over the border. They were to take part in the execution of some *Heckenschützen* (snipers) who had fired treacherously on some German soldiers and hence had to be properly punished. As policemen they had to form the security cordon, while a Gestapo *kommando* from Tilsit would do the shooting. Although perplexed, Schmidt-Hammer nodded. He did not regard himself as a Nazi, he had never joined the party and throughout his life all he had ever done was to pursue his vocation, namely optometry and optical instruments, which he sold in a shop he had opened in Königsberg. Only by *force majeure*, due to the war, had he been called up on September 1, 1939, even though, probably because of his age – he was 32 years old – he was considered useful only for police service. Since then he had enjoyed a rapid career that within the space of a year, had taken him to the rank of reservist lieutenant and to his place of employment in Tilsit, as aide to Maj. Günther. For this reason, he saw himself as only a technician seconded to the police, professional enough to do his duty, but not particularly enthusiastic about the situation into which he had been thrown. Schmidt-Hammer was not a fanatic, he was not obsessed with party slogans. Of course, he understood the period his country was going through and therefore would not refuse to obey orders, but at the same time he was convinced that there were people much better suited than him for carrying out certain tasks. He was probably not even a very good policeman; in fact, some might have said he was not even a good German. Perhaps sensing his silent doubts, the major gave him some encouragement as he sent him on his way, referring to crimes, criminals and duties to be performed on higher orders: the very same concepts that he then repeated that morning, a few minutes before leaving. Gargždai was only a couple of kilometres over the border. On leaving Memel they had headed south, along the new road, and less than an hour later they had reached the border post at Laugallen just beyond which they stopped at a road junction in the middle of the countryside, a few hundred meters from the first houses.

The place was crowded with people they had never seen before. There were men from the Gestapo in Tilsit and others from the Laugallen frontier post wearing *feldgrau* uniforms, and then also members of the SD armed with automatic weapons, bearing the typical diamond on the left forearm. Everyone seemed to be following the orders of a burly SA Colonel, who looked rather agitated and was engaged in a discussion with an officer of the civil administration who Schmidt-Hammer recognized as being the Kreisleiter of Memel, Werner Grau. Not far away stood the mayor of Memel, Brindlinger, along with a number of civilians who had arrived in their cars. Schmidt-Hammer went up to the group of officers headed by the SA Colonel who, according to what Günther had told him, was to give him orders for the operation. Certainly it was a paradoxical situation: while he, Werner, was forced to be there but would gladly have preferred to be elsewhere, many other, anonymous civilians who had nothing to do with what was going on, had gone there voluntarily, as if drawn by morbid curiosity to watch an obscene show. In a sense, the whole situation reminded him of circus games in ancient Rome, where enthusiastic spectators would come to watch cruel fights to the death. Schmidt-Hammer realized how obscene the whole business was when the Colonel informed him of a change of orders. Not for the better. They no longer simply had to keep watch over the group of snipers and cordon off the area where the shooting would take place, but they were also, by order of the Führer,[8] to take part in the execution together with the men from the platoon. That was what had been decided and that was what they had to do. Nervously, he walked with his platoon to a point a little farther to the east less than a hundred meters from the roadway, where some Gestapo men were standing in a circle watching over a large group of figures, some sitting on the marshy, mossy ground and others busy in digging a trench nearby. Werner had expected to find Russian men in uniform, maybe some political commissars, or some young hotheads from the *Komsomol* who had perhaps been mobilized by their leaders to cover the flight of their companions with sniper fire. He had expected, in short, to find guilty people, or at least people *worthy* of execution, which would make the shooting easier for him and his men. Werner Schmidt-Hammer had expected the enemy, but all he saw was a group of terrified civilians, elderly people with long beards who murmured incomprehensible litanies and teenage boys who were not yet old enough to be soldiers. Later, abandoned on the ground like a pile of rags, one of the victims was lying there shot through the neck, while other bodies – which looked like Russian soldiers in khaki uniforms – were transported by groups of Jews and thrown into a stretch of the long trench, amid orders and angry blows inflicted on those who were slower than the others. Close by the trench, standing out with his bushy beard and long black caftan, an old rabbi was taunted and beaten by some of the Gestapo officials. Schmidt-Hammer ordered the platoon to stop in order to check their weapons. A few meters back down the road he had seen the burned bodies of two German soldiers waiting to be taken away. Perhaps it had been decided to set an example so that it would not happen again, or perhaps, who knows, that group of Jewish prisoners actually had something to do with the ambush. Perhaps the Jews really were enemies. Whatever the explanation, one thing Werner Schmidt-Hammer was sure about – it was going to be a really dirty job.

ENDNOTES

1 Hilberg, *ibid.*, p.12.

2 This section is based entirely on the KTB of Oltn. Gerhard Riebel of 3/Polizei-Bataillon 322 for the days of June 7, 9 and 10, 1941, published in Ernst Klee/Volker Riess: "Schöne Zeiten". Judenmord aus der Sicht der Täter und Gaffer, Frankfurt am Main, 1988, pp.19-21. Every factual detail is therefore accurate but some artistic license with regard to the language has been used in the narrative.

3 From Dino Buzzati: *The Tartar Steppe*, Godine Books,

4 This section is based entirely on the biography of Rottwachtmesiter Hans Hespe, reconstructed by Karl Schneider under the title *Zwischen alle Stühlen. Der Bremer Kaufmann Hans Hespe im Reserve-Polizeibatallion 105*, Bremen, 2007.

5 In his first memo, submitted to the *Entschädigungskammer* of the Court of Bremen in 1951, Hans Hespe uses the word "Mördergrube", borrowing the German term used to translate Jesus's words to the merchants in the temple. In English:: "My house shall be called a house of prayer; but ye have made it a den of thieves." (Matthew 21, 12-17). In the more general sense, Hespe means something like "making his heart into a receptacle for horrors". Schneider, *ibid.* p. 27

6 This section, as with section two of the epilogue, *Reaching the Night*, is to be considered *abstract*, in that it makes no precise mention of any particular unit, apart from some general references to Polizei-Battailon 307, which moved from the River Bug to the River Dnepr between June and September 1941, after having perpetrated the massacre at Brest Litovsk. Both of these sections represent a metaphorical evocation of a journey towards and across barbarism, taking their cue from Joseph Conrad's masterpiece. In this sense, some of the themes addressed by Conrad seem to match the path of genocide undertaken in this case by the police battalions in Russia: the colonization of the east, the claim to be bringing the light of Nazi *civilization*, the dream of omnipotence, the abandonment of moral laws, the sense of the immanence of death, the madness that progressively takes hold of the protagonists, as well as the barbarization – the darkness – that came to overwhelm the formerly civil symbols of the empire right up to its final defeat.

7 This section is based entirely on the reconstruction carried out by the Court of Ulm during the trial against the commander of the Polizeidirektion "Memel", SA-Oberführer Bernard Fischer-Schweder and others – LG Ulm, Ks 2/57 dated August 29, 1958, and against the alarm platoon leader of the KdSchupo "Memel", R.Ltn. Werner Schmidt-Hammer – LG Ulm, Ks 2/57 dated Novermber 3, 1960. See Curilla, *ibid.*, pp. 136-143, Joachim Tauber: *Garsden, 24 Juni 1941.* In *Annaberger Annalen 5/1997*, pp. 117 ff.

8 Shortly before the execution, Fischer-Schweder, SA colonel and Chief of Police for Memel turned to Schmidt-Hammer to suggest that he explain to his men that the victims "were to be shot on Hitler's orders for committing crimes against the Wehrmacht (Sie werden wegen Vergehen gegen die Wehrmacht auf Befehl des Führer erschossen)." Curilla, *ibid.*, p 140, Joachim Tauber, *ibid.*, p. 126, Helmut Langerbein, Hitler's death squads. The Logic of Mass Murder, College Station, 2003, p. 163.

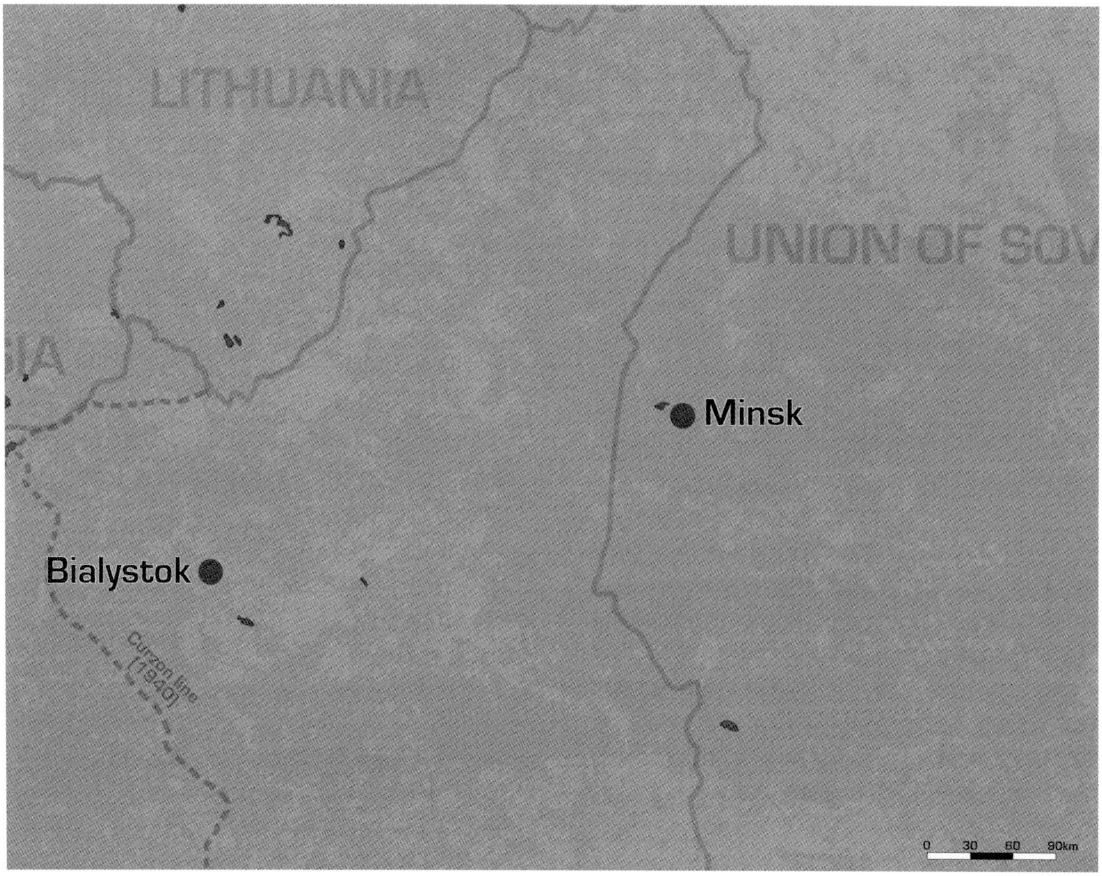
LITHUANIA
UNION OF SOV
SIA
Minsk
Bialystok
Curzon line
(1940)
0 30 60 90km

CHAPTER ONE

"UNFORGETTABLE FIRE"

BIALYSTOK, JUNE 27, 1941

The city and its houses, from its foundation to its top,
I destroyed, I devastated, I burned with fire.

Sennacherib, Babylonia, 689 BC

1.1 INTRODUCTION
In the area of Bialowieza, July 11, 1941

On 26 and 27 June 1941, Major Weis personally led his companies to clean up the wooded area on both sides of the Sokoly to Bialystok road and when clearing up the forest south of the city, he worked tirelessly under fire from enemy snipers. He personally, together with his battalion, was always on hand to help. The clearing-up action carried out by his battalion helped to pacify the city and the surrounding areas in a relatively short time. He is considered worthy of decoration.[1]

We do not know exactly where they were, or whether it was morning or afternoon. However, we do know from photographs[2] that it was a clear day; we can imagine that it was a little muggy, as summers often are in that area of north-eastern Poland on the southern border of Lithuania, on the edge of the great Belarusian plain. It was probably a simple yet engrossing ceremony: in a clearing in the trees one can see at least one company lined up behind its officers, and in front of them, some Wehrmacht masters of ceremonies holding the decorations and reading the award proclamation. In the foreground one can make out Generalleutnant Johann Pflugbeil, commander of the 221st Sicherungs-Division, intent on pinning an Iron Cross on the breast of a policeman standing to attention, his pride visible on his face. On the policeman's left wrist, above the blacks cuffs of his uniform, one can make out an armband with the inscription *Deutsche Wehrmacht*, which in the summer of 1941 was the distinguishing mark of the police battalions that had been added to the Wehrmacht security divisions. Just behind the decorated policeman one can see some of his fellow policemen, armed with cameras, as they try to immortalize the scene from other angles.

From the photograph it is not possible to recognize the decorated policemen, but this is, after all, a detail of little importance, since he was probably one of the seven members of Polizei-Bataillon 309 which on that day, July 11, 1941, was being awarded just recognition for their war deeds.

The war against the Soviet Union had begun only 19 days earlier, but already numerous decorations had been awarded, adding to the battalion's list of achievements and boosting the morale and pride of the men serving in it.

But there was one problem: up to that moment Polizei-Bataillon 309 (Cologne) had not yet seen action. It had not taken part in clashes with the enemy, or indeed any military operations worthy of note. All it had done was make a peaceful advance towards the east in the wake of several front line units that were some way ahead of it. The battalion had not engaged in any bloody fighting, nor apparently had it suffered any losses. It had crossed the border shortly after June 22, entered a town without a fight and likewise without a fight had left the town a few days later. Then, it had calmly spread across the forest of Bialowieza, where seven of its men had finally been given their reward, to the satisfaction of all.

We do not know exactly where they were that day, or whether it was morning or afternoon. But we do know what those policemen had done to merit their award.

1.2 BEFORE THE HURRICANE

According to the data provided by the 1936 census, there were about 100,000 inhabitants in Bialystok – a Polish city of ancient traditions situated at the crossroads between the Baltic world, the Germanic area and the Slavic territories. Of these inhabitants 42,482 were Jews[3], who formed one of the most flourishing Ashkenazi cultural communities in the entire region of north-eastern Europe; there was much Zionist ferment and the Jewish labor movement was strong[4]. During the previous decades this community had gone through many adventures and much hardship beginning with the Russian pogroms of June 1, 1906, which had led to the death of 70 Jews and the looting of hundreds of shops and houses[5]. Relations between Poles and Jews had worsened with the latter falsely accused of having fought alongside the Bolshevik militias, right up to the troubles of the summer of 1920[6]. Finally, there had also been the Soviet invasion in September 1939, after which the Bialystok area had been annexed to the SRSF of Belarus, with the Jews once again singled out by the Poles as supporters of the Red Army.

In fact, more than demonstrating their support for the Soviets, the Jews of Bialystok – and Polish Jews in general – had chosen the lesser of two evils. The news brought by the thousands of refugees who crossed the line of demarcation with the territories occupied by Germany left little doubt about what was preferable – from the point of view of the Jews – between the outright racial persecution imposed by the Nazis and the political and ideological oppression imposed by the Soviets. In the latter case, leaving aside the class conflict between proletariat and middle class – the class to which many Jews belonged – there was no preconceived intolerance on the part of the communist system against *Jews* as such. They could therefore aspire – at least in theory – to a less precarious coexistence than what they would have to face under the Nazi yoke. Based on this simple reasoning, then, tens of thousands of Jews poured from the General Government into Soviet territory between the fall of 1939 and early 1940. As early as November 1939, in Bialystok there were approximately 33,000 refugees[7], which meant an unsustainable logistical burden for the town administration.

This exodus from west to east, which then ceased and in part flowed back during the early months of 1940, was one of the causes that fostered the negative stereotype of *Judeo-Communism*, especially in the collective imagination of the Polish population: a stereotype that would later be picked up effectively by Nazi propaganda. In fact, although many Jews, especially younger Jews, actually managed to make their way in the maze of Soviet bureaucracy, as well as in the armed forces and police, the situation that many hopeful refugees actually faced in the Soviet Union was very different from what they had imagined. Paradoxically, the first to be affected by the NKVD were Jews who were members of the banned Polish Communist Party, accused of Trotskyism, followed by the members of the Bund and the main exponents of religious institutions: the latter not so much in the context of anti-Semitic persecution – which did not form part of the ideological framework of the Soviet regime – but because of the overt hostility of the regime towards *all* religions, seen as an incompatible element that disrupted relations with the state. Within these terms then, while on the one hand anti-Semitism was widespread during the last years of the so-called Second Polish Republic, it basically ceased to exist under the Soviet system[8], on the other, the Jewish community of Bialystok still had to endure unrelenting political persecution by an omnipresent and paranoid regime. During subsequent deportations – the last of which took place on the eve of *Barbarossa* – there were probably several thousand Jews in Bialystok regarded as *enemies of the state* who were transferred inside the Soviet Union (to Kazakhstan and elsewhere), while others in the meantime – and at least as long as this was possible – had reached Lithuania or had voluntarily left for other parts of Russia. Overall, then, considering the algebraic sum of *arrivals and departures*, including displaced persons and refugees, the Jewish population of Bialystok on the eve of *Barbarossa* had probably reached 50,000 inhabitants[9]. Of these, for all the reasons mentioned above, only a minority could actually be regarded as favorabale to the Soviet regime, as opposed to the vast majority – some disillusioned and partly *broken in* by history – who were able to adapt to the circumstances despite the many difficulties. This disproportion makes the equation between Jews and Communists clearly approximate and instrumental, albeit no less effective as propaganda, first in its extremist Polish form and later at the service of the Nazi regime.

1.3 BEYOND THE BARRIER

They had left Ostrolenka immediately after June 22, 1941, headed towards the bridges over the Narew; on the other side of the demarcation line was Soviet territory. Only a few weeks earlier, in late May, they had been transferred from Radom, in the General Government, following agreements reached on April 16 between Himmler, Daluege and Wagner, the general quartermaster of the OKH. These assigned a police battalion to each of the nine security divisions of the Wehrmacht ordered to take part in the initial phase of *Operation Barbarossa*. For this reason, the policemen who made up Polizei-Bataillon 309 (Cologne) now had to share the road with the Silesians of the 221st Sicherungs-Division, whose task it was, starting from Ostrow Mazowiecka, to secure the rear of the Fourth German Army as it headed for Belarus[10]. In particular, in the words of the divisional commander, Gen.Ltn. Johann Pflugbeil, the battalion had been assigned the task to "clear the city of Bialystok of Russian stragglers and the population hostile to Germany, and to act to maintain peace, security and order inside the city"[11]. Essentially this was a new task for Polizei-Bataillon 309, which previously had been mainly used as a garrison unit. It was, in fact, a newly formed battalion, built around a group of *police recruits*, including those born in the years 1909-1912[12], who had been transferred to Radom and Pionki, Poland, on September 23, 1940. Before June 27, 1941, there is no information indicating its involvement in any war crimes. What is certain is that it was subjected to several hours of political indoctrination before its entry into Soviet territory. This included watching anti-Semitic films[13]: this was fully in line with the ordinary training programme as indicated for police battalions – which set aside only two or three lessons a week of *weltanschauliche Schulung* – certainly too little to put them on a par with the ideologically elite units such as the Einsatzgruppen. Nevertheless, only a few hours after having set foot on Soviet territory, this battalion was responsible for a massacre perpetrated in cold blood and in such a brutal manner as to suggest the presence of specific factors, without which the situation – which then degenerated into genocidal chaos – would hardly been able to manifest such perniciousness.

In fact, apart from a recognized basic ideological background – probably confused, but enough to form a valuable motivational underpinning for many of the massacres perpetrated by the police battalions – what is undoubtedly significant is the specific role played by general situational dynamics. These had the effect of changing, depending on the occasion, the initial approach to the killings, especially at a stage – at the beginning of summer 1941 – when the final genocidal project had not yet emerged in all its details and was therefore *still* being operated according to standardized mechanics[14]. In the specific case of Bialystok there were probably psychosocial variables that acted as a trigger and catalyst within the existing ideological culture medium.

This was nothing other than a moral short circuit, which may have affected many if not most of the men in Polizei-Bataillon 309. For the first time in their lives, these men found themselves in a position to exercise almost absolute control over their surroundings, beyond the reach of any existing legal or social constraints. Their behavior was guided only by the political, social and cultural stereotypes that had been fostered in the police force, not so much through the short and sketchy ideological indoctrination their unit had received as through their previous full immersion (as citizens only recently called to arms) in the "racial body (*Volkskörper*)" of National Socialist society, com-

A group of Bialystok Jews rounded up between August 15 and 29, 1943, during the liquidation of the ghetto. Note, in the background, the deployment of German troops, probably from Polizei-Regiment 26, which took part in the action from the start.

plete with its superficial but nonetheless all-embracing ideological conditioning. Then there was the fact that the men of Polizei-Bataillon 309 found themselves in a position where they could exercise enraged but rewarding *absolute power* over individuals like the Jews, who until then had been cast in a negative role. On top of this came, on the one hand, a total absence of control by the higher command (both regimental and divisional), who proved to be totally apathetic and incapable and unwilling to curb the excesses of their subordinates, and on the other there was also the open complicity of the intermediate commands (company and battalion), who legitimized and were in effect the driving force behind the behavior of their men. In many of the succession of massacres that occurred between the summer of 1941 and the fall of 1942 policies and procedures became gradually more and more clearly defined, in some ways more professional and subordinated to a (relative) operating discipline imposed from above: the victims were forced to step forward, often after having laid their clothes to one side so they could be reused, they were lined up or made to lie down in the pit, often according to a certain geometry so as to make optimal use of the space, and were then shot with coordinated firing procedures (at least in the early stages of the massacre). This pattern was designed to create a psychological barrier between the victims and perpetrators, who could thus feel part of a complex depersonalized mechanism and this helped lessen the individual effects of a possible emotional involvement. What happened in Bialystok was the opposite, with the members of Polizei-Bataillon 309 taking part in a massacre that was almost a sacrificial, tribal and collective rite, in which, far from being rejected, the emotional and in a sense metaphysical component was positively sought as an integral and inseparable part of the rite itself. To sum up, in all probability the opportunity to do something extraordinary, in a certain sense something absolute in terms of power, something that broke the mould and that served to bind the men to each other, thus lending the as yet inexperienced battalion a sort of blood identity – was the motivational dynamic that drove the Bialystok massacre, combined with the knowledge that they could do so with impunity thanks to the legitimacy guaranteed by the higher command[15] and the basis provided by the ideological hinterland. This was not, however, the structured and in some ways *professional* perspective of the Einsatzgruppen, but the more superficial, politically indifferent and generic – and for this reason much more popular – typical view of large parts of the German people and thus also of the police battalions recruited from among the general population. In this sense, the fact that those who perpetrated this crime were not genocide professionals but ordinary men with no previous criminal experience, without a specific ideological indoctrination or mission plans to orientate them to do so, not yet corrupted by the progressive brutalization of the conflict and in a peaceful environment such as the city of Bialystok that had been occupied without a fight, if anything makes the event even more dramatic, and shows how fragile and osmotic the barrier between moral rectitude and abomination can be.

1.4 UNFORGETTABLE FIRE

Given a friendly welcome by some of the Polish population, Polizei-Bataillon 309 entered Bialystok on the morning of Friday June 27, 1941, with orders to support the 2nd Sicherungs-Regiment in cleaning up the city from any Russian stragglers and anti-German elements. The battalion was organized as follows:

- Bataillon Stab: Maj. Ernst Weis
- The 1 / 309 under the command of Hptm Hans Behrens
- The 2 / 309 under the command of Oltn. Johann Hohl
- The 3 / 309 under the command of Oltn. Rolf-Joachim Buchs

We also have the names of other officers belonging to the battalion: Ltn. Gorgs, commander of the fourth platoon of the 1 / 309; Ltn. Theo Oldenburg, commander of another platoon of the 1 / 309; Ltn. Wilhelm Porschen, commander of the second platoon of the 3 / 309; Ltn. Heinrich Schneider, commander of the fourth platoon of 3 / 309. Two of these companies, the 1 / 309 and the 3 / 309, entered Bialystok on June 27, some time between nine in the morning and noon, and set up in the marketplace. They were followed in the afternoon by the 2 / 309, which arrived after skirmishing sporadically with some Soviet rearguard soldiers[16]. It is not clear at this point who decided how subsequent events were to develop, although there are no doubts about the fact that, some days earlier, Weis had passed on to his company commanders the so-called *Kommissarbefehl*, relative to the killing of the captured Soviet political commissars: this order could have served as further legitimacy for subsequent events. In any event, around midday of June 27, Behrens and Buchs ordered the two companies gathered in the square to proceed with searching Jewish quarter[17], which was then surrounded by a cordon of policemen. In this first phase, marked by the crackling of automatic weapons, grenades exploding against doors, screaming and pleading, humiliation and brutality, there were dozens of victims among the Jews, including some children[18] and hospital patients who could not be transported[19]. In several cases, those who refused to open the door or who were tardy in doing so were killed on the spot before the eyes of their families. With these methods, by the early hours of the afternoon, all Jewish males of military age had been forcefully rounded up and made to leave their homes, often by means of blows inflicted with rifle butts. Behrens, in particular, apparently gave instructions about which Jews should be killed on the spot, which should be carried off to be shot and, finally, which were to be brought to the marketplace or the synagogue, chosen as collection points for victims rounded up in the district[20]. Houses were looted, as well as synagogues and prayer houses and a liquor store was broken into, which led to many of the police officers coming under the influence of alcohol, including the battalion commander, Weis. According to witness statements given by former members of the battalion to the public prosecutor in Dortmund, many Poles collaborated in the *Jew hunt* by indicating to the police the houses inhabited by their Jewish fellow citizens and other possible hiding places[21]. There were cases of elderly Jews whose beards were burnt as *punishment* for not being able to dance to the lively rhythm imposed by their persecutors[22]; others were killed randomly, and soon the streets began to be littered with corpses[23]. At least ten Jews were shot in the back of the head by two policemen of the third platoon of the 3 / 309, under the eyes of their immediate superior, platoon leader Lieutenant Schneider[24]. At the height of terror, while the Jews were being pushed into the marketplace, two members of the community, one young and one elderly, went so far as to throw themselves at the feet of Pflugbeil, commander of the 221st Sicherungs-Division, begging him to stop the massacre. Incredibly, one of the policemen present at the scene opened the flies of his trousers and urinated on them[25]. The General had the policeman reprimanded and punished, but he made no effort to take control of the situation, which had by now degenerated completely. Some officers of the Wehrmacht tried to stop the massacre, but they were ignored[26]. According to several witnesses, both Wehrmacht soldiers and Jewish survivors, the violence and shootings went on for several hours until late in the afternoon[27]. In the midst of this tragedy there were also grotesque episodes, one of which happened to a team leader of the 1 / 309, Zugwachtmeister Moll, who volunteered along with seven other fellow soldiers to carry out the shooting of a group of 30 Jews. While escorting his victims to the place of execution on the outskirts of the city, he thought he heard the sound of an approaching Russian military march (actually the sound was coming from a gramophone inside a house). In panic, fearing the sudden return of the Soviets, Moll and his men abandoned their captives in the road and returned hastily to the city: they were, of course, very diligent to demonstrate their *martial virtues* against unarmed civilians, but clearly reluctant to do the same against Red Army soldiers[28]. Shortly after noon, while the *mopping up* continued and the number of arrests mounted, commander Behrens of the 1 / 309 (he was also deputy battalion commander) came to the market square to give the order to his officers to begin the shooting of the Jews who had gathered in the meantime. Dozens of them were taken to two sites selected for execution, where machine guns had been positioned – a mass grave dug in the park near the *Branicki*, the Government building, and a piece of land just outside the city[29]. Behrens himself, and platoon leader Schneider then went to the square where the synagogue stood, the Shulhoyf, where meanwhile 700-800 Jews had been brought, mostly men, but also many women with children who did not want to leave their husbands and fathers[30]. Then at dusk, while 100 or 150 men belonging mainly to the 3 / 309 – but also to the other two companies and to the Nachrichtenzug – formed a double security cordon around the synagogue, more policemen forced all Jews into the building, whose doors and windows were blocked from the outside with furniture and household goods and then subjected to machine gun fire. Fuel tanks were emptied around the edges of the synagogue, and even inside it, through the windows. Then, Behrens and Schneider[31] gave the final order. According to the indictment of the Dortmund public prosecutor, the terror of death spread everywhere, to the loud cries of the trapped Jews trying to escape[32]. The fire was started when grenades were thrown on to the petrol and immediately began to spread to the entire building, inside which could be heard the sound of sacred hymns and screams of terror. Some Jews tried to escape through the blazing door but were shot down by machine guns, while others who threw themselves out of the windows with their clothes on fire suffered the same fate when they landed in the square. At least six Jews were killed in this way by the police officers guarding the synagogue; they ended up being consumed by fire, human torches under the eyes of the Germans[33]. Several women at the windows held up their offspring begging for the children at least to be spared; they were targeted and hit by policemen standing guard outside. A young man who had escaped the flames asked in vain for pity, before being mowed down by a burst of machine gun[34], while others deliberately went to the windows, preferring to be shot rather than to die in the fire. A Jew took his own life by hanging himself from a column, while others tried to find refuge in some small storage rooms to the sides of the main room, choked by the smoke which soon invaded the entire synagogue. By a fluke, and with the help of the synagogue sexton who lived outside, two dozen Jews managed to get out through a side door at a moment when external surveillance was briefly relaxed. They, and perhaps another lucky few, were the only ones who managed to survive the synagogue fire[35].

This is the testimony of a Jewish citizen of Bialystok who escaped the massacre, given to the public prosecutor in Wuppertal on August 9, 1966:

I could observe closely – from about 20 yards away – how German officials placed explosives against the walls of the synagogue, even though the synagogue had already begun to burn. At the same time, hand grenades were thrown through the windows, causing a terrible din. I also saw a young man who tried to save himself by jumping from a window, who was killed by a shot fired from a German[36].

It took about half an hour for the tragedy to reach its epilogue. Then the screams stopped and silence fell. According to Norbert Simgen, President of the Court at Wuppertal, the screams of the victims burned alive inside the synagogue were heard up to 800 meters away, the shots up to two kilometers and the stench of burning human flesh over 400 meters[37].

While the synagogue and the unfortunate people locked inside it ended up being consumed in the fire, as a result of the summer heat the fire soon began to spread to neighboring wooden houses, and it was only at that point, faced with a situation now out of control, that the commander of the battalion Weis finally arrived on the scene and decided to order the fire to be put out[38]. However, despite the intervention of a unit of Wehrmacht engineers, most of the Jewish neighborhood around the synagogue continued to burn throughout the night so that even the Battalion's motor fleet, dangerously threatened by the fire, had to be driven away in a hurry. Amidst the flames and under the rubble of their collapsed houses, approximately another 1,000 Jews were killed. Briefly, the fire came very close both to the Government building, where General Pflugbeil had stationed the command of the 221st Sicherungs-Division, and a nearby hotel, which had become headquarters of the Sicherungs-Regiment 2, and which had to be abandoned[39].

In the course of that evening, when Pflugbeil finally decided to intervene by calling Weis for a debriefing, the latter could not say anything because he was completely drunk. Heinrich Schneider was in the same state – he was found in the middle of the road injured and unconscious from too much alcohol – as were many other members of the battalion[40]. Finally, after the flames had been subdued at the first light of dawn, it became clear that much of the neighborhood surrounding the synagogue had been completely destroyed. Overall, taking into account those who were shot in the mass graves, the victims of the collapsed and burned houses and those burned alive inside the synagogue, at least 2,000 Jews from Bialystok died on June 27, 1941. The next day, Saturday, June 28, working groups composed of Jews and Poles and supervised by staff of the battalion proceeded to recover the bodies, many of them burned or charred to the point where they literally had to be scraped off the ground with shovels and put into sacks[41]. It took three days and 20 wagons to transport the remains of the victims to the Jewish cemetery, where they were buried in a mass grave.

1.5 CRIMES WITHOUT PUNISHMENT

In 1959, based on testimony given in the case against Polizei-Bataillon 322[42], an investigation was initiated by the ZStL into the events of Bialystok of June 26, 1941, from which emerged the involvement of an *unspecified* police battalion, under the orders of a certain *Maj. Weiss*. In short, using the information that came into the possession of the *Sonderkommission* of the LKA Baden-Württemberg, it was possible to identify the unit, Polizei-Bataillon 309, as well as its commander, namely Maj. Ernst Weis of Stettin, who moved to Mönchengladbach at the end of the war, where he lived on a lieutenant colonel's war pension. In April 1960, the ZStL drafted an initial report on the investigation, contained in the file 205 AR-Z 20/60, from which emerged eleven suspects, including Buchs and Schneider. At that point, as the statute of limitations was approaching the final date of May 8, 1960[43], procedures were initiated for opening a formal investigation, resulting in the sending of the files to the public prosecutor in Mönchengladbach, Weis's place of residence. Weis was identified as the main figure among the 30 ex-policemen who at that point in time – May 1960 – made up the list of suspects. Later, while the case against Weis was dropped after his death in August 1964[44], investigations against the other police officers of the battalion – almost all residents of North Rhine-Westphalia and many of whom were still in service at various police authorities – were continued by the Sonderkommission of the LKA NRW Düsseldorf led by Kriminalmeister Ernst Woywod, called upon by Dortmund public prosecutor Schaplow in October 1961 to help compile the dossier StAwDo 45 Js 21/61. Amid great difficulties, due to a climate of silence and lack of cooperation, the gathering of evidence and the interrogation of suspects and witnesses – including several Jewish survivors living in Israel – continued until May 8, 1967, when the formal indictment was finally issued by the Dortmund public prosecutor against 14 members of Polizei-Bataillon 309, those who could be indicted on a precise charge[45]. They included the commanders of the 1 / 309 (Behrens) and the 3 / 309 (Buchs), the platoon commanders Porschen and Schneider and ten other policemen[46]. The allegations made by the prosecutor centered on murder, accessory to murder and aggravated arson. The first hearing was scheduled for October 10, 1967.

This trial – LG Wuppertal 12 Ks 1 / 67 – was intended by the president of the court Norbert Simegenia to be of particular importance, both from a legal and media standpoint, given the large number of defendants, the presence among the prosecution witnesses of some survivors from Israel, the symbolic choice of the place where the hearings were held – the main hall of the Wuppertal Polizeipräsidium[47] – and the fact that seats had been reserved for the media among the public.

Things, however, were not to go according to plan, and also the interest of public opinion soon subsided, as other news items attracted their attention. Begun on October 10, 1967, the trial took place following the thread of the depositions by 250 witnesses, many of whom were very reticent[48], and ended on March 12, 1968, with mixed results. From the beginning, for health reasons, Hans Behrens had been excluded from the trial[49], and the case against Heinrich Schneider was also terminated after he committed suicide in his cell only a few days after the start of the hearings. At that point, the following sentences were passed for the other 12 defendants[50]:

- life sentence for Buchs, Schaffrat and Rondholz acquittal for Morgenbesser, Porschen and Thomas; remission of sentence for Eberhardt, Fuchs, Herweg, Ihrig, and Leinemann Schütte;

Later, these results, of little significance in themselves, were revoked in subsequent appeals and revisions: first by a decision of the Bundesgerichtshof, BGH 3 StR 337/68 of May 13, 1971, which commuted Rondholz's life imprisonment to four years in prison. Secondly came the decision by the Court of Wuppertal, 12 Ks 14/71 dated May 25, 1973, which upheld Buchs' and Schaffrat's appeal and recognized that they had only been accessories to murder, which meant the lifting of their life sentences and the new sentences of four and six years, respectively; terms which they had already served[51]. This ruling was made final in 1975, when the last appeal by the Dortmund public prosecutor was rejected by the Bundesgerichtshof, BGH 30 StR 193/74 according to the decision of January 29, 1975.

The following are short biographies of the main perpetrators of the massacre of Bialystok:

WEIS, Ernst: born in Szczecin on June 20th 1894. Major in the Schutzpolizei and first commander of Polizei-Bataillon 65 from September to November 1939. He was later transferred to the command of the Polizei-Ausbildungs-Bataillon "A" / Polizei-Bataillon 309 and served with this unit in Radom, Poland, from September 1940 to May 1941. With regard to the events at Bialystok, he probably issued the order to proceed with the raid on the Jewish quarter – which was then circulated to the companies through his subordinates Buchs and Behrens – but it is unclear whether this was in written or oral form. Also unclear is what his actual role in the massacre was. Called to Gen.Ltn. Johann Pflugbeil for debriefing on the evening of June 27, he was found drunk. Nevertheless, on July 11, 1941, for the *operation* he carried out he was awarded the Cl. 2 Iron Cross by Gen.Ltn. Johann Pflugbeil himself. He moved to Mönchengladbach after the war and was identified on the basis of information obtained from the *Sonderkommission* of the LKA Baden-Württemberg. He was interrogated for the first time about the events in Bialystok in 1960. He denied any involvement in the massacre, admitting only to have heard *rumors*, but relating to other units. He died in August 1964, while he was being subjected to preliminary investigations by the public prosecutor of Mönchengladbach[52].

BUCHS, Rolf-Joachim: born in Kaiserswerth, near Düsseldorf, on September 12, 1914. Volunteer in the Wehrmacht and member of the SS from 1934, he became a police officer cadet in 1936. Lieutenant of the Schutzpolizei, he took part in the Polish campaign and in operations in France. Commander of the 3 / 309, according to the indictment issued by the public prosecutor in Dortmund, he did not take an active part in the blockade of the synagogue and the subsequent fire, but arrived later, with events already in progress. However, he did nothing to prevent the policemen of his company from taking part in the massacre, nor did he order them to stop firing at the synagogue windows. He was thus accused of being an accessory in the depraved and cruel murder of at least 800 people. Personally, he merely waited for the screams inside the synagogue to cease and the smoke to clear, "thus losing the opportunity to behave like a human being"[53]. On one occasion, urged by a captain of the Wehrmacht to put an end to the massacre, he refused to obey on the grounds that he did not recognize his authority over him. In another case, he freed a Jew who begged him to spare his life[54]. For the Bialystok *operation,* on July 11, 1941 he was awarded the Cl. II Iron Cross by Gen. Ltn. Johann Pflugbeil. Re-admitted to the police after the war, in 1953 he became commander of the police in Solingen and then, from 1957, Chief Commissioner (*Polizeihauptkommissar*) and instructor for civics [sic] at Landespolizeischule in Düsseldorf. Under investigation by the public prosecutor in Dortmund, he was remanded in custody from September 1965 to the beginning of 1966, and was then suspended from police service in the following March[55].He was found guilty of killing at least 700 people by arson and sentenced to life imprisonment. On appeal, his sentence was commuted to four years in prison.

BEHRENS, Hans: born in Rehna, Mecklenburg, on September 13, 1895. Captain of the Schutzpolizei. Member of a Freikorps in the period immediately following the end of World War I, he enlisted in the police during the Weimar Republic. Commander of the 1 / 309, according to the indictment issued by the public prosecutor in Dortmund, during the massacre he ordered several of his subordinates, including Friedrich Rondholz, to shoot at least 250 Jews, in various places in the city. He was responsible for the order to set fire to the synagogue. For the Bialystok *operation* he was decorated with the Cl II Iron Cross. by Gen. Ltn. Johann Pflugbeil on July 11, 1941. Promoted to the rank of major, he subsequently became an official supervisor (*deutsche Aufsichts-Offizier* - DAO) for the Lithuanian Polizei-Bataillon 9 and was later moved to the Netherlands. Sentenced immediately after the war to six months in prison by a British military court, in 1951 he became a lecturer in criminal law at

Kiel Landespolizeischule. He held this position until September 30, 1955, when he was finally discharged with full pension rights having reached the rank of superintendent (Polizeirat).[56] Indicted by the public prosecutor in Dortmund, the case against him was dropped soon after the start of the trial for health reasons

SCHNEIDER, Heinrich: born in Wuppertal-Barmen on 8 October 1914. Afrter enlisting as a volunteer in the Landepolizei at Münster in 1934, he took part in the invasion of Poland in September 1939 and was then transferred to Cologne, with the rank of Leutnant der Schutzpolizei. Assigned to the Polizei-Ausbildungs-Bataillon "A", he became commander of the fourth platoon of the 3 / 309. At the beginning of the action at Bialystok he ordered his men to go from house to house to arrest all Jewish males, and he himself personally killed at least five Jews during the roundups. Along with Behrens he was said to have given the order to set fire to the synagogue. He returned to Münster in September 1941, and served in Lyon, France, from March 1943 to 1945. For the Bialystok *operation* he was decorated with the Cl II Iron Cross. by Gen.Ltn.Johann Pflugbeil on July 11, 1941. A prisoner of war, he was released by the Americans in 1946 after a short period of denazification. In the following years he tried many times to be reinstated in the police in Cologne but was rejected as *unsuitable for active duty* because of his injuries. Entitled to a war pension from 1954, he was added to the list of suspects of the public prosecutor in Dortmund and underwent the first of his 16 interrogations regarding the events of Bialystok on January 2, 1963. Placed in custody in June, he was released on bail pending trial. In the indictment of the public prosecutor in Dortmund he was charged with seven murders, perpetrated deliberately for petty reasons. Recognized by several witnesses as a fanatic anti-Semite, he was again arrested ahead of the trial, but committed suicide in his cell a few days later, on October 14, 1967, mentally overwhelmed by the weight of the accusations[57].

PORSCHEN, Wilhelm: born in Grefrath, near Mönchengladbach, on February 12, 1907. Lieutenant, commander of the second platoon of the 3 / 309, he gave orders to his platoon to surround the synagogue and to fire at anyone who attempted to escape. After the war he became a police instructor in Schleswig-Holstein and was then transferred to the Kriminalpolizei at Bergheim / Erft (NRW)[58]. Tried by the Court of Wuppertal, he was acquitted after the trial with a ruling of March 12, 1968.

HERWEG, Josef: born in Urbach near Cologne, on February 7, 1914. Polizeiobermeister. Leader of the first platoon of the 3 / 309, he took part with his men in cordoning off the burning synagogue[59]. Tried by the Court of Wuppertal, the sentence imposed on him on March 12, 1968 was remitted.

THOMAS, Wilhelm: born in Cologne on December 4, 1914. Polizeimeister. Leader of the machine-gun section of the 3 / 309, he took part with his men in the cordoning off of the burning synagogue[60].Tried by the Court of Wuppertal, he was acquitted at the end of the trial with a ruling of March 12, 1968.

RONDHOLZ, Friedrich: born in Neu-Isenburg, near Darmstadt, on October 22, 1913. He joined the police in 1934 and was assigned to the Polizeiverwaltung in Cologne in 1935. Sergeant. Transferred to the Polizei-Bataillon 309 just before *Barbarossa*, he was a member of the fourth platoon of the 1 / 309. At the massacre in Bialystok, during a road patrol by his platoon, he proceeded, "intentionally and with premeditation (*vorsätzlich und mit Überlegung*)" and without any order from his superior, Ltn. Gorgs, to execute with shots to the head four unarmed Russian prisoners of war who had already surrendered and were kept standing with their faces to the wall and their hands up: he was found guilty of this crime by the court of Wuppertal. For the Bialystok *operation* he was decorated with the Cl. II Iron Cross by Gen.Ltn. Johann Pflugbeil on July 11, 1941. A prisoner of war, he was released by the British in 1946 and was readmitted to the police in 1947 at the rank of Polizeiobermeister. He was suspended from duty in 1965 after investigation by the public prosecutor[61]. Sentenced to life imprisonment for the murder of four Russian prisoners and as an accessory in 13 other murders, when the Bundesgerichtshof reviewed his case, his sentence was commuted to four years because of the "special state of emotional arousal (*einen Gewissen Erregungszustand*)" provoked in him by the previous discovery of some killed and maimed German soldiers, which caused him to seek revenge on prisoners captured[62].

SCHAFFRAT, Wilhelm: born in Beggendorf, near Aachen, on October 11, 1912. After being rejected by the SS in 1940 for physical reasons, he was assigned to Polizei-Bataillon 309 and then admitted to the Waffen-SS in January 1943 following the lowering of enlistment standards. During the roundup in Bialystok he took five Jews, one by one, to his comrade Forern, for him to kill them individually. For the Bialystok *operation* he was decorated with the Iron Cross by Gen.Ltn. Johann Pflugbeil on July 11, 1941. A prisoner of war, he was released in the summer of 1947. In the indictment presented by the public prosecutor in Dortmund, he was accused of deliberately perpetrating murderous actions for petty reasons[63]. He was found guilty of ten murders and sentenced to life imprisonment. On appeal, his sentence was commuted to six years in prison.

1.6 PARADIGMS AND ARCHETYPES

The massacre at Bialystok of June 27, 1941 is a particularly famous, and heinous, criminal event referred to in numerous articles and studies: among these, it is worth mentioning the chapter dedicated to it by Heiner Lichtenstein in his book *Himmlers grüne Helfer*, the essay by Michael Okroy "*Man will unserem Bataillon was tun ....*". Der Wuppertaler Bialystok-Proze– 1967/68, and also the relevant section in Goldhagen's controversial work *Hitler's Willing Executioners*[64]

Aside from its tragic notoriety, the *historical dynamics* that lay behind the massacre are still in part confused: that is to say, it is not yet clear whether it was an intentional and planned massacre, and if planned at what level of command, or if it was the result of an *improvised* action that came from below and may have escaped the control of its perpetrators. We will try in this section to suggest some interpretations related to ideology, causes, to intentional processes, and to the general environment and personal ideas to which the men of Polizei-Bataillon 309 were exposed. In this way we shall seek to demonstrate how the *experience of Bialystok* was not so much the result of a laboratory project, but rather a relatively random combination of different elements, among which should also be included the psychosocial dynamics we mentioned at the beginning. It must be pointed out first of all that this massacre was the first perpetrated by a police battalion on the Russian front. While many others would follow which were far more devastating in magnitude, the Bialystok massacre marked, so to speak, a fixed point relative to the involvement of the Ordnungspolizei in the Jewish genocide. In terms of number of victims, manner of execution, and the motivations given by the executors, Bialystok was an archetype, a kind of model for subsequent massacres, which served to demonstrate the genocidal flexibility of the Police units when faced with particularly cruel and large-scale events, well beyond the encouraging experiments in Poland in the fall of 1939[65]. The fact that by that time the ideological and racial question relating to Judaism in Germany was firmly established in the popular imagination – and consequently in the units that came from the people – was graphically demonstrated by the anti-Semitic inebriation that befell Polizei-Bataillon 309 on that day, June 27, 1941, well before any operational decision on the Final Solution had been reached. This inebriation marked a further lowering of the collective moral threshold and placed in the hands of the planners of the genocide a powerful new tool of destruction – the police battalions – which up until then had only been potential.

From this point of view the question of ideology,

stratified by years of cultural pseudo-education through second-rate but effective means, including the periodical *Der Stürmer*, films such as *Jud Süss* and magazines such as *Die Deutsche Polizei*, certainly had an important role in fostering the cultural climate in which the events of Bialystok could take place. At the same time, however, one cannot fail to note that this ideological tendency, in the specific case of Bialystok, came from below, that is to say, from the lower levels of an anonymous police battalion and was not dropped from the top management level by those real *laboratory products* known as the Einsatzgruppen. In this sense, it is as if the ordinary policemen had become aware of the need to reflect subjectively as a unit – understood as a micro-social nucleus – the crude macro-social ideological dynamics that collectively permeated the German people. This is a fact that can be read as a resounding success for the regime: being able to contanimate large sections of the population, who now responded to the ideological call almost of their own initiative, in the form of their representatives in uniform. After which, given the coarse crudeness of the ideological tools used at those levels, the brutal suitability of the battalion's response in action is no surprise: a medieval blaze, alcoholic stupefaction, and the disgraceful attitude of many of the officers and ordinary policemen.

Aside from micro-ideological factors, further dynamics can however be discerned in the Bialystok massacre which suggest a *sudden* event organized at lower levels of the hierarchy, rather than according to an *a priori* pattern. These dynamics are more similar to those of a pogrom – like those which were perpetrated a few days later in Jedwabne and Radzilow – than the massacres managed and organized on an almost *industrial* scale, like those of Babi Yar and Rumbula. We are speaking here of the dovetailing of personal responsibility and implied intentionality contained in the general directives the battalion received on the eve of *Barbarossa*, which transformed the overall picture into a game of Chinese shadows: visible in outline, but essentially evanescent in substance.

What appears certain is that, although the objective responsibility for the massacre clearly lies with many of the figures at the scene – from divisional commander Pflugbeil, who did nothing to prevent it, up to platoon leaders of the battalion working on the ground – it is nonetheless more difficult to attribute subjective responsibility. It is not entirely clear when and by whom the order was actually issued to proceed with the execution of Jews gathered in the square and to set fire to the synagogue. In reply to the objections of a Wehrmacht captain faced with the tragedy going on before him, Behrens spoke – probably falsely – of orders from above, while at an investigation – apparently superficial and without consequences for the perpetrators – initiated by the 221st Sicherungs-Division into the causes that led to the uncontrolled spread of the fire, all the officers of the battalion responded – with obvious hypocrisy – *that they knew nothing about it.* Weis, in his mystifying report, stated that the synagogue fire was caused by the accidental explosion of an anti-tank missile, thus declining any personal responsibility[66]. Finally, for obvious propaganda reasons, a journal for German troops at the front attributed the event to an air raid. In the midst of this carousel of self-absolving interpretations, it now seems certain that no order was ever issued by the Wehrmacht command – under whose authority the battalion formally stood – for the arrest and execution of the Jews of Bialystok. For this reason, Weis would have been the one to order the searching of the Jewish quarter on the basis of his own ideological views and the general orders received before *Barbarossa*, while the final decision about the fate of the prisoners was probably left in the hands of his two company commanders, who from the beginning of the *action* must have opted for an implicit genocide solution, without considering alternatives other than a massacre[67]. In other words, there was no *explicit and formal* order issued *from above*, but what the police were supposed to do, or what was expected of them, would have been understood[68]. From this perspective, the Bialystok massacre was the result of the *personal initiative* of Behrens and Buchs, endorsed by Weis, who in an environment that was becoming more and more chaotic and out of control – and finding himself barely in control of his own actions as he was under the effects of alcohol – would have left a *free hand* to his two subordinates. At the same time, the genocide solution adopted by the two company commanders would not have been unexpected, given the consciousness, widespread among the members of the battalion, about the fate that awaited the Jews in the war[69]. It is equally likely that the lack of explicit orders was the cause of this operational anarchy that swept through the battalion from commander down to the last policemen, who found themselves having to *improvise* in their pursuit of their genocidal inclinations. In utter confusion, reinforced by the guilty inaction and indifference of those who, like General Pflugbeil and his officers, would have been in a position to intervene to put an end to the slaughter[70], it is actually quite difficult to find any trace of a planned massacre: on the contrary, there seems to have been a rather clear desire on the part of Behrens and Buchs to put into effect, in their most extreme form – encouraged and legitimized by Weis, that is, hindered neither by him nor others – the implications contained in a series of directives that had reached the battalion in the days before the start of *Barbarossa*. In particular, before June 22 the personnel of the battalion received both the *Kommissarbefehl*, relative to the killing of all captured Soviet political commissars, and the so-called *Erlass Barbarossa*, which approved "collective reprisals against civilians (*kollektive Gewaltmassnahmen*)" and offered a guarantee of impunity for those who perpetrated them. These were accompanied by the observations Weis made to his officers about the beginning of the war against Judaism and the Jews, who were to be eliminated without exception, regardless of age and sex[71]. To these directives were added the afore-mentioned orders issued by Gen.Ltn. Pflugbeil on June 1941: Moreover, in the hours before their entry into Bialystok, the bodies of 25 soldiers that had been tortured and mutilated – probably by the retreating Soviet soldiers – had been discovered by men of the 1 / 309 and 3 / 309 companies[72]. This horrific episode may have helped to strengthen – by means of a specious and distorted interpretation of the relationship between the event and those responsible for it – the genocidal frenzy of the perpetrators of the Bialystok massacre. That the Bialystok massacre was carried out using improvised methods also seems confirmed by the fact that no transport plans for taking the victims out of the town had been prepared, nor were there plans for a site to keep them even temporarily[73], as well as the total absence – despite the hot weather – of any preventive measures designed to stop the fire from spreading. As a matter of fact, the synagogue fire spread *beyond the safety limit* and even jeopardized the battalion's motor fleet, as well as the actual command of the 221st Sicherungs-Division. It appears, from this point of view, that the safety limit was interpreted by many of the policemen somewhat flexibly, to say the least. According to the testimony of a member of the battalion, given to the ZStL, some of his fellow soldiers prevented local volunteers – alarmed by the fire spreading to the wooden houses of the Jewish quarter – from helping to put out the fire, seen not so much as a worrisome *side effect*, but as a *welcome setback* to be greeted with satisfied comments, in that it got rid of a few more "deutschfeindliche"[74]. In such a context of automatic ideological reflexes, implied intentionality, personal feelings and a situation that was out of control, it is quite possible, therefore, that the men of Polizei-Bataillon 309 may have felt effectively in possession of a large degree of autonomy and discretion in interpreting the rather vague orders they had received, without the need for further requests or written and formal orders. In this sense, if we want a conclusive summary, we could speak of the Bialystok massacre as the seemingly oxymoronic product of induced spontaneity, which however, made clear the potential of emotional distance between perpetrators and victims. This potential could be expanded appropriately and projected into a strategic systematic dimension in which the act of genocide was no longer the result of chance but of a wide-ranging project. Accordingly, what in the case of Bialystok might appear as a momentary emotional withdrawal on the part of the perpetrators, basically the result of local events, came to be the archetypal paradigm of a destructive model; not so much because of the way in which these destructive events were later replicated, but rather in terms of the emotional dynamics and in particular the complete lack of empathy between hunters and *prey*, seen only as dehumanized and harmful elements to be neutralized once and for all, by means of the social prophylaxis of genocide[75].

1.7 DEMIGODS OF DEATH

Even given the diversity of interpretations, the common factor in the literature relating to the events of Bialystok on 27 June 1941 is the fact that no *formal and explicit* order was issued regarding the treatment of Jews captured during the raid. After that, in both cases – either if the massacre is to be attributed to the decision of a single commander (Weis) who had "properly understood and anticipated the wishes of the Führer"[76] or if the only question the executioners *might* have asked themselves regarded the technical aspects of the massacre (burning, shooting or otherwise) and not whether it was right or wrong[77] – what is certain is that it was a hellish slaughter. A slaughter perpetrated with especially brutal methods, and this despite there having been no provocative or hostile act directed against the battalion by the Jewish population; nor were any weapons or other illegal material found in the Jews' looted homes[78]. It is probable, therefore, that a deadly chain of causes and events set off the spiral of genocide, perhaps even beyond what might have been the perpetrators' original intentions, and that the orgy of violence during the raid ended up fuelling itself, right up to its tragic epilogue – an epilogue that at that point would even have been inevitable. That is to say, at some point in the early afternoon of June 27, 1941, intentionally or not, the men of Polizei-Bataillon 309 crossed a moral threshold, entering an area where the destructive tendency became uncontrollable. There is, indeed, something aberrant, degenerate about the way the massacre was carried out. An explosion of idolatrous and savage violence, sublimated in the flames of the blaze. This was not only a purifying conflagration, the product of minds blinded by anti-Semitism – as Goldhagen writes[79] – but rather something like an ancestral reflection, a recourse to fire as a ready source of destructive power, by a tribal horde engaged in a sacrilegious ritual of death[80]. In this act of genocide, one notes something deeper, something that goes beyond the *simple* application of an ideological theorem or racial prejudice, something that has its roots in the very essence of post-Neolithic civilization: namely the *exercise of power* as such, which becomes absolute through unlimited, pseudo-divine control over men and things[81]. During those long hours of complete moral degeneration, the policemen from Cologne elected themselves to the role of demi-gods, dispensers of death. Aside from the simple dominance of certain ideological schemas, something else stopped working: social rules and conditioning, the sense of individual and collective ethics, civil education, the vision of good and evil: none of this had meaning any more, and probably it could not have had meaning, for the new demi-gods, narcissistic and temperamental creators of their own amoral dimension, situated outside common sense and guided only by the rule of caprice[82]. From this point of view it can thus seem *almost reductive* to press within the boundaries of anti-Semitism – which is at any rate the result of a long, albeit dark, rational cultural process – an event that seems to be a sublimation of ancestral violence, the exercise of unlimited and inhuman destructive ferocity. An event that truly showed a return to the heart of darkness, to idolatry imposed by the cruel demigods of death through the levy of the wild fire of the Holocaust, from whose ashes was meant to rise a new social order in a new historic civilization – the Thousand Year Reich, which in those days of 1941 was delivered up to the judgment of History, erecting its ramparts above a necropolis of burnt bones and shattered buildings.

ENDNOTES

1 Sicherungs-Regiment 2. Proposal to award the Iron Cross I Class to Major Ernst Weis, 2.7.1941: Weis "Ernst, Stettin 20.6.1894, Major der Schutzpolizei, Pol.-Btl. 309, e.K.I des Weltkrieges. Major Weis hat am 26 und 27.6.1941 persönlich an Ort und Stelle seine Kompanien zur Säuberung der Waldstücke beiderseits der Strasse Sokoly-Bialystok und bei der Säuberung des Waldes südlich der Stadt und in derselben eingesetzt und unermüdlich im feindlichen Heckenschützenfeuer eingegriffen. Er persönlich und seine Bataillon waren stets hilfsbereit zur Stelle. Die Säuberungsaktion seines Btl. hat dazu beigetragen, dass Stadt und Umgebung in verhaeltnismässig kurzer Zeit befriedet wurde. Er ist der Auszeichnung würdig. gez. Ronicke, Oberst und Rgts.-Kdr." Mallmann/Riess/Pyta, p. 74, HIS, p. 594.

2 Of the two photos we have of this episode – one a mirror image of the other – the first is reproduced in Mallmann/ Riess/Pyta, p. 76 and the second, the one described here, belongs to a private collection.

3 Bender, p. 19.

4 Okroy, p. 301.

5 Bender, pp. 15-16. The pogrom was apparently planned and carried out by a group of Russian extremists belonging to the Hundred Blacks organization, with the support of the police and units of the Czarist army and went on for three days, during which time there were also clashes between the pogromists and groups of Jews, probably Bundists. Subsequently, the local Russian authorities tried to place the blame on the Polish population, who had in fact kept out of the affair.

6 The accusation levelled by the Polish military commander who entered Bialystok after the retreat of the Bolshevik units proved to be unfounded; however, it helped fuel the popular idea of "Judeo-Communism" (Żydokomuna)

7 Bender, p.59.

8 The situation in the former Polish territories annexed to SRFS Ukraine – Galicia in particular – was different. Here, due to a combination of other factors, anti-Semitism persisted as an underlying but ever-present phenomenon.

9 Bender Bialystok, p. 189.

10 Lichtenstein, p. 73. Indictment by the Dortmund public prosecutor's office. StAwDo, Anklageschrift, May 8, 1967.

11 Mallmann/Riess/Pyta, p. 70: "Pol.Batl. 309 wird Sich.Rgt. 2 für Säuberung der Stadt von russischen Versprengten und deutschfeindlicher Bevölkerung und zur Aufrechterhaltung der Ruhe, Sicherheit und Ordnung innerhalb der Stadt Bialystok unterstellt». Befehl Sich.Div.221/Ia v. 27.6.1941, BA-MA, RH 26-221/12b; vgl. PB 309 an 1. und 2.Komp. v. 27.6.1941, BAB, R 20/58.

12 The battalion had been founded on 19 September 1940, converted from a training unit, the Polizei-Ausbildungs-Bataillon A "Köln". Sonderbefehl nr. 106 Kdo d.Schupo Köln vom 19/9/1940.

13 According to the testimony of Ltn. Heinrich Schneider, the battalion was shown the Jud Süss, the infamous anti-Semitic film, all the rage for propaganda purposes at the time. Mallmann/Riess/Pyta, p. 71, Westermann, pp. 175, 284.

14 See, for example, the motivations behind the massacres at Brest Litovsk and Kamenec Podolski, in chapters two and four of this book.

15 A circular issued by the Ic office of the 221st Sicherungs-Division on June 19, 1941, states: "The troops of the Red Army are opposed to us not only from a military standpoint, but also as political enemies. According to the Judeo-Bolshevik doctrine, they will not use only military methods. The men must be prepared for this [and] if necessary, resort to drastic measures, with appropriate harshness and ruthlessness – also in regard of the enemy population." Westermann,p. 174, original German text in Mallmann / Riess / Pyta, pp. 70, 178.

16 Bender, p. 90, Okroy, p. 301, Klemp Osteuropa, p. 279, Lichtenstein, p. 74. Indictment by the Dortmund public prosecutor's office, StAwDo, Anklageschrift, May 8, 1967.

17 Klemp Ermittelt, p. 262, Klemp Osteuropa, p. 279, Lichtenstein, p. 74. Indictment by the Dortmund public prosecutor's office, StAwDo, Anklageschrift, May 8, 1967.

18 Westermann, p. 175.

19 Kemp Ermittelt, p. 263, Bender p. 91.

20 Bender, p. 31

21 *Ibid.* pp. 91, 315, Curilla, p. 515.

22 Klemp Ermittlet, p. 263, Curilla, pp. 512-513, Goldhagen, p. 201, Bender, p. 91.

23 Goldhagen, p. 201. The final report of Polizei-Bataillon 309 dated 1 July, refers to 230 bodies picked up on the streets. Curilla, p. 518, BA-MA, Film S 57076, Gefechtsbericht des Pol.Bat. 309.

24 Klemp Ermittlet, p. 263, Curilla, p. 513.

25 *Ibid.,* p. 263, *ibid.,* p. 514, Goldhagen, p. 201, Bender, p. 91. In addition to being morally reprehensible, this disgraceful attitude on the part of a subordinate before his superior has to be regarded as intolerable at the very least from the point of view of military discipline – a concept, that ought to be uppermost in the mind of any good officer, which Pflugbeil clearly was not.

26 Klemp Ermittlet. p. 263, Curilla, p. 514.

27 Klemp Ermittlet, p. 263, Mallmann/Riess/Pyta, p. 72. Testimony of Elias Z., a survivor, given on July 5, 1966 to the Dortmund public prosecutor's office.

28 Curilla, p. 514, Lichtenstein Wuppertaler, p. 625, Lichtenstein, p. 74. Indictment by the Dortmund public prosecutor's office, StAwDo, Anklageschrift, May 8, 1967.

29 Bender Bialystok, p. 189.

30 The exact number of Jews inside the synagogue varies according to the sources. According to what was established in the sentence at the first trial in Wuppertal against Buchs and the others, there were 700 victims (800 according to the indictment); according to the estimates obtained during the second trial in Wuppertal against Buchs and Schaffrat, the number was 500.

31 Curilla, p. 515, Bender, p. 92, Okroy, p. 302. Lichtenstein, p. 74. Indictment by the Dortmund public prosecutor's office, StAwDo, Anklageschrift, May 8, 1967.

32 Klemp Ermittelt, pp. 263-264.

33 Goldhagen, p. 203.

34 Curilla, p. 516.

35 Bender, p. 92.

36 Mallmann/Riess/Pyta, p. 73.

37 Lichtenstein, p. 81.

38 Curilla, p. 517.

39 *Ibid.*

40 Klemp Ermittelt, p. 264, Curilla, p. 517.

41 Lichtenstein Wuppertaler, p. 622.

42 See Chapter 5.

43 The statute of limitations, which came into force 15 years after the end of the war, covered murder, grievous bodily harm resulting in death and accessory to murder (Totschlag, Körperverletzung mit Todesfolge und Beihilfe zum Mord). Okroy, p. 308.

44 Klemp Ermittelt, p. 267, Klemp Osteuropa, p. 279.

45 The original 23 accused were reduced to 14 who were put on trial, while charges against a further 162 were dropped.

46 Lichtenstein, pp. 69-72, Lichtenstein Wuppertaler, p. 620.

47 Okroy, p. 302.

48 Excerpts from the testimonies the cross-examination by the president of the court Simgen, have been published in Lichtenstein Wuppertaler, pp 662 ff.

49 Curilla p. 510, Klemp Ermittelt, p. 267, Okroy, p.302.

50 Okroy, p. 302, Lichtenstein pp. 88 and ff. Sentence by the court of Wuppertal. LG Wuppertal, 12 Ks 1/67, March 12, 1968.

51 Okroy, p. 317. LG Wuppertal, 12 Ks 14/71, May 24, 1973.

52 Okroy, p. 308, Klempr Ermittlet, p. 262.

53 El Pais, December 7, 2009.

54 Goldhagen, p. 202, Curilla, p. 514.

55 Klemp Ermittlet, p. 265, Lichtenstein, pp. 70-71. Indictment by the Dortmund public prosecutor's office, StAwDo, Anklageschrift, May 8, 1967.

56 Klemp Ermittelt, p. 265, Lichtenstein, pp. 70-71. Indictment by the Dortmund public prosecutor's office, StAwDo, Anklageschrift, May 8, 1967.

57 Klemp Ermittelt, p. 263, Curilla, p. 513, Okroy, pp. 312-313, Lichtenstein, pp. 69-70, 75. Indictment by the Dortmund public prosecutor's office, StAwDo, Anklageschrift, May 8, 1967.

58 Klemp Ermittelt, p. 265, Lichtenstein, pp. 72, 77. Indictment by the Dortmund public prosecutor's office, StAwDo, Anklageschrift, May 8, 1967.

59 Lichtenstein, pp. 72, 77. Indictment by the Dortmund public prosecutor's office, StAwDo, Anklageschrift, May 8, 1967

60 *Ibid.* pp 72, 77, Indictment by the Dortmund public prosecutor's office, StAwDo, Anklageschrift, May 8, 1967.

61 *Ibid.* pp. 72, 76.

62 *Ibid.* pp. 90-91. Sentence passed by the Court of Wuppertal. LG Wuppertal 12 Ks 1/67, March 12, 1968.

63 Mallmann/Riess/ Pyta, p. 72. Testimony by Alfons S. Lichtenstein, p. 70. Indictment by the Dortmund public prosecutor's office, StAwDo, Anklageschrift, May 8, 1967.

64 See the bibliography for this chapter.

65 Among these must be mentioned the massacre at Ostrow Mazowiecka on 11 November 1939, during which 364 Jews were shot in retaliation by a unit of Polizei-Bataillon 11, as well as the numerous executions carried out by Polizei-Bataillon 61 or by police units subordinate to the EG zbV of Woyrsch in the autumn of 1939. In addition, of course, there were also the massacres whose victims were Poles.

66 Curilla, p. 518.

67 Klemp Ermittelt, p. 263, Okroy, p. 302. In his testimony Buchs stated that there was no explicit order to massacre the Jews in Bialystok, but only general instructions whose implicit meaning was clear to everyone. Klemp Osteuropa, p. 280.

68 Klemp Ermittlet, p. 263, Klemp Osteuropa, p. 280.

69 Lichtenstein Wuppertaler, p. 622.

70 Pflugbeil could have intervened at any moment. For example, he could have agreed to the requests of the two Jews on their knees before him and who were humiliated, or during the shootings carried out in the park in front of the government building which housed the command of the

221st Sicherungs-Division, hit by ricocheting bullets that even threatened to burst through the windows. Pflugbeil reacted to this inconvenience by ordering the firing squad to move further into the park. The trial at Wuppertal was unable to gain a clear picture of the role played by the units of the 221st Sich.-Div. According to the testimony of a policeman, some Wehrmacht soldiers shot tracer bullets on to the petrol, which contributed to setting off the fire. Klemp Ermittelt, p. 264, Klemp Osteuropa, p. 281.

71 Browning, p. 13, also Okroy, p. 301.

72 Curilla, p. 151, LG Wuppertal II 12 Ks 14/71, 24 May 1973 against Buchs and Schaffrat, p. 20, LG Darmstadt. 2 Ks 1/75, 25 February against Rondholz, p. 21.

73 Klemp Ermittelt, p. 263, Klemp Osteuropa, p. 280.

74 Goldhagen, pp. 203, 545. One of the policemen exclaimed: "Let it burn, it's a nice little fire", while another expressed his appreciation of the spectacle with the words: "Splendid, the entire city should burn down."

75 On the concept of momentary or chronic "emotional withdrawal" and the dehumanization of the enemy, see Erich Fromm, The Anatomy of Human Destructiveness, pp. 162-163.

76 Browning, p. 14.

77 Goldhagen, p. 202.

78 Testimony given by policeman Hubert H., Mallmann/Riess/Pyta, p. 72.

79 Goldhagen, pp. 202-203.

80 On the concept of tribalism in relation to the police battalions, see § 5.6, Closed communities and microdynamics.

81 Cf. Erich Fromm, The Anatomy of Human Destructiveness, pp. 210-211, which quotes the inscription composed by the Assyrian King on the destruction of Babylon: "The city and its houses, from its foundation to its top, I destroyed, I burned with fire. The wall and the outer wall, temples and gods, temple towers of bricks and earth, as many as they were, I razed and dumped them into the Arakhtu Canal. Through the midst of that city I dug canals, I flooded its site with water, and the very foundations thereof I destroyed. I made its destruction more complete than that by a flood."

82 Among the caprices of the demigods must also be counted the power of grace, to be dispensed parsimoniously and at one's own discretion. As in the case of the Jewish father of three children who begged Buchs to spare their lives. In this case, Buchs, possibly pleased with this implicit recognition of his omnipotence, granted the request, leaving the man free to go, one imagines with a wave of the hand and a slight nod.

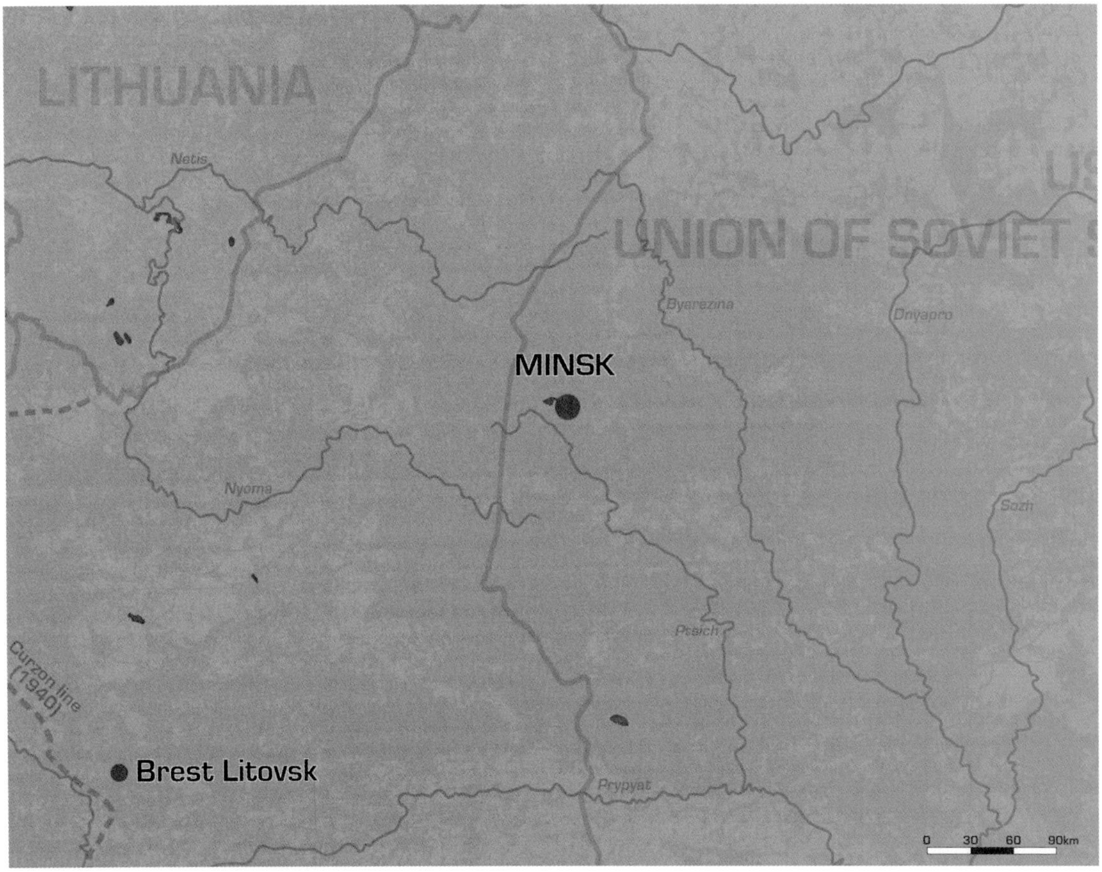
LITHUANIA
Netis
UNION OF SOVIET
Byarezina
Dnyapro
MINSK
Nyoma
Sozh
Psich
Curzon line (1940)
Brest Litovsk
Prypyat
0 30 60 90km

CHAPTER TWO

"BESONDERS SCHWERE EINSÄTZE BEVORSTÄNDEN"

GENOCIDAL DEBUT FOR POLIZEI-BATAILLON 307 BREST LITOVSK, JULY 13, 1941

Nach meinen eigenen Gedanken, im Zusammenhang mit meinen damaligen Handeln befragt, muss ich ganz offen erklären, dass die Handlungsweise jedes einzelnen von uns der eines Mörders gleichkommt.

Heinrich Meier, Polizei-Bataillon 307[1]

Her name was Sheine Feige Janowich and she was a Jew. She was born in Brest Litovsk in 1886 and in Brest Litovsk she met her death 55 years later.

No picture is left of her, no one is left to remember her voice, only a short note, jotted on a document kept in the archives of Yad Vashem[2].

But we do know the circumstances leading to her death: hers and that of 4,000 more Jews, that day, in Brest Litovsk, on July 13, 1941.

2.1 POLICE AND POLICY

A former Tsarist frontier fortress at the confluence of the rivers Bug and Mukhavets, the city of Brest Litovsk fell into German hands in the hours following the start of *Barbarossa*, upon the action of the Wehrmacht's 45th Infantry Division and consequent withdrawal of the Soviet garrison in the fortified town built on the river islands.

Of the approximately 50,000 residents recorded by the Polish census of 1931, over 21,000 formed a Hasadic Jewish community of ancient traditions devoted to trade and craft [3], dating from the mid-fourteenth century. As a result of historical events related to the partition of Poland this community was increased further, probably in proportion to the total population of the city, which in September 1939 had come close to 60,000 dwellers.

All of them, but especially *briskers* Jews, lived with apprehension of the entrance into the city, between June 22 and 23, 1941, of the first German troops, soon followed by Einsatzkommando 7b led by SS-Sturmbannführer Günther Rausch, who, in the short period of his stay in Brest, from 26 to 28 June, found the time to uphold several "unspecified police measures *(sicherheitspolizeiliche Maßnhmen)*»[4].

In the days following, with the battle still raging in the area of the fortress[5], the city was also reached by a battalion of police attached, along with two other similar units, to a regimental group called Polizei-Regiment "Mitte", that answered orders directly from HSSPF Erich von dem Bach[6].

It was Polizei-Bataillon 307, established on October 3, 1940 in Lübeck, from a training unit already used for several months in Poland, in the Biala Podlaska area, where, among other tasks, it had become familiar with practices of "racism, ethnic cleansing, land reform on a racial basis, segregation of Jews and forced labor"[7]: all, of course, proportionate to 1940 levels which, although already quite high in terms of virulence, were not yet close to those tragically degenerated into in the catastrophic post-*Barbarossa* massacres[8].

The battalion was organized into three companies under the command of Maj. Theodor Stahr, with Oltn. Hans-Albert Salzinger as battalion adjutant and commander of 3/307. We also have the names of some of the other officers, including commander of 1/307, HPTM. Grube, of 2/307, Oltn. Siegfried Klocker and two platoon commanders: Ltn. Friedrich Niehoff (1/307) and Ltn. Max Kayser (of 3/307)[9].

We do not know the level of ideological enthusiasm shown by the battalion staff, formed by men born between 1909 and 1912, but only that of some officers, five of whom were also SS members (the three division commanders and two of the platoon leaders)[10]. It must be said, to that effect, that the likely membership to the NSDAP of much of the enlisted personnel, ranking or not, must be regarded only as an indicator of relative significance in terms of political loyalty. Actually joining the party – *a mass organization* – did not necessarily mean sharing ideology and objectives, but could in many cases conceal, especially among older age groups, an opportunistic choice dictated by the need to adapt to the times and bring to one's own advantage the social benefits deriving from the close alignment with the dominant thought, and also by the necessity to avoid suspicious attention that inevitably was reserved to ideologically *non-compliant* subjects.

The case of police officers who were members of the SS, of course, should be looked upon under a different perspective because this was an *elitist organization* whose membership implied a careful selection and a high degree of ideological loyalty. However, we only know that a small part of the battalions' officers belonged to the SS, while there is no such data available about the battalion's staff.

Consequently, beyond the clues that being part of the *300 Series* imply, there is insufficient evidence to deem Polizei-Bataillon 307 as particularly ideological or unequivocally linked to the Nazi doctrine[11]. In fact, having been constituted mainly through the mobilization of Wachtmeister personnel – i.e. reservists in their thirties born around 1910, with a cultural upbringing of the Weimar era and called into service in late autumn 1939 – these *Series 300* battalions cannot be simplistically ascribed to any ideological élite, but at most to an area generally attributable to the radical right and not necessarily National Socialist[12]. What we have here is a group of men in their full adulthood, advocating an ideal of strict order and consequently disciplined, inclined to be faithful not so much to a precise party theory, but rather to a rigidly conservative, conformist and reassuring idea of State. In their role as servants of the State, the obedience of these men was primarily for the State itself and, by extension, for the government that represented it. That said, the fact that in that historical phase the leaders of the regime had promoted a lucid, logical and insane desire to amalgamate State, government and party into one ideological and social entity with obvious repercussions on the role of the Ordnungspolizei and its positioning in relation to the National Socialist doctrine. This is hardly surprising as this had been a major goal of the Nazi totalitarian system from the beginning. In that respect, the common Ordnungspolizei – intrinsically an entity of the State of a non-political nature – certainly ended up choking in the deadly embrace of the iron political will of the regime, through a long series of ethical compromises signed in the name of a shared (in)morality. This does not mean, however, that the work of indoctrination carried out from April 1937 had been completed, or that it had proved so effective as to make the Ordnungspolizei a monolithic *ideological phalanx*: what is certain is that the outbreak of the conflict caught the Ordnungspolizei in a phase of transition, and that Himmler's subsequent efforts to strengthen the ideological training clashed with the compelling and increasingly stringent operational needs of the units[13]. And the fact that the Ordnungspolizei were still in midstream in the imminence of the conflict, is confirmed by a sentence by Daluege, spoken on September 15, 1938, less than a year before the invasion of Poland: "*It will be only a matter of time* before the entire police force unites in a permanent structure with the SS"[my emphasis – author's note][14].

In the case of police battalions, connivance with the regime was therefore the poisoned fruit of a regressive path, along which the ideological theorems widespread in Nazified German society – including State anti-Semitism – remained in the background, behind a complex mosaic of *social algorithms* (situational mechanisms, intergroup relations, stereotyping of *the other*, micro-dynamics within the units, personal interpretations, etc..), which played a considerably significant role in the relation between police battalions and the Jewish genocide, which is illustrated in some of the next paragraphs.

2.2 IN THE LAND OF MILK AND HONEY

Coming from Biala Podlaska, just beyond the border of the River Bug, Polizei-Bataillon 307 had been subordinated directly to von dem Bach's HSSPF through the *Stab* of Max Montua's Polizei-Regiment "Mitte" in view of Barbarossa, thus it did not formally depend on any Wehrmacht command, except for contingent and temporary tactical requirements. In that role it made its entry into Brest Litovsk between July 2 and 3, 1941[15] and for a few days it engaged in security activities, during which different executions of alleged spies, snipers, looters, political commissars and some women were perpetrated[16]. In this phase, the battalion was temporarily attached as reinforcement to 221. Sicherungs-Division[17].

In fact, the actual genocidal debut for Polizei-Bataillon 307 occurred in the week between July 6 and 13, 1941, or, more likely, on Sunday, 13[18], and took the form of a meticulously planned and executed slaughter, completely different from the Bialystok massacre of June 27, which had been so chaotic and improvised. In other words, all those episodes of *criminal fantasy* that had made the Bialystok massacre so disorganized did not reoccur in Brest, where everything went according to the plan, in more stages, precisely and orderly, accompanied by preventive and false reassurance to the Jews about the willingness of Germany to transfer all detainees – fit men aged between 16 and 60 – to work in Germany[19].

Under this plan the city was divided into sectors, each of which was assigned to one of the companies and combed in succession, with each platoon deployed along a road and organized into two teams in charge of searching the homes located to the right or the left.

The action, which lasted for several days, usually began between seven and eight in the morning, the Jews being forced to leave their homes and sent under escort, with all their luggage, up to a single collection point near the central prison, where they were then sorted into groups, in the courtyards in front of the lodgings of the individual companies. Then, approximately around noon and after handing their luggage to the Germans – *who would later send them to the workplace* – the unsuspecting Jews were boarded onto trucks leaving for the execution spot[20]. With this system, over 4,000 victims could be conducted to an orderly death within two or three days[21], with breaks between one shooting and the other, frequent rotation of the firing squad personnel, suspension of activities to allow the policemen to eat their rations, and the strawberries with milk and other goodies which were also distributed[22]: a particular that indicates a certain degree of attention by the battalion commanders to the moral and material welfare of their men, so scrupulously committed to perpetrate a bloody carnage. And this episode appears so tragicomically grotesque in how it accompanied the Jews of Brest Litovsk to their fate of death, almost in a kind of blasphemous biblical paraphrase: "Go and gather the elders of Israel and say to them, The Lord God of your fathers came to me saying: I raise you from affliction of Egypt, and will bring you up [...] in a land flowing with milk and honey"[23].

In any case, beyond the more or less ordered and *rational* procedures of its execution, the slaughter quickly assumed brutal connotations. The Jews were kicked and beaten on their way to the pits, while the firing squads, apparently formed only by volunteers, quickly started to lose the accuracy of their shots, so that an ever-increasing number of Jews, even only slightly wounded, ended up falling into the pit on top of those who already had been shot, often fainting and ending up being *buried alive* by the next group of victims. The most unfortunate ones languished in slow agony, many of them did not die from the wounds they received but were suffocated by the bodies of the slain, after many hours if not days.

According to the memories of at least two police officers, after a day of shootings one could distinctly hear the cries for help from the wounded left in the pit, which continued to rise even after the second day of shootings. Only in some cases the wounded received the coup de grace[24]. In the face of such atrocities there was no apparent reaction of enthusiasm from the policemen, but neither of evident rejection. No one would refuse to perform his duties, nor would claim to have done so in the testimonies that these men gave before the ZStL twenty years later. There are not even reports of cases of *post traumatic stress* among the perpetrators for whom, let's remember it, this was the their first mass genocide action[25]. Simply, at least according to available data, Polizei-Bataillon 307 officers would experience the event in a state of seemingly *hypnotic trance*[26], thus managing to overcome with surprising ease the impact of the horror. *Ordinary men*, probably beyond all expectations, had become *willing executioners*.

We will now look at some details of the involvement of individual companies in the bloodshed.

2.2.1 – 1/POLIZEI-BATAILLON 307

Between 07:00 and 08:00 hours, while part of the company proceeded in the cordoning of the sector assigned, the staff of one of the platoon stormed one house after the other, rounding up Jews and gathering them, with their luggage, in the middle of the road. After that, in groups of 50 and unaware of their fate, the victims were escorted up to a square near the prison, where they remained awaiting the end of the raid. At about noon, while half of the company was called back to their quarters, presumably to eat their rations, the other half was left to guard the Jews until, in the early afternoon, the trucks arrived.

Onto each of them, 30 or 40 Jews were loaded, for a trip that lasted 15 to 20 minutes, up to an open, sandy area. Here, the victims were taken down and marched to the top of a low hill surrounded by a double cordon of police, where, during the morning, a large mass grave had been dug by another group of 60 Jews. Once the excavation work had been finished, these men were shot in the head by a police *kommando* and were now lying in the pit, in full view of the new victims.

Then, in groups of ten, the Jews were walked closer to the edge of the pit having to face their executioners, and were then shot by firing squads consisting of two groups of ten policemen. Many of the victims were given the coup de grace, others, who had fallen by the edge, were rolled into the ditch.

The executions went on until dusk. They were then suspended until the following day.

2.2.2 – 2/POLIZEI-BATAILLON 307

The raiding modalities of 2/307's own sector were identical to those of 1/307. The victims of this battalion were gathered in the courtyard of a building - a school or an army barracks- and then loaded onto 13 trucks.

After a 20-minute drive the vehicles stopped near a rolling terrain, covered with patches of vegetation, where there was a long trench - probably a Soviet anti-tank ditch - topped with a mound of sand and surrounded by a cordon of policemen.

TThen, having been beaten with sticks and rifle butts, the Jews were brought down from the trucks and pushed in groups on top of the embankment, where a firing squad of 2/307 in charge of the shootings was awaiting.

In this case too, shootings were suspended in the afternoon and resumed the day after.

2.2.3 – 3/POLIZEI-BATAILLON 307

In the case of 3/307, mopping up operations would begin at 03:00 hours and were completed in about three hours, with the victims and all their baggage gathered in a schoolyard in front of the company's quarters.

Then, from early afternoon until about 17:00 or 18:00 hours, the Jews were loaded onto trucks which shuttled between the school and a large rolling terrain near the River Bug, about a half hour away, with old Soviet bunkers and two or three anti-tank ditches.

As the trucks arrived at their destination, the victims were driven off in groups of ten and pushed to the edge of one of the ditches, where a *kommando* of 20 policemen taking orders from a platoon commander was awaiting them. Each victim was killed by two policemen and every quarter of an hour the entire *kommando* was replaced by another team. The executions, some 600, continued until sunset, after which they were suspended and then resumed the next day.

Overall, 3/307 would shoot 1,200 ÷ 1,500 Jews, including a dozen women who chose to refuse to leave their husbands and join them in death. We do not know for sure, but it is likely that among them there was also Sheine Janowich Feige, wife of Shmuel.

2.3 FACTS AND ACTS

The following are excerpts from documents related to the investigations which resulted in the process of Lubeck, from the final report written up in 1964 by ZStL, then forwarded to the Prosecutor of Lübeck for preliminary investigation v. Salzinger and others [27].

> *The executions were perpetrated in the south of the city of Brest Litovsk, beyond the fortifications, in a land of sand dunes. Getting there from the city center would take around 15 minutes. The hills were covered with low vegetation and the soil was sandy. At least 12 ditches had been dug, which had the following dimensions: 32-feet long, 8-feet wide and 9/13-feet deep. Each hole could contain up to 600 bodies. The excavated soil had been piled up at both ends. No lime chloride or other disinfectants were available. Some of the Jews were transported by trucks, whilst others were marched from the city in a long column which was then stopped about 330 yards from the graves. Once here, they had to hand over their bags, which were piled in an open space. After that, divided into groups of about 50, they were taken to the edge of the pits and forced to lie with their bellies to the ground along both sides, so that only their heads would stick out over the edge of the pit. Standing behind each Jew there would be a shooter, armed with a Gewehr 98 with fixed bayonets. The gun was pointed at the victim's head, resting the bayonet on his neck, so that the bullet hit the nape at an angle of 45 degrees. In this way, the entire upper part of the skull was ripped away by the blow. In several cases, however, if the gun's inclination angle was too wide, or if the victim's head jerked upwards at the moment of the shot, the bullet would hit the neck. In those cases, officers or platoon leaders intervened with their guns, to give the wounded the coup de grace. Then, the gunner threw the body into the pit, pushing it by the feet.*

The first day, these executions continued uninterrupted until early afternoon. At the beginning 10-12 people at a time would be shot. However, this uniformity could not be maintained for long and shooting sequences soon became very irregular. The Jews were brought to the mass grave with their clothes on and they were not ordered them to remove them. This description of the massacre is taken from the detailed testimony of former police officer Heinrich Meier, who was part of a firing squad and took part in the shootings.

> *According to testimonies given by other members of his company, in some cases the Jews had to dig the pit under the supervision of the policemen. According to other members of the battalion, themselves part of the firing squads, in some cases the Jews were lined up at the edges of the pit and two policemen would shoot each of them, one aiming at the head and the other at the heart.*
>
> *That evening the members of the battalion that took part in executions would receive a special ration of strawberries and cream.*
>
> *The numerical evaluations of the participants involved in the shootings vary from a minimum of 6,000 to a maximum of 10,000 victims. A benchmark for evaluating the total number is the excavation of at least 10-12 ditches, each capable of holding at least 600 bodies. The shooting went on for at least three days. Radio Moscow said 5,000 people were killed in this operation. The EM of July 24, 1941, reports the liquidation of 4,435 people [...].*
>
> *[According to the testimony of the platoon leader] J., who belonged to a firing squad, during the shooting in which he took part, 10 or 12 women were also killed. These women had not been arrested, but had voluntarily decided to follow their husbands, and would not part from them even when their men were lined up in front of the trench in order to be shot, so they were shot too. In one case, at the grave where he was, four women were lined up. [The witness] does not remember to have seen any children. In those groups of victims where women had followed their husbands, it also happened that some couples remained embraced until a few moments before the shooting, right before the platoon commanders forced them to separate. Hence, the women took their husbands' hands and died with them.*

The member of a firing squad, Manthey, confirms having seen some women among the victims. There would be also a woman with a child, who voluntarily joined her husband in death. In his testimony Hanke reports of some injured Jews down in the pit who did not receive the coup de grace, and remembers personally witnessing horrific scenes.

The following is a summary of the facts as reconstructed by the Prosecutor of Lübeck on the basis of testimonies given by several former officers of the three battalions[28] during the preliminary investigations that would lead to the request for the indictment of upon Salzinger and others, presented to the Court of Lübeck on September 21, 1970. Each testimony reflects, of course, the specific viewing angle of the witness and for that reason, being an action which lasted several days, in different shooting-locations, there may be differences with regard to timing, methods, techniques and the description of details[29].

[First company (1/307)]

Since morning, in this guarded area, a pit 50 to 65-feet long, 6-feet wide and 3-feet deep, was excavated by a group of about 60 Jews. Once this work was completed, the 60 Jews were shot by a firing squad formed of 15 men. The Jews were forced to line up along the edge of the excavation, turned inward and with their backs to the firing squad. Some of them were not mortally hit, yet they fell into the pit. They were then killed with the coup de grace inflicted by individual members of the firing squad.

Then, in groups of ten, the other Jews were brought to the trench through an embankment of sand placed beyond the security cordon and were lined up along the edge of the pit, facing the inside. Then, on the firing order given by the platoon leader, they were killed by a firing squad composed of 20 men, but only half of whom were shooting, placed at a distance of 15 to 30 feet.

The Jews who did not fall into the pit were thrown in by some members of the company in charge of this task. The Jews who were not killed immediately received the coup de grace [...]. The execution lasted until sunset. [...]

The operation lasted until the afternoon and was completed with the arrival of the victims already held in prison. It is possible that there were between 2,000 and 3,000 victims. During the operation we wouldn't be told of a Judenaktion but of an intervention that would prevent future killing of German soldiers. Among the arrested there were Jews, Poles, Russians, and also Russian soldiers caught in civilian clothes. They were considered former soldiers because of their shaved heads.

The next morning the company was ordered by the battalion to provide a firing squad. Hauptmann Grube then asked for volunteers. There were so many he would be spoiled for choice.

Together with Hauptmann Grube and half the company, the 50-60 volunteers chosen went to the execution spot, located a few miles away from Brest Litovsk, towards the Bug. There was a flat terrain with an old anti-tank ditch. There, he [the accused Niehoff, N/A] ordered his men to cordon the entire area, from a distance of over half a mile. The guard posts were in sight of each other. After the security cordon had been formed the first truck arrived with the prisoners. These men, Jews but not exclusively, were brought from the prison under the supervision of other members of the company. A Russian colonel was among them. Approximately, six to eight prisoners at a time were brought to the pit and everything happened very quickly. They were all clothed and were aligned on the long side, their backs turned inward. The shooting was carried out on command from a distance of 15 feet by a firing squad comprising six to eight men. After running the task, he (the accused N.) [Niehoff, N/A], was replaced by Hauptmann Grube and other NCO's.

The shooting lasted from 09:00 hours until late afternoon. Only men were killed. According to his estimates about 1,500 people were killed. At times during the shooting, battalion commander, Maj.

Stahr and physician Dr. Sprengerm would show up. The doctor had to examine whether all those who had been shot were dead, or if a coup de grace was necessary; if so, that was delivered by the doctor himself or by the shooters with their rifles.

[Second company (2/307)]

The transport was carried out with 13 company cars. Each vehicle was filled with about 30 Jews, some of which were forced on board through the blow of truncheons and rifle-butts [...] and two or three guards watching them. The Jews were then forced towards the pit, again with repeated blows inflicted by men on guard in order to encourage them to go faster [...].

While the witness H. says that the firing squad was divided in two parts, each of which shot at groups of 12 Jews lined up in front of them, along the ditch, the witness M. [Heinrich Meier, N/A] talks about 10 or 12 Jews who had to lie flat out, leaning their heads over the edge of the pit. Behind every Jew there was a shooter who stood armed with a rifle with fixed bayonet, and leaned the point of his bayonet on the neck of the victim and then pulled the trigger. The shooter would then throw the victim's body into the grave, by his legs. About 1,500 Jews were killed this way [...].

On completion of the shooting the second company members returned to their quarters. The action, for this company, lasted for two or three days.

[Third company (3/307)]

The execution site consisted of two or three graves, each 100-feet long, 6-feet wide and 10-feet deep. The Jews were forced towards each of them in groups of ten. Once there, they had to align along the ditch, their backs inward. Then they were shot by a firing squad of the company, consisting of 20 men, from a distance of 30 feet. Every Jew was targeted by two company members, who aimed at the head and the heart. Every 15 minutes the firing squad was replaced by another platoon. After the end of the executions, the bodies were covered with shrubs and sand [...]. The use of the third company, as revealed by the investigations, did not last only one, but two, or even more than three days in a row [...].

The trip ended in an area outside the city, where three ditches had been dug, each 60-feet long and 15-feet wide. Upon the arrival of the firing squad these ditches already contained many bodies covered with sand. The firing squad consisted of 12 men in two lines, who shot 12 Jews. During the execution, the accused S. [Salzinger, N/A] was going back and forth and oversaw the whole operation. During this second day about 600 Jews were killed.

In addition to the reconstruction made by the Prosecutor of Lübeck, it may be interesting to read the exact testimony given by 2/307 police officer Heinrich Meierto to the same prosecutor:[30]

That morning we were awakened at 03:00 hours. The execution day was probably July 10, 1941. At first we were ordered to muster, equipped with our "98" guns and ammunition. Our task was to bring to the streets all the Jewish men of the neighborhood. They were allowed to wear their clothes and have as many pieces of luggage as they could carry with them. We were told that the Jews would be sent to work in Germany...

The roundup of the Jews and their gathering in the streets of the Jewish quarter went on until 06:00 hours. A part of our battalion was sent, by the trucks, to the execution site. The rest of the unit was left to watch the Jews who were going to be sent there.

The site was located south of Brest Litovsk, beyond the fortifications, and looked like a terrain with wavelike dunes. It took about fifteen minutes to reach it from the city center. When we arrived, at about 06:30 hours, we were approached by an SS unit, certainly a company. The SS soldiers, armed with machine guns, had cordoned a circular area of 650 yards in diameter. In addition to the SS there were also members of the SD, in gray uniform. Judging from what I learned later, after the execution of men these units would also take care of women and children, who had been taken by the SS to the execution site after noon. These soldiers were also equipped with automatic weapons.

There were twelve trenches 33-feet long, 8-feet wide and 10/13-feet deep. I believe that each grave could hold 600 bodies. In order to avoid misunderstandings regarding the number of Jews shot that day (which, before, I figured as 10,000), I want to stress that about 6,000 Jewish men were shot during the action I have described. From speeches heard later I learned that their total number was 10,000.

We did not have lime chloride or other disinfectants. Shortly after our arrival, a long column of Jews came from the city. It was stopped about 330 yards from the trenches. While the Jews set down their luggage, the platoon commanders designated the soldiers to be assigned to the firing squad. Then we were explained how the shooting had to be performed.

According to the instructions we were given, the Jews had to be brought to the trenches in groups of 50 and forced to lie face down, on both sides, so that their heads protruded beyond the edge of the pit. Behind every Jew was a soldier armed with a "98" gun with fixed bayonet. The execution was to happen this way: the tip of the bayonet was to be leaned on the victims' nape.

After that, the gun had to be tilted to an angle of 45 degrees, then they pulled the trigger. It often happened that the entire upper part of the skull was stripped away, along the path of the bullet. From time to time, if the shooting-angle proved too large, or in the case the victim's head had jerked upwards during the shot, it could happen that the bullet would only rip through the neck [without causing death, A/N]. In these cases an officer or the platoon commander had to intervene with a gun to give the victim its final blow.

We, the soldiers, had to throw their bodies in the trenches, but there was nobody who cared to pile up the bodies on the bottom. The execution lasted until the afternoon, with these procedures. At first, on the long side of each pit men were shot ten or twelve at a time. After that it became impossible to maintain that uniformity, and the sequences of shooting became more disorderly.

The Jews were brought to their grave with their clothes on and they were not forced to remove them. The action ended at four in the afternoon, then we were taken back to our quarters with the trucks. For that day our work was completed.

As far as I remember, during that day we received no food and, of this I'm sure, no alcohol. We didn't pause once.

We were not told to keep secrecy on the action but I do not think that we, the policemen, discussed it after the executions; if we did, then it was only in condemnation.

Virtually all the Jews that I talked about accepted their fate with stoicism and heroic self-control. I personally lived the action as in a trance and could not help but be amazed by the behavior of the Jews. According to my current point of view, questioning myself about my actions at that time, I must admit in all honesty that the actions committed by each of us were no less than murder.

2.4 TEAMWORK

While there seem to be no doubts about how the roundup and execution of the victims was carried out, the historical circumstances that led to the massacre should instead be framed in a broader context.

Regardless of the effective date of the massacre, that the Court of Lübeck places in the period between July, 6 and 13, 1941, it is generally accepted that this was an operation conducted in harmony between the authorities of the Wehrmacht, those of the SS and those of the police, each of which played their role and provided their own structures.

It was the command of Division 221.Sicherungs of the Wehrmacht who would forward, on July 7, 1941, the request for a company of Polizei-Bataillon 307 to be used in the FK 184 area of Brest Litovsk (Maj.Gen. Stubenrauch) to HSSPF von dem Bach, as the division was unable to ensure the safety of deposits and the cleansing of the city using only its own manpower[31].

Then, in the hours that followed von dem Bach's positive response (July 8)[32] and the arriveal of reinforcements sent by 162nd Infantry Division, raids and *sanitizing* operations were carried out, both in the urban area of Brest Litovsk and its surroundings. In fact, according to a statement by Max von Schenckendorff, Berück Mitte on July 9, 1941, "the systematic mopping up of several locations, which include Bialystok and Brest Litovsk" was started "with the collaboration of SD and Ordnungspolizei units»[33]: this was done, apparently, so that the Wehrmacht could ensure the security of their rear lines, including the taking of hostages and the participation of military units in "mopping up operations by the police (*Durchsuchungsaktionen der Pol.*)"[34].

Then, on July 11, after a visit to Bialystok by Himmler and Daluege, Montua, the commander of Polizei-Regiment "Mitte", passed an order by vom dem Bach to Polizei-Bataillone 316 and 322 that authorized "the execution of all male Jews of Bialystok aged from 17 to 45, for being guilty of looting". In the following hours this order was extended to Polizei-Bataillon 307 of Brest Litovsk [35].

It is obvious that such an order represented a real *license to kill* because it imposed a precise racial distinction (Jewish men) in the face of an overly generic crime (looting). Furthermore, not including any measure against possible non-Jew looters, it insinuated the devious equation *looters = Jewish*, as well as its natural evolution *Jews = looters*. Thus, Montua's order could be interpreted in its broadest sense by the most *zealous* police officers, and possibly be extended to other age groups and categories of victims including - why not? - even women who, as wives, could easily be considered *accomplices* of their husbands.

The last piece of the great criminal mosaic that was forming was put in place with the inspection of Daluege, von dem Bach and Montua in Brest Litovsk, which probably took place between July 12 and 13, in a repetition of what had happened in Bialystok a few days before. And indeed, in his speech to Polizei-Bataillon 307, Daluege stressed that "particularly difficult tasks were now approaching (*Besonders schwere Einsätze bevorständen*)»[36].

Then, with everything in place and the rounding up happening at the usual hours, the carnage could begin: and it began punctually on the morning of Sunday, July 13, 1941.

We have mentioned so far the fundamental role played by Polizei-Bataillon 307: however, it is still worth repeating as it was not just the policemen who were involved in the massacre of Brest Litovsk, but also - as already mentioned - the other infrastructures in the city, that took part with their tactical assets. In particular, for the transportation of victims from Brest Litovsk to the execution sites, Wehrmacht trucks were used, plausibly provided by FK 184, i.e. belonging to the fleet of 162nd Infantry Division, stationed in Bialystok during those days[37].

Moreover, according to Heinrich Meier's aforementioned testimony, at the site of the massacre there was an unidentified SS unit, probably a company, and a small SD group: in this case it could have been a detachment of Einsatzkommando zbV "Brest" sent from Krakow's BdS Schöngarth, formed with personnel drawn from KDS "Lublin"[38].

2.5 EXCEEDING THE LIMITS

Apart from the typical historical dynamics that led to the massacre of Brest Litovsk, it is worthwhile to point out some psychosocial causes included in two axes of the four-angle model (self-construction of the identity of perpetrators and perception of the victims as "the others") proposed by James Waller as a possible explanation of the ordinary origins of extraordinary human evil[39]. Social marginalization was probably one of these causes that in our case, however, is to be seen, paradoxically, in reverse.

It is a fact that social marginalization, progressively enforced upon Jewish communities through the Judenpolitik from 1933 in Germany and from September 1939 in the occupied territories, and the objective and physical isolation in which the Israelite citizens of the Reich found themselves – being as they were, set aside as alien entities to most of the members of the so-called Aryan society – have been two basic premises to the transition to Vernichtungspolitik[40].

Furthermore, it is paradoxical how similar dynamics ended up involving – albeit on different ethical and objective grounds – many units of the Ordnungspolizei which, transferred from their original Reich sites to the eastern territories, found themselves operating in a tactical and social context deeply modified by the ongoing conflict. We are not trying, of course, to venture obscene parallels between victims and perpetrators, but to identify some of the mechanisms that amplified each other and helped to shape a devastating genocidal synergy.

2.5.1 – Dein Freund, dein Helfer

Let's reflect, in particular, on the social habitat that surrounded the Ordnungspolizei units, both those training in barracks and those acting on the territory, in the immediate pre-war and early stages of the conflict.

Unlike those structures of the regime more directly related to the party - especially Sipo-SD - executives of police battalions and agents of municipal police (with the usual exceptions) were not yet deemed of a political caliber sufficient to make them true *warriors of ideology*, i.e. particularly indoctrinated individuals. They still belonged, in their majority, to that category that Browning identifies as *ordinary men*, who represented the transposition in a military context of the social, ideological and behavioral patterns typical of pre-war German society. In this sense, the Ordnungspolizei *average executive* reflected the *average German citizen*, with his vices and virtues, his strengths and flaws.

This mutual identification was only a first step, the first and immediate consequence of the broader effort of the regime to radically reorganize the Ordnungspolizei, not only from the structural point of view of the *container* - something that proved relatively easy to succeed in between 1936 and 1939 - but also and above all of the *contents*, through the *genetic transformation* of the Ordnungspolizei from an inherently apolitical State institution to an outright political tool available to the regime. To achieve this result the regime identified two areas of intervention in the medium / long term, both having to do with loyalty: the political-ideological loyalty of all the Ordnungspolizei staff on the one hand, and the social loyalty of the institution towards citizens on the other.

Thus, while the desired *political and ideological loyalty* of all the staff represented the sealing ring between the Ordnungspolizei and the regime - a slow process that required longer individual indoctrination (*Weltanschauliche Erziehung*) - *social loyalty* became the faster connecting link between the Ordnungspolizei and the people, as well as the essential prerequisite in order to close the circle, with the people adapting to the plans laid out by the regime.

The Ordnungspolize thus became a central system of transmission between the regime and the people: a system that could be punitive/repressive in case of a negative/hostile approach of the citizen toward the establishment, and rewarding/friendly otherwise. The first variable applied to the marginal fringes of the outcasts, the misfits and the non-conformist, who were to be distanced and punished, and the second variable was associated to upright citizens, orderly and willing, examples to be rewarded and identified with.

Through a positive social loyalty of this type, summarized in the *Freund und Helfer* project – a powerful tool of political marketing rather than an abstract ideological issue – police officers could be perceived by the population – and, presumably, that is how they perceived themselves - as *guardians of the State* (and not so much of the establishment) in their position of *citizens in uniform*: that is, guardians of the law, welfare and collective security, to be addressed with the fearful deference in any case due to the representatives of the executive authority, but at the same time, with the quiet confidence granted to friendly private members of the community (*Freund*), amicably available to all, for any need (*Helfer*). This mechanism strengthened, in the officer, the reassuring conviction to be working for their fellow citizens, who awarded him proper appreciation and respect, and in the meantime allowed the Ordnungspolizisten to differentiate themselves from their colleagues in the Security Police: on the one hand the *helpers*, on the other the *oppressors*, *velvet glove* and *iron fist*, *good cop* and *bad cop*.

The attempt by the Nazi regime to reorder the Ordnungpolizei by connecting it to the people for their instrumental ends was giving good results. Benefiting from it were not just executives of the Schupo and the local police who were working in closer contact with the citizens by virtue of their operational role to, but also members of the urban units who lived locked in their barracks, whose integration in the communities in which they served was actually favored by the recruitment carried out on a local basis, which allowed the policemen of these unit to be deployed in their home town, or at least not far from it.

Hence, in such a context the policemen could in no way feel alien to the civilian population, even after Berlin legislated, in June 1936, on the rationalization and centralization of the various regional police forces: a structural event that, had it been poorly managed, could easily lead to a kind of *elitist* isolation, similar to the one that permeated certain circles of the Wehrmacht, linked as they were to the Prussian military traditions and consequently quite detached from a social and civilian context. Furthermore, probably as a *strategic option*, the Ordnungspolizei was chosen to represent the good face of the regime to the citizens, thanks to a popular background whose roots were not so much in Nazi ideology, but rather in Germanic sternness - *Treue, Gehorsam, Disziplin, Vaterland*. These concepts, of a familiar and traditional nature, not ideological, were confirmed and strengthened after the beginning of the conflict, also through the influx of thousands of police reservists in their thirties, redrafted from civilian life: mature individuals with their own families, professionally stable and not prone to that political frenzy that could eventually characterize the next generation of German youth, brought up in full Nazi environment - *Volk, Reich Führer*. In other words, Ordnungspolizisten adhered perfectly to that social and para-ideological image that had made the Ordnungspolizei so similar, in the collective imaginary, to the icons depicted in propaganda posters issued during the annual celebrations of the *Day of German Police* [41].

This situation remained stable until September 1939. Then, almost as in a huge demonstration in the field of the *social identity theory* developed decades later by Henri Tajfel[42], the beginning of the conflict and the invasion of Poland completely changed the the dynamics of the relation between the police battalions - social entities (*ingroups*) - and the various external groups (*outgroups*) with which they began to deal in the new territories.

2.5.2 – *Keine Freund, keine Helfer*

The massive deployment of police battalions in Poland starting from September 1939, presented the Ordnungspolizei with a situation that was almost unprecedented, but introductory to its involvement in the Jewish genocide. In a nutshell, we witness a convulsive high opinion of their own group - the battalion - from the police officers who formed it and a subsequent exasperated comparison between themselves and the surrounding social reality. In this sense, upon examining the historical and political macro-causes that led to the genocide and the different situations that took place on the various fields of death, we must add a series of unusual inter-group events among individual battalions and an external environment radically different to the familiar one that they had left in Germany.

The objective isolation from the environment around Ordnungspolizisten was probably one of the many impulses that provided fuel to the spiral of genocide, especially in conjunction with other schemes - stereotypes, prejudices, ideological models, religious and cultural conditioning, etc. – that they were already saturated with. Once they found themselves far away from the conformist German reality, they felt they could rely only on themselves: a logic only partly correct, which manifested itself through the strengthening of internal bonds of community within the unit and through the devaluation of all that was left outside of the group by comparisons that (for many reasons) could only be discriminatory. Such process evolved through three subsequent stages, and was made easier by several objective factors.

From the perspective of the police officers the issue was to face not only the obvious outwardly differences between westernized German Jews and so-called *Ostjuden* - which inevitably accentuated their sense of alienation among these unusual Jewish communities and the *ordinary Aryan* that the policeman believed to represent [Meeting Phase] - but also to handle a situation where the police department as a group - and by extension the individual officers who were part of it - was no longer seen as a factor of friendship and support (friend and helper), but rather as a hostile element of oppression. From being a community member, appreciated and respected, the policeman became a *foreign body*, hated and feared, received with suspicion and isolated in guarded garrisons, with only little contact with the civilian population except for official purposes taking place in a perspective of repression rather than aid.

In such a context, the unit/group became, for the policeman, his own moral community, a rare island of familiarity, security and entertainment (*Gemütlichkeit*), the only safe harbor amid a distrustful and hostile Slavic and Judaic sea to whom, in turn, he reciprocated distrust and hostility. This approach, so superficial because it was generated from a position of strength and therefore did not need further analysis, could not go beyond a gross devaluation of *the other*, directly proportional to the need to *be as one* with their fellow soldiers, and a boorish confirmation of abused but pervasive stereotypes with which, especially in the occupied Eastern territories, Jews and Slavs were classified.

Hence the creeping in of a kind of *siege mentality* (paradoxically specific to the *ghetto mentality* that plagued the Jews [43]), exacerbated by tactics and military needs, that caused the onset of a strict separation between the groups [Isolation Phase] - in this case between occupiers and occupied - i.e. impermeability of the first toward the second, and subsequent disruption of those mechanisms of empathy and knowledge that a proper and peaceful (and not only pacified) context would help both groups to recognize each other. It is a mentality in which the erosion of ethical and moral limits commonly accepted and respected, until that moment, appears not only feasible but also quite likely.

In such a *poisoned* environment, characterized by the disappearance of the reference point between the unit and its ideal environment, and a stiffening of relations between occupier and occupied with its subsequent spiral of stereotyping, prejudice, mutual suspicion, resentment and hostility, the passage to an open conflict between the groups [Break-point Phase] can be extremely quick. Under such conditions, the consequence of the general barbarization of a brutal war fought with the cruelest means is the almost inevitable and utter rejection of the opponent. They are not only seen as an enemy to be defeated on the basis of factors more or less objective - political and economic in the first place - but also viewed as a true *abomination* placed outside of any moral community, to be removed by any means through a work of *social reclamation*. A reclamation that, in the context in which they found themselves to act, the *ordinary men* were able to carry out with relative ease, having gone beyond their moral threshold through a process of moving forward toward the adaptation to the *tribal conformism* in which they were immersed, one step after another, with increasing docility and zeal and always minor resistance [44]. Until the final moral apocalypse.

2.6 AS ROADSIDE VICTIMS

The first investigations on the massacre of Brest Litovsk took place in the early sixties by ZStL and the outcome is in the collection of 26 testimonies of former members of Polizei-Bataillon 307, stored in ZStL 204 AR - Z 82/61 v. Salzinger and others.

Then, in 1964, the files were passed on to the court

of the city of competence, Lübeck, which, through proceedings Staw Lübeck - 2 PJs 189/64 VU-Antrag vom 9.9.1965, requested the opening of preliminary investigations against four members of the battalion[45]:

Salzinger, Hans-Albert: born May 1, 1910 in Munich. Battalion adjutant at Stab/307. After the war he reached the rank of major in the Bundeswehr. He retired before the trial, and was investigated by the Prosecutor of Kiel on February 24, 1965.

Niehoff, Friedrich Wilhelm: born September 2, 1914 in Oldenburg. Commander of the first platoon of 1/307. After the war he reached the rank of Chief Inspector (*Polizeihauptkommissar*). Still in service in Bremervörde when the trial began, he was investigated by the Prosecutor of Kiel from October 16, 1964, for, among other things, intentionally and deliberately killing two Russian peasants from Mogilev and Slutsk. In order to hasten the death of one of the two who had only been wounded after being shot, Niehoff ordered that a heavy stone be thrown onto the victim's chest[46].

KAYSER, Max Erich: born 27 August 1913 in Tilsit. Commander of the first platoon of 3/307. After the war he reached the rank of police captain (*Polizeihauptmann*). He retired before the trial, and was investigated by the Prosecutor of Kiel from September 14, 1966.

KLOCKER, Sigfried: born November 10, 1911 in Dornbirn, Austria. Commander of 2/307. Later transferred to the Waffen-SS, he became commander of the Second Battalion of the Waffen-Grenadier Regiment der SS 30 (14. Waffen-Grenadier-Division der SS). After the war he reached the rank of Chief Inspector (*Polizeihauptkommissar*). Still in service in Bottrop when the trial began, he was accused by the Prosecutor of Kiel to have perpetrated the murder of 40/50 Jewish women and five or six (or 10) Jewish children in the Slutsk area between July 26 and 30, 1941 and to have taken part in the execution of 100/200 male Jews in the Mogilev area between Klichev and Gorodishche in September / October 1941. During his interrogation of October 31, 1972, before the Prosecutor of Dortmund, Klocker *candidly* asserted that he had learned only at the time of the action that "it had anything to do with the shooting of Jews". With regard to his professional skills, he was regarded positively by his superiors. In fact, his service record describes him as "skillful and devoted unreservedly to the cause of the Nazi State"[47].

All these preliminary investigations were completed five years later, when, with proceedings StAw Lübeck - 2 PJs 189/64 vom 21.9.1970, the Prosecutor of Lübeck requested the Court of the same city the indictment of the four suspects.

Moreover, at the same time, on the basis of the documentation provided by the Prosecutor of Lübeck, the Prosecutor of Dortmund opened an additional investigation against Niehoff and Klocker, in relation to crimes committed after the massacre of Brest Litovsk.

In 1970, accepting the request of the Prosecutor of Lübeck, trhough proceedings LG Lübeck III AR 118/70 2 Js 189/64 the trial v. Salzinger, Niehoff, Kayser and Klocker was opened by the Court of Lübeck. This process, however, was closed a few months later, on March 23, 1971, with a bewildering ruling that erased the request of the prosecution of *murder and complicity in murder* and converted it into *manslaughter*: a type of offense that granted the immediate return to freedom of the four suspects, on the grounds that the charge was subject to a prescription term of fifteen years[48]. Basically, with this decision, the Court of Lübeck put more than 4,000 civilians shot in mass graves on a par with victims of a traffic accident.

As for Niehoff and Klocker, however, the file of the Prosecution in Dortmund was still open.

In 1971, with proceedings StAwDo 45 Js 6/71, the Prosecutor requested the indictment of Niehoff before the Court of Lübeck and, in 1972, the indictment of Klocker before the Court of Essen.

Again, in the first case Lübeck declared itself incompetent and with ruling Lübeck LG III Str 38/71 2 Ks 1/71 of December 21, 1971, Niehoff was acquitted[49].

As for Klocker, the last of the defendants, the matter took on a disturbing aspect.

In 1972, in fact, after the request for indictment in Essen, Klocker was granted the suspension of the proceedings for health reasons. Then, once the proceedings re-started in 1973, the person that should have been the principal witness for the prosecution committed suicide, hanging himself just two days before the decisive hearing. Meanwhile, another of the witnesses decided to recant his previous testimony against Klocker[50].

On May 15, 1973, in the absence of all possible evidence against him, Klocker was released, with ruling LG Essen Js 45 6/71 22 53/73.

In order to draw a comparison with the baffling decision of the Court of Lübeck, it is worth reading an excerpt of the opposing unequivocal conclusions of the Prosecutor of Lubeck, released on July 9, 1965 and included in the request for indictment, filed two months after to the same court[51]:

> *The killing of Jews was illegal. Given the mode of the execution it is to be presumed that both the administrative decision to proceed with the action of Brest Litovsk and the shooting of people, have been implemented on the basis of racial grounds. The perpetrators of this massacre were aware, without a need for further confirmation, of the illegality of their actions. The main defendents accused of the murder carried out actions typical of voluntary homicide. The main defendants have planned and prepared the massacre [...]. Their conduct can be ascribed, in many ways, to the case history covered by § 211 of the Criminal Code* [52]. *The main reasons given by the perpetrators, in particular racial hatred, were based on violations of human dignity so severe as to be considered particularly reprehensible and thus regarded as despicable.*

2.7 CONSIDERATIONS

Based on all the elements described so far, we can draw some conclusions about the dynamics that, synchronized as they were in a *perfect storm*, made possible the slaughter of Brest Litovsk. From the following list – essentially similar to an Ishikawa diagram, with slaughter as *effect* – we can see the existence, from the outset, of a deep interaction between local initiatives and orders coming from above[53], i.e.:

- the presence of more or less explicit orders from the top hierarchies of SS and Police, as well as the physical presence in the territory of the same top hierarchies;
- The role of Max von Schenckendorff, an advocate of the theory according to which «*Der Jude ist der Partisan, der Partisan ist der Jude*»[54];
- the occurrence of certain military needs, although basically used as excuses, in the area of Brest Litovsk, such as surveillance of deposits, protection of communication lines, presence of stray Soviet soldiers attacking the rear lines, etc..;
- the specific characteristics of Polizei-Bataillon 307 – a unit of the so-called *300 series* - i.e. belonging to that group of battalions that were rightly or wrongly regarded as the operational (but not necessarily ideological) élite of the Ordnungspolizei, with all the consequences that could arise from this position;
- the presence and possibly the intervention in the action, of a strongly ideological unit, such as Einsatzkommando zbV "Brest", an offshoot of Schöngarth, a radical anti-Semitic;

Then, to these situational causes, specific to the case of Brest Litovsk, there must be added other types of dynamics more generally applicable to each genocidal event perpetrated during the summer/autumn of 1941. Such dynamics derived from both the overall political and historical atmosphere, and from *inter-group* and *intra-group* factors related to the role and activities of police battalions, in this case Polizei-Bataillon 307:

- The propaganda against the eternal Judeo-Bolshevik enemy that was rekindled between June 21 and 22 by the distribution of 800,000 copies of the proclamation of Hitler's "Soldaten der Ostfront!" among the troops awaiting the attack order.[55]

- The appearance of the well-known *Freischärlerpsychose*, especially in the circles close to the Wehrmacht. This "*psychosis of an insurgence*" was not only a legitimate military concern, but an obsessive projection of a reality that was feared in the same measure as it was virtual, at least in that phase, as it included political, ideological and racial aspects and tended to feed itself geometrically inside a sort of endless vicious circle: a deadly spiral, in which it became essentially impossible to distinguish rationally between friends and enemies and anything in between, with the consequent application of brutal solutions Manichaeism would be proud of.[56];
- personal reasons affecting each man differently, depending on the specific experience, level of education, social and cultural background, peculiarities in character, weakness of individual defenses with respect to the influence that crept in through ideological propaganda, internalization of stereotypes, etc..;
- The micro-dynamics internal to the unit (*intergroup* causes), which were not easy to ignore and that we shall refer to in one of the next paragraphs[57];
- I*ntra-group* causes: i.e. relations between external environment and perpetrators – specifically Polizei-Bataillon 307 – who, for the first time, were basically put in a position in which they could *exceed the limits* by reacting with a preventative act (the massacre) to an alleged Jewish threat: such threat went beyond the sphere of the *perceived imaginary* and reached the level – please allow us the oxymoron – of a *real imaginary*.

In conclusion, the perfect alignment of all these factors produced a devastating result. As Mallmann correctly pointed out, this result was not a *bureaucratic* massacre, or an *industrial* extermination, rather a "situational radicalization of the enemy (*situativen Radikalisierung des Feindbildes*)"[58]. In other words, it was the dramatic *evolution and rationalization* of the impromptu facts of Bialystok, the next step along the road that in a few months would lead to the final Solution, i.e. the planned application of a *method* to achieve an *objective*.

The Jews slain in Brest Litovsk on July 13, 1941 and in the following hours were at least 4,000. Among them, according to the executioners' testimonies, there were several women and children.

Through a grossly approximate study of the numbers, we can say that over a weekend almost 20 % of the Jewish community of Brest Litovsk was erased, a figure that rises to a terrifying 40 % when taking into account only the male part of the population. In practice if we assume that the core of an average family consisted of at least five members, therefore, probably 4,000 households making a population of about 21,000 Jews (1931 data), we come to the conclusion that basically, every family lost an immediate relative: be it a father, a husband or a son. Moreover, since the victims belonged mainly to the most vigorous and productive part of the Jewish population, their disappearance dealt a devastating blow to the entire community, not only in the short term, but also and especially in the perspective of a future demographic advancement of the community itself, which was basically prevented or at least greatly reduced.

In social terms, in other words, beyond the immediate painful losses, a massacre of this scale amounted to prepare, in the long run, the extinction of a community that had lived in the area for centuries, with all its' human and cultural heritage.

To be fair, we doubt that in those chaotic early weeks of *Barbarossa* there were specific calculations behind the murderous hand of the architects of the genocide, on a visit to Brest Litovsk. We rather think of a convergence, on a general framework, of spurious and instrumental dynamics designed to meet small-scale *needs*, which probably were not yet part of a precise and broad extermination strategy, but that, like many small tributaries of a great river, contributed to nourish its flux and flow.

Moreover, it should also be said that the victims of July 13 would find little consolation from the understanding of the overall and specific plan, regardless of the calculations made and not made. Neither would the victims of the next few weeks: in fact, it would only be a matter of days before the application of a new wave of massacres swept over the traumatized *Briskers*, and this time it would be at the hands of the Sicherheitspolizei.[59].

After which, all those who somehow survived until autumn 1942, were forced to wear the Magen David, the *brand of infamy*[60].

Sheine Janowich Feige and 4,000 more victims, at least, would be spared from that.

ENDNOTES

1 "According to my point of view of today, if I think of what I did back then, I must admit, in complete honesty, that the actions carried out by each of us, were no less than homicide". Kohl, pp. 224-225.

2 See *Yad Vashem. The Central Database of Shoah Victims' Names.*

3 *Encyclopedia Judaica*, p. 1362, Browning Policy, p. 124.

4 Browning Policy, p. 118, Curilla, p. 848.

5 Officially, the citadel was declared as "taken" by the command of 45.ID on July 8, 1941. In fact, sporadic fighting and snipers' activities continued until almost the end of the month: only on July 23, actually, the last defenders were overwhelmed. Gerlach, p. 546.

6 In addition to Lübeck's 307, Polizei-Regiment "Mitte"was also formed by Polizei-Bataillon 316 (from Recklinghausen) and 322 (Vienna): with comparison to 307, the latter two operated further north, in the Bialystok area, were they perpetrated a brutal massacre between July 12 and 13, 1941. See Kopitzsch, pp. 264-265.

7 *«Faktisch bedeutete dies ein Praktikum im Sachen Rassismus, eine Einübung ins Projekt der etnischen Säuberung und "völkischen Flurbereinigung", der jüdischen Ghettoisierung und Zwangsarbeit»*. Mallmann Einstieg, p. 85.

8 In the Biala Podlaska area, personnel of the battalion would carry out the execution of death sentences ruled by the local Standgericht, while other likely activities included escorting Jewish forced laborers to the Belzec *Arbeitslager* that they were being deported to.

9 Lichtenstein, p. 168.

10 Mallmann Einstieg, p. 83, Klemp Ermittelt, p. 250.

11 See Browning Policy, p. 118, where unlike battalions of regular series, hastily assembled in September 1939, largely drawing from VPS, Polizei-Bataillon 307 is quoted as a unit reasonably trained and formed by carefully selected individuals, just like a good part of battalions of the *300 Series*. However, having been constituted primarily around Wachtmeister personnel - i.e. reservists in their thirties in conscription classes of 1910, with a cultural upbringing typical of the Weimar era and redrafted just after the start of the war - these *300 Series* battalions, cannot generally be ascribed, in our view, to any ideological elite.

12 Even in 1933, the percentage of police officers members of NSDAP barely reached 0.7 % (approximately 700) of the entire police force under the Weimar government. Westermann Soldiers, p. 43.

13 According to a circular issued by Himmler in 1937, the ideological indoctrination included a weekly lecture held by SS members, as well as a monthly meeting on matters concerning the National Socialist doctrine. Then, starting from 1940, daily sessions should be held within the units: in fact, everything was reduced to no more than three weekly meetings, lasting 15 or 20 minutes each, the actual efficacy of which leaves ground for doubts. Westermann Soldiers, p. 45.

14 *Ibid.*, pp. 45, 64. Daluege's phrase unintentionally confirms how the work of amalgamation, evidently ideological as well as structural, was a project still in progress, which certainly could not be completed before the start of the conflict.

15 Curilla, p. 570, Browning Policy, p. 119.

16 Overall, about twenty shootings were carried out, among which, probably, several Jews. Curilla, pp. 570-571.

17 221.Sicherungs-Division produced its own police battalion, Polizei-Bataillon 309, that in those days had been deployed in the Bialystok and Bialowieza area. See Chap. 1.

18 Mallmann Einstieg, p. 84, Browning Policy, p. 121. According to Gerlach, p. 546,the massacre was perpetrated on July 7; three to four days before the arrival of the battalion in the city. According to Westermann, the raid was carried out on the morning of July 9. According to the testimony of policeman Heinrich Meier, reported in Kohl, p. 224, the execution day was July 10 – see Chapter 2, note 30. According to Longerich, p. 350, the massacre took place on July 12. According to Curilla, p. 571, the shootings began on July 13.

19 Curilla, pp. 571-572. See Browning Policy, p. 121, where the testimonies of several policemen are quoted. Also Westermann, p. 176.

20 Hüttmann, p. 22.

21 In total the three companies shot no less than 4,000 Jews, as well as about 400 Russians and Belarusians. These numbers are substantially confirmed in the request to open a preliminary investigation made on April 9, 1965 by the Prosecutor of Lübeck v. Salzinger and others (StAw Lübeck - 2 PJs 189/64 VU-Antrag vom 09.09.1965), which puts the number of Jews killed at 3,000 ÷ 4,000. Furthermore, these figures originate

from the EM 32 of July 24, 1941, which relates the killing by Ordnungspolizei staff of 4,435 people, including 400 Russians and Belarusians, in the locality of Brest Litovsk: «*In Brest-Litovsk hat die Ordnungspolizei mit Unterstützung des dortigen Einsatztrupps 4.435 Personen liquidiert*». Klemp Ermittelt, p. 252, Mallman Einstieg, p. 84.

22 Curilla, p. 55, Browning Policy, p. 121, Mallmann Einstieg, p. 85, Hüttmann, p. 23.

23 The Book of Exodus, 3, 16-17. Who knows if some of the perpetrators, upon receiving their reward after slaughtering innocent civilians, remembered this Bible passage, and maybe smiled in the face of the tragic irony of such a paradox...

24 Mallmann Einstieg, p. 85. Testimonies of E.M., December 9, 1964 and of E.S., August 28, 1964 given to ZStL, 204 AR-Z 82/61.

25 Mallmann Einstieg, p. 85.

26 Probably Robert J. Lifton would have liked the "state of trance" description that police officer Heinrich Meier referred to in his following testimony, for his theory of doubling. See Robert J. Lifton: *The Nazi Doctors: Medical Killing and the Psychology of Genocide*, New York, 1988.

27 Hüttmann, p. 23, Lichtenstein, pp. 184-186, Kopitzsch, p. 265. ZStL 204 AR–Z 82/61 v. Salzinger and others.

28 Hüttmann, pp. 24-25. The testimonies of 26 police officers of the battalion had been collected from ZStL 204 AR-Z 82/6 and then transmitted to the Prosecutor of Lübeck for the opening of preliminary investigations. According to the testimonies, there are differences in details regarding mainly particular dates, times and methods of the executions, which reflect different moments of the massacre, as well as the frequent rotation of staff of the three companies, from time to time assigned to *Erschiessungskommandos*. There is no need to remember how each testimony photographs the personal perspective of each witness, which is not necessarily identical to that of other witnesses, especially in terms of the difference in space and time in the global context of the massacre.

29 StAw Lübeck – 2 PJs 189/64 vom 21.9.1970, Ziffer 3.

30 Heinrich Meier's testimony is reported in Kohl, pp. 224-225. His English version is published in Gitelman, pp. 281-283.

31 Mallmann Einstieg, pp. 84, 87. Literally: «*zur Sicherung der Lager und Säuberung der Stadt*». BA-MA, RH 26-221/12. The request of 221.Sich.-Div. to von dem Bach was based on the two reports that the division command had received on July 5 by Stubenrauch and Stahr, according to which, «there was a desperate need of more troops», to guard the deposits and the hundreds of rail wagons captured, loaded with equipment, and to counter Soviet stragglers. Browning Policy, p. 119 – NARA T-315/1667/358-9, 374-6.

32 Westermann, pp. 176, 284. *Der HSSPF zbV beim Berück Mitte. Betr.: Säuberungsaktion in Brest. 8.7.1941.* BA-MA, RH 26-221/12a.

33 Browning Policy, p. 120, Mallmann Einstieg, pp. 84, 87, Kopitzsch, p. 264. «*Zehntagemeldung Berück 102 an OKH vom 9.7.1941: Unter Zuhilfenahme der dem Befehlshaber zur Verfügung stehenden Kräfte der Orpo und des SD ist mit dem systematischen Durchsuchen der grösseren Ortschaften, insbesondere von Bialystok und Brest begonnen worden*».

34 See von Schenckendorff's order to 221.Sich.-Div. of 9.7.1941 - NARA T 315/1667/357. Browning Policy, p. 120. In a first phase, immediately after the entry of German troops in Brest Litovsk, three or four thousand inmates previously taken prisoners by NKVD had been released, provoking protests by Nebe, commander of EGB, who maintained that the release would deprive the occupation authorities of a powerful tool of repression. The releases ended around July 5. Curilla, p. 571. On the NKVD arrests in the annexed areas of eastern Poland and western Ukraine, see Bogdan Musial: *Konterrevolutionäre Elemente sind zu erschiessen.*

35 Bef.Kdr. Pol.Rgt.Mitte Ia 15 34, 11.7.1941: «*Auf Befehl des HSSPF zbV beim Berück Mitte, sind alle als Plünderer überführten männlichen Juden im Alter von 17-45 Jahren sofort standrechtlich zu erschiessen*». STAM, StAwBo, nr. 9647,1,Bl.38. The inspection of Himmler and Daluege in Bialystok took place on July 8, 1941 and ended with a dinner attended by, besides the two of them, von dem Bach, Max von Schenckendorff, Montua, Waldow and Nagel (commanders of Polizei-Bataillone 316 and 322) and several other Wehrmacht and SD officials. The arguments of discussion during dinner are not known: the fact is, however, that after this meeting, at least 3,000 Jews were shot in Bialystok on July 12, followed the next day by 4,000 in Brest Litovsk. In view of this, to speak of a coincidence seems unsound, to say the least. See Westermann, p. 176, Mallmann Einstieg, p. 84, Browning, pp. 15-16, Browning, Origins, pp. 268-269. See also Angrik / Voigt / Ammeerschubert / Klein, pp. 334, 374, where WL's testimony to ZStL - AR-Z 52/59, Bd.II, Bl.41, is reported, according to which: "Himmler was unhappy about the low number of Jews arrested and required a more decisive action to that effect."

36 Curilla, p. 571. Also Longerich, p. 350. Present at that inspection were also Otto Winkelmann, chief of Ia office of Hauptamt-Orpo and Paul Riege, BdO of "Krakau". Hüttman, p. 22. The day of the inspection is not certain; it could have taken place between July 9 and 13, hence even before that of Bialystok.

37 Gerlach, p. 547. Also Westermann, p. 176, Browning Origini, pp. 271, 678.

38 Curilla, pp. 571, 860, 862. Gerlach, p. 547. Two SD detachments, one destined to Brest Litovsk and one to Pinsk, with a total of about 30 men, had been mobilised as early as July 2, 1941, on the orders of BdS "Krakau", Eberhard Schöngarth.

39 James Waller: *Perpetrators of Genocide: An Explanatory Model of Extraordinary Human Evil.* In Journal of Hate Studies, vol. 1, 2001.

40 See for example Bauman, pp. 173 ff.

41 SeeKenkmann/Spieker, Bildteil, in particular pp. 44-51.

42 See Henri Tajfel: *Human Groups and social categories. Studies in Social Psycology*, Cambridge, 1981.

43 See § 8.6.4.

44 See for example, the moral decline which police reservist Hermann Gieschen was subject to, a member of Polizei-Bataillon 105, who, in letters to his wife, in the short space of a few weeks, shifted from the sarcasm of the early days to his superiors, to the initial piety towards the Jews he met, to the anonymous passivity towards the events that happened around him and finally the pride for the brutal actions that he was performing. Ludwig Eiber: «*... ein bißchen die Wahrheit» Briefe eines Bremer Kaufmann von seinen Einsatz beim Reserve-Polizeibataillon 105 in der Sowjetunion 1941.*

45 Lichtenstein, p. 168.

46 Klemp Ermittelt, pp. 252-253.

47 *Ibid.*, pp. 253-254.

48 Lichtenstein, pp. 169-170, Klemp Ermittelt, pp. 379-380, Curilla, pp. 569-570.

49 Justiz und Verbrechen Lfd 764, Klemp Ermittelt, pp. 252-253, Curilla, p. 380.

50 Klemp Ermittelt, pp. 253-254, Curilla, p. 380.

51 Hüttmann, p. 48.

52 «Murder for despicable reasons *(Mord aus niedrigen Beweggründen)».*

53 Browning Policy, pp. 116, 118.

54 On Max von Schenckendorff and his repressive policies see HIS, pp. 462, 469, 580.

55 Mallmann Einstieg, p. 85.

56 *Ibid.*, p. 86. Let's remember that on July 3, Stalin had announced on the radio the beginning of the Great Patriotic War and the partisans' uprising in the rearlines: an event that certainly fed the "psychosis of insurgency" – something that was unjustified in that area and in that phase of the occupation.

57 See § 5.6, *Closed communities and microdynamics.*

58 Mallmann Einstieg, pp. 85-86.

59 Between July and September 1941, 4,403 more victims were to be counted in Brest Litovsk, the majority of which, probably, Jews: EM 43 of 5.8.1941 (1,280 victims); EM 47 of 9.8.1941 (510); EM 56 of 18.8.1941 (1,296); EM 66 of 28.8.1941 (769); EM 78 of 9.9.1941 (548). Browning Policy, p. 124.

60 See *Pinkas Hakehillot Polin – Brest*, pp. 226-237

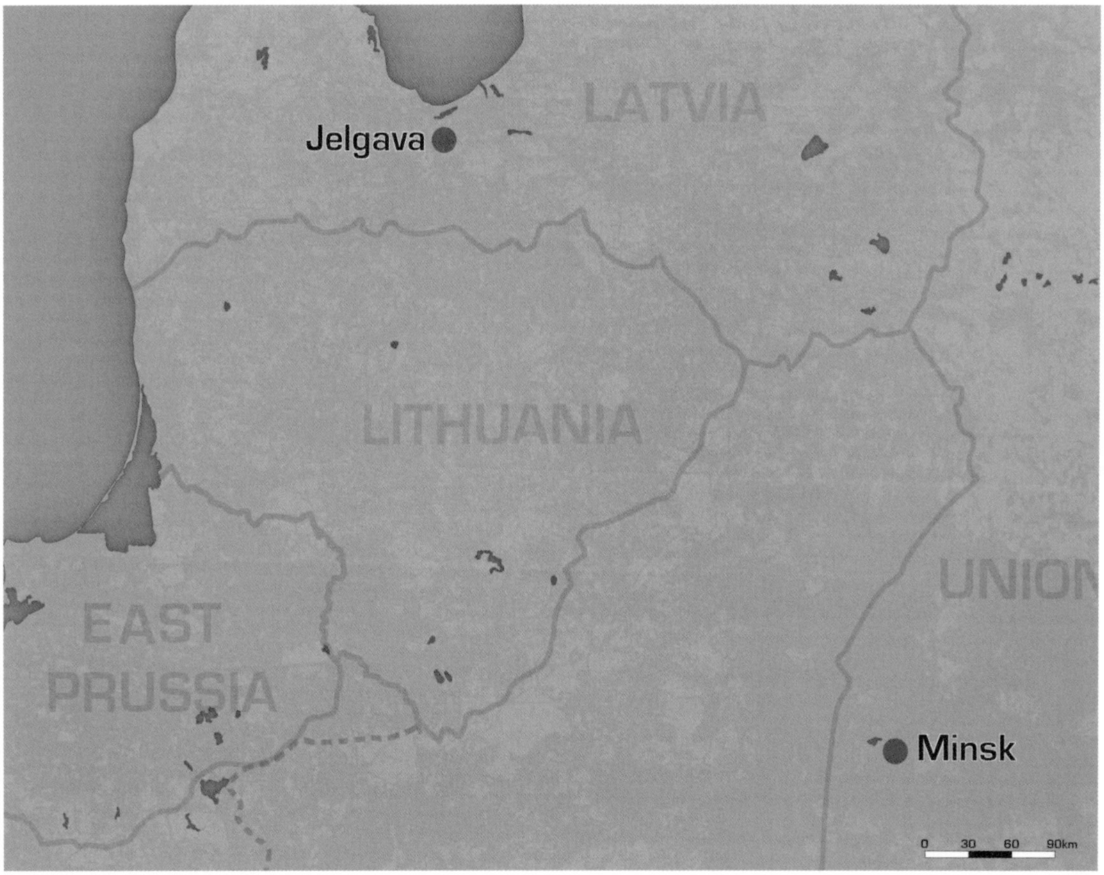
LATVIA
Jelgava
LITHUANIA
EAST
PRUSSIA
UNION
Minsk
0 30 60 90km

CHAPTER THREE

"MARTINS VAGULANS AND THE DESTRUCION OF JELGAVA'S JEWRY"

JULY-AUGUST 1941

Though this be madness yet
there is method in't

William Shakespeare – Hamlet, Act 2, Scene 2

Of course, the whole point of a "Doomsday
Machine" is lost if you keep it a secret!

Stanley Kubrick – Dr. Strangelove

3.1 INTRODUCTION

The destruction of European Jewry which occurred during WWII through the various *technical* stages in which the Final Solution can be divided – at least in theory - is somehow symbolized not only, of course, by the extermination camps, but also by the large mass killings in which tens of thousands of Jews were butchered in the eastern territories by shootings in common graves, especially during the summer / fall of 1941. Among these, to name just a few of the most brutal, we remember Babi Yar (33,000 victims), Rumbula (25,000), Kamenec Podolski (23,600) [1] and Rvno (15÷21,000).

However, we must add to these slaughters, so apocalyptic in terms of victims, an almost infinite number of, so to speak, *peripheral* executions, which led to the disappearance of hundreds of medium and small communities, often of ancient tradition, with their cultural and economic fabric often dating from the late Middle Ages,. That was the case, for example, in Lithuania, where about 95 % of pre-war Jewry was destroyed[2], and also Belarus, Ukraine, Galicia and Latvia, where almost entirely on sight, about 65 % of the Jewish population was exterminated[3].

In this sense, the disappearance of large Jewish communities living in major cities of Eastern Europe ended forever that Jewish cosmopolitanism of merchant origin; perhaps the most impacting and immediately noticeable, if not somewhat superficial, aspect of eastern European Jewry. Instead, the annihilation of small communities throughout the various territories, geographically distant from major economic centers, irretrievably destroyed that fragile but tenacious texture represented by the culture of *shtetl*, typical of Yiddish-speaking Ashkenazi Jewry. That culture somehow represented the most intimate and mystical vision of European Judaism, one in which values and traditions could still prevail over secularism and materialism of Western imprint that by then was quite rife in large eastern urban centers too.

Therefore, if large urban communities could, in general, represent the modernist *reason* of the Eastern Europe Jewish world, small towns preserved its *traditional* consciousness that *in any case* was inevitably destined to die out gradually over time, but to which the Final Solution dealt the death blow, with a brutality that was matched only by its troglodytic coarseness.

However, despite its devastating impact on the *vitality* and the *historic spirit* of European Jewry, the Final Solution in the periphery is still an aspect only partially focused on. This is due, among other aspects, to a lack of accurate data, which could help define its magnitude in terms of modalities, times and numbers. The result is that individual local events, confined to small communities and remote areas, ended up disappearing because they were merged into a more general contextualization.

An example of this situation is given by the events that involved the Latvian Jewish community of Jelgava (Mitau in German). The knowledge we have about its destruction is still rather fragmentary and partial. In this chapter we have tried to trace its contours, as far as possible.

3.2 JELGAVA

With regard to Latvia, the social composition of the local Jewish community eventually settled as late as the second half of XIX century with the arrival in Riga - outpost to the west – of a growing number of Israelites coming from other provinces, to the point where the about 44,000 Jews living in the city in 1935, represented over 46 % of the entire Latvian Mosaic community[4].

And indeed because many Jews of different origins and backgrounds moved and settled in a relatively short time into one small geographical area, the Jewish community of Latvia saw its strict theological and historical differences gradually fade into one large *melting pot*[5].

After Riga, the other two major Jewish centers were in Daugavpils, Letgallia (about 11,000 people) and Liepaja, on the Baltic (about 7,000).

Apart from these urban realities, which accounted for about 68 % of Latvian Jewry, there were numerous smaller communities scattered in other provinces, including Jelgava, where out of a total population of 34,000, approximately 2,000 were Jews, almost all of which, apart from a few tens of Latvian citizenship, were partly Germanized, speaking German and Yiddish, mainly traditionalist and observant[6]. With regard to their political orientation, the majority of Jews in Jelgava eligible to vote in the elections of 1925, had expressed their support for Zionist movements: a trend that would remain substantially unchanged over the following years and that was only interrupted by the Soviet occupation in the summer of 1940 [7]. When that happened, logically, some Jews were co-opted into the local Soviet administrative apparatus and were then placed, on June 25, 1941, in a battalion of the Latvian militia (with K.Ulpi as commander, K.Žubīti as political commissar), hastily assembled around Komsomol youth, members of the Communist Party local branch, factory workers and a group of refugees from Lithuania: in all not more than 273 men[8] among which, obviously, the Jews could only be an absolute minority, certainly consistent with the percentage they represented within the total population of the region (about 6 %).

In any case, this battalion survived only from June 25 to the afternoon of June 26, when in the midst of an uncontrolled chaos that left the territory in

A view of Jelgava during the days of German occupation.

anarchy, the general evacuation of all Soviet military and administrative apparatus was ordered in Jelgava [9]. In the chaotic hours that followed about a thousand Jews, many of whom were from Latvia or other parts of Lithuania, fled Jelgava - where in the meantime a citizens' committee of self-defense had been formed by anti-communists, nationalist elements and young students. In their escape, these Jews headed partly to Riga and partly, probably, toward Russia[10]: it is reasonable to assume, then, that some, or many of these, could be considered more sympathetic with the Soviet regime.

All others, by choice, or necessity, decided to remain in Jelgava. Of those, very few survived the summer of 1941[11].

3.3 VAGULANS

In the colorful patchwork of auxiliary groups who voluntarily joined the Germans in the early days of *Barbarossa*, a prominent place - more for its intrinsic qualities than for its durability - was occupied by the so-called Kommando "Vagulāns". Formed in Jelgava on June 29, 1941, it gradually spread to most of Zemgallia through a network of local commands with which it continued to operate until mid-August, when it was finally dissolved and reorganized in a different form.

The experience of Vagulāns is specific, if not unique, for its peculiarities. It fits into that gray area where, particularly in certain areas of the Baltic and in Galicia, local auxiliary groups, more or less spontaneous, directed by other factions and with different margins of autonomy, took up arms, not so much and not only to use them against the rearguard of the Red Army, now within reach, but also in order to perpetrate violent activities. With the Soviet political oppression as a political background that linked them, their actions almost always degenerated into *organized pogroms*, persecutory events, as well as acts of racial genocide, invariably directed against the Jewish population[12].

The case of Martins Vagulāns is emblematic. Andrew Ezergailis, perhaps the first to have characterized Vagulāns, describes him so[13]:

"Vagulāns graduated from the University of Latvia in 1934 with a degree in agronomy, but he had spent most of his working life prior to the occupation as a journalist with a variety of newspapers in Bauska, Jelgava, and Riga. He was a member of a fraternity and had been a member of the Pērkonkrusts prior to the Ulmanis coup. The similarities between Nazi and Pērkonkrusts anti-Semitism perhaps were sufficient for Stahlecker and Vagulāns to reach an understanding about the Jews. Vagulāns did not disappoint Stahlecker".

It is not clear how Vagulāns made contact with Stahlecker. According to the version that he confided to an acquaintance, Latvian lawyer Rudolfs Turks, member of SD [14], the two met *casually* on the highway to Riga and from here the two would start an acquaintance built on trust. Stahlecker would then place Vagulāns in charge of organizing a core of Latvian SD auxiliaries in Jelgava[15].

A second, different version, proposed by Pavlovičs[16], portrays Vagulāns as no more than an opportunist and ambitious adventurer, who, finding himself in the Meitene area, near the border with Lithuania, soon after June 22, managed to get in contact with the command of the German XXVI Army Corps, which commissioned him to organize security in Jelgava. At that point, thanks to the written authorization, in the late afternoon of June 29, Vagulāns would show up to the city committee – which was vaguely trying to take the most urgent measures for the safety of the city, by now basically left to its own devices[17] – and apparently without objections would proclaim himself «Jelgavas drošības dienesta štāba priekšnieku *(Sicherheitsdienststabführer Stadt Jelgava)*». According to this version of events, the first contact between Vagulāns and Stahlecker would occur around July 2, that is, a few days before the arrival in Jelgava of an EGA detachment, namely Teilkommando "Becu", conveying specific instructions relative to the beginning of anti-Jewish persecution in the city and the district [18]. At that point, having revealed himself as one of the few local leaders willing to *get their hands dirty*

German troops in Jelgava. Summer 1941. Note the Latvian National banners on both sides of the street. In the Baltic and in Ukraine, at times, the local people welcomed the Germans very warmly.

with such matters, Vagulāns would become Stahlecker's Latvian referent in the Zemgallia district, despite the discontent of FK 818, that saw him as little more than an incompetent, unable to provide both ordinary administration of the territory under its jurisdiction – including food supplies to the troops, which were totally disorganized and inadequate – and to ensure the road network was useable – essential for connecting with Riga and still roamed by groups of Soviet stragglers on their way to Russia as well as Lithuanian criminal gangs. For this reason, according to Pavlovičs, the Wehrmacht would tolerate Vagulāns only because, driven by his innate anti-semitism, he proved willing to take on even the most inadmissible assignments, including the deportation of all Jews in Jelgava and the surrounding areas of controlled residence. It seems that this last measure was wanted by FK 818 (and not the SD), in order to remove the Jews from areas considered *sensitive*, such as the bridges on the Lilupe river, in obedience to that sort of *paranoid obsession* that overwhelmed Wehrmacht's rear-line commands[19]. In other words, according to Pavlovičs, Vagulāns was a *useful idiot* (or rather a seedy adventurer)[20], tolerated by the Wehrmacht and maneuvered by Stahlecker, and with little support among the local ringleaders outside Jelgava.

These dynamics, however, are interpreted differently by Ezergailis, who suggests that Vagulāns may have been an SD operative before Barbarossa, and may have begun his mission in Jelgava precisely because he held that role, providing in fact one of those ephemeral operational commands that Ezergailis identifies as "Self-Defense Commandantures (Selbstschutz-Kommandantures)»[21].

In this sense, Vagulāns' settling in the city and his immediate assumption of all powers in the chaotic vacuum left by the Soviets and not yet filled by Sicherheitspolizei - whose first core, Teilkommando "Becu," arrived in Jelgava only within the first ten days of July - would be too quick to be casual[22]. It was so quick, in fact, as to be able to organize, the very next day, June 30, and perhaps with Stahlecker's consent, the release of the first issue of Nacionālā Zemgale, a newspaper published and edited by Vagulāns himself, which became the organ through which he began to issue orders and decrees, as well as the megaphone to spread his anti-Semitic hysteria.

For these reasons it cannot be excluded that Vagulāns, perhaps through old adhesions with members of Perkonkrusts fled to Germany in July 1940, or perhaps through some *Volksdeutsche* Latvian immigrant in the Reich, could actually have been in contact with SD since before *Barbarossa*, and that they had hired him, equipped with their own political directives and then left him on stand-by awaiting a favorable opportunity. Opportunity that would come in the small hours of June 22 when Vagulāns, after going into hiding, could join a group of Latvian partisans operating in the Eleja area, along the border with Lithuania, not far from Meitene. Then, he would provide the Germans with information about Red Army units in the Jelgava area which he, in turn, received from an acquaintance, Arturs Neparts, a student at the Institute of Science of Jelgava and leader of an underground student group[23].

In this context, if, as it seems, there actually was a meeting between Stahlecker and Vagulāns, along the road which leads from the Lithuanian border to Riga, via Jelgava (probably around June 29), it seems unlikely that it happened fortuitously. On the contrary, it would seem quite deliberate, arranged in order to define the further development of a project that already existed and was outlined in general terms; something that wouldn't leave much room for improvisation or spontaneity. In other words, in his march towards Riga, Stahlecker intended to organize, with Latvian personnel, an SD territorial network, naming the individuals responsible at local level: so, besides Jelgava, auxiliary SD branches unofficially called *Selbstschutz Kommandantures*, would also be activated in Bauska, Tukums and Jēkabpils, as well as many other places in Latvia[24].

Stahlecker remained always rather vague with regards to the execution of Jews and never openly ordered them, and actually it is not known what arrangements he made with Vagulāns. What is certain is that it is very reasonable to suppose that Stahlecker, whose command of Riga was only twenty / thirty miles away from Jelgava, gave his prior approval, or at least tacit approval, to the events that occurred in Jelgava in July / August 1941, which led to the annihilation of the local Jewish community. The same consideration goes for the ideological line adopted by *Nacionālā Zemgale*, day by day more violently anti-Semitic, to the point of self-congratulation in its last issue dated August 15, for the expulsion of the Jews "the creators of the world's misery" from the city, implemented with "exemplary support of German soldiers".

According to Ezergailis then, it is rather unlikely that Stahlecker did not give a kind of *prior blessing* to Vagulāns, who, from the day after his installation in the premises of the Prefecture, in Liela iela 42, began building his organization. This organization was mainly based on an initial group of 10 or 15 subjects that had already served in the pre-war Latvian police, in the paramilitary and civil defense organization Aizsargi, and in the cores of armed national partisans who had taken to the streets in those days. In fact, with an article published on June 30 in the columns of *Nacionālā Zemgale*, Vagulāns announced the establishment of his command – the equivalent of a security police – and ordered the recall to arms of all policemen and Aizsargi who were in service in the city until June 15, 1940 (the date the Soviet Union had invaded the Baltic States). At the same time, a number of regulations were issued regarding urban security, assignment of identification bracelets to the staff[25], possession of weapons, press censorship, price-control, seizure of vehicles and application of the laws of war (shooting) for offenders: all measures that, in the extraordinary and chaotic situation that Latvia experienced during the final days of June 1941, could be considered rather ordinary, but that confirm the full grip on power and the authority of Vagulāns upon Jelgava and its suburbs within the short time-frame of 24 hours. Obviously, anti-Jewish measures were added immediately to these early regulations; announced on June 30 by Vagulāns through a rant on the *Judeo-Masonic conspiracy* centered around the Protocols of the Elders of Zion. These measures came to light with the decree of July 3, which required the dismissal of Jewish workers from factories, commercial activities of public interest and the various city institutions. This early harassment was followed by a second two days later, which focused on prohibiting Jews from visiting theaters, cinemas, museums and public parks[26].

It was estimated that Kommando "Vagulāns" may have reached, at the height of its strength, a force of about 300 men, a hundred of which in Jelgava and the rest dispersed in a network of commands extending to the neighboring districts of Bauska, Tukums and Jēkabpils, apparently operating from July 5, as confirmed by Vagulāns himself through an article published two days later by Nacionālā Zemgale at the end of a tour of inspection in various locations. The same article highlighted, in emphatic tones, numerous problems encountered in those detached branches about organization, leadership and lack of respect for the orders issued by the central Command.

As for Jelgava, where the *kommando* had its own headquarters, different structures were created[27]:

- Central control of Vagulāns and s cretariat, in *Liela iela* 42
- A guard unit
- A command center for the urban area of Jelgava
- A coordination center for the detached commands
- A command of criminal police
- A command for treasury and seized valuables
- A command for the seizure and management of properties
- A command for the management of economic matters
- A command for controlling prices and black market
- A *Kommandantur* for concentration camps
- An investigative command
- A command for the registration of Jews
- A passport office
- A special task units

Reading this structure within the frame of the general context, we get a sense of the ambition that revolved around Kommando "Vagulāns", which was allowed to expand within certain limits, until it evolved into something very similar to a real security structure on a local scale, parallel to the DS. At some point, however, something stopped working.

On August 18, 1941, two days after announcing the end of the Jewish community in Jelgava with his usual anti-Semitic hysteria in the columns of *Nacionālā Zemgale*, Vagulāns was removed from command and replaced by Valdis Jursons, who also assumed control of the newspaper that was then renamed simply *Zemgale*[28]. As for the operational structure of the *kommando*, this was kept intact in its broad outlines, but rearranged into an ordinary Schu-Einzeldienst district police (and not as an auxiliary security police force), with all the political significance that went with it. With regard to Vagulāns, consistent with his attitudes, he would not find anything better to do than enlist in Kommando "Arajs", only to be incarcerated in Riga's main prison in 1943 for the rape of a Jewish woman in Minsk[29].

Several hypotheses have been advanced on the reasons that led to the replacement of Vagulāns. Only one, namely that his anti-Semitic fury went beyond any limits imposed by the Germans, has been ruled out as improbable, given the support that the Germans ensured and would continue to ensure to Arajs and his henchmen. All the others seem fairly likely and do not necessarily contradict each other:

- The first and most plausible one is that the function of Vagulāns may have been considered *exhausted* once the situation in the city and the district was more or less normalized and, especially, after completing the destruction of the Jewish community of Jelgava[30]. We do not actually know what agreements he made with Tahlecker on June 28, but it is possible that they were restricted to the short-term only and to the execution of the *dirty work*. As a matter of fact, that would be in line with the short-lived and limited role of the other *Selbstschutz Kommandantures* established in

Latvia during the first six weeks of the occupation. In that respect, having allowed Vagulāns to enlist in Arajs' group and maintain links with the SD (see § 3.7), suggests that the replacement was not his *ultimate fall* before the eyes of his controllers, rather that he was put in a position to decide his own fate, after completing the *mission* in Jelgava.

- The second possibility is that Vagulāns may have proved to be unmanageable and potentially dangerous because he was a nationalist. The fact that after August 16 his group ended up reorganizing itself as a sort of auxiliary police force along the lines of Schu-Einzeldienst, losing those attitudes of political police that so far had distinguished it, is quite significant. In that respect, it is no secret that the directives coming from Berlin, that Stahlecker had to apply, adapting them into a difficult context, did not include the presence of armed auxiliary entities that were not entirely under strict political and operational control by the Germans who, actually, as early as July 8 imposed the dissolution of all partisan groups formed spontaneously after June 22[31]. Given that, Vagulāns' evident ambition to turn his mishmash of thugs into something politically significant would be something impossible to tolerate beyond a certain limit. Another clue to this effect could be the removal, as of August 18, of the adjective "*Nacionala*" from the head of the newspaper, which was thus reduced to a more innocuous and generic "*Zemgale*".
- A third possibility – advanced by both Ezergailis and Pavlovičs[32] – is that Vagulāns was deemed professionally unfit to play a leading role in a condition "of stabilization", that is; a condition that was not an emergency. Hence, regardless of the level of his political and ideological loyalty, he was replaced by Hptm. Jursons because the leading of a police structure at district level was something too complex to be left to an amateur, and, as far as experience goes, Vagulāns could not claim any, except from being a mediocre journalist and political agitator.
- A final hypothesis, advanced by Ezergailis [33] relates to possible incompatibilities between Vagulāns and Gebietkommissar Walter von Medem, newly appointed to the civil administration in the Jelgava district by Reichkommissar Lohse. A few days after taking charge on August 12, 1941[34], von Medem wrote a stern memorandum in which he endorsed the full responsibility for the killing of Zemgallia Jews to "those crazy Latvians", probably as a response and refutation to an article that appeared in Vagulāns *Nacionālā Zemgale* on August 15, in which such *credit* was given primarily to the Germans[35]:

This is Vagulāns' version:

> *Jelgava is now Jew-free, a small sign announces it at the entrance of the Zemgallia metropolis. This sign is enough to acknowledge – and to inform all citizens of Zemgallia – [...] that the builders of the new order – the German soldiers – have demonstrated exemplary faith in the support and ensuring the success, [namely] the expulsion of that race of people, originators of all miseries in the world.*

This is von Medem's:

> *The brutality and resettlement emanated primarily from the Latvians, and were directed against local Jews and Communists. The Latvian people has freed itself of the Jews with spontaneous hatred, and there was also a bloody showdown with local Latvians elements.*

We do not know for sure what the starting point was for the conflict between von Medem and Vagulāns. However, for a person of noble but decayed lineage, such as Walter-Eberhard, Baron von Medem – who, with the impudence of a king in his personal domain had begun to exercise his power in the district from the spectacular *Jelgavas pils*, the Palace built by Bartolomeo Rastrelli that had been home of the Dukes of Courland – the competition from a small local *plebeian* ringleader such as Vagulāns could hardly be tolerated. Add to this von Medem's likely personal resentment and desire for revenge against the *ungrateful* Latvians in general, and we have a plausible framework for the rapid collapse of the power system exercised by Vagulāns in Jelgava and surroundings[36]. In any case, whatever the motivations that led to his withdrawal, the fact remains that after Vagulāns' intervention, the so-called *Jewish question*, at least in the District of Zemgallia, could effectively be considered *solved*.

Let's see how.

3.4 PREPARATIONS

According to the June 30 edition of *Nacionālā Zemgale*, Jelgava fell into German hands without a fight, at 14:30 on June 29, soon after being reached (at 12:50 hours) from the vanguard of a motorcycle troop of the 61st Infantry Division, in charge of keeping open the bridges south of the city. According to that article - then re-released on July 6 on the basis of a piece written by German war correspondent Frank Götze - the Latvian population warmly welcomed the German troops[37]. Then, within a few hours, Stahlecker and Stab/EGA crossed the city and, on June 30, reached Pardaugava, a suburb of Riga on the south bank of the Dvina, and finally Riga itself the following day (July 1)[38]; on the same day Jelgava was chosen as headquarters of Feldkommandantur 818 led by Maj. Schaefer, who, however, took the assignment only on July 6, leaving for a few days a power vacuum in the city and county, at least with regard to the Wehrmacht's authority: a vacuum that was occupied firmly by Vagulāns and his men[39].

At this point, according to the information available – mainly to the acts collected during the process of Cologne v. Adelt and Becu (members of Einsatzkommando 2) – the only Sicherheitspolizei unit to enter Riga after Stahlecker would be Alfred Becu's Teilkommando, that arrived between July 2 and 4, 1941. During the same days the EK2, led by Rudolf Batz, also arrived in the city. Batz then gave orders to Becu to establish a small group of men in Jelgava in order to proceed with the elimination of all potential opponents - including of course the entire Jewish component of the local population[40] - and to support (and presumably keep an eye on), the activities of Vagulāns' auxiliaries.

Based on this calendar, the presence of Stahlecker in Jelgava can be put at no later than June 29, that is shortly after the meeting with Vagulāns, and, probably, shortly before the burning of the synagogue that occurred *two or three days after* the entry of German troops into Jelgava. This was one of the first acts perpetrated against the Jewish community and in this case, probably carried out by a few small detachments of EK2 that were still in town, perhaps in order to give Vagulāns and his men a *practical demonstration*[41].

A succinct account of the synagogue arson – that probably occurred on the night between June 29 and 30, or alternatively between June 30 and July 1 – was given on October 16, 1970 before the Court of Cologne by Arturs Tobiass, a Latvian citizen who witnessed the aftermath of the lighting of the fire because his home was only a few hundred yards away from the synagogue, so after hearing a massive explosion, at around midnight, he ran to see what was happening:

> *"When I arrived the synagogue was in full blaze. The onlookers said that the Germans had started up the fire with gasoline and hand grenades. It was not longer after that I saw a group of Jews approaching. No longer can I remember whether they were only men or whether women also marched along. On both sides of the group, five meters apart, marched uniformed men in German steel helmets. It is difficult to estimate how many Jews were in the group. There could have been 100 to 200 persons. The Jews disappeared in the darkness and I went home.*
>
> *The next day I talked to a neighbor who lived next door to the synagogue. He told me that the rabbi had refused to leave the synagogue and the Germans had killed him. He was left lying, and burned in the synagogue. I also heard that either there were Jews burned in the synagogue or that excesses were committed to the group of Jews marching by the burning synagogue. I must too say that I stood in the back of the crowd of onlookers.... As the Jews were marched by the burning synagogue, I heard Latvian onlookers commiserate with them [...]. At*

this event I heard no expression or activities of anti-Semitism among the Latvians"

So, Jelgava's synagogue pogrom was not perpetrated by some lawless band of Latvians, but an act hatched by German personnel in uniform against a group of Jews who, presumably, had gathered inside the synagogue to seek shelter or perhaps to discuss what to do. Indeed, Latvian civilians who witnessed the fire would have expressed sympathy for their Jewish fellow citizens[43].

With regard to the Jews arrested after the fire, their fate is unknown. According to Kaufmann, during the early days of occupation there were several shootings of Jewish individuals or even whole families[44] – probably in the region of some tens of people – but he does not report any indication suggesting a mass execution – which the shooting of 100 or 200 people obviously would have been. Therefore, it is plausible that the Jews arrested that night were confined for the most part in the same buildings destined to become part of the ghetto to which all the other Jews of Jelgava were to be deported within the first week of occupation[45].

The confinement under surveillance of Jelgava's entire Jewish community is confirmed by the orders issued by Vagulāns through the columns of *Nacionālā Zemgale*. In fact, immediately after ordering all owners of buildings to provide the security police with lists of tenants (July 1) and after banning Latvians from any commercial or exchange agreement with Jews (July 3), Vagulāns produced yet another drastic discriminatory measure, ordering all Jelgava Jews to leave their homes, as well as their jobs, by July 5, and go to the ghetto buildings assigned to them. At that point, the buildings used for forced segregation were placed under surveillance by Vagulāns' men.

The witness, Arturs Tobiass, confirms this particular [46]:

4 NACIONĀLĀ ZEMGALE Nr. 5. Piektdien, 1941. g. 4. jūlijā.

Anordnung

Mit Bekanntmachung dieses Anordnung den 3. Juli 1941, gebe ich den Auftrag in Fabriken, Industrie- und Handels-Unternehmen und in allen Behörden ohne Ausnahme sofort alle jüdischen Arbeiter und Angestellte zu entlassen.

Für die Durchführung dieses Anordnung mache ich die Leiter der Unternehmen verantwortlich.

Bei Ubertretung dieses Anordnung werden die Schuldigen nach Gesetzen der Kriegszeit zur Verantwortung gezogen.

1941. 3. Juli
Mitau

Sicherheitsdienststabsführer
Stadt Jelgawa (Mitau)

Rīkojums

Sākot ar šī rīkojuma publicēšanu 1941. g. 3. jūliju, uzdod visās fabrikās, rūpniecības un tirdzniecības uzņēmumos, kā a visās iestādēs bez izņēmuma nekavējoši atbrīvot no darb židus — darbiniekus un strādniekus.

Atbildību par rīkojuma izpildīšanu uzlieku uzņēmumu atbi dīgiem vadītājiem.

Rīkojuma nepildīšanas gadījumā vainīgie tiks saukti pie a bildības pēc kaŗa laika likumiem.

1941. g. 3. jūlijā
Jelgavā

Drošības dienesta priekšniek

Anordnung

Die jüdischen Einwohner, welche Wohnungen und Arbeitsstellen in unten genannten Strassen und von denen eingeschlossenen Rajonen haben, müssen bis zum 5. Juli 1941 18 Uhr ihre Wohnungen und Arbeitsstellen verlassen.

Driksa — Zwejniek — Lapskaln — Kasernen — Oberst Briedis — die ganze Doblenische Strasse — Wall-Strasse — Litauische Strasse bis Platone Strasse, längst der Eisenbahn bis zur Aa und das ganze Neu-Mitau auf den rechten Ufer der Aa.

Sicherheitsdienststabsführer
Stadt Jelgawa (Mitau)

1941. 3. Juli
Mitau

Rīkojums

Židu tautības pilsoņiem, kuŗu dzīvokļi un darba vieta atrodas zemāk minētos pilsētas valdes ieslēgtos rajonos un iela līdz 1941. g. 5. jūlijam pulksten 18 nekavējoši jāatstāj.

Driksa — Zvejnieku iela — Lapskalna iela — Kazarmes ie — Pulkveža Brieža iela — Dobeles iela visā gaŗumā — Vaļņ iela — Lietuvas iela līdz Platones ielai — Dzelzceļš līdz Lie upei un visā Jaunās Jelgavas daļā labā Lielupes krastā.

Drošības dienesta priekšnieks

1941. g. 3. jūlijā,
Jelgavā.

Anordnung

Mit dem 5. Juli 1941 ist es jüdischen Einwohnern verboten Theater, Kino, Anlagen, Museen und andere Veranstaltungen zu besuchen.

den 2. Juli 1941
Mitau

Sicherheitsdienststabführer

Rīkojums

Sākot ar 1941. g. 5. jūliju židu tautības pilsoņiem a liegts apmeklēt teātŗus, kino, publiskus parkus, mūzejus citas mākslas iestādes, kā arī sarīkojumus.

1941. g. 2. jūlijā
Jelgavā

Drošības dienesta priekšnieks

Some of the anti-Semitic decrees implemented by Vagulāns through the columns of Nacionālā Zemgale of July 4, 1941. In particular, the prohibition to attend cinemas and theaters (2/7), the order of abandonment of dwellings (3/7) and the dismissal of Jewish workers from factories and businesses (3/7).

"I heard that the Jews were assembled in a building on my street that stretched along to the fish market. The house was near the Kielupe River. The house in which the Jews were assembled could have accommodated only a small part of the Jelgava Jews, it was guarded by an ex-sergeant of the Latvian Army and other Latvians, as he [the sergeant] told me. I cannot remember anything special about the Jewish confinement, because the ex-sergeant who told me was frequently very drunk".

Hence, if, as it seems, Vagulāns and his acolytes were unrelated to the synagogue attack, they could soon find a *remedy* to this deficiency, as following events would demonstrate.

3.5 ANNIHILATION

Stahlecker's EM 40 of August 1, 1941, reports that by that date 1,550 of Jelgava's surviving Jews had been *eliminated*: a figure consistent with the previous summary reported by *Nacionālā Zemgale* on July 29, according to which 1,200 Jews had been *expelled* from the city. A few days later, on August 15, again from the columns of that newspaper, Vagulāns announced the *disappearance* of Jelgava's Jewish community. Further downsizing of the time frame within which the massacre was perpetrated is provided by a letter written by Wachtmeister Hermann Gieschen, to his wife Hanna on July 20, 1941. He was a member of Bremen's Polizei-Bataillon 105, that was in transit in Jelgava on its way to Riga[47]:

We marched for about 60 miles, and we are now on Latvian territory, about 25 miles away from Riga... The small town where we are is very pretty. Life has resumed its course. The refugees have returned ... The Jews are all away. There are more Jews in Mitau. I do not know where this pack is, they probably went out to work in the fields ... [sic!] Moreover, the Mitauer Hof was opened, a large new hotel, several officers live there. You can also have lunch there... prices are quite low. Riga too is a beautiful and orderly town. You can tell it has a Germanic imprint. Everybody is friendly and clean, wide streets, beautiful buildings, nice shops and fine restaurants.

The data derived from these sources makes it reasonable to frame the annihilation of Jelgava's Jews in a period between the first and second ten days of July, largely coinciding with the stay in the city of TK "Becu," which lasted for at least a week, from about July 4. All this is further confirmed by signs bearing the *Mitau judenfrei* announcement, placed on the different entrance points to the city a few weeks after the occupation began[48].

To outline the period in which the *liquidation* of Jelgava Jews occurred is important in trying to establish the responsibilities and the context in which such uprooting was perpetrated. From the available data it seems that Becu's *Mordkommando* and Vagulāns auxiliaries shared responsibilities. Probably, while the first had been sent to the town in order to give orders and supervise, the latter executed such orders, after having carried out, as early as June 30, shortly after their settlement in Jelgava, all the preparatory *work*: marginalization and identification of Jews and their subsequent imprisonment within specific areas.

In Jelgava, as in much of Latvia, mass executions would begin only *after* the establishment of so-called *Selbstschutz-Kommandantures* by the Germans, essentially formed around members of partisan groups, such as Vagulāns', who had taken up arms in the days of the Soviet retreat from the country. Approximately 700 of these operating entities were set up at local level throughout Latvia. They were, on the one hand, subject to the Wehrmacht's territorial structures (*Orts* and *Feld-Kommandanturen*) and on the other available, when necessary, to take on anti-Jewish activities, in the role of a genocidal workforce for SD detachments [49]. Most of these *Kommandantures* were involved in the Jewish genocide, and it is a fact that, for about six weeks, from June 22, 1941 onwards, many of them held a significant role especially in rural areas, where it would otherwise be difficult for Sicherheitspolizei to intervene with only the few units available to them in Latvia. In any case, these structures were *creatures* of German imprint, which disappeared by fall 1941, once the provinces were eventually rid of Jews, and the occupation authorities decided they could be disbanded[50]. For this reason, the Jewish genocide in Latvia should not be read as a spontaneous and *endogenous* phenomenon generated by the Latvians' resentment towards the Jews dating back to the period of Soviet occupation: it was rather the result of *exogenous* pulses launched by Sicherheitspolizei branches and under their close supervision.

One *proof* of this is Stahlecker's angry reaction of August 6, 1941 before the most pragmatic guidelines on the *treatment* of the Jews outlined by Lohse, newly-appointed Reichkommissar Ostland, who he felt was *guilty* of not taking into account the new possibilities offered by the eastern territories to "solve the Jewish question by a radical treatment (radikale Behandlung der Judenfrage)[51].

Another *proof* is Stahlecker's jotting, on the same memorandum, regarding the need to discuss the matter only *by voice*, not being appropriate to do so in writing, as a matter concerning "fundamental orders from higher authorities of Security Police"[52].

Last *proof* is the substantial failure, admitted by Stahlecker himself, of the attempt to incite the Latvian population to perform anti-Jewish pogroms immediately after the entry of German forces into the country[53]. Such admission does not deny but actually confirms the optimistic impressions that Stahlecker recorded, with deliberate ambiguity, in EM 40 of August 1, 1941, about the completion of some (allegedly) *self-cleansing* actions by the Latvians, including the *removal* of 1,550 Jews in Jelgava (an action in fact directed by the Germans). In other words, the failure of *spontaneous* pogroms had the effect of bringing the burden of solving the so-called *Jewish question* in Latvia (and elsewhere) back into Nazi hands.

That said, the subordinate role of Latvian perpetrators with respect to their German controllers does not rule out the proven responsibility of certain sections of the local *intelligentsia*, probably a very *noisy* minority – such as student associations, newspapers like the *Nacionālā Zemgale*, intellectual extremist circles, etc.[54] – for helping to exacerbate the most intransigent pulses among the population through *cries of pain*, manipulation of episodes and distorted reading of events, and also for relying on the widespread climate of uncertainty and the objective difficulties produced by the sudden and unexpected *regime changing*. A poisoned environment, typical of any situation of exasperated, anarchy-prone turbulence – like that of Latvia in the short period of hiatus between the Soviets' escape and the entry of German troops during which all that non-ideological mix of violence, abuse, opportunism, expediency, tricks and destitution – failed to lead to *pogroms* or mass-executions. It was, however, instrumental in the creation of that mephitic social habitat suitable to facilitate the transition from discriminatory anti-Semitism to eliminationist anti-Semitism in the short span of a few weeks or even a few days, as in the case of Jelgava.

The acts of the trial of Cologne provide some details on what happened in the days of the massacres in Jelgava.

As reconstructed by investigators, the group of Sipo-SD, composed of nine EK2 members and acting on Alfred Becu's orders, supported by a dozen officers of the first half platoon of 1/Polizei-Bataillon 9 led by Wilhelm Adelt, went from Riga to Jelgava in the days immediately following July 4. Right from the start, following instructions from Batz, Becu made contact with Vagulāns and provided him the support of his firing squad[55].

This is Adelt's testimony recalling his first encounter with Becu[56]:

> *As soon as we arrived in Riga my 12 men and I were assigned to an SD Sonderkommando of about equal strength, commanded by SS-Sturmscharführer Becu, who was completely unknown to me, who ordered us to follow him and his group, not telling us why or the destination. Then, early in the afternoon we reached Mitau, where we took our quarters. I placed part of my group to guard the lodgings.*

By then, with the imprisonment of Jews in the buildings assigned to them (July 5) already completed, all that was left to do was proceed with their *liquidation*.

It is not clear, in fact, if the Jews' *liquidation* occurred through one single mass-shooting or in various stages during the month of July. Comparison of the limited data available seems to confirm the second hypothesis, because that would commit a smaller number of men compared to one large action: it should be remembered that besides the few German policemen commanded by Becu and Adelt, only about a hundred of Vagulāns' auxiliaries, including the administrative staff, were available in Jelgava. Therefore, it is possible that every *action* was aimed at one single group of ghetto-buildings, and then on to the next only when the previous one had been *emptied*.

Here is an excerpt of the proceedings of the preliminary investigation initiated by the Prosecutor of Dortmund v. Adelt and Becu[57]:

> *In July 1941, after the entry into Riga of much of Rudolf Batz's EK2, an SD kommando and members of 1/Polizei-Bataillon 9 were sent to Mitau (Jelgava), in order to liquidate the Jews, together with lettischen Selbstschutz. Acting under Adelt's orders was a group of 1/Polizei-Bataillon 9, while the entire kommando was led by Becu. The executions of Jews in Mitau (men, women and children), were perpetrated every day for about a week or so, at a former firing range a few kilometers away from the city. The members of Polizei-Bataillon 9 were partly used at checkpoints and in part also in the firing squads. The firing squads took orders from Becu and sometimes Adelt too. After this task, the kommando was shipped back to Riga.*

As reported by Latvian civilian Tobiass to the Court of Cologne, the shootings began two or three weeks after the occupation, that is, around mid-July[58]:

> *"About two to three weeks after the German occupation I saw a truck full of Jews, consisting of men and women, I think, drive out of the city. It was not clear to me what was happening to the Jews. It was the talk of the town, even if it was not said publicly, that the Jews would be killed.... I heard from various sources that the Jews were killed on the shooting practice field of the Jelgava infantry regiment. This shooting range in Latvian, was called šaujamlauks. The field was about two kilometers south of Jelgava, not far from the Jelgava-Šiaulai road".*

One of Becu's pieces of evidence that he gave to the Prosecutor of Berlin, reveals some details on how Jelgava's executions were perpetrated. In particular, by his own admission, he received from the Latvian an initial list of Jews already arrested and shot by the Latvians themselves, excluding a group of about a dozen still locked in a bunker near the firing range. After the arrival of Becu and his men, they too were taken out in groups of five and shot in a nearby trench. The shootings would then continue every day for several days. About a hundred victims were shot by the firing squad commanded by Becu himself, who gave orders to his men using a whistle. In the absence of Becu, the platoon received orders from another police NCO (probably Adelt). The Latvian auxiliaries at the scene escorted the victims, cordoned off the area and covered the pits[59].

A detailed confession given by Adelt in 1968 before the Court of Cologne confirms both the place and the modality of executions, which would occur over several days in a row, for a total of at least 500/600 victims[60]. Previously, in a testimony given to the Prosecutor of Dortmund in 1967 in which he stated that sometimes he was forced to replace Becu at the command of the firing squad because he was ordered so, Adelt did not fail to underline the difficult relations between him Becu, and more generally, between the policemen and the SD[61].

> *I would have to monitor the area, so that no unauthorized person could approach the execution place. Becu told me clearly that the victims were Jews...*
>
> *So we went along with the SD men near the shooting range. The place was about one or two miles out of town, in an open field bordered on one side by a stream and by a forest on the rear. It was slightly wavy and looked like a firing range training field with protective walls of sand. I placed my men at the entrance, keeping them at a distance, and then*

I inspected every sentry post to make sure that everything was in order.

I do not know either how or from where Jews were brought to the place of execution, at least I did not see that on the first day. The two following days the executions continued in the same place, with Jews being led to the pits by Latvian auxiliary policemen, who were wearing bracelets and were armed with rifles. Among the Jews there were mostly men, but also women and children. As far as I could see, the pits had not been excavated before.

The condemned (the Jews I mean), had to dig their own grave, after which they were pushed up to the edge and lined up in groups of eight or ten, facing the pit. The executors were SD members, placed at a distance of between fifteen and twenty-five feet. They shot the victims with bolt action rifles. Some SD men shot while crouched on one knee, others standing. How many victims each of them shot, that I could not say. The order to fire was given by Becu. Some of the condemned fell immediately into the pit, some did not. All those who had not fallen directly were thrown into the pit by the next group of prisoners. I do not know if all of them were already dead or not but I remember Becu himself walking along the edge of the pit and firing some coup de grace. The victims were in the vicinity of the pit, waiting to be killed in the same way, group after group. In between the shootings no soil was thrown to cover the corpses and only in the end the pit was covered by the Latvians. The pit was between sixty and one hundred and sixty feet long and six-seven feet deep. Every day a new mass grave was dug by the prisoners.

During the three days of shooting between 500 to 600 people were killed. The prisoners had to remove their clothes, but I did not see if this was true for women. The clothes were piled up and taken away by the Latvians. Valuables, money and jewels, obviously, had to be delivered. But it was also possible that the Jews did not have anything of value on them. Becu said that Jews should be killed because they were not compatible with the Nazi regime, and that all Jews, in general, were to be uprooted.

Such was the general dynamics of the executions on the basis of the evidence, each issued from their specific viewing angle, but all agreeing in its essential aspects. At least four of these executions were identified by the Court of Cologne, through the comparison between these and other individual accounts attached to the pleadings[62]:

1.

In particular, during the first day of executions, at least 80 Jews would be shot – men, women and children. While some of the men, guarded by Latvians, proceeded to dig the graves, the other victims were locked in a bunker, surrounded by policemen. Then, once the digging was finished, the victims were brought out in groups of five, forced to remove their clothes up to the inner linen, and then they were shot by a firing squad consisting of both SD members and Latvian auxiliaries. Each victim was taken at gunpoint by two executioners, one aimed at the head and the other at the heart. The fire order was given by Becu. It is possible that some of the victims were not Jews.

After the first day of shootings the policemen would be rather gloomy, so gloomy, in fact, that the SD men would offer them tasty food and many alcoholic beverages.

2. – 3.

Two more executions were perpetrated the next day or a few days after the first: one in the morning and one in the afternoon, with a total of about 80 victims – men, women and children – and in the same way. In this case also alcoholic beverages were distributed to the policemen. At some point, the commander of the firing squad cried out to the victims who were about to be shot: "Look up: there is your Lord Yahweh."

4.

Jelgava was not the only theatre of massacres. In at least another town of the same district, about 10 to 15 miles away, 40 or 50 Jews were shot, including women and children, and perhaps even some non-Jews. This execution was perpetrated mainly by SD personnel, but some 1/9 police officers also joined in. The victims, kept enclosed in a barn guarded by Latvian auxiliaries, were killed with pistol shots on the edge of a mass grave. Among the victims was a woman in advanced pregnancy. After the execution, the policemen who had fired – six at least – were particularly depressed.

3.6 BODY COUNT

Given the fragmentary nature of the information available, it will probably never be established with absolute accuracy how many Jews were the victims of the genocide in Jelgava and its surroundings.

Assessments have been made and even *exact* figures provided, including those, excessive and unrealistic, estimated by the Soviet Extraordinary Commission in 1945, which numbered the victims as 5,964. In fact, the number of Jews who lost their lives in Jelgava and its immediate vicinity was probably under 2,000, almost all killed in July / August 1941.

A good starting point for attempting an estimate of the casualties is the 1935 census which counted 2,039 Jews living in Jelgava[63]. Of these, about one thousand managed to escape before the Wehrmacht's arrival in late June 1941, as reported in the columns of *Nacionālā Zemgale* on July 29[64], partly replaced by many others who flocked to the city driven out from the provinces and also from Lithuania in order to escape the German vanguards, or forcibly resettled during July on Vagulāns' order[65]. Therefore, assuming similar numbers between *arrivals* and *departures*, it is plausible that the number of Jews in Jelgava, in the early days of German occupation remained roughly stable compared to the 1935 census.

Secondly, we should consider the 1,550 Jews killed, indicated by Stahlecker in his August 1, 1941 report and substantially confirmed by the columns of *Vagulāns Nacionālā* Zemgale (1,200 victims).

At this point, adding together the victims of the four executions positively identified by the Court of Cologne (1÷4), we come to a clear first number of at least 200 Jews murdered by the *kommando* policemen and the Latvian auxiliaries *on Becu's direct order*, in Jelgava and its surrounding area[66]. This can be compared to a total number of victims that was probably almost ten times as high[67], as partly confirmed by various testimonies given at the same court, including Adelt's (which reports 500/600 victims in three days) and those of other police officers of TK "Becu" (which report a total number of victims close to 1000).

Between the numbers reported by Vagulāns and Stahlecker (respectively 1,200 and 1,550 victims) and those upon which the Court of Cologne had to base their objective assessments (200), there is room to speculate over the existence of another far-reaching destructive event (in the order of several hundred victims) that police officers might also have been involved in or, possibly, a certain number of *minor* shootings, some of which possibly were perpetrated only by Vagulāns' men before or after the departure of TK "Becu" and for this reason cannot be found in the testimonies. All this of course, is influenced by the limited information available, which does not allow us to establish the precise dynamics of events.

Apart from all this, however, what is certain is that the Jewish community of Jelgava was destroyed and the city declared *Judenfrei*. And even allowing for the survival of perhaps 350 Jews after the summer of 1941[68], we are back to a death toll exceeding 1,500, which coincides with the number reported by Stahlecker on August 1, and easily compatible within the gross total of 3,576 civilians – both Jews and non Jews – killed in the Zemgallia district, also confirmed by Stahlecker in his further summary report dated October 15, 1941[69].

3.7 NO-MESIS

After the dissolution of his small power system in Jelgava and its surroundings, Vagulāns would become part of Kommando "Arajs", for a time and with assignments unknown, possibly related to communication with EK2, together with SS-Hauptsturmführer Arnold Kirste: a name that we shall come across again soon. Then, on an unknown date, Vagulāns left Arajs and was sent to Minsk, probably as attaché to the group of interpreters led by Otto Libram[70], or maybe to the Latvian company at the dependence of KDS "Weissruthenien", a company that, among other tasks, was used until October 1943 in the Maly Trostenez extermination camp[71]. Vagulāns' presence in Minsk is confirmed by a charge for the rape of a Jewish woman, for which he was repatriated in 1943 and locked up in Riga prison. At this point, and for the rest of the conflict, Vagulāns disappears. All that is certain is that soon after the war he managed to immigrate to Australia where he died in 1982, locked in a psychiatric hospital[72].

We know something more about the fate of Adelt and Becu.

What we do know is obviously related to the case launched on July 8, 1968 by the Court of Cologne (Köln LG 24 Ks 1/68), at the request of the Prosecutor of Dortmund (StAwDo 45 Js 18/65) and on the basis of those files collected as early as the late fifties that had allowed the opening of preliminary investigations against three EK2 members on June 20, 1966: Adelt, Becu and the above mentioned Arnold Kirste[73]. The investigation of the latter, however – former EK2 deputy commander and then in charge of liaising between Rudolf Batz and Viktor Arajs – was deleted a few months later, on February 14, 1967, despite his obvious involvement in all the criminal events that linked to one another EK2, Kommando "Arajs," Bikernieki's *killing field* and the slaughter of Rumbula and despite the fact that he was summoned several times to testify against his former comrades. Also, Kirste would have been directly involved in the formation of TK "Becu" and then of course informed of what the duties of that unit in Jelgava were[74].

However, for the two remaining suspects, the Court of Cologne granted a request for trial, which was upheld on October 5, 1967 by the Prosecutor of Dortmund with the new file StAwDo 10 Js 64/67 which reads, about Adelt[75]:

> *Polizeimeister Adelt Wilhelm, born September 2, 1914 in Obermeinitz, district of Sprottau, is under investigation for murder since February 14, 1967, by the District Court of Cologne. Adelt is accused, as commander of a group of the first platoon of the First Company of Polizei-Bataillon 9, to have performed, during a shooting perpetrated under the supervision of the co-defendant Becu, the lockdown of the area through the members of the unit under his command, to have temporarily led the firing squad and to have finally completed an action in which he had taken part as a subordinate.*

These were the motivations through which the Court of Cologne formalized the charge of complicity to the murder (*Beihilfe zum Mord*) of at least 163 victims to Adelt, and at least 200 to Becu. Despite the gravity of such crimes, however, the ruling that followed was incredibly lenient: it summed up to only a three-year sentence for Becu and 18 months for Adelt. This verdict was finalized on July 1, 1969, by judgment of the Bundesgerichtshof, 2 StR 184/69.

Regarding Adelt, his biographical notes are contained in the binders of the Prosecutor of Dortmund, StAwDo 45 Js 18/65, filed with the State Archives of Münster. They state that after being captured by the British in Norway at the end of the war, Adelt was released on August 20, 1946. He was then refused readmission within the police force, and worked in Berlin as a chauffeur from 1947 to 1953 but then, at his second request, he was reinstated in service as Oberwachtmeister in a compound in the Steglitz district of Berlin on August 1, 1953. After that, he was definitely discharged on May 10, 1967 after the opening of the case v. him and Becu[76]. He was then arrested on January 3, 1972 and imprisoned in Moabit prison. Although minor, the sentence imposed by the Court of Cologne was further mitigated after an appeal for clemency for health reasons advanced on September 21, 1972 by his daughter at the Ministry of Justice of North Rhine-Westphalia, which agreed to the detainee spending the rest of his sentence on parole. In the end, on April 9, 1976 Adelt obtained forgiveness by the Court of Cologne[77].

Regarding Becu, the available biographical news describes him as a career policeman, born August 28, 1902 in Bendorf, near Koblenz, who served in the Prussian Schutzpolizei from 1923. He remained in service also after Hitler's rise to power, attaining the rank of Wachtmeister in 1935. A Party member from May 1, 1933 and SS member from May 20, 1939, on June 1, 1935 he was transferred to the Security Police as a member of Erfurt's Gestapo, with the Kriminalassistent rank in Referat IIa. Transferred to Weimar's Gestapo in 1941, in May of that year he was included among Sicherheitspolizei's officials assigned to EK2[78].

He reinvented himself as a mechanic after the war. The Court of Cologne deemed him socially not dangerous, so after the sentence he was placed behind bars in the Attendorn prison on March 12, 1970, but he was granted a series of benefits deriving from this privileged status, including two licenses to spend time with his family within the first year of detention. Moreover, in January 1971 the same director of the penitentiary requested approval for suspension of the imprisonment. This request was approved and he was placed under house arrest in a housing structure controlled by the same prison. At that point, after a last and fruitless appeal by the Prosecution, the Court of Cologne decided the final commissioning of Becu's freedom, once half the original sentence had been served: something that promptly happened, Becu being "released" on September 12, 1971[79].

3.8 CONSIDERATIONS

For a number of years scholars of the Jewish genocide, especially *regional* genocide, have been agreeing on one point: without the active support of a wide plethora of units, entities and auxiliary structures recruited in the occupied territories, the practical realization of the extermination by the Nazis would have encountered many more difficulties and taken a significantly longer time.

However, some circles of a *reductionist* inclination, support the theory of a so-called *parallel Holocaust*, which was perpetrated soon after the start of Operation *Barbarossa* in some areas of the Soviet Union, and especially in Galicia and the Baltic by local populations and in response to the brutal communist oppression imposed by Moscow between 1940 and 1941. According to this theory, such a violent and *spontaneous* reaction would culminate in pogroms, acts of brutality and mass executions perpetrated on the basis of *dynamics which were endogenous and completely independent - albeit parallel - from the racial policies hatched in Berlin*. This is a rather specious vision, restricted to some specific situations, whose objective limitedness does not allow us to go beyond the acknowledgment of a theory[80].

The truth is, there was a massive involvement of local units and armed groups in the destruction of countless Jewish communities, but in almost all cases, it was *directed* or at least *inspired from outside*, especially when referring to systematic and organized actions. As early as June 29, 1941 in fact, confirming his verbal orders of June 17, Heydrich sent a message to Einsatzgruppen commanders, emphasizing that:

> *Self-cleansing actions implemented by anti-Jewish and anti-communist circles in the lands to be occupied should not be hindered in any way. On the contrary, they shall be intensified, led on the right track if necessary, but without leaving any trace, in a way that these "self-defense groups" could not refer to any orders or any political aims and objectives in the future [...]*[81].

However, despite Heydrich's expectations, cases of collective violence perpetrated against the Jews by local people and recognized as *genuinely* spontaneous, were extremely limited and largely insignificant in the general *economy* of the genocide. Irrelevant, in fact, to the point that Stahlecker himself, on October 15, 1941, in a report to Berlin on the situation in Ostland, was forced to admit that it was not possible to solve the *Jewish question* only through pogroms[82]. An admission confirmed by his following report of January 31, 1942 where he states that:

After the Judeo-Bolshevik terror – during which a total of 33,038 Latvians, had been deported, arrested or killed – one would expect a widespread pogrom by the population; on the contrary local forces spontaneously eliminated only a few thousand Jews. In Latvia, therefore, it was necessary to proceed with extensive round-ups by Sonderkommandos and with the help of Latvian auxiliary police units (usually family members of murdered or kidnapped Latvians) [...][83].

In Latvia, more than elsewhere, attempts to induce *spontaneous* pogroms among the population in the early days of occupation resulted in total failure, to the point that it was necessary to proceed with the activation of organized auxiliary groups to achieve those results that the lynchings had not obtained on their own[84]. Hence the sudden activation of semi-official units to take care of *dirty work*, that could be *dismissed*, or not, depending on the circumstances and that ultimately could share – or even bear in full – the heaviest historical, moral and legal responsibilities in case things did not go the right way[85].

One of such groups was that led by Vagulāns. Tomašuns' view is that Vagulāns was a mediocre, ambitious and unscrupulous adventurer, who presumably placed personal profit on top of every other consideration, except perhaps for his open, staunch anti-Semitism.

At the same time, these features could be easily used to the advantage of those who, like Stahlecker and his *entourage*, were in charge of introducing *Judenpolitik* to the Baltic and therefore were searching for the workforce required to achieve this goal.

It appears obvious that this could not happen without the existence of a basic plan hatched in broad terms in Berlin, and applied with the appropriate *adjustments* to different local situations. In fact there were too many similarities in dynamics, times and methods, from the Baltic to the Black Sea, in the rapid process that during the summer of 1941 caused the *Judenpolitik* to evolve into *Vernichuntgspolitik*. There are too many connections to think that the Jewish genocide could be due only to a simple series of coincidences, or to a kind of point of no return that was a consequence of the progressive barbarization of the conflict on the Eastern front, and therefore something that had not been planned in advance and only partially desired. Too many mechanisms were at work to not think of a pre-existing design, perhaps not developed in the details, but certainly outlined in its essentials and gradually modeled on the evolution of situations[86].

It has been alleged, by those who advocate the theory of *genocidal randomness*, that the absence of specific written orders reveals the non-existence of a prior project of extermination.

Well, we think exactly the opposite. The repetition of situations, almost in photocopy, in operational and social contexts very different from each other is a clear indication of the existence of general guidelines, evidently originated from a single source. In other words, taking the facts as a starting point and proceeding backwards, it is possible to reconstruct both the original plan and the will that gave life to all this and, additionally, albeit empirically, obtain all missing circumstantial evidence no longer obtainable for various reasons. Arnold Kirste's deposition seems to lead to this conclusion. He maintains that in Bad Schmiedeberg, during the days before *Barbarossa*, there was already an awareness by both Batz (EK2) and Jäger (EK 3), about what their role would be in relation to the so-called *Jewish question* in the Soviet Union, even in the absence of an incontrovertible written order. In this sense, according to Kirste, both officers would decide to act "according to how things evolved"[87].

The destruction of Judaism in Latvia was accomplished in a few weeks thanks also to available individuals like Viktor Arajs, Roberts Stiglics, Herberts Teidemanis, Martins Vagulāns and others. Each of them, in the general context of the genocide, had a role that proved to be more or less important and destructive, but that was, however, the result of a deliberate annihilating will, methodically applied as soon as it became clear that so-called "self-cleansing actions (*Selbstreinigungsaktionen*)" would not achieve significant results[88].

The annihilation in the Latvian province began early, long before any sign of barbarism or any indication of difficulties in military operations on the eastern front could be glimpsed. That is, long before anything that could lead to an allegedly *inevitable* Final Solution. Instead, it began immediately, destroying even communities of a medium size such as that of Jelgava, in concentric waves that from the periphery closed toward the center of the country, until the Rumbula apocalypse.

To paraphrase Shakespeare, there was a method to the annihilating madness of the pale principles of genocide. Method, not randomness.

And the Arajis, the Stiglics, the Teidemanis, the Vagulāns, the police battalions and the SD departments were the tools applied to this method. Using yet another quotation, they were "the doomsday machine".

This quotation should not be seen as excessive, because it was an entire world that was erased in just a few weeks.

The world of the Jewish communities of Latvia.

ENDNOTES

1 See Chap. 4.

2 See Arūnas Bubnys: *The Holocaust in Lithuania: an Outline of the Major Stages and their Results*, Amsterdam, 2004, p. 214.

3 Ezergailis, p. XIX.

4 In 1824 the number of Jews living in Riga was 513. This figure increased to more than 5,000 in 1867, 14,000 in 1881 and almost 34,000 in 1913. Ezergailis, p. 60.

5 Until the second half of the nineteenth century Latvian Jews were divided in two main sects: the *Misnaggedim*, observant of the Torah, speaking Yiddish and German, residing mainly in Courland and Zemgallia and partially Germanized, and the rabbinic Hassidim, speaking Yiddish and Russian, residing mainly in Letgallia and largely Russified. Both groups, however, belonged to the sphere of Orthodox Judaism, as opposed to Haskalah secularism introduced in the late nineteenth century that, in Latvia, had its center in Riga.

6 See Tomašuns, p. 163, who provides 1935 census data, with the Jews of Jelgava divided according to their citizenship.

7 See *Pinkas Hakehillot Latvia v'Estonia*, pp. 158-159.

8 Pavlovičs, pp. 136-137.

9 Pavlovičs 2003, p. 111.

10 *Ibid.*, p. 137.

11 On considerations about numbers and losses of Jelgava's Jewish community, see § 5.

12 See for example § 12.3.

13 Ezergailis, p. 156.

14 Rudolfs Turks was a Latvian lawyer who got in touch with Stahlecker on July 1, 1941, a few hours before Riga's fall into German hands. Soon after he moved on to serve Otto Libram, head of unit III-SD, of EK2/KdS "Lettland", and was later sent to Minsk, with the rank of lieutenant, leading a team of interpreters.

15 See Ezergailis, pp. 156-157. A German liaison officer, in contact with EK2's Stab, would work together with *Vagulāns*.

16 Juris Pavlovičs: *Okupācijas varu maiņa Zemgalē 1941. gada vasarā: Jelgavas apriņķis 1941. gada jūnija beigās – jūlija sākumā.*

17 Pavlovičs pp. 139-140. An emergency committee for the city had been formed from June 27 around a group of local notables, who started a security service to ensure essential services and prevent lootings in factories and shops in the city. This service was essentially formed by students of the local training college who would wear a yellow armband.

18 Pavlovičs, pp. 144-145.

19 *Ibid.*, p. 147.

20 *Ibid.*, p. 134.

21 See Andrew Ezergailis: *Pašaizsardzības komandantūru loma holokaustā*, published in 2000 in *Latvija Otrajā Pasaules Karāq. Starptautiskās konferences materiāli.* Some traces of this concept can be also found in Ezergailis' previous work: *The Holocaust in Latvia* of 1996, pp. 154 and 225 ff.

22 As reconstructed by the Court of Cologne, Teilkommando "Becu" was deployed to Jelgava a few days after the arrival in Riga of EK2, between July 2 and 4, 1941. See Curilla, p. 289, Tomašuns, p. 170.

23 Tomašuns, p. 164. With regard to Neparts, after initially following Vagulāns to Jelgava, he abandoned him in July and moved into the ranks of anti-German resistance. He was arrested by SD and stayed in Salaspils, Sachsenhausen and finally Neuengamme prison camps. Immediately after the war he became president of the Association of Latvian resistance movements (LPKDA), established in Detmold with permission of the British military government and then immigrated to the United States in 1950.

24 Lasmanis, p. 267.

25 On July 31, 1941, again in the pages of *Nacionālā Zemgale*, Vagulāns ordered, for his men, the adoption of uniforms with Aizsargi ranks and insignia, together with a bracelet with Latvian national flag colors, stamped with a Feldkommandantur 818 seal.

26 Tomašuns p. 165, Lasmanis 2003, p. 290.

27 Ezergailis, p. 158.

28 Previously, on July 11, 1941, with news released the day after by *Nacionālā Zemgale*, Jursons was appointed commander of Jelgava's district police by Gebietkommissar von Medem. It is easy to read in this appointment that vom Medem celebrated bypassing Vagulāns, an indirect attack on Vagulāns himself, who thus saw his authority reduced to the urban area of Jelgava only.

29 Ezergailis, p. 169. On the Germans' moral depravity in Minsk and their alcoholic and sexual excesses, see Browning Origini, p. 311.

30 Stranga, pp. 25-26, Stranga Holocaust, p. 214.

31 *Ibid, ibid.*

32 Ezergailis, p. 124-125.

33 *Ibid.*, pp. 161-162, 170.

34 Ezergailis Versions, p. 71.

35 *Ibid.*

36 Walter-Eberhard Alexander Albert Freiherr von Medem was the descendent of a noble German family from Courland. One of his forefathers, Ordenmeister Konrad Medem von Mandern was probably the founder of the first fortress of Mitau-Jelgava, its construction dating back to 1265. Wealthy landowners until the end of WWI, in the turbid months after the October Revolution and the independence of Latvia, their properties were nationalized in 1920, after the agrarian reform imposed by the new Latvian government, despite that their young scion Walter-Ebehrard had actively participated in the 1919 War of Independence and the capture of Riga, as commander of Freikorps von Medem. Walter-Eberhard was born in Liegnitz, Silesia, May 4, 1887 and became a member of the Stahlhelm immediately after returning to Germany from Latvia in 1920. He joined the Nazi Party and was a member of the SA, reached the rank of SA-Oberführer and the rank of Leiter der Personalstelle in Frank's Civil Administration, in the General Government, before being appointed Gebietkommissar in Jelgava: a position he held from August 12, 1941 until the Germans retreated from Latvia, in summer 1944. He died in Prague, probably executed, on May 9, 1945. See also Eksteins, pp. 135, 170.

37 Tomašuns, pp. 164-165, Pavlovičs, p. 141. According to EM 11 of July 3, 1941, Stahlecker entered Jelgava on June 28, 1941, accompanied by Stab EGA. See Krausnick/Wilhelm, p. 173.

38 Ezergailis, pp. 150, 168. Stahlecker's entry of Riga is reported in EM 12 July 4, 1941.

39 Pavlovičs, p. 146.

40 Curilla, p. 289. Conclusions of the Court of Cologne – LG Köln 24 Ks 1/68 vom 8.7.1969.

41 Ezergailis, p. 157.

42 *Ibid.*, p. 227.

43 *Ibid.*, p. 227, Tomašuns, p. 171. The fact that it was Germans, and not Latvian auxiliaries who were eventually given German helmets, is evident from the fact that Vagulāns' auxiliaries - which until then were only fitted with a bracelet with the national colors over civilian clothes - began to wear the Aizsargi uniform only from July 31. And in any case it is rather unlikely that the Latvian witness Arturs Tobiass, may not have recognized Latvian uniforms in the glow of the flames, albeit from a distance.

44 Kaufmann, p. 111. According to Kaufann, in addition to some local civilians, among the murderers there were also Latvian Volksdeutschen returning from Germany.

45 Ezergailis, pp. 226-227. To this effect, warehouses or abandoned factories near the fish market, around the train station and the southern part of the city were used.

46 *Ibid.*, p. 227.

47 Eiber, p. 72. On Gieschen see Chapter 2, note 44.

48 Kaufmann, p. 111, Tomašuns, p. 171.

49 Stranga Holocaust, p. 166. In the early days of Barbarossa, partisans would form at least thirty groups, with a total of about 6,000 men. Most of these were co-opted-in *Selbstschutz Kommandantures*, at least until July 8 when the order to disarm issued by Stahlecker against Latvian insurgents did not persuade many of these people, disillusioned by the German attitude, to give up cooperation.

50 Stranga Holocaust, p. 166.

51 Ezergailis, p. 206, Browning Origini, p. 322. The English translation of Stahlecker Memorandum of August 6, 1941, is reproduced in Ezergailis, p. 378-380. Lohse's guidelines insisted on the exploitation of Jews through work, not to mention genocidal hypothesis: a utilitarian view of the environments present in the Ministry of Occupied Eastern Territories, which clashed with the ideological vision, then escalated in exterminationist, of the RSHA.

52 Ezergailis, p. 207, Browning Origini, p. 322. In his memorandum of August 16 Stahlecker uses the term «*grundsätzlichen* [...] *Befehlen* [*von höherer Stelle*]», to define the "fundamental orders" regarding the *Jewish question* received by the regime leaders. He uses the same words also in his following report filed in Nurnberg as 2273-PS. See attachment n. 6. Evidently, this is no coincidence; rather an indication of Stahlecker's willingness, in dealing with the *Jewish question*, to make constant reference to arrangements from Berlin, which in all probability he received only orally. Such arrangements then confirm that the choice regarding extermination by the regime leaders may have been taken, in Ostland at least, earlier than August 16, 1941. Around the same time, following a meeting held on August 12 in Ukraine between Himmler and Jeckeln, the latter gave way to a drastic acceleration of the great massacres in Ukraine, starting from Kamenec Podolski's. See § 4.4. Hence, those early days of August 1941 represent the moment when the final choice to solve the *Jewish question* through extermination, taking advantage of the isolation and distance offered by the large spaces of the East, was probably taken in Berlin.

53 See Report Stahlecker *of* January 31, 1941, IMT Nuremberg, Document 180-L, partially reproduced in Attachment 2. See also Stranga Holocaust, p. 159.

54 Stranga Holocaust, p. 167. By the second half of 1941 as many as 43 newspapers and magazines were published in Latvia, one of which was the notorious propaganda and anti-Semitic pamphlet *Tēvija* (Riga), *Kurzemes Vārds* (Liepaja), *Tālavietis*

(Valmiera) and *Daugavas Vēstnesis (*Daugavpils). Zellis, p. 237, Ezergailis, pp. 165, 166, 171.

55 Testimony by Alfred Becu given before the Court of Cologne. Ezergailis, p. 226, Klemp Sibirien, p. 296.

56 Klemp Sibirien, p. 294.

57 *Ibid*, p. 296. Acts of StAw Dortmund, March 9, 1965.

58 Ezergailis, pp. 227-228.

59 Klemp Sibirien, p. 296-297. Testimony given by Alfred Becu before StAw Berlin, 1 P Js 362/59 (k).

60 Ezergailis, p. 228. Longerich, pp. 333, 671. Adelt's testimony was originally given before ZStL on July 21, 1959 and is confirmed by another policeman, Karl Becker, who was part of the surveillance cordon and gave a total of 160 victims, women and children included, at the end of an execution day.

61 Klemp Sibirien, p. 294.

62 Curilla, pp. 92, 289-291. Conclusions of the Court of Cologne – LG Köln 24 Ks 1/68 vom 8.7.1969.

63 Tomašuns, p. 163, Ezergailis, p. 403. There were, specifically, 2,004 Latvian Jews and 35 Jews of other citizenships.

64 According to Tomašuns, p. 163, several Jelgava Jews looked for refuge in Riga, where they ended up being trapped and sharing the same fate as Riga's Jews. So, they became genocide victims not in Jelgava, but in Rumbula.

65 Ezergailis, p. 226.

66 Tomašuns, p. 170.

67 Ezergailis, p. 226.

68 Despite Jelgava being formally declared *Judenfrei*, probably in late July 1941, some Jews would survive until at least January 1943, including a group of 289 who worked for the district commissioner. Moreover, according to the EM 96 dated September 27, 1941, 45 Jewish patients of Jelgava's psychiatric hospital were shot on September 2, while others, on the run from Riga, met the same fate on an unknown date. Tomašuns, p. 172.

69 *Ibid*., p. 162. EM of 15.10.141.

70 SS-Sturmbannfüher Otto Libram, commander of Abtelung III of KdS "Lettland". Later trasferred to KdS "Weissruthenien". He was killed by a partisan in 1943. Ezergailis, pp. 56, 57, 152, 168, 382.

71 The presence of a Latvian division in Maly Trostenez is confirmed by Curilla, p. 268 and Gerlach, p. 187. This division would be included in a training battalion consisting mainly of Baltic, Rumanian and Hungarian *volksdeutschen* that would be part of that group of divisions so-called *Schutzmannschaft der Sicherheitspolizei* (SMdS). See Birn, pp. 306-308.

72 Ezergailis, p. 169. Testimony given by Ēriks Pārups, former Latvian army officer, then took up Nazi resistence.

73 Klemp Sibirien, p. 297.

74 *Ibid*. In the organizational chart of EK 2/KdS "Lettland", Kirste was Vice-commander of Abteilung IV – Gestapo, directly subordinated to Rudolf Lange. In the absence of Lange, he was the main liaison officer with Arajs. He was summoned to testify in the trial v. Arajs himself. Ezergailis, pp. 152, 187, 190, 223, 231, 243, 245, 382, Curilla, pp. 120, 278. Born in Jarotschin, Poznan region, August 4, 1901, between 1940 and 1941 he served in Lublin's Gestapo and then, after the start of Barbarossa, as liaison officer between Arajs and EK2. Promoted SS-Sturmbannführer on April 20, 1942, he was later transferred to Breslau's Gestapo. After the war he remained in the police force reaching the rank of Regierungsinspektor.

75 Klemp Sibirien, pp. 292-293.

76 *Ibid*., pp. 295-296.

77 *Ibid*., p. 297.

78 Gräfe/Post/Schneider, p. 536.

79 Klemp Sibirien, p. 297.

80 Bogdan Musial, who also analyzed and highlighted the relations between the Soviet occupation of eastern Poland and the Baltic in 1940 and the rise of anti-Semitism among the same populations when German troops entered the same territories, bluntly dismisses the hypothesis of an independent anti-Jewish policy by those administrative entities established by the Nazis in the Baltic, which he calls puppet-states. Musial, pp. 685-686.

81 Musial, p. 656. *«Der Selbstreinigungsbestrebungen antikommunistischen und antijüdischer Kreise in den neu zu besetzenden Gebieten ist kein Hindernis zu bereiten. Sie sind im Gegenteil, allerdings spurenlos auszulösen, zu intensivierten wenn erforderlich in die richtigen Bahnen zu lenken, ohne dass sich diese örtlichen "Selbstschutzkreise" später auf Anordnungen oder auf gegebenen politische Zusicherungen berufen können»*.

82 Ezergailis, pp. 203, 232.

83 Musial, p. 660. NMT Nürnberg, vol. XXX. Doc. 2273-PS, p. 73-74. *«Nach dem Terror der judisch-bolschewistischen Herrschaft – es wurden insgesamt 33.038 Letten verschleppt, verhaftet oder ermordet – ware ein umfassendes Progrom der Bevolkerung zu erwarten gewesen. Tatsachlich wurden jedoch durch ein-heimische Krafte nur einige tausend Juden aus eigenem Antriebe beseitigt»*. See attachment nr.6.

84 Musial, p. 660.

85 Hilberg, p. 328.

86 See Ezergailis, p. 204.

87 Testimony given by Arnold Kirste, present at the interview between Batz and Jäger, given before the Prosecutor of Hamburg, StAw Hamburg, 147 Js 31/67, on March 31, 1966, during pre-trial procedures v. Bruno Streckenbach, director of Amt I of RSHA. Angrick/Klein, pp. 49, 57.

88 Musial, p. 660.

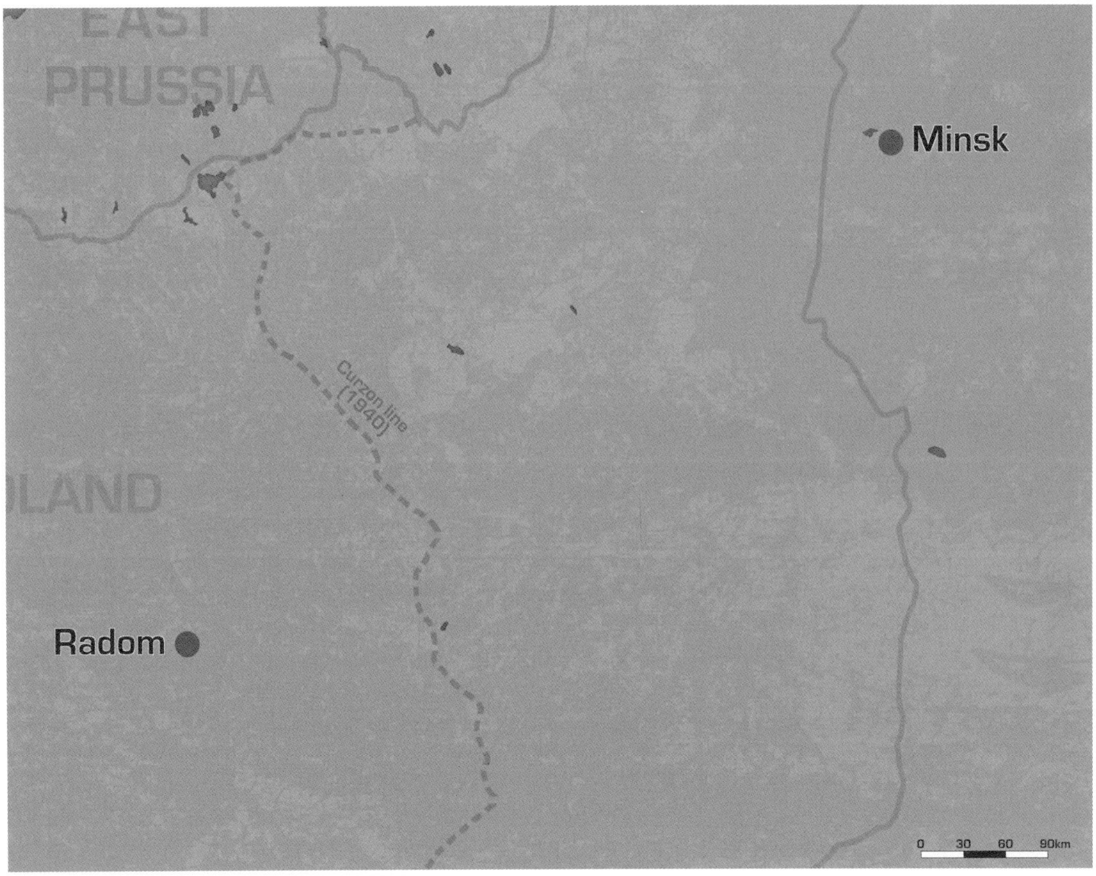
EAST PRUSSIA
Minsk
Curzon line (1940)
OLAND
Radom
0 30 60 90km

CHAPTER FOUR

"SEHT EUCH DIESEN MANN AN"

KAMENEC PODOLSKI, AUGUST 27-29, 1941

Die Liquidation dieser Juden
bis zum 1.9.1941
durchgeführt zu haben

Friedrich Jeckeln, August 25, 1941[1]

4.1 INTRODUCTION

God's work. Coming from the north, along highway H09 from Ivano Frankovsk and climbing along the switchbacks that lead up to Yablonitsky, what we see is God's work. The unique landscape of conifers that accompanies the 3,054 foot rise up to the mountain pass, the storm-water run-off of the Tisza and Prut valleys leaves the road and follows the trekking paths to the back of Mount Hoverla, with a peak reaching over 6,500 feet, in a universe of rather barren rocky ridges, its flow chaotic but of unparalleled breadth, like a balcony located above the mouth of the narrow Chorna Tysa valley. Beyond the pass, down to the south, between highway and railroad, the little village of Körösmezo – Jasinya in Ukrainian – introduces, from the east, the spectacular Swidowiec complex. In Körösmezo, on a small hill almost at the center of the village, the remains of an old Jewish cemetery with hand-carved tombstones, corroded by moss and surrounded by weeds, mark the passage on this land of a small Jewish community now disappeared. Further south, continuing along the H09, before reaching the border crossing to Romania at Velyyky Bychkiv's mountain pass, lies the small town of Rakhiv, about twenty miles from Körösmezo, which marks the geographical center of Europe, or, at least, it did so according to old Austro-Hungarian self-centered measurements.

The center of Europe, the heart of the continent, a place of pride for the cartographers of the dual monarchy who marked this as the extreme eastern boundary of their empire. A place surrounded by an environment of unparalleled beauty, slow pace and ancestral peacefulness. An ideal boundary, like a cusp, reaching to western Magyars, southern Romanians and eastern Ukrainians. A place that should be a meeting-point. A true work of God.

But this work, which was to be God's, was taken away from Him. The heart of the continent stopped beating for several days in July 1941, and the transcendent beauty of those places probably suggested only a biting regret for the thousands refugees huddled in terrifying conditions on trains speeding to what was the Ukrainian border, as shown on the frontier drawn during that furious summer. That meeting point became a passage point, a last leg of a hellish odyssey bound to finish a short distance ahead, beyond the Dniester, near Kamenec Podolski. An odyssey that would take more than 23,000 Jews – mostly Ruthenians, but also Slovaks, Ukrainians, Poles and Romanians – to meet their tragic fate in a desolate bomb-scarred field, on the western edge of the great plains of Ukraine.

4.2 ALIENS

The *appeasement of Munich* marked the zenith of Nazi expansionist policy implemented by means other than military and led to the dismemberment of Czechoslovakia, between November 1938 and March 1939. One of the negative effects that it caused was the destabilization of the boundary structure of all Central and Eastern Europe, and the subsequent *alienation* of large ethnic minorities enclosed within the borders redrawn by agreements between the various powers playing the *great game* of territorial ethnical/political revision. Of all minorities involved, the Jews almost inevitably ended up *footing the dearest bill*, finding themselves deprived of their old citizenship from one day to the other, without automatic right to a new one.

In particular Hungary, the recipient of major land acquisitions by the First Vienna Award (November 2, 1938) and its subsequent invasion of Sub-Carpathi-

A view of Körösmezo in the Thirties.

Yablonitsky Pass in the Thirties. In the background, immediately past the forest, Körösmezo can be spotted.

an Ruthenia (March 1939), will deal with this phenomenon[2]. This situation was further aggravated in September 1939 by the German and Soviet invasion of Poland – which produced the flight of thousands of Polish and Galician Jews to Hungary – followed on August 30, 1940, after the Second Vienna Award, by Hungary's acquisition of the entire Romanian northern Transylvania[3]. Another group of Jews was finally forced to Hungary in April 1941 after the annexation of Yugoslavian Bačka (Bácska)[4]. The result of these territorial annexations was the growth of the Hungarian Jewish community from about 400,000 surveyed within Trianon's border of 1939 (4.3 % of the population), to 725,000 (4.9 %) within 1941 new borders. Moreover, with Hungary's *Third racial law* of August 2, 1941, 100,000 Jews converted to Christianity, 10 % of whom living in the annexed territories were counted as Jews[5].

In one way or another, over time, a large proportion of the more than 325,000 annexed Jews were able to obtain Hungarian citizenship. In 1941, however, 20 % of Jews living within the new Magyar boundaries (about 145,000) were still without citizenship[6]: this number included the majority of refugees coming from third countries. According to various estimates, in September 1939 – hence before the annexation of former Romanian and Yugoslav territories – only a tiny percentage of the approximately 15 to 35,000 Jews that fled to Hungary from the Reich, Austria, Poland, Czechoslovakia and Galicia, managed to obtain a new citizenship from the government in Budapest or, alternatively, a temporary residence permit or a transit permit to Palestine[7]. However, while refugees from third countries were gathered in internment camps, those Jews already living in border areas that were being annexed to Hungary (southern Slovakia, Transylvania, Ruthenia, etc..), continued to live in their homes, more or less undisturbed.

This situation continued until the beginning of *Barbarossa*, when the already precarious status of Jewish residents within the new borders of Hungary reached its breaking point. In fact, following a proposal launched on July 12, 1941 by two leaders of the anti-Semitic KEOKH[9], on the following August 2 the so-called Third racial law was approved by the Council of Ministers in Budapest, which authorized the expulsion of all Jews without Hungarian citizenship living within the borders of Hungary: in all, about 145,000 people[10]. The area of expulsion chosen was that part of Soviet territory under Magyar military administration, beyond the eastern border of Carpathian Ruthenia.

Once the red tape was dealt with, starting on July 14, the "expulsions of recently infiltrated Russian and Polish Jews"[11] began, with particular focus on Jews exiled from Poland and those living in Ruthenia and in former Romanian Maramureş communities[12]. Many Slovak Jews and even some groups waiting for Hungarian citizenship, but who had not yet received the final documents, were included in this number too. The expulsions were particularly violent in Ruthenia. They were perpetrated by the Hungarian gendarmerie at short notice, the deportees were allowed to bring minimum possessions with them, and had to hastily crowd in the railway cattle cars in which they were transported directly to Körösmezo, the location chosen as collection point before the final push across the border. From here, according to the plan, teams of trucks would shuttle back and forth, carrying 1,000 Jews each day to Kolomyia, which was Galician territory but still, temporarily, in an area of Hungarian military administration[13]. From here, finally, in columns of 3-400, escorted by Hungarian gendarmes, the deportees would be driven beyond the Dniester, in the area of the German military administration, and forced to walk to Kamenec Podolski and other places referred to as final destinations (Buczacz, Czortków and Stanislaviv)[14]: one last exodus, almost biblical, which put the long columns of Jews, exhausted from the march and the scorching heat, at the mercy of gangs of Ukrainian militiamen, free to impose their predatory law and murder all those who resisted the robberies[15]. Not infrequently, once arrived near the Dniester, the groups of prisoners were simply abandoned in the open countryside, free to go wherever they wanted, but with the threat of being brought before a firing squad if they dared to return to Hungary.

Among the few survivors of the deportation of stateless Jews in the summer of 1941, was Leslie Gordon, a Polish Jew of Canadian citizenship, who gave his dramatic testimony during the Eichmann trial in Jerusalem. An extract of his evidence that focuses on the phases of deportation to Kamenec Podolski is reproduced in Appendix 1.

1.3 GUESS WHO'S COMING FOR DINNER?

The Hungarian showdown, implemented without prior agreement with Berlin, put the German occupation authorities before a *fait accompli.*

Further south, along the southern course of the Dniester (an EGD area), the long columns of Rumanian Jews expelled from Moldova by Bucharest troops were violently pushed back by German soldiers guarding the bridges[16]. Hungarian Jews on their way to Kamenec Podolski, via Kolomyia (Galicia), however, were allowed to enter Ukraine; this was probably due to lack of orders to stop them by the local German commands (the area was under the command of 444. Sicherungs-Division and EGC) as well as the state of utter confusion in which the administration of German SS and police in Galicia was in: after taking over from the Hungarians, at the beginning of August, it evidently was unable to organize its *filter* at the border with Ruthenia[17]. Further confusion to this picture was brought by occasional initiatives taken by individual local governments as in the case of Brzezany's Kreishauptmann, who used the Ukrainian militia to repel from its *kreis,* Hungarian Jews who had arrived there[18].

It wouldn't take long, however, before Germanic military authorities manifested concern for the continued influx of Jews from Hungary.

Indeed, as early as July 28, a telex message sent by 444.Sicherungs-Division's command to Berück "Süd", Karl von Roques, requested that the Budapest government re-admit Hungarian Jews, because of discontent spreading among the Ukrainian population[19]. Such complaint, however, had no effect, because of the sharp rejection given by the Hungarians (July 30)[20].

The next day, July 31, in a message addressed to the above-mentioned division, Kamenec Podolski's FK 183 warned about the possible spread of epidemics among the Jews left to their own devices and deprived of any provisions, requesting their removal[21]. Further communication by FK 183, dated August 13, again addressed to 444.Sicherungs-Division, insisted on the need to implement all the measures necessary to deal with refugees, who by now had become an intolerable burden for the city[22].

This is evidence given by a Hungarian soldier stationed in Kamenec Podolski between August 18 and 19, 1941:

> *"Many Jews here, especially women, are in rags, but have red-painted lips and ask for bread in exchange for jewelry. They'd give anything for a little bread. Some are dragging their steps, desperation on their faces, others are crawling on the road, collapsing from exhaustion and hunger. Some others bandage the wounds on their feet with rags torn from their clothes. The Jewish quarter of town is filled with Jews, many are coming from Budapest: they live in unspeakable, indescribable filth, wearing little clothing. The streets reek and in some houses there lie unburied corpses. The waters of the Dniester are contaminated here, and dead corpses float adrift, washed out from the river bank*[23].

Thus, while German military authorities were facing an unexpected and difficult to solve problem, which represented, by their compulsive point of view, a threat to the lines of communication and a source of disorder in the rear[24], the Hungarians were trying to speed up expulsions of the Jews *in surplus* from their *storage area,* so as to get rid of them completely before that part of Galicia that they administered was annexed to the General Government. As a matter of fact, up to 14,000 Jews were deported to various parts of Galicia by August 10, rising to 15,567 on August 19; however, only 3 or 4,000 more arrived by the end of that month as by then the border had been closed [25].

This dead-end situation, the result of conflicting interests, threatened to fall upon the unfortunate Jews.

They were the unwelcome *guests* of two quarrelsome diners.

4.4 COLUMBUS' EGG

Until that moment Gyula Spitz had been a lucky man.

A Magyar Jew, born in Budapest, but unlike most of his coreligionists, instead of the Mandatory Labor Service he had been conscripted into the Hungarian army and assigned to a Honvéd regular unit as truck driver, from 1940 to 1942[26].

In this role, between August 27 and 28, 1941 he was sent to Kamenec Podolski, where he witnessed the walk of long columns of Jews escorted by German troops, directed to an open field outside of town. From inside his vehicle, Spitz was able to secretly shoot some photographs currently stored in the archives of USHMM[27]. Apparently, they are the only images available of what happened during the phase immediately prior to what was "the first five-digit massacre of the Final Solution"[28].

So what else had happened?

According to the schedule established by Berlin based on the eastern advance of Heeresgruppe "Süd", those areas of Western Ukraine already firmly in German hands, namely Volhynia and Podolia, would switch on September 1, 1941 from the Wehrmacht's military administration to the civil administration of Erich Koch, Reichkommissar of Ukraine (RKU)[29]. However, some of these territories, including the regions of Zhitomir and Kamenec Podolski, that had been subject to Soviet rule for decades, were regarded by an *astute* think-tank in Berlin, as more *Bolshevized* than the Lutsk and Rovno western regions of Ukraine, annexed to the USSR in 1939. The reaction of the Nazi leadership and military hierarchies to this condition was as autistic as always, wrapped up as they were in their *Freischärlerpsychose*. Thus, they saw it fit to deploy the most indiscriminate and drastic measures, including collective reprisals and mass-hunting against the Jews, summarily indicated as Bolsheviks tout-court. This distortion was blatantly surreptitious, reminiscent of Pavlovian-Lombrosian theories, aimed at delineating the *supreme Jewish enemy* through the synthesis of non-overlapping categories, namely the political and the ethno-religious. This synthesis had already borne fruit during those weeks with the rapid transition from selective executions of adult male Jews in the first days after Barbarossa, to the indiscriminate killings carried out with the gradual progress of the advance eastward; in Novograd Volynski (Zwihal), for instance, where a great number of Jewish women and people as young as sixteen were liquidated on July 25, 1941, on orders given by HSSPF Friedrick Jeckeln[30] and in Stara Kostantinova, which had become Jeckeln's temporary seat, where 139 Jewish women had been shot on August 20[31].

In such an alchemy of ideological automatisms and ongoing exterminating inclinations, the tendency to seek out a rapid and definitive solution to the problem of thousands of Hungarian Jews who continued to flock to the Kamenec Podolski ghetto – where in the meantime, considering the local population already present, the conditions of survival had become desperate – is not surprising.

Indeed, the solution, probably unexpectedly, came on August 25 in Vinnitsa, at the *Chef der Abteilung Kriegsverwaltung bei Generalquartiermeister des Heer*, where the many high-ranking officers attending a meeting[32], approved the proposal made via telephone by Jeckeln – who was not present – who volunteered to solve the *Jewish problem* of Kamenec Podolski with his own methods before the scheduled date. The minutes of the meeting, drawn up on August 27, leave no doubt about Jeckeln's intentions:

> *About 11,000 Jews were driven across the border from Hungary, near Kamenec Podolski. During previous negotiations no agreement was reached for the repatriation of these Jews. Therefore, the HSSPF (Ogruf. Jeckeln), hopes he'll manage to complete the liquidation of these Jews before September 1, 1941*[33] *[my emphasis – authors note].*

Obviously, besides freeing the undecided Wehrmacht officers of a seemingly unsolvable problem, Jeckeln's *providential* intervention was also a way of earning personal credit with Himmler. From this point of view, actually, the issue of Jewish refugees from Hungary came at the right time: a ploy to appease Himmler's discontent against his eastern *proconsuls* Prutzmann and Jeckeln, both guilty of not having acted up to that moment with the necessary resolve and not having kept him sufficiently updated on the situation of the executions in their respective *protectorates*. At this point, the report that Jeckeln had been called to make before Himmler on August 12, 1941, seems preliminary to the acceleration of the genocidal campaign in Ukraine[34].

In this sense, the extermination of thousands was the simplest solution to the convergence of different instances with these desperate people, guilty only of being Jewish and who, considering their state of total exhaustion could in no way pose a threat. It was the *Columbus' egg* for Himmler, Jeckeln and of course the Wehrmacht, which would be relieved of a considerable logistical weight without paying toll[35].

The swift adoption of the proposal made by Jeckeln, who was given the green light without any objection by the many participants in the meeting, leaves no doubt about the position on the matter taken by the highest authorities of the Wehrmacht in Ukraine. In other words, the Wehrmacht leaders and the civilian officers gathered in Vinnitsa, chose to delegate the *Jewish issue* in Kamenec Podolski to the SS and the police the Pontius Pilate way, endorsing *de facto* the final extermination inclinations[36].

4.5 A SLOW DEATH RACE

Conscious of his own means, Friedrich Jeckeln made sure he'd keep his promise and more.

Believing that the Hungarian Jews were not a large enough target, he extended his *attention* to local Jews, who lived in segregation in the Kamenec Podolski ghetto since it was established, on July 20, 1941. In practice, we should take as a starting point the approximately 14,000 Jews in the city in 1939 on the eve of the conflict (38 % of the total population). If we deduct those who expatriated to Hungary during this period in order to escape the Red Army, that is, those who escaped into the Soviet Union after June 22, 1941 in order to escape from the Nazis, and if we add the deportees expelled from Hungary in July and August , we reach a total of at least 28,000 Jews herded into the Kamenec Podolski ghetto in August 1941, half of which were of Hungarian origins[37]. Jeckeln's axe would fall upon all of them.

The Kamenec Podolski ghetto could be considered completely temporary, as it did not provide the housing and logistical support needed to sustain such a large number of inmates. On the initiative of FK 183, the ghetto perimeters were set within the old town, with the historic fort at its center and accessible only through a single guarded bridge. The Jews living in other parts of town and in nearby villages such as Orinin, Chemerivtsi and Smotrich[38], had to move, with only 110 pounds of baggage each, into those small dwellings inside the ghetto walls that had been made available by Hungarian families who were relocated outside the ghetto. Then the Hungarian Jews began to come in, filling up beyond measure - with all the obvious consequences in terms of lack of food and hygiene - an area that had been designed to hold only local Jews on a temporary basis[39]. And again, unlike in Poland and the Baltic, there is no evidence sustaining the intention to set up ghettos in Ukraine, but only *temporary stocking centers* for Jews, while looking for alternative solutions.

So, while in Kamenec Podolski the ghetto was created in the old town, in other Ukrainian locations they used collective farms, bombed buildings, warehouses, disused factories (Kharkov) and even cattle cars (Cherniakhiv)[40] for that purpose: buffer solutions, that provided excuses and inevitably foreshadowed radical measures. The precarious housing conditions imposed on the Jews was obviously accompanied by a logistic precariousness: food supplies to the ghettos, in particular, were not a priority at all for the Wehrmacht. That, together with restrictions of any kind imposed on the Jewish community, relegated inside a circle of walls, substantially meant a sentence of death by starvation. From this point of view, the alarmed communications sent by FK 183 about the deplorable conditions of the Kamenec Podolski ghetto are streaked with cynical hypocrisy in their solicitation of any form of solution to an existing problem that could drag on for months should it not be resolved in one way or another. Those enclosed in the ghetto were lacking the most basic means of sustainment and denied even small economic activities that had been allowed in other ghettos elsewhere that could give them some sort of benefits or some hope to survive through hard work. Instead, they were reduced to begging for a piece of bread, locked up in overcrowded slums, forced to live among garbage and diseases, sometimes with the unburied corpses of their relatives. What the Jews of Kamenec Podolski and their Hungarian coreligionists were forced to endure during their brief detention in that ghetto – about forty days – was probably something very similar to a *slow death race*, a state of sheer decay. They were deliberately pushed by the German authorities beyond the limits of survival, which enabled the elegant officers of the Wehrmacht to be offended, with unparalleled cynicism, by a problem that they created and against which, at that point, they were urging the resolution through the adoption of the most drastic measures[41]. Needless to say, Kamenec Podolski was not an exception but the rule, at least in Ukraine, where in late summer 1941 the ghettos, transient and ephemeral, never came to represent an opportunity for survival, albeit precarious, but a means to facilitate the Final Solution, a death trap from which escape was virtually impossible[42].

4.6 DEEDS, NOT WORDS

To reach the ambitious goal he had vowed, Jeckeln needed deeds to turn his words into actions. And he did so with unrepenting determination.

Once he was given the green light by the military authorities who met in Vinnitsa, Jeckeln reached Kamenec Podolski in a Fiesler Storch, and immediately started preparations for the massacre, aided by his deputy, SS-Brigadeführer Gerret Korsemann. They, together with a few Wehrmacht officers, would witness the massacre from atop a low hill overlooking the mass graves[43]. This is a particular that indirectly confirms that FK 184 had full knowledge and gave their approval to the entire operation. Clearly, they had been informed by Jeckeln, just like the Hungarian military authorities, who for the next four days (until August 31) would still have held the administrative responsibility for the area of Kamenec Podolski[44].

Despite the experience gained in the many massacres perpetrated in previous weeks in Kovel and Vinnitsa, Jeckeln's task was not an easy one: the number of Jews he had planned to liquidate in such a short time available was very large and he lacked units to perform the action.

The location of choice, known as *Porokhovye sklady*[45], fell on a vast slightly undulating field about five miles north of Kamenec Podolski, riddled with craters from an earlier bombing that could usefully be used as makeshift mass graves.

As for the units, it was immediately evident that the choice was quite limited: first in line was Stabskompanie / HSSPF "Russland- Süd" which followed Jeckeln in his movements on the field. This unit operated as the commanding core and escort unit[46] and probably represented the only security police unit involved in the massacre, given the presence in other areas of various EGC detachments[47]. In addition, there was one contingent of Ukrainian auxiliaries recruited from FK 184, plus a platoon of Hungarian engineers formed by Danubian Swabians, that possibly was made available by the Magyar military authorities for surveillance tasks around the area of the massacre[48]. However, this amount of manpower was still too little to complete the operation on schedule. Then Jeckeln's problems were solved by a police battalion stationed in Khmel'nyts'kyy (Proskurov), about 90 miles north of Kamenec Podolski, where it had arrived on August 27 from Tarnopol, Galicia.

This battalion had been formed in February 1941 in Berlin-Spandau, and was immediately considered as "available (*zur Verfügung Chef der Ordnungspolizei*)". As such, after its entry into Soviet territory, in mid-August in the Przemysl area, Galicia, it had been placed under Jeckeln's command as *"a division for special uses (zur besonderen Verwendung)"*[49].

Leading the battalion was Maj. Kurt Dall, who took over precisely during those days. The division commanders were HPTM. Alfred Weber (1/320), HPTM. Hans Wiemer (2/320) and HPTM. Heinrich Scharway (3/320). The first two divisions took part in the massacre from August 27, while the third, that had been bringing up the rear, arrived at the massacre location on August 28 at about noon: it too, however, had time to participate in numerous shootings.

Kamenec Podolski would not be the first *Säuberungsaufträge* for Polizei-Bataillon 320. It had aLready taken part, a few days before (August 20), in the massacre of 439 Jews in Stara Kostantinova[50], although only in a supporting role to 1. SS-Infanterie-Brigade. It was a *novice* division, so far only marginally involved in genocidal actions, nevertheless, it managed to become the main force behind a terrible massacre of defenseless civilians *ex abrupto.* This was something that was not enough to cause any outwardly perceptible particular reaction or emotional trauma in the policemen that perpetrated it, except in a single case of conscientious objection by policeman Herbert H., acknowledged and accepted by his division commander Scharway.

This is the testimony given by Herbert H., given to ZStL, 204 AR-Z 48/58 on January 15, 1960[51]:

> *I remember a speech of our commander Scharway in front of the deployed division, during which he informed us that the entire battalion would be used in a Jewish action in Kamenec Podolski. From his speech it was clear that the Jews would be shot. His words were meant to be an ideological indoctrination for us, and that is why they were unequivocal on how the Jews had brought disorder in the world, how idle they were and how necessary it was to eliminate them. I do not remember, now, his exact words, but this is what he meant. However, his words were meant to convince us of the necessity of such measures [...]. Scharway, in his speech, also said that nobody would be forced to take part in the shooting [...]. After the company was ordered to break ranks, I went to Scharway and asked him in private to be exempt from taking part in the action [...]. I called his attention to the Hague Convention, which forbade the killing of defenseless people and the fact that this did not go well with my conscience. I also made him note that I had been taught the Hague Convention during my training in Eilenburg. Scharway then replied only that he considered me ill, and for that reason, I did not have to join the Jewish action: "Okay, Herbert, you are exempt," he said. I am not aware if other members of the division were exempted in the same way, but I did not have the impression that there was anyone else among them that felt as I did after Scharway's speech. It seemed to me, to be the contrary; that everyone had agreed on that measure as a necessary evil [...]. I cannot even say if after the speech our officers were feeling moody or depressed...*

According to Herbert, he was the only member of his company who refused to shoot. Probably unbeknownst to him, there were other similar episodes throughout the battalion, but even so, it would still be rare, isolated cases in the midst of a not enthusiastic but consenting, mass of at least 500 policemen. Of course, among all these, only a minority, possibly among the officers, could be included in the category of so-called *true believers*, against a large majority of individuals involved in what Otto Dov Kulka calls "passive complicity"[52]: a condition that went beyond mere indifference to the fate reserved to the Jews, and that would best be described as reluctance to take part in burdensome acts which were deemed as necessary.

This was probably the most advanced consensual line that all police battalions involved in the Jewish genocide converged upon. Let's remember that they were not cheap products of ideological nature, but the result of complex social alchemies: "Peculiar, but not at all exceptional. Rare but not unique. [Not so – authors note] an inherent attribute of modern society, neither a phenomenon alien to it"[53]. Certainly this phenomenon was not exclusive to the German people, but rather the entire human population, within specific conditions. In this sense, we agree with Christopher Browning's opinion, that the overwhelming majority of perpetrators were not ordinary Germans, but rather more tragically, countless ordinary men[54].

4.7 SARDINENPACKUNG

Kamenec Podolsky would be the most dramatic pogrom to date, becoming the point of no return on the road to the Final Solution. Jeckeln planned the action over several days, during which the victims, gradually rounded up in the ghetto, would be brought out in long columns to the place of the massacre under the close supervision of police officers who, at this stage, were to play security tasks only. Then, the executions would be carried out mainly by Stabskompanie / HSSPF[55].

The Jews, of course, were not told about the real purpose of the operation. Instead, they were advised to prepare their personal baggage, linen and spare clothes for a transfer elsewhere. According to the testimony of a police officer, many of the Jews approached him hoping to be told what their destination would be[56.] The columns included women and children, while the elderly, unable to move independently, had to be carried on improvised stretchers.

The victims' illusion disappeared with the slow approach of the columns to the execution spot, in the middle of a rather bumpy ground, surrounded by a first cordon of policemen, beyond which they could see many people and hear the crackle of automatic weapons.

Once past this barrier, the victims were ordered to gather in large groups surrounded by other policemen, and every time a new column was arriving from the city, the perimeter of surveillance of the group widened to include several thousand people[57].

The victims were then ordered to undress and leave their clothes and baggage on the ground, after which, in small groups, they were forced closer to the pits scattered everywhere.

These were, in fact, funnel-shaped bomb craters, which could reach a diameter of 65-100 feet and a depth of 15-20 feet, in which firing squads were awaiting, usually formed by four men holding submachine guns. In some of these platoons there were policemen too.

According to the aforementioned testimony by Herbert H., member of 3/320, Scharway, the company commander, would hold a short speech to his men, about the need to proceed with the elimination of the Jews which he described as "idle and originators of world disorders"[58] before the executions. At the same time, Scharway also informed that he would not order anyone, individually, to take part in the shootings. Despite that, apart from one single case, no other policeman would pull back or object[59].

What happened then was something very similar to a circle of hell.

For many hours, without pause, after being pushed to the edge of the pits groups of Jews were forced to jump into the craters and then lie directly on the bodies of those who preceded them, only, in an inverted position, so as to optimize space: it was the so-called "sardine cans (*Sardinenpackung*)" method, created by Jeckeln. Then, the victims were killed with single shots to the head, or sometimes with hasty bursts of automatic weapons. In some cases the executions took place with the victims left standing, killed at close range[60].

The only degree of tolerance towards the executors was shown if some of them had failed, or were no longer able to kill children: in that case he could ask to be replaced, get out of the pit, have a sip of brandy and then, eventually, return to his post[61]. In other cases, the executions were to continue unabated, as reported by witness Hermann Krüger, a member of Jeckeln's personal staff who, together with his colleagues Johannes Lüschen and Willi Wedekind [62,] continued to kill, plunged into the pit, for at least one or two hours uninterruptedly; he could leave only after other police officers arrived to the spot in order to replace his team. That day, August 27, the executions went on without a break from 10:00 to 16:00 hours[63].

There were no doctors to establish the victims' death. Some who passed out after receiving only a wound could sometimes regain consciousness under the bodies of the slain just to languish in agony or, if luckier, to receive the coup de grace. There were also cases of wounded who begged their tormentors to kill them[64].

This is the testimony by Hermann Krüger, given on September 22, 1941, to ZStL 204 AR-Z 13/60[65]:

I was involved, at the end of August, in the great Kamenec Podolski massacre. I remember that many Jews were killed. The Jews were shot in several funnel-shaped ditches. Probably it was bomb craters. The ditch I had been assigned to, had a diameter of 65-100 feet and a depth of 15-20 feet. As soon as our journey to the place of execution began, Jeckeln ordered Lüschen, Wedekind and I to be ready. We knew we were going to an execution. When we arrived, the killings had not yet started. Several firing squads had been prepared, each consisting of four men. One of these platoons was formed by me, Lüschen, Wedekind, and a policeman we did not know. We were equipped with submachine guns, probably made in Czechoslovakia. The place of execution was cordoned off by a police division. The firing squads were formed by policemen and SS members. The Jews arrived in a long column. At that point Jeckeln ordered me, Lüschen, Wedekind and the other policeman to take position at the bottom of a crater. The Jews began to enter the pit. Even though some of them remained standing, they were generally made to lie down, then we would kill them with shots to the nape. There were women and children, but I only shot men. We went ahead without interruption. I tried several times to get out of the pit, because I was beginning to crack, but each time I was ordered back inside. All in all I had to shoot for about an hour or two. Then we were replaced by a police kommando. I cannot say exactly how many were Jews I had to shoot. Maybe 50 or 100. There was no doctor to determine that the victims were really dead. I still remember a wounded, unconscious Jew. When he regained consciousness he began to scream, crying to be killed. Only then he was given the coup de grace. I also remember a girl, aged about 20, and a boy, aged about 12, who begged Sturmbannführer Meyer for their lives, telling him they were not Jews. Meyer then spoke with Jeckeln and the two were released. I still remember that kid: he jumped by joy when his life was spared, the girl was very happy too. The first day the execution went on from 10am until 4pm.

A brief image of the massacre reached us through the words of Ukrainian auxiliary Ivan Pavlovich Tchaikovsky, given during his interrogation on May 15, 1944 in a Soviet prison[66]:

> *I took part three times in the execution of peaceful Soviet citizens ... The first time on August 28, 1941, when no less than 4,000 citizens of Jewish nationality were shot in Bialanovka, on the outskirts of Kamenec Podolski. We, the Schutzmännern, were placed around the Jews, to guard them and to prevent any escape. The Jews were naked, and in groups of five or six had to run to the pit where two Germans shot them ... Many people asked me to help them escape, but I pushed them back each time.*

Another testimony of the Kamenec Podolski massacre is given by Gabor Mermelstein, a surviving Jew, a driver, like Gyula Spitz, and member of a Hungarian military unit:

> *"As we approached to the border town of Kamenec Podolski, we began to hear intermittent gunfire [...]. I suspected that this operation must have been of a greater magnitude than the ordinary minor executions perpetrated by the Nazis.*
>
> *The gunfire became louder, and soon we encountered a group of women, so we stopped the convoy to ask them what was happening. In voices broken with sobs, the women told us that a little further away, people were being slaughtered by the hundreds. I asked them if the victims were Jews. They answered amid wails and uncontrollable weeping, that both Jews and Poles were being murdered. So we drove for about two miles in the direction of the gunfire, until we came upon the edge of the forest. Here we saw hundreds of naked people. We slowed down and began moving along a line of birches – a little further from it, we saw a mass of naked corpses. The contour of the forest turned in a semicircle and suddenly we came within sight of a quadrangular ditch, lined with people on all four sides. It was here that hundreds of innocent people were being slain by the monotonous round of machinegun fire.*

I will never forget what I saw and what I felt: the terrified faces, the unresisting bodies, heaps of men, women and children consciously staggering to their graves. My reaction was a combination of panic, outrage and inconsolable pain [...].

As the slaughter continued, the drivers of the convoy – eighty percent of who were Jewish – started to cry in their driving seats. The German officer sitting next to me noticed that I was weeping. He looked at me placidly, glancing at my yellow armband, and said: "Why do you cry?". I responded: "How could I possibly not cry when I'm facing this?". "Oh, don't worry", he said, "there are still plenty of Jews in the world"[67].

That is how thousands of Jews died.

4.8 TÄTIGKEITEN ABGESCHLOSSEN

Three days later, the terrible massacre was over. According to the daily telexes that Jeckeln sent to Himmler, with copies to RSHA, HA -Orpo and KS-RFSS, 4,200 Jews were shot on August 27, 11,000 on August 28 and 7,000 on August 29[68].

However, in spite of the results obtained, as far as Jeckeln was concerned, something had not worked.

He was annoyed, probably at the attitude shown by some officers of Polizei-Bataillon 320: not only had they not forced their men to take part in the massacre, but they had also authorized some 3/320 officers to get away from the pits after committing only a limited number of executions. Obviously - although there does not seem to be have been a single defection in the Battalion ranks[69] - the mere fact not all his subordinates had taken part in the carnage totally and unconditionally was enough to send Jeckeln into a rage: a reaction proven by the violent altercation that he had after the massacre with Maj. Dall, commander of Polizei-Bataillon 320[70].

There is also a trace of this discontent in the August 29 telex in which, correcting his earlier posts of August 26 and 27, Jeckeln proudly wanted to give credit for the entire genocidal *performance* to his Stabskompanie, declassing Polizei-Bataillon 320 to mere tasks of monitoring and escort[71].

However, it was not over yet.

After the shootings, probably on the evening of August 29, Polizei-Bataillon 320 was sent back to its headquarters in Khmel'nyts'kyy (Proskurov). From here, during the following day, some of its divisions were involved in another massacre in Min'kovtsy, a town about nine miles southeast of Proskurov. At the same time, some other patrols were recalled to Kamenec Podolski, both to prevent scavenging of corpses by Ukrainians plunderers and to hunt or to inflict the final blow to any possible survivors [72].

At that point, with a summary report sent to Himmler on August 30, Jeckeln claimed for his Stabskompanie the final credit for 23,600 killing [73]:

"The figures for Stabskompanie HSSPF Russland Süd should be completed. The number of Jews liquidated in Kamenec Podolski has risen to 23,600."

Jeckeln's pride was now satisfied.

4.9 BEFEHLSNOTSTAND

The Kamenec Podolski carnage did not go unnoticed.

In the weeks that followed it, rumors of the massacre began to circulate in free Europe and in the United States where the *New York Times* gave notice of it on October 26, 1941, while in London the *London Institute of Jewish Affairs* talked about it during November[74].

Paradoxically, despite its sad notoriety, neither the authors of the massacre (*Täter*) nor their accomplices (*Gehilfen*), were ever summoned to answer for their crimes before the law, although it looked like something was going to happen [75].

In 1958, with process 204 AR-Z 48/58, a voluminous file against KdS "Rowno", Polizei-Bataillon 320 and Polizei-Kompanie "Ostland" (Polizei-Bataillon 33) had been opened by the ZStL for a series of crimes committed in Ukraine between 1941 and the end of 1943: among these, the slaughter at Kamenec Podolski.

According to Ludwigsburg, these crimes saw the direct involvement of Polizei-Bataillon 320, which could then be charged with murder (*Mord*) and complicity in murder (*Beihilfe zum Mord*). In particular, the officers and NCOs of the battalion, including Alfred Weber, former commander of 1/320, and Hans Wiemer Polizeirat, former commander of 2/320 and still in active service at the Polizeipräsidium Recklinghausen, would have played a major role in the crimes.

With these assumptions, during 1961 ZStL requested the Prosecutor of Dortmund to proceed with the opening of preliminary investigations v. *Wiemer und anderen*; the investigation was actually started with file StAwDo Js 45 7/61.

It was clear from the outset that the investigation was going to be very complex, because as many as 400 police officers were summoned, the majority of whom belonging to Polizei-Bataillon 320 and the others to Polizei-Kompanie "Ostland". Of the 131 policemen summoned to testify in the prosecution, as many as 128 denied any direct involvement in executions, while only three admitted to it.

At that point, after several months of investigations and hearings, on January 16, 1962, the Public Prosecutor of Dortmund concluded that: contrary to Ludwigsburg's assumption, most of the defendants were found guilty only of participation in support activities during the massacres, a kind of secondary complicity, which according to the legal interpretation still applied to Nazi crimes back then, was not considered punishable. Therefore, many of the 363 defendants were declared not punishable.

With regard to those not included in this number, a special file (StAwDo 45 Js 23/63), was later opened on about thirty of them, all members of Polizei-Kompanie "Ostland". Further investigation was ordered on Hans Wiemer, the main defendant, by the Court of Dortmund.

Further investigation that led to nothing: through the decision of December 13, 1962, the Prosecutor of Dortmund decided that the questionable *Befehlsnotstand* legal artifice, namely the alleged impossibility of disobeying orders, could be considered applicable to Wiemer. That guaranteed the suspension of the investigation on the defendant.

Ludwigsburg applied against this decision requesting the reopening of the investigation to the Court of Dortmund in February 1963, but did not succeed. The last word on the whole affair was pronounced on April 23, 1963, by Attorney General Hamm, who ultimately upheld the decision of the Court of Dortmund and put an end to the investigations.

By German laws, no-one was guilty for the Kamenec Podolski massacre.

4.10 CONSIDERATIONS

Quoting Klaus-Michael Mallmann, the slaughter of Kamenec Podolski is a true "quantum leap (*Sprung qualitative*)"[76] in the process of the annihilation of European Jewry. It was not, in fact, only a brutal but somehow *controlled* massacre, like the ones that had preceded it, which were perpetrated on the basis of specious but somehow *expendible* reasons in that they tended to hit targeted areas of the Jewish communities involved (adult males of military age, *intelligentsia*, pro-Soviet elements, etc.).On the contrary, Kamenec Podolski represented a new phase, which could be said to have a *genocidal intent*. *Before* Kamenec Podolski there had been random massacres, relatively spread and limited, along the axes of the troops' advance eastwards. *After* Kamenec Podolski there was no need to draw a *distinction*, there was no need to have *reasons* other than annihilation for the sake of it.

The more inconsistent the situational background outlined during the meeting of August 24 in Vinnitsa appears – with its excuse to justify the massacre (Judeo-Bolshevik threat, security of communication lines, inability to sustain the refugees, etc.) – the more the intention to leave the experimental stage of *selective* genocide in order to enter the *systemic* stage of genocide seems real.

- Kamenec Podolski is the political will to begin to *resolve*, once and for all, the so-called *Jewish question* by methods that were not political, but methods of annihilation: in this sense and perhaps for the first time, it is possible to distinguish in an evident way, the transition from the so-called *Judenpolitik* to the *Vernichtungspolitik*, thanks also to the implicit collaboration – or, better said, the non-opposition – of some important Wehrmacht leaders. Somehow, in the rapid decision-making process that led to the massacre, a clear desire to establish a point of no return on the road to the Final Solution can be envisaged. After that, it remains unclear at which level of the hierarchy chain this *input* actually started: it is not clear if this process was ascending; from Jeckeln to Berlin to *anticipate a will*, or descending; from Berlin to Jeckeln, to turn a theory into reality.

- Kamenec Podolski is the outline of functional mechanisms - operational, tactical and technical, as well as political – of a strategy of mass destruction. It *inaugurates* the season of *killing fields*, the great *indiscriminate* massacres on the Eastern Front: in just a few weeks in fact, the *five-digit* bloodsheds of Berditchev (September 15-16), Vinnitsa (September 19-20), Babi Yar (September 29-30), Dnepropetrovsk (October 13-15), Rovno (November 6-8) and Rumbula and Kharkov in December / January 1941-1942 would be perpetrated. In autumn 1941, in essence, the will to exterminate of decision-making structures - in Berlin as in the suburbs - and the operational capabilities of the divisions called to implement it - in other words the *production of death* - reached unparalleled peaks, exceeded only during the *permanent* genocidal phase of the gas-chambers, launched in spring 1942. The fundamental role played by the Ordnungspolizei in each of these massacres, that by now had become an indispensable *fußvolk der Endlösung*, should be stressed[77].
- Kamenec Podolski widens the genocidal horizon. Until then the massacres in Ukraine and Belarus had targeted primarily (albeit not exclusively) male Jews, in part members of the so-called *intelligentsia* of alleged pro-Soviet sympathies. Kamenec Podolski was the starting-point for the systematic slaughter of women and children too. In other words, no more *biological exemption* to death was ever again granted by the perpetrators, who could then cross the threshold of systemic genocide[78].
- Kamenec Podolski is when genocide *goes international*: it goes beyond the borders of the Nazi Empire and expands into other countries. Genocide becomes *complicity*, or perhaps more accurately, open collaboration: not only by individual groups of villains as had happened before and was happening in the same period in Lithuania and Latvia, but by governments, such as those in Hungary and Romania[79], who were allies but certainly not subdued. Genocide enters, for the first time, the category of things that are feasible, leaving behind the ideological abstraction in which it had been hitherto confined. Genocide now becomes *the solution*.
- Kamenec Podolski means answers. Reactions to the massacre are assessed on the widest scale possible, both for perpetrators and victims, and the result of this assessment is that, in fact, there would be no reactions: victims would be led to an orderly death and executioners would obediently fulfill their ignoble task. Whether it was due to an ascending or a descending mechanism, the result did not change: the experiment was positive, by and large.
- Kamenec Podolski, finally, is the clear perception of how the alienation and marginalization in which Judaism had been led to precipitate during the long years of ideological bulimia that followed the rise of Nazism, was inversely proportional to the feeling of empathy that executioners felt toward their victims. That is, it was now clear how the idea of the *Jew* as an obstacle to be removed through a real work of *social reclamation*, had been internalized. From this point of view and in relation to the so-called *Jewish question*, as Jan Kershaw noted: "The depersonalization of the Jew was the real success of Nazi policy and propaganda"[80].

And to understand this concept, there could not be a better example than what an officer of Polizei-Bataillon 320, said to his men, pointing at a Jew who was sadly walking to his execution: "*Seht Euch diesen Mann an. Das ist ein typischer Jude, den man ausrotten muss, damit wir Deutschen leben können*".

"Look at this man. He is a typical Jew: he must be uprooted so that we Germans can live" [81].

ENDNOTES

1 "The liquidation of these Jews will take place by September 1, 1941". HIS, p. 132, Hilberg, pp. 830, 964, Gerlach/Götz, p. 74.

2 Through the *First Vienna Award* (November 2, 1938), Hungary received part of southern Slovakia (the so-called *Felvidék*), inhabited by approximately 68,000 Jews. In March 1939, 78,000 more Jews living in Sub-Carpathian Ruthenia *(Kápátalja)* were added to them. Brahm, p. 29. The acknowledgment of Hungarian citizenship to all these people was prevented by Hungary's *Second Racial Law* of May 1939, which denied naturalization to all Jews unable to demonstrate a proved residence of their ancestors in Hungary since 1848. Gerlach/Aly, pp. 44-45, Hilberg, p. 829.

3 Through the *Second Vienna Award* (August 30, 1939), Hungary received the entire Rumanian northern Transylvania, where about 140-160,000 Jews were living. Musial Persecutori, pp. 677, 692, Brahm, p. 29.

4 After the dismemberment of Yugoslavia, April 1941, Hungary received the territories of Bácska and Baranja, inhabited by approximately. 14,000 Jews. Brahm, p. 29.

5 Braham, p. 29, Musial Persecutori, p. 677.

6 Gerlach/Aly, p. 53.

7 These Jews had been let into Hungary since 1938, with permission of the Interior Minister, Ferenc Keresztes-Fischer, urged by the Jewish office for Palestine. The project was to provide temporary asylum to refugees who were waiting for the result of their applications for emigration to the Middle East. In fact the project was stalled and refugees found themselves stuck in Hungary. Braham, p. 32.

8 *Külföldieket Ellenőrző Országos Központi Hatóság.*

9 The two, Ödön Martinides and Árkád Kiss, won the support of the Hungarian Defence Minister, Károly Bartha and the Chief of General Staff Henrik Werth, who persuaded the Prime Minister Bardossy about the goodness of their project.

10 In fact, the expulsion from Hungary of Jews without citizenship had already been envisaged by the *Second Racial Law* of May 1939, with notifications of expulsion duly delivered to the recipients. Then, not finding any country willing to accept the deportees, the expulsions were postponed every six months, until Operation Barbarossa made available the vast spaces of occupied Ukraine. Evidence by Pinchas Freudiger – The Trial of Adolf Eichmann, Session 51-04, Volume III.

11 Directive of KEOKH, July 12, 1941. Brahm, p. 33.

12 On the expulsions from Maramureş see: Gross/Cohen: *The Marmaros Book. In Memory of 160 Jewish Communities*. Tel Aviv, 1983 [*Sefer Marmarosh; mea ve-shishim kehilot kedoshot be- yishuvan u-ve-hurbanan*].

13 The Galician districts of Stanislaviv, Horodenka and Kolomyia remained under Hungarian military administration from July 1, 1941 to the beginning of August, when they were formally annexed to the General Government. Pohl Ostgalizien, p. 49, Pohl Krüger, p. 2/24, Gerlach/Götz, p. 221.

14 Brahm, p. 33. Particularly mocking was the fate of about a thousand exiles, who miraculously survived the massacre of Kamenec Podolski because they were diverted to Stanislaviv. They would not escape, however, the dramatic Blutsonntag Stanislau (October 12, 1941) a few weeks later. Gerlach/Götz, p. 221, Pohl Ostgalizien, p. 109.

15 Brahm, p. 33.

16 Namely SK 10b on the Mogilev-Podolski bridges and Einsatzkommando 12 on Yampol's. At one point, towards the beginning of August, the troops of Bucharest forced a column of Rumanian Jews beyond the Dniester, near Kamenec Podolski: again the attempt failed due to the intervention of a detachment of SK 10b (TK "Schuchart"), coming from Mogilev-Podolski. Angrick, p. 202. On the vicissitudes of Rumanian Jews expelled from Transnistria see Angrick Escalation.

17 From the beginning of August 1941, when Galicia was annexed to the General Government and until October 13, the role of SSPF "Lemberg" was contended by Friedrich Katzmann - supported by the governor of Galicia, Lasch - and Carl-Albrecht Oberg - sponsored by HSSPF "Warsaw". The latter prevailed, but the position remained vacant for at least two months. It is likely that in this confused situation, the executive power regarding the so-called *Jewish question* was handled by Helmut Tanzmann, leader of Einsatzkommndo "Lemberg", although he was only officially appointed KDS for the District of Galicia from September 1, 1941. See Pohl Ostgalizien, pp. 84-86.

18 Pohl Ostgalizien, p. 109.

19 HIS, p. 129. *«Juden von Ungarn aus Ungarischen Konzentrazionlagern mit Lkw. in die Gebiete Buczacz, Czortków, Kamenec Podolski abgesetzt. Ukrainische Bevölkerung beunruhigt. Diese Juden müssen unbedingt zurück. Sich.Div. 444 bittet Ungarn entsprechende Weisung zu erteile»*. BA/MA RH 22/5.

20 HIS, p. 129. *«Es handelt sich um Juden, die keine ungar. Staatsbürger sind u. die vor 2 Jahren sich vor d. Sowjets nach Nordostungarn geflüchtet haben. Diese werden jetzt in ihre Gegend wieder zurückgebracht»*. BA/MA RH 22/5.

21 HIS, p. 132, Mallmann/Riess/Pyta, pp. 84, 181, Pohl Ukraine, p. 29. *«Die Zahlreichen Juden wurden vermehrt durch Zuzug der aus Ungarn ausgewiesenen Juden, von welchen etwa 3000 in den letzten Tagen hier ankamen. Ihre Ernährung stösst auf grosse Schwierigkeiten; auch besteht Seuchengefahr. Sofortiger Befehl über ihren Abtransport ist dringend erwünscht»*.

22 Lower Ghettoization, pp. 122, 299. Communication by FK 183 to 444.Sich.-Div. of August 13, 1941. USHMM RG11 01 M13, 1275-3-662.

23 Ungváry, pp. 177-178.

24 Brahm, p. 33, Angrick Escalation, p. 18/33.

25 Breitman, p. 64, Brahm, p. 34, Angrick, p. 199, Angrick Escalation, p. 18/33, Gerlach/Götz, p. 221, Pohl Ostgalizien, p. 109. Of all the deportees from Hungary, about 13,400 were from Ruthenia and at least 4,000 came from other areas of the country.

26 Spitz's luck ended shortly thereafter; he was arrested by the Gestapo and sent to Mauthausen, where he died. He managed, however, to deliver the photographs and the narrative of the events he witnessed to his son Ivan.

27 See also HIS, p. 133.

28 Brahm, p. 34

29 Mallmann/Riess/Pyta, pp. 85, 181. KTB Berück Süd/Ia v. August 23, 1941. BA/MA, RH 22/3, Breitman, p. 64.

30 In total, about 800 Jews – men and women aged between 16 and 60 – were shot by a detachment of 1. SS-Infanterie-Brigade. Curilla, pp. 94, 901, Pohl Ukraine, p. 28, Lower, p. 4. About Novograd Volynski see Jeckeln's Einsatzbefehl dated July 25, 1941: NARA RG 242 T-501/R 5/000559-60.

31 Longerich, pp. 376, 686. EM 59 dated August 21, 1941.

32 The meeting was attended by Generalquartiermeister Eduard Wagner, Maj. Hans Georg Schmidt von Altenstadt (Chef der Abt. Kriegsverwaltung), Ministerialdirigent Justus Danckwerts (Leiter der Abt. V Verwaltung, in der Abt. Kriegsverwaltung), Oberst Ernst-Anton von Krosigk (Chef der Generalstabes bei Berück "Süd", Regierungpräsident Paul Dargel (Vertreter der Reichkommissar Koch), Oberregierungsrat Dr, Walter Labs and Hptm. Dr. Otto Bräutigam. The latter two were officials for the Ministry of Eastern territories. Jeckeln, it seems, was not present and submitted his proposal by telephone. HIS, p. 132, Angrick Escalation, p. 23/33, Angrick, p. 203.

33 *«Bei Kamenetz Podolsk hätten die Ungarn etwa 11.000 Juden über die Grenze geschoben. In den bisherigen Verhandlungen sei es noch nicht gelungen, die Rücknahme dieser Juden zu erreichen. Der HSSPF (SS-Ogruf. Jeckeln) hoffe jedoch, die liquidation dieser Juden bis zum September 1, 1941 durchgeführt zu haben»*. HIS, p. 132, Hilberg, pp. 830, 964, Gerlach/Götz, p. 74.

34 Mallmann Endlösung, p. 454, Lower, p. 4.

35 Angrick Escalation, pp. 23-33, Gerlach/Götz, p. 74. Jeckeln had an opportunity to obtain the quota of victims needed to climb the particular standings of perpetrators of genocide, appeasing Himmler, while Roques was tasked with solving the logistical problem of supplies, getting rid of a large number of "unnecessary breadeaters (*unnutzer Esser*)", while maintaining good relations with Jeckeln. Mallmann/Riess/Pyta, p. 85.

36 Lower Ghettoization, p. 124-125.

37 Mallmann/Riess/Pyta, p. 85, Lower Ghettoization, p. 124.

38 Arad Holocaust, pp. 166, 566.

39 Lower Ghettoization, p. 124-125.

40 *Ibid.*, p. 126-127.

41 *Ibid.*, p. 127.

42 *Ibid.*, p. 129-130.

43 Angrick Escalation, pp. 24-33, Pohl Ukraine, p. 31.

44 Pohl Herrschaft, p. 258.

45 Arad Holocaust, pp. 166, 566.

46 Stabskompanie/HSSPF "Russland-Süd" was formed by Jackeln's bodyguards *(Leibwache)*, a squad of guards *(Wachzug)*, an administrative core, drivers and ordinances. See Mallmann/Riess/Pyta, p. 85. The firing squads that played a predominant role in both the massacre at Kamenec Podolski and that at Rumbula (Latvia, November 30 and December 8, 1941) were selected among them. Hilberg, p. 317, Ezergailis, p. 242.

47 HIS, p. 135, Pohl Ukraine, pp. 30, 63. The only EGC member in Kamenec Podolski was SS-Sturmbannführer August Meyer, who acted as liaison officer between Jeckeln's staff and EGC itself. Actually, other divisions of the security police were detached not far from Kamenec Podolski, but they didn't take part in the slaughter. In particular, there was a detachment of Schöngarth's EG zbV in Tarnopol, that in late August had pushed back a column of Jews sent over the River Dniester by a Hungarian battalion, while from early August an EGC kommando was stationed in Chernov, that was in charge of keeping Romanians and Ukrainians separate. Angrick, p. 192, Angrick Escalation, pp. 11/33, 18/33, Hilberg, pp. 830, 964, Pohl Ostgalizien, p. 109, Headland, p. 131. According to Arad Holocaust, p. 165, also an EGC detachment of about thirty men took part in the massacre.

48 Brahm, p. 34, Pohl Täter, p. 213, Pohl Ukraine, p. 29, Klemp, p. 285, Breitman, p. 64, Longerich, p. 377.

49 Klemp, p. 284.

50 Curilla, pp. 618, 793, Longerich, pp. 376, 686. On August 1941, in Stara Kostantinova, the battalion would act as support to 1. SS-Infanterie-Brigade, who massacred 439 Jews (300 men and 139 women) found guilty (EM 59 of August 29) of failing to comply with work orders, sabotaging crops, starting a black market in stolen cattle, mistreating Ukrainians civilians and being *impertinent* [sic!]. The battalion's involvement in this bloodshed is confirmed by a report of HSSPF "Russland-Nord", dated August 20, 1941. See also Hilberg, p. 317.

51 Mallmann/Riess/Pyta, pp. 85-86.

52 See Otto Dov Kulka/Aron Rodrigue: *The German Population and the Jews in the Third Reich*. In Yad Vashem Studies XVI (1984), p. 430.

53 Bauman, p. 163.

54 Browning Ordinary, p. 54.

55 Breitman, p. 64.

56 Testimony given by Wilhelm W., Mallmann/Riess/Pyta, p. 87.

57 *Ibid.*

58 *«Dass die Juden die Unruhe in die Welt gebracht haetten, dass sie arbeitsscheu seien und beseitigt werden müssten».* Testimony given by Herbert H., Mallmann/Riess/Pyta, pp. 85-86.

59 *Ibid.*

60 Testimony given by Hermann Krüger, HIS, pp. 135, Mallmann/Riess/Pyta, pp. 86-87.

61 Testimonies given by Herbert Stephan and Karl Raddatz, Angrick, p. 204, Angrick Escalation, pp. 24/33, 25/33.

62 Lüschen, Wedekind, Krüger and others were part of Jeckeln's personal staff since the Braunschweig days and also during the Ukrainian massacres of 1941 (Stara Kostantinova, Berdičev, Krementchug, Krivoi Rog, Dnepropetrovsk and Kamenec Podolski), and kept that role also after Jeckeln's transfer to Riga in November. According to the scarce information available, Willi Wedekind, born on December 1, 1913, died of head injuries sustained during an air attack on August 14, 1944. As for Kruger, he was called to testify during the investigation of ZStL 204 AR-Z 13/60 v. Degenhardt and others. The file was then forwarded for preliminary investigation to the Prosecutor of Kiel, 2 Js 269/65, and then filed July 28, 1971 because of Degenhardt's death, which occurred four days earlier. As for Johannes Lüschen, we only know that he was Jeckeln's personal driver. See Angrick/Klein, pp. 156, 164, 460.

63 Testimony given by Hermann Krüger, HIS, p. 135, Mallmann/Riess/Pyta, pp. 86-87.

64 Testimony given by Hermann Krüger, HIS, pp. 135.

65 *Ibid.*

66 Arad Holocaust, pp. 166, 566.

67 Mermall, pp. 126-127. Gabor Mermelstein (Gabriel Mermall) was luckier than Spitz. After serving in a Hungarian labor division until 1943 he managed to escape in early 1944, together with his son, hiding in a Ruthenian forest, where he survived with the help of a Hungarian logger until the return of Soviet troops.

68 Angrick, pp. 203-204, Angrick Escalation, pp. 24/33.

69 Witness Herbert H. would request and obtain permission to be excluded from the shooting by his division commander Scharway. Mallmann/Riess/Pyta, pp. 85-86.

70 Curilla, p. 925, Pohl Ukraine, pp. 31, 63. Testimony given by Ottmar L.

71 *«Fernschr. vom 29.8.41: Erfolge:* [...] *Stabskompanie erschiesst erneut 7.000 Juden, somit Gesamtzahl bei der Aktion in Kamenec Podolski liquidierten Juden rund 20.000. Änderung zu Tätigkeitsbericht vom 26 und 27.8.41: statt Pol.Batl.320 setzen: Stabskompanie; i.d. Meldung vom 27.8. statt 5000, 11000. Pol.Batl.320 was nur zur Absperrung eingesetzt».* HIS, p. 134, Krausnick/Wilhelm, p. 189.

72 Breitman, pp. 64-65, 265. Decrypted message of September 2, 1941.

73 *«Nachtrag die Zahl der durch Stabskompanie HSSPF Russland Süd. In Kamenec Podolski liquidierten Juden erhoeht sich auf 23.600».* HIS, p. 134, Breitman, p. 64.

74 Bankier, pp. 1121-1122.

75 Klemp, pp. 287-289.

76 Mallmann/Riess/Pyta, p. 85.

77 Polizei-Bataillon 45 was involved in Berdičev, Polizei-Bataillone 45 and 314 in Vinnitsa, Polizei-Bataillone 45 and 304 in Babi Yar, Polizei-Bataillon 314 in Dnepropetrovsk, Polizei-Bataillone 315, 320 and part of Polizei-Bataillon "Ostland" in Rovno, Polizei-Bataillon 22 in Rumbula and Polizei-Bataillon 314 in Kharkov.

78 Browning Origini, p. 302.

79 On the role of the Rumanian Government in the Jewish persecution of summer/autumn 1941, see for instance Jean Ancel: *The Jassi pogrom – June 29, 1941;* Radu Ioanid: *The Deportation of the Jews to Transnistria;* Andrej Angrick: *Rumänien, die SS und die Vernichtung der Juden.* See also Angrick Escalation, quoted in the bibliography.

80 See also Jan Kershaw: *Hitler, the Germans and the Final Solution*, pp. 184, 199. Jerusalem/London, 2008.

81 Testimony given by Wilhelm W., Mallmann/Riess/Pyta, p. 87.

Two Hungarian policemen together with German soldiers. Magyar police had a fundamental role in the deportation of Jews from Hungary, both in 1941 and 1944.

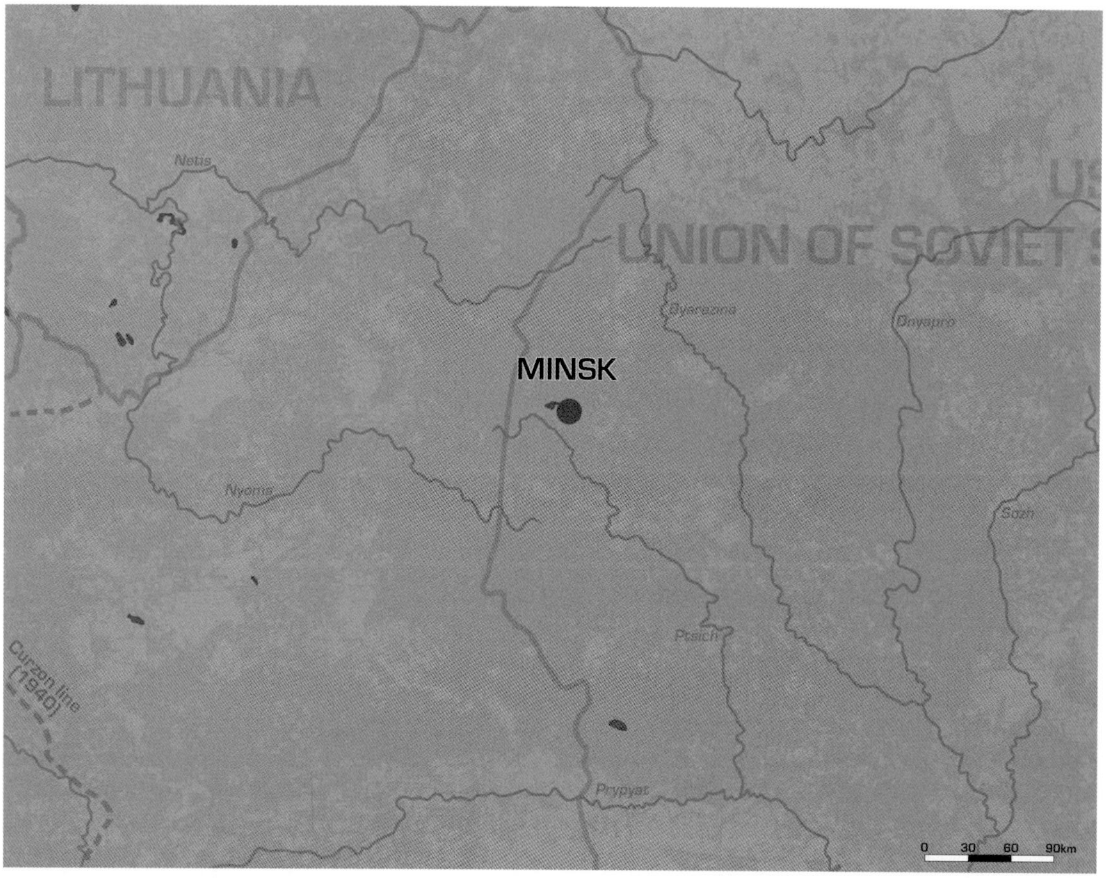

LITHUANIA
UNION OF SOVIET S
US
MINSK
Netis
Nyoma
Byarezina
Dnyapro
Sozh
Ptsich
Prypyat
Curzon line
(1940)
0 30 60 90km

CHAPTER FIVE

"HERREN DES TATORT"

POLIZEI BATAILLON 322 AND THE SLAUGHTER OF MINSK SEPTEMBER 1, 1941

Fragezeichen auf Fragenzeichen gab es,
ohne daß der Berg von Schuld kleiner wurde.
Was übrigblieb,
müssen ganze Serien schlechter Gewissen,
nicht nur schlechter Gedächtnisse sein.

From an article in Rheinische Merkur, 1963.[1]

5.1 DIVIDE ET CAEDE

Daumanstrasse, Schirokaja-Strasse, Masyukovshchina, Drosdy, Puschkin-Kaserne, Maly Trostenez…

From July 1941, all these places - streets, villages and boroughs within the urban area of Minsk or in its immediate vicinity - began to appear more frequently in the reports submitted by those units that had been commissioned to guard and run them: initially, regular units of the Wehrmacht, then Wacht or Landesschutzen-Bataillone, or Sicherheitspolizei cells[2]. They were temporary lagers, labor or prison camps, detention and killing centers, forming a complex of concentration camps without equal, where tens of thousands of civilians, prisoners of war, communists and former Soviet administration executives had been locked up since the days that followed the entry of German troops in Minsk, which occurred on June 28, 1941[3].

Soon after, the Jewish ghetto too would follow and become part of that repressive and destructive universe.

According to a reliable estimate, about 10,000 Jews in Minsk managed to escape from the ghetto, reaching the forest and joining partisan groups[4]: that means – calculating the existence of the ghetto at about 820 (from July 20, 1941 to October 21, 1943) – a daily average of about a dozen successful escapes. This was possible thanks to a widespread network of complicity established among Jews and Belarusians, between *the inside and the outside*. This complicity existed on the basis of an identity perceived as *common* by the majority of both communities and surmounted the unproductive and often fatal opposition among the Jews and the local people, built on ethnic and political grounds, that, was however, was quite widespread in many other areas of occupied eastern Europe. From this perspective, the situational context of the Minsk ghetto represents an exception due to an accumulation of simultaneous factors, essentially tied to the ideological and social dynamics initiated by the Soviet regime, particularly in that part of Belarus with Minsk as its capital, which was historically part of the USSR.

Unlike other Soviet territories, both of recent annexation like the Baltic, former Polish Western Belarus and Galicia, or characterized by the presence of cells that maintained a cultural identity despite the fierce policy of denationalization carried out by the Stalinist regime - especially in Ukraine - Belarus did not have its own consolidated ethnocentric vision, nor the historical, ethnic and linguistic instruments which could foment it in the short-term. Generally speaking, Belarus continued to perceive itself as an offshoot of Moscow, where the nationalist ideology of the early century - so virulent in other areas - had found but little adherence from political parties of minor importance and support[5].

In such a context then, it was relatively easy for its people, especially those living in urban areas and belonging to the younger generations, to accept the Soviet internationalist ideology, with its vision of solidarity and overcoming of barriers between classes and ethnic groups: a vision that had led to good social integration between the Jews and the rest of the population, resulting in the marginalization of anti-Semitism and inter-ethnic animosity in general.

This reality, so specific with comparison to the complex ethnic, social and political mosaic of occupied Eastern Europe, favored, during the war, an onset of bonds of solidarity – hardly conceivable elsewhere – between the Belarusian Jews enclosed in the ghetto and the Belarusian Belarusians living outside of it. It produced a reasonable degree of acceptance towards the fugitives who escaped from the Minsk ghetto by the partisan units operating in nearby forests who gave them an alternative (precarious but still preferable to the fate of the ghetto). This support to the fugitives was not given in other places, like Lithuania or Ukraine, where the local population tended to not look kindly on them, and often spied on them in exchange for a reward.

Evidently, such an osmotic situation, in terms of inter-ethnic relations, put into serious difficulties the Nazi conception, so coarsely Manichaeistic, of confrontation between groups, based on the elevation of some at the expense of others through the application of abstract racial theories and for instrumental reasons related to the dynamics of the occupation. This ploy could be and certainly was quite successful in places that were historically and culturally structured, such as the Baltic, Ukraine and in part, even Poland (with its 1939 borders) but much less so in Belarus, where right from the start the Germans had a hard time drawing the line between desired *friends* (ethnic Belarusians) and perceived *enemies* (Jews and Russians), by using for that purpose only schematic race theories held valid in Berlin, but that proved insufficient in that particular reality.

Also, political dynamics, mixed with race relations, added a further element of fluidity to a situation with no stable and defined reference points: the lack of a solid foundation of nationalism, the lack of grip on the urban population of the logics based on anti-Soviet and anti-communism, and difficulties in fomenting anti-Semitic positions in Central and Eastern Belarus, hindered the consolidation of Nazi rule. The Germans were not perceived as liberators from the Soviet yoke – as had happened in the Baltic, in Galicia, in Ukraine and in several areas of former-Polish Western Belarus – but as a form of oppression tout-court, where one existing form of *domain* was being replaced by an even

Minsk, autumn 1941: German soldiers, two policemen among them, parade a group of visibly worried Jewish religious men as a trophy. Note the tallit, the prayer shawl, that two of them were forced to wear, probably in order to improve the scenographic effect of the photo.

more alien and illegitimate one[6]. Certainly, in Belarus as elsewhere, the Germans could count on a vast reservoir of collaboration from which to draw recruits for the auxiliary police, but at the same time the pro-Soviet partisan reaction was widespread, whereas it had been very marginal – if not unheard of – in Galicia, the Baltic and Western Ukraine. Moreover, difficult as it was for the new rulers to foster anti-Semitic pogroms even where anti-Semitism could be said to be relatively common, it was almost impossible in Belarus, where the Nazis came to be perceived as *barbarians* and *hangmen*, while the Jews – despite Berlin's wishes – continued to be considered by the local population as human beings *no more and no less than the Belarusians themselves*[7].

Right from the start, in Minsk and in major cities of central and eastern Belarus, the Germans found themselves having to deal with an atmosphere of suspicious wait, low empathy and ambiguous and reluctant cooperation from the local population. This attitude, together with the absence of anti-Semitic flare-ups – such as those which took place in Kaunas, Lviv, Boryslaw and other locations[8] – probably contributed to feed an obsession for security by the Nazi occupation forces, inclined as they were to confuse the cautious prudence of the population with an overt opposition – of which the Jews were, of course, a part of. In the summer of 1941, however, the armed opposition was still to come, and when it did, it would be completely disorganized, with limited means and limited, at least in the beginning, only to the politicized and pro-Soviet sectors. The occupation forces – Wehrmacht, SS or police acting together – reacted to such opposition in nuce, by meeting *terror with terror*; be it through the rude and uneducated attitude of the arrogant ruler upon the ruled, reduced to the status of helots through the essentially predatory and colonial approach of the military units against the indigenous population, the violent intolerance towards all forms of dissent, not only the dissent of an ideological nature, but also that deriving from objective problems. The worry was not to conquer hearts and minds, but to reset them, but they obtained in return the opposite result which only served to multiply the reasons for opposition, in a virtually endless repression/reaction vicious circle. In the cities they proceeded with mass arrests of males of military age. In Minsk, around the beginning of July, the *entire* male population aged between 15 and 45/50, both Belarusian and Jewish, was deported to Drosdy prison camp, about three miles north of the city, to be submitted to an ideological *screening* during which, among the Jews, some 3,000 so-called *intellectuals*, professionals and elements of alleged communist faith, i.e. members of the Soviet apparatus, were selected and then shot[9]. Then, while the surviving Jews were detained in the camp, the Belarusians were allowed to return to their homes: a concession that was meant to draw a line between Jews and Belarusians, inducing into the latter the relief of preferential treatment, but that, on the other hand, confirmed the people's perception of the *barbarian nature* of the new rulers, who had very poor influence over them, and were very generous in dispensing brute force.

Rural areas too were affected by repeatedly destructive waves of repression, which, although aimed primarily against Jews, involved a growing number of *gentiles*. According to Christian Gerlach, as many as 85-90 % of the victims of the anti-partisan war in Belarus was made up of Belarusian peasants who, with time and the spread of the insurgency from winter 1941, became the main target of Nazi repression[10]. In the eyes of the population, then, the first genocidal wave of summer/autumn 1941 ended up coming together with anti-partisan repression, only confirming the exclusively *terroristic* approach of the new rulers who, for their part, soon found themselves having to deal with a situation that had gradually become unmanageable. The units, always too few to obtain complete control of the territory, but numerous enough to feed the spiral, ended up having to operate in a context of growing hostility; a hostility not whispered but patent, not potential but real hostility, no longer elitist but popular. Scattered over a huge territory, the garrisons became overwhelmed by a sort of encirclement-syndrome, which they responded to by applying indiscriminate and draconian methods. The obsession with security spread from urban areas – inclined to be more politically advanced – to the countryside, eventually involving the farmers, who at first were passive and fatalistic but then found themselves having to choose, reluctantly, between the hammer of repression and the anvil of insurgency. The forest became a hotel for partisan groups; the villages became recruitment areas and objectives of spoliation for both contenders, the links between town and countryside were strengthened by the growing number of civilians that moved from the intolerable conditions of the first to the second, where food could be easier to find, and survival chances could be higher[11]. Together with the fugitives, ideas were also moving. These ideas brought Communist propaganda, albeit fainted within patriotic ideals, and as months went by what had been, after all, a phenomenon limited to the pro-Soviet ideological sectors eventually stretched to epidemic proportions, especially in central and eastern areas of the country. In their reckless and ideological Manichaeism and because of their disastrous failure to deal with dissent by methods other than simple criminal repression, the Nazis turned into dangerous fighters those who initially, as defined by Nechama Tec, were but simple *inactive dissenters*[12] and, paradoxically, ended up becoming victims of their own ideology[13].

Culturally incapable of structuring a rational non-ideological response to the issues that arose after their entry into Belarus, the Nazis were limited to react in only the most simplistic and counterproductive way. The assimilation of Jews and peasants to communists and partisans, including them in a single unsolvable circular equation, with dramatic consequences: not only for the Jews who were the first and designated victims, but also, in the medium term, for the rest of the population – and especially for the perception that this population was forming against its new rulers.

5.2 PREAMBLE

The decision to establish the Jewish ghetto in Minsk was taken on an autonomous initiative of local Feldkommandantur 812 (Oberstleutnant Karl Schlegelho-

A group of Jews in Minsk, 1941. Note the yellow mark on the chest and the back. Source: Bundesarchiv.

fer), by order issued on July 19, 1941. This was just a few weeks before the shifting of powers, in Western Belarus, including its capital Minsk, from the Wehrmacht Military Administration to the civil rule of the Generalkommissar Wilhelm Kube (August 31).

In accordance with Schlegelhofer's arrangements, the entire Jewish population still living in Minsk (about 85,000) had to move to a slum area northwest of the town, close to the old Jewish cemetery, within five days from the issuing of the order[14]. At the same time, the Judenrat was established, its task being the registration of the residents, or, at least, those who had survived the first decimation of alleged communists Jews, so-called *intellectuals*, and those considered to be *anti-German*, carried out in the prison camp of Drosdy, towards the beginning of July[15].

The executions perpetrated in Minsk during the early weeks of July had been somehow *improvised* and uncoordinated, but they were based on potentials of danger perceived as real, or determined by specific conditions. The establishment of the ghetto was aimed at concentrating a whole category of potential victims (the Jews) within the circumscribed boundaries of a zone in which shooting was both tolerated and encouraged. In July 1941 then, the city of Minsk became the focal point (Schwehrpunkt) of the persecutory, selection and annihilation activities, perpetrated in Belorussia by EGB[16], in close cooperation with Ordnungspolizei units, kindly offered by HSSPF Erich von dem Bach: among these was Polizei-Bataillon 322, two companies of which had just entered the city.

After that, thanks to the shifting of powers to the civil administration, the various police bodies were able to define – once and for all – their own specific expertise with regards to the ideological and annihilation warfare: expertise that until that moment had been successfully shared with Wehrmacht security and rear units.

With a few exceptions, it is documented how most genocidal actions that took place in Belarus between July/August 1941 and following months were carried out through the coordinated use of both Sichereits and Ordnungspolizei units: this can be partly attributed to the direct intervention of the highest SS and Police ranks, who, at that time, were frequently inspecting the units.

As happened in Bialystok and in Brest Litovsk on July 12 and 13, and as would happen in Mogilev on October 19, in Minsk too the intervention of a higher rank (Daluege in this case), had a direct relation to the subsequent carrying out of a slaughter. This slaughter, as we will see later, was in no way *justified* by any military or security logic, but followed a *sheer* genocidal perspective, and precisely because of that, probably required further *encouragement* from the top.

Such encouragement punctually arrived on August 29, when Chef der Ordnungspolizei, Kurt Daluege, and HSSPF von dem Bach met in Minsk. The next day, the order for a Jewish action in the ghetto in coordination with SS-Obersturmbannführer Hans-Hermann Koch of the EGB was issued to Gottlieb Nagel, commander of Polizei-Bataillon 322[18]. The action was launched on August 31, 1941, after informing the commanders of companies 1/322 and 3/322.

5.3 AUSTRIA FELIX

The unit that was called to perpetrate the first *reduction* of the Minsk ghetto was an Austrian battalion with German cadres, formed in Vienna-Kagran from a training unit on April 15, 1941. This battalion had already been given the opportunity to show its genocidal tendencies since its entry into Soviet territory – between July 5 and 6, 1941 –, carrying out the second massacre of the Jewish community of Bialystok (July 12)[19]. This is the structure of the three divisions of the battalion in August 1941:

Bataillon-Stab: Maj. Gottlieb Nagel, Adj. Oltn. Josef Uhl;

Kraftfahrzeugstaffel: Hptm. Frömsdorf;

Nachrichtenzug;

1/322: Hptm. Reinhold Jörke;

2/322: Hptm. Sigfried Binz (since July 1941);

3/322: Oltn. Gerhard Riebel.

Erich von dem Bach (center) while inspecting a police unit in Minsk, around 1943. On his right HSSPF "Russland -Mitte" Curt von Gottberg. Source: Bundesarchiv

The events that unfolded thereafter follow the monotonous pattern of a well-rehearsed scenario.

On July 31, 1941, while the personnel of the 3/322 division cordoned off the ghetto, 1/322 policemen, together with Sipo officers and one NSKK company, carried out a door-to-door roundup of all Jews aged 15 to 60, often whipping and hitting them with sticks[20]. They were pushed up to a previously bombed square – probably the inner courtyard of the prison of Minsk – where most of the women with their children were separated from the men and later sent back home: with the exception of a group of 64 women who, apparently, had been caught not wearing the yellow star *inside their homes*. After which, about 700 Jews remained under surveillance in the Minsk prison, where they spent their last night[21].

That same evening, coming from Bereza Kartuska, the 2/322 division arrived in Minsk, in order to join operations on the following day. It had been called in to *reinforce* the depleted ranks of the battalion; weakened by an unusually high percentage of men that had fallen ill (79, about 16 % of the total[22]).

According to reconstruction by the Court of Freiburg during the proceedings v. Uhl, Riebel and Hülsemann, at this point in time the battalion personnel and high ranks hadn't been informed about the real goal of the action. Only in the evening of that August 31, Nagel instructed battalion Adjutant Uhl to proceed with the organization of two firing squads, to be used the next day. Replying the objections raised by Uhl, Nagel explained he was receiving orders from Montua, commander of Polizei-Regiment "Mitte", who, in turn, was receiving orders *from above*. Consequently, according to this logic, the *resulting* need to obey orders until they were changed implied that none of them would have been considered responsible for what happened in the following hours[23]. This assertion, which for obvious reasons was widely popular with the battalion, would be the core of *Befehlsnotstand*, the legal artifice which meant the alleged impossibility to disobey orders, that years afterwards would be so generously applied by Western Germany's Courts to many of the defendants prosecuted for war crimes.

The following day, September 1, after spending the night in the open courtyard of the prison, many of the Jews arrested the previous day were loaded onto the Kraftfahrzeugstaffel trucks, that shuttled them towards a kind of marshland area, not far from town, where some common graves had previously been dug. At the same time the remaining victims, with the addition of another group of about 200 Jews[24] – probably arrested a few days before and detained in the same jail –were lined up and forced to march towards their fate.

As well as the firing squads, awaiting them were also Sichereitspolizei executives and a few officers of the Battalion-Stab, among which Nagel and Uhl, the latter being particularly distressed and reluctant, as he had been ordered to witness the massacre by Nagel himself[25].

As the trucks reached the common graves – at least three had been dug and they were large enough to contain several hundred corpses – the victims were forced to descend in small groups through a specially designed slope made of soil that ran to the bottom of the trench, where the firing squad was in wait.

In order to speed up operations, the trucks approached the edge of the pits in reverse, so that the victims could be unloaded directly onto the slope. The procedures were carried out among shouts and confusion, one of the platoon leaders of 3/322 in particular, Oberleutnant Rasche – his anti-Semitism being well-known – would regularly beat the victims with blows of his stick, in order to *encourage* them into the ditch[26].

At that point, the victims were ordered to lie down, face to the ground, while behind them the firing squad lined up rifles pointed at the necks. Then the platoon commanders gave the order to fire.

Overall, 914 executions were perpetrated by Polizei-Bataillon 322, including the 64 women imprisoned during the roundup. According to the KTB of 3/322, the firing squad of this division killed 330 of these victims, among which 40 women[27]. All the others were obviously murdered by 1/322 firing squad.

In parallel with this action, carried out by Polizei-Bataillon 322, another slaughter would be perpetrated during the same hours, or maybe several days later, in the Minsk ghetto, at the hands of EK 8, supported by men of Feldgendarmerie and, possibly, also by Ordnungspolizei personnel, with a total of 2,278 more victims[28].

The following is evidence by Ltn. Friedrich Soier, former commander of 3/322's second platoon, given on October 19, 1965, before Department 18 of the Austrian Ministry of the Interiors, and transmitted to ZStL that was investigating the case[29]. The evidence given by this officer seems more meaningful and credible, compared to the reluctant statements released by his German comrades: this is because, since 1957, the repression of Nazi crimes in Austria had been closed *de facto*, and although the terms of prescription for murder had been formally abolished in 1965, this measure did not have any practical effect that could worsen Soier's position.

His words were:

Firstly, all around the ghetto a line of policemen was deployed, mainly formed by personnel of the battalion. After which, SD members and police officers – including myself – entered the ghetto and ordered the Jews to leave their homes. Those who did not obey voluntarily, were forced out.

The Jews were pushed up to a square, previously targeted by bombing [probably the inner courtyard of the prison of Minsk, N/A]. Among them were not only men, but women and children too.

I don't remember exactly who was in charge of watching over the Jews gathered in the square. In any case, immediately after the roundup, our division was loaded onto the trucks and we were sent back to our quarters.

The Jews remained in the square all night. Then, the next morning, when we returned to the square, most women and children had been already released. At that point, about 1,000 Jews had remained in wait in the square, men and women, but especially men.

Our company had just three or four trucks, so as many Jews as possible were loaded onto each of them, together with a few policemen: these comrades had to guard the prisoners, after which they were used to form the execution squad.

After that we travelled out of Minsk for a few miles, and then we arrived at an open field north of the highway. There was a slightly hilly terrain, where three trenches had been dug, 10 – 15 yards in length, 2 yards in width and 3 yards in depth. High-ranking SS officers were present at the killing field.

The pits I mentioned before had clearly been planned or dug by people who were already experienced in the execution of large numbers of victims, because one side sloped to the bottom, so that the Jews didn't have to jump inside from the edge, but they could run down the soil ramp directly towards the bottom of the pit.

The trucks approached the pits in reverse, and once they were close enough to the edge, the Jews were forced off. In each of the three pits there were 12 policemen that formed the firing squad. The Jews had to run towards them in groups of 12, so that each policeman had a victim in front of him.

The Jews had clothes on, they were ordered to lie down at the bottom of the pit, face to the ground. In the trench I was in, the firing order was given by Oltn. Rasche, who shouted: "1 - 2 Fire!". Then, the sound of a round of bullets being fired was heard.

At a certain point, I was ordered by Oltn. Ri[ebel] - but it could have been Oltn. Rasche - to shoot dead those that had only been wounded. I think this happened in three cases, when I saw some Jews that, although mortally hurt by the bullet, were not dead yet.

Then, when Rasche was called out of the trench, I was ordered by Oltn. Ri[ebel], to take command of the firing squad in that pit, which I did, giving the order to fire twice. Eventually, Ltn. Busche arrived to replace me.

That day, 350 Jews of both sexes, mainly men, were killed in the three common graves where the firing squads of our division had been sent.

I want to emphasize that, during the executions, no unnecessary acts of cruelty were perpetrated.

After the first group of Jews was loaded off, the trucks went back to the square to bring other victims. How many times they travelled back and forth, I don't remember, but I do not think this happened very often.

None of the SS-men present on the killing field took part in the executions.

The following is an excerpt of the KTB of 3/Polizei-Bataillon 322[30].

August 31, 1941

15:00. Jewish action in the Minsk ghetto completed. Ninth division [3/322, N/A] in charge of cordoning the ghetto, while seventh division [1/322, N/A], NSKK division and SD performed the searches. All Jews aged 15 – 60 were imprisoned, as well as all women not wearing the compulsory yellow mark on their clothes. Overall, 916 Jews of both sexes were imprisoned[31].

September 1, 1941

05.30. Shooting of the Jews imprisoned the day earlier carried out, about 6 miles east of Minsk, north of the highway Minsk-Smolensk-Minsk. Three firing squads were formed. 9th division's firing squad [3/322, N/A] shot 330 Jews in total (40 women)[32].

5.4 HERREN DES TATORTS (MEN OF THE CRIME SCENE)

As far as the judicial path of the Polizei-Bataillon 322 is concerned, a good reference work, very useful for in-depth examination,[33] is the article written in 1986, 25 years after the facts, by Alfred Aedtner, former *Kriminalhauptkommissar* and member of the *Sonderkommission der ZStL*, and published in the weekly magazine *Der Spiegel*. The following is a limited summary of salient facts and biographical notes of some key figures in Polizei-Bataillon 322 [34] in the 1941 summer/autumn bloodsheds, Minsk included.

Maj. Gottlieb Nagel: Born 1892 in Württemberg, a war volunteer in 1914, police service in 1920, member of the NSDAP from May 1, 1933, SS-Sturmbannführer from December 1, 1940. Commander of Polizei-Ausbildungs-Bataillon «Wien-Kagran» from February 1941 and of Polizei-Bataillon 322 until August 1942. As a prisoner of war, he was subjected to de-nazification in 1948 and was finally dismissed from service. After the war he lived in Stuttgart and died in November 1978[35]. Very strict with discipline and respect for authority, but also popular with his subordinates – to the point that he was nick-named "Papa Nagel" – during the first Bialystok action of July 18 and the Minsk action of September 1, it seems that, urged by his battalion Adjutant, he tried to raise an objection to the improper use of policemen in the firing squads. However, his complaints were confined to a rather superficial level, and they never cast a doubt about the battalion's active participation in the slaughters. On the contrary, Nagel was always very careful that the orders he received and, in turn, gave, were executed unconditionally, and demanded the presence, by his side, of all his officers, including Uhl[3]6, during the bloodsheds.

Oltn. Josef Uhl: Born 1909 in Gaggenau, Baden. Member of NSDAP and the SS. The holder of a commercial enterprise affected by the 1929 financial crash, he joined police service in 1930. A Schutzpolizei NCO, he became lieutenant in 1939, after passing a course at the Academy. Promoted to Oberleutnant and instructor in a police school, he was Nagel's Adjutant at Polizei-Ausbildungs-Bataillon «Wien-Kagran» (later Polizei-Bataillon 322) from January 1940 to March 1942. Promoted to captain in January 1943, he requested and obtained permission to be transferred back to a police school, and then took back control of a division at a police regiment engaged on the Russian front. Held in Soviet captivity for a short time after the war, after 1946 he was readmitted to police service as Personalreferent at the Interior Ministry of Baden and then, from 1958, as director of Personalabteilung of Landespolizeidirektion Südbaden. After the war he was domiciled in Freiburg[37]. According to his own testimony, given to the Prosecutor of Freiburg, in his position as Battalion Adjutant he would accompany his battalion commander Nagel during inspections at the places of massacres, including Bialystok and Minsk, remaining shocked and *paralyzed by terror*: that is why he would urge Nagel himself to remonstrate with Max Montua about the misuse to which the battalion had been assigned, receiving reassurances and promises, but very poor results in practical terms. For this reason, disgusted by the massacres, he applied for transfer to another position, which was eventually granted in March 1942. Uhl's evidence, supported by other statements, was considered convincing by the Court of Freiburg, which therefore acquitted him of all charges[38].

Hptm. Reinhold Jörke: Member of NSDAP. Polizeihauptmeister from May 1, 1933. SS member. Commander of 1/322. Of socialist tendencies, he had been described as *SPD-Bonzen* in a report written on him by SS-Allgemeine-Standarte 35 of Kassel[23]. He died a few years after the war, before the beginning of the Freiburg trial[39]. Strict at ensuring the execution of orders by his subordinates and insensitive to any kind of objections and critics, within Polizei-Bataillon 322 he was also officially responsible for legal matters *(Gerichtsoffiziere)*[40].

Lippmann, Hermann: born 1906. In the police service from 1929, member of the NSDAP, SS member from autumn 1939. Captain, commander of 2/322 until July 1941. He died a few years after the war, before the Freiburg trial[41].

Hptm. Sigfried Binz: Born 1898. Member of the NSDAP. Police service since 1920. In spring 1933, NSDAP-Kreisgericht Berlin-Spandau opened an investigation against him for having fraudulently pre-dated his militancy in the NSDAP to 1928 and declared his real belonging to *alter Kämpfer*. SS member since autumn 1939. Captain from July 1941 and commander of 2/322 in replacement of Hermann Lippmann. He died a few years after the war, before the beginning of the Freiburg trial[42].

Oltn. Gerhard Riebel: Born in Darmstadt, Hesse. Member of SS-Allgemeine from 30 April 1933. NSDAP member. Transferred to SS-VT in April 1939. Initially a theology student, he then opted for voluntary military service. Graduated from SS-Junker-Schule in 1938 with the rank of SS-Obersturmführer. In 1939, aged 24, he was transferred to Schutzpolizei as an officer in active service with the rank of Oberleutnant. Commander of 3/322. Domiciled in Darmstadt after the war, he remained in police service as Steuerinspektor at Bensheim an der Bergstrasse (Darmstadt, Hesse)[43]. During the Bialystok massacre of July 18, 1941 he took personal command of his division engaged in the roundups, although he maintained that he had not had, until then, a clear perception about the motivation of the *action*. Indeed, according to what he stated before the Court of Freiburg – probably for opportunistic reasons which, however, earned him the recognition of *Befehlsnotstand* – he would abhor the treatment meted out to Jews during the massacre in Minsk without, however, intervening to stop the excesses of his subordinates, among which was deputy division commander, Oltn. Rasche. Apparently, during the following massacre at Mogilev, Riebel would make sure that unnecessary suffering to the victims was avoided, organizing the executions in an orderly and professional manner: something undoubtedly years away from the bestial ethylic anarchy that the Lithuanian auxiliaries had fallen into – and that he had authority to stop, but decided not to – but certainly not quite so consolatory from the victims' point of view[44].

Rasche, Erich: born June 23, 1916. NSDAP member since the age of 17. An SS member, he remained in the Wehrmacht for a year beyond the compulsory military service. Discharged from the army, he took a course at an SS officers' school, after which he entered the police academy. Assigned to an Einsatzgruppe during the invasion of Czechoslovakia, he was later transferred to Polizei-Bataillon-Ausbildungs "Wien-Kagran" and then became commander of the platoon 3/322 with the rank of Oberleutnant, and Riebel's deputy in command of the division. A fanatical Nazi and anti-Semitic, Rasche commanded a firing squad during the massacres of Bialystok and Minsk and proceeded in person to inflict numerous death blows to the victims left wounded in mass graves, even threatening punishment for those subordinates more reluctant to take part in executions or hesitant to pull the trigger. During the massacre, it seems, he volunteered to escort the Jews to the common graves, inflicting violence and brutality upon them on the way[45]. He was killed in action near Mogilev on December 2, 1942.

Hülsemann, Heinz Gerd: A police volunteer, he initially followed the normal training procedure, and in 1941 passed a course for officers, gaining the rank of lieutenant. Transferred to Polizei-Bataillon 322, he became platoon leader of 1/322 and after the war he spent four years in Soviet captivity. After his release he served the police again, at the Ministry of Interior of Nordrhein-Westfalen from 1954 and then with Siegen's police authorities from 1961, with the rank of Polizeiobermeister[46]. Commander of a firing squad during the Mogilev massacre, he would maintain a professional attitude during the shootings, without indulging in excesses and brutality: in this respect, his statements before the Court of Freiburg were considered convincing, so he too was granted the benefit of the Befehlsnotstand[47].

Suspicions of a possible involvement of Polizei-Bataillon 322 in war crimes and mass murders emerged in 1958 during the investigations of Bavarian LKA against Erich von dem Bach, that led to the hearing, as ordinary witnesses, of several former policemen of the battalion. Consequently, in 1960 those early clues were transmitted for competence – by virtue of the residence in Stuttgart of the main suspect, namely former battalion commander Gottlieb Nagel – to the Baden-Württemberg LKA that, through the Sonderkommission der ZSTL (folder ZStL 202 AR-Z 52/59), requested the opening of preliminary investigations, as well as issuing arrest warrants for Nagel and the Battalion Adjutant Uhl to the Public Prosecutor of Stuttgart. Both arrests were made on October 6, 1960 in Stuttgart and Freiburg[48], while further investigations followed (ZStL 202 AR-Z 650/61), as new witnesses (about one hundred) were summoned to the hearings. In this way, between February 1961 and February 1962, the arrests of Gehrard Riebel and Gerd Hülsemann were made; the latter a former platoon leader of 1/322 and still in service as Polizeiobermeister at Siegen's Kreispolizeibehoerde[49]. After which, albeit among difficulties and reticence, in May 1962 the request for indictment v. Nagel, Uhl, Riebel and Hülsemann was delivered by the Public Prosecutor of Stuttgart to the Court of Stuttgart.

At that point however, Nagel's defense attorney – certainly as a defense strategy – requested the intervention of the First Instance Chamber at the Court of Stuttgart (*Schwurgericht*) because of his client's alleged health reasons. Nagel had already claimed his non-involvement into the charges he was accused of by describing himself to the Court as a former battalion commander whose authority before the officers of his own divisions had been strongly weakened by repeated intrusions of regimental commander Montua and Einsatzgruppe B commander Nebe, to the point that he was almost deprived of control of his own unit.

This situation, he maintained, made him a powerless valet, unable to prevent the use of his men in firing squads: a valet, however, who was well-known to his subordinates bu the nickname "Man of the crime scene" *(Herr des Tatorts)*[50].

In any case, the deletion of the position of the main defendant meant that the entire file had to be transferred by default to the Prosecutor of Freiburg, city of residence of the second main defendant, namely Oltn. Uhl.

Finally, after a new series of investigations due to recantations, amendments and memory-blanks by the witnesses, a new indictment request was issued in February 1963 against the three remaining defendants (LG Freiburg, 1 Ks (AK) 1/63), against which the convictions requested were inexplicably mild and extremely weakened in terms of responsibilities, compared to that of Stuttgart: five years for Riebel, three years for Hülsemann, investigated for complicity in one hundred murders, and acquittal for Uhl, who was also granted economic compensation for the period spent in preventive detention[51].

Nevertheless, although scarcely significant, these requests too were rejected on July 12, 1963 by the Court of Freiburg, that on July 12, 1963, issued a ruling of complete acquittal, based on the questionable legal principle of *Befehlsnotstand*. Equally, even the following appeal presented by the Prosecutor of Freiburg was rejected for the same reasons by the Bundesgerichtshof, with ruling BHG - 1 StT 498/63 of January 14, 1964.

It was not over yet.

The discovery in the archives of Prague in January 1965, of the war diary of Polizei-Bataillon 322, with all its unquestionable contents, gave ZStL another chance to reopen the proceedings and request the prosecutor that had jurisdiction – in this case the Prosecutor of Darmstadt, residence of Gerhard Riebel, now risen to the role of main defendant – the opening of new preliminary investigations (folder ZStL 202 AR-Z 6/65). In 1966, with folder LG Darmstad 2 Js 376/65, the request of Ludwigsburg was upheld by Darmstadt, that proceeded with the investigations v. Riebel and 19 other policemen - who, until that moment, had been considered ordinary witnesses - and, again, v. Uhl, charged with three further indictments of murder.

This time the investigations lasted for about six years. Then, the final word was given by the Court of Darmstadt through the final verdicts on February 2, 1972, April 27, 1972, and October 2, 1972, that again based on *Befehlsnotstand* or *Putativenotstand*, finally acquitted all defendants and buried for the second time the about 10-11,000 victims – 9,000 of which were Jews – assassinated by Polizei-Bataillon 322 personnel during its service on the Eastern front.

5.5 EPITAPHS

Here are some significant statements made by police members of Polizei-Bataillon 322, given to investigators who were questioning them.

Testimony given by Gerhard Riebel to ZStL AR-Z 52/5:

> *I remember an inspection by General Daluege at the POW camp at Bialystok, where I was serving together with my front unit. I asked him a question about the tasks that my battalion had been assigned to, telling him that I believed them to be in contradiction with my feelings as a soldier. His reply was a rebuke that made it clear to me that he, Daluege, categorically expected all his officers and soldiers' unconditioned obedience to orders, to which we were bound by the oath of allegiance*[52].

Testimony given by Josef Uhl to ZStL AR-Z 52/59:

> *Even then I didn't approve of the extermination actions against the Jews because I didn't think it was right to shoot someone just because they are Jews, that is, a member of a specific race. But I must say that at that time we saw it as something normal to single out the Jews as responsible for our misfortunes, as well as the war. Therefore I did not feel guilty in any way, because being as such actions were arranged by the Government, as far as I was concerned the Government itself was taking full responsibility for them [...]. As a civil and State servant, I had been educated to unconditioned obedience towards the Government and the Constitution. Moreover, all of us had taken the oath of allegiance. As a consequence, I could recognize nothing else except obedience to orders and to the Government authority. That is why I have never tried to avoid my duty, nor to refuse the implementation of an order, even when this implied my presence at, or participation in, an execution*[53].

Testimony given by A.S. (1/322) to ZStL AR-Z 6/65:

> *He (Jörcke) sharply drew our attention to the fact that any order had to be executed entirely and without objection, and that anyone who preferred to disobey would be sent before an SS court and surely sentenced to death*[54].

Testimony given by E.Sch. (3/322) to ZStL AR 6/65:

> *There were several cases of comrades refusing to take part in the shootings. Sometimes I did too. And there were no consequences for me or the other objectors from our commanders; we were simply used for other tasks. No one was ever threatened with punishment or the firing squad*[55].

Testimony given by F.L. (2/322) to ZStL AR-Z 6/65:

> *As far as I know, not one member of my division ever volunteered for a shooting. However, I must say that there were some individuals within the division who were prey to some kind of blood thirst. I don't mean by that that they would have fun during the shootings, only that these subjects were used any time an action of this type would be organized*[56].

Although indicative of a widespread mentality, or at least of a strategic defense during the trial, the emphasis placed by several policemen on the alleged necessity to obey orders then is revealed for what it is: specious and fallacious. Indeed, the weakness of some statements to that effect (Riebel, Uhl...) - and by extension the weakness of the concept of *Befehlsnotstand* - was underlined by Adalbert Rückerl, ZStL director, in his book *NS-Verbrechen vor Gericht*, which documents how there has not been one single case of a policeman having to pay with jail or death by firing squad for his refusal to kill a Jew[57]. At most, the threat of punishment, court-martial and even death by firing squad (Jörke) was used as an *incentive* to induce obedience in the greatest possible number of policemen, lest many of them could have asked to be exempted from executions with deleterious effects on both the result of the action and the morale of the unit, especially in those who would choose to obey. In short, facts prove this was only a biased stereotype. This is confirmed not only by the statements of E.Sch., but also several cases of blatant disobedience to orders which had no dramatic consequences, except some angry verbal response: Maj. Heinrich Hannibal's refusal to concede Polizei-Bataillon 303 to Jeckeln, for the massacre at Vinnitsa on September 19, 1941, for example[58].

More than threats then, it would seem that it was conformism, together with a misguided sense of camaraderie towards their fellow soldiers that induced many reluctant policemen who, otherwise, would rather not be involved, to take part in executions. In other words, between units and in particular between police battalions, a *tribal spirit* emerged, that was one of the necessary conditions upon which the idea of the Jewish genocide found their sound and willing executioners.

5.6 CLOSED COMMUNITIES AND MICRODYNAMICS

German Ordnungspolizei came to be after the great reorganization that had begun in the mid-thirties and had brought state centralization of different local and regional police branches into a unique, national police body. An operative and ideological path that has already been described in valuable essays[60], this reorganization gave life to a seemingly monolithic entity, but it didn't alter the primeval essence of individual police departments, that continued to be recruited on a strictly regional base. Personnel of reserve battalions, in particular, continued to come from the same geographical area, or at most from neighboring urban centers in case a single city could not provide a sufficient number.

This method could have devastating effects on a single community if a military reverse caused the annihilation of an entire department, but on the other hand it consolidated bonds within the battalion, as men coming from the same environment tended to reconstruct the complex web of relationships, habits and even contrasts that they had in civilian life. It could happen that contingents of *strangers*, who were sometimes integrated at some battalions in order to complete the ranks, were viewed as outsiders by their peers[61]. Inevitably, as the conflict went on the various differences tended to be being forgotten, but a precise geographical identity, especially within the units, was maintained as far as it was possible, at least in the first period and as long as the progressive arrival of replacements as a result of losses did not eventually dilute the original tissue.

The result of this structure was the creation of real *closed communities*, enclaves of *gemütlichkeit* with habits and rules that were not written but still influential in terms of individual behavior towards the rest of the group. Beyond the obvious military discipline, which often was enforced by officers who did not necessarily belong to the same community, but were strangers, the ranks acted by creating *micro-dynamics*, which proved to be particularly effective, and were not easy to evade.

Thus, if bearing common hardships, sharing everyday ordinariness and being in the same situation are all factors that help foster solid bonds in any military unit, in the case of police units they were further strengthened by the common origins and by the prospect of being able to meet again, if lucky enough to survive the conflict, once back to civilian life. In the latter case, having failed to comply with group rules or to fulfill some duty or task - whatever it was - in front of their colleagues and fellow villagers, basically meant betraying the group in the immediate and, in perspective, taking the risk of being considered bad or unreliable members of the community.

In this sense, it seems appropriate to talk of a real *tribal bond* developed within a police unit, where the lack of an individual inevitably fell back on other members of the group, with consequent risk of social isolation for the *traitor*. It is quite evident that in a situation where the bonds of camaraderie were essential to withstand the rigors of such a lawless conflict, the feeling of being criticized by his comrades, pointed out as the weakest of the group, *frowned upon* and isolated, could be a hardship too much to bear. An example of such a dynamic can be found in the case of the massacre at Józefów, perpetrated by Polizei-Bataillon 101 on July 12, 1942.

In his work on Polizei-Bataillon 101, Browning explains that about 80 % of unit members took part in the total extermination of 1,500 Jews in Józefów and that only a dozen policemen (about 2 %) had asked openly to be exempted from executions before the massacre. He quotes conformism as one of the main reasons for this high level of participation, as retreat from executions would have meant *losing face* in front of their colleagues. While explaining this high adhesion with a different shade, Browning reports how the evidence given after the war by several police officers involved in the slaughter, invariably focused on the need *to make a team* with their peers and how, in contrast, it lacked any hint of ideology or anti-Semitism as a reason to justify their participation in the massacre. It is possible that this omission reflected a general attempt by the defendants to minimize their responsibilities against the prosecutor who was questioning them. Therefore, they regarded it as more convenient to be perceived as temperamentally weak, a group of cowards in a herd, rather than as racist and anti-Semitic individuals. However, it is also true that admitting to being anti-Semitic at a time when anti-Semitism was dogma amounted to nothing more than a confession of conformity, fully in line with the general context: something that, consequently, could also help to dilute one's ideological positions in a sea of similar situations. By principle, to recognize one's self guilty of a crime largely shared with others is easier than to admit publicly one's own weakness. Moreover, nothing would have prevented the defendants to describe themselves as redeemed citizens, in the hope to obtain a benefit out of it, during the proceedings. Therefore, beyond the expected general condemnation that this admission would generate, to declare themselves anti-Semites could be a viable short cut and perhaps, the reason why the defendants did not admit to that, was because the personal reasons exposed during the proceedings were truthful in this respect, and the ideological thrust beyond their involvement in the massacre of Josefòw was a minor one.

Beyond the specific example shown by Polizei-Bataillon 101, it is plausible that the same type of behavior may have been repeated on a more general scale, even by other police departments that participated in brutal murders, but for which no detailed analysis is available. It is possible that in front of the recurrence of similar environmental conditions, given the same parameters, the reactions of persons called into question may have been similar.

In the case of the police battalions, belonging to a closed community would be a particularly strong motivational thrust, paradoxically capable of arousing guilty feelings, not by those who perpetrated the slaughter, but by those who did not, as their refusal caused greater, unneeded distress to their peers. What we see here is a reversal of ethics, the onset of a distorted moral concept: agreeing to carry out a mass-shooting not because it was deemed right – it would have been so if ideological motivation was behind such action – but because it was deemed necessary. And even if an action might seem despicable it was certainly more tolerable if it could be shared by the entire community. Within the unit they could find the solidarity of comrades and the opportunity to remove the weight of horrible visions of death that populated genocidal missions, but also received the impulses to renew this deadly spiral.

Community then became a shield, a *gemütlich* environment to escape to after an execution – have a drink with fellow soldiers and possibly crack jokes of a vulgar humor, certain to be surrounded by peers who would share the same destiny. At the same time, the more events were experienced and shared the more the community became her own worst enemy. Day after day, shooting after shooting, that reality, so objectively distorted, faded into ordinary. The ethics, continuously subverted, ended up being accepted, the only difference being a moral boundary pushed a little further away.

5.7 CONTEXTS AND CAUSES

Compared to many other bloodsheds that had already been, or would be soon perpetrated in the Soviet Union, the Minsk massacre of September 1, 1941 was of a comparatively reduced magnitude: 914 victims, 93 % of which were males aged between 15 and 60 – that is, belonging to a category potentially able to represent a menace – in addition to a small group of women, arrested because they were *allegedly* found without the *Judensterne*, hence *guilty* of a misdemeanor according to the occupiers' rules[62]. This might suggest a kind of aimed and *selective* slaughter, somehow based on *expendable pretexts* and, therefore, scarcely contaminated by ideological and/or racial motivations. The truth is the situation was completely different. Let's examine it from two points of view:

- From a contextual point of view, what we have in Minsk, is the picture of an *upcoming genocide*, in many ways experimental and comparable to the *actions* carried out during the same weeks in Bialystok (July 12) and Brest Litovsk (July 13). These followed the inspections that the highest ranks of the SS, the police, and others, made in various area of the Eastern front. Actually in Minsk, as well as Daulege and von dem Bach, the ceremony for the shifting of powers from military to civilian authorities was also attended by Reichkommissar Lohse, Gen. von Schenckendorff, Generalkommissar Kube and BdO "Ostland" Jedicke[63]. And it's a fact that in the summer of 1941, the simultaneous presence of more leaders in a recently conquered place – even if characterized by different degrees of ideological approach as they were – saw the execution of brutal slaughters against the Jewish population as a consequence: that happened in Bialystok, in Brest Litovsk, in Mogilev, and in Minsk. In a way it was as if, through its physical presence on the field, the leadership wanted to verify the feasibility of the extermination choice and then fix points of no-return, basically *genocidal cornerstones*, then develop around them in different ways, timing and intensity – depending on local circumstances – the subsequent phases of the annihilation of Jews. Himmler himself, during his visit to Minsk in mid-August 1941 wanted to spend part of his time witnessing *de visu* a certain number of executions and assessing the feasibility of different killing methods a very short time before the executions took place, a thing that makes the causal link between the two seem obvious.

Being a capital city, Minsk was the largest of the Soviet cities under Nazis control at that time and included a large Jewish minority, which would not be easy to get rid of quickly (or maybe it was not appropriate to do so, at least in the first phase). This could be because it was immersed in a non-Jewish majority that was largely hostile or doubtful towards the new rulers, with only a minority favorable to them. It would have taken time to get to the complete genocide, and balanced decisions in order to avoid counterproductive effects. Nevertheless, from the Nazi point of view, a signal in that direction was needed, so that the heterogeneous players of the dynamics of genocide, the active ones and the passive ones, could perceive it. A signal that would mark the point reached and frame the next steps along the way to the Final Solution. Basically, the decision makers needed time to oil and synchronize the mechanisms of destruction and possibly fill, with the imminent arrival of Jews from the Reich, the void left by those who would be exterminated first[65]. At that point, once the general objectives were set by the central leadership, the local authorities would be in charge of putting them in practice, choosing the time and manner deemed most appropriate and on the base of their *limited* experiences until that moment.

In particular, in the remote regions of Eastern Europe it would be the most external elements of the genocidal world that would provide their contribution, namely the local collaborationist administrations and the auxiliaries, and the level immediately above them, represented by civil and military German structures of occupation. All those groups of perpetrators – such as police forces and some units of Waffen-SS and the Wehrmacht – who followed, were marching alongside, and in part were replacing the advance that depended on the Einsatzgruppen, that by now had reached the extreme limits of their mission[66]. In this sense, it was not the presence of new more or less ideological units that fueled the spiral of genocide, but rather the opposite: it was the expanding of the genocidal horizon in progress to require the influx of new units suitable for the purpose. In other words, just as any good management allocates resources as the direct result of a strategic plan, in *Project Genocide* too the choice of extending the effects of destruction was followed by new energies flowing in the system. New energies that would provide that vast destructive manpower that the Einsatzgruppen inherently lacked were indispensable to transfer the idea of genocide by the *selective* plan to a systemic one[67]. The Minsk massacre was a relatively small piece of this major project. It was useful, though, to complete that model of *culture of genocide* to which different units and heterogeneous structures would be called to give their active contribution of death to – at least until new methods of extermination, more rational in their criminal purpose, and less psychologically challenging for the executioners, were introduced[68].

- If we look at the causes that could have led to the Minsk action on September 1, 1941, the motivations of non-ideological type, suggested by objective problems, are very weak and biased. The alleged necessity to eliminate so-called *intellectuals* – speciously listed as a potential source of danger – loses its value in the case of the Minsk massacre simply because the entire Minsk Jewish intelligentsia had already been exterminated or placed in a position to do no harm, as confirmed by EM 32 of July 24, 1941[69]. Among them were many members of the Communist Party of Belarus or subjects in some ways related to the old regime, who were identified one by one in the Drosdy camp and the central prison in Minsk and shot immediately after. Some, apparently not considered dangerous, had been allowed to survive, locked up in the ghetto, others, who somehow had managed to escape the ideological screening, had to camouflage within the great mass of ordinary Jews, with almost zero resources and freedom of movement. Apparently, German authorities could not have precise knowledge of these scattered survivors, persuaded as they were to have carried out a *thorough investigation* of the suspects, according to the same words reported on EM 21 of July 13, 1941[70]. All this, of course, unless they wanted to replace God, paraphrasing the Book of Genesis and crushing fifty innocent people to find one culprit[71].
- The level of danger posed by those who, among the Jews of Minsk, could actually be called active ideological opponents was rather unrealistic, certainly more potential than concrete. On the eve of Barbarossa, there were just over 8,000 members of the Communist Party, as well as around 23,000 young members of Komsomol, out of a registered town population of 239,000 souls[72]. Only some of them were Jews, and they had already been decimated by the July massacres. The same intellectuals were essentially wiped out, except for doctors and engineers who were deemed necessary. The underground movement in the ghetto then – divided into a few small autonomous groups, completely unaware of each other until at least autumn 1941 – gathered around a few dozen workers and students without financial resources and operational doctrine, chaotically busy mainly organizing escapes to the forests around Minsk, and inclined to give priority to a strategy of survival before any initiative meant to actually cause damage to the Nazis[73]. Also, the creation of the ghetto in itself made it easier to control all those who, rightly or wrongly, could be considered as potential opponents. A boundary wall was never built around the Minsk ghetto, but a simple fence patrolled by security guards, which remained relatively permeable, having placed *all the eggs in one basket*, and having identified them by an unequivocal trademark, made it pretty easy to restrict the potential danger, and avoided the *discomfort* of having Jews wandering in the rear.

The massacre of September 1, 1941 then, was very unlikely perpetrated for security reasons, not even of a preventive nature. It hit the Minsk ghetto at a time when the Jewish underground cells present in it were still in their embryonic stage, uncoordinated and totally isolated from outside Belarusian groups[74]. Also, had it been adopted in a counter-insurrectional perspective, the German *action* would certainly have had the effect of decapitating the Jewish Resistance structure, something that did not happen: on the contrary, during the following weeks the clandestine network within the ghetto managed to develop and weave contacts with the outside. For this reason, the coup of September 1, 1941 was launched in the dark, not in order to suppress a perceived danger, but purely as ideological terrorism.

Paradoxically, the result obtained by the Nazis was the opposite of that intended. After the establishment of the ghetto, many young Jews who thought they'd manage to survive – albeit in a *bantustan*, faced with the mortal danger posed by looming German actions – ended up joining the clandestine groups in order to escape toward the partisan units operating in the forest. It was a slow, endless trickle, which damaged the Germans more than a non-ideological approach to the problem would have; a direct result of the colonial policy applied by the Nazis in Belarus, arrogant and counterproductive, brutal and catastrophically ineffective.

Perpetrated during the transitional phase from systemic to selective genocide regardless of its magnitude and individual motivations, the Minsk massacre was a single frame of a destructive project in progress, which would soon be revealed in all its' entirety.

According to Browning's words: "In the first six months of the war against the Soviet Union, the «material» was «tested» and «opportunities» were «used», as envisaged by Heydrich in his Prague speech of October 2, 1941"[75]. Minsk, from this point of view, was a chance taken; all it took to proceed with the murder of 914 Jewish civilians were a few policemen and several hours.

Of course, the complete genocide of a people took much longer and many more resources. But that day, September 1, 1941, in Minsk, a small step was taken. A path of destruction had been traced.

ENDNOTES

1 "A lot of questions were made, but the mountain of guilt did not become smaller. All that is left now is not just bad memories, but lumps of bad conscience". Aedtner, p. 86.

2 Kohl, pp. 78, 91, Gerlach, pp. 506-508.

3 In the Minsk area about ten prison, transit and extermination camps were already or were shortly to be activated (Maly Trostenez): Kollasstrasse, Logoisker-Strasse, Stalag 352 prison camps, Güterbanhof and the aviation camp should be added to the ones mentioned.

4 Epstein, p. 41.

5. Belarus' first whimpers of independence came to be in February 1917 during the days of the collapse of the tsarist monarchy and persisted until November 1918, when the defeat of Imperial Germany deprived the Belarusian National Committee of the only, ambiguous political and military support it could rely on. Remaining isolated, the Belarusian government (Rada), that in the meantime had taken office in Minsk, was overwhelmed and forced into exile by the Bolshevik counteroffensive, following which the Soviet Socialist Republic of Belarus was proclaimed.

6 Epstein, p. 79.

7 Epstein, pp. 60, 297. Report by Maj. Doven, Wehrmacht-Befehlshaber "Ostland", to Reichkommissariat "Ostland".

8 On the pogroms of Kaunas and Boryslaw, refer to Chap. 6, § 2 and 12, § 3.

9 Epstein, pp. 80-81. After the selection by kommandos of EGB, GPF and probably EG zbV (TK "Bonifer") the prisoners were transported to a cave in the camp's surroundings and then shot. Curilla, pp. 463-464, Gerlach, pp. 507-508.

10 Gerlach Olocausto, p. 292, Gerlach, p. 913.

11 On depopulation of the cities see for instance Mogilev's case when the Red Army returned. Only a few more than 10,000 inhabitants were left on June 1944, from the ca. 110/113,000 living in town on the eve of Barbarossa. Kohl, p. 142. See Chap. 6 for more details.

12 Tec, p. 1025.

13 Dean, p. 119.

14 Gerlach, pp. 523-524, Kohl, pp. 246-247.

15 Around early July, the entire Minsk male population aged between 15 and 45 was deported to Drosdy's prison camp, about five kilometers north of the city, in order to undergo an ideological screening, during which ca. 3,000 Jews – both civilians and prisoners of war – were singled out as intellectuals, professionals and "of allegedly communist faith", that is, members of the Soviet apparatus. Epstein, pp. 80-81. After the selection by kommandos of EGB, GPF and probably EG zbV (TK "Bonifer") the prisoners were transported to a cave in the camp's surroundings and then shot. Curilla, pp. 463-464, Gerlach, pp. 507-508. See EM 21 of July 13, 1941, reporting on the establishment of the camp and the *liquidation* of 1,050 Jews after a *careful screening*. After which, as reported by EM 32 of July 24 "the entire Minsk Jewish intelligentsia had been liquidated". This report (July 22) had been advanced by a communication by Nebe to Heeresgruppe "Mitte", according to which "Minsk Jewish intelligentsia is no more *(in Minsk gibt es keine jüdische Intelligenz mehr)*". Gerlach, p. 509. Drosdy's camp was *emptied* by July 19, after the deportation to the West

of POWs and the release (July 10.12) of a good share of Belarusian civilians and Jews who survived the selections. The other prisoners – several thousand civilians, including many non-Jews – were transferred to Masyukovshchina's camp (Stalag 352).

16 Gerlach, p. 549.

17 One of these exceptions was the massacre at Bialystok of July 27, 1941, perpetrated exclusively by an Ordnungspolizei battalion. See Chap. 1.

18 AVAK, p. 342. Longerich, p. 370. Gerlach, p. 228, identifies Koch as a commander of SK 7c (before VK "Moskau") of EGB. Indeed Koch's position as of July 1942 isn't clear: however, if he was in charge of coordinating the action in the Minsk ghetto, it is possible that he was a referent of section IV.B 4 of the same EGB, hence an SK 7b officer. Manfred Ziedler, *Der Minsker Kriegsverbrechen Prozess vom Januar 1946*, p. 228, refers to him as *an officer in an EGB Sonderkommando.* Born in 1914, Koch was captured by the Soviets at the end of the war and was processed in Minsk together with 17 other defendants between January 15 and 19, 1946. Sentenced to death, he was executed on January 30, 1946.

19 This massacre, which involved Polizei-Bataillone 316 and 322, was followed a few days later by the synagogue massacre, perpetrated on June 27 by Polizei-Bataillon 309.

20 Curilla, p. 556. LG Freiburg I AK 1/63 of July 12, 1963.

21 AVAK, p. 342, Breitman, p. 50, Curilla, p. 555, Klee/Dressen/Riess, p. 28, Klemp, p. 291.

22 AVAK, p. 342, Breitman, p. 50.

23 Curilla, p. 556, Langerbein, p. 141.

24 Breitman, p. 50.

25 Langerbein, p. 141. It seems that Uhl asked Nagel for permission to step away from the pits, but only obtained it a half-hour after the executions had begun. LG Freiburg I AK 1/63 of July 12, 1963.

26 Curilla, p. 556, Langerbein, p. 141.

27 Klee/Dressen/Riess, pp. 28-29. KTB 3/322, 1.9.41. Curilla, p. 557.

28 EM 92 of September, 23, 1941, Curilla, p. 557, Longerich, pp. 370, 683. It is not clear if this total of 2,278 victims includes the 914 of September 1. It seems plausible that, being as this action was carried out by Ordnungspolizei alone, the number reported on EM 92 could refer to the total of victims *produced* solely by EK 8 during its specific intervention.

29 In ZStL: 202 AR-Z 6/65 Bd. II, Bl. 391ff of September 19, 1965. AVAK, pp. 344, 379. As far as the shootings are concerned, see Longerich, p. 683, who quotes the statement of another policeman, Alois Fischer, released before the ZStL on October 27, 1965.

30 Klee/Dressen/Riess, pp. 28-29.

31 *Ibid.* KTB 3/322 of August 31, 1941, 15:00. *«Durchführung einer Judenaktion im Ghetto der Stadt Minsk. Die 9.Kompanie übernahm die äussere Absperrung, während die 7 Kompanie, NSKK Kompanie und der SD, die durchsuchung vornahmen. Es wurden alle Juden im Alter von 15 bis 60 Jahren festgenommen. Darüber hinaus alle Jüdinnen, die nicht den vorgeschriebenen gelben Fleck and ihren Bekleidung trugen. Ingesamt wurden festgenommen und ins Polizei Gefängnis überführt: 916 Juden beiderlei Geschlechts».*

32 *Ibid.* KTB 3/322 del September 1, 1941, 05:30. *«Durchführung der Execution der am Vortage festgenommen Juden etwa 10 km ostwärts Minsk, nördlich der Autobahn Minsk-Smolensk-Moskau. Es wurden 3 Executionskommandos gestellt. Das Kommando der 9 Kompanie erschoss ingesamt 330 Juden (davon 40 Jüdinnen)».*

33 Alfred Aedtner: *An Ort und Stelle erschossen*. Der Spiegel 44/1986, pp. 76-99.

34 See also Klemp, p. 292-294, that, essentially, follows the legal part of Aedtner, as well as AVAK, pp. 362-366.

35 Aedtner, p. 81, AVAK, pp. 352, 382.

36 Langerbein, pp. 140-141.

37 AVAK, pp. 352, 382, Langerbein, pp. 129-130, Liechtenstein, pp. 60-61.

38 Langerbein, p. 141.

39 AVAK, pp. 352-353, 382. Report of 35. SS-Standarte to SS-Abschnitt XI-XVIII dated March 24, 1933.

40 Langerbein, p. 143.

41 AVAK, pp. 352-353, 382.

42 *Ibid.*, pp. 352, 382.

43 *Ibid.*, pp. 352-353, 382, Aedtner, p. 76, Liechtenstein, p. 61, Langerbein, p. 132.

44 Langerbein, pp. 141-142. On the slaughter of Mogilev and the role played by Ukrainian auxiliaries, see § 6.5.

45 *Ibid.*, pp. 141-142.

46 Liechtenstein, p. 61.

47 Langerbein, p. 143.

48 The arrest of Nagel was followed by that of Aedtner and two other colleagues. The next day, upon the decision of the Prosecutor of Stuttgart, the subject was released on payment of a deposit of 2,000 DM.

49 *Ibid.*, pp. 80-81. Following his release after four years in a Soviet prison Hülsemann returned to Germany where, again, he served the police, at the Ministry of the Interior of Nordrhein-Westfalen. Lichtenstein, p. 61.

50 AVAK, pp. 354-355. The cunning inconsistency of Nagel's arguments is demonstrated by the behavior of Maj. Heinrich Hannibal, commander of Polizei-Bataillon 303, who, in a

similar situation in Vinnitsa, had rejected the use of his men in firing squads, having a violent altercation with Jeckeln, without suffering retaliation.

51 Aedtner, p. 84.

52 AVAK, p. 353: *«Ich erinnere mich eines Besuches von General der Polizei aluege bei mir im Gefangenlager in Bialystok, bei dem ich um eine Verwendung bei einem Fronttruppenteil nachsuchte und mit der Begrünung, dass ich mit dem Einsatz und Aufgabengebiet, wie er meinem Bataillon zugewiesen sei, mit meinem soldatischen Empfinden im Widerspruch stände. Als Entgegnung musste ich eine Rüge in Empfang nehmen, dergestalt, dass mir Daluege kategorisch erklärte, dass er von seinen Offizieren und Polizeisoldaten erwartet, dass sie die ihnen übertragenen Befehle bedingungslos ausführten, an die sie sich durch ihren Eid gebunden fühlten».*

53 *Ibid.*, p. 354: *«Schon damals habe ich die gegen die Juden durchgeführte Ausrottungsmaßnahme als nicht richtig angesehen, weil ich mir sagte, man kann doch niemand erschießen, nur deshalb, weil er Jude ist, also einer bestimmten Rasse angehört. Ich darf jedoch daraufhinweisen, daß damals propagiert wurde, die Juden seien an unserem Unglück schuld und die Juden seien verantwortlich für den Krieg. Ich habe mich jedoch nicht irgendwie belastet gefühlt, weil die Maßnahmen schließlich von der Staatsführung angeordnet waren und ich davon ausging, daß diese Staatsführung eben auch die Verantwortung für die Maßnahmen zu tragen habe [...]. Als Beamter und Staatsdiener war ich zu unbedingten Gehorsam und z. Treue gegenüber Regierung und Verfassung erzogen. Schliesslich hatten wir alle einen Diensteid geleistet, dar uns verpflichtete. Ich kannte demgemäss nicht anderes, als den Anordnungen und Befehlen der jeweiligen Regierung zu gehorchen. Deshalb habe ich auch nicht versucht, mich um die Ausführung von Befehlen, insbesondere um die Mirwirkung beziehungsweise Anwesenheit bei Erschiessungen zu druecken, zu umgehen oder schliesslich regelrecht zu verweigern».*

54 *Ibid.*, p. 356: *«Er (Jörcke) machte uns eindringlichst darauf aufmerksam, dass die Befehle hundertprozentig und bedingungslos zu erfuellen seien, weil jede Befehls-verweigerung unnachsichtlich nach sich ziehe, dass der Mann vor das SS- und Polizeigericht gestellt werde, wo er zweifellos mit der Todesstrafe zu rechnen habe».*

55 *Ibid.*, pp. 358, 384: *«Es haben sich manchmal Kameraden geweigert, an Erschiessungen teilzunehmen. Darunter war auch ich einige Male. So wie man mir nichts tat, von der Fuehrung aus, so ging es auch anderen Befehlsverweigerern, wir wurden eben anders eingeteilt. Es wurde also nicht mit irgendwelchen Strafmassnahmen gedroht, schon gar nicht mir Erschiessungen».* E. Sch. Was platoon leader of 3/322.

56 *Ibid.*, p. 360: *«Soweit mir bekannt ist, habe sich vorerst zu den Erschiessungen keine Kompanienangehörigen freiwillig gemeldet. Hingegen muss ich sagen, dass es einzelne Kompanienangehörigen gegeben hat, die von einer Art Blutrausch erfasst waren. Ich führe das aber nicht darauf zurück, dass sie sich an den Erschiessungen ergötzten, sondern vielmehr darauf, dass es bei solchen Aktionen immer etwas zu organisieren gab, was von diesen Leuten dann ausgenützt wurde».*

57 Aedtner, p. 85, Westermann, p. 236, Kwiet, p. 87.

58 Klemp Ermittelt, pp. 54-57, Westberg, p. 81, Curilla, p. 935. Maj. Hannibal reached the zenith of his military career with the rank of SS-Brigadeführer und Generalmajor der Polizei, commanding a Kampfgruppe in Western Prussia in January 1945. He died in Hamburg, aged 82.

59 See for example § 1.6, *Paradigms and Archetypes, §8.6, Objective Genocide* and § 13.8, *The Midas Touch.*

60 In particular Edward **B. Westermann:** *Hitler's Police Battalions. Einforcing Racial War in the East*, Lawrence, 2005.

61 See for example the case of policemen Wilhelmshaven and Rendsburg attached to Hamburg's Polizei-Bataillon 101, not to mention the Luxembourgers assigned to the same battalion. Browning, p. 44.

62 It should be mentioned that their "misdemeanor" took place inside their living spaces, and not in a public place, which proves how specious the motives of those who carried out the arrests were.

63 Gerlach, p. 568.

64 Browning Origini, pp. 294-295, 323-324, 364-365.

65 Jews from the Reich started to arrive in Minsk between November 8 and 28, 1941. In order to make space for them, about 11,000 local Jews were shot between November 7 and 20. Browning Orgini, pp. 316, 402-403.

66 On the multi-level structure of Nazi totalitarian system, see § 8.6.1, *Sfera.*

67 For a deeper insight into various aspects of genocidal dynamics, see § 8.6, *Objective Genocide.* Also Browning Origini, p. 241.

68 See for instance, Gen. Maj. Refzlaff, IdO "Wien", on the eve of departure from Vienna of Polizei-Bataillon 322 (June 6, 1941): "every man of the battalion should understand that he must treat Slavic people as a member of the master race, and prove to be a real German *(daß sich jeder vom Bataillon bewußt sein soll, den slawischen Völkern gegenüber als Herrenmensch aufzutreten und zu zeigen, daß er Deutscher sei)"* Aedtner, p. 89. Browning Origini, p. 244 Also Westermann, p. 2, Curilla, p. 546, Kwiet, pp. 78-79, Breitman, p. 45.

69 See Chapter 4, note 15.

70 Einsatzgruppe received the order to search the camp, together with Geheime Feldpolizei. Only those who managed to prove their innocence in all charges, and that they were not involved, politically and criminally, were let go. All the others were kept in the camp and carefully screened, after which 1,050 Jews were liquidated. Others are executed on a daily basis". EM 21, July 13, 1941, EGB, Minsk.

71 Book of genesis 18, 22-32.

72 Epstein, p. 110. 73 According to the author, the great majority of Komsomol did not take part in active resistance, and tried to go unnoticed by the Germans.

73 *Ibid.,* pp. 73 ff. Apart from the ghetto escapes, clandestine groups were able to develop some propaganda activities, mostly based on leafleting, listening to Soviet radio and getting in contact with Belarusian partisan groups active outside the ghetto. At the height of its expansion, perhaps, the clandestine network within the Jewish ghetto in Minsk reached 450 permanent members, divided into groups of ten.

74 Coordination between clandestine groups inside the ghetto was established during October 1941, while the first contacts between the ghetto and the city were started by some young Jews only between late October and early November 1941. Epstein, pp. 114, 118.

75 Browning Origini, pp. 312, 318.

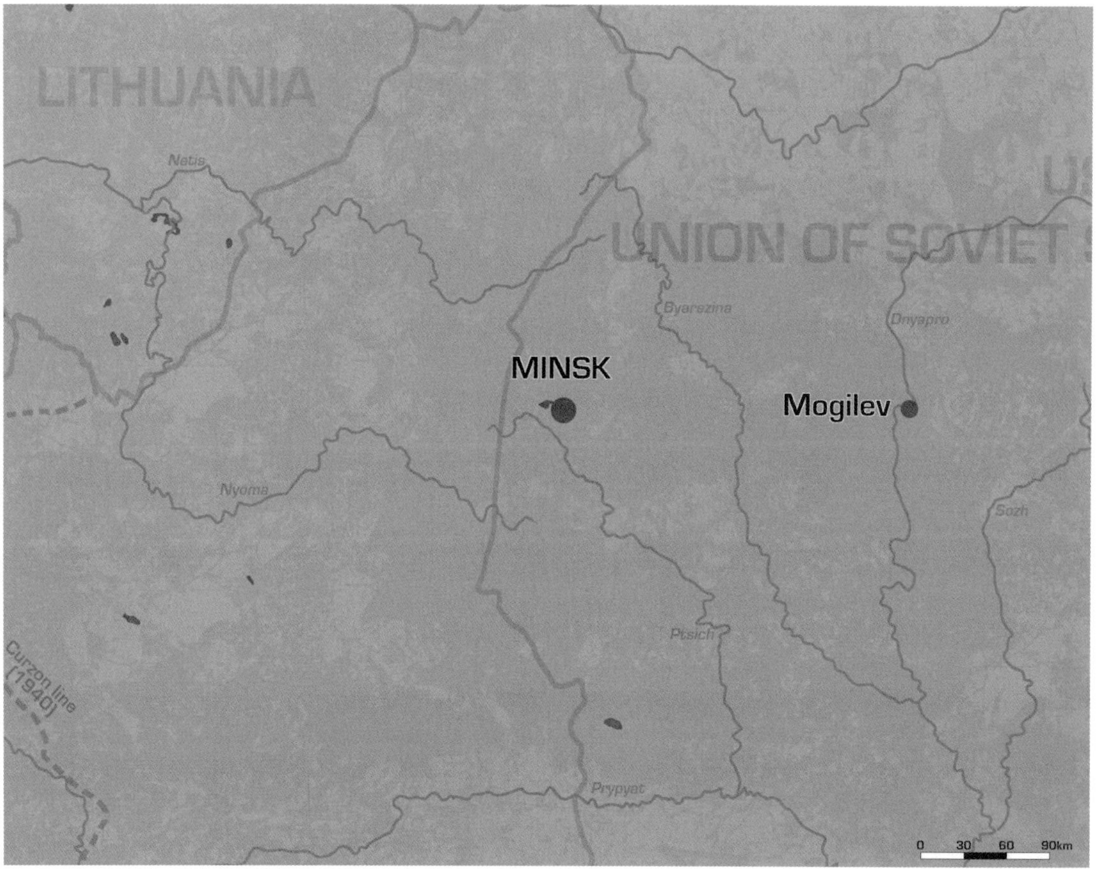
LITHUANIA
UNION OF SOVIET S
US
Nalis
Byarezina
Dnyapro
MINSK
Mogilev
Nyoma
Sozh
Ptsich
Curzon line (1940)
Prypyat
0 30 60 90km

CHAPTER SIX

"DOUBLE ENTRY"

ORDNUNGSPOLIZEI AND THE DESTRUCTION OF THE JEWISH COMMUNITY OF MOGILEV OCTOBER 1941

Der Tod, den wir ihnen gaben,
war ein schöner, kurzer Tod

Polizeisekretärs Walter Mattner,
October 5, 1941[1]

6.1 INTRODUCTION

According to German journalist Paul Kohl, author of a report-book written at the end of a trip to the Soviet Union in 1985[2], almost one-third of the population of Mogilev – a town located along the Dnieper River in Eastern Belarus – did not survive the first three years of German occupation. This is a dramatically high percentage which can produce devastating effects on any social ecosystem, as well as being consistent with the available demographic surveys that report an average depopulation rate of 60 % per year[3]. A percentage of the 10,000, mostly young civilians who were deported to forced labor in Germany, and an unknown number of refugees that followed the Red Army retreat in July 1941, or who were subsequently forced to abandon the city to seek refuge in the countryside – where apparently there were greater chances of survival – must be added to the total of deaths, which he estimates at around 40,000, mostly caused by shootings. In general, therefore, of the approximately 110/113.000 inhabitants present in Mogilev on the eve of Barbarossa, 10,000 or so would still be counted by the time the Soviets returned, on June 28, 1944[4]: among them, essentially, there were no more Jews.

Indeed, by the time the German troops entered the city, the Jewish community of Mogilev – which counted about 19,700 members in 1939 – had already been reduced to about 7,000[5] as a consequence of the evacuation of the Soviet army, which the vast majority of them followed. Of these 7,000 Jews, 6,000 were massacred in the course of two slaughters perpetrated on October 2 and 19, 1941. Then, there were more victims in the weeks and months that followed, up to an almost total obliteration, estimated on at least 90 %[6] and confirmed by the announcement of a virtually *Judenfrei* Mogilev, triumphantly reported by EM 133 on November 14, 1941.

These numbers show percentage-wise, the part of the Jewish community that remained in Mogilev and was subject to Nazi rule, suffered almost triple the amount of losses compared to those inflicted on the rest of the local population. This fact is rather important because it demonstrates once again the implicit existence of a precise will of *sheer* annihilation, on the basis of brutally ideological/racial grounds, which had priority over the various situational dynamics that in some cases could have motivated an excuse for a massacre. If anything, in Mogilev these dynamics sided with, but certainly didn't replace, the strategic direction plotted at the highest level of the decisional hierarchies.

The path laid at the base of this *success* was very smooth and quick.

6.2 UNDER THE LENS

In late July 1941, just after the entrance of the Wehrmacht into Mogilev (July 26), war correspondent Rudolf Kessler, a member of Propagandakompanie 689, attached to 15th Infantry Division, filmed a total of 104 frames currently stored at Bundesarchiv Berlin. These frames, of excellent quality, depicted members of the Jewish community in three different contexts. These were: the getting in line, the march and the activities of a work brigade equipped with shovels and brooms, engaged in collecting war remnants and other military equipment abandoned by the Soviets; the census of the population by the Ortskommandantur and finally; the transfer of some families with their household goods from one part of the city to another[7].

In this set of frames, several of which are deliberately designed as close-ups. This was done in order to make those depicted almost caricature-like, responsive to the stereotypical image of the Jew used in propaganda films of the regime. There are some interesting details, including the presence of non-German auxiliaries in charge of supervising the work brigade and the staff of the Wehrmacht coordinating their work, as well as the task of large *Magen Davids* being sewn onto the clothes of Jewish forced laborers.

Kessler's frames represent a relic of considerable interest, not only for their content, but because they document, with plenty of close-ups and medium close-ups, the last moments of a historical community destined to disappear within a few weeks, still unaware in those early days after the occupation, of the fate they would endure.

Indeed, in those images, the expressions on the faces of most Jews forced to work could be defined as fearful uncertainty or anxious wait for the future, while others seem to hint at a confused astonishment or suffering resignation. There is hardly a trace, except perhaps in one case, of what could be read as a feeling of anger because of the obvious humiliations to which those portrayed – mostly adult and older men – were submitted. The mockery of the *masters* towards their victims seems to be one of the main themes, especially in the segment focused on forced labor, itself consisting of two different sequences.

In the first sequence, the long column of Jews, shaggy and dirty, their clothes ragged and tattered, made to carry their brooms like rifles on their shoulders, approximately lined-up in improvised rows, proves to be a true parody of an orderly and martial military unit aimed at suggesting to the target audience of the film a merciless confrontation with the young and disciplined German soldiers in their clean and flawless uniforms, who actually appear in some of the images.

Through an operation of sophisticated and subtle propaganda, and without a hint of any episode of overt brutality, the photographer then succeeds in conveying his subliminal message, based on the ruthless comparison – one-way of course – between a mass of subjects implicitly portrayed as *stupid* underdogs, to be observed with curiosity and disgust (Untermenschen), and an *élite* of rulers (Herrenvolk), the likes of which, obviously, the spectator of those images was meant to feel a part of. Also, these images were structured in a way that reminded of "*der Ewige Jude*", the virulent feature movie/documentary that had been shown only a few months before in all cinemas of the Reich, whose stylistic narrative, made of similar contrasts and comparisons, was the highest possible expression of such denigration of the Jews.

But the theme of humiliation in Kessler's work reaches its peak in the second sequence, where he shows a large group of Jews sewing large Stars of David on their garments. Apart from the clearly derisive caricature made by representing a group of men engaged in a traditionally female task such as sewing, with the intent of weakening the role of the Jew male in the collective imagination of the Aryan spectator, what is particularly striking in these specific images, is the choice of the protagonists. Selected among those with the most pronounced somatic features, or those with specific physical singularities – such as one clear case of dolichocephaly – and always associated with shots from top to bottom, with the obvious effect of crushing and deforming the perspective, the result is a sequence of purposely grotesque images, meant to cause reactions of astonishment and physical repulsion in the target viewers.

All this was consistent with the policy of dehumanization and marginalization of the Jew, implemented by the regime since the end of 1939 in Poland, and introductory – in a perspective of *social remediation* – to their ultimate eradication[9]. The Jews' ultimate eradication would then assume a real character of salvation for the whole Arian humanity that would become *finally purified*, to quote Goebbels, of its *waste products*. Accordingly, in the specific case of Mogilev, it would take only a few weeks before the passage from the filmic representation of the *clinical problem* constituted by the local Jews, to the drastic resolution of the same through *mass euthanasia*[10].

6.3 CHARACTERS …

Although the process that led to the annihilation of the Jewish community of Mogilev was, in general, fairly rapid and obstacle-free, the tactics behind the dynamics that fueled the destructive sequence are still not completely defined. It is not clear whether the choice to take the initiative to proceed with the annihilation of the ghetto was made by Erich von dem Bach, in his role as HSSPF, or by the Nebe / Bradfisch tandem, as leaders of EGC / EK8 in direct contact with Berlin, nor can we forget the responsibilities of the local Wehrmacht authorities, in relation to their specific tasks.

What is clear, beyond all, is that a number of factors, different from each other but still sufficient to reach an explosive mass, combined and created the conditions to put into practice the abstract theories of annihilation that were being plotted in Berlin. A sort of devastating mixture formed by General der Infanterie z.V. Max von Schenckendorff as commander of the rear lines in the "Center" area (Berück "Mitte") [§ 6.3.1], Obergruppenfüher Erich von dem Bach as HSSPF "Mitte" [§ 6.3.2], and lastly Otto Bradfisch, commander of Einsatzkommando 8 [§ 6.3.3]. For different reasons, these three characters were to be found in Mogilev in October 1941.

In late summer 1941, while the campaign of annihilation of German Jews – and to that effect the *final phase* of the Jewish genocide – had not yet started, the total destruction of the so-called *Ostjuden* was already in full swing: first target in a progression of concentric circles starting on the Eastern outskirts of the *empire* – Ukraine and Belarus in particular – that would soon reach the Baltic and the General Government and then the metropolitan Reich.

Likewise, the annihilation of the Eastern Jews had progressed through subsequent phases, each coinciding with the crossing of a different and more brutalizing threshold of morality. The last of such phases had been the mass extermination in Kamenec Podolski, that included women and children, during what is considered the first *five-digit* massacre of the Final Solution, perpetrated on the orders of Jeckeln between August 27 and 29, 1941[11].

The same moral threshold was trespassed immediately after in Ostland, for example, with the massacres of Minsk (September 1) and Kaunas (October 28-29) and a series of other *actions* of varying magnitude, perpetrated here and there in Belarus, Lithuania and Latvia. Hence, the double massacre of Mogilev is part of a sequence that had already been tested and was advancing well. But with a difference. While so far the largest killings had occurred mostly in areas subjected to civilian administration, the Mogilev massacre was one of those cases where the destruction of *an entire community* was perpetrated in an area of military administration. Also, it did not occur in the days immediately following the occupation, perhaps using the excuse of retaliation (as Babi Yar, for instance, was argued to be), but *coldly*, many weeks after the entry of German troops into the city, in a steady, ordinary situation, under no real emergency or threat, and obviously with the approval of Wehrmacht's senior authorities, including Max von Schenckendorff, Befehlshaber des Rückwartigen Heeresgebietes "Mitte", settled in the city during August[12].

Thus, the Wehrmacht's responsibilities in the Mogilev massacre - as well as Charkov a few months later - are quite evident, and inspired by a number of *reasons,* real or fake[13]:

- an undeniable lack of food supplies with which to support the Belarusian people in the city, although this problem was easing somewhat as a consequence of the ongoing migration to the surrounding countryside;
- lack of adequate housing;
- the will to stop the smuggling of food by local farmers, through which the Jewish population was trying to provide for their subsistence;
- concern for the safety of the rear lines, at a time when the offensive against Moscow was about to be launched.

All these requirements, considered essential by the Wehrmacht, would be sufficient for von Schenckendorff to welcome von dem Bach's order to proceed with the annihilation of the Jewish community, through a first *action* scheduled on October 2, 1941.

6.3.2 – *Erich von dem Bach, HSSPF "Mitte"*

There are two interpretations in relation to the dynamics that led to the massacre. According to a first reading of the events, it was von dem Bach who issued the order for the destruction of the Jewish community of Mogilev[14] barely a week after the establishment of the ghetto, which occurred on September 25. Thus it is plausible that the idea of the massacre could have been pondered long before the publication of the order itself, and that the establishment of the ghetto in itself was only a temporary expedient. It is possible therefore, that von dem Bach was pushed to this decision because of factors related to his HSSPF role.

Firstly, the need to *live up to* the genocidal activism of his colleague Jeckeln in Ukraine - far ahead of him on the road to resolution regarding the Jewish question - may have led von dem Bach to want to show Himmler, who was expected to visit the city on October 23[15], a completely Jew-free Mogilev through the massacres of October 2 and 19. Secondly, von dem Bach might have been moved, on purely ideological grounds, by the desire to *completely* eliminate the Jews *at least* from the city that had become the seat of its main command[16]. Thirdly, the need to consolidate his position using the so-called Jewish question as a means to counter, in the same way, the powerful issue of the *partisan question* that von Schenckendorff was addressing. From this point of view, and in consideration of the role played in Western Belarus by the military duo Walter Braemer and Gustav von Bechtolsheim (Wehrmacht-Befehlshaber "Ostland" and commander of the 707th Infantry Division respectively), the consolidation of the position of von dem Bach with comparison to von Schenckendorff's in Eastern Belarus would mean a readjustment in the overall balance of powers, at that time too favorable to the Wehrmacht in the Central Russian operational field[17].

Therefore, faced with the necessity to acquire political clout, it is plausible that von dem Bach may have seen it fit to capitalize on the genocidal impulses that were being theorized in Berlin, putting them into practice through a campaign of annihilation of the Jews from entire areas of Eastern Belarus[18], supported by Sicherheitspolizei and, in particular, by Otto Bradfisch's Einsatzkommando 8, which would have the role of *prompter* in this dynamic.

6.3.3 – *Otto Bradfisch, Einsatzkommando 8*

The second interpretation of events directly involves Artur Nebe, EGB's leader. On September 9, 1941, after a ten-week advance, Einsatzkommando 8 had to stop their march eastwards into Mogilev, as they were waiting for the unlocking of the Smolensk front. In such a static situation, the unit – whose command line, by principle and in a context of operational fluidity, passed through Nebe's Stab / EGB to get directly to RSHA in Berlin – had to operate directly in contact with von dem Bach's HSSPF. Certainly then Nebe ended up coordinating operations with von dem Bach, not so much in a subordinate position, but as equals, because of the delicate role that he was required to perform.

Hence, it is possible that it was Nebe who ordered Bradfisch to destroy the Mogilev ghetto, in agreement with von dem Bach, who, responding to a request made by Bradfisch himself, would authorize the use of Polizei-Bataillon 322, stationed in the city. At that point, once he obtained the reinforcements requested, Bradfisch would take over the entire operation with his EK8[20], thus becoming one of the main characters behind the bloodsheds of October 2 and 19, 1941.

In any case, regardless of the transversal nature of the decisions that were the basis of the double massacre at Mogilev, the involvement of EK8 in *both* crimes is documented, although some sources do not confirm explicitly involvement in both actions, but only in the second one[21].

In addition, we should consider the overall context in which Bradfisch found himself operating. Although he had small detachments advancing further on to the east and southeast – in Smolensk, Vitebsk and Gomel around November 5 and then up to Roslavl and Bryansk in December – Bradfisch and his EK8 kept their main center of operations in the region between Orsha, Mogilev and Bobruisk, because of the ending of the German advance in Central Russia which followed the failure of the offensive against Moscow *(Unternehmen Taifun).*

Consequently, the presence of the unit in the same area for a relatively long period, was certainly functional to a "cleansing of the territory (*Säuberungsaktion*)" more accurate than the disordered, patchy sequence of murders perpetrated during the rapid advance of summer and autumn 1941: a cleanup that allowed, through EM 133 of November 14, to declare Mogilev "virtually free of Jews (*als fast judenfrei bezeichnet*)"[22].

However, regardless of how the decision-making process at the base of the destruction of the Mogilev ghetto evolved, its practical realization involved a number of perpetrators belonging to different units and organizations, which were mobilized for action in two stages. The following paragraphs examine the protagonists of the two massacres [§ 6.4], and how they performed their criminal actions [§§ 6.5 & 6.6].

6.4 ...AND INTERPRETERS

The Nazi concentration camp system in the Mogilev region in late summer 1941 reproduced the triangular pattern upon which such repressive and occupational apparatus was based: 1) a group of camps for prisoners of war run by the Wehrmacht and particularly its 286.Sicherungs-Division[23]; 2) a camp for civilian prisoners controlled by HSSPF "Mitte"[24]; 3) the Jewish ghetto established on September 25 and formally run by the city administration, but in reality under control of Einsatzkommando 8[25]. Obviously, being focused on the two slaughters of October 2 and 19, this chapter will only deal with the events related to the Jewish ghetto, even though the camp for civilian prisoners numbered several hundreds of Jews selected among the members of Mogilev's community or taken from the various villages of the area, who were killed with various kinds of excuses.

It is not clear, in fact, when the segregation of the Jews of Mogilev was decided upon. Probably, the first restrictive measures were taken up by the Wehrmacht in August, through a decree of Stadtkommandantur with which the concentration of all Jews in the Podnikolje neighborhood was ordered. This was an order which was never implemented because of the objective impossibility to execute it. After that, in September, the Jewish Council asked Bradfisch, through the local administration of Belarus, for an expansion of the area to be allocated to the future ghetto. The answer was positive, but the necessity of having to complete the relocation of the entire community by September 25 wasn't fulfilled. This dynamic would prove that it was Bradfisch, a few days after the entry of Einsatzkommando 8 into the city, who ordered the establishment of the ghetto, probably after an agreement with von dem Bach and with the authorities of the Wehrmacht. Then, once the annihilation of the ghetto was decided upon, von dem Bach himself, in his role as HSSPF, would authorize the mobilization of the units necessary to action, including Polizei-Bataillone 316 and 322, Polizei-Kommando "Waldenburg", 5/NSKK-Verkherskompanie "Berlin", a contingent of Ukrainian auxiliaries and Einsatzkommando 8 with extra platoons from 2/Polizei-Bataillon 9.

6.4.1 – Einsatzkommando 8

At the time of its activation, this Sicherheitspolizei unit, a part of Einsatzgruppe B, comprised 11 officers and 141 other ranks commanded by Bradfisch, mostly members of the Gestapo and Kripo, as well as some elements of SD. A detachment of policemen belonging to the second and third platoons of the second company of Polizei-Bataillon 9 in Berlin was also added. Tactically, EK 8 was divided into six autonomous Teiltruppen, distributed in different areas: therefore it is legitimate to think that only a part of this staff – in addition to the one directly under the command of the group (the Stab / EK 8) – was in Mogilev on the occasion of the two massacres, with the rest of the unit scattered among other places. In any case, regardless of the presence or absence in Mogilev of all its detachments, EK 8 remained heavily involved in both October 1941 slaughters (and others committed later), to the point that after the war, the facts of Mogilev were to be found in the binders of prosecutors of both West Germany and the DDR, helping to form the accusations against the group in subsequent indictments in the courts of Chemnitz (DDR), Frankfurt, Kiel and Munich[26].

6.4.2 – 2/Polizei-Bataillon 9

Unit of Ordnungspolizei, twin of division 4/9 involved in the Simferopol bloodshed (see § 9.3). At the start of Barbarossa, Hptm. Helmut Gantz's 2/9 had spread three platoons among the detachments of EGB: in particular, the Einsatzkommando 8 and 9 had received, respectively, first platoon (Ltn. Paul Dinter) and third platoon (Hwmst. Richard Neubert), with which they moved eastward, along separate routes, to Minsk. Then, in early August, the third platoon was detached from EK 9 and assigned to Bradfisch's EK 8. Both platoons arrived in Mogilev around mid-September and were involved in the destruction of the ghetto: the first platoon in the massacre of October 19, the third platoon in both massacres.

6.4.3 – Polizei-Bataillon 316

Stemming from a training unit (Polizei-Ausbildungs-Bataillon "Recklinghausen") this battalion was created in Bottrop and Gelsenkirchen in December 1940 and was assigned on the eve of *Barbarossa*, as second battalion, to Polizei-Regiment "Mitte". Commanded by Maj. Heinrich Hoecke (1/316, Hptm Walter Nord; 2/316, Hptm. Hermann Kraiker; 3/316, Htm. Otto Petersen), it was heavily involved in the Jewish genocide in the days that followed its entry into Soviet territory, with an estimated death toll of at least 10,000 victims[27]. According to Martin Hölzl, who can be described as the battalion's *biographer*, a blood-red line follows the entire story of Polizei-Bataillon 316, and this line is Jewish genocide. For this reason, in some of his most recent works, the battalion is considered as a real "personal reserve (*persönliche Einsatzreserve*)" for von dem Bach, who seems to have allocated EK8 as an "emergency unit"[28]: a situation confirmed by Hoecke himself, who once stated that "the battalion could be called into action at any time, at Bradfisch's request"[29]. In the postwar some members of the battalion – including Kraiker – were investigated for war crimes and then indicted before the Court of Bochum[30]. In Mogilev the battalion was involved in the slaughter of October 19, but not that of October 2. At the beginning of Barbarossa, a unit of Nuremberg's NSKK was added to the battalion. This unit, though, seems to have joined the surveillance of civilian prisoners at SSPStOF's "Mogilev" lager, and not the October slaughters.

6.4.4 – Polizei-Bataillon 322

Stemming from a training unit (Polizei-Ausbildungs-Bataillon "Wien-Kagran"), this battalion was formed in Vienna in April 1941. On the eve of *Barbarossa* it was assigned, as *third battalion*, to Polizei-Regiment "Mitte" commanded by Maj. Gottlieb Nagel (1/322, Hptm. Reinhold Jörke; 2/322, Hptm. Siegfried Binz; 3/322, Oltn. Gerhard Riebel). It was widely used in genocidal activities with an estimated death-toll of 8-10,000 victims[31]. It too was completely at HSSPF von dem Bach's disposal. Once in the Mogilev area, between September 7 and 8, it was temporarily assigned to Berück 102, Max von Schenckendorff, who made it available to Sicherungs-Regiment 2 of 221. Sicherungs-Division, for anti-partisan tasks. Actually, after carrying out numerous shootings of Jews, alleged insurgents and their helpers in the villages around Mogilev throughout September, the battalion was soon called back by von dem Bach and entrusted to take part in the October 2 slaughter, but not in the October 19 massacre. After the war numerous members of the unit were investigated and then indicted before the Courts of Freiburg and Darmstadt[32]. At the beginning of *Barbarossa*, a unit of Stuttgart's NSKK (Hstuf. Bauer) was added to the battalion. This unit, though, doesn't seem to have taken part in the massacre but was placed in charge of the surveillance of Judenlager (probably adjacent to SSPStOF's camp for civilian prisoners) where the around 1,000 Jews who survived the destruction of the ghetto were confined.

6.4.5 – Polizei-Kommando "Waldenburg"

A small unit of Ordnungspolizei, with the numbers of a reinforced platoon, it was established in Waldenburg, Silesia, in early October 1941. It was commanded by Revierleutnant Willi Schulz and counted 25 to 30 officers, both on active duty and reservists. Relocated to Mogilev around mid-October, it was meant to train a unit of local auxiliaries in the local garrison of Schutzpolizei (KdSchupo Mogilev – Hptm. Win.). Eventually, following the decision to keep Mogilev and the rest of Eastern Belarus under the Wehrmacht's military administration, instead of annexing it to GKWR, the *kommando* could not be assigned to the tasks it was created for. So, after being placed in the charge of Hptm. Win, it was made available to SSP-StOF "Mogilew" (Oberstleutnant Hubert Kölblinger), and given surveillance duties for sensitive targets, including the concentration camps for civilian prisoners run by Kölblinger himself, as of November 1942. Mobilized for the annihilation of the ghetto, it took part in the massacre of October 19, but not that of October 2. After the war, Schultz was investigated and then indicted before the Court of Detmold[34]. In addition to co-responsibility for the murder of at least 3,600 Jews during the massacre, in the weeks and months that followed the kommando took part in additional actions in other locations and in individual executions, for a total of nearly 3,800 victims[35].

6.4.6 – 5/NSKK-Verkherskompanie "Berlin"

A unit of *Nationalsozialistische-Kraftfahrkorps*, this division was established in Berlin on Himmler's decree of May 17, 1941[36]. It was attached to Polizei-Regiment "Mitte" at the beginning of *Barbarossa.* The unit depended directly on Polizei-Bataillon 307, which was the *first battalion* of the same regiment, for logistic support. Comprising only 65 men (compared to a planned workforce of 110 elements), the division took orders from NSKK-Oberstaffelführer Niedenzu and was divided into three platoons. Relocated at first to Minsk, around mid-October 1941 the division was moved to Mogilev where, during November 1941, it replaced 7/NSKK-Verkherskompanie "Nuremberg" in the surveillance of the lager for civilian prisoners. Of the three NSKK divisions assigned to the three battalions of Polizei-Regiment "Mitte", the Berlin division was the only one to be involved in the destruction of the Mogilev ghetto, having taken part in the massacre of October 19[37].

6.5 TAKE ONE: OCTOBER 2, 1941

The dynamics of the decision-making process that led to the destruction of the Jewish community of Mogilev are not yet fully clear. What seems to be clear, however, are the events that involved the executive levels, accurately reconstructed by the Court of Freiburg during the trial v. Uhl, Hülsemann, Riebel and other members of Polizei-Bataillon 322[38].

It seems that in the hours before the massacre of October 2, Oberstleutnant Max Montua, commander of Polizei-Regiment "Mitte", sent the operation order to Maj. Nagel, commander of the battalion, which was the larger unit in term of numbers stationed in Mogilev during those days, thus able to perform such assignments. Then, the Viennese policemen were joined by members of EK8, von dem Bach's Stab and also a unit of Ukrainian auxiliaries.

Then, while the Jewish ghetto was surrounded, as customary, by a cordon of policemen, a Sicherheitspolizei squad and about 20 Ukrainian auxiliaries proceeded to carry out the round-ups, dragging all the Jews they could find from outside, regardless of their age, sex or health conditions. All those unable to walk, those who somehow tried to react to the round-up, running or hiding wherever possible, were killed on the spot. According to a report by Hptm. Riebel, commander of 3/322, 65 Jews were executed, "moved by vile and cowardly fear, they tried to hide in any possible corner, [thus making] it very difficult to pull out of their holes those filthy elements *(Schmutz starrenden Elemente)*[39].

After five hours, once the round-up was complete, the victims were lined up and forced to march to an old truck factory just outside town, the Dimitrov-Automobilwerke, and then locked up to spend the night there, in one or more of its abandoned warehouses.

The morning after, adults and children were separated and then transported - mainly through trucks belonging to KfZSt of Polizei-Bataillon 322 (Hptm. Frömsdorf) - to near a long anti-tank ditch dug in an open field, where the execution squads formed by staff of the three divisions of the battalion, and Ukrainian auxiliaries, were already waiting. Other policemen formed the security cordon surrounding the site of the bloodshed, and others were in charge of forcing the Jews off the trucks and then escorting them to the edges of the trench.

The execution procedures, at least in the beginning, had been methodically planned, but could change according to the division. As for Jörke's 1/322, a squad of 10-15 men had been taken from each of the three platoons that made up the division, with the task to carry out a certain number of shootings, after which the staff of that squad was replaced by other members of the same platoon, so that each policeman shot the same number of Jews. Riebel's 3/322, however, was the only execution squad, formed of 24 men, who were never replaced, but had the advantage of shooting the same victim in pairs. Commanding the squad was Oberleutnant Rasche, 3/22 platoon leader, who counted the Jews to be pushed into the pit and then gave the order to fire. At times, when the victims didn't seem particularly quick to enter the ditch, he *encouraged* them with blows of a stick.

Initially, during the intervals between one execution and another, the bodies of the victims were covered with soil, but as the procedure went on faster, such operation became sporadic, to the point that the new victims were forced to lay face down, directly on the bodies of those who had been shot before them.

The following testimony comes from W.G., a 3/322 policeman, given to a ZStL investigator[40]:

One day we were ordered to get on a few trucks, carrying with us the ordinary individual equipment: rifle, helmet and gas mask. There were several of these trucks, each with 20-25 men on board: they were passenger trucks, with seats, probably seized by battalion K-Staffel. Oblt. Rasche, an officer of the battalion, led the Kommando [...]. We were not told a thing about the reason and the destination of the journey. Normally, before any operation, we were given explanations.

We passed through slightly undulating terrain - how long and how far we were I can no longer remember - up to a system of ditches that I would describe as a long and wide trench, about six-foot deep, where finally we stopped [...]. I saw several officers, some with feldgrau SS uniforms. I recognized the SS staff because of the Totenkopf on their caps [...]. In addition to Rasche there were also more police officers, who might have been higher-ranking than Rasche, but I cannot be sure of this now. In any case I didn't know them and they probably belonged to some other unit [...]. Some policemen forced men and women down from some trucks and then took them to the pit. Rasche steadied us, divided us into groups of five and each group was positioned at a point along the edge of the pit. While forming the firing squad Rasche told us, with his emphatic way of speaking: "These are partisans, partisans, partisans ...". He might also have said: "These are partisans and communists," or "communist partisans." Then, when the firing squads took their place, Rasche ordered: "Aim, Fire!"

The victims were forced to lie face down on the bottom of the pit [...]. After the first few were shot, their bodies were covered with soil, I cannot remember exactly whether by the police, by Germans of another unit, or by the Russians. Then the next victims were brought forward and Rasche ordered to fire again. I remember Rasche, pistol in hand, walking back and forth along the edge of the pit. I am not able to say, though, if he shot or if he didn't. Question: "Were you aiming before shooting? Do you think that those people were dying instantly?"

Answer: I think I aimed at the victims' heads. I can't say that for sure though. I can't even remember how many I had to shoot before I was replaced. While the victims were being covered with soil we were given the time to walk around and smoke a cigarette. During the shootings alcohol was never distributed in my sector [...]. If I'm not wrong I had to shoot for about an hour, or an hour and half, before I was replaced. But I couldn't tell how long the whole operation lasted [...]. I couldn't realize whether among the people shot or those yet to be shot there were Jews, or not. The people to be shot, men and women, were all adults. I didn't see children and elderly among them. If there had been, then probably I would have doubted that they really were partisans [...]."

The apex of brutality was reached in the stretch of the trench assigned to Ukrainian auxiliaries who, constantly replenished by liquor, were very soon completely inebriated and no longer able to coordinate with each other. At that point, the executions were perpetrated in utter confusion, as they were firing individually with atrocious fun, especially children, who were taken from the trucks and literally thrown into the pit from a distance of several meters. In some cases, a few Ukrainians, it seems, tried to hit the children with volleys of automatic weapons before they reached the bottom of the pit. All that was happening a short distance from the Polizei-Bataillon 322 execution squads – still obedient to their shooting discipline – but the German officers of the battalion witnessing this situation, among which Otln. Riebel, commander of 3/322, made no attempt to restore discipline in the drunken mob. Even the order that Riebel himself gave to the truck drivers to stop at a certain distance from the pits so that the victims could not see too clearly what was happening a little further on, is likely to be due to considerations relating to security rather than by a burst of humanitarianism, as was claimed by Riebel in self-defense before the Court of Freiburg[41].

The killing of children was also perpetrated by some members of Stab / HSSPF "Mitte", in the presence of von dem Bach himself. Von dem Bach, it seems, planned from the beginning the killing of women and children and it was probably in order to avoid such a burden to the police units that this task was entrusted to the Ukrainians [42]. The brutality of these auxiliaries was such that even some of the battalion policemen were disgusted by it, among which G.B., a 1/322 member[43], and his colleagues E.C.[44] and R.F.[45]:

G.B.'s testimony:

I remember clearly the Ukrainians, already drunk, who kept drinking and singing. They wore Russian brown uniforms [...]. The shootings weren't executed at a specific order, but indiscriminately, every Ukrainian for himself. I have witnessed, during this action, children being thrown in the air by the Ukrainians and hit by exploding bullets, like pigeon shooting (wie Tontauben abgeschossen wurden).

E.C.'s testimony:

Among the Ukrainians there was an SS or SD officer, with several scars on his face. He brandished a long leather whip with which, every now and then, he would punish people. I remember how he raged vehemently on a 13, maybe 15-year old girl, when she started crying out loud as soon as she got down from the truck. This officer whipped the girl so hard that she dropped dead, soaked in blood. The same officer had unlocked the truck that the children had gotten out of. As soon as the children, who were aged between 3 and 19, had got off the truck, they were grabbed by some Ukrainians who threw them in the tank ditch where other Ukrainians opened fire on them.

R.F.'s testimony:

At the shooting site there was a Ukrainian unit that was constantly given vodka. We saw that almost all those soldiers were drunk. The Jews were brought to the pit by trucks. Then we saw members of SD pushing people off the trucks. As far as I remember there were men, women and children and newborn babies too. I saw, from a distance of about 60 meters, uniformed Ukrainians catching the babies and/or the children by their legs, throwing them in the air and shooting at them like clay pigeons.

No other event during the operations in the Soviet Union was so impressed in the memories of the battalion's members, as the f Mogilev massacre[46], during which, according to the KTB OF Polizei-Bataillon 322 dated October 2, 1941, 2,208 Jews were shot dead. Of these, 378 were murdered by 1/322 and 555 by 3/322. In his testimony, one Kraftfahrzeugstaffel member said he could not eat or sleep for three days after the slaughter. The same would happen to many of his colleagues[47]. Riebel himself, while trying to emphasize the case for the defense before the Court of Freiburg, seems to really have been shocked by the bloodshed of Mogilev and said that from that moment on "he could no longer believe in goodness." Similarly, Hülsemann described the situation as "repugnant"[48].

In that respect, it seems plausible that the events at Mogilev might have represented the psychological breakpoint of the battalion. From that moment on, in fact, it wouldn't again be destined to mass executions of Jewish women and children, but only to *ordinary security operations*, during which, however, single or group shootings of alleged partisans, including several wouldn't be spared them.

In order to solve once and for all the so-called Jewish question then, the time had come to replace the divisions. The time had come to call in Polizei-Bataillon 316.

6.6 TAKE TWO: OCTOBER 19, 1941

> *On October 19, 1941, a large-scale operation against the Jews was carried out in Mogilev, with the support of Polizei-Regiment "Mitte": 3,726 Jews of both sexes and all ages were liquidated during this action. "These measures have been deemed necessary because since the beginning of the occupation of Mogilev by the German troops, the Jews have not only ignored the authority of the occupying forces, but in spite of all measures taken, they have also continued their anti-German activities (sabotage, partisan support, refusal to work, etc..), to a point and with such insistence that, in order to restore order to the rear, it was no longer possible to tolerate all this".*

These are the surreal motivations that, with EM 13 of November 14, 1941, the final bloodbath of Mogilev's Jewish community was justified. Surreal motivations that inspire two questions: indeed, one wonders: 1) how and by what means, the Jews of Mogilev, already annihilated by the massacre of October 2, would be able to carry on so stubbornly their alleged anti-German activities from within a closed and guarded ghetto, to the point of posing no less than a *threat* to the rear 2) how could their stubborn refusal to fulfill the obligations of work be conciliated with those images taken back in July / August 1941 of a resigned group of Jewish workers, by war reporter Rudolf Kessler and already described in section 7.2.

It is quite clear then, that the October 19 massacre was nothing but the *conclusion of the job* started on October 2 and divided into two stages, probably for organizational reasons.

The operational dynamics that brought along the almost complete annihilation of what remained of the Mogilev Jewish community were almost identical[49]: the same authorities that decided the action, the same, if not greater, violence used during the executions. And the same victims once again; men, women and children, shocked and beyond help.

What changed were some of the characters in charge of perpetrating the executions, now represented by Polizei-Bataillon 316 instead of Polizei-Bataillon 322, by members of Polizei-Kommando "Waldenburg" that had been brought there and by the fifth detachment of Berlin NSKK.

Again, the description of the events comes to us in the form of court acts, in this case from the Court of Bochum[50], which state that the sanitary cordon and the roadblocks, set up by Polizei-Bataillon 316 and Polizei-Kommando "Waldenburg"[51] around the perimeter of the ghetto, signaled the start of the action. Then, squads of Ukrainians stormed the houses and forced the Jews to gather in the streets under the surveillance of SD staff and the battalion policemen, mostly belonging to units 1/316 and 2/316. There was no exception and, as customary, many sick people who couldn't be transported and elderly who couldn't move were *liquidated* on the spot.

The victims were divided among adults and children and were brought inside a factory on the outskirts of Mogilev, where they spent their last night.

The carnage took place the following morning, in an open space in the forest a few kilometers away from Mogilev on the way to Belynichi, near some long Soviet tank ditches or shorter and rounded pits. The execution squads, already there, were formed by staff from Polizei-Bataillon 316 – particularly from 1/316 and probably also 2/316 divisions – from EK8 and from non-German auxiliaries, all organized to open fire on command with volleys of rifle or, in some cases, individually, with automatic weapons. At the location, it seems, there were also different members of Polizei-Kommando "Waldenburg", apparently only as spectators and with no active role in the shootings[52].

In this case too, as happened on October 2, the execution times, rather strict at first, were progressively slowed until a confusion of individual shootings. These were mostly against women and children, as they wouldn't keep still and quiet in front of their executioner. One such girl, it seems, completely traumatized, staggering on her feet over the bodies of her family members was shot and killed by a policeman to whom she had in vain asked for pity[53].

There would be cases where some victims who were being held captive in a building waiting for their turn, were forced to strip off all their clothes, or down to their underwear, and then escorted to the shooting spots.

The Ukrainians in particular, while walking their victims to the pits, would use great violence, especially against women and children: several mothers were silenced forever while holding their babies in their arms, while in other cases some children were wrenched off their mothers and literally thrown into the ditch, often aimed at by other Ukrainians, in the attempt to hit them while in air[54].

According to the Court of Monaco in the case against Bradfisch[55], several members of Polizei-Bataillon 316 had asked to be exempted from the shootings, while others - among those who had not taken part in any previous execution - had fainted in disgust. The large number of such requests would actually cause delays in the shooting times, with victims forced to also endure the excruciating wait for their turn. In contrast, according to numerous testimonies given during the investigations that were later used in the Court of Bochum, only volunteers among the policemen would take part in the shootings.

In any event, it seems that even Polizei-Bataillon 316 may have come very close to its psychological breaking point. As a matter of fact, there seems to have been cases of policemen in the pits, so out of control, prey to a sort of murderous frenzy, shooting the corpses that drenched them. Some Jews lying at the bottom of the pit were wounded but not dead, they would be hastily covered with soil and then submersed by other *layers* of victims. According to one witness, in Mogilev there was no organization and coordination of the killing procedures: anybody could shoot and kill at will, and above all "children were thrown into the pits as trash" *(Kinder wurden wie Müll in die Gruben geworfen)*[56].

The Jews of Mogilev who survived the massacres of October 1941 numbered about a thousand[57]. Craftsmen, who were deemed essential, and some of their families, had been segregated in a work camp – at times indicated as Judelager – built in the area of the Dimitrov-Werks factory, probably adjacent to the civilian prisoners' camp activated on September 29, 1941 and run by SSPStOF "Mogilew"[58]. The establishment of the camp, however, didn't stop the progressive annihilation of the survivors, 279 of which were shot on October 23, the day of Himmler's visit to Mogilev. Over the following weeks there were many other victims: these killings elevated to at least 7,500 the total of Jewish victims in Mogilev and its immediate surroundings.

For them all, after the war, there was essentially no legal compensation.

In fact, a documentation file on the crimes committed by Polizei-Bataillon 316 on the Eastern Front was launched by ZStL as early as the end of the Fifties, with the opening of file 202 AR-Z 168/59. Then, with grounds to proceed considered sufficient, Ludwigsburg sent the file to the Central Office for the prosecution of Nazi crimes to NRW Ministry of Justice, at the Court of Dortmund, where it was filed as StAwDo 45 Js 2/61. At that point the Court of Bochum could finally open the preliminary investigations against Hermann Kraiker and nine other members of Polizei-Bataillon 316, integrating a previous investigation launched by LKA NRW (*Sonderkommission "Agata"* – 16 Js 13/59 of September 15, 1960)[59].

After about four years, on February 25, 1966, the Prosecutor of Bochum requested to open the case. But, after two more years of hearings, indictments and guilt pleas, in April 1968 the same prosecutor requested the acquittal of Hermann Kraiker and nine other defendants, on the basis of the *Befehlsnotstand* legal artifice, which sanctioned the non-punishment for those crimes committed in alleged *impossibility to disobey orders*: a request which was upheld by the court in June 1968, with freedom restored to all 60 defendants[60].

It is interesting to note how, after 1945, up to 116 former members of the battalion remained in the police service at the various local governments of West Germany. The procedural vicissitudes that involved some members of Polizei-Bataillon 322, also acquitted, by the Courts of Freiburg and Darmstadt, on the grounds of Befehlsnotstand, were essentially identical[61].

As for Polizei-Kommando "Waldenburg", only one of its' members, namely its commander, LTN. Willi Schulz, was found guilty by the Court of Detmold - LG Detmold, 2 Ks 2/66 and sentenced to six years and six months imprisonment on October 11, 1967[62]. Only, the crimes that Schulz was found guilty of had nothing to do with the Mogilev massacre. These were in relation to a certain number of shootings perpetrated at other sites (mainly Grodjanka), but also in Mogilev itself, in June 1942, inside the work camp for civilian prisoners. Hence, in this case too, no one was guilty of the Mogilev massacre.

Therefore, in spite of years of preliminary investigations, hundreds of witnesses called and questioned and countless hearings sustained, Western Germany's justice system proved to be completely ineffectual with regards to the involvement of Ordnungspolizei divisions in the facts of Mogilev. The 10-year imprisonment sentence imposed by the Court of Munich on Otto Bradfisch on July 21, 1961 (LG München I, 22 Ks 1/61)[63], seems to be nothing but a palliative measure with substantially zero value in terms of legal compensation because that conviction included the whole sequence of crimes perpetrated by Einsatzkommando 8 in Central Russia, between June and December 1941, with the double Mogilev massacre considered as only *one of them*. Therefore *diluting* the whole lot of the crimes into one big *melting pot* produced the paradoxical effect of historical disempowerment of the single events with respect to the global context.

6.8 CONSIDERATIONS

The description of Mogilev's events comes from the acts of two different Courts: the Court of Freiburg regarding Polizei-Bataillon 322 (October 2) and the Court of Bochum regarding Polizei-Bataillon 316 (October 19), both deriving from two separate investigations undertaken by ZStL in 1959. Hence, with being the crime scene common to the two killings, it is likely that investigators and prosecutors of both cases helped each other, especially in relation to the common elements, such as environmental and operational context, dynamics, decision-making and more. In any case, we're talking about different perpetrators at different times - although close – so it seems likely that the investigators had to follow distinct paths, in particular with concerns to the testimonies of participants in the two bloodbaths, as neither of them took part in both actions.

In spite of that, the picture painted by the two Courts is incredibly similar, with details and particulars – especially on the methods used during the executions and the brutality of the Ukrainian auxiliaries – that could be quite simply applied to either of the two massacres. The similarities are so striking that they might as well be read as a *continuum*.

However, the structure of the two independent investigations is not weakened by that. As a matter of fact, under no circumstance, or only extremely unlikely, could such testimonies could have had an influence on each other because they were given by former Ruhr policemen in one case, and former Austrian policemen on the other, therefore a cross-check of the veracity of the testimonies, with all their similarities, strengthens the individual significance of each investigation.

All this allows us to reconstruct how events unfolded, but also to prove how irrevocable and firm the will to solve the *Judenfrage* was; through the indiscriminate extermination of every sector of the Jewish population, regardless of age, sex and health condition, and - consequently - without there being any connection to any *sign of danger*, real or alleged, from the victims against the occupiers.

In addition, the extermination of women and children of a tender age demonstrates the existence of an unparalleled project of annihilation, strengthened by the incredibly brutal methods adopted to *sever the problem at the root.* Had it occurred only during the first massacre, the use of Ukrainian auxiliaries excited by alcohol, with their uncontrollable inclination towards violence, could have been - perhaps - only a misjudgment by their German controllers: an accident that may be suppressed with appropriate disciplinary action and by no means to be repeated. But the Ukrainians also took part, possibly with even greater brutality, in the second bloodshed; that makes explicit the willingness by top decisional spheres to use every means available to achieve their goal quickly. The nature of such a goal then could not, in any way, be improvised, but it must necessarily have originated from a project which evolved as time passed. Step by step, it took real shape and was put into practice, resorting to criminal fantasy and impromptu makeshift means – such as the Ukrainian auxiliaries.

Clearly such a situation, rich in genocidal intentions but poor in means suitable for the purpose, could not last long: there was a risk of damaging the efficiency of those units - such as Polizei-Bataillon 322 – which up to that point had adjusted to the criminal need, but were now reaching their breaking point. This was a problem that was highlighted by Montua, commander of Polizei-Regiment "Mitte" to RFSS Heinrich Himmler during his last visit, on October 23, in a finally *Judenfrei* Mogilev. A problem that the Reichsführer responded to by announcing the imminent readiness of *alternatives* to shooting *(andere massnahme)*[64]. A problem that would soon be solved through gas chambers and extermination camps[65].

After Mogilev, mass-shootings in common graves wouldn't stop; they went on for another few months until spring 1942. After Mogilev, though, the time had come to begin a new phase[66], which would go beyond all that criminal improvisation and would bypass that sort of genocidal anarchy that was now showing all its limitations.

What had been accomplished so far in Soviet Union in terms of *Judenfrage* was a lot; a lot, but not enough. The time was right for new decisions.

6.9 EPILOGUE

There are faces difficult to avoid, and there are words impossible to misunderstand.

The faces, so tragic and painful, so confused and bewildered, so uncertain and alarmed, are the faces of the Jews, depicted by war correspondent Rudolf Kessler. Real faces, grotesque at times, their features pronounced, full of an expressivity that maybe the photographer himself didn't want to portray, ambitious as he was in the attempt to capture the negative prototype, the stereotype incarnate to associate to the evil idealization of the *Süss Jew*, or the grotesque depictions of the *Wandering Jew*. These faces may be unpleasant but they are real, in opposition to the positive and plastic beauty of Leni Riefenstahl's Aryan models, so aesthetically splendid and so extraordinarily inexpressive.

The words, on the contrary, so brutal and bewildering, so corny as to sound plain stupid, are the words of a German policeman, Polizeisekretärs Walter Mattner, in the letters that he wrote to his wife soon before and soon after the October 2 bloodshed, that he took part in together with the rest of Polizei-Bataillon 322[67]:

October 2. I was assigned a special operation (zu einer Sonderaktion gemeldet). Tomorrow, I will have the chance to use my gun. I will have 28 bullets, but probably that won't be enough [...]. That's because there are 1,200 Jews too many in town (in eine Stadt zuviel sind), that must be crushed (und umgelegt werden müssen). By the time I'm back home, I shall have some nice stories to tell you. But that's enough talk about them, I wouldn't want you to think I have become too bloodthirsty.

October 5. I was there too, the other day, when the great bloodshed happened. When the first truck arrived my hands were shaking a bit, while shooting; then I got used to it. After the tenth truck I was aiming calmly and shooting precisely at the many women, children and newly-born babies too. I kept in mind that I have two children at home too, that these hordes (diesen Horden) would treat them exactly the same way, maybe ten times worse [...]. The children were thrown in large arcs in the air (Säuglige flogen in grossen Bogen durch die Luft) and we shot at them in mid air, before they fell into the water of the pit. Let's get rid of this scum (Nur weg mit dieser Brut) that triggered war all over Europe. I'm already eagerly awaiting (Ich freue eigentlich mich schon) our return home, because many say that after that, the turn of our Jews is next (Juden dann kommen unsere heimischen dran). Well, I've already said enough.

Perhaps, in his own way, Walter Mattner too was a victim. His words, so horribly sincere, give a measure of how many and what limits can be overcome, day after day, execution after execution, until the final overthrow of ethics. The complete loss of contact with moral reality that shines through Mattner's words, entirely separated from the objective reality that he continues to describe so coldly and (apparently) in full consciousness, seems to testify to the presence in him of a real emotional short circuit. This may have made him too, a victim[68].

But, beyond this historical, social, ethical and rational view-point, one difference is clear: the difference between real victims and real executioners, between their faces and their words.

ENDNOTES

1 "The death we gave them, it was a quick and clean death". See Gerlach, p. 588, Browning Origini, pp. 309, 507.

2 Paul Kohl: *Der Krieg der deutschen Wehrmacht und der Polizei 1941-1944. Sowjetische Überlebende berichten.*

3 Compared to the original population of 110/113,000 on the eve of Barbarossa (June 1941), in November 1942 the city counted almost 35,000 inhabitants (a decrease of about 68 % in 17 months), reduced to 15,000 by the end of 1943 (February 1944, 63 % decrease) then 10,000 in July 1944 (34 % decrease half-yearly). Gerlach, p. 419.

4 Kohl, p. 142.

5 Gerlach, p. 587.

6 The thousand survivors of Mogilev's Jewish community were liquidated between October and December 1941, during four executions, with about 650 victims in total. Gerlach, p. 591.

7 Bundesarchiv Berlin, Bild 101 I 138 1083 03>; 101 I 138 1084 02>;101 I 138 1091 06>.

8 Sponsored by the Ministry of Propaganda *Ewige der Jude* collects, in the form of a pseudo-documentary, the film footage shot in Poland immediately after the occupation. Structured around the starkest anti-Semitic stereotypes, the film was broadcast for the first time to the German public on November 28, 1940.

9 On the anti-Semitic propaganda campaign, implemented through films or images provided by Wehrmacht's Propagandakompanien, see Friedländer, pp. 45-51.

10 Friedländer, pp. 45-46.

11 See Chap. 5.

12 Indeed, retaliation against the Jews of Mogilev had been perpetrated by a unit of the Wehrmacht a few days after the occupation of the city, in response to the killing of a German officer by a woman in a Russian uniform. Following this killing, about fifty Jews, aged between 20 and 45, were imprisoned and later killed by an Infanterie-Regiment 81 firing squad. HIS, pp. 150-153. The October 1941 massacres - that had nothing to do with this episode – weren't even *justified* by a similar deed, which might have been used as an excuse, but were committed purely and simply by a genocidal desire *tout-court.*

13 Gerlach, p. 592.

14 *Ibid.*, pp. 578-588, LG Bochum, 15 Ks 1/66, p. 437, Curilla, p. 560.

15 Browning Origini, pp. 314, 376.

16 The ambition to *cleanse* Jews from the *capital* of his domain, making *air breathable for the Germans*, was not new, as Governor General Hans Frank had called for an extensive operation to evacuate the 50,000 Jews of Krakow during a meeting on April 12, 1940. Browning Origini, p. 145.

17 On the role of 707.ID, led by Braemer and von Bechtolsheim, see HIS, pp. 468-474

18 Browning Origini, p. 300.

19 Krausnick/Wilhelm, p. 182, Curilla, p. 435.

20 LG Freiburg, 1 Ak 1/63, p. 446. Curilla, p. 560.

21 In particular, the *explicit* participation of EK8 in the October 2 massacre, was not observed by the Court of Bochum (Bochum LG, 15 Ks 1/66), during the trial v. Kraiker. This is probably due to the failure to mention the same EK8 - in relation to the events of October 2 and 3, 1941 – in the KTB of Polizei-Bataillon 322, in which only von dem Bach's Stab/HSSPF, the 3/322 and the Ukrainian auxiliaries are mentioned. By contrast, confirmation of the involvement of EK8 in the October 2 massacre comes from Hauptwachtmeister Richard Neubert's evidence, commander of the third platoon of 2/Polizei-Bataillon 9, who was assigned to EK8. Curilla, p. 435.

22 EM 133, November 14, 1941, Gerlach, p. 592, Curilla, p. 437, Browning Origini, p. 411.

23 It was referring to Dulag 185, 127 (from February/March 1942) and 203, as well as Stalag 341. Kohl, pp. 141 and 291.

24 Gerlach Extermination, p. 62. This camp had been activated in late September 1941 in order to imprison all those – mainly civilians – who were not destined for one of the POW camps. Operationally, the camp was placed under the control of SSPStOF "Mogilev", Oberstleutnant Kölblinger and was guarded by Polizei-Kommando "Waldenburg" at first and then by an NSKK unit. Gerlach, p. 591.

25 Gerlach Extermination, p. 62.

26 Curilla, pp. 426-428.

27 Klemp Ermittelt, p. 282, Hölzl, p. 271, Curilla, pp. 830-831.

28 Gerlach, p. 541, Klemp Ermittelt, p. 280.

29 Gericht der BRD, LG München I, July 21, 1961, 22 Ks 1/61, VII/1b – JuNSVe, Lfd.Nr. 519.

30 LG Bochum, 15 Ks 1/66, June 5, 1968, v. Kraiker and others. Curilla, p. 527.

31 Curilla, pp. 830-831, Klemp Ermittelt, p. 294.

32 LG Freiburg, 1 Ak 1/63, July 12, 1963, v. Uhl, Hülsemann and Riebel; LG Darmstadt, 2 Js 376/65, February 2, 1972 and October 2, 1972 v. 19 battalion members. Curilla, p. 545. For more details see § 5. 4, *Herren des Tatorts*.

33 Hochstetter, p. 464.

34 LG Detmold, 2 Ks 2/66, February 16, 1967, v. Schulz. Curilla, pp. 342-343.

35 Curilla, pp. 830-831.

36 Hochstetter, p. 460.

37 *Ibid.*, p. 463.

38 LG Freiburg, 1 Ak 1/63, pp. 446-449, Curilla, pp. 560-561, Gerlach, p. 588.

39 Curilla, p. 560, Breitman, p. 66. See Report Riebel, pp. X-XI.

40 AVAK, pp. 347-348, 380. ZStL AR-Z 6/65, Bd. II, Bl. 339-343.

41 Langerbein, p. 142.

42 AVAK, pp. 348, 380. Testimony by H.G., aide at Stab/HSSPF "Mitte" given to ZStL AR-Z 152/59, Bd. II, Bl. 1034-1036.

43 AVAK, pp. 349, 380. Testimony by G.B., given to ZStL AR-Z 6/65, Bd. III, Bl. 773.

44 *Ibid.*, pp. 349, 381. Testimony by E.C., given to ZStL AR-Z 6/65, Bd. III, Bl. 639.

45 Mallmann/Riess/Pyta, p. 139. Testimony by Rudolf S., given to ZStL AR-Z 6/65, Bd. III, Bl. 715.

46 AVAK, p. 349.

47 *Ibid.*, p. 350.

48 Langerbein, p. 143.

49 Gerlach, p. 590, quoting some evidence, suggests that all the approximate 7,000 Jews of Mogilev may have been transferred to Dimitrov-Werke on October 2 when the first massacre took place. The victims of the massacre of October 19 then, were taken directly from the factory, and not the ghetto, where by then there were no Jews.

50 LG Bochum, 15 Ks 1/66, June 5, 1968, v. Kraiker and others, pp. 438-527.

51 LG Detmold v. Schulz, p. 22. Curilla, p. 343.

52 Curilla, p. 343.

53 *Ibid*, p. 539.

54 Contrary to Bochum's, during the trial v. Bradfisch, the Court of Monaco mentions a Belarusian auxiliary unit, or a contingent of Russian militia. Curilla, p. 538.

55 LG München I, July 21, 1961, 22 Ks 1/61, Curilla, pp. 539-540.

56 Evidence given by Alfred H., given to the Prosecutor of Bochum – StAwBo 9526, Klemp Ermittelt, pp. 282.

57 Gerlach, p. 590, Gerlach Extermination, p. 62.

58 *Ibid.*, p. 590, *Ibid.*, p. 62.

59 Klemp Ermittelt, p. 279, Hölzl, p. 449.

60 Klemp Ermittelt, pp. 279-280.

61 For a more thorough assessment of the procedural events of Polizei-Bataillon 322, see § 5.4.

62 Curilla, pp. 342-343.

63 *Ibid.*, pp. 426-427. Besides Bradfisch, two EK8 *teilkommandoführers,* Wilhelm Schulz and Oskar Winkler, were also convicted of complicity in murder, and given seven years and three and a half years in prison respectively.

64 Breitman, p. 75. Evidence given by von dem Bach's aide-de-camp, present at the meeting. See Browning Origini, p. 376.

65 Indeed, the gas vans in Mogilev were previously used for the first time towards the beginning of September, for an experimental gassing of more than 500 mentally ill people. Browning Origini, p. 295.

66 *Ibid.*, p. 300.

67 Gerlach, p. 588, Browning Origini, pp. 309, 507.

68 Mattner assigned to Mogilev's SSPStOF, was investigated in Vienna in 1947 and 1964, without reaching a conviction. Browning Origini, p. 50.

Unit of Polizei-Bataillon 12 on the Leningrad front. January 1942.

PHOTO SECTION 1

Memebers of Polizei-Bataillon 101 in Lodz, summer 1940.

Schutzpolizeireviere members in Vienna.

Leningrad Front: member of Polizei-Bataillon 102 while inspecting the wreckage of a destroyed Soviet tank.

Weapons training for men of a police battalion in Tilburg, Holland.

Norway: gunnery training with an old MG 08 machine gun.

Police unit training long-distance shooting with Steyr Solothurn S-100.

Policemen of an unidentified unit interrogating a suspected partisan, probably in Poland.

Gunnery training for police departments with Mauser rifles mod. 1898a.

Norway: member of Polizei-Bataillon 255 in gunnery training with excellent Czechoslovak ZB 26 machine gun.

Policemen in shooting training with obsolete 13 MG "Dreyse" in a former Czechoslovak bunker. Around 1940.

Saybusch (Ostoberschlesien): members of a motorcycle police battalion during a training break. Note the MP 28 II held by the policeman in the foreground.

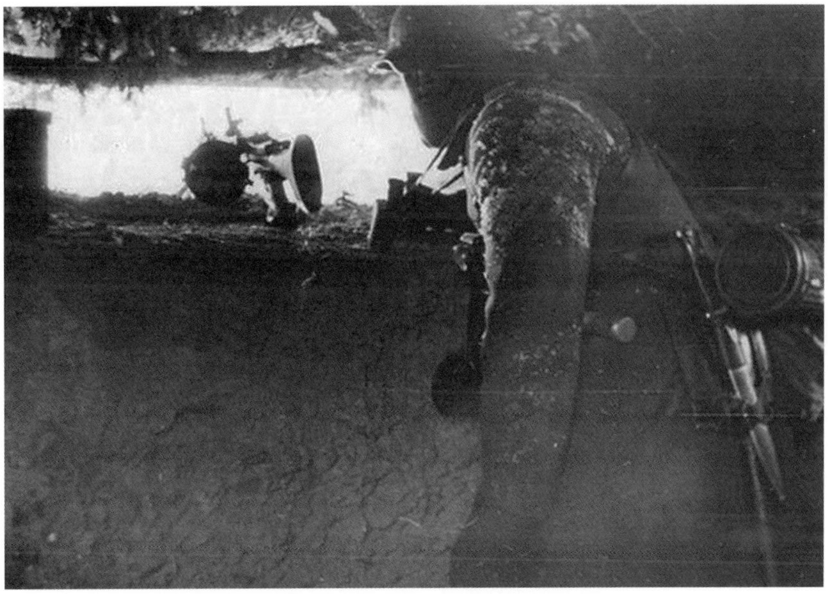

Police guard in a bunker. Probably Northern Russia.

Member of Polizei-Gebirgsjäger-Regiment 18.
Note the mountain boots and the Edelweiss on the cap.

Rock-climbing training for Polizei-Bataillon 302 men in Norway.

Polizei-Nachrichten-Kompanie member in action.

Polizei-Bataillon 121, January 1942: difficult conditions on the Leningrad front.

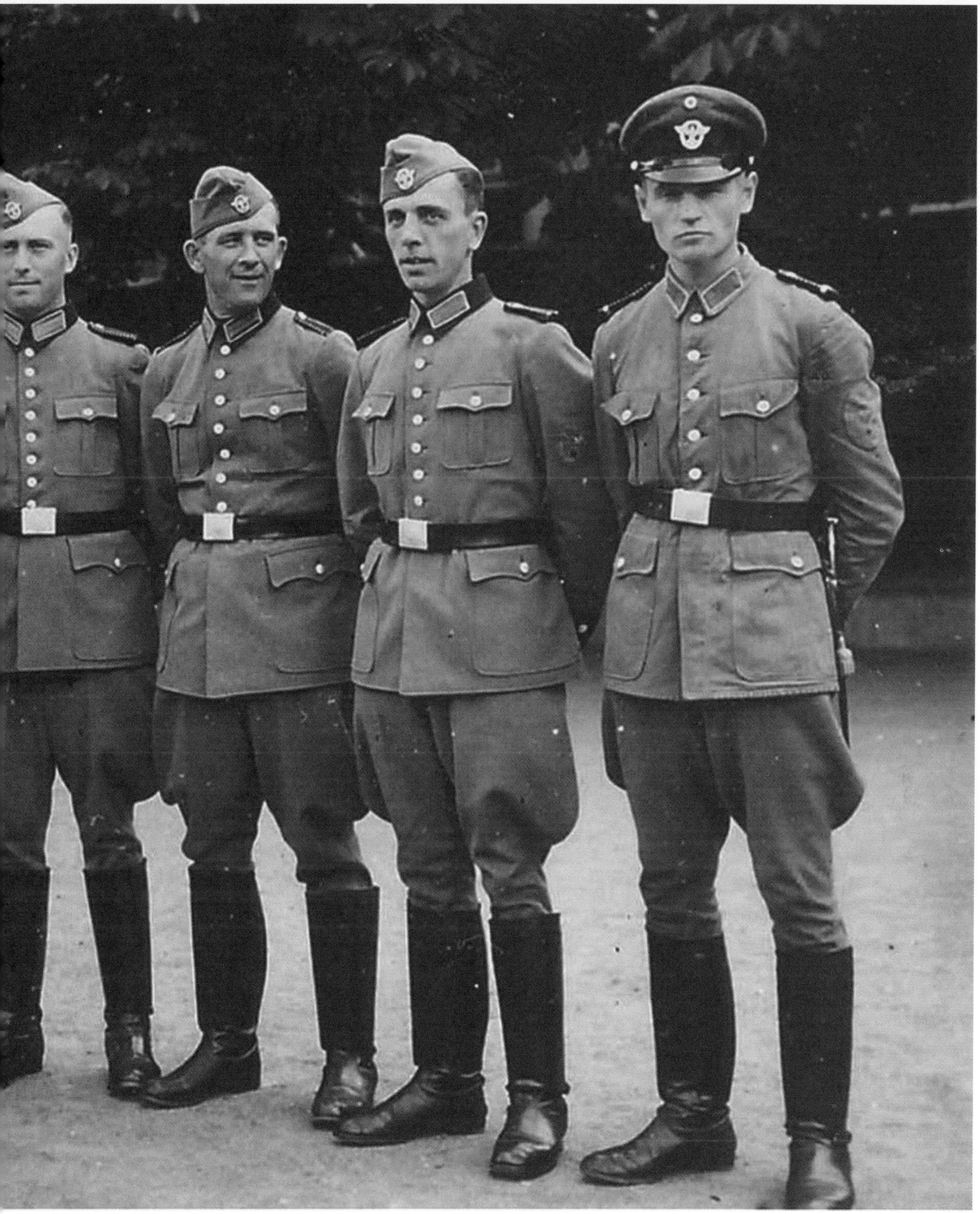

Members of Polizei-Bataillon 102.

Convoys of Polizei-Bataillon 255 struggling with "rasputiza" on the eastern front. Probably autumn.

Entrance of a police unit somewhere in Czechoslovakia. Maybe 1939.

Würzburg's sanitary team 131, with their omnipresent Kübelwagen. Note the banded shield, symbol of the battalion, just below the license plate.

Police unit training somewhere near Berlin. Note the mix of uniforms worn by the officers.

Police battalion in Norway.

Members of a Schutzpolizeireviere.

Schutzpolizeireviere members in front of their Mercedes truck.

"Freund und Helfers": coffee break for two Schutzpolizisten in Berlin.

A nice image of a group of policemen on board a vessel in navigation along a channel.
On their arms, above the eagle, the word "Berlin" is readable.
That identifies them as members of Berlin's Schutzpolizei.

Officers of an unidentified police battalion in Klattau (Protectorate), 1940.

Police unit leaving from Stettino's port.

Lunch break for a unit of Polizei-Bataillon 302 in Norway. Note the Edelweiss on the cap of the first man squatting to the right.

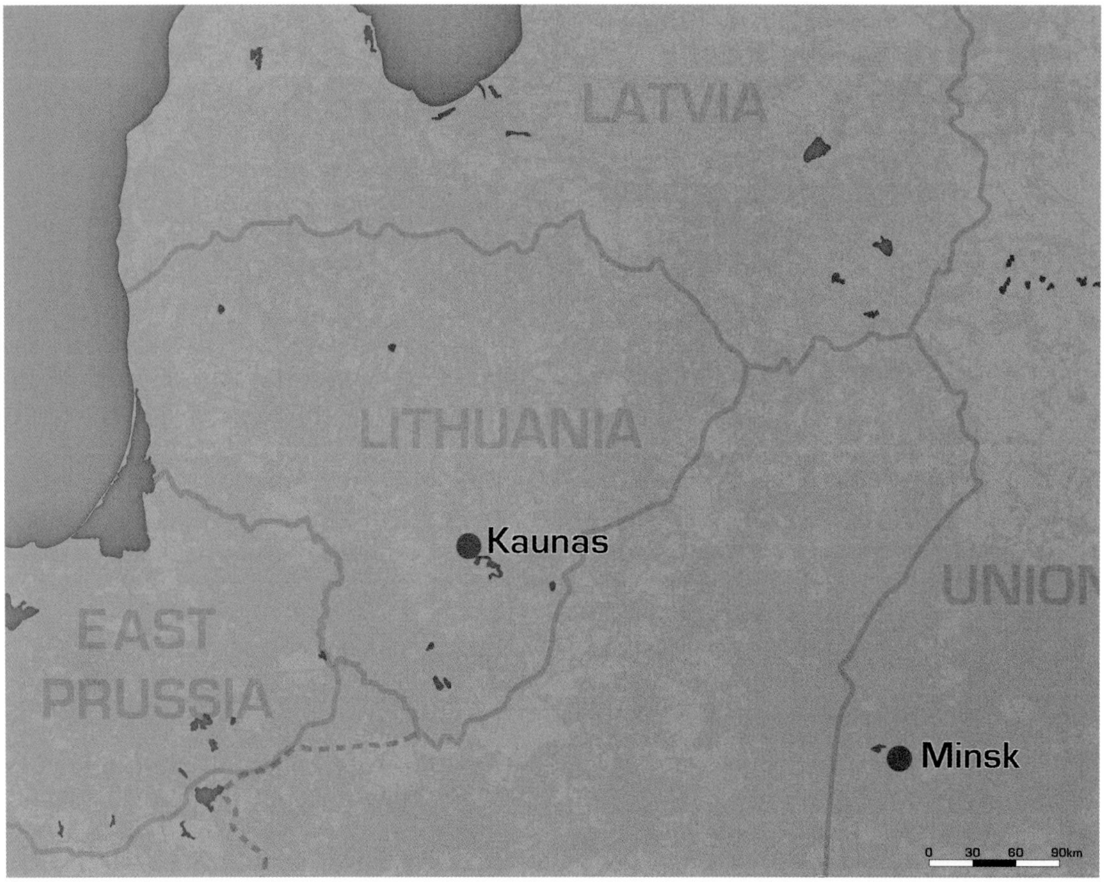
LATVIA
LITHUANIA
Kaunas
EAST
PRUSSIA
UNION
Minsk
0 30 60 90km

CHAPTER SEVEN

"GROSSE GHETTO, GROSSE AKTION"

KAUNAS, OCTOBER 28 – 29, 1941[1]

"It wasn't worthwhile
living for more than sixty years,
in order to witness
a day like this….."

Elchanan Elkes,
Kaunas, October 28, 1941

Eine art «ausforstung»
vorgenommen worden sie…

Heinrich Schmitz,
Wiesbaden, February 28, 1962[2]

"Tuesday morning, October 28 was rainy. A heavy mist covered the sky and the whole ghetto was shrouded in darkness. A fine sleet filled the air and covered the ground in a thin layer. From all directions, dragging themselves heavily and falteringly, groups of men, women and children, elderly and sick who leaned on the arms of their relatives or neighbors, babies carried in the mother's arms, proceeded in long lines. They were all wrapped in winter coats, shawls, or blankets, so as to protect themselves from the cold and the damp. Many carried in their hands lanterns or candles, which cast a faint light, illuminating their way in the darkness. Many families stepped along slowly, holding hands. They all made their way in the same direction – to Demokratu Square. It was a procession of mourners grieving over themselves. Some thirty thousand people proceeded that morning into the unknown, towards a fate that could already have been sealed for them by the bloodthirsty rulers.

A deathlike silence pervaded this procession tens of thousands strong. Every person dragged themselves along, absorbed in their own thoughts, pondering their own fate and the fate of their family whose lives hung by a thread. Thirty thousand lonely people, forgotten by God and by mankind, delivered to the whim of tyrants whose hands had already spilled the blood of many Jews.

All of them, especially heads of families, had equipped themselves with some sort of document, even a certificate of being employed by one of the ghetto institutions, or a high school graduation diploma, or a German university diploma – some paper that might perhaps, perhaps, who knows, bring them an "indulgence" for the sin of being a Jew" [...][3].

7.2 TWO MONTHS EARLIER

The Jewish population of Kaunas had been the victim of three different *actions* in the days before and after the ghetto was formally institutionalized, on August 15, 1941[4]. During the course of such actions at least 2,550 Jews had been taken from their homes and shot at Fort n. IV by Lithuanian auxiliaries of TDA-Batalionas. Specifically, according to the *Jäger Report* of December 1, 1941, the executions took place on August 2 (205 Jews and four Lithuanians), August 9, (534 Jews) and August 18 (1,811 Jews and one Polish). Before the beginning of August, however, an even greater number of Israelites – between 8 and 10,000 – had been *liquidated* in the city in what was later labeled as "the most extensive series of mass executions of unarmed civilians that ever took place in Lithuania until that moment"[6]. In total, within only 54 days of occupation, from June 25 to August 18, approximately one-quarter of the whole Jewish population of Kaunas – which numbered 40,000 people before *Barbarossa* – had already been killed during the genocide, mainly through organized mass-shootings. This percentage would then increase to around 95 % before the Red Army returned, in July 1944[7].

The progressive decimation of the Jewish community had begun during the early hours of the occupation, in the form of so-called *pogroms*, perpetrated by squads of Lithuanian extremists wearing distinctive armbands. Such squads were formed by civilians who benefited personally from these actions and were spurred on by former army men who reorganized themselves as local police: all this was approved and supported by EGA personnel [8]. These pogroms, which were the result of negotiations between Stahlecker and the leaders of Lithuanian activists in Kaunas – among which Algirdas Klimaitis and Bronius Norkus – caused the death of approximately one thousand Jews, nearly all of which were murdered in the Vilijampolė district between June 25 and 27, 1941 [9]. However, this first phase, uncoordinated and improvised, was rather short and finished before the end of June in order to give way to the next phase, characterized by mass-imprisonments of the Jewish population, the institution of what came to be known as a "temporary concentration camp for Jews"[10] at Fort no. VII in Kanaus, and the systematic shooting of many thousands of imprisoned Israelites at the same Fort no. VII as well as at Forts no. IV and IX.

Within such context, the mass-shootings began on June 30 and continued until late November, mainly at the hands of the firing squads of TDA-Batalionas, which had been placed in charge of the surveillance of the forts on rotation. As a matter of fact, in several cases the presence of TDA-Batalionas men as guards of the forts coincided with the implementation of mass-slaughters. Such was the case, for instance, with the 6th/TDA at Fort no. VII on July 9 (38 victims), with the 3rd/TDA at Fort no. VII on July 19 (26 victims), with 5th/TDA at Fort no. IV on August 2 (209 victims), with 4th/TDA at Fort no. IV on August 9 (534 victims) and again with 5th/TDA at Fort no. IV on August 18 (1,812 victims). Furthermore, post-war testimonies have shown that 1st/TDA took part in shootings on an almost daily basis[11], while for some time 5th/TDA was placed under the direct command of SK1B for the executions in rural areas around Kaunas, during which hundreds of people were killed[12]. Eventually, the number of executions committed resulted in a major health problem, worsened by the summer heat and impossible to conceal because of the unbearable reek coming from the common graves which were barely covered with a layer of soil. This was on top of the danger of epidemics among the inmates detained in the forts under intolerable hygienic conditions, as well as the possible contamination of rivers and aquifers, something which led to a ban on swimming in rivers around the city[13].

Nevertheless, the mass-slaughters and pogroms of the first two weeks of occupation had produced the result of *reducing* the number of Jews destined to be locked up in the ghetto, the establishment of which had been announced by Stahlecker on July 7, 1941, under the disguise of restoring *security* and *order* in Kaunas. Under the decree, issued on July 10 and bearing the signatures of Bobelis, the Lithuanian military commander of Kaunas, and Palčiauskas, the mayor of the city, the Jews' relocation would have to be completed by August 15. The chosen area; a suburb of wooden houses behind the Neris River where 5-6,000 Jews and 8-10,000 non-Jews (who were to be relocated elsewhere) were living until that moment, would then receive a total of at least 30,000 people, with the result of doubling the population density and further worsen the already fragile health conditions[14]. At this stage, demoralized and broken after the violence suffered during the first few weeks, the Jews looked upon the establishment of a ghetto in an area of the town reserved for themselves as the only way to obtain relative safety from dreaded raids by overexcited Lithuanians[15].

The forced relocation of approximately 25,000 people took place as planned, before August 15. On this day the perimeter of the ghetto was isolated from the rest of the city. A further barbed-wire fence divided the interior of the ghetto in two parts: the *Kleine Ghetto* (small ghetto) and the *Grosse Ghetto* (large ghetto), which were crossed by a street *(Panerių gatvė)* whose access was off-limits to the Jews. The two parts were connected by a wooden bridge which loomed over this street, while surveillance was taken care of by the third division of Polizei-Bataillon 11, supported by Lithuanian auxiliaries[16].

Once the *Indian reserve* had been sealed off with fences and armed guards, the inmates were given a few days' truce, something which made them hope that the situation couldn't get any worse. The events that unfolded during the following weeks would prove that this was far from the truth, and that the Jews of Kaunas had been locked up not so much in just a ghetto, but in a deadly trap.

Armed Lithuanian activists in Kaunas, July 1941. At least one of them is wearing the armband with the national colors.

7.3 TWO DAYS EARLIER

The drama was staged in the afternoon of October 25, 1941, as SS-Hauptscharführer Helmut Rauca, responsible for Jewish Affairs at the Gestapo of Kaunas, entered the offices of the *Judenrat*. Without hesitation, he informed the terrified members of the Council about the decision to proceed with a rationalization of the workforce in order to prevent any competition between those who held the work-permits issued by the civil administration – the so-called *Jordansheine* – and those who didn't. It was for this reason that the latter would be relocated and isolated inside the small ghetto, while the workers and their close family members, who stayed in the large ghetto, would receive larger food rations. As a consequence of this decision, photographs of all those considered fit to work would be taken[17]. This operation would take place by calling out loud the workers' names at a public gathering called for 06:00 hours on October 28 in *Demokratenplatz*. Hence, the *Judenrat* had to spread the news to the population immediately through a decree, making sure that everyone, with no exceptions – thus including the disabled and the newly-born babies – obeyed the order. Obviously, Rauca's dreadful endnote implied that all those who did not show up would be shot on sight by the patrols in charge of house by house searching[18].

Not surprisingly, the assembly order caused panic with the entire Council, which proceeded to present a petition to Rauca. This petition proved to be fruitless, as Rauca assured about the absence of any ill-will on his side[19]. The Council then tried to find further information which could shed light on his real intentions. They obtained disturbing clues: surreptitious contacts with the Lithuanians had unveiled alarming news of how Russian prisoners of war were digging large mass graves at Fort no. IX[20]. Furthermore, during the same hours, highly selective special permits began to be distributed directly from the Gestapo offices to a few skilled workers engaged in the repair works at the airport or at particularly important factories; all these were signals which left little room for optimistic interpretations with regards to Raucas' real intentions. Eventually, after lengthy consultations and disputes within the Council and after receiving the decisive opinion of Avraham Shapiro[21], Chief Rabbi of Kaunas, in the late morning hours of September 27, the *Judenrat* decree was inevitably made public to the population of the ghetto.

It was the hardest choice the *Judenrat* could make, as it imposed the sacrifice of the most vulnerable members of the community in order to save all the others. The decision, supported by religious texts consulted by Rabbi Shapiro, was probably inevitable, also in view of the complete lack of preparation of the community if faced with the prospect of resistance to Rauca's order. In that respect, Kaunas was a typical example of the dramatic and controversial choice of the *lesser evil*, which meant that a few would survive for yet another day – and that a few lucky *Daniels* would avoid the *lion pit* – but at the same time this decision implied a devastating ethical/religious dilemma, which resulted – as in the case of Lachwa of September 1942 – in an almost *masadic* self-sacrifice, weapons in hand, of the entire community[22].

The events at Kaunas unfolded in a different way than those at Lachwa: in Kaunas the *Judenrat* had to choose to sacrifice nearly ten thousand people so that at least as many would survive. Given such great numbers the choice was an almost inevitable one, and it was reinforced by the fact that – cynical though it may sound – those who were chosen as survivors belonged to the youngest and most *productive* sphere of the population and as such – at least theoretically – they offered the greatest potential for a renewal of the community which the predestined victims, mostly elderly and sick, were no longer able to guarantee.

In a way, even in that dimension of (un)living which the (un)reality of the ghetto represented, accepting the selection imposed by the Nazis was the last desperate effort that the Jewish community made in order to hope that there could be a future and preserve itself for as long as possible through the protection of the traits which were necessary for survival. Though reluctantly, through the lacerating consent to martyrdom of its least essential part, the community was experimenting a sort of social Darwinism on itself: if on the one hand the community could find a philosophical/religious justification of this decision in the writings of the Maimonides about keeping alive the highest possible number of Jews in order to not interrupt the continuity of Judaism (in his search for answers, Rabbi Shapiro most certainly reflected upon such writings during the night before). On the other hand it led to anthropological patterns of safeguarding the community which existed in various cultures, and whose symbolical representation, in the case of the Jews, is embodied by the ritual of the *scapegoat* as described in Leviticus 16.

From this point of view, the choice that was imposed on Kaunas (about 40 % victims in order for the remaining 60 % to survive) seems different from the one imposed on Lachwa, where the Nazi *generosity* spared the lives of 30 (sic!) craftsmen, selected from a population of about 2,000 souls (1.5 %). In both cases, hard as it may have been, the choice was essentially forced upon the Jews: in Kaunas to keep the right to live on, in Lachwa to reclaim the choice of how to die. And both cases witness the will of the Jewish community to resist. This is obviously so Latchwa, with its armed struggle, but also in Kaunas, because of its desperate determination to keep alive that fragment of Judaism in front of the by then obvious wish of the Nazis to eradicate it once and for all.

It's difficult to imagine the overwhelming thoughts of the thousands of Jews in those few hours between the publication of the decree of the *Judenrat* and the appointment with the destiny Rauca had in mind for them. As a matter of fact, none of them could know for sure what was going to happen in *Demokratenplatz*: there was of course a sense of impending tragedy, but it was impossible to outline the contours and the extent of it, and certainly there was also the unspoken hope of each of them of being spared what they probably dared to fear.

Most probably, many of them spent the night praying or bidding farewell to their family members; some, it is believed, clung to the logic of reason to counter the effect of a terrifying event – "How can this really be happening? Has God really forsaken us?". Others spent the night reading the sacred texts, the prophetic visions of the Apocalypse, or perhaps the interpretation of the fate reserved to the unworthy of God, such as the one described in Psalm 49.14. But certainly, logically, that fate could not have had a rational manifestation in the objective reality, especially if established in the same world which had given birth to great men the likes of Kant, Goethe or Schiller. Indeed, we can only guess the intimacy of how they lived those night hours before the round-up of October 28, but beyond any Reason – thought upon or just desired – the processions of mourners who walked out of their homes at dawn, darkness and sleet all around them, in the glow of trembling flames, opened a passage between the real and the unreal, between the world of the living and the transcendence of Sheol, with death at their side as the last shepherd.

7.4 INGLORIOUS BASTARDS

It was a small and diverse party of efficient and zealous individuals that decided, organized and eventually perpetrated the majority of massacres in the Kaunas ghetto in the summer of 1941. According to Lithuanian historian Arūnas Bubnys, on September 23, 1941, Karl Jäger's Einsatzkommando – which had been stationed in Kanaus since June 29 – was officially transformed in the central command of Lithuania's Sicherheitspolizei, that is to say in "Litauen" KdS [23]. Inside, SS-Oberstrurmführer Martin Kurmis was appointed commander of Abt.IV (Gestapo) of the so-called *Jewish question*. However, around mid-October, he was replaced by SS-Hauptsturmführer Heinrich Schmitz[24]. Up until that moment Schmitz was Jäger's deputy at Stab/EK 3 and during the following months he would accept great responsibilities behind the destruction of Lithuania's Jews.

Among others, two NCO's who had served in the infamous – and now disbanded – Rollkommando "Hamann" were employed directly by Schmitz and were transferred to the Abt.IV. They were SS- Hauptscharführer Helmut Rauca, who had been Hamann's deputy, and SS-Hauptscharführer Josef Stütz [25]. Rauca, who would later become commander of Section 4A3 (partisan movements) of the "Litauen" KdS, was named by Jäger "commissioner for Jewish affairs (*Beauftragter für jüdische Angelegenheiten*)" in Kaunas; this position would basically grant him the right of life and death over the ghetto-dwellers, as during the raids, he would be supervising the selections of the victims to be shot[26].

SS-Hauptsturmführer Fritz Jordan had basically the same role to Kaunas' civil administration that Rauca had as responsible for Jewish affairs. Through his position, he was responsible for the imposition of various vexatious and surreal anti-Jewish decrees[27], as well as for the release of work-permits to the ghetto-dwellers which were the only glimmer of temporary survival for those who received them[28]. Lastly, appointed by the Lithuanian city mayor Kazys Palčiauskas[29] to serve as middleman between the city's authorities and the *Judenrat*, was Jordan's direct associate Mikas Kaminskas, a civil collaborationist employed by the municipality of Kaunas. A slavish bureaucrat, Kaminskas played his part of official mouthpiece, transmitting orders to the Jews of the ghetto without showing any empathy towards them whatsoever. Indeed, he did remarkably well when it came to helping plan *actions* against the ghetto, among which those of August 18 and October 6, 1941, despite his personal reassurances to the members of the Jewish Council[30].

Apart from the leaders who planned the events and the key personnel who supported them, what was needed to execute materially the *Jewish actions* on the field was, according to Klaus-Michael Mallmann's appropriate definition, the so-called *fußvolk der Endlösung*[31], that is to say a genocidal workforce large enough to reinforce the low aliquots of Sicherheitspolizei. In the case of the Kaunas massacre of October 28, 1941 that workforce was well represented by the third division of Polizei-Bataillon 11 acting under the orders of Hptm. Alfred Tornbaum[32], aided by a contingent of Lithuanian auxiliaries brought in from Major Kazys Šimkus' PPT-Batalionas 1 *(Litauische-Hilfspolizei-Bataillon 1).* Šimkus was a former officer in the Lithuanian Air Force who went on to lead an auxiliary battalion recruited in the early days of the German occupation which had already been used by EK 3 in the mass-executions at Kaunas' forts[33].

7.4.1 – *Polizei-Bataillon 11*

The German division which proved to be most directly involved in the Kaunas killings was Polizei-Bataillon 11. Originally a battalion from Königsberg, Eastern Prussia, it was created as early as September 1939 and, especially during the early months after Barbarossa, it was destined to become one of the most destructive tools of genocide used by the Ordnungspolizei. As a matter of fact, apart from Kaunas – which they reached in late June 1941 – this battalion was responsible for a real extermination campaign in the Minsk province, where two of its divisions were transferred from October 6, 1941 until approximately mid-November, together with the Lithuanians of PPT-Batalionas 2 led by Maj. Impulevičius[34]. Polizei-Bataillon 11 was commanded by Maj. Franz Lechtaler, a 51-year old Rhenish who was believed to have socialist ideas[35], and after the war was sentenced to two years' imprisonment by the Court of Kassel, for the massacres committed in Belarus[36].

For some time Polizei-Bataillon 11 represented the main German unit available to FK 821, even after the transfer of power from the Wehrmacht's military administration to Reichkommissar von Renteln's civilian administration, proclaimed in Lithuania on July 17, 1941. The role it played in Kaunas was crucial. Until the appointment of his superior, KdO Engel, which took place in September, Lechthaler was, in fact, the Ordnungspolizei's highest-ranking officer in Kaunas. He also had a prominent role in the complex German hierarchical ladder deployed in the city.

In view of this situation, the allocation of tasks directly related to the so-called *Jewish question* to Polizei-Bataillon 11 and its commander Lechthaler happened almost automatically. Such tasks included surveillance of the ghetto, which the battalion conducted from mid-August[37], and the escort of Jewish *Arbeitskommando* who had to go daily from the ghetto to work locations outside of it, including Aleskotas' airport.

Actually, the decision to use Jewish workforce, which implied the issue of work permits – the so-called *Jordanscheine* – that the civilian administration delivered to all workers[38], was the discriminating factor of the selections between the ghetto-dwellers. They were divided into those who were able to work and those who weren't, those who were productive and those who were *useless*; in a nutshell, those whose lives would be spared for a little longer and those who would be killed immediately.

It's interesting to note how, after Lechthaler's departure for Belarus with half of Polizei-Bataillon 11, Tornbaum's 3/11 battalion was basically made available to KdS "Litauen" Jäger, evidently as a result of an agreement with KdO Engel, to whom the battalion kept referring to, but only for routine administration[39]. For everything else, and particularly for its actions concerning the *Jewish question*, Tornbaum's battalion could be considered as a real genocidal cohort, as were its two units (2/11 and 4/11) which, at that time, were in Belarus, and engaged in wreaking havoc and causing destruction among the Jewish communities in the Minsk province[40]. In his book Tory describes the police chief and eager executor Alfred Tornbaum:

> *Tornbaum was the embodiment of a typical German gendarme. He expressed great interest in arts, in philatelic collections, and in valuables in general. He was a sadist, fond of listening to Listzt's rhapsodies played by an artist, only to rob him afterward of his piano. He was a police dog, who forced women to undress, so that he could then conduct gynecological examination on them while, at the same time, beating them severely. This police inspector who plundered and looted treasures from the Jews, repaying them with blows on all parts of the body; this broad-shouldered man in his grey uniform and shining boots, feared by his own subordinates; this [was] Tornbaum, who had thought that his rule over us would be indefinite [...]*[41] "

Another testimony of Tornbaum's cruelty during a raid in the ghetto is offered by Joheved Inčiūrienė, a surviving Jew, who was a 17-year old girl at the time of the events described:

> *He walked in our room, gun in hand. He forced us to open the wardrobes where we kept our winter clothes and ordered a Jew who accompanied him to load our clothes, together with two suits that belonged to my father, onto the trucks waiting in the courtyard. (After he had left), I saw through the window our clothes being loaded onto the trucks, then, all of a sudden, Torbaum shouted to the middle-aged Jew who had carried our clothes without hurry: "Dance, you Jew!". Not understanding what the German was ordering him to do, the Jew kept still. Then Tornbaum pointed the gun at him and shot him point-blank*[42].

7.4.2 – PPT-Batalionas 1

Among the Lithuanian units acting in Kaunas in the summer/autumn of 1941, PPT-Batalionas 1, led by Maj. Kazys Šimkus, played a key-role in the resolution of the so-called *Jewish question*. It was a squad formed on August 7, 1941 from the restructuring of the former TDA-Batalionas, itself formed in Kaunas on June 28 by Lithuanian personnel previously in service with the Red Army, and by groups of nationalist insurgents who received orders from Bronius Norkus and Kazys Šimkus[43]. Greatly oversized because of the numerous enlistments, this battalion – widely used since the beginning of July in the shootings perpetrated in the forts under the orders of Jäger's EK3 – had been reorganized on the following August 7 and divided into three smaller formations, namely; PPT-Batalionas 1 which stayed under Šimkus' command; PPT-Batalionas 2, led by Antanas Impulevičius (who was later transferred to Belarus) and PPT-Batalionas 3 commanded by Maj. Antanas Švilpa.

As for PPT-Batalionas 1 (*Litauische-Hilfspolizei-Bataillon 1*, in German), it originated from former divisions TDA third (1/PPT 1, Oltn. Anatolijus Dagys), fourth (2/PPT 1, Ltn. Bronius Norkus) and fifth (3/PPT 1, Hptm. Juozas Truškauskas)[44]. All these divisions had already taken part in the July/August 1941 executions at Fort no. IV (3/TDA, Ltn. Juozas Barzda) and in the province (Rollkommando "Hamann" – 4/TDA Ltn. Norkus) and continued perpetrating genocidal activities during the following weeks[45].

More specifically, the entire battalion was involved in the massacre of October 29. Its men were used to cordon off the ghetto during the selection, in house to house searches, in the escorting of columns of Jews to Fort no. IX and in the following execution of victims, perpetrated mainly by the third division (3/PPT 1). Overall, from July to December 1941, the 1/PPT-Battalion would be responsible for at least 26,000 executions[46].

7.4.3 – PPT-Batalionas 3

The restructuring that had given birth to the PPR-Batalionas 1 and 2 had left a number of men unassigned. These men were used to create the seventh division of TDA-Batalionas which, on August 7, 1941, was used to form the nucleus of PPT-Batalionas 3, into which two other newly-created divisions converged. Ltn. Antanas Guselis (Gudelis) was appointed commander of the 3/PPT – formed from the 7/TDA –. He would replace Antanas Švilpa, who had become commander of the battalion.

Beyond the documented evidence on crimes committed or not by the battalion, the orders given to the guards around the village of Vilijampolė, as to how they should act in a way that *not one Jew could move away from the fence that cordoned off the ghetto* were clear and unequivocal.

Relocated to Kaunas during the time of the actions of autumn 1941, this battalion was certainly used for ghetto surveillance. There was, however, no concrete evidence confirming its direct involvement in the massacres of the Jews of Kaunas[48]; only circumstantial evidence, which the Wiesenthal Center cited when moving to have Guselis charged with war crimes in February 1999. After the war, Guselis fled to Adelaide, Australia. The Wiesenthal Center asked the Lithuanian government to proceed with the extradition request to the Australian one, or at least to start a trial in absentia.

June 25, 1941, during the days of Vilijampolė's pogrom. Lithuanian National activists aboard a T20 "Komsomolez", a former Soviet artillery tractor. Men like these converged in great numbers in TDA-Batalionas. Notice the armband worn by the first man from the left. Source: Bundesarchiv.

7.5 DEMOKRATENPLATZ: OCTOBER 28, 1941

On October 28, soon after dawn, after completing the round-up of the ghetto-dwellers in Demokratenplatz[50], teams of Lithuanian auxiliaries began house to house searches, looking for any hidden Jews: these Lithuanians were coordinated by a squad of German officers under the command of Hauptwachtmeister Blask[51]. In the meantime, a security cordon had been drawn around the entire perimeter of the ghetto by the other 3/11 officers, who were armed with machine guns. Behind them, on the hills overlooking the Jewish ghetto, many Lithuanian civilians had assembled to watch the *show*.

The wait for the crowd of Jews to be amassed inside the square lasted until 09.00 hours. Finally Schmitz, Rauca, Jordan and Tornbaum appeared before their victims, already divided into groups according to the workplace of the family men[52]. All around them, at the corners of the square, machine-guns were placed, as other officers of Tornbaum's 3/11 and Lithuanian auxiliaries rallied around the anxious crowd.

Now, the selection could begin.

Let's read Tory's testimony[53]*:*

"The columns of employees of the ghetto institutions and their families passed before Rauca, followed by other columns, one after another. The Gestapo man fixed his gaze on each pair of eyes and with a flick of the finger of his right hand passed sentence on individuals, families, or even whole groups. Elderly and sick persons, families with children, single women, and persons whose physique did not impress him in terms of labor power, were directed to the right. There, they immediately fell into the hands of the German policemen and the Lithuanian partisans, who showered them with shouts and blows and pushed them towards an opening specially made in the fence, where two Germans counted them and then reassembled them in a different place [...].

When some old or sick person could not hold out any longer and collapsed on to the ground, the Lithuanians set upon him instantly, kicking him with their boots, beating him, and threatening to trample him underfoot [...].

Rauca directed the job of selection composedly, with cynicism, and with the utmost speed [...]. Throughout the selections he did not exhibit any sign of fatigue or sensitivity at the wailing, pleas, and cries, or at the sight of the heartrending spectacle which took place before his eyes when children were separated from their parents, or parents from their children, or husbands and wives from each other [...].

From time to time, Rauca feasted on a sandwich [...] or enjoyed a cigarette, all the while performing his fiendish work without interruption.

When a column composed mostly of elderly people, or of women or children appeared before him, he would command contemptuously: 'All this trash to the right!' or 'All this pile of garbage goes to the right!'. To Dr. Elkes, when he tried to intervene in an attempt to save their lives, he would say: "Wait, you'll be grateful to me for having rid you of this burden" [...].

Now and then Rauca would be handed a note with a number written on it, copied from the notebook kept by the German who diligently applied himself to the task of recording the number of Jews removed to the small ghetto [...].

The selection was a protracted affair. Hungry, thirsty, and dejected, thousands of people waited for their turn from dawn [...]. Those who were weak – those who could not withstand the psychological tension and the bodily torment – collapsed and breathed their last even before their turn came to pass before Rauca.

It was beginning to grow dark, yet thousands of people remained standing in the square. Captain Jordan now opened another selection place; he was assisted by Captain Tornbaum. Rauca could count on this pair without reservation [...].

The selection was completed only after nightfall, but not before Rauca made sure that the quota had been fulfilled and that some 10,000 people had been transferred to the small ghetto. Only then were those who had passed through the selection, and had remained standing in the square, allowed to return to their homes [...]. One-third of the ghetto population had been cut down. The sick people who had remained in their homes in the morning had all disappeared. They had been transferred to Fort no. IX during the day.

The square was strewn with several dozen bodies of elderly and sick people who had died of exhaustion. Here and there, stools, chairs, and empty baby carriages were lying abandoned.

On his way back Dr. Elkes muttered: "It wasn't worthwhile living for more than sixty years in order to witness a day like this....".

7.6 AUTUMN DAWN: OCTOBER 29, 1941

The dramatic selection of October 28 had moved nearly 10,000 Jews, mostly elderly, sick, children and unlucky unemployed from the large ghetto to the small, dilapidated ghetto around Sajungosplatz, previously emptied of its inhabitants during the October 4 action[59].

Even though most of them had no hope whatsoever, all of them could not be sure about what the future held for them: so much so that some of them began discussing how to organize their survival in the new sector.

Every illusion, however, was brutally shattered at dawn on that October 29, when Tornbaum's officers and Šimkus' Lithuanians stormed the houses of the small ghetto, forcing the Jews to line up and march towards Fort no. IX, about four kilometers away. The weakest and those who were unable to move, among which many women with children, were put aboard the division's trucks[60]. Then, as the thousands of victims started walking, a symphony of tears, prayers and groans began to rise, higher and higher, filling the entire column, from top to bottom. The *Grosse Aktion* of the small ghetto of Kaunas was reaching its climax.

Let's keep reading Tory's words[61]:

"It was an autumnal, foggy and gloomy dawn when German policemen and drunken Lithuanian partisans broke into the small ghetto, like ferocious beasts, and began driving the Jews out of their homes [...]. The partisans barked out their orders to leave the houses and to line up in rows and columns. Each column was immediately surrounded by partisans, shouting "Forward march, you scum, forward march", and driving the people by rifle butts out of

the small ghetto toward the road leading to Fort No IX. It was the same direction that the Jews had been led away in the "action" commanded by Kozlowski on September 26, 1941, and in the "action" of the liquidation of the small ghetto on October 4, 1941. The same uphill road [...] to a place from which no one returned.

It was a death procession [...]. Column after column, family after family, those sentenced to death passed by the fence of the large ghetto. Some men, even a number of women, tried to break through the chain of guards and flee to the large ghetto, but were shot dead on the spot. One woman threw her child over the fence, but missed her aim and the child remained hanging on the barbed wire. Its screams were quickly silenced by bullets [...].

The procession, numbering some 10,000 people, and proceeding from the small ghetto to Fort No, IX, lasted from dawn until noon. Elderly people and those who were sick, collapsed by the roadside and died [...]. Thousands of curious Lithuanian flocked to both sides of the road to watch the spectacle, until the last of the victims was swallowed up by Fort No. IX.

In the fort, the wretched people were immediately set upon by the Lithuanian killers, who stripped them of every valuable article – gold rings, earrings, bracelets. They forced them to strip naked, pushed them into pits which had been prepared in advance and fired into each pit with machine guns which had been positioned there in advance. The murderers did not have time to shoot everybody in one batch before the next batch of Jews arrived. They were accorded the same treatment as those who had preceded them. They were pushed into the pit on top of the dead, the dying, and those still alive from the previous group. So it continued, batch after batch, until the 10.000 men, women, and children had been butchered. Villagers living in the vicinity of the fort told stories of horrors they had seen from a distance, and of the heartrending cries that emanated from the fort and troubled their waking hours all day and night [...]".

The path of the columns along to Fort no. IX began in the early morning of October 29 and went on for hours until late afternoon. Inside the fort everything was ready, waiting for the first victims. All cells had been emptied and the prisoners transferred to Kaunas' main prison. Large mass graves had been dug by two hundred Russian prisoners of war on the western side of the fort. Led by Jäger himself, a numerous contingent of Sicherheitspolizei officials, accompanied by at least fifty Lithuanians led by Šimkus and his aide Barzda had arrived from Kaunas. Machine guns had been placed along the mass graves and a security cordon had been drawn around the fort[62]. Standing still on Kanaus' hill, eight kilometers away from the city centre, Moloch was waiting patiently for Cabiria to arrive.

The description of what happened at Kanaus' Fort no. IX on that October 29, 1941 has reached us through the dramatic testimonies of Kuki Kopelman – then a boy of thirteen – who incredibly survived because he was assumed to have died under the bodies of other victims, and Ignas Veliavicius-Vylius – Lithuanian head-officer of Fort no. IX – who both witnessed and took part in the carnage.

This is Kopelman's story[63]:

"German and Lithuanian guards stood at the entrance with several large dogs straining at their leashes, barking and snarling furiously. We were pushed through the gates.

Several trucks were standing inside the courtyard, their engines running. They often backfired and it sounded like shots. A young German officer addressed us: 'In spite of all the ridiculous rumors, you're going to be transported to working camps in the east. You will shower and then be issued working clothes. Undress and leave your clothing here'.

He spoke in civil tones, and in spite of all we knew about this death factory he almost sounded convincing.

Whatever spark of hope we felt was extinguished when we heard a long burst of machine-gun fire and distant screams. The Germans heard it too, for they raised their guns and pointed them at us.

'Quickly you Jews! Undress and into the showers! You're just hearing the backfire of some trucks', the officer shouted […].

But no one moved, no one seemed able to move a muscle. The officer calmly walked up to an elderly who was standing near the front, drew his Luger and shot him in the face. When he fell to the ground his head opened up and his brains poured out into the mud.

Suddenly everyone was undressing. When you're about to die, even a few minutes seem precious, as if another second might bring a reprieve […].

What followed was a nightmare in slow motion. Every tiny detail will stay burned in my memory forever. On the officer's signal the Germans and Lithuanians launched themselves at us. 'Run, run, you Jew swine', they shouted, lashing out at us with sticks and rifle butts, their dogs attacking the slow-moving ones, tearing pieces of flesh from their legs and buttocks. We started running in a wild panic with the guards and dogs after us […]. Then as we rounded a corner we saw dozens and dozens of machine guns mounted around an open field. They were firing long bursts into a huge pit. I could hear screaming from inside […]. Lithuanians and Germans with rolled up sleeves and red faces were loading and firing into the mob. You could see the yellow flashes from the barrels, and a veil of blue smoke drifting over the field. It was a scene out of hell itself. There were hoarse shouts, and women's shrill screams, and children and babies crying and dogs barking. It stank of sweat and urine and excrement as terrified bodies just… let go. I saw one bearded man standing by the pit, shaking his fists at the sky and screaming. 'Jews! There is no God! There is a devil sitting up there!' He looked a lot like my old rabbi. Blood was streaming down him and they kept shooting at him, but he kept standing there, screaming at the sky. Then we were at the pit. It looked like thousands of bodies, one on top of another, screaming and writhing, begging the Germans to finish them off. A vision of hell. A vision of hell.

We were right in front of the guns. Bullets were buzzing around me like angry bees, but all I felt was the crush of the mob behind me […]. Then I felt a weight fall on my head, knocking me into merciful oblivion".

And this is Ignas Veliavicius-Vylius' testimony[64]:

The Jews who were brought to the fort were not registered. Ten of those who escorted the Jews to the pits came to me from time to time in the courtyard of the fort and I would hand over groups of a hundred – men, women, children and the elderly, without being concerned with their family names. People were lined up in columns of four abreast and taken from the gate of the fort towards the pits. At a certain distance from the pits, they were told to take off their outer clothing and move towards the pits. They were then pushed into the pits and forced to lie down while being shot.

The first groups lay in the pits which were full of water. Whoever did not obey the order to lie down was beaten with sticks, the butts of rifles, and thus forced to lie down in the pits. This scene of murder and shooting was horrible. The guards abused their victims. The more stubborn elements among the Jews were already beaten on the way. Throughout the day one could hear the sound of the victims' groans and shouting as well as the weeping of women and the cries of little children. The women carried their babes in their arms and held the hands of the other children. They crawled into the pits and lay down on the hundreds of corpses of those who had been killed earlier while awaiting their own end.

At the same time, there was a sort of rally in the courtyard. Speeches were addressed to the waiting Jews calling on them to go to their death upright, with heads held high. There were others who shouted slogans to activate a revolutionary struggle for freedom. These demonstrations helped me to keep order, as some of the people were listening to the speeches while others, that is the majority, prayed, despite the sound of weeping that did not stop. Eve-

ry ten minutes, another hundred were taken from the place.

Towards evening, with the approaching darkness, the mass slaughter came to an end. The pits were full. The victims lying in the pits were not covered with earth. Among the dead, there were still children, men and women who had not died. They lay beneath the dead corpses and groaned. I saw many wounded men and women covered with blood, trying to crawl out of the pits in order to escape. But the guards caught them, beat them and forced them to return to the pits where they were finished off with bullets.

When the murderers finished shooting the Jews, Jaeger's Gestapo men and Shimkus's police loaded the dead onto trucks and took them away. On the following day, the remainders of their belongings were also taken, in order to distribute them among members of the Nazi party. The pits were later on covered with ash by the prisoners of war who were returned to the fort from the "Yellow Prison". The earth covering the pits did not rest for some time after that. Hundreds of the wounded lying there were moving about at death's door.

That day, 9,200 Jews were exterminated: 2,007 men, 2,920 women and 4,273 children. This is confirmed by Karl Jäger in his final report of December 1, 1941, which reads: "clearing from the ghetto of superfluous Jews *(Säuberung des Ghetto von überflüssige Juden)*».

7.7 WAITING TIMES

After the war, of all the main culprits of the massacres perpetrated in Kaunas in the summer / autumn 1941, only three found themselves having to answer for their actions during an interminable legal process, which was started by ZStL towards the end of the Fifties with

Kaunas' Jewish neighborhood, around 1939. Source: Bundesarchiv.

the collection of information files. This process ended about thirty years later with the death in jail from an incurable disease – while still awaiting trial – of the last of the major defendants of that investigation: Helmut Rauca. The same man who only a few months before had finally been extradited to Germany from Canada, the country where he had lived undisturbed from December 30, 1950 until May 20, 1983[65].

Regarding the fate of two of the other major culprits of the massacre, namely Jordan and Šimkus, the former had been killed on the Eastern Front on August 2, 1942, while the latter had taken refuge in Australia, where he is believed to have died on June 10, 1968[66]. The body of Ltn. Juozas Barzda of Kavolių, Zarasų district, adjutant of the battalion led by Šimkus, heavily involved in the massacres at Fort no. IV in July / August 1941 and then, up until late October also involved in Lechthaler's genocidal campaign in Belarus with PPT-Batalionas 2 led by Impulevičius, was found and identified on January 15, 1945. His body was found in Lake Platelai, where he probably landed at the end of an unfortunate parachute jump which took place in December, at the beginning of a sabotage mission behind Soviet lines[67].

The following is a brief history of the judicial process regarding investigations conducted by the Prosecutor of Frankfurt between 1959 and 1983.

1959: The Prosecutor of Frankfurt receives from ZStL the file relating to Schmitz and other EK3 members: the dossier is referred to as ZStL 207 AR-Z 14/1958 (Schmitz). The Prosecutor of Frankfurt classifies the dossier as StAw Frankfurt am Main 4 Js 1106/59 v. Heinrich Schmitz et al.

1961: On September 27, 1961, the Prosecutor of Frankfurt requests the Court of Wiesbaden to open a preliminary investigation (StAw Frankfurt am Main VU-Antrag v. EK 3) v. members of PB 9, PB 11 and EK3 including Rauca, against whom, a few days earlier (September 21), an arrest warrant in absentia had been issued. Heinrich Schmitz is placed in custody

1962: (February): concerning the massacre of October 28 and 29, 1941, on February 28, 1962 Heinrich Schmitz makes the following statement to the Prosecutor of Frankfurt: "It was a sort of "thinning". This word, now, may sound terrible, but it describes quite well what happened then. Some 10,000 Jews were selected according to principles of usefulness and good health. And about 10,000 of them were actually killed. *(Eine art ausforstung vorgenommen worden sie. Dieser Ausdruck hört sich jetzt fürchterlich an, aber er bezeichnet ziemlich treffend das, was damals geschah. Es wurden etwa 10.000 Juden ausgewählt nach dem Grundsatz der Nützlichkeit und auch der Gesundheit. 10.000 wurden damals auch tatsächlich umgebracht)*»[68].

1962: (November): In November 1962, the proceedings by the Court of Wiesbaden begin. Schmitz commits suicide in his cell. Avraham Tory is called to testify as prosecution witness. His diary is accepted as evidence against the prosecutor[69].

1966: March 27: The Prosecutor of Frankfurt requests the Court of Wiesbaden to drop the charge made v. officer G.B., member of 3/11.

1966: (August): Through the sentence LG Wiesbaden 4 Js 1106/59 – 7 VU 3/61 of August 22, 1966, the Court of Wiesbaden approves the request of the Prosecutor of Frankfurt to drop the charge v. officer G.B., member of 3/11.

1971: The Court of Wiesbaden, with sentence LG Wiesbaden 4 Js 1106/59 - VU 3/61 of December 6, 1971, drops the charge v. the other members of Polizei-Bataillon 11 placed under investigation, including Alfred Tornbaum, as well as that of four EK3 members. According to the bewildering court ruling, "the only function Tornbaum had was to select the victims, not knowing what the result of his actions would lead to. Also, his presence in the ghetto, in the course of both actions, does not automatically lead to consider that Tornbaum was partly responsible for what happened, nor does it demonstrate his support for the actions"[70]. During these days, the Prosecutor of Frankfurt receives evidence about Rauca's presence in Canada.

1973: Further ruling by the Court of Wiesbaden issued on January 28, 1973, LG Wiesbaden VU 3 / 61-4 Js 1106/59 of January 28, 1973, also drops the charge v. those PB 9 members still under investigation.

1982: Federal Germany's authorities request Rauca's extradition to the Canadian authorities. Rauca is arrested by the RCMP on June 17, 1982. Avraham Tory is called to testify v. Rauca in Toronto; again, his diary and other documents are accepted as proof.

1983: Following the extradition to Germany of Helmut Rauca (May 20, 1983), the Prosecutor of Frankfurt issues an accusation against him on August 26, 1983 (StAw Frankfurt 50/4 Js 284/71 of August 26, 1983 v. Rauca), after which Rauca is arrested and placed in custody in Kassel. Already gravely ill, Rauca dies in prison before the trial begins on October 29, 1983.

7.8 CONSIDERATIONS

The carnage of Kaunas on November 28 and 29, 1941 seems to put an end to the brief and bloody path that after the early weeks following *Barbarossa* had unraveled along a theory of massacres that were relatively selective and almost *improvised*, scattered along the axes of the advance of Einsatzgruppen and subsequent reinforcements represented mainly by police units. The Kamenec Podolsky massacre of August 27 to 29 represented the crossing of the threshold of the *systematic* variant of *itinerant genocide* which had preceded, then accompanied, its *permanent* phase, centered on the extermination camps of Belzec, Sòbibor and Treblinka, which were opened in the spring.

In that respect Kaunas did not represent a turning point in the Jewish genocide but rather consolidated the trend to expand enormously the category of victims, which now included to an increasing extent – and without any will to confuse all those who did not seem *immediately* useful, according to the arbitrary judgment of the perpetrators – not only those who could be considered dangerous, sick or unfit, but also people who were fit or young but for some reason didn't have a work permit. Kaunas didn't represent the extermination of an *entire* community – something that would happen shortly afterwards in Rumbula, in Latvia or in Chacov (Ukraine) – but it came very close: Kaunas shows how the road to the Final Solution, the aptly defined *Weg zur Endlösung*, was being taken in great strides and in a totally natural, consistent and functional way[71].

For several reasons the carnage of Kaunas cannot be considered as *the* tragic historical symbol of the Jewish genocide, unlike Rumbula. The apocalyptic power of the numbers (about 25,000 victims in two days), in addition to witnessing the obliteration, without one single exception, of an entire Jewish community – Riga's – make Rumbula the epitome of itinerant genocide not so much because of the destructive dynamics that were produced during the massacre, but rather as a psychological moment of no return. It was also a dress rehearsal and final verification of *feasibility* – given its magnitude – of a strategic choice, the genocidal choice, seen as a method of social engineering put into practice in order to solve once and for all the Jewish question. For this reason after Rumbula there was only desert: the next step, besides the huge mass graves hidden in the forest, would have been taken only by the long columns of victims brought to the gas chambers.

In Kaunas, on the other hand, where the victims of the October 28 - 29 slaughter were about one-third compared to those of Rumbula and where somehow the ghetto managed to survive for about thirty-two more months, there was a powerful, yet only hinted at, combination of all those genocidal dynamics that had emerged in the course of the previous killings in different ways, but almost never at the same time.

- In Kaunas the selection was premeditated, planned and applied, first on the weaker and more vulnerable, then on the children and youngest people (about 45 % of the total), as well as on women, the sick, the elderly and those who did not have a work permit: that is to say all those categories which were deemed *unnecessary* because they were unproductive, and which then became prime targets for a rational annihilating strategy. In other words, if genocide had to be, there was nothing more cynically logic than to begin by getting rid of the most useless ones, preserving for purely utilitarian purposes only those who were immediately able to be useful through their work. Speaking of which, let's recall what Rauca said to Elkes during the selection: "You'll see, you'll thank me afterwards for freeing yourself of all this weight."
- In Kaunas the selection did not occur on a nominative basis, eventually discarding the list of some opponents considered dangerous, but through an arbitrary process valid for all, based only on the *eye of the master*, the same process that would later be used countless times on the platform at Auschwitz. That is to say; those fit to be exploited until they dropped on one side and the *unnecessary* to be eliminated without hesitation on the other. In this respect, Kaunas was ahead of the times and a precursor to the selective methods which would later be used in extermination camps.
- In Kaunas, the logic and the methods typical of extermination camps were also applied during the process of killing, with endless waves of naked Jews being walked beyond the gates of the fort to be mowed down by machine guns in mass graves: a system that had nothing different, except the cause of death – bullets instead of gas – from the one applied, for instance, at Sòbibor and Treblinka, where other endless columns of equally naked Jews were passing the threshold of the tunnels that led to the gas chambers. Therefore, if *technically* Fort no. IX cannot be defined as an extermination camp, *in practice* it worked as such. By extension, the same *Grosse Ghetto* of Kaunas can be said to have served the same function as Sòbibor's Field no. 1, where all those Jews not destined for immediate gassing would survive because they were deemed fit to work. In other words, somehow, the organizational and structural system of *Aktion Reinhardt*'s death camps had been anticipated by the complex of imprisonment and massacre represented by the forts and the ghettos of Kaunas[72].
- In Kaunas, as well as in Rumbula, in the camps run by Aktion Reinhardt and in many brutal massacres in Belarus and Ukraine, there was a large collaboration with local auxiliaries, actively used as a workforce in the firing squads, during the escorts and at roundups. Some of them could perhaps have been driven to act against the Jews by feelings of revenge, linked to *endogenous* political / ideological reasons dating to the period of Soviet occupation. But when they all found themselves to be used solely as material executioners with orders from above, without a say in the matter[73], they leveled these feelings to those of their German controllers. Let's say it: the same hopeful nationalistic Lithuanian administration, although aiming for their own goals (even if unrealistic) contributed decisively to the destruction of Judaism in Lithuania; not only did they not oppose the genocidal solution imposed from above, but they adopted it wholly[74], thus falling into a bleak state of moral, and not only political, allegiance to Berlin.
- Kaunas saw what we might call a *community of purpose*. In fact, it was not only the Sicherheitspolizei, through the "Litauen" Office of Jewish Affairs of KDS IV B 4 – institutionally set for the task – to be involved in the decimation of the ghetto, but also the Ordnungspolizei, the German civil administration that reported to SA-Brigadeführer Hans Cramer, the Lithuanian civil administration led by mayor Palčiauskas and the ubiquitous militarized auxiliaries under the command of Šimkus. This proves the application of a synergic strategy in order to optimize the resources, where all these institutions provided a relevant contribution at the same time as they pursued their immediate objec-

tives. This is indicative of a genocidal decentralization, with Berlin at the core of a system which is reproduced in large scale in the periphery, breaking into a thousand semiautonomous trickles functional to the same global design[75].

- In Kaunas there was no *operational need* related to security, neither was there a pretext for retaliation related to the execution of such a massacre, not even the grotesque *justification* that had been made during the so-called *Aktion-Kozlowski* of September 26[76]. There was just a willingness to proceed with the gradual destruction of the ghetto – *thinning*, that was the term used – based merely on genocidal intentions. Even the declaration made by Schmitz to the Prosecutor of Frankfurt about the *principles of usefulness and good health* as the reason behind the selection goes in that direction: that generation of Jews that the Nazis had *put their hands upon*, had to be the last; not another birth would be tolerated in the ghetto[77], all family ties, all community bonds, the passing-on of traditions to the children and the young, the assimilation of the memories of the elderly, the solidarity among generations… all of this had to be severed once and for all. The river had to be gradually dried up until it withered away in the moment when even the last *useful* Jew would cease to be deemed as such.

According to accepted estimates, almost 95 % of the Lithuanian Jewry, meaning about 200,000 people, did not survive the Final Solution[78]: the highest percentage within the boundaries of occupied Europe. In Kaunas alone, except for the few who managed to run away before the Wehrmacht arrived, of the approximately 40,000 Jews who were in town in June 1941, only 2,000 had survived by the time the Red Army returned, in July 1944[79].

The numbers of this catastrophe leave little room for interpretation and sophistry.

One can quibble about the dynamics, roles and methods through which all this happened, but one cannot deny that there was a clear political will aimed at crushing the Lithuanian Jewry on grounds which were purely ideological and racial. This will was pursued from the first to the last day of the occupation, even during the long *delay tactic* of the period spanning December 1941 – March 1943, during which the *biological selection* produced by the unbearable conditions of the ghettos replaced the mass executions.

One can argue about the context in which this catastrophe was perpetrated and the relationships that could or could not intervene between the different components of the Lithuanian society and the outside influences that conditioned them, but the fact remains that for over three years, from June 1941 to July 1944, a substantially defenseless part of the population, reduced in physical and logistical conditions that made it impossible to react in any way, was scientifically, constantly and relentlessly persecuted and annihilated, taking advantage of power relations that could not have been more unbalanced.

One can argue about the sufferings endured by the population of Lithuania during the Soviet occupation before *Barbarossa* and certainly acknowledge them, as well as looking at the feelings of revenge that broke out when that domain ceased to be, but at the same time the so-called theory of *two genocides* is by no means acceptable. Neither is the brutal generalization that in a sort of collective blame wished to expand to the entire Lithuanian Jewry – which was basically and mostly Ashkenazi and practicing – the guilt of certain segments of the same pro-Soviet Jewish community of Lithuania or even the *imported guilt* through the wrongdoings of those *Soviet* Jews members of the NKVD or other repressive organizations who were sent to Lithuania in 1940 as part of the occupation forces, and who were basically atheists and internationalists. The latter is a one-way justificatory and self-absolving theorem which has its roots in Nazi propaganda and was rightly denounced as *troglodytic* by members of the contemporary Lithuanian culture itself[81].

All this can be discussed, but it cannot be denied that the Lithuanian Jewry, which for centuries had been a cultural and economic crossroads straddling the Baltic, Germanic and Slavic worlds was irretrievably erased in the space of thirty-seven months, at the hands of a rough but lucid annihilating will.

We want to close with this passage taken from: *The Vanished World of the Lithuanian Jews*[82]:

> *"The remarkable Lithuanian Jewish community, which once occupied a prominent place in the Jewish world and stood out as a unique part of the world Jewry, is no more. All that remains is memory".*

The memory carved in the rocks of the Valley of the Communities at Yad Vashem.

ENDNOTES

1 This chapter contains excerpts of Avraham Tory's volume: *Surviving the Holocaust. The Kovno Ghetto Diary*, which in turn is the editorial revision, complemented by historical notes and updates, of the diary written at the time of the events described by Tory himself, a surviving Lithuanian Jew and secretary of the *Judenrat* in the Kaunas ghetto from 1941 to 1944. So, in the next few paragraphs I will include some passages taken directly from this work, which is not only a personal diary, but a real historical chronicle, minutely detailed, to the extent that it was accepted as primary evidence in the course of three different legal proceedings for war crimes or for the revocation of citizenship in cases brought before the courts of Wiesbaden (Germany), Tampa (Florida, USA) and Toronto (Canada), v. members of Nazi political and military administration of Kaunas, believed to be co-responsible for the Jewish genocide in Lithuania in the years between 1941 and 1944. Consequently, for a thorough knowledge of the facts relating to the Kaunas ghetto, see Tory's volume, which this chapter draws largely upon, especially for the description of the events of October 28, 1941. See Avraham Tory: *Surviving the Holocaust. The Kovno Ghetto Diary*. Introduction by Martin Gilbert and historical notes by Dina Porat. Cambridge, Massachussets, 1990.

2 "It was a sort of *thinning*". Dieckmann, pp. 448, 466.

3 Tory, p. 49.

4 Dieckmann, p. 443.

5 *Ibid.*, p. 442.

6 Dieckmann/Sužiedėlis, p. 54. According to the EM of July 11, 1941, up until that day 7,800 Jews had been *liquidated* by shootings carried out by Lithuanian *kommandos*. This number includes the approximately 1,000 Jews killed in Kaunas during the pogroms of the early days. These shootings were perpetrated by the Lithuanians of the TDA-Batalionas, by personnel of SK 1b and by a contingent of policemen from Polizei-Bataillon 9, incorporated to the EK3. See Dieckmann, pp. 442, 463, Dieckmann/Sužiedėlis, p. 55-57.

7 The number of surviving Jews which greeted the return of the Soviet Army in Kaunas in July 1944 was around 2,000. Dieckmann, p. 439.

8 Dieckmann/Sužiedėlis, p. 30 onwards, particularly pp. 32, 36-37. The flats of the Jews killed or jailed were systematically raided by the *pogromists,* who were often sure about the correct addresses thanks to the information received from Lithuanian landlords about their Jewish tenants.

9 Dieckmann Pogrom, pp. 359-360, Dieckmann/Sužiedėlis, p. 42. Information on how Stahlecker instigated the pogroms can be found in his report *Gesamtbericht Einsatzgruppe A, bis zum 15 Oktober 1941*, in IMT Blue Series, vol. XXXVII, p. 672 – Doc. 180 L. As for Bronius Norkus, See Chapter 8, note 14. Information on Algirdas Jonas Klimaitis, is scarce. From what is known he was a journalist, a fanatic anti-Semite, who voluntarily led a group of companions who acted in complete independence from the *same* will of the LAF *(Lietuvos aktyvistų frontas)*: the provisional government of the Lithuanian Prime Minister Ambrazevičius. According to Michael MacQueen, Klimaitis managed to find safety in Germany, where he was found living under a false name at the end of the Seventies. Subjected to preliminary investigations by the Prosecutor of Hamburg, he died before he could be brought to trial. In 1992 his son Algirdas was accused and jailed by Lithuanian authorities as a suspected KGB agent. MacQueen, pp. 97, 102.

10 Dieckmann/Sužiedėlis, p. 52-53. This provisional concentration camp for Jews had been created inside Fort no. VII on June 30, 1941 in order to find a remedy for the lack of space inside Kaunas prison and was placed under the administrative responsibility of Jurgis Bobelis, the Lithuanian military commander of Kaunas.

11 Stang, pp. 143-144, Jäger Report in Bartusevičius/Tauber/Wette, pp. 303-304, Dieckmann/Sužiedėlis, p. 57. The commanders of the divisions of TDA-Batalionas in the time-span examined were: 1/TDA: Hptm. Bronius Kirkila until July 12 (who committed suicide) and then Hptm. Povilas Pukys; 3/TDA: Oltn. Juozas Barzda; 4/TDA: Hptm. Viktoras Klimavičius; 5/TDA: Hptm. Juozas Truškauskas.

12 Dieckmann/Sužiedėlis, p. 57.

13 *Ibid*, p. 59. KTB of Wirtschaftskommando "Kauen"

14 Tory, pp. 16-18.

15 *Ibid.*, pp. 60-61.

16 Curilla, p. 154, Tory, p. 39, Dieckmann, p. 443.

17 Curilla, p. 173, StAw Frankfurt am Main, 50/4 Js 284/71 of August 26, 1983 v. Rauca.

18 Tory, p. 43-44.

19 According to the reconstruction of the Prosecutor of Frankfurt, Rauca assured the members of the Judenrat about his intention to get to know the population of the ghetto and to gather information about their employment opportunities. Curilla, p. 173, StAw Frankfurt am Main, 50/4 Js 284/71 of 26.8.1983 v Rauca.

20 Faitelson, pp. 137, 139. The Jews who benefited most from these permits were those who belonged to the so-called "Lipzer Brigade", who were engaged in reconstruction works in the buildings occupied by the Gestapo in Kaunas.

21 Abraham Duber Kahana-Shapiro, born in 1871 and deceased on February 27, 1943. Chief Rabbi of Kaunas and important figure among Lithuanian Rabbis. At the request of the Judenrat, he accepted the tragic responsibility to have the last word on the fate of the ghetto, which had been made clear by Rauca's irrevocable order. Despite being ill for a long period, he survived the decimation of the ghetto and died in his bed on February 27, 1943.

22 The reaction to the massacre of the Jews of Lachwa is referred to in Chap. 14.

23 Bubnys, *Vokiečių okupuota Lietuva*, p. 78.

24 Stang, pp. 60, 98. Before Barbarossa, Martin Kurmis had taken a colonial police course at the PAI school of Tivoli, Italy, between November 1940 and March 1941, learning, among other things, the most effective methodologies to deal with indigenous tribal populations. Probably because of this training, in 1944 he was included in a mission of intelligence / sabotage in southern Iran, aimed at organizing strikes among the workmen unloading cargoes with U.S. lend-lease supplies direct to the Soviet Union and to convince local chieftains to perform acts of sabotage and guerrilla warfare against the convoys and the line connecting to the Caspian Sea.

25 Between July and October 1941 Rollkommando "Hamann" had sown destruction among the Jewish communities of Lithuania, killing around 53,000 civilians. See the *Jäger Report* in Bartusevičius / Tauber / Wette, p. 303-308, Stang, p. 158-160. Largely formed of Lithuanian auxiliaries, its cadres also included a small group of German non-commissioned officers: apart from Hamann, Rauca and Stütz, the names of SS-Hauptscharführer Porst, Salzmann, Mack and Planert are mentioned. See Curilla, p. 309. The Rollkommando Hamann was dissolved in early October 1941, shortly after the perpetration of its last massacre in Žagarė, south of Vilnius (October 2).

26 Stang, p. 98.

27 The grotesque order of August 10, 1941, which forbade the Jews to walk the streets with hands in their pockets (sic!) says it all. Benz/Kwiet/Matthäus, p. 185.

28 Jordan, who also ranked SA-Obersturmführer, was the director of Hauptabteilung Politik II and was directly subordinate, as the representative for the ghetto, to HS-Brigadeführer Hans Cramer, head of the German civil administration of Kaunas (*Stadtkommissar*). Jordan died at the front on August 2, 1942. He had been transferred there following an altercation with his superior. See Dieckmann, pp. 443, 463, Neumann, p. 147, Tory, p. 38.

29 Born in 1907 in Žagarė, Kazys Palčiauskas was mayor of Kaunas from June 25, 1941 to May 1942 and was then appointed director of a food cooperative by the Germans. He fled to Germany in 1944, when the Red Army returned to Lithuania and after the war was hired as a clerk by a German company that worked for the US Army. Having obtained the certificate of *Displaced Person* in 1949 by the International Refugee Organization (IRO), he was acknowledged as suitable for emigration to the United States on a favorable opinion of the *Displaced Person Commission* and the investigators of the CIC and could then apply for the entry visa to the U.S. at the American sub-consulate of Amberg (Munich), which he obtained after an interview with the Vice-Consul. Palčiauskas reached the United States on April 19, 1949 and the following July 18, he applied for citizenship, which he eventually received in 1954. Living in St. Petersburg, Florida, he was tracked down by OSI and charged, on June 15, 1981, of collaboration with the Nazis and in particular of "shared responsibility in the persecution of civilians, in the confinement of over 20,000 Jews in the ghetto, in the confiscation of Jewish property and in the emission of orders of deportation". Subjected to the process of denaturalization on December 6, 1982 before Tampa's District Court, on March 23, 1983 he was stripped of his American citizenship in the first instance. This verdict was subsequently confirmed by the following appeal before the Eleventh Circuit Court of Appeal on June 18· 1984. As a result, at the request of the OSI, deportation proceedings were opened before the Immigration Court, with the first hearing set for February 18, 1985. The subsequent judgment ruled Palčiauskas to be expelled from the territory of the United States: judgment later confirmed by the *Board of Immigration Appeal* and in line with the opinion of the

U.S. Immigration and Naturalization Service. This expulsion judgment was appealed by Palčiauskas before the Eleventh Circuit Court of Appeal on August 26, 1991, a few months before he died of a heart attack in St. Petersburg on January 7, 1992. Allen, pp. 9-10, Palčiauskas' Sentence, *The New York Times*, June 16, 1981 and December 7, 1982, *Orlando Sentinel*, January 10, 1992, Ryan, pp. 358-359.

30 The action of October 6, 1941 ended with the shooting at Fort no. IV of 534 so-called *intellectuals*, who had been ordered by Kaminskas to report for a simple filing job. Instead, the *action* of October 6 was directed against the small ghetto, from which at least 1,600 people were taken, then shot at Fort no. IV.

31 See Klaus-Michael Mallmann's article: *Vom Fussvolk der "Endlösung". Ordnungspolizei, Ostkrieg und Judenmord*. Tel Aviv, 1997.

32 Curilla, pp. 151, 174.

33 See § 8.2.

34 See § 8.2.

35 Mann, p. 266.

36 Curilla, p. 150. LG Kassel, 3a Ks 1/61 of January 9, 1963.

37 During an exchange of messages between Himmler, Prutzmann and Reichkommissar Lohse, dated August 24, that is a few days after the establishment of the ghetto (August 15), the use of Lithuanian guards in support of 3/ Polizei-Bataillon 11 - which had been engaged in the surveillance of the ghetto for several days - was authorized. Breitman, pp. 78, 271.

38 On September 15, the first 5,000 work permits were handed over to the Jewish Council which distributed them on the basis of the lists compiled by the offices of Fritz Jordan, with a limitation of "not more than one certificate per married couple". The tragedy was that the work permits bore the names of the holders and therefore could not be transferred to anyone, therefore these certificates protected only the direct owners of the work permits, while around them all their closest family members - children, spouses, parents - as well as more distant relatives, could be subject to *free hunt* during the selection. Tory, pp. 36-37.

39 Engel, appointed KDO "Litauen" around mid-September 1941 and Lechthaler, commander of Polizei-Bataillon 11, had a conflict concerning the management of Lithuanian auxiliary units, which until then had been controlled by Lechthaler, but whose command Engel was now claiming in view of his new role. The conflict was resolved by BDO Jedicke, firstly with a compromise and then by transferring Lechthaler to Belarus (October 6), along with two divisions of his battalion (2/11 and 4/11). Instead, battalion 1/11 remained in Lithuania, at Marijampole, while, as already mentioned, Tornbaum's 3/11 was placed at the command of Sicherheitspolizei. Stang, p. 187.

40 1/11 (HPTM Vanselow), the last of the four divisions of Polizei-Bataillon 11, stayed in Marijampole during summer / autumn 1941 and joined the rest of the battalion in Vitebsk, Russia, in late December of the same year.

41 Tory, p. 403.

42 Inciuriene, pp. 203-204.

43 Bubnys Hilfspolizeibataillone, p. 119.

44 *Ibid.*, p. 119, Dieckmann/Suziedėlis, pp. 31-32, 50-51.

45 Bubnys Hilfspolizeibataillone, pp. 119-120. Regarding the involvement of 4/TDA in the massacres of Rollkommando "Hamann" see § 8.2, *Band of slayers*.

46 Bubnys Hilfspolizeibataillone, p. 120, Bubnys Holocaust, p. 11.

47 Bubnys Holocaust, pp. 16-17. 1/PPT 3 was commanded by Hptm. Andrius Juškevičius, 2/PPT 3 by Ltn. Justinas Pakalniškis.

48 Bubnys Hilfspolizeibataillone, pp. 122-123, Bubnys Holocaust, p. 17.

49 Antanas Gudelis, born in 1911. A member of the third "Dragoons" Lithuanian regiment, on the eve of the Soviet invasion, he enlisted in the TDA-Batalionas on July 17, 1941 and was assigned to the seventh company as Švilpa's deputy; he was promoted to commander of 3/PPT on September 1, 1941. He emigrated to Australia in 1949 and obtained Australian citizenship in 1958. Living in Adelaide, he was accused by the Wiesenthal Center of having taken part in massacres in the Lithuanian town of Kupiskis between July and August 1941, as well as in the forts of Kaunas and in other places in early September (Leipalingis, Seirijai and Simnas); for that reason he was subjected to investigation by the Australian SIU between 1989 and 1991, but was acquitted for lack of concrete evidence. Then, in July 1999, his name was included in an investigative dossier opened by the Attorney General of Lithuania, which, however, was closed because Gudelis died on September 12, 1999. Singer / Grossmann, p. 497, Zuroff's interview to ABC, February 28, 2000.

50 Despite its name, in autumn 1941 Demokratenplatz was a large uncultivated area on the northern edge of the ghetto. It was later converted to agricultural use.

51 Curilla, p. 175.

52 *Ibid.*, p. 173. StAw Frankfurt am Main, 50/4 Js 284/71 of August 26, 1983 v. Rauca. According to the Prosecutor of

Frankfurt, Rauca and the others arrived in the square at around 07:00 hours.

53 Tory, p. 51-55.

54 This detail was confirmed by the Prosecutor of Frankfurt: StAw Frankfurt am Main, 50/4 Js 284/71 of August 26· 1983 v. Rauca: StAw Frankfurt am Main 4 Js 1106/59 of March 27, 1966, v. Heinrich Schmitz.

55 The term *partisans* is used by Tory to refer to the Lithuanian collaborationist groups who placed themselves at the service of the Germans. Therefore, this word must be understood in this way while reading this chapter, as it is used in strict adherence to the original text.

56 Elchanan Elkes (1979-1944), President of the *Judenrat* of Kaunas' ghetto. He died in Landsberg's concentration camp, Germany, on October 17· 1944.

57 According to one testimony, at some point in the evening, Rauca left the square and was replaced by Ltn. Iltmann, commander of a platoon of 3/11, who oversaw the selection of the last 5 or 6,000 Jews. This officer would prove to be quite *generous*, selecting only about thirty particularly sick and frail elderly men. Curilla, p. 174.

58 According to the Prosecutor of Frankfurt, those who died of exhaustion and were left on the square numbered between 10 and 15. StAw Frankfurt am Main, 50/4 Js 284/71 of August 26 1983 v. Rauca. Stang, p. 103, maintains that there were 30 victims.

59 See Chapter 7, note 30.

60 Curilla, p. 175, StAw Frankfurt am Main 4 Js 1106/59 of March 27, 1966, v. Heinrich Schmitz.

61 Tory, pp. 54-59.

62 Faitelson, pp. 152-153.

63 Ganor, pp. 175-176. Kopelman's testimony was published by his childhood friend Solly Ganor (Zalke Genkind) in his book *Light one Candle. A Survivor's Tale from Lithuania to Jerusalem* [ed.ted.: *Das andere Leben. Kindheit im Holocaust*]. Soon after its release, Ganor's book caused controversy concerning certain points of the story. The dispute was soon put to rest after Barbara Distel, the well-known historian and movie director of the Dachau memorial museum for over thirty years got involved, siding with Ganor.

64 Faitelson, pp. 154-155.

65 Margolian, pp. 113-114.

66 Kazys Šimkus: born in Riga (Latvia) on September 9, 1905. Graduated from a teaching school on September 7, 1925, he completed officer training at a military police school. Transferred to Naval Aviation he obtained a pilot's license on April 14, 1927. Promoted to Captain on November 23, 1932, he obtained the rank of Major on November 23, 1938 and was assigned to the command of the 4th bombers' Squadron. Discharged on July 2, 1940 after the Soviet invasion of Lithuania, he enlisted in TDA-Batalionas and became its commander on July 24, 1941, replacing Andrius Butkūnas. He held command of PPT-Batalionas 1 from August 7, 1941 until March 1942, that is during the period of the killings of Kaunas. Šimkus fled to Germany on a plane in October 1944 when the Soviet Army was advancing in Lithuania. In 1949 he managed to emigrate to Australia with his family and was accepted into the refugee camp of Bonegilla (Victoria), from which he immediately disappeared at some point in 1949, after being recognized by a young Jewish survivor, also resident there. He would then reside in Geelong (Victoria) and then in Melbourne, where he died on June 10, 1968. In the early nineties his name was included in a list of 38 Lithuanians residing in Australia deemed to be members of the TDA-Batalionas and placed under investigation by the Special Investigations Unit. In 1993, at the time of the redaction of SIU's final report, 18 suspects - including him - were dead.

67 Barzda Juozas, born in Kavolių, district of Zarasų, platoon commander in a Lithuanian infantry regiment on the eve of the Soviet invasion. Leader of a clandestine student resistance group active at the University of Kaunas. Member of Stab/TDA-Batalionas from June 28, 1941. Commander of 3/TDA-Batalionas from July 3, 1941 and then of 3/PPT-Batalionas 2 from August 25. He was replaced from the latter position by Hptm. Juozas Uselis and assigned to the Stab/PPT-Batalionas 2, with which he was transferred to Belarus at the beginning of October. Recalled to Kaunas at the end of the month and appointed Battalion's aide of Kazys Šimkus' PPT-Batalionas 1 he was transferred to Litauische-Schu-Bataillon 302 in 1944, as commander of the third company. Member of Lithuanian anti-Soviet resistance and commander of the partisan group "Vanagas" from August 19, 1944.

68 Dieckmann, pp. 448, 466.

69 Tory was called to testify, his diary acknowledged as evidence, in the hearings of Wiesbaden v. Heinrich Schmitz (commander of Abt. IV Gestapo of KdS "Litauen"), of Tampa v. Kazys Palčiauskas (mayor of Kanaus) and of Toronto v. Helmut Rauca (Schmitz's aide).

70 Curilla, p. 177. LG Wiesbaden, 4 Js 1106/59 – VU 3/61 of December 6, 1971.

71 Christopher R. Browning, *Der Weg zur Endlösung. Entschedungen und Täter*. Bonn, 1998.

72 Regarding the organization of the camps of Aktion Reinhardt, see Yitzhak Arad: *Belzec, Sobibor, Treblinka. The Operation Reinhardt Death Camps.*

73 The same Lithuanian *pogromists* who acted in the early days of *Barbarossa*, some of which were absorbed into militarized auxiliary units (including Šimkus') and that according to one theory *should demonstrate* an anti-Semitic attitude of the Lithuanian population completely independent of anti-Jewish policies applied from Berlin and powerfully implemented at the same time as the Soviet withdrawal from the country, become essentially irrelevant in the *general economy* of the Jewish genocide: in fact, the victims of pogroms (more organized than spontaneous), which took place in Kaunas in late June 1941, were no more than a thousand, as noted by Dieckmann / Sužiedėlis, p. 43. Basically, the theorem of an alleged political vendetta by the natives against the *Judeo-Bolshevik* oppressors is entirely misleading, as it applies only to some individual episodes spanning a very limited time-frame which took place in a political, operational and situational context in which the presence of the Sicherheitspolizei units - or at least their *inspiring* influence from outside - cannot be underestimated.

74 Bubnys Outline, p. 215.

75 For further information on the topic of genocidal decentralization, see § 8.6, *Objective: Genocide.*

76 The so-called Aktion-Kozlowski of September 26, 1941, which caused the death of 1,608 Jews, would have been committed as a *reprisal* for a gunshot from the side of the ghetto, in the direction of a certain Willi Kozlowski, a 3/11 officer on duty guarding the outer perimeter. The sheer ratio of the reprisal - 1,600 victims for a shot that did not reach the target - goes far beyond any conceivable proportions infinitely superior to the Sühnequote of 100 hostages for every German killed, applied in Serbia and already considered *a limit* in itself. This is enough to prove the obvious pretense of such justification.

77 See Rauca's order to the Judenrat of July 24, 1942: "Pregnancies and births are forbidden in the ghetto. Every pregnancy must be interrupted. Any woman in a state of pregnancy will be shot". Benz/Kwiet/Matthäus, p. 205.

78 Bubnys Outline, p. 214.

79 Dieckmann, p. 439.

80 Just to give an idea of the conditions that the ghetto-dwellers were subjected to, here is a list of the main food products that each of them was entitled to *weekly*, as per Stadtkommissar Cramer's order of August 26, 1942: 25 oz. of bread, 4.4 oz. of meat, 4 oz. of flour, 2.5 oz. of surrogates, 1.8 oz. of salt. The rations of bread and meat were rather *generously* doubled and supplemented by the addition of 0.7 oz. of fat to those Jews employed as workers for the Germans. Benz / Kwiet / Matthäus, p. 207. Cramer's Order to the Jewish Council of Kaunas, August 26, 1942.

81 Tomas Venclova, quoted by Leonidas Donskis, in the introduction of: *The Vanished World of the Lithuanian Jews,* p. X.

82 Alvydas Nikžentaitis/Stefan Schreiner/Darius Staliūnas: *The Vanished World of the Lithuanian Jews*, p. 1.

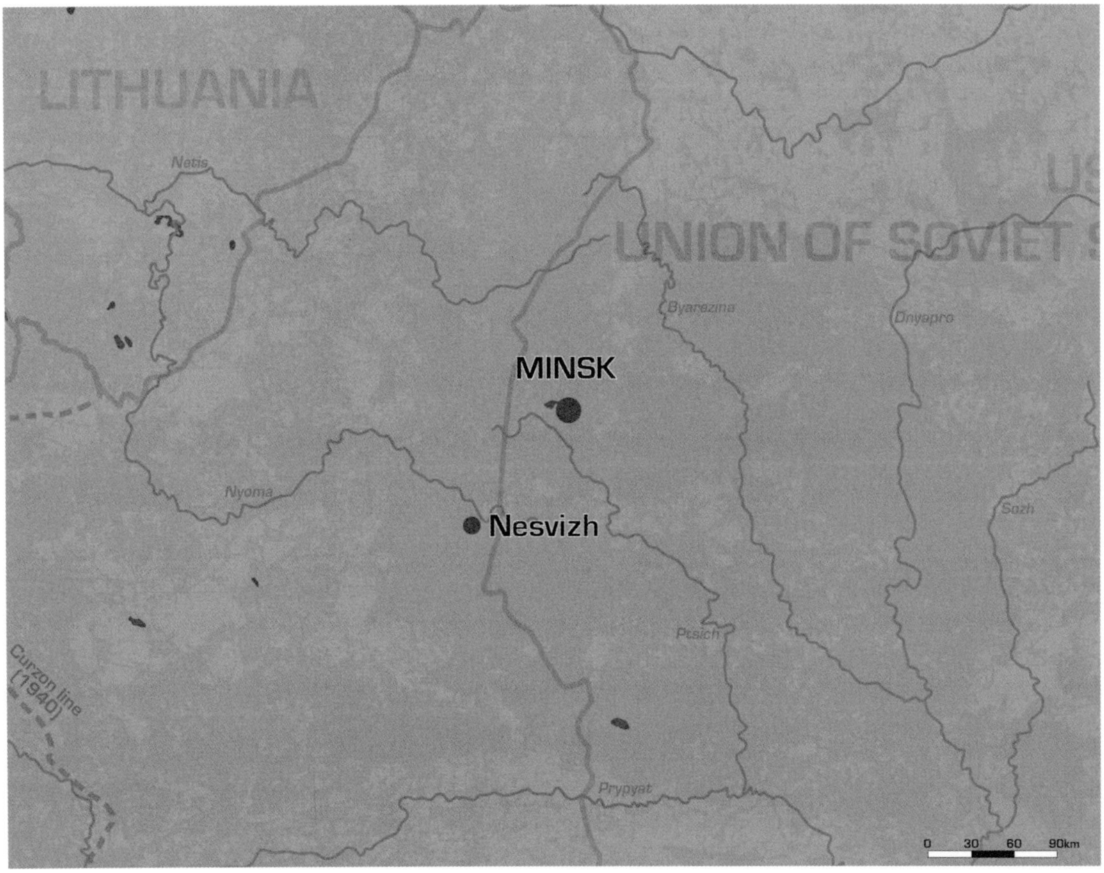
LITHUANIA
UNION OF SOVIET S
US
Neris
Byarezina
Dnyapro
MINSK
Nyoma
Nesvizh
Sozh
Ptsich
Curzon line (1940)
Prypyat
0 30 60 90km

CHAPTER EIGHT

"DAS FLACHE LAND IST VON JUDEN ZU SÄUBERN!"

«EINSATZGRUPPE LECHTHALER» AND THE SLAUGHTER OF NESVIZH OCTOBER 30, 1941

Überall da, wo die Juden unschaedlich gemacht worden sind, ist anscheinend Ruhe eingetreten.

Lagerbericht des Reserve-Polizei-Bataillon 11, October 21, 1941[1]

8.1 INTRODUCTION

Hammond, Indiana. US District Court, June 18, 1997

> *It is hereby ORDERED, ADJUDGED and DECREED that the naturalization order of this court entered February 17, 1955, granting United States citizenship to Kazys Ciurinskas is REVOKED AND SET ASIDE, and that Certificate of Naturalization No.7262096 is CANCELLED. It is further ORDERED that Kazys Ciurinskas shall, upon receipt of this order, SURRENDER Certificate of Naturalization No.7262096 to the Attorney General.*
>
> *The Clerk shall send a certified copy of this order and the Clerk's final judgment entry to the Attorney General. 8 U.S.C. § 4451(f).*
>
> *SO ORDERED.*

The sentence was as heavy as a stone and left no room for doubt or different interpretation of what the precise meaning of the few laconic lines with which Judge James T. Moody, of Hammond's District Court, had ruled his fate: revocation of citizenship, or, in bureaucratic terms, denaturalization. A single word that had the power to present devastating scenarios in front of him. He could certainly make an appeal against it, but, objectively, with very little hope of success. Those facts, coldly described in the pages of the ruling, nailed him to his past, which although very remote and almost forgotten, now resurfaced together with the very real prospect of him paying his dues.

Forty-eight years had passed since that October 24, 1949, when, coming from Europe, he had finally landed in New York. In the previous months he had gone through the lengthy red tape required to obtain entry visas to the United States as a Displaced Person, and all went smoothly: in May 1949 he had requested assistance from the International Refugee Organization which, on July 7, had granted him the longed-for DP-Certificate. He had then been questioned by CIC investigators, to whom he described his life as a mill worker in Kaunas, Lithuania, between 1936 and 1944, after which he had requested an entry visa for the United States to the American consulate of Blutzbach, Germany, where he had moved after the war. He had been interviewed by the vice-consul, who had finally approved his application on July 15, 1949. Then he had finally entered the United States, and had become an American citizen on February 17, 1955.

From that day he had lived quietly in Crown Point, Indiana, until the OSI men found out about him and opened the window on his past, on that long-gone autumn of 1941when his unit, Litauische-Schu-Bataillon 2 of Kaunas, was transferred to Minsk, Belarus. It was to that point, according to the Court of Hammond, that his original sin was to be traced back to.

We do not know for sure if Casey Kazys Ciurinskas, a building contractor in his second life in the USA and a member of a genocidal Lithuanian battalion during his first life in Eastern Europe, did actually actively participate in any execution, or if he was guilty of any war crimes. Neither the OSI investigation, nor the trial at the Court of Hammond could give a definitive answer on that[3]. What is certain is that Ciurinskas lied about his past when applying for an entry visa to the U.S., continued lying when he obtained the American citizenship a few years later and persisted in the lie even before the Court of Hammond, almost until the end, until the undeniable dark side that had enveloped his previous life - and that he had tried to keep hidden - was revealed in all its evidence, crumbling the castle of lies upon which he had built his second life. At that point, with the dissolution of the agreement based on trust between him and his adopted country at the time of entering the United States, the conditions that allowed him to remain in the country, including retaining his new nationality which was fraudulently acquired, also fell. From this point of view, if he did or did not participate in massacres took a backseat with regards to his belonging to a genocidal unit. This was not something that automatically made him a war criminal, but still sanctioned his "acquiescence towards activities and conduct contrary to civilization and human decency", such as to cast doubt on his "good moral character"[4] and thus to preclude his right to reside in the United States.

This mechanism hit many members of the Litauische-Schu-Bataillon 2 who had fled into American territory after the war. In fact, because the main concern of the administrative procedure was denaturalization, and not the allocation of *legal misconduct* onto the defendants, the criminal and *genocidal nature* of Litauische-Schu-Bataillon 2 - understood as an operating entity - was *transferred* to all its members taken as individuals, given the fact that they could not and did not want to change their individual orientation within *that* collective criminal reference system represented by the same battalion. Beyond his personal actions, Ciurinskas was then charged with regards to his *moral guilt*, or even more abstractly, his *metaphysical guilt*[5].

Regardless of whether or not Ciurinskas was personally and legally guilty, the actions of the Lithuanian battalion of which he was part of from late June 1941 to April 1942, are widely documented and can be summarized in the total of 14,000 to 17,000 victims in the period between early October and mid November 1941, i.e. the roughly six weeks during which the unit was located in Belarus, in the Minsk area, supporting two German companies of Polizei-Bataillon 11.

8.2 BAND OF SLAYERS

What arrived in Minsk at the beginning of October 1941 was the tactical evolution of an auxiliary Lithuanian battalion formed as early as June 28, 1941, which had passed through a series of renovations. It was originally formed around a core group of 150 nationalist volunteers and former militaries, members of two partisan groups (led by Kazys Šimkus and Bronius Norkus) used by Erich Ehrlinger of Einsatzkommando 1b for the surveillance of a prison camp in Fort n. VII [6]. Thanks to new recruitments during the days that followed its creation, however, it quickly rose in numbers to the point that, as early as July 4, it constituted a *Selbstschutz –Bataillon*, by German terminology, (a *Tautines Apsaugos Batailonas Darbo* -TDA- in Lithuanian), composed of as many as 724 elements in five companies, initially led by Andrius Butkūnas and then by Kazys Šimkus from mid-July[7].

The presence of this battalion is reported in EM 19 of July 11, 1941, which quotes that Sicherheitspolizei in Kaunas used a special unit (*Sonderabteilung*) of 250 Lithuanian auxiliaries to carry out executions (*Executionen*), particularly within the old fortifications and also outside the city[8]. Obviously, among the victims, which included communists, Soviet officials and political commissars, there were also Jews. Executions would be preceded and followed by copious libations of vodka by the executioners: as a matter of fact, alcohol – and, more generally, discipline - was a constant and unresolved issue among unit members, despite the punishment threatened and inflicted by both Butkūnas and his successor Šimkus[9]. In addition, at least in the early days, other forms of slackness including looting and violence against Jews, which often degenerated into brutal murders, were tolerated. Arbitrary arrests and unjustified summary executions were a daily ritual until at least July 11, when commander Butkūnas finally resolved to prohibit that kind of abuse, under the threat of draconian punishments[10]. This was in some part at the urging of the German military command in Kaunas that was worried about the mess caused by these actions and the negative repercussions on the same operations performed by Jäger's EK3.

With these measures, and others implemented in the following days, the anarchic improvisation of the *willing* but still amateurish Lithuanians was finally set aside, leaving room for the intervention of the disciplined and methodical German professionals of the Sicherheitspolizei. In this sense, during Jäger's strict management, TDA- Batalionas was duly co-opted as genocidal workforce in executions, especially at forts n. IV and n. VII and in Kaunas' central prison, to the point that in many cases, during the shootings, the intervention of German staff was limited to the infliction of death blows. In general, the executions took place in mass graves, the victims stretched out or kneeling on the bottom and the Lithuanians opening fire from above, standing on the edge of the pit, in some cases with machine guns[11]. From the comparison between the data shown in the companies' worksheets in July / August 1941 and the data reported in the well-known *Jäger-Bericht* of the same time, the presence of personnel drawn from different Lithuanian companies to Kaunas' forts n. IV and n. VII is clear on at least six different occasions, during which the massacre of a total of 3,174 Jews and 17 communists was perpetrated[12].

However, it was not only in Kaunas that TDA-Batalionas was able to fulfill its genocidal role in the summer of 1941; in fact they perpetrated a long series of massacres in the province, in support of Rollkommando "Hamann"[13] – a small detachment of Jäger's EK3 – to which, since June 29, a platoon of about sixty Lithuanian auxiliaries taking orders by Ltn. Bronius had been attached. This was probably the same partisan unit he was the leader of immediately after the start of Barbarossa[14]. This detachment, which then became the fourth platoon of 4/TDA, was considered, within the battalion, "a special unit (*Spezialabteilung*)"[15], used as genocidal workforce in rural areas around Kaunas, where no EK3 stable detachments had been implanted. Indeed, the massacres detailed in the aforementioned *Jäger report* perpetrated by Rollkommando "Hamann" and the Lithuanians between July 7 and October 2, 1941 – including that of Užusaliai, in which Kazys Ciurinskas also took part– with a total of 52,922 victims, were no less than 62[16].

The dynamics of the preparation of the Final Solution in Lithuania in the summer of 1941, as well as the *technical methods* applied to the perpetration of the massacres are well-known and detailed[17]: an exhaustive batch of information which leads us to identify Lithuania as both the experimental ground on which the Nazi program of annihilation was tested, and to recognize the genocidal actions that were perpetrated here as precursors of the continental Final Solution[18]. In this regard, it should be emphasized how the fine network spread in Lithuania by Sicherheitspolizei, only in part reinforced by the gradual onset of Ordnungspolizei units and facilities (including Polizei-Bataillon 11 commanded by Franz Lechthaler, arrived in Kaunas in early July) obtained a highly *significant result* in terms of victims - mostly Jews - in relation to the forces available. Such a result, obviously, would not have been achieved without the massive use of auxiliary Lithuanian units whose utilization by German controllers represents an achievement in the rationalization of available resources, as well as an excellent example of *business management* applied to the field of Jewish genocide.

In fact, if we look at the procedures, the execution of victims in the province was perpetrated mainly by the Lithuanians of Hamann's *kommando*, often supported by cores of local self-defense groups, who were assigned the tasks of searching for the victims as well as the surveillance of them and the preparation of the mass graves in the targeted areas. In other words, a task typical of skilled workers, who were flanked by few German elements assigned to the *kommando* in functions that were mainly clerical (coordination, control and management of field operations). One step above the ladder were the mid-level *executives*, such as Jaeger and Hamann, responsible for the entire genocidal project within their territories through decision-making, in particular with regards to the achievement of the *target* of victims, strategic planning according to the time and resources available, the choice of target areas and the issuance of the orders regarding the whole operation[19].

Within this semi-managerial scheme, such auxiliary units found themselves relegated to the role of mere material executors, free of any decision making power, and along way from being able to represent a movement of widespread popular reaction to the wrongdoings of Soviet occupation, i.e. a political phenomenon to be reckoned with. On the contrary, in the light of the tasks which they were meant to perform, these units reflected their supremely abstract *status* as real *non-entities* as intended by Bentham, created in order to produce among the Lithuanian population the instrumental belief of the existence of a situation which in fact was only imaginary, namely the coveted return to national autonomy, something that in deeds was immediately stifled by Nazi colonialism.

Under this point of view, the activation of TDA-Batalionas and its extensions worked very well as a *decoy* because the perception of this illusion was initially very strong, especially among nationalists, who enlisted in large numbers during July / August 1941, to the point that the six companies of TDA-Batalionas with a total of 874 men as of July 6, eventually became seven in August, more than twice the standard number of any ordinary German infantry battalion. All this despite the high rate of desertions and requests for leave that between July 5 and 11, had involved no fewer than 117 men, largely as a reaction to genocidal activities in which the battalion was constantly engaged[20].

This abnormality, combined with the German uncertainty regarding the political significance of keeping such a large number of men in one single structure, led to the splitting of the battalion which, on August 7 – a few days after the transfer of power from military to civilian administration – gave life to *Pagalbinės Policijos Tarnibos Batailionas 1* (PPT) and *Pagalbinės*

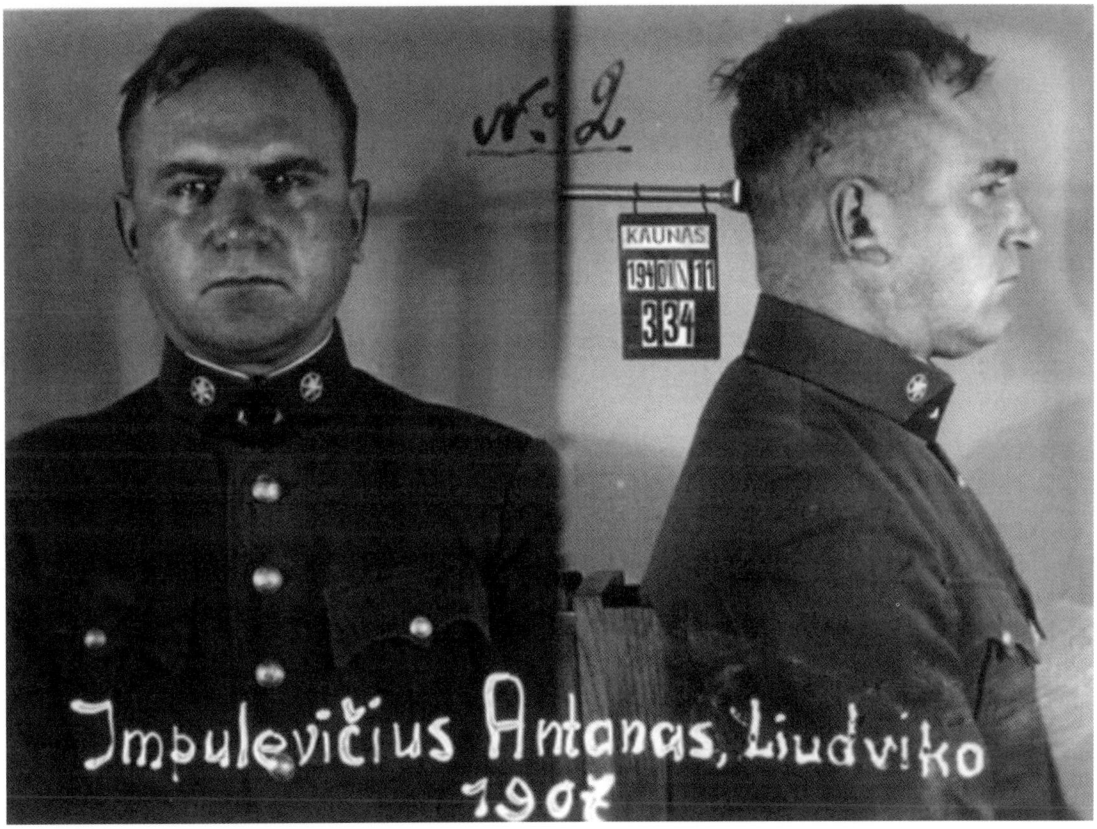

Antanas Impulevičius, wearing the uniform of the officials of the Lithuanian Army in 1940, after his arrest by NKVD. Switching to the Germans' side in late June 1941, after the war he fled to the United States, where he died in 1970.

Policijos Tarnibos Batailionas 2. These units were commanded by Kazys Šimkus, (with former third, fourth and fifth TDA companies), and Antanas Impulevičius, with former TDA first (Ltn. Zenonas Kemsura, 1/PPT 2), second (Oltn. Juozas Krištaponis, 2/PPT 2) and sixth (Juozas Uselis, 3/PPT 2) companies respectively[21]. These battalions were identified in German as *Litauische-Schu-Bataillone 1 and 2*[22] and, as of Oct. 5, 1941, were both placed under Franz Lechthaler's authority. Only Impulevičius' battalion, though, was sent to Belarus, together with two companies of Polizei-Bataillon 1. Among those who left for Minsk on October 6, was Kazys Ciurinskas, a member of the second company[23].

With the transfer to Belarus, the genocidal parable of TDA-Batalionas and its offshoots was going to reach a climax: born enthusiastically in the days of the Soviet retreat from Kaunas as a cluster of guerrilla units, it had been co-opted in the mass-executions of Kaunas and its province through its detachments, to the point of becoming a bunch of willing executioners, perhaps tellingly, often drinking a lot[24]. The unit, however, became so accustomed to genocidal practices that they could actually be asked to perform the same task - after *completing the work* in Lithuania - beyond national borders.

8.3 DOMINUS IN TERRAM

We have already mentioned in Chapter 7 the role played by Franz Lechthaler and his Polizei-Bataillon 11 in the resolution of the *Jewish question* in Kaunas. However, his function as *dominus* concerning also the management of Lithuanian auxiliaries, and the conflicting relationship that he had with the newly-established KdO "Lituanien", which was probably the origin of his transfer to Belarus, is worth a mention in this section.

The transfer of power from the Wehrmacht military administration to the civilian one of Reichkommissar von Renteln, which occurred on July 17,[25] carried a reorganization of military structures, hitherto focused – in Kaunas – on Feldkommandantur 821 (Gen.Maj. Robert von Pohl)[26] as the main security entity in the urban area and surrounding district. For unspecified reasons, the expected activation of a general command of Ordnungspolizei for Lithuania (KdO) only took place in mid-September. Therefore, in this period of interregnum, Lechthaler found himself having to play the role of *pro-tempore* KdO, by virtue of his rank and his unit which, at that stage, was the main German unit at the disposal of FK 821. All that was enough to also get control of Lithuanian auxiliary units, as per instructions received on July 30 by Wehrmacht-Befehlshaber "Ostland" Gen.Ltn. Braemer. Lechthaler gave notice of the new situation to the Lithuanian military commander of Kaunas, Stasys Kviečinskas, in two dispatches sent on August 6 and 7, informing about the project to split TDA-Batalionas and the need to obtain unconditional respect of orders, together with the battalion's assignment of a new name, from TDA to PPT[27]. Kviečinskas himself was appointed liaison officer of the Lithuanian battalions for KdO by a subsequent order issued by Lechthaler dated November 25, 1941.

The ambivalence of Lechthaler's role as *acting on behalf of* KdO and holding the KdO position becomes rather confused as this position was actually occupied by Maj. A. Engel, in mid-September 1941[28]. On October 5, in fact, a few days after the arrival of Engel in Kaunas, a compromise was found between the two for the *subdivision* of the two Lithuanian battalions already established or about to be established: Lechthaler would get control over *Litauische-Schu-Bataillone 1, 2* and *3* (PPT 1, 2, and 3), while Engel would get control over the new *Litauische-Schuma-Bataillone 4* and *5*[29]. However, it was evident that this dualism was rather byzantine and difficult to sustain over the long term. Thus, the following day (October 6) BDO "Ostland" Jedicke sent Lechthaler the order to move to Belarus with two companies of Polizei-Bataillon 11 and the entire Litauische-Schuma-Bataillon 2[30]. It is plausible, from this point of view, that Jedicke's decision was dictated by a desire to strengthen Engel's position in Kaunas because soon after on December 16, 1941, Engel's supremacy was finally confirmed by a notice sent to Lechthaler, who had recently returned from Minsk with his men[31].

According to a report (*Lagerbericht*) regarding Polizei-Bataillon 11 filed on October 21, 1941, there were 775 men accompanying Lechthaler in Belarus: of these, 314 belonged to the two companies of Polizei-Bataillon 11 (2/11 and 4/11) and the others to Litauische-Schuma-Bataillon 2[32]. Reading what BDO Jedicke announced from Riga on October 17 their task was to "fight partisan groups in connection with the Wehrmacht"[33]. That was the theory; in practice, things did not go exactly that way.

In fact, as confirmed in the same report of Polizei-Bataillon 11, as many as 4,142 "hostile elements (*deutschfeindlichen Elemente*)" were *liquidated* by German policemen and Lithuanians auxiliaries in the period between October 14 and 21 alone - that is to say during a *single week* of operations - with *no losses suffered* [!]; no dead, no wounded[34]. This is a very *remarkable* result, which confirms the effectiveness of Lechthaler's men against opponents who were obviously unarmed. From this point of view the genocidal expertise accumulated in Lithuania in previous weeks was proving particularly useful.

Indeed, the role of Lechthaler and his men in Belarus was one of support to a real campaign of annihilation disguised in terms of security operations, initiated by commander of 707.ID Gustav von Bechtolsheim in his new role as military commander of GK "Weissruthenien", to which Lechthaler's units were also subordinated[35]. It seems that this campaign, instigated by von Bechtolsheim, was agreed upon with Wehrmacht-Befehlshaber "Ostland" Braemer, and, probably, "Berück Mitte" Max von Schenckendorff, each in his own territory or jurisdiction[36]. The relocation of Lechthaler in Belarus - probably the response to a request made by Braemer[37] - was how BDO Jedicke himself did not miss the opportunity to earn political points, while at the same time addressing the *controversy* of Kaunas. Thus, it seems clear that the genocidal campaign launched in GK "Weissruthenien" in autumn 1941 originated from a common ground of responsibilities attributable to the Wehrmacht, but the leading roles, in terms of active participation in the massacres, were actually performed by the experienced German and Lithuanian perpetrators of Lechthaler *dominus*.

8.4 QUIET NEIGHBORS

In his testimony given on May 16, 1960, during the preliminary investigation that later flowed into the process of Kassel, one of the defendants, Willi Papenkort, former commander of 2/Polizei-Bataillon 11, labeled *Aktion Judenrein* the genocidal campaign hatched to *solve* the problem of Jewish ghettos in Western Belarus, i.e. to eradicate from the territory, according to the official version, the threat posed by so-called Judeo-Bolshevism[38]. This campaign was triggered by an obsession with security by the rear-line commanders of the Wehrmacht, often mixed with deep anti-Semitic prejudices – whose origin dated back to the political troubles of 1919-1923 and the territorial questions along the eastern border, especially in Upper Silesia – more than by a real threat represented by partisan groups; which, in truth, was always somewhat relative within the borders of GK "Weissruthenien". The following remarks by historian Hannes Heer, effectively summarizes the political-ideological vision common among senior ranks of the Wehrmacht:

> *The Jews and the partisans had taken over the role of the Spartakists, the first name of the German Communist Party, in all their insidious metamorphoses. The ghettos, created by the generals seemed more and more like breeding grounds for conspiracy and uprising: fleeing from the threatened massacre, the Jews transmitted the poison of disintegration into Russian villages*"[39].

Instead of trying to understand the social dynamics that favored the spread of the insurgency, let alone trying to *predict* the mechanisms of cause / effect between occupier and occupied, of all possible solutions to this problem, the vision that prevailed, simplistic and specious as it was, is summarized in a report by von Bechtolsheim on November 5, 1941: "The Jews, without exception, are in all respects identical to the partisans"[40]. Inevitably, the result of such a theory, albeit untried but easy to understand, was an unexpected similarity of purpose between the alleged military needs of the Werhmacht and the political and ideological approach of SS and Police structures, which produced a violent genocidal campaign in rural areas of Western Belarus. For about a month, from October 1941 to early November, within the territory under the administration of Felkommandanturen 812 (Minsk) and 250 (Baranovichi), Lechthaler's men from detachment "Schlegel" of EK8 – (*Nachkommando*) – perpetrated a long series of massacres on an almost daily basis: Uzlyany/Dukora (8/10), Rudensk (9÷11/10), Kliniki (13/10), Smolevichi (14/10), Logoysk (15/10), Pleschchenitzy (16/10), Minsk (16 and 18/10), Koydanovo (21/10), Molodechno (26/10), Slutsk (27-28/10), Kletsk (30÷31/10) and finally, Nesvizh (31/10)[41]. As regards the final action, it was perpetrated by Ortskommandantur "Neswish" of Oberfeldwebel Anton – with 20/30 soldiers of 8./IR 727 within its ranks – in collaboration with the Lithuanian auxiliaries of PPT-Batalionas 2, with a detachment of Polizei-Bataillon 1 and elements of the local Belarusian infantry.

Besides those mentioned, in other cases the massacres of autumn 1941 in the GK "Weissruthenien" were also actively performed by units of 707.ID, and by the German territorial gendarmerie. In Mir, for example, (November 9, 1941), the action was performed by the staff of the Ortskommandantur of Stolpce (Oltn. Ludwig Göbel), supported by Belarusian auxiliaries; in Slonim (November 14), men of 3/Polizei-Bataillon 69 and 6./IR 727/707.ID were called in, supported by members of Gendarmerie-Posten "Slonim", staff of KDS-Außenstelle "Baranovichi" (Waldemar Amelung), Belarusian auxiliaries and an unidentified detachment of Latvians or Lithuanians, possibly commanded by Amelung. In Novogrudok (December 5), the seventh company of IR 727/707.ID was called in[42]. In other words, because *Aktion Judenrein* was not inspired by Sipo-SD or by the political authority of HSSPF / SSPF as in eastern Belarus, but by the rear-line commanders of the Wehrmacht[43], participation in the massacres was quite varied and each time performed by the units available at the time.

The fact remains, however, that in the roughly four weeks in which Lechthaler and his men were stationed in Belarus, it was those men of Polizei-Bataillon 11 and PPT-Batalionas 2 who represented the bulk of *weltanschauungstruppen* which went on to form something very close to a real additional *Einsatzgruppe*.

A few years later, after the war, it was precisely this role, i.e. the awareness of having been used as mere instruments of genocide by their Germans controllers, that influenced many members of the PPT-Batalionas 2 – who fled to the West as *Displaced Persons* and could not return to Soviet-reoccupied Lithuania – in the misrepresentation and / or concealment of their *wartime* past at the time of the investigative procedures for issuing entry visas to the United States and elsewhere. Some decades later however, after the opening of archives in Eastern Europe, the past re-emerged for many of them, which resulted in proceedings for denaturalization, as with Ciurinskas.

For each of these refugees it is almost impossible to prove *beyond a shadow of a doubt* a precise personal criminal responsibility in relation to specific criminal cases. All of them took part in at least one of the actions with roles and actions that probably varied each time. Nevertheless, because proceedings for denaturalization are regulated by the Civil Code, and not the criminal one, such cautiousness is irrelevant for the establishment of the existence of a fraudulent administrative offense made in intentional bad faith such as immigration in the absence of necessary requirements. Therefore, opposing all legal countermeasures during the hearings by the various defendants was essentially futile.

Let's remember some of them:

8.4.1 – Stab/Litauische-Schuma-Bataillon 2 – Maj. Antanas Impulevicius

GRABAUSKAS, Juozas: born 1920. Lieutenant. Enlisting in CT-Batalionas on July 11, 1941 he became commander of the fourth platoon of 2/PPT-Batalionas

2 on the following August 27. He was transferred to Belarus with the rest of his unit, through Order Document n. 42 dated October 6, 1941[44]. He took refuge in the United States after the war and lived in Chicago working as a chemist. His identity was uncovered by OSI investigators and he was accused of illegal immigration and thus deprived of American citizenship. Subject to deportation proceedings, Juozas *Joseph John* Grabauskas voluntarily returned to Lithuania in late October 1993, before the court decree[45]. According to the allegations made against him by the OSI, during a massacre he inflicted the coup de grâce to the victims that were only wounded by the firing squad[46].

IMPULEVIČIUS, Antanas: born January 28, 1907 in Panevezys. Released from military school in 1925 as a company commander, he was attached to the command of the 2nd Lithuanian Infantry Division, with which he served from November 1933 to October 1934. A graduate at the officers' staff School in June 1937, he was arrested by the NKVD after the Soviet invasion. Released in the early days after *Barbarossa*, as of June 28, 1941 he became deputy commander of TDA-Batalionas (PPT-Batalionas 2 from the following August 7). Transferred to Belarus in October to November 1941 and a member of General Plechavičius' *Lietuvos vietinė rinktinė*, after the dissolution of that organization by the Germans in May 1944, he managed to reach Germany the following October, escaping the Red Army. Emigrated to the U.S. in 1949, he was tried in absentia by a Soviet court and sentenced to death *in absentia*[47]. An American citizen from 1964, residing in Philadelphia, he changed his name to Antanas Impulionis [8]. Moscow's request for extradition was rejected by the U.S. government. He died in Philadelphia on December 4, 1970. Antanas Gecevičius (see § 8.4.2) was a member of Stab / TDA-Batalionas who, like Impulevičius, was transferred to 1/PPT-Batalionas 2

PUKYS, Povilas: born 1914. Adjutant of TDA-Batalionas, on July 14, 1941 he assumed command of the second company, replacing the deceased HPTM. Bronius Kirkila. On the following August 25 he was appointed aide to PPT-Batalionas 2. After the war, Pukys found refuge in New Zealand under the name of Jonas Pukas. He was identified in Auckland in 1989, after Efraim Zuroff of the Wiesenthal Center transmitted a list of suspected war criminals to the New Zealand government. Investigated by a team led by Detective Senior Sergeant Wayne Stringer, Pukys was not prosecuted due to a lack of sufficient evidence to convict him and his file was closed in 1992. He died in 1994. During the two interrogations he was submitted to, led by Stringer himself in April and June 1992, Pukys denied any involvement in war crimes, merely conceding, reluctantly and contradictorily, his role as a *riding instructor of German officers*, and his position as a mere eyewitness. In that capacity, amidst confirmations and denials, he would have *witnessed* the massacre of Minsk during which, according to his own words, at the time of the executions, the Jews "would yell like gooses" [sic]. While acknowledging his presence in the city in the days of the massacre, along with another 70 or 80 fellow soldiers, he denied being aware of the massacre in Slutsk. In the course of their investigations in Israel and Lithuania, New Zealander investigators Stringer and Kevin Marlow recovered circumstantial evidence about the participation of Pukys in the massacre that took place in the Lithuanian town of Užusaliai (the same that Ciurinskas also took part in) and heard various testimonies most of which were reluctant or insufficient. In any case, in the opinion of Stringer, "if there was a culprit, that was Pukys". Among the witnesses heard in Lithuania was Juozas Aleksynas, one of the accusers of Antanas *Gecas* Gecevičius. In turn, Pukys was questioned in Auckland regarding the case of Gecas by Scottish investigator, Chief Inspector John Montgomery[49].

8.4.2 – 1/Litauische-Schuma-Bataillon 2 – Ltn. Zenonas Kemsura

ALEKSYNAS, Juozas: born 1914, corporal of 1/PPT-Batalionas, a member of Antanas *Gecas* Gecevičius' platoon. Residing in Vilnius, Lithuania, he gave his testimony to the Lithuanian public prosecutor Valentukevicius, engaged in preparing the dossier for the extradition of Gecas, submitted to the Ministry of Justice of Scotland in February 2001. According to his testimony, the battalion was transferred to Belarus "in order to exterminate the Jews", but any such action would take place "with the participation of the Germans". In this respect Gecas, who was fluent in German, "would receive orders directly from the Germans and act accordingly"[50]. During another testimony given to New Zealand investigators in the case against Povilas *Jonas* Pukys, Aleksynas confirmed the presence *of the entire battalion* during the Slutsk massacre with the staff of the three companies taking turns shooting the victims in the mass graves[51].

GECEVIČIUS, Antanas [Gecas]: born May 26, 1916 in Jokuliai, Memel area (Klaipeda). A cadet of the Military Academy of Lithuania from September 1937, he received the rank of second lieutenant in the Air Force in August 1938. He went into hiding after the Soviet invasion and joined TDA-Batalionas with which, between July 4 and 6, 1941 he participated in the executions perpetrated on Jäger's orders in Fort n. VII of Kaunas, as well as in the Garliava massacre of late August / September 1941. Promoted to lieutenant on July 30, he was appointed commander of the third platoon of 1/PPT 2 with which he was transferred to Belarus and then involved in the mass-killings at Dukora, Koydanovo and Slutsk[52]. According to the testimony of former comrades - including Juozas Aleksynas, corporal of 1/PPT 2 - collected by the Lithuanian Public Prosecutor during the compilation of the dossier for his extradition from Scotland, in all these cases Gecevičius would give the order to fire and would personally carry out several shootings with his gun[53]. He was awarded the Iron Cross, probably on a date following the dissolution of the battalion operated by the Germans, in February 1944, and became attached to an ancillary unit operating in Italy, from which he then deserted in September of the same year together with a large group of fellow soldiers, probably a whole company of 160 men, many of whom were also members of PPT-Batalionas 2. In November, he enlisted in the Polish forces of General Anders, and was probably attached to the 2nd Independent Polish Commando Company and received a decoration for his bravery[54]. Once he reached Britain in 1946 along with Anders' Polish men, he was demobilized in 1947 in Johnston, Renfrewshire, near Glasgow. A British citizen from 1956, he lived in Edinburgh under the name of *Gecas*, and worked as an engineer in the mining sector – possibly developing links with government sectors during the miners' strikes in 1973 – and obtained the retirement pension in 1981. Traced in 1986 by an investigator of the Wiesenthal Center, he was the target of an investigative proceeding by the *Crown Office War Crime Unit,* led by Chief Inspector John Montgomery, regarding at least 10 murders, which was followed in 1987 by a journalistic investigation by STV (Scottish Television), which made public the story of the *quiet neighbor* Gecevičius *Gecas*. Then, despite the emergence of authoritative voices to the contrary, in 1994 the judicial investigation of the *Crown Office* was closed in the context of the *War Crime Act*, having been unable to gather concrete evidence on *Gecas'* involvement in criminal actions. Among the witnesses was also Povilas Pukys, questioned by Montgomery in Auckland, New Zealand, in 1992. After being dismissed, the investigation against *Gecas* was re-opened on July 27, 2001, following a request for extradition by the Lithuanian government. The extradition was rejected by the *Crown Office* on September 4, 2001, because of *Gecas*'s failing health, confirmed by independent appraisals. Gecas died in hospital a few days later, on September 12, in the aftermath of a heart attack. According to unconfirmed KGB documents, for a certain period Gecevičius *Gecas* had links with the British MI6[55]. Not to be confused with Vytautas Gecas, rifleman, a member of 2/PPT-Batalionas 2.

KATINAUSKAS, Motiejus: born 1914. Rifleman. Member of 1/TDA-Batalionas from July 22, 1941, when the battalion was split he was assigned to 1/PPT-Batalionas 2 and then transferred to Belarus, with the rest of his unit, through Order Document n. 42 dated October 6, 1941 [56]. After the war he managed to reach the United States, where he changed his name to

Matthew Katin, with residence in Norwood (Mass.), not far from his former comrade Vytautas Gudauskas (former 2/PPT-Batalionas 2), with whom he shared the following process of denaturalization. Tracked down by OSI investigators, on November 9, 1984, he was accused of illegal immigration in the United States and was then subjected to proceedings for the revocation of citizenship. In May 1989, the proceedings against Katinauskas was still being debated amid legal skirmishes concerning the modalities of acceptance, by the court, of testimonies given by Soviet citizens residing within the USSR, as had been requested since July 1985 by OSI lawyer John Loftus. The objections to such testimonies by the defendants' lawyers (Neil Hartzell of Sherin & Lodgen), had basically blocked the progress of the proceedings until the beginning of 1989[57].

NAUJALIS, Juozas: born 1919. He served in the Lithuanian Army from 1938 to 1940 and returned to civilian life in July 1940. Then, in early August 1941, he volunteered in TDA-Batalionas as a member of the First Company[58]. Promoted to corporal, he was assigned to 1/PPT-Batalionas and transferred to Belarus on October 6, 1941 with the rest of the battalion[59]. Apparently engaged in Minsk on garrison duty from November 1 to 14 he was assigned to the Koydanovo garrison. He deserted the battalion in November 1943 and was captured and sentenced to one year in prison, after which he was deported to Germany as a forced worker[60]. He remained in Germany after the war, where he obtained on May 16, 1949, the coveted status of *Displaced Person* from DPC, which allowed him to apply for an entry visa to the United States, which he obtained, entering the United States the following August. A resident of Cicero (Ill.), in the Chicago area, he was tracked down by OSI investigators, to whom he gave a sworn statement about his assignment in October 1941, to a guard unit employed solely in the surveillance of the railway station in Minsk. Accused of collaboration in the persecution of Jews as a member of a battalion in the service of the Nazis, in October 1995 he was called to give evidence in order to clarify his position before the Immigration Court. Having failed to produce what was required of him, and having never requested American citizenship, in April 1997 he received a deportation order to Lithuania. After an initial appeal rejected by the *Board of Immigration Appeal* (BIA), Naujalis then turned to the Court of Appeals for the 7th Circuit (Judge Richard A. Posner), the hearing set on September 28, 2000 and the decision confirming the judgment of expulsion was issued on February 15, 2001[61]. Following that judgment Naujalis declined to appeal to the Supreme Court and obeyed the order of expulsion on March 15, 2001. After his return home, the Director of the *Special Investigation Division* of the Public Prosecution of Lithuania, Rimvydas Valentukevicius, who in turn had opened an investigation on Naujalis, confirmed that he had still not found evidence in relation to his possible criminal conduct during his period of service with the PPT-2 Batalionas[62].

8.4.3 – 2/Litauische-Schuma-Bataillon 2 – Oltn. Juozas Krištaponis

BUDREIKA, Juozas: born 1917. Enlisted in TDA-Batalionas, he was assigned as a gunner to 2/PPT-Batalionas 2 on August 1941 and was then transferred to Belarus with the rest of his company the following October 6, as confirmed by Order Document n. 42 dated October 6, 1941[63]. In 1958 he managed to reach the United States, where he obtained citizenship in 1967. A resident of Gulfport, Florida, he worked as a chef. He was tracked down by OSI investigators, who opened the proceedings for denaturalization against him. In September 1994, after admitting before OSI his fraudulent and illegal entry into the U.S., he agreed to return voluntarily to Lithuania even before seeing his U.S. citizenship revoked. As agreed, Juozas *Joseph* Budreika left the United States for Vilnius on May 14, 1996. A few days later, on May 28, the District Court in Tampa (Judge Steven D. Merryday) formally sanctioned his denaturalization. He died in 1996, shortly after his return to Lithuania[64].

GECAS, Vytautas: born 1922 in Naumiestis, district of Taurage. A fusilier, member of 2/PPB-Batalionas 2 from July 7, 1941 he was transferred to Belarus with the rest of his unit, as confirmed by Order Document n. 42 dated October 6, 1941[65]. He found haven in England in 1947, and in August 1962 he requested the entry visa to the United States at the U.S. consulate in Liverpool and obtained a temporary permit for four months. Consequently, he reached U.S. territory on October 23, settling first in Chicago and then, from 1989, in Sunny Hill, Florida. Investigated by OSI investigators from July 25, 1991, on September 12 of that year he refused to respond to the long list of questions about his past in Europe between 1940 and 1944, and also failed to provide documentation as to the regularity of his entry into the U.S. Refusing to do so again a year later before the Judge of the District Court of Northern Florida and despite the obligation laid down in this direction by the Court of Appeals – whose judgment was confirmed by the Supreme Court in 1997 – on May 4, 1999, Gecas was jailed for 18 months in Pensacola (Fl) for contempt of court. After his release he was subjected to the procedure of expulsion by the OSI, during which he finally admitted to have participated, together with his unit, in several murderous actions in Belarus. Expelled from the United States, he returned to Lithuania on August 31, 2003[66].

GUDAUSKAS, Vytautas: born April 22, 1918. Member of 2/PPT-Batalionas 2, he was transferred to Belarus, as confirmed by Order Document n. 42 dated October 6, 1941[67]. After the war he managed to reach the United States, where he obtained American citizenship and resided in Gilbertville (Mass.), not far from his former comrade Motiejus Katinauskas (former 1/PPT-Batalionas 2), with whom he would share the court case that was to follow. He was discovered by OSI investigators and charged with illegal immigration. The first hearing in the trial for his denaturalization was held on June 1, 1984 at the Federal District Court in Boston[68]. In May 1989 the proceedings against Gudauskas were still being debated amid legal skirmishes related to the modalities of acceptance, by the court, of testimonies given by Soviet citizens living in the USSR, as required since July 1985 by OSI lawyer John Loftus. The objections to such testimonies by the defendants' lawyer (Randolph Tucker of Hill & Barlow), had basically blocked the progress of the proceedings until the beginning of 1989[69]. Gudauskas died on November 15, 1997 in Old Furnace, Worcester (Mass.), without having been expelled from the United States.

JUODIS, Jurgis: born 1911 in Kaunas. A member of 2/PPT-Batalionas 2, he too, like Ciurinskas, was subjected to the process of denaturalization by the District Court in Tampa (Fl). Becoming a member of TDA-Batalionas, on June 28, 1941, Juodis was appointed commander of the third platoon of 2/PPT-Batalionon 2 on August 27, 1941. Transferred to Belarus in October / November 1941, he took part in the killings at Rudensk and Slutsk. He took refuge in the United States in 1954 and obtained American citizenship in 1955. A resident of St. Petersburg Beach, Florida, he made a name for himself as a successful painter. Accused of "arrest, detention and murder of unarmed Jews and other civilians in Lithuania and Belarus" he was investigated by the OSI as of October 26, 1981 for entering the U.S. illegally, but died after 1985, before the trial had begun[70].

KLIMAVIČIUS, Jonas: born August 29, 1907 in Marijampole. Lieutenant, platoon commander of 2/PPT-Batalionas 2 he was transferred to Belarus with the battalion on October 6, 1941[71]. He was in Germany after the war with *Displaced Person* status, and managed to reach the United States on May 14, 1949. An American citizen from 1954, he initially resided in Long Island and then in Wells, Maine, working as an engine driver. OSI investigators tracked him down and interrogated him for the first time in July 1983. On May 30, 1984 he was formally charged with "collaborating in the persecution of Jews and other civilians, as a member of a police battalion controlled by the Nazis" and for entering the U.S. illegally on the basis of false statements knowingly issued when he obtained the entry visa. Subpoenaed to provide documentation in his favor, he had his U.S. citizenship revoked by the Court of Portland (Ma), on September 28, 1987, having failed to provide what was needed of him[72]. Following a further appeal by the defense, the decision of Judge Gene Carter was overturned in July 1988 by the Court of Appeals in Boston that planned a new hearing for December 12, 1988. Then, a few days before the trial, following an agreement signed with Eli Rosenbaum of OSI, Klimavičius agreed to renounce his American citizenship and committed to providing OSI with information on other PPT-2 Batalionas' former comrades already resident in the Boston area (Kisielaitis and Gudauskas), in exchange for his deportation order being revoked. The agreement between Rosenbaum and Klimavičius was signed on Monday, November 28, 1988[73].

KRIŠTAPONIS, Juozas: born March 1, 1912 in Uzulenis, Ukmerge district, nephew of former Lithuanian President Antanas Smetona. Lieutenant in the 2nd Infantry Regiment of Lithuania, after the Soviet invasion he was automatically transferred to the 184th Infantry Division of the 29th Army Corps. A Red Army deserter, he joined the TDA-Batalionas in Kaunas and from August 1, 1941, became commander of the second company, attached to Batalionas PPT-2. Transferred to Belarus, he became involved in the genocidal campaign: according to one witness, on the occasion of the Rudensk massacre he exempted 15 or 17 of his men from participating in executions, accepting their objections[74]. He returned to Kaunas and remained in command of the company until September 30, 1942, when he was assigned to Litauische-Schu-Bataillon 252. A member of Lietuvos Laisvės Armijos, he went into hiding when the Red Army returned in August 1944. In December 1944 he was appointed commander of the partisan district of Vytis. He was killed in battle by NKVD troops on January 12, 1945, in the Uzulenis forest.

MAČIUKAS, Mamertas: rifleman, a member of 2/TDA-Batalionas from July 7, 1941, he was assigned to 2/PPT-Batalionas 2, with which he was transferred to Belarus in October / November 1941 [75]. He fled to Canada after the war, and was subjected to a denaturalization process that ended with Mačiukas' voluntary departure from the country and subsequent revocation of his citizenship on April 30, 1998.

MINEIKIS, Antanas: born 1917, he enlisted in PPT-Batalionas 2. He was assigned to the second company with which he was sent to Belarus on October 6, 1941, through Order Document n. 42 dated October 6, 1941[76]. Later, probably in early 1944, after the dissolution and disarmament of the battalion by the Germans, Mineikis was transferred to a Lithuanian auxiliary unit relocated in Italy from which, along with many other comrades, he deserted at the end of the year to join the Polish troops of General Anders. Attached to the 2nd Polish Independent Commando Company, he reached England in 1946 with the rest of the Polish forces and was granted British citizenship in 1956[77]. Soon after, he moved to the United States. A resident of Gulfport, Florida, he became an American citizen and ran a motel until OSI investigators tracked him down and subjected him to denaturalization proceedings. In his sworn statement, Mineikis admitted his participation, in several cases, to the transport by trucks of civilians, including women and children, to mass graves, as well as witnessing the shootings. Stripped of American citizenship in January 1992 by the U.S. District Court in Tampa, Mineikis returned to Vilnius, Lithuania, on September 15, 1992 having received the deportation order from the immigration judge in Miami. In 1993, on grounds of failing health, his case was finally closed due to lack of evidence from the Lithuanian Public Prosecutor in charge of investigating war crimes. Admitted to a nursing home, he died from the aftereffects of a stroke on November 24, 1997[78].

8.4.4 – 3/Litauische-Schuma-Bataillon 2 – Hptm. Juozas Uselis

BENKUSKAS, Henrikas: born April 5, 1920 in Kaunas. Enlisted in TDA-Batalionas, he was assigned to 3/PPT-Batalionas 2 as a gunner and was then transferred to Belarus, as confirmed by Order Document n. 42 dated October 6, 1941[79]. After the war he managed to reach the United States in 1949. A resident of Chicago, he never requested U.S. citizenship. Tracked down by OSI investigators, on March 25, 1984 he was accused of "having taken part in the executions of Lithuanian Jews in the Kaunas forts, as well as being involved in the imprisonment and murder of Jews and other unarmed civilians and Soviet prisoners of war in the Minsk-Borisov-Slutsk area"[80]. He underwent a deportation procedure formally launched on June 2, 1984[81].

KISIELAITIS, Juozas: born November 23, 1920. Enlisted in PPT-Batalionas 2, he was attached as a rifleman to the third company and was then transferred to Belarus, as confirmed by Order Document n. 42 dated October 6, 1941[82]. He fled to Germany in 1944 after the Soviet return to Lithuania and at the end of the conflict was admitted to a *Displaced Persons Camp* and then managed to immigrate to Canada in 1948, abandoning his wife and his son in Lithuania[83]. A Canadian citizen from 1953, in 1963 he moved to the United States, to Worcester (Mass.), where he worked as a tailor until 1981, when he was tracked down by OSI investigators. Forced to admit his identity during his first interrogation due to the documents shown to him by Eli Rosenbaum, on May 24, 1984, Kisielaitis was formally accused of "having taken part in the arrest, detention and murder of civilians in Lithuania and Belarus". Then began the procedures of deportation from the U.S. and order of presentation in Boston before the immigration judge, scheduled for November 5, 1984[84]: an obligation which was followed, on April 29, 1985 by his announcement of voluntary return to Canada. He returned first to Burlington, Ontario and later to La Salle, near Montreal. Consequently, OSI sent a record of Juozas *Joe* Kisielaitis' file to RCMP, but no further steps were initiated by the Canadian *War Crime Unit* and in 1987, Kisielaitis received confirmation that the authorities in Ottawa were not intending to deport him due to of the lack of evidence against him. This situation was confirmed by Kisielaitis himself, repeatedly approached by local journalists interested in his case[85]. On February 15, 2001 his attempt to reenter Fort Lauderdale, United States, was blocked right from the start by U.S. immigration officers who were waiting for him at the airport in Montreal.

8.5 NESVIZH, BELARUS

His name was Anton Specht. He was a young, handsome son of a hat seller in Lindenberg im Allgäu, in the Bavarian Alps. He commanded an infantry platoon of the 8./IR 727, which formed the Ortskommandantur garrison of Nesvizh, a village of about 7,000 inhabitants south of Minsk, more than half of which were Jewish. He and his fellow soldiers had arrived in this village at the end of August, with the rest of 707. ID, to handle the situation at the rear, and had begun to immediately implement the usual discriminatory measures upon the large Jewish community that had remained in the village. Until then, however, his task was a *routine* one: the village, small and tidy, gathered around a dozen streets and enriched by an imposing sixteenth century castle, was occupied by the Wehrmacht as early as June 27[86] and up until then there had not been acts of irreparable brutality. Consistently with the general situation, life in Nesvizh had continued to progress within tolerable limits and without turmoil, both for the Polish and Belarusian population and for the Jews themselves, who of course were affected by *customary* harassment but not yet by systematic violence.

Due to that, when on October 29 Specht transmitted to the Judenrat the order for the entire Jewish community to assemble in the marketplace[87] the Jews did not consider it, nor did they want to consider it, the prelude to an imminent disaster, but *only* as a further act of harassment by the occupation authorities towards their community. Only a few days earlier, the Judenrat had managed to pay a huge ransom in gold and money in exchange for the release of 200 young Jews who had been taken as hostages[88]. The most common hypothesis among the Jews waiting was that of yet another depredation, perhaps through the systematic looting of homes left unattended. Ortskommandantur explained that it was a necessary measure aimed at the verification of individual documents[89]. On the other hand, they may have interpreted the rally of the whole Jewish community, at least 4,500 people, in an almost reassuring way: despite the knowledge of some disturbing clues, including the recent excavation by Polish workers of two long trenches near the castle Radziwill[90], they did not consider feasible, *reasonably*, a *coldly* calculated mass murder of such proportions[91]. Certainly, during those hours, all members of the Jewish community of Nesvizh shared a feeling of uncertainty.

Wearing their best clothes and armed with all their documents, the Jews began to gather in the market square, after leaving inside their homes – as per orders – the sick and the elderly that could not move, whose names and addresses had already been communicated to the German authorities[92]. Punishment for those who would not comply with orders was not the usual one: this time they would be shot on the spot.

The square, approximately the size of a football field, filled up quickly with the Jews. In one corner, amid chairs and tables about 25 or 30 people had gathered, including members of the Judenrat, Oberfeldwebel Specht and some Wehrmacht soldiers. Local Belarusian policemen guarded the Jews in the square and regulated the influx of the columns of Jews going in, while the remaining Ortskommandantur German staff had formed checkpoints all along the roads leading to the city.

From the very beginning what was to be a simple document check took on the semblance of a real selection: the best craftsmen; saddlers, shoemakers, tailors, blacksmiths, glass makers and weavers, identified on the basis of a list, were gathered in a part of the square together with their families members, while all the others – in the grip of increasing anxiety and impending sense of tragedy – were left in place [93].During the selection process the trucks arrived, in columns from the direction of Slutsk, and men in a uniform that was unfamiliar got out of them. Someone among the Jews, listening to their words, realized they were Lithuanian. The newcomers formed a cordon around the square and then proceeded to transfer to a school, guarded by Belarusian gendarmes, the few hundreds of artisans and their families selected for survival: a total of less than 600 people[94] who, immediately after the massacre of their fellow Jews, went to form the core of the Nesvizh ghetto.

We do not know exactly which company of PPT-Batalionas 2 took part in the action, nor whether there was also a direct involvement by the staff of Polizei-Bataillon 11: however, it seems sure that German policemen took part in the surveillance of victims around the common graves and that there were German officers also among those who gave firing orders to the firing squads.

The shootings began immediately after the selection of the craftsmen and occurred in two different places. Most of the victims who were able to walk – almost all those gathered in the square – were brought to the mass graves dug in the park of Radziwil castle. The invalids, the sick and elderly people left in their homes were taken by special *Räumungskommandos*, who loaded them aboard the trucks and transported them up to an open field outside of town, along the road to Snov[95].

According to the testimony given by a German soldier, member of Ortskommandantur, who witnessed the action, execution procedures took place very quickly. Coming from the market square, about ten minutes away, the Jews were lined up and forced to walk to the castle park up to a certain point, about twenty yards away from the mass graves, where they had to remove and leave their clothes. All around German policemen watched this phase of the operation and took custody of the victims' money, watches and valuables. Then, wearing only their underwear, the Jews were forced towards mass graves in groups of 25 and lined up along the edge of the trench. Behind them, the firing squad, consisting of 30, 40 or perhaps even 50 Lithuanians, carried out the shootings on the officers' commands.

The same procedure was applied to group after group of Jews. The sound of gunfire was clearly audible even from a fair distance away and reached the columns of victims still walking along the road; then, they would see the two mass graves that stood out in full view of the Jews in the process of removing their clothes. The shootings continued for several hours, without hindrance, without any pretensions of secrecy or attempts to resist by the victims. During the day the echo of gunfire also reached the Jews selected to survive and still confined in the village school[96].

Overall, on October 30, 1941 up to 4,000 Jews were shot[97]. Their possessions, clothes and furniture left in the abandoned houses were sold in the following days to Belarusian and Polish peasants. For the survivors, 600 between the craftsmen and their families, the doors of the ghetto were opened. It was destined to survive until July 1942, when, faced with the prospect of an almost total decimation, the Jewish underground, formed in Nesvizh as early as September 1941, chose the path of armed uprising, using fire, iron bars and bottles of acid.

8.6 OBJECTIVE GENOCIDE

Nesvizh was just one of the steps, and not even the bloodiest, in the genocidal campaign perpetrated in Belarus by *Einsatzgruppe "Lechthaler"* in October / November 1941. As such, it resembles one of dozens of massacres, all quite similar *technically* and in some ways *anonymous*, that went on without interruption for over a year between the beginning of Barbarossa and autumn 1942, in Belarus, Ukraine, the Baltic and Poland: in other words, what happened in Nesvizh was the application of an almost standardized genocidal model, developed as a condition for the existence of a new ideological system (§ 8.6.1.), realized by an organizational structure of a managerial type (§ 8.6. 2), powered by rather precise internal dynamics (§ 8.6.3) and characterized by the painful acceptance by the victim (§ 8.6.4).

8.6.1 – Sfera

Within Arendt's totalitarian universe, which she defines as having an "onion-like structure" the massacre of Nesvizh, as well as most of the executions perpetrated by mass-shootings between summer 1941 and spring 1942 in the Soviet Union, appear as *waste products*. In this context, these executions are the practical consequences of actions taken by the outermost layer, i.e. the one placed at the greatest distance from the nucleus, hence from the center of power embodied by the *leader, custodian* of the *totalitarian verb*. Power is structured in rings, each of which is characterized by a degree of *ideological purity* that tends to pollute as it moves away towards the outer layers. In an ideal sense, the loss of such *purity*, from the inside towards the outside, appears as an intrinsic feature of the totalitarian architecture. In this way, essentially, the inner circles of the system, compared to the outer ones, appear as ever-increasingly elitist and dogmatic, ascetic and deified and placed above responsibilities, as almost metaphysical entities. At the same time, in a practical sense, the deterioration in quality can be seen as a logical consequence linked to the impossibility of obtaining the maximum ideological tension generated from the core by an increasingly larger audience of heterogeneous perpetrators. Being immersed in the concrete reality of the situations more than anyone else, rather than complete adherence to the tenets of ideology, the direct perpetrators found themselves having to deal with objective problems: the infinite diversity of specific events, propelling individual forces and a variety of individual cases. Eventually, all these individual and peripheral dynamics and central directives merged into one bloody magma. In other words, the great design that represented the cornerstone of the Nazi totalitarian model: the solution of the Jewish question was steeped in ideological mystique when it remained a theoretical elaboration on the leaders' clean and tidy desks. But all this ideology was gradually lost when the time came to actually give substance to the theorems and stability to the system, by putting the *ideal enemy*, the *eternal Jew*, in a condition to cause no harm. When eventually all these genocidal orders were passed on from one layer to the next until they reached the most external one, that of the zealous executors, all these elaborations turned into the filthy reality of the mass graves. From this point of view, the mass-shootings constitute a sketched and experimental attempt – whose ultimate evolution was represented by the implementation of the extermination camps through successive refinements of the method of genocide – that the Nazi regime adopted to realize its own vision of the world: a utopia that could not be realized without the annihilation of the *perceived evil* and the consequent triumph of a revolutionary social model, built around a *new man* totally in line with the system from every point of view: ethnic, political and social.

Evidently, such an ideal society *in embryo*, could not be brought out of nothing: it required a constant process of adapting of methods and ideas, to which war gave only the perfect setting, but not the cause or the pretext. Rather, the conflict offered an opportunity to accelerate the design by starting the application of new eugenic and social models, both in terms of *construction of the new* and *deconstruction of the existing*, through the field-testing of new hypothesis of *solution*: it is sufficient to think of the social engineering creativity centered around the transfer of *Volksdeutschen*, or the planned colonization of part of Poland or the Crimea, or the *Lebensborn* project. All these models were *constructive* of the new. Let's now consider the annihilation of disabled people through *Aktion T4*, the marginalization and social exclusion of the non-compliant through methods that could be legislative (racial laws), executive (camps) or social (ghettos) and the physical destruction of entire categories deemed *harmful*. All these models were *deconstructive* of the existent.

Within such a giant fresco aimed at the quasi-divine creation of the totalitarian Nazi ideal, the process could not be linear or free of obstacles, but ended up going through experiments, tactical retreats and temporary changes of direction. Just like the system of concentration camps came to represent, in *deconstruction*, the zenith of Nazi totalitarian society, so the mass graves were its rough sketch, a waste product of pre-production soon replaced by the industrial efficiency of the extermination fields: the contact point between the two methods was the *massive production of corpses*[98].

In this respect several paths could be chosen but there was only one goal. For this reason, the removal of *evil* represented by the Jewish enemy was not a choice conditioned by circumstances, or simply a reaction to the radicalization of the conflict, or even the convergence of situational dynamics out of control, but an *existential condition* of the regime, indispensable to the realization of the utopia. After that, the executive procedures were adapted to the path chosen in a managerial perspective, through phases, times, places and actions that were semi-independent but always consistent with the implicit *ideal*.

8.6.2 – *Symbiosis*

In addition to the application of a theorem, the Jewish genocide was a concentrate of actions. In this sense, there was a need for the intervention of leaderships at all levels to prepare the strategic outlines aimed at achieving results through operational planning, instructions to key personnel, proper motivational climate, indications of a general nature but functional to an end, individual initiative and even *intuitive application of the perceived wishes* of the leader. At the same time the need for the action of the workforce to be consistent towards the goal set – albeit in a jungle of personal logics, autonomous motivations, trivial impulses, individual profits, coarse mechanisms – also became the essential element for the general pattern to be put in conditions to operate.

From this point of view the *solution of the Jewish question* does not seem to have been different from a management by objectives (*MbO*), in which the strategic direction theorized by the leadership of any organized structure is put into effect by the consistent actions of the material performers called to reach the goal. Consequently, it is very unlikely that many different types of performers, acting as a team but independently of each other, adopt identical schemes in the absence of adequate information about the nature of the goal to be achieved, the strategic direction from the leadership and the context of an environment favorable or non-hostile. In other words, the two parts of the structure – leadership and staff – are symbiotic and functional to one another, unable to stand separately except in limited and sporadic cases.

Adopting such a scheme on the Jewish question, it is evident that the leadership of the Reich and the perpetrators of the genocide have been operating in synchrony on the basis of a shared goal, despite coming from different directions: i.e. where there was slaughter, there was planning, in the same way as the accomplishment of a business result is directly related to the choices made beforehand in order to reach it[99].

The final result is therefore sufficient to confirm axiomatically the substance of a project. The execution of the genocide demonstrates the existence of a genocidal will, regardless of the presence or absence of written orders. In other words, it is not the *smoking gun* to confirm the existence of a murder, but rather the presence of the slain victim that makes the murder action obvious.

As we mentioned before, the fact that *Project Genocide* may have passed through various phases and subsequent *improvements* as less bloody alternative options were set aside, proves the existence of a logic of *work in progress* within a process of *ongoing radicalization*, i.e. a complex operational dynamic aimed at a goal, in which both the leadership and the workforce, each within its own field, shared the responsibilities of the final result.

8.6.3 – Decadence

With regard to the workers, the slaughter of Nesvizh is paradigmatic of how far the executive bases were from each other – in terms of ideological purity – compared to the theoretical dogmatism of the core that by now was diluted by the operational contingencies of those who were to apply these dogmas in real life.

The actions perpetrated by Lechthaler's units in Belarus belong to the outermost layer of the Nazi totalitarian regime, much more to the outside than those of Einsatzgruppe B, which had preceded them by only a few weeks: we witness the passage from Weltanschauungstruppen's criminal idealism, be it real or perceived, to the brutal coarseness of Vernichtungstruppen, the *quality* level of whose perpetrators is drastically lower. The brilliant young SD, the élite products of a "generation without limits (*generation des Unbedingten*)"[100], were replaced by a bunch of mercenary auxiliaries, so the ideological schemes, if there ever were, are turned into pure filth and doctrine is reduced to carnage. Enthusiastic Lithuanians, already patriotically enrolled into a national battalion, are dragged out of their environment and agree to their conversion into mercenaries of genocide, exterminating people who had no relation to them whatsoever, no bond, no resentment, no interest. The battlefield on the Eastern Front thus becomes a laboratory for the experimentation of new forms of social and physical annihilation and the reality of the ghettos offers the solution of a prolonged death, and provides an alternative to the immediate annihilation in mass graves.

With the use of large numbers of auxiliaries, and reserve staff in the case of police battalions, we witness how the doctrinal abstractions theorized in Berlin lose their ideological thrust: the operational bases, ever-increasing in numbers, proportionately move away from the core and incorporate new parameters specific only to themselves and reprocess the ideological material by simplifying it and adapting it to their local and individual specificity. The running order does not change, but the crew can change: once the first impulse is given and the basic patterns are outlined it is no longer needed to stubbornly insist on the ideological and racial purity of a small élite of enthusiast perpetrators. Instead, it is sufficient, and perhaps more convenient, to extend the radius of tolerance, co-opt different energies, find new *human material* to fit the needs of the project regardless of its obvious lower quality, as long as it is able to *perform the job* successfully. Lechthaler's Lithuanians, as well as the reservist henchmen of Polizei-Bataillon 11 were not an élite, nor a mob either: they were, if anything, individuals who chose to free themselves of their own capacity of judgment, tucking away in the comfortable dimension of non-thought, or, in the best case – to quote Arendt – diverting their instinctive piety towards a self-absolving sympathy of their inner selves, compelled by their sense of duty to accept horrible deeds[101].

There does not seem to have been, except in rare cases, a moral vindication by the ordinary perpetrators during the course of their *work*, although nothing made it impossible. At most there were acts of visceral disgust, physical repulsion which often resulted in the permission to leave the firing squad or was repressed through the ingestion of alcohol during and after the shootings; we do not know yet how many of these episodes can be attributed to genuine moral suffering. What is certain is that the perpetrators were not of course unaware of the gravity of their acts; they lacked the will to let it emerge. In the early post-war years, for example, the Lithuanians deliberately lied during interrogations in order to obtain entry visas to the United States, which proved their clear ability to discern, activated on command: the same capacity that only five or six years earlier they had obviously carefully numbed and that was the cause, decades later, for the immigration authorities to charge them all for lack of *good moral character*.

8.6.4 – Destinies

Elaborated by the system, coordinated by the management and implemented by the workforce, *Project Genocide* clamped around the victims' throat like the jaws of a vice. It could be argued that it was something inevitable, considering that the victims were the ultimate target and the end product of the project itself. From this point of view the slaughter of Nesvizh was no different from many other massacres perpetrated elsewhere, and it is precisely this closeness that gives us food for thought.

Since early post-war the slaughter of Nesvish has been remembered and recounted by the survivors, some of which – such as Shalom Cholawsky – would take part in the first revolt of a Jewish ghetto in Belarus, organized in Nesvizh on July 21, 1942 by the survivors of the massacre of October 1941[102]. In this sense the dramatic life-span of the Nesvizh ghetto – opening with a massacre and ending with a riot – fits in the too short casuistry in which the will to fight in order to refuse the fate already written for them by others prevailed among the Jewish inmates. The same refusal to oblivion was also chosen by the *condemned to death* of Lachwa (it will be described in Chapter 14) and is the manifestation of a different possible reality, a viable alternative to the passive acceptance of a planned destiny. The uprising of Nesvish also represents the viability of an armed resistance, despite the impossible conditions of the ghettos, to oppose not only their captors, but also to reject the choice of the *lesser evil*, almost always followed by those Jewish Councils that were so severely stigmatized by Arendt who defines them – probably generalizing excessively – as "one of the darkest chapters in all that dark matter"[103].

Beyond the unreasonable hope of success, which objectively seemed completely unlikely, an armed uprising could open a way to salvation for some of the condemned, but above all, it would give the opportunity to *exit the ghetto*, which was not only a visible barbed wire barrier, but a psychological condition and even a form of reassuring self-isolation. Armed resistance, revolt, rejection of total surrender, would be a way to break free from what Bruno Bettelheim calls "the ghetto mentality"[104]. A mentality that made the Jews, already physically confined, prisoners also to a principle of inertia and that ended up feeding the vicious circle that their tormentors imposed on them: a spiral that brought them closer and closer to destruction, and that at some point Abba Kovner chose to break up, refusing to accept the same fate that had swept away most of the ghettos and rejecting his fate as a *sheep to the slaughter* already written for him[105].

However, even if the end there was a reaction, until that time the choice of the inmates of Nesvizh had been the same as that adopted by the victims of other massacres and deportations, namely the acceptance of fate imposed by the cruel demigods of death.

It is certainly ungenerous – and yet it has been done – to identify the passivity of the Jews as one of the causes of their destruction. The episodes of daily survival that constantly put them to the test, the sacrifices they found themselves having to make every day to overcome all kinds of obstacles, the choices they faced, the moral strength shown... all this is probably more than enough to witness the existence of resistance *in deeds*, which did not manifest itself in armed rebellion against the enemy, but in a prolonged reaction to the death of the ghetto: a reaction that counters the heavy accusation of *surrender to the instinct of death* made by

Bettelheim himself[106]. Nevertheless, while this reaction of life – which did happen – prevented the Jews from becoming complicit to the tormentors in their lives, their non-reaction at the time of death – which also happened – made them essentially defenseless *before their death*. In other words, precisely in order to give a final meaning to the abnegation demonstrated by the victims in life, the so-harsh trials passed through the years and the incredible hardships endured would probably have deserved a different dismissal at the time of their deaths. But for most of the victims it was not so, almost all of them simply let their tormentors *bring* them to their death, orderly stacked in a mournful, poignant procession: the final act of that leveled and spectral *society of the dying* that was spreading from the death camps to the ghettos and that was nothing but a *magnanimous*, pseudo-divine concession, by those who had deliberately worked their deaths one day after another. In this respect, having left the right to manage their deaths to others was probably the victim's biggest defeat.

At the end of his work, Raul Hilberg quotes the testimony of Hermann Friedrich Graebe, a German engineer who witnessed the Dubno massacre, given during the Nuremberg trial of the Einsatzgruppen[107]. It is worth pausing on a particularly significant passage [Graebe's complete testimony is reproduced in Annex 3].

> *"During the 15 minutes that I stood near the pit I heard no complaint or plea for mercy. I watched a family of about eight persons, a man and a woman, both about 50 with their children of about 1, 8 and 10, and two grown-up daughters of about 20 to 24 […]. The father was holding the hand of a boy about 10 years old and speaking to him softly; the boy was fighting his tears. The father pointed towards the sky, stroked his head, and seemed to explain something to him […]. I well remember a girl, slim, and with black hair, who, as she passed close to me, pointed to herself and said '23'.*
>
> *I walked around the mound and found myself confronted by a tremendous grave. People were closely wedged together and lying on top of each other so that only their heads were visible. Nearly all had blood running over their shoulders from their heads. Some of the people shot were still moving. Some were lifting their arms and turning their heads to show that they were still alive. The pit was already 2/3 full. I estimated that it already contained about 1,000 people. I looked for the man who did the shooting. He was an SS man who sat at the edge of the narrow end of the pit, his feet dangling into the pit. He had a tommy-gun on his knees and was smoking a cigarette. The people, completely naked, went down some steps which were cut in the clay wall of the pit and clambered over the heads of the people lying there, to the place to which the SS men directed them. They lay down in front of the dead or injured people; some caressed those who were still alive and spoke them in a low voice. Then I heard a series of shots".*

That father, who comforted and protected his son to the last, the young woman who spoke, the dying that caressed each other kept intact their extraordinary dignity, but waived the privilege – which they also could have had – to decide on their death. Some others, however, those few who fought back, claimed that privilege for themselves, regaining possession at the time of their death of their *uniqueness* that the executioners had attempted in every way to erase.

8.7 EPILOGUE

O'Hare Airport, Chicago, May 12, 1999

They had battled as long as it was possible, with every weapon at their disposal. They had invoked the Fifth Amendment, turned to the Board of Immigration, appealed to the Court of Appeals without success. Every attempt was in vain. Only a month earlier, on April 15, the last assault had proved fruitless. By confirming the previous sets of proceedings with a deportation order, Judge Anthony D. Petrone of the Immigration Court in Chicago, had planted the last nail in the coffin of a case that had dragged on for too many years since that March in 1993. It was then, when at the District Court in Hammond, Illinois, OSI pathfinders had filed a request for postponement on seven charges against him, all centered around the crime of illegal immigration into the United States. It was then that his ordeal had begun, and was now really coming to a close – at least in the United States. Sure, they could still appeal to the Supreme Court's Judgment of God, but with almost zero chance of success, as his lawyer had confirmed by extending his arms and as, just a week earlier, his own former comrade Gečas, thrown in jail in Pensacola for refusing to answer questions from the judge... had proved.

At that point all he could do was surrender to the inevitable.

Too quickly; he had to prepare the luggage, the few things he would bring back with him, not many more than he had brought with him when he had left Blutzbach, Germany, fifty years earlier. Too quickly; he had to get accustomed to the new reality of *not* having managed to become someone else. Too quickly, he had to surrender to the idea of giving up everything he had built during half a century of hard work. Too quickly, the plane that they had already made sure he would board, would take him back *home* to Vilnius, Lithuania, where he would finally re-find himself, or rather, that forgotten part of himself that once he had left on Eastern Europe's rubble fields. It was the past returning, with its shadows, with its ghosts. Maybe it was not right, perhaps they should have let him live out his last years in his quiet town near the lake. Maybe it was not worth the trouble to exhume the past, the old faded memories of a long-gone era. Or maybe it was right. Maybe it was not revenge but justice, the cosmic nemesis that nobody could escape. He had received a lot from the theater of life and without paying the entrance fee. That fee was now being claimed, now that the show was over and he was just about to exit the theatre. He, *Casey* Ciurinskas, did not know what was right and what was wrong, just as he had not been able to understand it in those distant years, when, wearing his uniform, he saw viewers get up from the velvet chairs and stand still in front of him, one row after another, directed prematurely to the exit. Even then, *Casey* Ciurinskas had not been able to say whether it was right or wrong. And now his turn had come; soon, it would be him reaching out, walking past the smiling cashier of the last show. The very moment he passed before the stern airport agent at the *check-in*, the exact moment he heard him say "*Casey* Ciurinskas" he realized that would be the last time that someone would cripple his name like that.

That moment would be the very last of the new life he had wanted for himself as: Kazys Ciurinskas, the *American*.

ENDNOTES

1 "Calm has apparently been restored wherever the Jews were placed under conditions to cause no harm". (*Lagerbericht*) Report of Polizei-Bataillon 11, reproduced in HIS, p. 472.

2 USA, Plaintiff, v. Kazys Ciurinskas, Defendant, No 2:93 CV 97JM, June 18, 1997. Quoted as *Ciurinskas' Sentence*.

3 See memorandum of OSI Senior Trial Attorney William Kenety, in *Outstanding Public Interest Lawyer in Action – OPIA. Harvard Law School.* In fact, in the sentence of Judge Moody, Ciurinskas was found guilty of certain participation in a reprisal action in Užusaliai, in the Jonavos' area, Lithuania, on September 11 and 12, 1941 which ended with the shooting of 43 civilians. The shootings were carried out by Rollkommando "Hamann", aided by Lithuanian auxiliaries, and it is not certain whether Ciurinskas took part in the shootings. See Ciurinskas' Sentence, § 50÷54, *Jäger Report,* Bl. 4, in Bartusevičius/Tauber/Wette, p. 306.

4 Ciurinskas' Sentence, Count VI.

5 On the concepts of moral guilt and metaphysical guilt, see Karl Jasper, *La questione della colpa.* Milan, 1996.

6 Stang, pp. 117-118, Bubnys Holocaust, p. 8. Ehrlinger had entered Kaunas with EK1b on June 28, 1941, in the footsteps of the Wehrmacht, and then left on July 2, after the arrival of Karl Jäger's EK3, to whom he handed over the task.

7 Bubnys Holocaust, pp. 7-8, Bubnys Hilfspolizeibataillone, p. 119, Stang, p. 123.

8 Stang, p. 122, EM 19 of July 11, 1941.

9 Between July and August at least 36 members of the battalion would be dishonorably discharged for alcoholism or insubordination. *Ibid.*, pp. 128-129.

10 *Ibid.*, pp. 129-130, Dieckmann/Sužiedėlis, p. 60.

11 Stang, pp. 133, 142-143.

12 The massacres were perpetrated on July 9 and 19, August 2, 9 and 18 in the presence of detachments brought by the 3rd,

4th, 5th, 6th and 7th companies of TDA-Batalionas. Stang, pp. 143-144, *Jäger Report,* Bl. 1 and 2, in Bartusevičius/Tauber/Wette, p. 306.

13 According to Stang, p. 160, and Bubnys Hilfs "Polizeibataillone", pp. 120-121, RoKo "Hamann" was an *ad-hoc* sub-division, composed of about ten Sipo German officers, called in time after time to run genocidal actions in rural areas around Kaunas. This detachment – whose personnel was not permanent – was part of that Teilkommando comprising about 40 men, led by Joachim Hamann, that was made to incorporate EK3, and that originated KdS "Kaunas". Among the executives that Hamann led we should mention SS-Hauptscharführer Helmut Rauca, who was also his deputy commander. On Rauca see Chap. 7, *Grosse Ghetto, Grosse Aktion.*

14 Born in Liepaja on December 20, 1914, a Lithuanian Air Force pilot in 1940, he took the leadership of a partisan group in the days of the Soviet retreat from Lithuania. A member of Voldemaras' ultranationalist movement, he became platoon commander of 3/TDA and was then transferred to 4/TDA as leader of the special unit *(Spezialabteilung)* aggregate to RK "Hamann". Eventually, in late August 1941, he was officially made commander of 4/TDA. A close friend of Stahleckers', he was an alcoholic and probably a drug addict – according to his father's post-war declarations – and committed suicide in early 1942, after his transfer in the Pskov area. Stang, pp. 158, 175-177. It seems that Norkus was among the nationalist officials who negotiated with Stahlecker between June 25 and 27 – soon after his entry into Kaunas – the instigation through the local population, *albeit with great difficulties,* of *spontaneous* pogroms against the Jews. See Dieckmann Pogrom, p. 359-360, Dieckmann/Sužiedėlis, p. 42. On Stahlecker's instigation to pogroms, see Stahlecker's report *Gesamtbericht Einsatzgruppe A, bis zum 15 Oktober 1941,* in IMT Blue Series, vol. XXXVII, p. 672 – Doc. 180 L.

15 See Stang, pp. 158-160, that quotes the names of the 57 platoon members.

16 According to Bubnys Holocaust, p. 14, not all the 62 slaughters mentioned by Jäger would see the participation of RoKo "Hamann" and the Lithuanians attached to it: in some cases the executions would be perpetrated directly by the local auxiliary police, probably on orders coming from Kaunas.

17 For an examination of the dynamics that led to the Final Solution in Lithuania see Dieckmann/Sužiedėlis, especially p. 67 onwards in connection to the events in the province. For the description of execution modalities adopted by RoKo "Hamann", see Stang, pp. 161 onwards.

18 Dieckmann/Sužiedėlis, pp. 67-68.

19 As for *cadres and workforce* of the genocide, see Chap. 13, *Räumung in Radom.* On the execution modalities of the slaughters by Rollkommando "Hamann", see Stang, pp. 161-163.

20 Bubnys Holocaust, p. 9, Bubnys Hilfspolizeibataillone, p. 119.

21 Knezys, s.p.

22 In February 1942, after a general reorganization, Litauische-Schuma-Bataillon 1 and 2 were renamed. Respectively, 13 and 12. Stang, p. 186. Former TDA seventh company was attached to *Pagalbinės Policijos Tarnibos Batalionas 2* together with two newly-formed companies. This battalion was later renumbered Litauische-Schuma-Bataillon 11 (Antanas Švilpa).

23 Ciurinskas' Sentence, 60a, Stang, p. 238. Originarily, Ciurinskas was a member of 5/TDA and was transferred to 2/TDA on July 15, 1941.

24 Stang, p. 167. Testimonies given to ZStL.

25 *Ibid.*, p. 56: *Erlass der Führers über de Verwaltung der neu besetzen Ostgbiete,* 17.07.1941. Von Renteln's actual settlement in Kaunas took place on July 28.

26 Dieckmann Pogrom, p. 358.

27 «In agreement with the order by Militärbefehlshaber "Ostland", I take on the command of Lithuanian Order Service and all partisan detachments, as of July 30, 1941». Arad, p. 237, Stang, p. 185, Knezys, s.p.

28 Stang, p. 187, Bubnys Hilfspolizeibataillone, p. 118.

29 Stang, p. 187.

30 HIS, p. 471. Jedicke's communication to Reichkommissar Lohse of October 17, 1941.

31 Stang, p. 187. Engel's communication to Lechthaler of December 16, 1941 in which the *only temporary* subordination of Litauische-Schuma-Bataillone 1, 2 and 3 to Polizei-Bataillon 11 was reaffirmed (italics by me: author's note).

32 HIS, p. 472. According to Breitman, p. 79, 284 Germans and 463 Lithuanians were relocated to Belarus, while Klemp Ermittelt, p. 110 and Gerlach, p. 612, maintain that there were, 326 and 457 respectively.

33 HIS, pp. 138, 471: *«Es ist Aufgabe dieser Kräfte, in Verbindung mit der Wehrmacht die gemeldeten Partisanen-Abteilungen zu bekämpfen».*

34 *Ibid.*, pp. 472-473.

35 See the brutally anti-Semitic statements pronounced by von Bechtolsheim in August 1941, quoted in Heer/Naumann, pp. 64-65.

36 Braemer, von Bechtolsheim and von Schenckendorff were all radical anti-Semites. They all wanted, for reasons that

were different, albeit matching in parts, to *free* Belarus from the Jews, both Western Belarus (under civilian administration) and Eastern Belarus (under military administration). Heer/Naumann, p. 69-71. On von Schenckendorff's role in the annihilation of the Jews of Eastern Belarus, see § 6.3.1.

37 Heer/Naumann Extermination, p. 78.

38 Heer/Naumann, p. 69, Heer/Naumann Extermination, p. 78, Klemp Ermittelt, p. 110.

39 Heer/Naumann Extermination, p. 67.

40 *Ibid.*, p. 66.

41 Gerlach, pp. 612-613, Ciurinskas' Sentence, 63a-i, Dean Participation, p. 285, Breitman Auxiliaries , s.p.

42 Curilla, pp. 612, 898, HIS, p. 144, Bericht, p. 67.

43 Gerlach, p. 618.

44 File Kisielaitis, author's archive, nr. 11/557-9, nr. 3/557-2. See also Stang, p. 210.

45 *The Register Guard,* November 6, 1993.

46 *Los Angeles Times,* January 4, 1998.

47 Wyman/Rosenzweig, p. 341.

48 Allen, p. 32.

49 *The Sunday Star Times* (Wellington), March 19, 2006.

50 *Scotland on Sunday,* December 23, 2001. Interview with Juozas Aleksynas.

51 *The Sunday Star Times* (Wellington), March 19, 2006.

52 *Scotland on Sunday,* December 16, 2001. Interview with Valentukevicius, director of the *Special Investigation Division* of the Lithuanian Public Prosecution, on the reasons behind the request for extradition of Gecas. *The Herald* (Glasgow), September 5, 2001.

53 *Scotland on Sunday,* December 16, 2001. Interview with Valentukevicius. Testimonies given by Juozas Aleksynas and Motjeus Paranas Migonis (Miegonis). *The Independent, July* 18, 1992. See also the list of 2/PPT-Batalionas member names, in File Kisielaitis, author's archive.

54 *The Independent,* July 6, 7 and 8, 1992.

55 *The Daily Mail,* February 20, 2001, July 28, 2001, September 13, 2001, *The Mirror,* July 27, 2001, September 12, 2001, *Daily Record,* September 13, 2001, *Sunday Mail,* October 14, 2001, *The Guardian,* September, 3 2001, *Scotland on Sunday,* December 16, 2001.

56 File Kisielaitis, author's archive, n. 109/557-9, n. 136/557-2. See also Stang, p. 203 who refers to him as *Motiejus Kalinauskas.*

57 *The Ukrainian Weekly,* May 28, 1989.

58 Juozas Naujalis, Petitioner, v. Immigration and Naturalization Service, Respondent, No A 7 258 120, September 28, 2000. Quoted as Naujalis' Sentence. Also Stang, p. 205.

59 *File Kisielaitis,* author's archive, n. 50, Naujalis' Archive § I.

60 Naujalis' Sentence § I.

61 Naujalis' Sentence § I.

62 *The Weekly Crier* 4/2001 – April 2-9, 2001.

63 *File Kisielaitis,* author's archive, n. 260/557-9, n. 293/557-2.

64 *Los Angeles Times,* January 4, 1998, *The Jewish Post & News,* May 29, 1996.

65 File Kisielaitis author's archive, n. 244/557-2.

66 Reinmann, pp. 195-196, Gečas' Sentence, I onwards.

67 File Kisielaitis, author's archive, n. 308/557-2.

68 *The New York Times,* June 2, 1984.

69 *The Ukrainian Weekly,* May 28, 1989.

70 Stang, p. 210, Zuroff, pp. 63, 241, Ryan, p. 355, *NYT,* October 27, 1981, File Kisielaitis, author's archive, Allen, p. 8.

71 File Kisielaitis, author's archive, n. 16.

72 *The Lewiston Daily Sun,* September 30, 1987.

73 *Ibid.*, December 1 and 2, 1988.

74 Hilberg, pp. 1155-1156, 1188. Testimony given by Martinus Kaciulis on August 16, 1982 to the US District Court of Tampa, during the process of denaturalization of Jurgis Juodis.

75 File Kisielaitis, author's archive.

76 File Kisielaitis, author's archive, n. 316/557-2.

77 *The Independent,* July 6 and 7, 1992.

78 *The New York Times,* September 17, 1992, *Los Angeles Times,* January 4, 1998.

79 File Kisielaitis, author's archive, n. 400/557-9, n. 444/557-2.

80 Allen, p. 11, Ryan, p. 353.

81 *The New York Times,* June 2, 1984.

82 File Kisielaitis, author's archive, n. 413, n. 459.

83 *Chicago Tribune,* April 9, 2002.

84 Allen, pp. 13-14, *Canadian Jewish News,* September 6, 2001.

85 *Canadian Jewish News,* September 6, 2001.

86 Cholawsky, p. 185.

87 Dean, p. 45, HIS, p. 139. Nesvizh *Judenrat* was created on June 30, 1941 upon orders from the local Werhmacht commander. A lawyer from Warsaw named Magalif was placed as President. Cholawsky, p. 185.

88 Around mid-October, about 200 young hostages were selected from among the male Jews forced to gather in the market square, and their liberation was forced on the *Judenrat* for a ransom of 500,000 Rubles and 5,5 lb. of gold. Dean, p. 44.

89 Dean, p. 45, Dean Participation, p. 286.

90 HIS, p. 139, Cholawsky, p. 186.

91 Dean, pp. 45, 183.

92 HIS, p. 141. Testimony given by survivor Chischin H.,

Dean, p. 45, Dean Participation, p. 286.

93 Dean, p. 45, HIS, p. 141. Testimony given by survivor Chischin H.

94 According to the sources, the number of Jews selected was between 560 and 585. Dean, pp. 45, 183, Dean Participation, pp. 286, 294, Cholawski, pp. 186, 199.

95 Dean, p. 45.

96 Testimony given on December 2 by August F. 1970 to ZStL, 202 AR-Z 116/67.

97 Curilla, pp. 171, 354, 897, Gerlach, p. 617-618, Cholawsky, p. 186.

98 Arendt Origini, p. 612.

99 See Peter Ferdinand Drucker: *Management: tasks, responsibilities, practices.* New York, 1994. In particular Chapters 8 and 9.

100 Michael Wildt: *Generation des Unbedingten. Das Führungskorps des Reichssicherheitshauptamtes. Studienausgabe.* Hamburg, 2003.

101 Arendt, p. 114.

102 See Moshe Lachovichy, *Churban Nieswiezh,* Tel Aviv, 1948; David Farfel, *Sefer Nieswiezh,* Tel Aviv, 1976; Shalom Cholawsky, *Soldiers from the Ghetto,* New York, 1980.

103 Arendt, p. 125.

104 Bettelheim, pp. 267, ff.

105 Israel Gutman, *Storia del ghetto di Varsavia*, p. 83.

106 Bettelheim, p. 278.

107 Hilberg, p. 1175. IMT Green Series, vol. IV, p. 446-447. On March 23, 1965 Graebe was acknowledged by Yad Vashem as Righteous among the Nations.

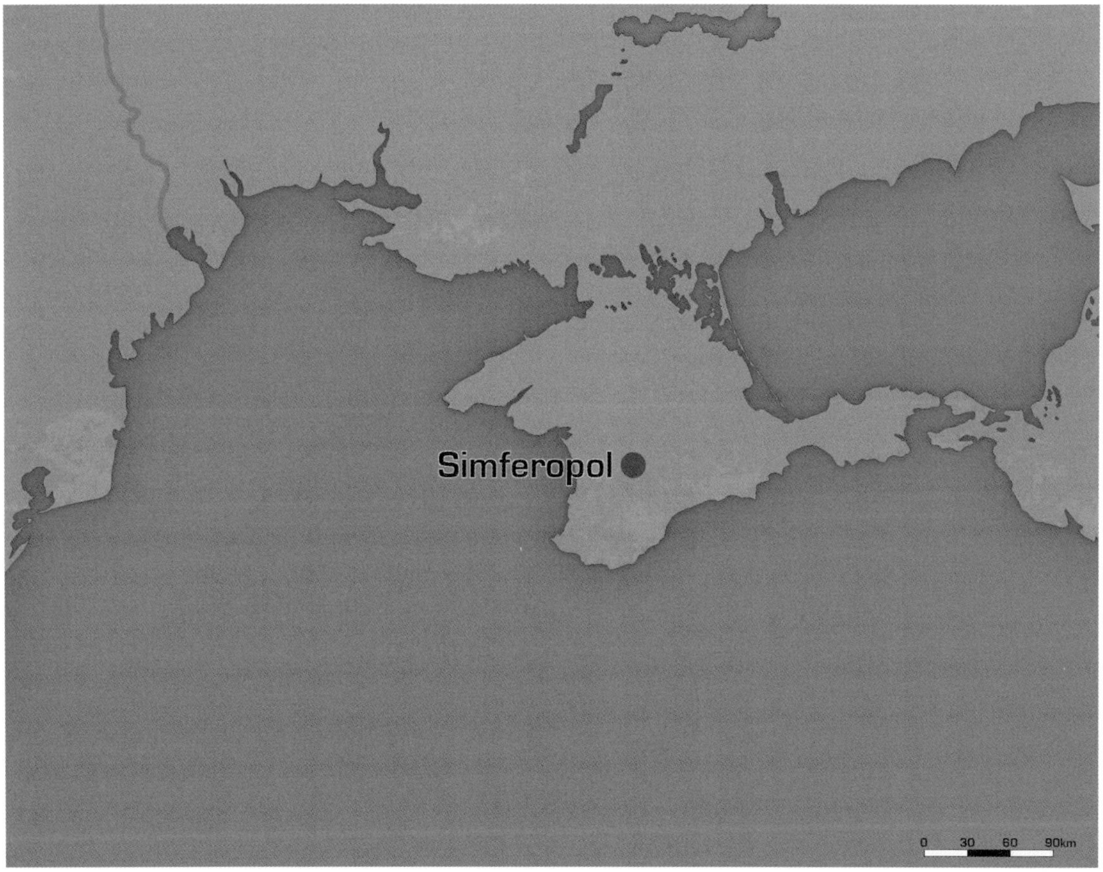
Simferopol
0 30 60 90km

CHAPTER NINE

"PEOPLE OF BERLIN"

SIMFEROPOL, CRIMEA, DECEMBER 9-13, 1941

Später kamen die Frauen und Kinder...

Albrecht Zöllner, Sonderkommando 11a
Court of Munich, June 26, 1962[1]

9.1 INTRODUCTION

The Skagerrak Strait, 30 minutes south of Larvik, late May 1942

They skirted the eastern edge of the deep sea keeping as far as possible to starboard to escape submarine dangers and they were about to leave the most dangerous area. They had left from Skeden, Denmark, that morning at the maximum speed that the old steamer allowed; 11.5 knots. In just under three hours they would reach the coast of Vesterøy, and then finally go into the relative safety of the Oslo fjord. Each of them was wearing a life jacket whose usefulness, if shipwrecked in such cold waters, was more theoretical than real. They only had to hope that they would not bump into an adventurous British submarine on patrol, or a drifting mine that would have broken the steamer in two like a walnut shell. Indeed, the handful of sailors from the Kriegsmarine who ran the ship did not seem particularly concerned. But then, they were seafarers, used to travelling dangerous routes. *They*, on the other hand, they were all *terrestrial*, more accustomed to great plains than to water in motion: the fact is, the mood of the men was not the best, though perhaps it would lighten once they reached firm ground. That too, however, left grounds for doubt.

Actually, for some of them this was the second trip to Norway. The first occurred about two years earlier, in May 1940, but the morale then – as the battalion veterans reminded them – was very different: there was enthusiasm, spirits were high, it was like the beginning of a great adventure. Two years later, however, everything had changed. The destination was the same, the service that they would be required to perform was identical, maybe even the ship – who knows – was the same as back then, judging by the rust ... Everything, at first glance, appeared unchanged as in a strange deja vu ... had it not been for Russia.

Between the two trips to Norway, there had been six months of Russian front; months of triumphal advances and dazzling victories, months of great battles and unforgettable exploits, months of manly glory and shining honor… for many, not for them. For them, things had gone a bit differently. And it was precisely that diversity that could now be detected on the faces of those men moistened by the salty waves that radiated from their nervous gestures and frowning dialogues. It was as if a shadow had settled on the battalion; they all sensed it but no one talked about it. As many as five months had passed since they were sent back to Germany, in January 1942, yet that shadow still loomed over their heads.

The first few weeks after their return passed smoothly: they had returned to Zamosc, Poland, where they reorganized and had no time to think, then they were transferred to Iglau, Moravia, and finally they returned to Berlin, where the entire battalion was basically disbanded so that its men could enjoy a long break. It was at that point, within the tranquility of their homes that problems began. Despite that the passing time was slowly moving them further away from Russia, memories stayed and images continued to resurface. To many they had become a constant, to others an obsession. Then someone from the top hierarchies had seen fit to rebuild the battalion and give its men a new mission: less important than Russia, but challenging enough so that the morale and efficiency of the unit would derive benefit from it. The snowy mountains of Norway had seemed like the right solu-

The arrival of Polizei-Bataillon 9 at Oslo's port on May 9, 1940. Source: Bundesarchiv.

tion, not only for those men, but also, probably, for reasons of opportunity. After Russia, in a way, Polizei-Bataillon 9 had become *cumbersome*, an ugly picture of itself reflected by a mirror. By turning the mirror, up there among the fjords, maybe that unpleasant image would disappear.

9.2 TOWARDS THE PRUT

Piatra Neamț, Rumania, July 23, 1941

They were painters, carpenters, bakers and confectioners, coopers, coachmen, gardeners and chauffeurs. They were mostly artisans. Many of them, born between 1908 and 1909, had found themselves unemployed in the period of the Weimar Republic and for this reason they had entered the police, which they left after a few years, between 1935 and 1936, to resume their old jobs. Thus, they had become reservists, and in that role were called up into service between 1939 and 1940 and annexed in a police battalion bearing the number "9" in Berlin-Spandau[2]. They had spent the first months of the war in Spandau as a garrison unit, with particular emphasis on close-combat training in urban areas. There had been rumors of their future use in activities of surveillance of facilities and crops, or other security activities: all *routine* tasks it seemed. No one was surprised by that, at least until the emphasis was placed on training simulations of arrest and shooting of hostages. At that point, officers had assured the most puzzled among the policemen that it was only a precaution in case some day they would be faced by the reality of war amd have to execute saboteurs or perform shootings in firing squads according to the ordinary trappings of military justice[3]: a plausible explanation, which no one objected to. Also, soon after, in May 1940, they had left for a nice period of service in Norway, where everything had gone well and where the battalion remained until January 1941 when it was sent back to Berlin to be reassigned to the monotonous garrison life.

However, in June 1941, someone at Hauptamt-Orpo eventually remembered them.

Berlin was filled with excitement in those days. Military units were reported to be leaving eastwards, for Poland: there was talk of big maneuvers, someone dared to speak out other assumptions, no one knew anything for sure. Once again, they were lucky.

Rather than Poland like many other battalions, they were sent to Bad Düben, Saxony, without receiving any explanation. Not far away, in Pretzsch Elbe, there was a border police school, where it was rumored that hundreds of officials from all over Germany had been sent to. They were not *Ordnungspolizisten* like them though, but agents of the Security Police, SD and Gestapo people, a Waffen-SS unit had also been spotted. Nobody quite knew what they were doing, but it was obvious that they were preparing for something.

As for them, they were annexed to the specialized school, which is why someone in the battalion had suggested an impending cycle of training operations in border areas, or at least some other assignment that might not be too demanding. If that was true, then it meant that their luck continued.

But then, in mid-June they were separated: the battalion was split and its three companies were each annexed to a special mobile squad formed by Sicherheitspolizei staff stationed in the Pretzsch school. It was rumored that they would all depart after leaving behind in Bad Düben their colleagues of the three machine gun platoons. There was quite a lot of drinking and farewell dinners, and many rumors that were not easy to give credit to. But above all, despite the passing days, no-one had told them what their tasks would be, or where they would be deployed, at least until Heydrich arrived in Pretzsch, on June 20, 1941 [4]: the strong ideological tone of his speech addressed to the officers and men gathered in the school, was what made it clear to everyone that their final destination was Russia.

They set off group after group within 24 hours along with their comrades of the Security Police, each company to a different area of the new eastern front: in the Baltic, in Belarus and Ukraine. Everyone except them and the three platoons of gunners that had all been gathered together in a new fourth company made of just over a hundred men, were held in Pretzsch to expect new orders. These orders finally arrived a few days later, through an unknown high-ranking RSHA official, a certain Otto Ohlendorf, who by then had become their new commander[5].

Surprisingly, however, they were not sent to Russia, as everyone expected, but to Romania, making a long tour through Moravia, Vienna, Budapest and Transylvania, to a remote village at the foot of the Eastern Carpathians. It was the village of Piatra Neamt, which none of them had ever heard of, but that, in those early July days, was crowded with Romanian and German troops of von Schobert's Eleventh Army Corps, heading to the front beyond the Prut, about a hundred kilometres to the east[6].

Here, before the final leap over the river and the Russian frontier, they were divided into platoons and half-platoons and sent to different points in their sector: thus, while the company command headed by Hptm. Hans Gabel was attached directly to Ohlendorf's Stab, three platoons of 4/Polizei-Bataillon 9 were divided among the various operational detachments of what – so they were told – was called Einsatzgruppe D. While he, Oltn. Karl Jonas, platoon commander, was assigned to SK11b led by Bruno Müller[7], his colleagues Ltn. Max Seeman and Ltn. Bernhard, both commanders of the half-platoons were assigned to Heinz Seetzen's SK 10th and Paul Zapp's SK11th respectively[8].

The departure from Piatra Neamt of the various detachments took place gradually, building on the progress of the eastwards advance made by the army corps, in whose sectors the same detachments were meant to operate. Thus, according to the plans of higher commands that Gabel gradually communicated to the different platoons, Seeman and his men headed northeast on July 4, up to the Romanian border city of Iasi and then on to Făleşti Balti[9]. Bernhard headed south, towards Bacau and Barlad, with the task of crossing the Prut and then heading to Chişinău[10]. As for himself, Jonas, he remained in Piatra Neamt for a few more days, waiting for the situation in southern Bessarabia to unblock. Finally, on July 22, Chief of Staff of the Eleventh Army, Ltn.Gen. Otto Wöhler, gave SK11b the authorization to move southwards towards Bolhrad with Tighina on the Dniester being the next destination. After much anticipation, their turn had finally arrived.

Karl Jonas made sure that all his men had taken their place on the trucks gathered in the square and then proceeded to the leading vehicle. Everything was in perfect order, but he noted some gestures which betrayed a certain nervousness among the men. He was not surprised by that: even though no one knew anything specific about the tasks they would face, everyone understood they were not going to Norway.

Just beyond the horizon lay the vastness of Russia, and even if only for that reason it was normal that a shadow of uneasiness would veil that feeling of *great venture* experienced up to that point: nothing, however, that could not be overcome after the first phase of acclimatization. Or so it was logical to expect.

Before him, after a few minutes, Jonas saw the convoy of SK 11b start to move. It was just past dawn on Wednesday July 23, 1941.

To their left, towards the east, behind the big tower clock of Stefan the Great, the sky was already clear. In front was the unknown; an *unknown land* lying beyond the misty confines of the Levant.

The embarking of Polizei-Bataillon 9 at Oslo station, May 1940. Source: Bundesarchiv.

9.3 SONDERFALL DER ENDLÖSUNG

The massacre of the Jewish communities of Crimea – including that of Simferopol – perpetrated in late fall 1941, represents a *special case* within the Final Solution. In fact, unlike other areas where the appearance of *Weltanschauungstruppen* meant the almost immediate annihilation of entire communities – or at best, their *reduction* – in the entire Crimea territory, the wave of killings was slowed in part by the particular ethnic composition of the population; something that, perhaps for the first time since the war began, put the commanders of extermination groups in serious difficulties with regard to the recognition of their potential victims. This problem could be resolved only by requesting the opinion of the racial experts in Berlin.

All this, however, happened in December 1941 Meanwhile, during their invasion of Crimea, the detachments of Einsatzgruppe D, which took part in the Simferopol massacre and the policemen of 4/Polizei-Bataillon 9 attached to them came to understand, without a doubt, what their main task would be[12].

9.3.1 – Sonderkommando 11b/ Polizeizug Jonas

They started to kill soon after crossing the Romanian border. In late July, the synagogue of Bolhrad was set on fire with the rabbi and some twenty Jews locked inside, while about 400 others were taken away on trucks and shot in the nearby village of Tabaki[13]. A few days later in Tighina, towards the beginning of August, at least 250 Jews, including women and children, were murdered in the course of several *actions* at the hands of the Romanians, the SK11b staff and the policemen of Jonas' platoon. During one of these executions which took place in early August Bruno Müller himself, commander of SK11b, killed a mother holding a child of about two or three years, *to set a good example* to his officers, among them Jonas himself, who in turn inflicted the death blow to many wounded Jews[14]. Shortly before he killed the woman and the child, Muller had urged his men with few but significant words: "She must die so that we may live"[15]. At that point, through such unambiguous examples and without any need for explicit orders, it was clear to all that the shooting of the Jews was the main task of the *kommando*[16]: a role that hitherto had been rather vague, but from then on was accepted and implemented by the staff, not without causing psychological problems from the very early stages[17].

After Tighina, in its advance eastwards, SK11b marked its genocidal path with the bloodbath of Odessa on October 23, 1941. This massacre was hatched by the Romanians, but saw the active participation of both SD staff and policemen, who proceeded to slaughter an unspecified number of Jews, but put at between 1,000 and 2,000[18]. The execution lasted several hours and was perpetrated around a large underground water tank. The Jews were led in groups to the lip of the siphon where they were killed by rifle shots to the neck. Those who did not fall into the tank after being shot and fell at the edge of the siphon, were pushed into it by the next victims. Periodically, at the behest of Oltn. Jonas, grenades were thrown inside the water tank into which many Jews, in an attempt to save their lives, had jumped before receiving the fatal blow. All of them were killed by the explosion amplified by the closed space of the tank[19]. During the execution, which took place in small groups, alcoholic beverages were served in abundance to the executioners, before whom the victims, particularly women, were forced to strip naked. Many of them were also hit with sticks or whips obtained from trouser belts or their equipment[20]. Incredibly, according to the testimony given by Johannes Schlupper, commander of a Teilkommando of SK11b, that of Odessa was *the most humane execution* in which he took part [sic!][21].

The Odessa massacre ended the first operational phase of SK11b on the Eastern Front. Towards the end of November 1941 it was ordered to reach Crimea. In the same period the unit commander, Bruno Müller, an unreliable alcoholic, was recalled to Germany and replaced by SS Obersturmbannführer Werner Braune[22], a protégé of Ohlendorf, who reached his new unit from Nikolajev, on the Black Sea, on November

20. A few days later, Stab/EGD with Ohlendorf and the core command of Hans Gabel's 4/9 made their entrance into Simferopol, followed shortly afterwards by SK11b[23]. The capital of Crimea, with its exotic and centuries' old ethnic mosaic, was to become the next target of the new *Khan*-like horde that was coming, but this time, from the west.

9.3.2 – Sonderkommando 11a/ Polizeihalbzug Bernhard

They had entered Ghitigeni, southeast of Bacau, on July 4, 1941. They carried with them an order issued by the command of the Eleventh German Army, which authorized them to proceed with the *raid of hostile elements*, and were headed for Chişinău, capital of Moldova, first target in their march eastwards[24]. Along the way, in Barlad, they had made contact for the first time with the *Jewish question*, but it had been almost exclusively a *divertissement*; they had given out a few beatings and whippings to those Jews too slow in carrying out the work assigned, *ordinary* humiliations and *little else*[25]: nothing, truly *irreparable*. Then, around mid-July, they crossed the Prut and with it the Soviet border. From that moment on, it was time to start *getting serious*.

The entrance of SK11a into Chişinău occurred on July 17, followed by a report from Zapp about the *special attention with respect to the treatment of Jews*[26], 9,000 of whom were still in town. In compliance, 68 of them, considered communists, were delivered to the kommando of a Feldgendarmerie unit, to be shot by a firing squad composed of policemen under the command of Ltn. Bernhard[27]. At the same time, many Jews were murdered on the streets by Romanian hireling soldiers, who had been granted a free hand by their commander, Tuodossi, in an orgy of violence that would raise the grievances of Zapp himself, concerned about the disorder and extreme *lack of professionalism* with which these abuses were perpetrated[28]. A few days later, around early August, 551 Jews, including 200 women, were shot by SK11a as a *reprisal* for the burning of a coal store, lit by an unknown hand[29]. In this case women were selected from within the newly created ghetto, while men were taken from the concentration camp where about a thousand Jewish men in Chişinău had been locked in the role of hostages (*Geiselreservoir*)[30]. At that point, after being registered under the guise of a labor service, the victims were brought to the graves and then shot: women first, men next[31]. In the firing squads there were also many Romanian soldiers, while the presence of Ltn. Bernhard during the registration process is confirmed.

Nikolajev, on the Black Sea, was the next stop for SK11a, heading there from Chişinău. The city at the mouth of the Bug was reached on August 18, 1941, and only a couple of days later, the SK11a performed the registration of Jews, which was followed by the establishment of a ghetto, at the request of the Ortskommandantur. Then, after Stab / EGD with Ohlendorf and Jonas at their command had entered the city, Ohlendorf and Zapp issued the order to the Judenrat to organize for September 14, the departure of 5,000 Jews from the ghetto, under the pretext of a job transfer *to other locations in Ukraine*. In anticipation of the operation, Ohlendorf arranged for reinforcements from an EK12 detachment coming from Cherson. Once the planning was complete, the day of the massacre came: men, deceived by false promises, were loaded onto Wehrmacht trucks and were then taken to a ravine about a mile away from the city where the shooting occurred; the day after, it was the turn of women and children. The executions lasted for three days, from early morning until 18:00 hours: two surveillance cordons were set up around the ravine, to prevent the arrival of visitors from neighboring villages and to block any escape attempt. On rotation, all members of the *kommando* were assigned to the firing squads: this precaution, however, did not avoid the occurrence of panic attacks among the executioners, including Ltn. Bernhard himself. According to testimonies given after the war, it was mainly members of the policemen platoon that were affected by post-traumatic shock and who, from that moment on, found themselves drinking heavily in an attempt to anesthetize their consciousness[32].

After solving the *Jewish question* in Nikolajev and the nearby town of Kherson[33], the genocidal actions of SK11a in southern Ukraine stopped for the rest of 1941. Crimea became the new operational area of the *kommando*, which began to send its advanced detachments in late October[34]: among these, Teilkommando "Scheuring", which was used during the Simferopol massacre on precise instructions by Ohlendorf[35].

9.3.3 – Sonderkommando 10a/ Polizeihalbzug Seeman

They had the first taste of Weltanschauungskrieg brutality at Iasi train station, where they had arrived in early July, from Piatra Neamt. They had opened a railroad car and seen them: hundreds of bodies piled on each other; men, women and children, horribly disfigured and already in an advanced state of decomposition. It was said that Romanian soldiers had done it; they entered the city before them, to rage relentlessly on the Jews, to kill thousands of them and deport many more. Some also said that it was the local people who started the pogrom, and then policemen and gendarmes had joined in too. In any case, before them was the result of an orgy of violence which had lasted for at least two days. Most of them were disgusted by such violence[36]. From this point of view, from the early days, the war on the Eastern Front had shown the German policeman its most brutal face.

The transition from mere spectators to protagonists, for members of SK10a, occurred a few days later in Bălti, fifty miles northeast of Iaşi, reached on July 10, and where by the middle of the month at least 75 Jews were executed by *kommando* staff, with the involvement of Seeman's police officers[37]. During one of these executions, asked by his men as to why he was shooting a Jew, Seeman would speak of "a demonstrative act (*Demonstrationszwecken*), needed to make it clear to all of them the type of situation they should expect in the course of further advance"[38]. These executions took place in the midst of such indiscriminate and brutal violence perpetrated by Romanian soldiers, that somehow they appeared minor and orderly events, as well as relatively small in number, given the fact that in those days of uncontrolled chaos, most of the Jews finally fled the city, taking refuge in the countryside[39].

After Bălti, which they left in late July, SK10a's next step on the genocidal path was Kodyma, just beyond the Dniester, the scene of a *preventive retaliation* to a plot allegedly hatched by young members of the local Jewish *intelligentsia*, which ended with the shooting of 98 Jews identified as Communists[40]. The shooting took place in a mass grave and even a Wehrmacht team took part in it. In addition to the 12 members of SK10a included in the firing squad, there were also some 41 policemen[41]. The execution was reported to AOK 11 from the command of XXX° Army Corps on August 2; in the meantime, another 175 Jews were arrested and held hostage in a Wehrmacht prison camp.

After Kodyma, around mid-August, SK10a reached the Beresovka area, about 40 miles north of Odessa, where at least 200 Jews were shot[42]. On this occasion, in the presence of Seetzen, Ohlendorf apparently uttered the following words: "this moment marks the beginning of the final solution to the Jewish question (*von der jetzt ab Endlösung Judenfrage*)"[43]. It is likely that a few officers of Seeman's platoon also took part in this execution.

Beyond Nikolajev on the Black Sea, where since September 18 Ohlendorf had established temporary EGD headquarters, SK10a proceeded slowly eastward. Between September and October its detachments were reported in Kakhovka, on the Dnieper, in Genichesk, on the Sea of Azov, in the entrance to the Crimean peninsula and in Melitopol, a little further north[44]. Then, during November, while the bulk of the unit was directed eastwards, first towards Mariupol and then in the direction of Rostov on the River Don, some small detachments kept further to the rear. One of these would be assigned to Werner Braune's SK11b and used during the Simferopol massacre[45].

In late October 1941, with Barbarossa progressively bogging down in the mud flats of eastern Ukraine, EGD operations in the area between the Dniester and the Dnieper basically ended. From that moment on the bulk of the kommando would move further east in the southern basin of the Don, where most men of EK12 and SK10a were stationed. But the *Crimean question* remained open; Ohlendorf had moved the rest of EGD and established his command in Crimea

Jewish victims of the Iaşi pogrom. At least 4,000 Jews were killed by the Romanians in Iasi, between June 27 and 29, 1941.

and it was here, prior to further advancement towards the Caucasus, scheduled for the next spring, that the so-called *Jewish question* had to be solved. There were the means and the will to do so. And for once there was also enough time. Enough time to make a *good job*.

9.4 BEFORE THE KRIMCHAKI

According to historian Warren Green, director of St. Louis Center for Holocaust Studies, "the Nazi policies in the Crimea illustrate the most perverse application of Nazi racism during the entire war period"[46]. These policies were focused on trying to identify the racial identity of various ethnic groups encountered by the Wehrmacht in Crimea, in order to decide whether or not to include them among the community of Mosaic descent (hence, ultimately, between the groups affected by the Final Solution). In this sense, Crimea, with its diverse ethnic and religious composition, often mixed and overlapping each other, presented substantial problems for theorists of race, especially with regard to particular communities of ancient Jewish ancestry who mixed over the centuries with people of Turkish-Tartar origin.

From this point of view, the opposite fate of two ethnically related groups such as Karaites and Krimchakis, is paradigmatic in showing the emptiness and inconsistency of the racial obsessions theorized in Berlin: on the one hand Karaites were substantially excluded – despite many questions which continued at least until August 1944 – from the trap of anti-Jewish legislation in Germany, with consequences in the occupied territories, including Crimea. On the other hand Krimchakis were placed among ethnic groups recognized as Jewish, with the subsequent destruction of the many thousands who were reached by detachments of EGD in Crimea. This happened despite the many similarities that related these two populations.

Both groups, in fact, had dwelled in the Crimean peninsula for a long time; Karaites moved there from the ancient Babylonian Jewish communities of IV century BC and Krimchakis probably from Constantinople, around I century AD. Both, in the course of time mixed with the local Turkish-Tartar populations to the point of borrowing their language (*Karaim* for Karaites and *Jagatai* for Krimchakis), that, however, they wrote in Hebrew characters. Both groups had mainly ended up having physical features which were essentially Mongolic and both professed the Jewish religion: Krimchakis observed rabbinical tradition while Karaites observed strict adherence to the Torah. There was a difference though, which probably ended up marking the fate of one group in the obsessive Nazi racial universe: in the late 18th century, on the basis of complex theological arguments, Empress Catherine of Russia had granted the disclaimer to the Karaites of their Jewish ancestry, with subsequent access to all rights and privileges that were denied to the various Jewish communities of Russia. This *status*, which guaranteed the Karaites their own ethno-religious uniqueness together with full Russian citizenship, was maintained in the two centuries that followed until the Karaites reached Germany after the October Revolution, through the many émigré who fled Bolshevik Russia. It was probably due to these historical assumptions that even in Nazi Germany, in January 1939, the Karaites were reconfirmed as not belonging to the communities of Mosaic lineage. Such *privilege* was a pass for their salvation.

Krimchakis, however, never disclaimed their Jewish origins, so they were considered Jews in all respects, albeit with some perplexity. Ohlendorf, who took office in Simferopol in mid-November, was the first to deal with the question of whether or not both these particular ethnic groups belonged to the Jewish religion. On December 5, 1941, overshadowed by doubts, he finally had to consult with Berlin on the matter, meanwhile suspending any decision in this regard.

The problem, in fact, went beyond the *simple* categorization of the two races in one direction rather than the other and ended up reflecting on the more general National Socialist policy towards non-Slavic nationalities of the Soviet Union, which was relatively benign in that it was adopted in an anti-Soviet prospect. As a matter of fact, the favorable reception given to their troops by the Crimean Tartars led the Germans to be cautious about any decision regarding race, in order not to lose this valuable support. The obvious physical and cultural affinities between the Tartars and groups difficult to categorize, such as Karaites and Krimchakis, imposed a more careful analysis of the issue and some caution in applying the extermination *tout-court*, precisely in order to avoid a possible adverse impact against the Tartars, who in the meantime were enlisting in large numbers in the auxiliary companies organized by the Wehrmacht.

On Ohlendorf's request, Office VII of RSHA, directed by Franz Six, attempted to resolve the difficult question on the basis of his own highly rough and approximate historical and anthropological knowledge.

However, as Angrick points out, it is conceivable that the final decision on the matter was taken by Himmler[47], also on the basis of reports sent to him by two of his representatives at that time on a mission in Crimea, in the context of an exploratory mandate in view of the proposed Germanic colonization of the peninsula[48]. We do not know the decisional process that led Himmler to accept the theory of the Kazhara ancestry of the Karaites, who were then seen as Turks who converted to Judaism and not as the Semites of Jewish faith: an historically questionable choice, which however saved the Karaites from Nazi persecution. Krimchakis, in contrast, were seen as the descendants of a group of Sephardic Jews fleeing the Spanish Inquisition around the XV century, hence *deserving* to share the fate of Eastern Ashkenazis[49]. In their case, obviously, mixing with Turkish-Tartar populations of Crimea was not considered a deterrent sufficient to prevent their extermination. In any case, by mid-December 1941, about 2,500 Krimchakis were *liquidated*, of a total population – at the moment of entry of German troops into Crimea – of a few thousand[50].

Ohlendorf was informed about Himmler's decision sometime within the first ten days of December: the date, in fact, is not certain, but it is plausible that Himmler's decision with regards to Krimchakis was taken in the period spanning from December 5 – the day when he received Ohlendorf's request – and the middle of the month, the date *by which*, according to EM 150 of January 2, 1942, the Jewish question was *solved* in Simferopol and other Crimean locations[51]. Ohlendorf's interrogation before the Court in Nuremberg shows that he received the order to exempt Karaites from the Final Solution directly from the race authorities in Berlin[52]: the denial to grant Krimchakis that sort of *racial immunity* implicitly sealed their fate.

Once the *green light* from Berlin was obtained, the usual procedures preparatory to the extermination also came into force in Crimea, including the blacklisting of all Jews in the city, which, in the case of Simferopol, was sent to the *Judenrat* on December 11, 1941[53]. Krimchakis were ordered to gather in order to be *registered* in a part of Simferopol different from that given to *ordinary* Ashkenazis: a mere formal and procedural difference that did not alter the substance of things but it drove them all towards an *ecumenical* extermination.

9.5 PEOPLE OF BERLIN

Questioned by his lawyer, Dr. Erich Mayer, as to who committed the slaughters of Simferopol in December 1941, Werner Braune, commander of SK11b, confirmed before the Trial of Nuremberg that his own unit – and in particular Paul Schulz's Teilkommando "Simferopol" with about 25 to 30 men – was among the main culprits of the massacre. He also added that because of staff shortages, some detachments from SK10b and 11a took part in the shootings, together with a police company that had arrived in Crimea precisely in order to replace the one used until then[55].

The time had come for 4/Polizei-Bataillon 9 to go back to Germany and for 3/Polizei-Bataillon 3 to replace it.

The small and large massacres in which the company had been involved since its entry into Soviet territory had become an almost daily commitment. This reality had in fact pushed almost all the police officers to require massive *turnover* with a different unit, so they could finally be called back to Germany, or at least moved to another area with a different assignment. Such treatment would be the same as that of the Sicherheitspolizei component of the *kommando*, that had already received a favorable staff turnover[55]. The problem of psychophysical breakdown of firing squad members was not something new to the top decision-makers in Berlin, so that by October 1941 both Himmler and Daluege had been made aware of the question by field commanders, Montua in particular[56]. As a means to avoid the situation becoming unmanageable, towards the beginning of December all four company commanders of Polizei-Bataillon 9, including Hans Gabel, were summoned to Berlin for consultations at Hauptamt-Orpo. After that, facing the evidence, the decision was made to withdraw Polizei-Bataillon 9 from Russia, sending in replacement Maj. Arthur Seidel's Polizei-Bataillon 3, also of Berlin. To do this, it was decided to stop Polizei-Bataillon 3 in Zamosc, Poland – originally it was destined for another area of Russia – and divide it into companies to be assigned to various Einsatzgruppen. Thus, once their replacements had arrived on the field, the exhausted men of Polizei-Bataillon 9 could finally go back home[57].

As for EGD, Gabel's 4/9 was replaced by Hptm. Kurt Holzlehner's 3/3 in a real hand-over that for only a few days would see the crossing on the killing fields of the new unaware executioners with the weary veterans of countless massacres.

Due to this mechanism, however, the impact for the police officers of 3/3 would be, if anything, even more traumatic than that suffered by their 4/9 colleagues. That is because during their slow eastward advance, between July and December, leaders of 4/9 had the possibility, up to a certain extent, to rotate the staff assigned to the firing squads, hence introducing their men to the reality of genocide relentlessly, but at least not all of a sudden. In some ways, this relatively gradual approach to such traumatic events, as spectators at first, then gradually turning into performers, was useful to 4/9 men at least in order to prepare for the crossing of the next threshold. A sort of moral mithridatism that, however, was not granted to 3/3 policemen. As a matter of fact, upon getting off the trains that brought them to Crimea via Zamosc, they were catapulted, probably barely realizing it, from the peaceful Berlin fall to the devastating reality of systemic genocide. They had no chance to get accustomed to it, no way to prepare for what was coming to them. The absent-minded vision and the perception of reality that they received as soon as the Poland / Ukraine border was crossed on their way southwards, was probably limited to the fast flow of the landscape through the windows of the train: a train that made them fall, within a few days, from the pleasant moments of rest on the *Unter den Linden* to the chilling daily routine of the mass graves filled with bodies and those suffocated by mud soaked with the victims' blood. Yet these men, *people of Berlin*, reservists like their comrades of Polizei-Bataillon 9, like them having served for several months in Norway between spring and autumn 1940, like them unaccustomed to the daily routine of death and mass killings, like them finding themselves having to point their rifles at the nape of trembling civilians on the edge of a ditch, or inside the ditch, as if plunged into one of Dante's hell pits… they too, like others before them, embraced that gun and hit their target, in dismay perhaps, but with discipline. Then they reloaded their gun and repeated the operation again and again… until it was over, at least for that day.

We do not know what those men were thinking while shooting at their targets, hitting and killing them. Here and there are fragments of their thoughts, often reassembled only after many years, before a federal prosecutor or during the questioning by a judge of the court.

Thoughts from the memory of Albrecht Zöllner, messenger of Stab SK11a, also mobilized during the massacre of Nikolajev of October 14, 1941[58]:

> *Then came women and children. During this execution there were indescribable scenes. I still remember when I had to shoot a woman who tried to protect her little boy keeping it close to the breast. I am not able to describe here in words what I felt at that moment. Soon after I had to shoot a 7 or 8-year old boy. When I pointed the gun at him the boy turned around to me, as if to ask for help. At that time I experienced a feeling of dismay, as if I was killing my own son and in that shock I was able to fire only after some time from the firing order. The shot missed. Then I had a nervous breakdown and had to be replaced immediately. That day I was only used to fill empty magazines of machine guns. Because of this breakdown in a few months my hair became prematurely gray.*

This was Zöllner, one of the many. He was not a criminal, and he was not a policeman. He was just a messenger of a genocidal kommando. He was not even from Berlin. However, there is reason to believe that his testimony, the feelings he had while killing that mother and son, could also be shared by those Berlin police officers, in their first or yet another act of death. There is reason to believe that, simply because it *could not* be otherwise, for the very fact of their *being* human beings. Yet, these human beings – *willing, trivial, common* depending on the interpretations – at some point lost their humanity: some for a short while, the time for a single killing, like Zöllner, others for much longer, perhaps they forgot about it forever. How all this was possible has been explained many times in brilliant essays and from different points of view. We now have a fairly clear picture of the various social, historical, political and psychological dynamics that helped to make this happen; but this is not the point. The point is that for a moment, one single moment or much longer, the humanity of these men, their own sense of morality and civil ethics, disappeared. Long or short as they were, those were moments of total obfuscation of values, of darkening of spirits and silencing of consciousness: this is exactly where the difference between all these men and their victims lies. Up to the very last, the mother who tried to defend her son holding him tight while facing a gun pointed at her, did not give up her *Humanity* and neither did the little boy, who turned in disbelief to his executioner, as if to reject the *inhumanity* of violence.

They stayed Human; those facing them lost their Humanity. For one single moment or for a lifetime.

9.6 DECEMBER MORN

The fate of Krimchaki and Ashkenazi Jews of Simferopol was sealed between Tuesday 9 and Saturday 13 December, 1941. There is no concrete evidence about the actual start of the massacre, which was launched against the Krimchakis first, *probably* on December 9[59] – presumably coinciding with the arrival of Himmler's decision about their fate. The massacre was then discontinued for a couple of days due to staffing problems, and was finally resumed on Thursday 11, when the Ashkenazis received the order to gather at specific sites in order to proceed with their registration. In any case, the action was completed within the first half of December[60].

As witnessed by Ohlendorf and Braune at the Nuremberg Trials, the request to proceed with the slaughter, i.e. to solve the *Jewish question* in the city before Christmas, would have been made as early as November 20, by the command of von Manstein's Eleventh German Army to Stab/EGD, and then discussed in early December during a conversation between Ohlendorf, Braune and Generalquartiermeister/AOK 11, Friedrich Hauck[61]. On that occasion, Hauck would provide EGD with vehicles, fuel and drivers, as well as a number of elements of Feldgendarmerie and GFP[62]. Consequently, Teilkommando "Simferopol" commanded by Paul Schulz (of SK11b), was mobilized in addition to the staff of 4/Polizei-Bataillon 9 available in the city: in relation to the latter, their involvement in the shootings was confirmed by several testimonies, given by several former police officers[63] or by Braune himself[64]. During this first phase, which probably took place on December 9, at least 1,500 Krimchakis were blacklisted and then sent to their deaths[65].

At this point, however, it seems that given the objective impossibility to proceed with the execution of many thousands of Ashkenazis as well, with only a few tens of men of TK "Simferopol", the action was suspended for about 48 hours, while they waited for reinforcements[66]. Indeed, the arrival in the city of 3/Polizei-Bataillon 3, which had been reported to have passed Odessa on December 10[67], was imminent, as was the arrival of TK "Scheuring" (of SK10b) and a detachment of SK11a. All these reinforcements were converging on Simferopol on Ohlendorf's precise orders[68]. In addition, AOK 11 also made available units of Feldgendarmerie-Abteilung 683 and GFP-Gruppe 647[69].

Once these reinforcements arrived, the operations of blacklisting and slaughtering could resume as of December 11, through the already mentioned transmission of the order to the *Judenrat*. As a precaution, in order to avert any possible suspicion and resistance, the victims were required to prepare all their luggage ahead of their transfer to another location. Then, once done with the blacklisting procedures, Wehrmacht trucks began to arrive.

Through snow-capped landscapes the victims were transported a few kilometers out of town, up to a tank ditch dug in the open, far away and not visible from the road, where they found waiting for them, among others, police officers of the 3/3, engaged in their first act of genocide. On seeing the Jews, these policemen immediately understood the reason why many of their colleagues in the 4/9 whom they had just met "were like crazy *(zum Teil durchgedreht waren)*"[70].

Immediately after the victims' arrival, shootings began, with Ohlendorf and Braune, by their own admission, supervising operations. On site were also Heinz Schubert (Ohlendorf's aide), Teilkommandoführer Paul Schulz and Gabel, commander of 4/9, with a half platoon of 10 or 15 policemen taking orders from Karl Jonas, and also, probably, Holzlehner, commander of 3/3[71]. Following is Karl Jonas' affidavit, given on September 3, 1947 before Rolf Wartenberg, investigative attorney of the Council of indictment during the Nuremberg trials against Otto Ohlendorf and the other Einsatzgruppen commanders[73]:

During my activity at EGD I once witnessed an execution. In December 1941 I was ordered to cordon off the execution site by Dr. Werner Braune, commander of SK11a. The execution site was six to ten miles outside Simferopol. Because of that, the victims were driven there by trucks. I took part in the blocking of the site only during the first day, then someone else took over. The cordoned-off area had a size of approximately half a square mile. Within the fenced area was a tank trap. The trucks drove past me and the victims were unloaded in the vicinity of the trench. Every now and then, while I was busy inspecting my unit – 10 to 15 men – I had the opportunity to look in the direction of the trench and observe that gathering of people. At around noon of the same day I got close to the execution site, the tank ditch, that was already partly filled with lying bodies. During my service with the shut-off team, I heard gunshots at regular intervals. I think I can say without a doubt that the bodies I saw lying in the tank ditch were those of the people who were driven to the tank ditch. Then I saw the trucks go back, empty. This is the only execution that I saw with my own eyes. However, I heard of a number of other executions by EGD comrades.

The access road was blocked to prevent the arrival of onlookers, while firing squads, consisting of a minimum of 10 to a maximum of 50 men – including Wehrmacht staff – took turns along one of the long edges of the trench. On the opposite margin, seven to ten feet away, their backs turned to the firing squad, groups of Jews including women and children were lined up in varying numbers, almost always standing, or kneeling, not wearing their heavy clothes and sometimes not even their shoes or their valuables, which they were forced to leave in a pile as soon as they got off the trucks, along the edge of the road[73].

At that point, the order to fire was given, which was followed if necessary, by the death blow, inflicted by NCOs of the firing squad. The bodies of those who fell along the edge of the pit were then pushed inside it by the next group of victims[74]. Periodically, after a certain number of executions, groups of Jews were forced to cover the bodies in the ditch with a thin layer of soil. They too were shot at the end of the day.

With this system executions lasted from December 11 to 13, with a death toll estimated at between 5,000 and 11,000[75]. As reported by Schubert at the Nuremberg trials, Ohlendorf's orders would be peremptory on the need to carry out the executions "in the most humane and military way" because, otherwise, "other methods would have a negative effect (*seelische Belastung*) on the morale of the men assigned to the firing squads"[76].

So let's see how this alleged *humanity* was applied, according to the testimony of Jean Breuer, a driver at the GFP-Gruppe 647, who took part in the shootings[77].

One morning, we – 25 to 30 men – received orders to take part in the shooting of Jews. A truck of our unit drove us to the execution site, about 10-15 miles away from Simferopol, if my memory is correct near a village along the road to Kerch. Our kommando was probably driven by NCO Berleb, who by then had already been promoted to sergeant [...]. Our vehicle came up to the SD command, near which several trucks with Jews on board – men, women and children – were already waiting with all their luggage. Led by some men of the SD, the column began to move. After we had stopped near the site, the SD ordered the Jews to get off the vehicles. They then had to leave their bags, their coats and their shoes by the roadside. The column, barefoot and guided by SD men was led through the snow to a trench dug about 300 yards away from the road. In the pit executions by an SD kommando were already underway. The SD firing squad was formed, as I recall of about 50 men, lined up along the trench, firing with machine guns on a group of Jews lined up on the other side of the trench.

The arriving Jews could see the whole procedure. There were harrowing scenes. The Jews began to cry, because they understood what was going to happen to them. I remember that during the evacuation one of us had reassured the Jews that they would only be transferred. After our arrival at the execution site, we were assigned to reinforce the SD firing squad and then we joined them. Then, on the other side, Jews were aligned with their faces turned toward the shooters. After the victims were put in place, an SD lieutenant gave us the firing order. Some of the victims immediately fell into the pit, while others fell and remained on the edge. The latter were then thrown into the pit by the waiting Jews. Inside the pit there were also Jews who had to layer the victims' bodies. If a Jew was wounded, but not mortally, SD men intervened to give the death blow, among which I remember a sergeant major with a submachine gun. Children, among adults, were killed in the same way. The shootings went on without interruption and when a line of Jews had been mowed down, another took its place. From a certain point onwards, fire was opened without even waiting for the order, automatically. We of the GFP were equipped with rifles and were then watched by the SD men so that we took aim when shooting. The execution site had been cordoned by SD people. Some Jews tried to escape and were killed by these men on watch.

From evidence such as Jean Breuer's, the public prosecutor of Munich was able to reconstruct the overall picture of the massacre at Simferopol, in the course of preliminary investigations against five members of the same GFP-Gruppe 647 (StAw München 112 Js 3/66) – which then ended up in a request for the case to be closed[78]:

The victims were driven to the tank ditch with blows of whips and scourges. They were then aligned facing the trench and shot in the back. In any case, the following victims could see before them the bloodied bodies of people killed before them. Children were separated from their mothers and murdered before their eyes. They were killed with blows to the neck and then thrown into the trenches.

Perhaps, as Braune wrote in his affidavit of February 24, 1947, victims were treated *humanely* by their captors. Perhaps there were none of those scenes perpetrated by brutal drunken auxiliaries. Perhaps there were no scenes of children being thrown into the ditches and hit by bullets in flight or whose skulls were crushed against a light pole. Perhaps those episodes of wild butchery and indiscriminate firing that characterized many of the killings described in previous chapters did not occur. Perhaps there were no executions of the sick in their beds. Perhaps there was no orgy of burning of synagogues with people inside. Perhaps there was none of that. Perhaps there was only a scrupulous and orderly distribution of death, a balanced and rational approach to the genocidal method in order to achieve the intended result, without indulging in unnecessary excesses. Perhaps it was the will to do *the job* quickly and efficiently, so as to minimize the emotional involvement of those who were called to kill. Perhaps it was so. But even if it was so, if every psychological load was purposely avoided as much as it was possible, then *implicitly*, in such a wilderness of empathy, that Humanity claimed by Ohlendorf and quoted by Braune, *could not* find space in any way. From that side of the ditch *there should not* be space, necessarily, on that December morning, for anything that was not the hypnotic repetitiveness of the mortal act carried out again and again, with eyes fixed within the horizon of the rifle sight. A soothing and numbing rhyme of gestures, at the same time antidote and narcotic against that overwhelming and desperate *need of life* expressed by those about to die. Raising the eyes from the rifle sight, *seeing* the victim instead of the target, would have meant to become *contaminated* by that desperate vitality on the other side of the pit; maybe someone did and perhaps some shots failed. Maybe a few moments of *Humanity* really did come off on that side of the trench too. Perhaps there were exceptions. Exceptions, not the rule. The rule was elsewhere and began where the line of sight ended: on the target. On the victim.

9.7 REDDE RATIONEM

The investigation into the crimes perpetrated by Einsatzgruppen (and by Polizei-Bataillon 9 which we will discuss separately) on the Eastern Front between June 1941 and 1943 is one of the cardinal points within the more general frame of accusations represented in Germany by the Nuremberg trials. The trial of the Einsatzgruppen, in particular, was held in front of an

American military tribunal (NMT) from September 29, 1947 to April 10, 1948 and ended with the death sentence for most of the major leaders who succeeded to the command of the four Einsatzgruppen and their sub-divisions. With regards to EGD, both Ohlendorf and Werner Braune were sentenced to death, while capital punishments were originally imposed on EGD's deputy commander Willy Seibert and to Heinz Schubert, but were later commuted to 15 and 10 years in prison respectively. Held just three years after the war and therefore still very much affected by the emotions emerging from the atrocities perpetrated by extermination groups, the trial of Einsatzgruppen was focused on the main figures and did not involve the many secondary characters involved in the massacres in different degrees, against which several Courts of West Germany began to move in the postwar investigations. The Court of Munich in particular, after ZStL's preparatory work, started a long series of preliminary investigations against the various sub-divisions of EGD. These investigations, which lasted for about a decade spanning the sixties and the early seventies, affected a large number of people, but only in a few cases could lead to processes with sentences of significant weight.

Regarding the December 1941 massacre of Simferopol, references and testimonies are filed in many cases initiated by the public prosecution of Munich, and in particular:

- StAw München I 22 Js 201/61, against Stab/EGD. According to Ohlendorf's affidavit of April 2, 1947, EGD's commanding core was made up of a limited number of executives. Among them, his deputy Willy Seibert, his aide Heinz Hermann Schubert, three medical officers (Schnopfhagen, Grohmann and Schröder), an economy executive, a telecommunications executive, a technical counselor and several employees and cadres. Moreover, the commander of 4/9, Gabel, was co-opted. The liaison officer between Ohlendorf and Stab/AOK 11 was Hstuf. Johann Seynstahl[79].
- StAw München I 22 Js 203/61, against SK10b, that ended with the conviction on March 22, 1972 of the three defendants: Sigfried Schuchart (5 years), Karl Finger (4½ years), Theodor Lipps (3 years). This department, that between mid-November and mid-December was relocated between Kerch and Feodosia, could have sent a small detachment to take part in the massacre of Simferopol, but there is no proof of this[80].
- StAw München I 22 Js 204/61, against SK11a, that ended on February 26, 1970 with the conviction of the unit commander Paul Zapp (life sentence) and two other co-defendants: Leo von der Recke (13 years) and Karl-Heinrich Noa (7 years). The case against the fourth defendant, Georg Möhlmeyer, was dropped.
- StAw München I 22 Js 205/61, against SK11b, ended on March 29, 1974 with the conviction of the three defendants: Rudolf Eschenbacher (5 years), Johannes Schlupper (4½ years) and Heinrich Winterstein (3 years).
- StAw München I 115 Js 4/66, against five members of GFP-Gruppe 647, later closed at the request of the prosecutor himself, despite the confessions given by all defendants. With regards to the unit, it was formed on September 10, 1940 and had been sent to France where it was attached to the 11th German Army in Romania. With a strength of about 80-90 men receiving orders from Feldkommissar Hermann Adalbert, in August 1941 it was initially used to block the influx of Jews who, being hounded by the Romanians, were trying to cross the bridges over the Dniester. It was then moved to Simferopol. It seems that on the occasion of the Simferopol massacre the department mobilized about thirty men who took part in the executions[81].
- StAw München I 112 Js 3/66, against Feldgendarmerie-Abteilung 683. This department was formed around early August 1939 in the Blücher-Polizei-Kaserne of Berlin, partly with staff of Schutzpolizei in service in Berlin, transferred from normal reveire activities, partly with elements of the gendarmerie of the Frankfurt am Main area, and partly with elements of the Wehrmacht. Deployed to

France in September 1940, it was later transferred to Krakov and then, in April 1941, to Targu Frumos, Romania, as part of the 11th German Army. The department entered Soviet territory on June 30, and reached Simferopol on November 14 with two companies, for a total of approximately 150 men. One of the companies, 2/683 took orders from SS-Hauptsturmführer Joachim Siedel, a professional police officer. In Simferopol the department was subordinated to Ortskommandantur I/853. The two companies took part in the slaughter of December 11-13, both in the round-up of the victims during the blacklisting and the following transportation on trucks, and forming the security cordon around the *killing field.* In both situations the department staff would use whips, sticks and dogs, so as to convince the most recalcitrant Jews to obey orders[82].

Here are brief biographies of some members of EGD and 4/Polizei-Bataillon 9 who were never prosecuted for war crimes, but by reason of their role and the departments they commanded, were allegedly involved in the slaughter of Simferopol.

SCHEURING, Adam: born March 13, 1899 in Veitschöchheim, near Würzburgj. SS-Obersturmführer. SS member from June 1, 1933, NSDAP member. Assigned to SK11a, he reached the Jalta/Eupatoria area around mid-November with the rest of his department, then, in early December, he was called back to Simferopol with a small detachment on Ohlendorf orders, in order to take part in the slaughter of December 11-13. Wounded in combat in 1942, he was awarded EK II. There is no indication of investigations for war crimes against him[83].

SCHULZ, Paul: born September 22, 1910 in Berlin. SS-Untersturmführer. Commander of Teilkommando "Simferopol" and, from early September 1942 Werner Braune's successor as commander of SK11b. Suspected of war crimes, his name was inserted in the StAw München I, 22 Js 202/61 dossier with regards to SK10a and in May 1962 the public prosecution of Munich issued a warrant for his arrest. After further investigations he was declared dead, his death having occurred in Leussow, near Neustrelitz, in June 1945[84].

GABEL, Hans: born April 4, 1909 in Magdeburg. Polizeihauptmann. Stahlhelm member since 1924, he joined the NSDAP on October 11, 1927. He served the SA from 1927 to 1935. He then enlisted in the police and took part in the occupation of the Sudetenland, Austria, Czechoslovakia and the invasion of Poland. A staunch Nazi and member of the SS from June 1, 1940, he became commander of 4/Polizei-Bataillon 9. Assigned to Stab / EGD he was, in the words of Ohlendorf himself, one of the few officers of his command – in addition to Braune, Schubert and Seibert – to which he assigned the task of supervising the executions. After 4/9's withdrawal from Russia and after only four weeks' leave, he returned voluntarily to the EGD, where, due to the illness of its commander Hptm. Holzlehner, he took command of 3/Polizei-Bataillon 3. Promoted to major and SS-Sturmbannführer, from spring 1943 he became Ia official at HSSPF "Serbien". Arrested in the post-war, he was released from a British POW camp in late 1946. Subjected to preliminary investigations by the public prosecutor of Munich in May 1962, his name was listed in the StAw München I, 22 Js 255/61 binder, then closed by decision dated March 6, 1963[85].

JONAS, Karl: Polizeileutnant. Born August 3, 1909 in Zminj, Istria. Having moved to Austria at the end of World War I, he graduated in Vienna in 1928. He then joined the illegal Austrian Nazi Party in 1935 and obtained his pilot license in 1936. He signed up to the Austrian police and remained in service in Vienna after the Anschluss. SA member from 1937 to March 1938, he joined the NSDAP and the SS and was admitted to a school for police officers in 1940. Promoted to Lieutenant in 1941, in April of that year he was assigned to Polizei-Bataillon 9 as a platoon leader in the 4/9. At the start of *Barbarossa* he was attached with his platoon to SK11b, where he remained until

December 1941, when the department was sent to Norway. It seems that he was awarded KVK II. Questioned as a witness at the Nuremberg trials against Ohlendorf, and by the public prosecutor in Munich in the investigation against SK11b (StAw München I 22 Js 205/61), it seems that he was never placed under investigation for war crimes[86].

SEEMAN, Max: Polizeileutnant. Born in the late nineteenth century he volunteered in the Navy during World War I and after 1918 he enlisted in the police and was assigned to the district of Berlin-Charlottenburg. He was then transferred, after a few months in the service of reviere to the Spandau suburb. He remained in service for about 20 years, then, in the autumn of 1939 he was assigned to Polizei-Bataillon 9 with the rank of Hauptwachtmeister. Placed in command of the half platoon assigned to SK10a, he was guilty – along with four of his colleagues – of the unprovoked execution of a Jew in Bălti *as a demonstration to his men*. It is uncertain whether or not he was together with the detachment of SK10a called by Ohlendorf to take part in the Simferopol massacre. He remained permanently assigned to the battalion until the end of the conflict. In 1969, already an old man, he was called to testify by the public prosecutor in Munich during the investigations against members of SK10a (StAw München I, 114 Js 17/65). There is no evidence about investigations against him for war crimes[87].

9.8 CONSIDERATIONS

In many ways the slaughter of Simferopol that took place from December 9 to 13, 1941, is comparable to that of Kharkov, which occurred between late December and early January 1942. Both, in fact, occurred in areas of military administration and in both cases the involvement of the Wehrmacht was crucial in the decision-making processes that led to the annihilation of the two Jewish communities. These were overwhelmed by the devastating convergence between the ideological fury incarnate of the mobile extermination units and alleged occupational issues handled by the army – rigidly anchored to their obsessions with security, even before any consideration regarding logistics. In this sense, although it was mostly Sonderkommando men who physically perpetrated the executions of Kharkov and Simferopol, it is equally true that the cooperation received from the local administrative structures of the Wehrmacht was absolutely necessary, with the army more than ever willing to provide logistical support and personnel to the extermination groups, in return for assumption of responsibilities by the latter in the execution of the *dirty work*. Not only that, in both situations it was the military commands that were first in raising the Jewish question in the two newly occupied cities. Stab / AOK 11 actually went as far as to solicit the solution with an explicit request to Ohlendorf's Stab in the case of Simferopol. On the other hand, the widespread tendency in von Manstein's army command was known even to the troops[88]. It comes as no surprise then, that as early as November 1941 – that is, a month before the slaughter – in a report to Korück 553 (Gen.Ltn. Heinrich Doehla) on the political situation in the city, Ortskommandantur I/853, responsible for the Simferopol district, already had full knowledge about the fate of the *remaining 11,000 Jews* who would be executed (*executiert*) by the SD[89].

Obviously, such foresight by a command of the lower level of an Ortskommandantur could not be random. It rather seems to confirm the existence, behind the scenes, of an unofficial line of conduct, inevitably inspired by higher levels of command in the Wehrmacht – in this case Stab/AOK 11 – aimed at the indiscriminate elimination of entire categories considered potentially dangerous. In other words, the idea of the Final Solution – in this case for alleged tactical reasons – would definitely be accepted by the army *too* – and not just by the ideological circle of the regime – to such a point that it spread to the lowest levels of military hierarchy. That said, the real *reasons* that prompted Stab/AOK 11 to request from Ohlendorf the solution to the *Jewish question* in Simferopol by Christmas 1941, remains an unresolved issue[90]. In this sense, the absence of a plausible causal link which may have stirred this disproportionate initiative by Stab/AOK 11 seems disconcerting.

As we shall see in the next chapter, the pretext used by Kharkov's Stadtkommandantur to proceed with the resettlement of local Jews in ghettos– and their subsequent annihilation by SK4a – was an attack whose victim was the commander of 68.ID, Gen. Georg Braun, along with some of his staff. On the contrary, nothing like that happened in Simferopol, where it rather seems that the physical elimination of the *entire* Jewish population took the shape of *preventive genocide*[91]. From this point of view the reasons – or rather non-reasons – given by Werner Braune in his interrogation before the Attorney Peter W. Walton about the possible causes at the basis of Stab/AOK 11's request are interesting: *maybe* [italics by me – authors note] military or strategic reasons, or issues related to the lack of housing or food – in any case, simple assumptions that Braune himself was not sure about[92]. Nothing, however, outlining any cause/effect relation, but only the application of preconceived mechanisms.

Apart from any more or less plausible motivational dynamics, what is certain is that instead of simply providing logistical support to the extermination groups, the army agreed to be fully involved in the genocidal action of Simferopol, up to the edges of the mass graves, through the use of no less than 180 men belonging to FGA 683 and GFP-Gruppe 647: one dependent on OK I/854 and the other subordinate directly to AOK 11[93]; an *uneasy* dependency, which outlines not only a tacit connivance with the same extermination groups, but an obvious high level of complicity of the Wehrmacht in the Jewish genocide.

9.9 EPILOGUE

Helmstedt, Lower Saxony, 11.30 hours, January 17, 1947.

They had traveled a lot in those last two years, though not of their will, and every time they were getting a bit closer to their homes. He could not tell exactly where they were now, but the feeling was that they had reached their final stage. They had left Norway in December 1945 as uninvited guests, after about three and a half years in the mountains bordering Sweden. A very long stay which had helped to ease the tensions accumulated in the past few months on the Russian front. In those three years, while everything around them changed, they remained calm and almost forgotten, until May 1945, when somebody told them that it was all over. Many began to think of their return home, to Berlin, although the letters they received made it clear that there was not much left of the city they had left that distant summer of 1941, a geological era earlier. Then, while everything was still confused, the Tommies landed in Norway and they found themselves prisoners of war, without any idea what their fate would be.

Eight months had passed until, between December 1945 and January 1946, they had been loaded aboard a ship and, to the relief of the Norwegian population, they had sailed for Germany, to the internment camp of Westertimke, near Bremen[94]. That was their initial stage, and already in those early, hectic weeks, many of them had begun to hope for an imminent release. As a matter of fact, some of them actually had been released, and in any case, mail from home came with some regularity: even if they would have to keep waiting, the situation was not intolerable. Sure, they were subjected to interrogations, but it was mainly the SS to be given the grilling: actually the Scots who supervised the field could almost seem as friendly with the Wehrmacht men and with those of the military police. Then, things changed.

On July 3, 1946 they were all transferred to Esterwegen, Emsland, which was said to be an internment camp for suspected war criminals[95]. Now they were gripped with fear: someone had begun to talk about processes, others a long period of political re-education as a condition for release, some were just waiting. As for himself, he tried to look around in order to understand the situation, and what he saw were men from other departments in addition to his, who all had something to fear: ex-officials of the security police, SS concentration camp guards. No-one, however, spoke happily of the past, nor was willing to admit anything. The CIC9, the field where they were locked, seemed to be a center of *filtering* and *screening* for prisoners considered dangerous, but every now and then someone went out; released, or more probably, in order to be transferred to some other field. They too, Polizei-Bataillon 9, had seen many fellow soldiers leave during the long weeks and months following their arrival in Esterwegen: some were set free, while many others, indeed, had succeeded in hiding their tracks in Norway, since the days of surrender. By then, only 247 men from the whole battalion were left[96]. He, Alfred Opielka, was still one of them. Despite that, he had cautious confidence, which he also expressed a few days earlier, on December 12, in a letter to his sister-in-law Marie. Actually, strictly speaking, the longer the time spent waiting the more things receded away and the possibility that mud resurfaced from the bottom of the pit were less and less. Or so they all silently hoped.

Then, the day before, January 16, 1947, at around ten o'clock at night, they were gathered suddenly in front of their barracks in the camp and quickly loaded onto trucks in silence. Many thought it seemed strange, someone scrawled letters quickly, everyone gathered their few belongings into a backpack and left. The ride was short. There was a train waiting for them in Oldenburg station and all around the aisles there were about sixty British military police officers who boarded the train with them on that convoy with tinted windows[97].

They left in the middle of the night, not knowing anything. There was no intermediate stop, just the uniform monotony of the journey, interrupted only by the regular passage of British military police in the hallway of the carriages. Until dawn. Then, at dawn, they noticed the sunlight filtering into the compartments, coming from the direction in which they were going. Some of them, suspicious, had then begun to calculate the path traveled by the hours of travel and the alleged speed of the convoy and made rough estimations of at least two hundred kilometers. The problem, however, was not the distance, but the direction of travel.

Eventually they stopped for a break that grew longer and longer. They saw the MPs move quickly through the corridor, they heard carriage doors open and close, they even seemed to hear the vehicle engines, screeching brakes and slamming doors from outside. By now, it was about 11:30 hours in the morning and they had been still for more than half an hour.

They heard the doors open and shut with a metallic thud once more and then the slight forward thrust of the train that started to move slowly. The voices came shortly afterwards, from the bottom of the carriage, at first confused and indistinguishable in the rattling of the movement and then more and more perceivable, as they came closer to their compartment. Finally, when they were just a few meters away, they all recognized. They were voices of a familiar language, the same language that they had already heard a few years earlier, in another time and another situation. It was the past returning, but this time as a nemesis: it was in Simferopol, shortly before returning to Germany, the last time they had heard someone speak in Russian[98].

ENDNOTES

1 «…and then came women and children». Testimony given by Albrecht Zöllner, StAw München I, 22 Js 204/61, dated April 26, 1962.

2 Angrick, p. 394.

3 *Ibid.*, pp. 397-398. Testimony given by reservist Eichelbaum, given to the public prosecutor in Munich, StAw München I, 22 Js 205/61 of June 25, 1964.

4 Angrick, p. 109.

5 *Ibid.*, pp. 109-110.

6 *Ibid.*, pp. 139-140, Angrick Escalation, p. 6/33.

7 Curilla, p. 807.

8 *Ibid.*, pp. 805-806, Angrick, pp. 178-179. The precise division of the half-platoons and platoons between EK and / or SK of EGD is not known. Until the beginning of July EGD was organized between Heinz Seetzen's SK10[th] and Alois Persterer's SK 10b (each of which had been assigned a half-platoon of policemen), Paul Zapp's EK 11 (a platoon) and Gustav Nosske's EK 12 (a platoon). Then in early July, EK 11 was in turn reorganized and divided in SK 11th (Paul Zapp) and SK 11b (Bruno Müller), to each of which half of the platoon previously assigned to EK 11 was attached.

9 Angrick, p. 163.

10 *Ibid.*, p. 169.

11 *Ibid.*, p. 186.

12 In the following pages we will resume the genocidal path of Sonderkommando 10a, 11a and 11b, in the July / October 1941 time-lapse, with particular reference to the role of cores of police officers detached within these structures. Instead, we will not take into account the other two EGD detachments, namely EK 12 and SK 10b, which had no role in the operations in Crimea.

13 Curilla, p. 806, Angrick, p. 189. Testimonies given before the public prosecutor of Munich, StAw München I, 22 Js 205/61, by former members of 4/Polizei-Bataillon 9: W.Z., W.K., W.B., and August Walloch, who took part in the Bolhrad action by guarding the synagogue from the outside and by pushing inside the Jews who later burned alive in the arson or were buried by the fall of the dome. Mallmann/Riess/Pyta, p. 153, testimony by Helmut A., member of SK 11b, given on November 15, 1961 to ZStL, 213 AR 1901/66.

14 Curilla, pp. 806-807, Angrick, pp. 187-189. One of these *actions*, with 155 victims is reported in EM 45 dated August 7, 1941. On Tighina's executions, see the testimonies given to the public prosecutor of Munich, StAw München I, 22 Js 205/61, by former members of SK 11b. In addition to that reported in the EM, there would have been two or three minor actions for a total of a hundred victims, as quoted in the testimonies of former police officers G.M. and W.B.

15 Angrick, p. 188, Angrick Escalation, p. 7/33, Mallmann/Riess/Pyta, p. 153. Testimony by Johannes Schlupper, given on May 11, 1962 ZStL, 213 AR 1901/66. Testimonies given to the public prosecutor in Munich, StAw München I, 22 Js 205/61, by former members of SK 11b. Müller's words, *«ihr müßt sterben, damit wir leben können», are basically identical to those pronounced by an official of* Polizei-Bataillon 320, during the slaughter of Kamenec Podolski: *«Seht Euch diesen Mann an. Das ist ein typischer Jude, den man ausrotten muss, damit wir Deutschen leben können»*. See § 4.10.

16 Angrick, p. 188, testimony by Johannes Schlupper, given on August 9, 1966 to the public prosecutor in Munich, StAw München I, 22 Js 205/61. LG München I, 115 Ks 6/71 of March 29, 1974, v. Schlupper and others.

17 *Ibid.*, p. 188. According to the testimony of Otto Fischer, member of SK 11b, soon after Tighina there would have been, among the members of the firing squads, a couple of nervous breakdowns that needed medical treatment.

18 *Ibid.*, p. 301, Curilla, p. 810. According to the indictment by the public prosecutor in Munich, StAw München I, 22 Js 205/61, vs. Johannes Schlupper and others, there were *at least* 500 victims.

19 Angrick, p. 300, Mallmann/Riess/Pyta, p. 153.

20 Mallmann/Riess/Pyta, p. 153, testimony by Ernst D., member of 4/Polizei-Bataillon 9, given on December 4, 1959 before ZStL, 213 AR 1901/66. Angrick, p. 300, testimony by Johannes Schlupper, given on May 10, 1962 before the public prosecutor in Munich, StAw München I, 22 Js 205/61.

21 Angrick, p. 301. Testimony by Johannes Schlupper, given before the public prosecutor in Munich, StAw München I, 22 Js 205/61. To quote Fromm, what we have here is a case of extreme sadism, of a sexual nature, with a desire for contempt and total control perpetrated by the tormentors upon their victims – specifically defenseless women, made even more vulnerable by their nudity – probably fuelled by alcohol, with a subsequent lowering of the moral threshold: certainly something extremely brutal and completely different to the disconcerting and self-absolving statements by Schlupper regarding the humanity of the executions. On Schlupper see Angrick, pp. 425-427.

22 *Ibid.*, p. 305.

23 Stab/EGD made its entrance to Simferopol during the first ten days of November 1941. See EM 132 dated November 12, 1941. SK11a followed between the end of November and early December. Angrick, pp. 323, 335.

24 *Ibid.*, pp. 169, 171.

25 *Ibid.*, p. 171.

26 Krausnick/Wilhelm, p. 199.

27 Angrick, p. 178, Curilla, p. 806.

28 Angrick, p. 179.

29 *Ibid.*, p. 185, Curilla, p. 806.

30 The Chişinău ghetto had been established around early July 1941 to segregate the around 9,000 Jews in town on the moment of the entrance of Romanian and German troops. It was guarded by units of the Romanian police force and also included a concentration camp from which Jewish men kept inside could be taken out in the event of a reprisal. Angrick, pp. 180-181.

31 It seems that the decision to include women was taken by Zapp, who was following oral instructions coming from Ohlendorf. Angrick, p. 181.

32 Angrick, pp. 241-251.

33 In the city of Cherson, southeast of Nikolajev, on a day between September 16 and 30, 1941, about 5,000 Jews had been slaughtered by SK 11a. Angrick, p. 251, Curilla, p. 809.

34 Krausnick/Wilhelm, p. 203. On October 29, a Vorkommando of SK 11a reached the area of Perekop while Simferopol was reached on November 5, by another detachment.

35 Angrick, p. 340, Curilla, p. 811.

36 Angrick, p. 147, Angrick Escalation, p. 6/33. Probably 4,000 Jews lost their lives in the Iasi pogrom, and at least as many died during the brutal deportations that followed the slaughter. Regarding the pogrom of Iași see Jean Ancel: *The Jassy pogrom – June 29, 1941,* Berlino, 2001.

37 Curilla, pp. 805-806, Angrick, pp. 164, 166-167. Testimonies by former police officers Hermann Joswich and Friedrich Schümann, given before StAw München, 22 Js 202/61, on March 21 and April 17, 1962. In particular, on July 11, ten Jews were shot as a reprisal for the attack suffered by a German vehicle. A second execution, with 20 victims, was perpetrated on July 15, followed a few hours later by a third, with 45 more hostages shot. Executions took place with the victims on their knees and shot through the neck.

38 Angrick, p. 164. Testimony of police officer Alexander Hülß, given on July 16, 1964 before StAw München, 22 Js 202/61.

39 Angrick, p. 166.

40 *Ibid.*, pp. 219-222, Curilla, p. 806, Krausnick/Wilhelm, p. 200. The allegation of conspiracy was made by a Ukrainian woman who eavesdropped on a conversation in Yiddish among some of the alleged conspirators. During the roundup of Jewish men and the subsequent selection of victims, however, it was not possible to identify any of the hypothetical conspirators and it was therefore decided to proceed with the execution of those who were identified as communists, in addition to the workers of a plant for bottling mineral waters, as potential poisoners [sic!]. The decision to go on with the shooting was taken by Wehrmacht's XXX.AK commander von Salmuth after a brief conversation with Seetzen.

41 Angrick, p. 222, Curilla, p. 806. The presence of police officers in the firing squad is reported in the testimonies of some 4/9 members.

42 *Ibid.*, pp. 234-235.

43 *Ibid.*, p. 235.

44 *Ibid.*, p. 236, Krausnick/Wilhelm, p. 201.

45 NMT Green Series, vol. IV, p. 327. Testimony by Werner Braune, Curilla, p. 811.

46 Green, p. 171.

47 Angrick, p. 328.

48 They were Oberkriegsverwaltungsrat Fritz Donner and Maj. Ernst Seifert of Wirtschaftstab-Ost, who stayed in Crimea from December 3 to 12, 1941. They were in Simferopol where they had a meeting with Ohlendorf on December 4. Angrick, pp. 328-329.

49 *Ibid.*, p. 330.

50 The number of Krimchakis still in Crimea in November 1941, when German troops arrived, is unknown. Since the Soviet census of 1926, about 6,400 Krimchakis had remained in the region. Many of them, however, managed to escape before the invasion. Green, pp. 171, 173.

51 NMT Green Series, vol. IV, pp. 185-186, EM 150 dated January 2, 1942: "Simferopol, Eupatoria, Alushta, Karasubazar, Kerch, Feodosia and other western Crimea districts were cleansed of Jews. From November 16 until December 15, 1941, 17,645 Jews, 2,504 Krimchakis, 824 gypsies and 212 communists and partisans have been shot. In total, 75,881 people were killed".

52 NMT Green Series, vol. IV, pp. 274-275.

53 Green, p. 172. The date of December 11 as blacklisting day for Simferopol Jews is reported in Benjamin West, *be-Hevlei Kiliya* [Pains of Destruction], Tel Aviv, 1963, p. 139.

54 NMT Green Series, vol. IV, p. 325.

55 Angrick, pp. 339-340.

56 See what happened to the staff of Polizei-Bataillon 316 and 322 during the slaughter of Mogilev, described in §§ 6.5 and 6.6.

57 Angrick, p. 340.

58 Angrick, p. 247. Testimony by Albrecht Zöllner, given before the public prosecutor of Munich. StAw München I, 22 Js 204/61, of April 26, 1962.

59 Angrick, p. 338, Curilla, p. 810.

60 NMT Green Series, vol. IV, p. 323. Testimony by Werner Braune.

61 *Ibid.*, pp. 215 (Braune), 251 (Ohlendorf), 292-293 (Ohlendorf), 324, 327 (Braune). Hauck, in this source, is wrongly quoted as *Hanck*. On Hauck, see HIS, p. 352.

62 Angrick Escalation, p. 22/33, Oldenburg, pp. 167-168, Stein, p. 354.

63 Curilla, pp. 810. Testimonies by E.V., E.D, and H.S., given before the public prosecutor of Munich. StAw München I, 22 Js 204/61.

64 NMT Green Series, vol. IV, p. 325. Testimony by Werner Braune.

65 Angrick, pp.338-339.

66 SK 11b had been divided into four Teilkommandos: "Simferopol", "Yevpatoria", "Alushta" and "Karasubazar", with a manpower ranging between 20 and 30 each. Simferopol's kommando, led by Paul Schulz, had 25÷30 men, including drivers and four police officers who led interrogations. NMT Green Series, vol. IV, p. 324. Testimony by Werner Braune.

67 Angrick, p. 340. Testimonies by Fritz Urbach and Heinz Hoffmann, given before the public prosecutor of Munich.

StAw München I, 22 Js 201/61, of December 9, 1963 and August 29, 1962.

68 NMT Green Series, vol. IV, p. 325. Testimony by Werner Braune.

69 Angrick, p. 341.

70 *Ibid.* See testimony by Walter Güsfeldt to the public prosecutor in Munich. StAw München I, 22 Js 204/61, dated October 2, 1963.

71 NMT Green Series, vol. IV, p. 325. Testimony by Werner Braune. Curilla, p. 811.

72 Affidavit Karl Jonas. NMT, Document NO-5272, September 3, 1947.

73 NMT Green Series, vol. IV, pp. 215, 300. Testimonies by Werner Braune and Otto Ohlendorf.

74 Angrick, p. 342.

75 The number of victims of the slaughter at Simferopol is not precisely known. Besides the 1,500 Krimchakis killed on December 9, at least another 5,000 Jews were killed. Curilla, p. 811. According to Braune's testimony during the Trial of Nuremberg, about half of the initial 10,000 Jews who were in the city managed to escape before the entry of German troops leaving at least 4 or 5,000 exposed to the genocidal action. NMT Green Series, vol. IV, p. 327. Testimony by Werner Braune. The truth is, according to a report by Ortskommandantur I/853 to Korück 553 dated November 14, 1941 (Hptm. Kleiner) as many as 11,000 Jews of the about 20,000 in the city on the eve of the war had remained there. Angrick, pp. 325-326. According to HIS, p. 175, about 10,000 Jews fell victim in Simferopol up until February 1942. According to Oldenburg, the victims were 13,000. In any case, by February 1942 the city was declared *Judenfrei*. Angrick, p. 343, EM 150 dated January 2, 1942. See chapter 9, note 45.

76 NMT Green Series, vol. IV, p. 582. Testimony by Heinz Schubert. See how Ohlendorf's alleged humanity was due as a need to preserve the morale of his men, not as a form of respect to the victims.

77 HIS, p. 177, Oldenburg, p. 168. Testimony by Jean Breuer, given before ZStL 213 AR 493/67 and included in the binder of the Public Prosecution of Munich, March 16, 1969.

78 Streim, p. 582.

79 NMT Green Series, vol. IV, p. 134. See Otto Ohlendorf's affidavit, NO-2856 dated April 2, 1947, Angrick, pp. 338, 416, 590.

80 NMT Green Series, vol. IV, p. 325. Testimony by Werner Braune.

81 Angrick Escalation, pp. 22/33, Oldenburg, pp. 167-168, 208, Streim, p. 581.

82 Oldenburg, pp. 66-67, Streim, p. 582. See also von Haken, *Spalier am Mördgraben,* on Zeit on line.

83 Angrick, p. 340, Curilla, p. 811, MacLean Field, p. 105.

84 MacLean Field, p. 111, Angrick, pp. 476 and 725.

85 NMT Green Series, vol. IV, pp. 46, 135, 537, 584. Testimony by Otto Ohlendorf, Angrick, pp. 96, 344, 395-396, Klemp Ermittelt, p. 101, Curilla, p. 956, MacLean Field, p. 59.

86 Angrick, pp. 342, 396, MacLean Field, p. 76.

87 Angrick, p. 396.

88 *Ibid.*, p. 338.

89 Kunz, p. 64, Stein, p. 354, HIS, p. 176, NMT Green Series, vol. X, p. 1259.

90 Stein, pp. 354-355.

91 On November 15, two weeks after the entry of German troops into the city, the explosion of a bomb in a building had killed or wounded eight German soldiers, while on November 29, two German soldiers were killed, one of them by stepping on a mine. In retaliation 50 male inhabitants of Simferopol (ethnicity unspecified) had been shot. Angrick, p. 333, Stein, pp. 356-357.

92 NMT Green Series, vol. IV, p. 328, Stein, p. 356.

93 Overall, about 400 people belonging to Stab/EGD (about ten), Stab/SK 11b (about 5), TK "Simferopol" (25 ÷ 30), TK "Scheuring" (probably about twenty), GFP-Gruppe 647 (25 ÷ 30), FGA 683 (about 150), 4/PB9 (a few tens), 3/PB3 (at least a hundred) and probably to a detachment of 11th SK (maybe ten), took part in the massacre: a considerable number, which establishes the victims/perpetrators ratio to an overall 27 to 1, that is 9 to 1 for each of the three days of the execution and that shatters completely the grotesque negationist theory of the nonexistence of the slaughter of Simferopol, based on obsolete theorems of Reginald T. Paget dating back to 1951, according to whom *only one SD company* would be objectively unable to massacre 11,000 Jews *in a single day of the executions* (on November 16 [sic]). See Stein, pp. 357-358.

94 Klemp Sibirien, p. 283. The internment camp of Westertimke was located within the area of a Kriegsmarine prison camp, liberated by the British in late April 1945. Run and supervised by Scottish departments, it began to receive German prisoners of war from April 29, 1945. It was later adapted to a camp for refugees fleeing the DDR.

95 *Ibid.,* p. 283. Following the end of the conflict, the prison camp of Esterwegen became a detention center for suspected war criminals awaiting trial and the phase of political re-education. Called CIC9, it was run by the British and

received a lot of concentration camp guards up until June 1946, when it reached a maximum of 2,600 inmates. Passed to the control of the German authorities as a normal prison, it was gradually abandoned by July 1950.

96 *Ibid.,* pp. 283-284. Coming from Westertimke, in July 1947, 260 police officers were transferred to Esterwegen. 13 of them were then released in the coming weeks, so in November there remained 247.

97 *Ibid.*, p. 285.

98 Of the 247 members of Polizei-Bataillon 9 that the British delivered to the Russians on January 17, 1947 and who were tried by a Soviet military court, 170 were found guilty and sentenced to imprisonment, of which 96 to 25 years hard labor in Bautzen prison. Those sentenced to between 10 and 25 years were instead imprisoned in Sachsenhausen until 1950 and then in other places. Then, towards the end of 1955 following the general amnesty proclaimed in May in the Soviet Union and during Adenauer's trip to Moscow, all those who were still detained in various Eastern German jails were released. Klemp Sibirien, p. 286, Angrick, p. 729.

Polizei-Bataillon 9 at Oslo train station, May 1940. Source: Bundesarchiv.

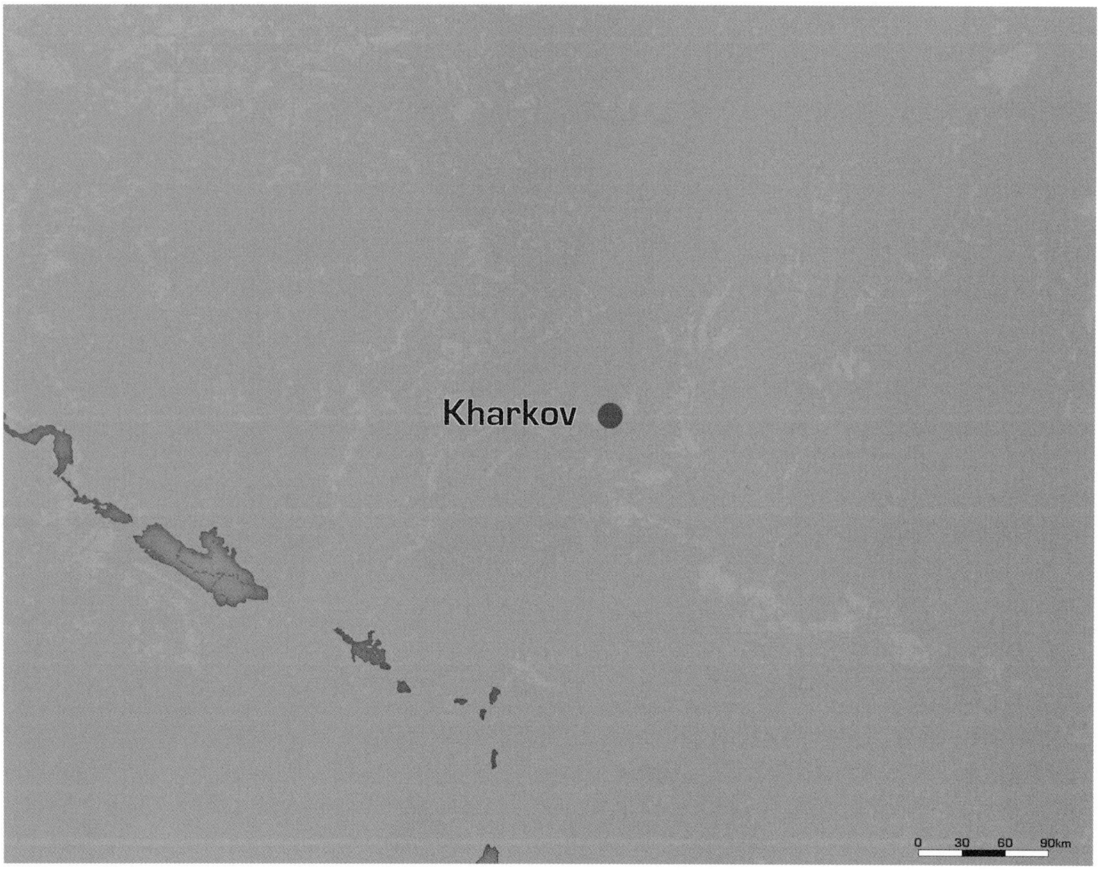
Kharkov
0 30 60 90km

CHAPTER TEN[1]

"BLOODY NEW YEAR"

THE MASSACRE OF THE JEWISH COMMUNITY OF KHARKOV DECEMBER 26, 1941 - JANUARY 7, 1942

Nach den bisherigen Erfahrungen
werden die Verbindungen zu den Saboteuren und Partisanen
in erster Linie
durch die jüdischen Bevölkerungteile Charkow's aufrecht erhalten

EM 153, 16.1.1942[2]

10.1 ON THE ROAD

Northern outskirts of Kharkov, December 15, 1941

It was -15 °C that morning in Kharkov and maybe it was snowing. Or maybe it had been snowing earlier and the freezing cold had formed an icy crust on the road that the wheels of the carts slipped upon: small overloaded wagons towed by small, worn out horses. Suitcases, household goods and shabby furniture were the load, and on top of everything were children, the sick, along with the elderly no longer able to walk.

The factory.

Sometimes a horse collapsed, spilling a load that no one could collect any longer, and killed or wounded the passengers that nobody could attend to anymore. There were dead people sprawled on the roadside, amidst crashed baggage. Dead and abandoned by those who were trying to survive, trying to stagger yet another step forward. Forgotten dead. Or maybe not. Maybe that night, someone would recite the Kaddish for them, provided they managed to get to the bottom of that damn icy road, in the final part of those fifteen kilometers, lost in the middle of nowhere and whipped by wind that led from the center of Kharkov to the factory.

Some Soviet bureaucrat, during one of the five-year plans of the thirties, had planned to build a tractor factory on the outskirts of Kharkov, to increase agricultural production. The land was fertile, the Donets flowed nearby. The Ukrainian plain could produce a lot, if well kept. And maybe it would.

But that winter of 1941 was a winter of famine. The factory, once teeming with activity, was empty, disassembled. Machinery had been quickly moved across the river, probably beyond the Urals. What remained were dilapidated buildings, empty skeletons with no value.

Given that, those useless skeletons might as well be filled. With grieving humanity. At least then, they would serve some purpose.

And that paradox: the plant to make tractors, which in turn should produce bread, filled with people on the brink of starvation. There was some irony in all this, something that sounded almost funny. It was akin to an act of revenge. Someone among his comrades of the 297th Infantry Division had once told him that it was the Jews who provoked the war. Well, if that was true, then perhaps it was only fair that they should pay the consequences. Philipp had a slight shiver: he blamed it on the icy wind.

Yet... all those thousands of Jews lined up, ragged, freezing... did not seem so dangerous. Indeed, they could even inspire pity. Even the guards around them, sunk in their overcoats, looked mostly bored and not particularly mean to the prisoners. They were Ukrainian auxiliaries, they spoke Russian just like those Jews they were escorting. Sometimes it seemed that they even mingled with them. And then there were the other guards: those of Sicherheitspolizei, or perhaps SS – it was hard to tell in those conditions. Steadfast, ugly people, it was better to stay away from them.

Philipp F. moved a few steps away. A few feet from him there was another dead on the roadside. An old man.

Yet another shiver. That damn icy wind.

10.2 EVACUATION

F. Philipp was in Kharkov that day in December 1941, with his comrades of the 297th Infantry Division of Vienna. They had arrived recently, but they would stay for a long time, until the following August, when they would cross the Donets with the rest of the Sixth Army, focusing on Stalingrad. Philipp, however, survived Stalingrad and some years later, in March 1961, gave his testimony, now kept in the archives of the State of Wiesbaden. He recounted his memories of that December morning and described in broad outline the context of those events that had led to many thousands of Jews – maybe 15,000, maybe more – being brought from their home in Kharkov up to an abandoned factory on the outskirts of the city and, a few weeks later, from here to a place called Drobitzky Jar, where they met their fate[3].

Stadtkommandantur of Kharkov, early November 1941

Those were days of famine. Upon withdrawing beyond the Don, the Soviets had taken away from the city everything that could be removed, so that nothing fell into the Wehrmacht's hands. A lot more had been destroyed and the number of inhabitants, about 800,000 before the war, had almost halved, partly following the retreating Red Army and partly fleeing to the countryside, where it was easier to survive. In November 1941 Kharkov was a ghost town, inhabited by about 450,000 people struggling to survive and that, meanwhile, had begun to die.

According to the fortnightly report of Stadtkommandantur, the German military administration settled in town in mid-October, 500 people died in Kharkov in just two weeks. Of these, almost 24 % died of starvation. This percentage would increase dramatically in the coming months, with the progressive exhaustion of stocks and the parallel increase of the cold, reaching a peak of 77,7 % in the second half of April 1942, that is 1,137 deaths from starvation on a total of 1,462[4].

This catastrophe, which would result in a total of nearly 12,000 deaths by starvation in the city, between December 1941 and September 1942 (out of a total of almost 20,000 victims – 59.6 % on average), was somewhat expected by the Wehrmacht, that did not manage, and did not want, to take any action.

During those October and November weeks the army command had been engaged in talks: there was much talk about how *not* to resolve the situation. Someone, actually, had the *brilliant idea* of suggesting the total evacuation of the city of Kharkov, in order to alleviate the Wehrmacht's stewardship from the worry of having to deal also with Russian and Ukrainian civilians. The campaign was immense, the first snow had not yet fallen and the Russian peasant was prudent and accustomed to life's hardships. Surely, many of them had hidden stocks, just as many had relatives or friends in town, maybe someone they owed a favor to: well, it was thought it was high time that these smart and *lucky* farmers reciprocated by welcoming into their *izbas* refugees evacuated from the city. In the end it was still a socialist sharing, a thing that the Bolsheviks were certainly used to.

So, they talked: talked about how to arrange the forced evacuation of 450,000 civilians with winter approaching, where to direct them, how to avoid obstructing the march of Wehrmacht columns on the road. But maybe they talked too much, because at some point someone had started to really ponder and reflect on ideas, to write reports. The good *idea* had not seemed as good anymore, contraindications emerged that went far beyond the possibility that it snowed in advance on the long columns of refugees lost in the steppes, or that *a few* thousand of them could even freeze to death on the road, or that, by altering the balance between town and country, the influx of all those displaced people could jeopardize an entire social ecosystem. No, it was nothing like that, but something much more important.

Poltava, German Sixth Army Command, November 6, 1941

Rudolf Paltzo[5] put down the two typewritten sheets dated November 6, 1941 that the diligent Ukrainian auxiliary lady had handed him for his signature. He was pleased with what he had read, and was certain that his superiors would have liked it. It could not be otherwise: his report contained truths to which he, Ic official at the Sixth Army Command had been called to give substance. Objective truths, very different from the theoretical abstractions developed in the office of the army quartermaster: like that lunacy to empty Kharkov, an entire city, of all its inhabitants... An absurd idea, conjured up by some idiot, accustomed to reason without using his brain.

How was it possible, for example, to think of bringing together the inhabitants of the city, many of whom were Russians, with the majority of Ukrainian peasants, without risking an uproar? Or to prevent the communist partisans, already active in that area, from finding a source of new recruits among the starving refugees? Overseeing all the villages was simply impossible, as it was unthinkable to oversee the entire perimeter of the city to stop those who would go back. There was a risk, after so many efforts to organize the evacuation, of being left at the starting point. Not to mention Bolshevik propaganda which would take advantage of the *fascist criminal deportation* by shouting it from the rooftops. Also, if they were forced to leave their homes, even the Ukrainians, who had welcomed the German troops so favorably, would end up turning their backs on them. It was not appropriate. It was not appropriate to add new problems to the many that already pestered the commands in the field[6].

The evacuation, therefore, had to be canceled. At most, residents could be asked to leave voluntarily, without forcing them, simply informing them that the Communist policy of *scorched earth* had left the stores empty and that, therefore, they should provide for themselves... unless, of course, they joined the Wehrmacht or any other military structure as auxiliaries, in which case they could count on the resources of the army to pass the winter [7]. That was a good idea that did not have any side effects: a feasible, practical, concrete solution to an objective problem. The few lines to the second paragraph of his report were also pragmatic. The Jews of Kharkov. They were a nuisance, no doubt about that. And political commissars, Communist Party activists, Soviet officials together with them: all people who could not be held in the city, let alone left free to move away somewhere. That horde had to be brought under control and watched over, preferably in an isolated place, all of them together somewhere they would not make trouble[8].

For them and them alone, forced evacuation was a necessary measure, which was to be executed without the slightest hesitation, as soon as possible. Certainly not because of the impending freeze, but as a safety issue, because the army did not want problems in their backline. Then, if during the evacuation it started to snow... well, that was just a false problem, actually, it could also be a convenient solution.

The evacuation of all those Jews, of course, would be a SD task. But those young, arrogant men, were too few and overworked, they would never make it without the Wehrmacht's support. Thus, it was necessary to get one's hands dirty.

Rudolf Paltzo took his pen and signed his report. Then, he called the auxiliary lady to give it to her.

She was young and pretty. It was worth to convince her to have Ersatzkaffe with him.

10.3 WELTANSCHAUUNGSTRUPPEN

Kharkov's western outskirts, November 19, 1941

They came quietly along mud-covered streets that looked like trails of a field. They were nervous. They had been deployed to that filthy, deserted, spooky city after leaving the bulk of their department in Poltava. They were called *vorkommando Kharkov*, "advanced Kharkov kommando": an ambitious title for a handful of men soaked with frost and dirty with *rasputiza*, that deadly sticky mash that inexorably blocked the axles of vehicles and forced them to incredible efforts to proceed further by just a few kilometers.

Yet, in the end, they had arrived. It was said that there were many thousands of Jews in the city who were unable to flee and now represented a problem. Still, they had to wait a few days before solving it, maybe a few weeks. Firstly, in order for other detachments of Sonderkommando 4a, scattered here and there between Kiev and Poltava, to have time to reach them and secondly because arrangements should have been made with those of the Wehrmacht who governed the city: despite everything, it was necessary to obtain their collaboration. There was bad blood with the army commands, the most they could get to was mutual forbearance. Yet, in that case, they needed to find a compromise. Kharkov was a long way eastwards in the Ukraine. It fell under military administration and because of that it was necessary that their movements were agreed upon with the local commands to avoid unpleasant misunderstandings, to rely on their logistical infrastructure in order to receive the necessary supplies and if necessary, to get some limited form of direct support. But above all, once all this was established, they should mind their own business: soldiers could go on playing war, because they, the men of Sonderkommando 4a, had a job to do and there must be no hitches.

But at the moment there was not much to do. His *vorkommando*, a dozen men in all, had to assess the situation, start making contacts, file reports, in particular about what had happened in town a few days earlier: there was talk of some bombs, hostages taken and killed, dead and wounded soldiers. It was even said that a general had been killed along with all his staff. The situation was confused and not very quiet at all[9].

However, he, Muller, was a simple SS-Untersturmführer, and did not have much power. To make arrangements with those *on the other side*, someone much higher up than him was needed. That someone would soon arrive.

Kiev, November 25, 1941

He wanted to send reinforcements to Kharkov, but the mud had prevented any movement: it was thus necessary that the temperature lowered a bit, so that the soil would give way to frost completely. At that point they would all be able to transfer there. For the moment he had to wait in Kiev with his command center, while the rest of the department, at least, had the opportunity to *finish the job* in Poltava[10].

But what worried him most was the situation in Kharkov: on November 14, several bombs, probably planted by communist saboteurs, had gone off destroying the general staff of the 68th Infantry Division. Thus, the command of 55th Army Corps of the Wehrmacht had ordered retaliation, demanding the arrest and shooting of hostages. The mayor of the city, Kramarenko[11], then ordered Orobšenco, head of the town's fifth district, where the bombs exploded, to proceed with the immediate selection of 50 civilians – Jews or communists, it did not matter – to be delivered to the Wehrmacht[12]. The order was carried out, yet the tension had not eased. Kharkov was close to the front and was a strategic point of great importance: there was a risk that the attacks multiplied, spreading panic and hostility among the population, a situation aggravated by the severe famine that gripped the city.

It was rumored that the general evacuation had been suspended; someone of the army command had changed his mind. However, that was not necessarily a bad thing; definitely there would be a big job to do, but at least it would end at once, without any need to go round the mud-buried villages in order to drive out every last small group of Jews. It would save time.

The same time that they were now losing waiting for the ice.

He had received radio news from Kharkov that tension was high within the Wehrmacht, they seemed to be preparing for something and some spoke of an imminent huge roundup: if that was true, then his arguments would find ears willing to listen. Unfortunately, Muller could not be more precise: rarely did officials confide in a sergeant, especially the *Prussians*, as he called the *poppies* of the Wehrmacht. That was why it was he who should deal with them.

Paul Blobel looked at the sky to the east: it was finally clear, clean, there were no clouds anymore. And above all it was beginning to get cold. That was good news. If that night it frosted, then they could leave the next day[13].

10.4 CONTACTS

Kharkov, November 26, 1941

He, his few men and fifteen vehicles arrived in Kharkov just before sunset, after catching up with the advanced detachment of Poltava along the road. Now, they were all there.

They had set off from Kiev at dawn, taking advantage of the sudden cold night and heading eastwards at breakneck speed. They had to stop two or three times, looking for alternative tracks, but overall it all went smoothly. They were lucky: if the darkness had surprised them while still on the march, surely the Feldgendarmerie would have forced them to stop and spend the night in some fetid izba, after kicking out the inhabitants. Things had gone well, in those cases there was always someone more nervous than the others and then the problem would be sorted out with weapons. It was not a problem to shoot some Russians – sometimes, actually, it was quite funny – but then they had to write reports, waste time, not to mention that some of his men could get hurt. Small troubles in fact.

This time though, they would be granted a refuge within four heated walls and he might even ask for an accommodation of his own. He felt he needed a drink and decided that would be that the best time to break the neck of that bottle of vodka that he had kept in his haversack. Later on though, when he would finally be alone.

First he had to get in touch with the Wehrmacht.

Paul Blobel stopped the Kübelwagen outside the Stadtkommandantur's offices.

A few days earlier, on November 4, he had met with Rudolf Paltz, Ic official of the information service at Poltava's army command. They had reassured him about the full cooperation of Kharkov's military commands, in order to definitely solve the *Jewish question* in the city[14]. At that point, all he could do was see for himself the value of that reassurance.

An aerial view of Kharkov, 1941. Source: Bundesarchiv.

In fact, there had been a promising start by the Stadtkommandantur, immediately after the bombs went off causing the death of General Braun: arrests, executions, removal of Jews from all public offices and reduction of their food rations. Then though, as usual, the *Prussians* had not gone any further, indeed, with a report dated November 19, the Stadtkommandantur had confirmed that whole series of preliminary measures, but had also reported that it had "postponed any further initiative against the Jews, so as not to alarm them too early, luring them out of their dens before the arrival of the necessary forces"[15].

All of this was a lie, of course. The Wehrmacht dandies did not want to get their hands too dirty and had decided to hand over the hot potato to him. To get rid of the Jews was convenient to all: the difficult part, however, was to find someone who would take responsibility.

So, once again, it was him and his few men that had to put things right.

10.5 GOING EAST

Kharkov, Ivanowka district, December 5, 1941.

They had come a long way since that late 1940 fall in Vienna when, having left Strebersdorf, they had boarded a train and headed north, towards Poland. It was a long time ago, no one really knew *how many*, but many lives had been consumed since.

Since the summer of 1941, after they were given orders to move eastward everything had happened very quickly. And, although no one could ever imagine it, it was precisely that very moment they faced the emptiness and the silence of the great Russian plain that the real journey began.

He remembered reading a book written by an Englishman many years before, some Conrad. It was about a man who, driven by the will to replace God, reached the end of the road and met his darkness; just like him, now it was them going to face their darkness, in that journey with destination nowhere surrounded by nothingness and horror.

The first time he had killed had been in July, in a village called Ljubomil, just inside the border[16]. That was the only time he remembered well. Then there was nothing, only a confused series of distorted images, as in a film played in fast forward: faces overlapping with other faces, places confused with other places. Villages passed that preceded villages to reach, deeper and deeper eastbound, the weeks turning into seasons and the only unchanging regularity of the rows of people lined up along the edge of a ditch.

There were no episodes or faces to remember or to take note of, but everything fragmented into interchangeable sequences. He became surprised, for example, when a few days earlier in Dnepropetrovsk[17], after watching him kill in anger a group of Jews who had already been lined up and were waiting to be executed, one of his comrades had asked him the reason of his fury while executing those victims whose fate was already sealed. He was not surprised by the act in itself, but rather because he had not had the perception of having done anything unusual[18].

And now he, the other kids in his company and the rest of Polizei-Bataillon 314 had arrived in that city, Kharkov, which was so far away that until that moment they had never even heard of it[19]. He did not know if that was the end of the trip or just an intermediate step. Nor, he wondered, if the time had come for him to meet his darkness or if he had already replaced God.

He, Oskar Josef Christ, did not ask himself any of this, besides there was no reason to do so.

This was just another place to be confused with more new faces to overlap.

10.6 BEFORE DAWN

Kharkov, December 14, 1941

They had a long discussion about what would be better to do in order to solve the problem, partly because a few days earlier, the army switched several parties for these talks. On December 3, in fact, the first Stadtkommandant of the city of Kharkov, namely General Erwin Vierow, had been replaced by Alfred von Puttkammer[20] commander of the rear lines, who was now responsible for taking decisions. It was obvious then, that so far there had been just a long delay, with consequent loss of valuable time. Not that they had wasted their time, not quite, at least: the census of the Jews was complete – there were many in the city, in spite of everything[21] – and, arriving from Dnepropetrovsk, Polizei-Bataillon 314, whose commander Maj. Otto Severth[22] had assured full cooperation, had now arrived thanks to their efforts. The problem, however, was that because time was going quickly, that would certainly be the last action of a *certain weight* until the following spring. While that could be a welcome break for the men, engaged non-stop since July, on the other hand it forced them to leave the job half done.

In addition, those two weeks of inaction had allowed them to perform the general service on two gas vans that had come from Poltava, and which were now ready to be put back in operation. He hated these old worn out vehicles: he had witnessed the opening of their doors in Poltava, and the vision of those bodies poisoned by gas and covered with vomit and excrement was not a pretty sight[23]. Had it been up to him, he would not even use them: the fact was, however, that in Berlin someone was infatuated with the idea of experimenting with alternative methods of execution to shooting, and since it was Berlin where everything was decided, all he could do was comply.

In any case, despite the methods that he would use at the appropriate time, what mattered was that the Stadtkommandant had finally decided to order, through posters on the city walls[24], the transfer of all the Jews of Kharkov to a place where they could be easily monitored, thus preventing the risk that they managed to escape the city or, even worse, that they went around planting bombs. With regards to the safety of the rear lines, the Wehrmacht did not seem to have doubts. After that, everything that would eventually happen to the Jews once they had been gathered and placed in custody, was something unspoken of, which spoke louder than a written report.

There were still several hours to go before dawn and Paul Blobel decided it was time for a last drink. They were going through hard times, and for a moment, while he uncorked the bottle, he wondered if History would remember him as a hero or a villain. He could not answer, but it wasn't so important after all.

He knew he was doing dastardly things. He knew he was doing great things.

10.7 VISIONS

Kharkov, in front of the Hotel Krasnaja, December 15, 1941

He had heard them coming in the early hours of dawn. First, a low murmur in the distance then gradually nearer, accompanied by a weary drag of steps that crumbled the crust of frozen snow. There were the cries of small children and the slow creaking of the wheels of the carts, often drawn only by the force of arms. Then he had heard voices. Stern orders barked angrily, in a language they had learned to recognize. Then, muffled thuds, like shots that cut down on soft surfaces. And more orders to drown the noise.

He hesitated to get close to the window – in those few weeks after the occupation he had understood that prudence was never enough. Then curiosity got the better of him: fortunately the darkening curtain was slightly away from the glass, so, from the outside, no one would have noticed any suspicious movement.

He remained in the shadows of the room and with extreme caution threw a glance across the glass, and then he saw them: they walked down the *Puschkinskaya* in long and slow columns towards the square in front of the Krasnaya Hotel, about 50 feet from his window. They were thin and pale. They were wearing ragged clothes and carrying suitcases, baskets and bundles, and were guarded by German and Ukrainian police officers. Then, when they were closer he recognized them: he recognized the yellow armband that the mayor Kramarenko had ordered the Jews to wear a few days before, and then he remembered the posters that were put up by the Stadtkommandantur all over the city walls, where it was ordered that by 10.00 hours on December 15 all Jews of Kharkov should gather, with their belongings, in the square outside Hotel Krasnaya, pending their *resettlement* in another area. Nothing else was specified; no reason, no destination: there was only the threat of immediate execution for all those who would not obey the order[25].

Dr. L.P. Nikolajew felt pity. He did not understand why everything was happening, or maybe he understood it all too well. He pulled further back in the shadow behind the curtain, when he saw two policemen who stopped just below his window. They were young, big and strong, they began to mock and beat up the Jews who passed before them. He heard them laughing and kicking an old lady while pulling the ears of kids. Then came a woman with a baby in her arms, who must have been about four.

He seemed to recognize her: maybe once, before the occupation, he had cured her of some illness. He had cured several Jews in Kharkov's hospital, a hundred years earlier... He saw the two policemen approaching the woman and heard the baby crying in fear. Then he saw the woman kiss the hands of the two policemen: maybe this time they would let her go.

He moved away from the window. He had seen too much and it was not prudent to look beyond.

Sure, he was Russian, he was a doctor, he thought he was useful, and perhaps he really was. It was better, however, to turn a blind eye, not to take any unnecessary risks. The idea was to write in his diary that he kept well hidden under a floorboard[26]. But he should have moved the curtain to receive the light necessary to write: it was too dangerous.

He stood still, undecided what to do, thinking that after all that was not his business: after all it was Jews, strange people ... Even among the Russians there was someone who hated them. Someone, perhaps, hated even the woman who kissed the cops' hands. Perhaps.

That night in silence. Yes, that night he would write in front of a candle.

It was cold in that room, and it would be nice to be able to make some tea. But he had run out of the blend and it was virtually impossible to find more out there. He resigned: besides, he doubted that a cup of tea would be enough to warm him.

10.8 IN THE FACTORY

Kharkov's Jewish ghetto, late December 1941

They had been ordered to guard the factory after the evacuation was completed, something that took a couple of days. Now, apparently, the situation was calm. Not everything, however, had gone smoothly.

During the exodus, apart from those who had died of exhaustion along the way, there had been robberies committed by groups of Ukrainians against the Jews in the columns: nothing particularly serious, but sufficient to create disorder, and because disorder was something that could not be tolerated, the Wehrmacht had carried out many executions: it was said that several hundred Jews had been killed for spreading lies against the German army[27] and that others, mostly the elderly and sick who were not able to march, had been taken by the teams responsible for rounding up the emptied flats. It was also said that these old men were then locked in the synagogue and left to die from starvation and the cold[28].

However things went, calm was now restored and his company, the first of Polizei-Bataillon 314 had drawn a security cordon all around the entire perimeter of the ghetto that he, Oskar Josef Christ, was about to finish inspecting with his team of police officers.

The ghetto. The new Jewish neighborhood isolated from the city. To tell the truth, it seemed a bit difficult to speak of a "new residential area for the Jews", as sometimes he happened to hear[29] because it was essentially crumbling shacks with no heating and no glass in the windows and lacking completely even the most basic services: more than a ghetto, it was something very much like a concentration camp, subject to a strict curfew which included the authorization to open fire without warning against anyone who was outside at night[30]. It also seemed that there was an outbreak of gastroenteritis inside the ghetto due to consumption of contaminated snow and that every morning twenty or thirty dead Jews could be counted[31]: another reason to maintain the quarantine around the factory by any means possible, including, of course, shootings in cold blood.

Actually, there were also other rumors in those days, rumors that preparations for a mass shooting were in progress: if they were true, then the problem would be solved *at the root*. Sure, he had heard such whispers ever since they had arrived in town about three weeks earlier; murmurs spread first among the troops and then among civilians, especially among the Ukrainians, many of whom also seemed in favor of punishing the Jews that way[32]. However, nothing had happened so far, nor was there other news after the evacuation, except, of course, the relief at not seeing *tramp* Jews roam around the city anymore.

He looked at his watch and realized there was still a little over an hour to go before the changing of the guard. Edelmüller's platoon would soon come to relieve Pütz's, and he, Christ, would go back to town. That evening he had an appointment he did not want to miss.

A few days before in a bomb shelter during a raid by Soviet fighters, he had met a young Russian girl. Her name was Vera, she had said she was a classical dancer in Kharkov's theater. He had proposed her to work for him as a cleaning lady, in the accommodation of the company and she had accepted. That morning, before going to the factory, he had informed the young lady that she should stay after the working hours.

There were cigarettes in his room, some candies and a bit of chocolate substitute that he had managed to obtain from a quartermaster friend of his.

For once, Oskar Joseph Christ, could afford to be generous[33].

10.9 DROBITZKY JAR

January 2, 1942

It was not difficult to escape from the ghetto. During the day, before the curfew, surveillance by those soldiers with the green uniform was relatively mild: it could not be otherwise as it was unrealistic to think to seal all the thousand possible escape routes of the factory's large area. Therefore, aware of this *handicap*, the guards were not as strict as they should have been.

The problem for the runaways – there had been several in those days – was where to go once they had left, and how to survive, both in the semi-deserted city gripped by famine and in the frostbitten countryside, with temperatures down to -20-25°C. Then they had to be wary of the Ukrainians, who in exchange for a bowl of flour and a bag of salt, often sold out the unsuspecting Jews who dared to knock on their izbas for help[34].

In other words, the ice desert that was all around them was an obstacle even more insuperable than German rifles.

Still, they had to try something. A few days before, around December 28, leaflets announcing the voluntary transfer to Poltava for all those who had wanted had been spread in the ghetto: this ad that was then followed by the boarding on trucks of a first group of about 500 people[35].

Many of them were wondering if it was better to agree to leave, rather than stick to languish in the factory, dying a little more every day. Many, in fact, had left. For him, however, to move to Poltava meant moving away from his wife – a non-Jew who lived in Kharkov together with their adopted son – and from the faint hope of being able to reunite one day.

For that reason, engineer S. Krivoruchko had remained in the ghetto.

That morning, however, the sentinels' cries told him that something was happening.

They had ten minutes to gather in front of the hut, hundreds of them, surrounded by a cordon of policemen who put them in a column and began to push them beyond the area of the factory, reassuring them about their destination: they, too, they said, would be moved to Poltava, where they would find better food and more comfortable accommodations. After all, they later added, it was just a little walk.

But then, a few miles beyond the last huts they had to leave the road and advance along a rough terrain.

It was then that they began to understand, when they began to see the first objects left on the trampled snow, and before them a double line of policemen standing on the edge of what seemed to be a big hole in the ground, at the end of which, from the opposite direction to the one they were coming from, machine guns could be seen.

There were trucks, at the mouth of the gorge, upon which the clothes of those who preceded them were piled up, and all around there were policemen and other Jewish groups intent on removing their clothes. By now they had realized that soon it would be over, within minutes their turn would come. Far away, beyond the walls of the gorge, muffled by the wind, bursts of machine guns and gunshots could be heard.

Then, in the unreal whiteness of the snow that fell in waves, Krivoruchko noticed that, not far from him, one of the trucks was about to leave. Perhaps, in all that confusion, if he was lucky, he could climb onto the back and hide amid the clothes. It would take just a moment.

He decided to wait for a group of elderly Jews who were approaching the mouth of the gorge like ghosts: they would hide him for a few moments from the sight of the guards. A few moments that could mean a lifetime[36].

They kept arriving in groups of several hundred, guarded by other police officers like him: definitely, that morning, someone had decided to make it big.

Despite being immersed in his overcoat Karl G.[37] was cold. It was maybe -20-25°C, with a freezing wind blowing from the north that made it even colder. The same wind that if anything, seemed to muffle the burst of machine guns, the gunshots and the screams coming from inside the gorge.

They had been mobilized early, just after dawn, he and the other men of his company of Polizei-Bataillon 314. They had been ordered to form a security cordon all around a large group of natural gorges in the ground, in the southeastern outskirts of Kharkov, near a village named Rogan. Other officers of the battalion, belonging to another company, had been instructed to remove the Jews from the ghetto, to escort them to the mouth of the gorge and then push them inside with blows of whips and sticks, after having forced them to remove their clothing.

Thus it began; SD firing squad opening fire on groups of Jews as they arrived in the gorges, and so it would continue, probably during the whole day, until the very last column arrived.

And there he was, in the midst of all this, his long woolen overcoat too thin to withstand those temperatures: nothing like the padded, fur-lined jackets that the Russians who were fighting to the north, on the Moscow Front, were said to wear. Yet, despite the cold and the endless hours, Karl G. considered himself lucky because he was not among those in charge of shooting. He and his fellow soldiers had to simply dismiss anyone not authorized to enter the execution area, all the while keeping an eye on the trucks that were loaded with the victims' clothes.

For that reason, that was basically a good day for him.

Karl G. casually observed a group of elderly Jews, half-naked and bruised by cold, who dragged their steps slowly a few dozen yards away from him, toward the mouth of one of the ravines: a long, sad column, big enough to hide the sight of a man who had just started to run for his life, toward one of the trucks parked nearby.

Shivering with cold, Karl G. balanced his weight first on one foot and then the other. He huddled in his overcoat and then turned his back to oppose a gust of wind colder than the others. No, he could not feel sorry for those freezing and tottering people in front of him. Maybe it was the cold, perhaps it was the habit, but all he wanted to do at that moment was to drink something warm, away from the icy wind that took his breath away.

The inside of the gorge was something like a circle of Dante's inferno.

He remembered watching the engravings of a French illustrator a few years before. They represented the Inferno as it really might be: the engravings were dark, full of shadings, claustrophobic, imbued with a romantic epic that turned the pain into something sublime.

But in that gorge there was nothing epic, romantic

or sublime. There was only pain. And the bodies mowed down by the machine guns.

They were about ten, he and his men, waiting for the Jews with weapons in hand. The policemen, a group of Austrians in green uniforms, forced them past the mouth of the gorge amid shouts and jostling in groups of 20 or 25, then it was up to them to make the Jews to lie down on the ground in neat lines and open fire, aiming at their necks.

This went on for nearly two hours, with some interruptions due to incursions by Soviet aircraft that also injured one of his men, and it would go on and on that day. Coming on the highway from Kharkov that morning, on a bus driven by the commander of his section, they had passed at least one pair of long columns, each consisting of hundreds of Jews, who, with their slow pace, would take a long time to cover the six miles that separated the tractor plant from the place where their destiny was being sealed.

Therefore, it was unlikely that all that would finish before the afternoon.

Viktor T.[38] used that moment of pause to light a cigarette. Several of his comrades were doing the same, some drank from a bottle of liquor while another was throwing up in the corner. It was a lousy job and he hoped he would not have to do it again in the days ahead. In the courtyard, in front of the building where they were housed in Kharkov, he saw two trucks with mechanics all around. He knew those sealed trucks well; he had already seen them in action in Poltava a few weeks before. That morning, for some reason, they had not been used, but it was likely that, as early as the next day, they could be back in operation, saving him and his comrades a lot of executions[39].

Until then, however, they were still the ones to wallow in blood mixed with snow.

He heard voices coming from the mouth of the gorge. They were starting to push them again.

Viktor inhaled two more quick puffs of smoke, threw away the butt, and together with his men headed for the group of Jews that had just been positioned on the gorge's edge. They were old.

He thought that at least it would be easier than having to shoot at children.

Paul Blobel couldn't be anything but satisfied: that morning everything was going well. Not that he ever doubted, there was no reason to doubt that, however, his experience taught him that in those situations there is always room for doubt, something that could hinder the smooth and somewhat monotonous flow of events.

But no, just like so many times before, history was flowing also on that snow-covered field. It was flowing in front of him, between the columns of the wretched, who slowly came from the factory and went to their deaths like robots.

On seeing those masses of individuals who, like sacrificial victims for the jaws of the god Moloch, meekly awaited their turn to cross the entrance to the gorge, beyond which the guns were ready, Paul Blobel felt a sense of irritation, because those Jews might have had a burst of pride, a reaction driven by anger, a less submissive attitude proving that they rejected the easy death that was offered them. They could have tried to rebel against the guards, unsuccessfully of course, but at least with pride. Yet, there was nothing. Only cries were coming from the marching columns. Someone sang psalms, many hugged each other, everyone obeyed. They were slowly disappearing without leaving a trace: History itself was wiping them out of History as a process of Darwinian selection. It was not his men or his machine guns opening fire killing them: no, those were mere details of a cosmic plan that went beyond the immediate and transcended the tools used.

Paul Blobel felt a sense of irritation, but it soon dissipated. It could be called fate, perhaps "inevitability of fate": what was certain was that History had chosen its own tools. And he was one of those tools, and that was their triumph. It was a struggle they were fighting, a battle in which will prevailed over indolence. The passivity of the defeated who accepted their fate was precisely the demonstration of the triumph of the victorious. They had gradually crept into the minds and imaginations of the victims, and little by little they had eroded their personalities and consciousness. It was not just physical death that they, the victorious, imposed upon the beaten, but something more absolute: it was spiritual annihilation[40], the right oblivion reserved for all those who renounce anger.

He felt that he needed a drink, so he decided to return to the *Kübelwagen*.

He got into his car and ordered his driver, Bauer, to head back to town, taking the Chuguyev-Kharkov road: his presence in Drobitzky was no longer necessary, and now things could go ahead as they were without him.

He pulled out the flask and loosened the top button of his coat. On that frozen, bumpy road it would take about twenty minutes before reaching the command center which meant plenty of time to relax.

Then he saw it, the last column, proceeding slowly on the outer edge of the road in the direction opposite to his. The car passed very close, nearly touching them. He saw someone staring at him through the window, looking at him with questioning eyes.

Paul Blobel looked away nervously and took another swig from the flask. While he closed it to order something to his driver, he realized that there was no need. Before him, sitting on the driver's seat, Julius Bauer had already accelerated.

They passed the column in a few seconds and lost it in the distance and in the damp sleet. Now it was really over. Blobel leaned his head against the edge of the back seat and closed his eyes. Yes, one thing was certain: that day would be remembered.

10.10 CONSIDERATIONS

The destruction of Kharkov's Jewry, which occurred from the last days of December 1941 until the first week of January 1942 during which about 15,000 people were killed, was not a random event, i.e. the product of a specific situation and not completely representative of a more general context. It was the result of a tangle of converging interests, fueled partly by an obsession with security and by the administrative inadequacy of the Wehrmacht's authorities. In addition, the desire to pursue policies of social and ethnic desertification of the conquered territory, not least by methods of genocide *tout-court* carried out by mobile units of mass murder, in this case represented by Paul Blobel's Sonderkommando 4a.

There seems to be no doubt that in that 1941/42 winter the Wehrmacht faced great hardships in terms of logistics and administration, due to difficult circumstances but also because of its inability and its choices. There are even fewer doubts about a clear willingness on the part of the hierarchies of the regime to address the complexity of the moment only through rudimentary, never-changing and preconceived ideological schemes of which the Einsatzgruppen, in summer / fall 1941, represented the essential practical realization.

The dull repetition – even in the presence of objectively changing situations – in the practical application of theoretical abstractions that were the basis for the formation of itinerant groups of extermination demonstrates the existence of a plan of annihilation as the main objective, which evolved over time and became gradually more and more sophisticated. It also confirms the absolute functional rigidity of the same itinerant groups, that appeared completely unsuitable to operate in an environment different from extermination and ideological clean-up, but instead were fully functional and responsive if placed in contact with the appropriate *primers* – the Jewish population in the first place – following a mechanism similar to a Pavlovian reflex applied in the field of ideology.

In other words, the raison d'etre of these groups – the main reason for which they were formed – was simply and only the achievement of ideological results through methods of a genocidal nature. Therefore, we can say that the Einsatzgruppen, militarily inadequate, poorly significant in number and scattered over an extremely wide territory, *should* not have, and, indeed, *could* not have, been used for purposes outside the range of their primary objective. Far from demonstrating an attitude of the Einsatzgruppen of a nature not only genocidal, the same rough sketches of *social analysis* that appear in lengthy reports drafted in the field and sent to Berlin on an almost daily basis, are fully consistent and functional with the raison d'etre of the same groups and their scope of action, taking shape as an ideological logging among layers of the population in the occupied territories, in view of subsequent *developments* in the politics of annihilation hatched in Berlin.

It was not always possible, for extermination groups, to intervene in person *to resolve the situation*: this is due both to their limited operational capabilities, and also because the Einsatzgruppen represented only *one* – but certainly not the only one, nor the first – of the evolutionary stages of a project of annihilation still to be defined.

It could therefore be necessary to have to use additional operating assets, more numerous and robust, able to take up the *genocidal legacy* of the extermination groups. Assets that were able to exploit the experience, the results and the lessons learned on the field, also in view of the ephemeral nature of these groups that were destined to disappear through a rapid process of territorialization.

In the specific case of Kharkov for example, there was a need for close collaboration between all the structures of occupation: Wehrmacht, Sicherheitspolizei (represented by Sonderkommando 4a), Ordnungspolizei through Polizei-Bataillon 314 and also the Ukrainian administration of mayor Kramarenko. Each of these structures, by virtue of their ability and their individual goals, helped shape the framework in which the destruction of the Jewish community of Kharkov was perpetrated. Thus, if the Wehrmacht's primary objectives were safety behind the lines and the need to relieve their logistical situation, the task of Kramarenko's administration was the relief of Ukraine's population through the allocation of all the scarce resources available, stealing them from others and especially from the Jews. At the same time, while the annihilation of Jews was Sonderkommando 4a's raison d'être (in Kharkov in this case), the police departments (Polizei-Bataillon 314 in particular) represented a further stage in the evolution of the itinerant genocide, still in connection with the Einsatzgruppen in that phase, but destined to supplant them in part, especially during the spring / summer 1942.

The tragedy of the Jews of Kharkov therefore, cannot be read as a product of chance, or as the result of a tactical need. In fact, it rather triggers in a lucid and coherent way that plan of multi-pronged annihilation started on the Eastern Front, and that throughout 1941 certainly saw the Einsatzgruppen as spearheads, actively supported by a plethora of willing followers.

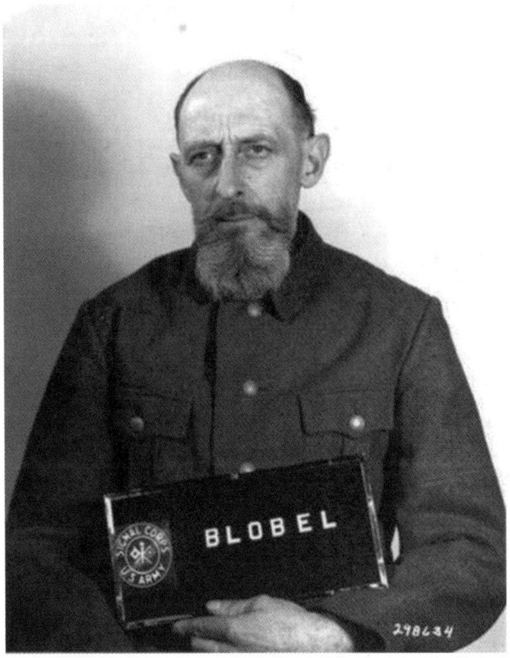

Paul Blobel, during the Nuremberg trial.

10.11 EPILOGUE

Kharkov, February 16, 1943

They came rattling in the late morning, overcoming the obstacles placed in the middle of the Susmskaja and then turned to the right, towards the square. They moved cautiously, but firmly, watching out for snipers: for this reason they had let the infantry down from the tanks, so that they could deal with any centers of resistance hidden inside those big buildings next to them, dilapidated and blackened by fire, the windows ripped open, but still solid and able to provide good protection to the defenders determined to fight.

It seemed, however, that the square was quiet and that was a piece of luck: to join the battle, room by room, in those immense concrete blocks that used to be Gosprom's complex, would require blood and precious time. Instead, Dzerzhinsk square seemed strangely quiet, almost suspended in its wait.

Some tanks had stopped at the mouth of *Nowj Prospekt*, others – including his – covered the two Gosprom blocks with their guns, while the infantry platoons had already begun to spread in the gardens on the south side of the square. The turret of his tank rolled slowly looking for threats that were not there and then stopped, while he gave a last look through the tank's view-slits. Then, he decided to emerge cautiously from the trapdoor: though tactical situations often required to fight inside, he was firmly convinced that the best location for a tank commander worthy of the name, was half-out, for that perception of the battlefield that view-slits alone could not guarantee.

Luckily there was no shot and even the riflemen, scattered in the snow behind every possible shelter, seemed to begin to believe that there would be no need to fight. Some of them approached the tank tracks, staying crouched: many were veterans who knew how to move and would not waste their lives unnecessarily, like freshmen. They moved in the wake of the tank that, in the meantime, had begun to move cautiously towards the big passage beneath Gosprom's central block.

It was then that he saw them, a small group of figures still and black, motionless in the corner, some fifty yards away from him. It seemed they had emerged from some unknown place, wrapped in clothes worn by the years, their faces pale and excavated. They did not carry weapons, and could not possibly represent a threat.

The tank moved and entered the passage. He continued to observe those motionless figures, now much closer: unknown but seemingly familiar, they were silently staring at themselves. There was an old man with an ancient face and he had memories of when he was still a child, in a small village of old izbas hundreds of miles from that large ghost town. He remembered a synagogue, the scent of incense and psalms now forgotten.

He ordered the tank driver to stop and fumbled in his haversack. All he had were a couple of packs of crackers and a tin of American beef. He threw them to him politely, without getting off the tank: he had no time to linger, neither to ask who they were.

The old man bent down to pick the food, continuing to stare.

He, Lieutenant Leonid Gorovitz beckoned with his hand. Then he struck a blow on the door of the tank's cupola.

"Davai, Ramil, Davai!" he ordered the driver crouched under him, on his uncomfortable little seat.

"Davai da!" He heard again from the small Uzbekistani tank driver, while the tracks resumed their rotations on the snowy slope to the west, towards the German front in retreat.

Kharkov, December 17, 1943. Results of the forensic commission[41]

Forensic experts have examined in Kharkov and surrounding area, the scenes of the crimes of the German fascist invaders and the sites where they carried out the extermination of Soviet citizens [...].

In the 13 mass graves opened in Kharkov and the immediate surroundings, a large number of bodies were found. In most of the graves, bodies were lying in extreme disorder, incredibly intertwined, forming human tangles difficult to describe. The bodies lie in such a way that they seem to have been offloaded, or simply piled up, but surely not buried in mass graves. In two of the pits in the Sokolniki forest, the bodies were found lined up in straight rows, face down, their arms bent at the elbow and their hands clasped around their faces or necks. All the bodies had bullet wounds to the head. This position of the bodies is not random: it is proof that the victims were forced to lie face down, only to be shot in that position. In the pits, where the bodies lie, and in those places where they were burned, forensic experts have found everyday items and personal effects such as purses, bags, knives, pots, cups, glasses, handbags etc. That detail, already revealed during the investigation – namely the fact that Soviet citizens had been deprived of their shoes before being murdered – has been fully confirmed by forensic examinations: in many cases, during the exhumation, the bodies that the experts have found were naked or nearly naked.

In order to verify which Soviet citizens were exterminated and how, experts have exhumed and examined 1,047 bodies in Kharkov and its vicinity. These include the bodies of 19 children and adolescents, 429 women and 599 men. The age range varies from two to seventy years [...].

The extermination of the Soviet people (both civilians and prisoners of war) was performed by means of carbon monoxide poisoning, shooting, use of fire and murder by hard and heavy blunt objects. All this has been established with absolute and irrefutable certainty, through the material collected during the preliminary investigations and subsequent judicial proceedings and has been tested with scientific objectivity by forensic experts.

The depositions of the accused and the testimonies say as in various parts of the temporarily occupied Soviet territory, the German fascist invaders have made use of specially equipped large vans, inside which Soviet citizens were killed by exhaust fumes containing carbon monoxide. Forensic experts have proved this fact beyond all doubt, examining for the first time the bodies exhumed in the city of Krasnodar and its vicinity. At the same time, the presence of carbon monoxide has been incontrovertibly confirmed by the combination of physiological, chemical and spectroscopic analysis of the blood found in the tissues and organs of the body. The same method of poisoning with carbon monoxide, as used in Krasnodar, was proved by forensic examinations to be the same as in some of the bodies exhumed in Kharkov [...].

The investigations and forensic examinations have determined that in addition to poisoning with carbon monoxide, the Germans have applied on a large scale, in the Kharkov area, mass shootings with automatic weapons, usually targeted to the back of the head, at the base of the neck and spine.

The examinations on the bodies have also proved that there were cases of killing through fracture of the skull and destruction of the cerebral cortex by means of hard and heavy blunt objects [...].

The German fascist invaders have tried to erase evidence of their crimes, especially poisoning by carbon monoxide, through the destruction by fire of the bodies of poisoned people. However, the results of investigations carried out have led to the discovery of charred parts of the skeleton in the bodies found in the cabins of Kharkov's tractor factory, which confirm the attempted destruction of bodies by fire [...].

After the German translation of the results of forensic experts, the President, Major-General Judge Miasnikov, closed the meeting of the Court.

ENDNOTES

1 The reconstruction of the events that led to the destruction of the Jewish community of Kharkov was drawn, by choice of the author, using a narrative scheme, with free interpretations of the scenic backdrop and the focus placed on the *flashbacks* of one individual character after the other within a frame of limited subjectivity of the characters themselves. Each event described is based on true events, rigorously documented, that occurred in the order they are presented and contextualized in their precise historical dimension. Therefore, all the people mentioned really existed, the only exception represented by Lieutenant Leonid Gorovitz, whose role, however, is entirely secondary. In this sense, whereas some contributions of the author of these lines might refer to the *setting* of the events described, it was the executioners and – especially – their victims, who wrote such dramatic script at the time.

2 "As in past experiences, the Jewish population of Kharkov has been in the forefront to entertain relations with partisans and saboteurs". HIS, p. 183.

3 Philipp F. was a member of 297th Infantry Division that arrived in Kharkov on November 1941 and was then destroyed in Stalingrad in February 1943. His testimony was given on March 23, 1961 and is kept at Wiesbaden's State Archive. HHStAW, 631a, 1856, p. 223-227. In HIS, p. 184.

4 Summary of Kharkov's Stadtkommandantur on the mortality of the population – December 1941/September 1942. USHMM – RG 31010M, R.7, 2982/4/390a, in HIS, p. 346.

5 Rudolf Paltzo, Oberstleutnant. Born October 29, 1904 in Löetzen, Eastern Prussia. He joined the Army after graduation and was appointed lieutenant in 1933. He was then transferred in 1939 to the Command Department of the Sixth German Army, where he took the role of information official (Nachrichtenoffizier). He stayed in this position until November 1942, was reported missing at Stalingrad and was subsequently declared legally dead in 1950. In fact, taken prisoner by the Red Army, he was sentenced to 25 years hard labor, only to be amnestied in 1955, when he could go back to West Germany. Suspected of war crimes he was investigated by some courts, but the records concerning him were finally closed in 1969. HIS, p. 183.

6 Rudolf Paltzo's opinion (AOK 6 Ic/AO) to Quartiermeister 2, Hptm. von Bila (AOK 6 Qu. 2) of November 6, 1941. In BA-MA, RH 20-6/494, Bl. 263f, reproduced in HIS, pp. 181-182.

7 In fact, this voluntary exodus took place on December 14, when about 10,000 selected persons (*Abwanderungswillige*), considered to be useful and potentially favorable to the Germans, were escorted out of town to the west, and housed in dwellings set up for that purpose. Before departure, through a careful *check-in* by SK 4a, several Jews who tried to abandon the city this way were identified and rejected. Angrick Kharkov, p. 122.

8 Rudolf Paltzo's opinion, Bl. 264.

9 On November 14, 1941, several bombs that had previously been placed in the building where 68th German Infantry Division had taken quarters were detonated by Soviet agents. The collapse of the building killed Gen. Maj. Georg Braun, the division commander, along with some of his general staff. See Angrick Kharkov, p. 120.

10 In Poltava, on November 23, 1941, supported by a platoon of Polizei-Bataillon 9, SK 4a's Vorkommando "Poltawa" perpetrated the execution of 1,538 Jews, using a gas truck. Testimony given by A.L. before the public prosecutor of Osnabrück, 17 Js 165/62. Curilla, p. 805.

11 Oleksey Ivanovyè Kramarenko. Born March 17, 1887 in Krementchug, chemistry teacher at the Technological Institute of Kharkov's University, he was appointed mayor by the German military administration on October 26, 1941. As a nationalist, he collaborated with the Germans in the repression against the communist movement and in the persecution of Jews, looking at the same time to ease the grip of famine on the Ukrainian population. For reasons not fully understood – apparently related to the discovery of Soviet spies in the offices of his administration – in the spring of 1942 the Gestapo began to look at him with suspicion and removed him from office on April 20. He was replaced by his deputy Semenenko. Accused of anti-German activities, the SD eventually arrested and executed him in August. See Friedrich, pp. 177. ff.

12 Friedrich, p. 158. The retaliation order included the arrest of 1,200 civilians identified as communists by district leaders (*Bezirkbürgermeister*) and their surrender to the commands of the 57th and 68th infantry divisions. Actually, given the tight time frame – within 20 hours after the explosion – the selection was extremely shallow and eventually involved a large number of non-communists, including many Jews. Fifty of the hostages were shot immediately after the arrest, followed by another 150 in the next few hours. The remaining 1,000 were detained in a concentration camp, with the threat of shooting 200 for each new bomb explosion. According to Stadtkommandantur, deterrence would prove *effective*. Angrick Kharkov, p. 120.

13 Paul Blobel: SS-Standartenführer. Born August 13, 1894 in Potsdam. An architecture graduate, he joined the NSDAP on December 1, 1931 and became an SS member. Transferred to SD in June 1934, he was appointed Sonderkommando 4a commander at the start of Operation *Barbarossa*: he held this position until January 13, 1942, when he was retired for *health reasons* related to his alcohol addiction. He returned to service as leader of the so-called Sonderaktion 1005, was arrested by the Americans after the war and tried at Nuremberg. Found guilty of crimes against humanity, he was sentenced to death and hanged in Landsberg Prison on June 8, 1951.

14 Friedrich, p. 159, Angrick Charkov, pp. 119-120. During the meeting, also attended by commanders of army corps, of divisions and of regional kommandanturen, it was decided to arrest en masse, for "security reasons (*Abwehrgründen*)" all the Jews of Kharkov and their isolation in a concentration camp was arranged for this purpose. The SK 4a would be mobilized for this operation. Because of its lack of numerical strength, however, it would gain support from the military units on site.

15 HIS, p. 183: «*Von irgendwelchen Maßnahmen gegen die Juden wurde bisher Abstand genommen, um diese vorerst nicht aus ihren Schlupfwinkeln zu locken, und vor Eintreffen der nötigen Kräfte nicht zu verstören*». Report of Kharkov's Stadtkommandantur dated November 19, 1941.

16 In Ljubomil, between July 21 and 22, the first company of Polizei-Bataillon 314 (Oltn. Oskar Josef Christ) had its genocidal baptism, taking part in two killings: as recon-

structed from ZStL during the preliminary investigations on Polizei-Regiment "Süd", the company 1/314, headquartered in a village near Kovel, would receive, in July, the order to make themselves available for a *SS-Kommando* with special powers, which was to arrive in a couple of days. And indeed, after the arrival of this *kommando*, the company was responsible to proceed with the roundup of all the Jews in the village, who were gathered and placed under surveillance. The day after, the shootings took place with the participation of company personnel. As reported in the diary of a 1/314 member on July 22, on that occasion 217 Jews of both sexes were shot, including women and children. Longerich, pp. 386 and 688. ZStL 204 AR-Z 1251/65 D. According to the Court of Traunstein, LG Traunstein 11 5 Ks Js 9437/78 dated May 26, 1982, against Karl Franz Wilhelm Bau., and Hans Her., as well as that of July 22 (215 victims), a further massacre, with 53 victims was committed in Ljubomil the day before (July 21), also with the participation of 1/314. See Curilla, p. 791.

17 In Dnepropetrovsk, on Jeckelnìs orders, the entire Jewish community was massacred between October 13 and 15, 1941, at the hands of Einsatzkommando 6 of Polizei-Bataillon 314 and Ukrainian auxiliaries. Curilla, pp. 797, 926, Mallmann Missgeburten, p. 81, Goldhagen, p. 285, Browning, p. 21, Hilberg, p. 320, Longerich, p. 379, Dean, p. 43, Krausnick / Wilhelm, p. 192, Westermann, p. 183, Pohl Ukraine, p. 37. With regard to the number of victims, the figures differ depending on the source: the *thousands* of Goldhagen become 15,000 for Hilberg, Mallmann and Westermann, passing through the 7/8,000 estimated by Browning and Longerich, and Dean's 10,000. At least 1,000 – more likely 5,000, and up to a maximum of 10,000 – is the number of victims conservatively estimated by the Court of Traunstein, LG Traunstein 11 5 Ks Js 9437/78 dated May 26, 1982, against two former members of Polizei-Bataillon 314. Klemp Ermittelt, p. 277. The victims reported in EM 135 dated November 19, the estimate deriving from an earlier report by Sonderkommando 4a dated October 13, are about 10,000. Hilberg, p. 407. With regard to the role of Polizei-Bataillon 314, the voluntary participation of men of all three companies of the battalion in the firing squads commanded by Oltn. Christ was established by the Court of Traunstein.

18 According to the testimonies given by 1/314 former police officers before the ZStL, at some point Oltn. Christ, the company commander, pulled out the gun and fired on a group of victims lined up and waiting for their execution, screaming at them. Testimonies given before ZStL 204 AR-Z 1251/65 D, Westermann, p. 185.

19 After three weeks spent in Dnepropetrovsk, Polizei-Bataillon 314 had reached Kharkov via Berezjaslav on December 5, 1941. See JuNSV, Band XXVII, Lfd.Nr. 663, p. 141.

20 Friedrich, pp. 121-122.

21 The result of the census of the Kharkov Jews, made by the various *Bezirkämter* before early December, was: 2,907 men, 5,405 women and 1,959 children, for a total of 10,271. Friedrich, p. 158. Thus, it is likely that during the following weeks those found in the communities searched in villages nearby were deported into the city.

22 Klemp Ermittelt, p. 439, Westermann, p. 184, Mehner, p. 326, Nix/Jerome, p. 259, JuNSV, Band XXVII, Lfd.Nr.663, p. 140.

23 Testimony given by Julius Bauer, Blobel's driver, before the public prosecutor of Darmstadt, StAw Darmstadt AZ: Ks 1/67 (ZStL 204 AR-Z 269/60, vol. 11, fols. 2390ff.). According to Bauer, Blobel ordered him to lead him to the site where the victims that had been loaded on the gas trucks in Poltava and had been inside those trucks, dead by poison during the whole journey, were going to be offloaded. When Blobel witnessed the opening of the doors, he looked away right after and ordered Bauer to bring him back. On the way back Blobel drank alcohol.

24 Rubinstein/Altman, p. 100: testimony given by the surviving Jewish engineer, S. Krivoruchko.

25 *Ibid.*

26 Dr. L.P. Nikolajew's diary on the German occupation in Kharkov, 1941-1943. ZStL, *Dokumentation UdSSR, Bd. 422, deutsche Übersetzung*. Excerpts published on: HIS, p. 180.

27 EM 164 dated February 4, 1942: «*305 Juden, die der deutschen Wehrmacht abträglich Gerüchte verbreiteten, wurden sofort erschossen*». Heer/Naumann, p. 281, Arad Holocaust, p. 191, HIS, p. 183, Krausnick/Wilhelm, p. 193.

28 Arad Holocaust p. 120. The Jews left to die that way would number over 400.

29 See EM 164 dated February 4, 1942, where the expression «*neuen Quartieren*» is used.

30 Friedrich, p. 160, Rubinstein/Altman, p. 100-101: testimony given by S. Krivoruchko. In the Kharkov *ghetto* the curfew was in force from 16:00 to 08:00 hours the next morning. Each violation was punished with death, without further warning. Arad Holocaust, p. 191.

31 Rubinstein/Altman, p. 100: testimony given by S. Krivoruchko. Also Arad Holocaust, pp. 191-192.

32 Arad Holocaust, p. 191.

33 According to the reconstruction by the Court of Wiesbaden, Christ met Vera Margascheva shortly after joining the battalion in the city and they had an affair that the superiors did not approve of. After being warned of the consequences that such an *inappropriate* liaison could cause him, Christ agreed to break off with the girl. In the meantime, however, she had found out she was pregnant. This was a problem for Christ, who took advantage of his sudden transfer to the front in March 1942, to ask two of his colleagues, Steinmann and Neubauer, to *resolve* the matter by murdering the girl. According to witnesses, the girl was taken on a pretext to a secluded place and finally killed with a gunshot. Despite the presence of about a hundred testimonies gathered by the prosecutor of Wiesbaden, the court held that it could not proceed against Christ as instigator of the murder, being as Steinmann and Neubauer were dead or reported missing and it being now impossible to recover the girl's body. By decision of February 23, 1968, LG Wiesbaden 2 Ks 1/67, the file against Christ was then closed. See also Der Spiegel 49/1967, pp. 38-41, Frankfurter Rundschau, 20.2.1968.

34 Arad Holocaust, p. 192.

35 Rubinstein/Altman, p. 101: testimony given by S. Krivoruchko.

36 *Ibid.*, pp. 101-102: testimony by S. Krivoruchko. After hiding among the clothes, Krivoruchko managed to jump down from the truck and then reach his wife in Kharkov. He had to stay in hiding for a few months and then roam from village to village until the Red Army returned to town, in February 1943.

37 Testimony given by Karl. G., member of Polizei-Bataillon 314, before the public prosecutor in Hamburg on November 9, 1964, StAw Hamburg 631 a, 1868, Bl. 2553, in HIS, p. 185.

38 Testimony given by Viktor T., member of a Sonderkommand firing squad, on June 25, 1960 before ZStL, 4 AR – Z 269/60, Bd. 1, Bl. 16.

39 *Ibid.*

40 Arendt, p. 20, quoting David Rousset, *Le jours de notre mort,* 1947.

41 *The People's Verdict: a full report of the proceedings at the Krasnodar and Kharkov German atrocity trials*, pp. 110-111.

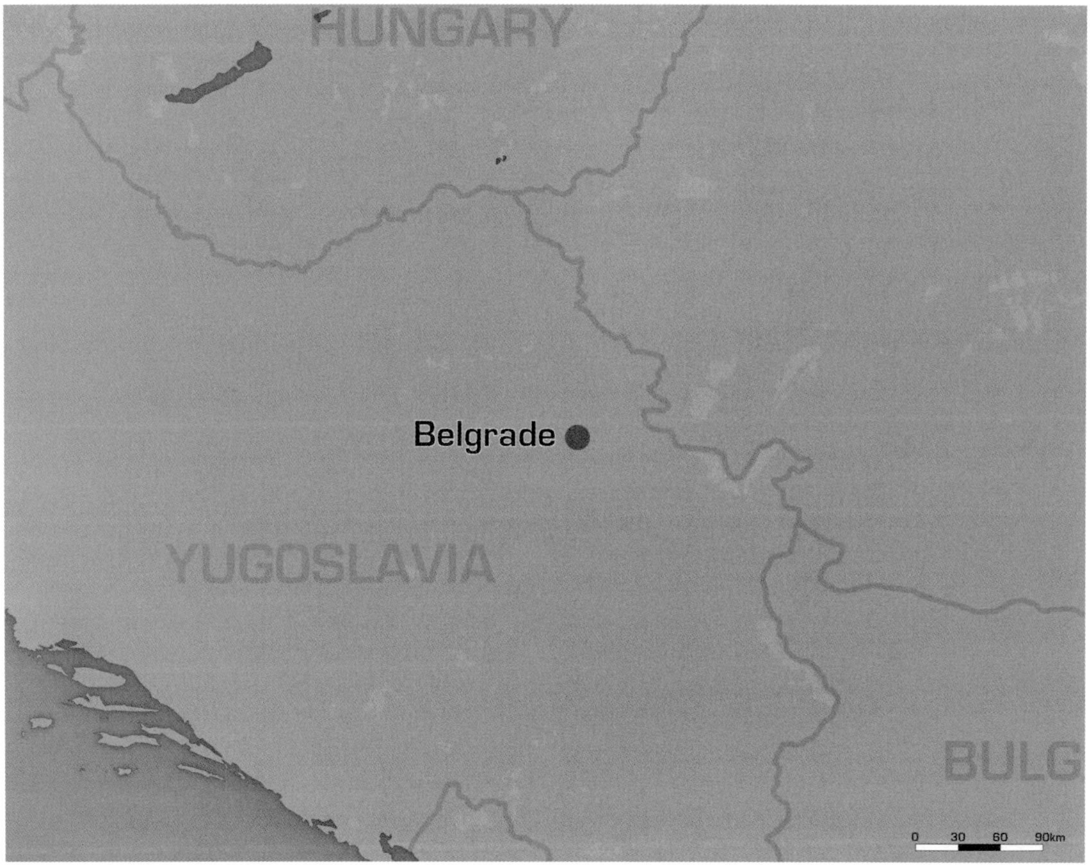
HUNGARY
Belgrade
YUGOSLAVIA
BULG
0 30 60 90km

CHAPTER ELEVEN

"LETTERS FROM SAJMISTE"

BELGRADE, SERBIA, FEBRUARY 1942

Mit den schärfsten Mitteln
die Ordnung wiederherzustellen!

Adolf Hitler[1]

11.1 INTRODUCTION

«*Serbien ist Judenfrei!*». These were the words chosen for the brusque telegram that Emanuel Schäfer, Chef der Sipo und des SD in Serbien (BDS), sent to the RSHA in Berlin to announce the resolution of the *Jewish question* in Serbia[2] in June 1942. The announcement, so essential in its brutality, implied the *disappearance* of at least 12,000 Serbian Jews, including nearly a thousand refugees from other parts of Europe[3] and was sent after completing the slaughter of women and children, implemented by means of a gas truck at the end of a long period of detention in the concentration camp of Sajmiste, in the outskirts of Belgrade. Women and children who in the early months of 1942, followed the fate of the male part of the Jewish population, quickly wiped out by firing squads during the autumn of 1941.

The destruction of the Jewish community of Serbia can be divided into two different stages according to methods of annihilation and – albeit in the abstract – to the driving forces that represented the motivational and ideological basis.

In a personal report to his superior Generaloberst Löhr, in August 1942, (Staatsrat) Harald Turner wrote, with obvious self-promotional pride, how Serbia was "the only country in which the Jewish and gypsies question had been solved (*Serbien eiziges Land und dem Judenfrage Zigeunerfrage gelöst*)"[4]. Turner had every reason to claim a similar *record*. In fact, in just a few months, from September 1941 to May 1942, the Jewish community of Serbia had been almost completely annihilated as a result of a deadly coming together of interests from the military authorities of the Wehrmacht, the SS and the police. Although these were animated by a partly different approach to the *Jewish question* – mostly related to the occupation policy for the first, and more ideologically oriented for the others – they eventually converged in everyday practice, influencing and mutually supporting each other, within a mechanism in which a sharp dividing line between the responsibilities of both sides does not appear as immediately perceptible.

In fact, on one hand, especially in the second phase of the winter of 1942 – the phase of extermination of women and children – the annihilation of the Jews of Serbia represents the local implementation of the Final Solution that had already started in other parts of Europe ever since the late summer of 1941. On the other hand, this crime was initiated and completed in a particular environment: that of Serbia, where the political and operational domain was not held by the SS and the police authorities, but by the military ones. Ever since the early months after the partition of Yugoslavia in April 1941, the military authorities had imposed a policy of occupation based on a vision of total domain, in which distorted and obsessive racial and ideological preconceptions – including those of a historical and traditional nature that originated from an ancient anti-Serb hostility – contributed to the contamination and orientation, along the axis of a seemingly endless and self-propelled spiral, of increasingly extreme and brutal tactical choices.

Thus, it was also inevitable that Serbian Jews, *dragged in* by abused theorems, became a prime target of repression by the Wehrmacht, together with communists, gypsies and nationalists, all included within an ideological *melting-pot*, confused and frayed, obtuse and counterproductive, as well as impossible to settle through the use of brute force alone.

In this respect, precisely because they were part of this multi-faced theorem, Serb male Jews were persecuted – and destroyed – during the first phase of the autumn of 1941, not so much in adherence to a strategic / ideological framework (*Vernichtungspolitik*), as instead occurred in other parts of Europe, but on the grounds of a tactical and situational context (*Okkupationspolitik*).

Obviously, such specificity does not relieve and does not deny in any way the choice by political leaders of the regime to implement, since summer 1941, the genocidal solution as concretization of their own ideological dogmas, in parallel with the engagement in a deadly war oriented along more conventional schemes of political and economic domination by the military hierarchies. Instead, the mix of tactical needs and ideological forces of the army demonstrates how the image of the *Jew* as a target to hit no matter what and regardless of any consideration had now been internalized, and shows how the annihilation machine was complex and multifaceted. It also shows that the habit to take the most extreme measures in complex situations, with the certainty of obtaining not only impunity, but outright approval, was widespread even between the rigid hierarchies of the Wehrmacht[5]. Given that, there was no need for explicit written orders to ensure that the intentions of the top men were translated into concrete actions by the local hierarchies, but only the will of the latter to adapt these wishes to their own needs, after extrapolating the implications. As a matter of fact, nothing is more ambiguous, but also equally significant, than the imperative *to restore order by the most drastic means*[6], issued by Hitler to General Franz Böhme, after having appointed him new general plenipotentiary in Serbia in September 1941.

There was evidence and there were implications. And there were those who were called in to interpret them. Franz Böhme, a Styrian from Zeltweg, was one of them.

11.2 ORGANISMS

The system of German occupation in Serbia was rather complex and redundant, articulated on a two-headed vertex controlled by the Wehrmacht that overlapped a hybrid structure of Army / SS and police at intermediate levels[7]. Only in September 1941, in order to overcome a certain decisional paralysis – and thus to react to the spread of the insurgency – top hierarchies were redefined, particularly with respect to relations between the military commander in Serbia (*Militärbefehlshaber*) and the commander of 65th Army Corps. There were several main characters – commands and departments – involved in the resolution of the *Jewish question* in Serbia:

11.2.1 – Militärbefehlshaber in Serbien

On April 20, 1941, three days after the capitulation of the Yugoslav army, OKH issued orders for the establishment of a military administration in Serbia within the borders of 1912, with the task of providing:

1) military security, through the departments of 65th Army Corps of Paul Bader's army (v. § 11.2.3);
2) administrative management through Verwaltungsstab des Militärbefehlshaber, commanded by Harald Turner (v. § 11.2.2). Activities of internal security, carried out by means of police departments, both civil and military, including Polizei-Bataillon 64 and Einsatzgruppe E (see § § 11.2.4 and 11.2.5) also fell to the latter.

On April 22, Luftwaffe General Helmut Förster was appointed as first military commander. He was replaced on June 2 by General Ludwig von Schröder, who died in a plane crash a few weeks later (July 28), and was replaced by another Luftwaffe man, Heinrich Dankelmann, who in turn ceded the post to Franz Böhme on September 18. On this occasion, the title of "military commander (*Militärbefehlshaber in Serbien*)" was replaced by that of "general plenipotentiary (*Bevollmächtigter Kommandierender General in Serbien*)". Whatever the title, that role, which represented the main German authority in Serbia, continued to remain firmly in the hands of the military until the end of the conflict; the only variation being the transition of competence from the aviation authority to the army authority. With regard to the involvement of this authority in the so-called *Jewish question*, it must be said that the first discriminatory measures – obligation to wear the Star of David, expropriations, forced labor, etc. – were imposed precisely by Militärbefehlshaber von Schröder[8], and then implemented by his successors; a thing that even in the absence of other factors – which, however, did occur –would be enough to nail the Wehrmacht, via his top military commander in Serbia, to its unquestionable historical responsibilities.

11.2.2 – Verwaltungsstab des Militärbefehlshaber

The civil administration of the territory as part of the task by the military commander / general plenipotentiary, was assigned, as of April 20, 1941, to the direction of Staatsrat, SS-Gruppenführer Harald Turner, who was referring directly to Stab des Generalquartiermeister at the OKH in Berlin. Turner's deputy was SS-Sturmbannführer Georg Kiessel. The main tool available to Turner for the imposition of his authority and the transmission of orders to the population were the four Feldkommandanturen formed by the Wehrmacht in Serbia: Belgrade (FK 599), Užice / Sabac (FK 816), Pancevo / Čačak (FK 610) and Niš (FK 809), which also had police and homeland security duties. For this same task Polizei-Bataillon 64 [9] was called in from Essen and Duisburg on June 30, 1941. Through the same Feldkommandanturen, or more accurately, through a liaison officer detached to each of them, the orders issued by the general plenipotentiary were sent to detachments of Fuchs' Sicherheitspolizei scattered throughout the area, which thus ended up liaising with Turner. As a matter of fact, it seems that Turner was also in charge of *Jewish affairs* in Serbia[10], superseding Fuchs and, *de facto*, acting as HSSPF; among his first acts in this area it is worth mentioning the order of June 22, 1941 imposing the Jewish community in Belgrade to provide a daily contingent of 40 hostages to be detained in the field of Topovske Supe, ready to be executed in case of retaliation[11]. Four months later, with his memo sent to Feldkommandanturen on October 26, 1941, Turner endorsed the final decision taken in those days by the top German military administration in Serbia, to proceed with the systematic extermination of Jewish men, leaving aside his previous project – unrealistic but not less lethal – to deport those same Jews to Romania[12].

11.2.3 – Höheren Kommando zbV LXV

In addition to the territorial administrative area controlled by the military commander, in the summer of 1941 the Wehrmacht in Serbia could count on mobile army units subject to the ordinary chain of command, on top of which was the 12th Army led by Field Marshal Wilhelm List, based in Thessaloniki, Greece. These units belonged to two different categories: firstly, there were three weak and inexperienced infantry divisions of occupation, 704th, 714th and 717th, specially constituted for the defense of the Serbian territory and on the other side three Landesschützen battalions were added, formed with senior staff and poorly trained, 562nd, 592nd and 920th, respectively divided between Feldkommandanturen 599, 610 and 809.

Both groups of departments were subordinated to a command, equal in rank to an Army Corps, called Höheren Kommando zbV 55 and led by General Paul Bader, who, until the reorganization in September 1941, was faced with an irreconcilable dualism with military commanders, all of the Luftwaffe, who succeeded in Belgrade from April to September and whom he had to refer to, at least theoretically. Then, with the appointment – advocated by List – of Army General Franz Böhme to general plenipotentiary, that operative and caste-like antagonism that Bader had opposed the generals of the aviation authority with, disappeared[13]. Regarding his involvement in the so-called *Jewish question*, Bader was the transmission belt of the repressive view implemented by Böhme and supported by List who, although neither a Nazi nor subservient to the regime, conceived the reaction to the insurgency as based solely on brute force, with hostage-taking, indiscriminate reprisals and terror as the main methods of punishment against the population. According to this rather coarse view, the identification between Jews and communists was considered something natural, not so much as ideological dogma, but as a rough mindset.

11.2.4 – *Einsatzgruppe E "Belgrad"*

Sicherheitspolizei was represented in Serbia by Einsatzgruppe E "Belgrad" led by SS-Standartenführer Wilhelm Fuchs, who, as early as April 2, 1941, had received an explicit order by OKH to consider as targets – in case of intervention in Yugoslavia – all enemies of the state including of course Jews, as well as communists, saboteurs and terrorists[14]. In other words, since before the invasion, Serbia's Jews had been consigned to the jurisdiction of the SS, with all the consequences that that represented[15].

Einsatzgruppe E, which hierarchically depended directly on the military commander, really enjoyed considerable autonomy; alternatively, in certain circumstances, it would act on behalf of and with input from Turner, who, in Serbia, represented the highest SS and police authority (at least until the entrance of HSSPF Meyszner in January 1942). In January 1942, on Heydrich's orders, Einsatzgruppe "Belgrade" evolved into BdS "Belgrade", SS-Obersturmbannführer Emanuel Schaefer coming from Cologne to replace Fuchs[16]. In that circumstance, Turner was stripped of his powers in relation to policing, while BdS "Belgrad" was subordinated directly to the RSHA in Berlin.

11.2.5 – *Polizei-Bataillon 64*

With Himmler's decree of January 5, 1942, a core command, destined to evolve a few weeks later into BdO "Belgrad" (Oberst May)[17] was formed in Serbia. Naturally, Maj. Adolf Joosten's Polizei-Bataillon 64, which was the first Ordnungspolizei department to arrive in Serbia, on June 30, 1941, fell under this authority. Placed at Turner's direct disposal, the battalion would also receive orders by Fuchs, detaching initially (July 1941) with the command and at least one company in Belgrade and the rest of the department in the sector of FK 816 (in Obrenovac, Šabac and Valjevo)[18]. In fact, between summer and autumn 1941, while the command was constantly kept in Belgrade, the tactical relocation of the various units of the battalion was rather frequent, both at platoon and at company level, with regular use of the departments in anti-partisan activities and especially reprisals and repression against civilians: these *actions*, in particular, saw the companies of the battalion involved in numerous shootings of hostages taken from concentration camps (especially that of Šabac). So, in the summer of 1941, numerous executions of hostages (communists and Jews) were perpetrated by 3/64 (Oltn. Otto Ehrmann) between Belgrade, Pancevo, Skela and Dedinje[19], while in autumn, 1/64 (Hptm. Adolf Gross) took part in the supervision and some executions of male Jews held in KL "Šabac"[20]. Then, at the beginning of 1942 all three companies of the battalion were involved in the massacre of women and children locked up in the Judenlager "Semlin" (Sajmiste), on the outskirts of Belgrade, during a genocidal campaign that would lead, basically, to the annihilation of the Jewish community of Serbia.

11.3 SUMMERTIME

The persecution of Serbian Jews began quietly a couple of days before the formal capitulation of the Yugoslav Army (April 17, 1941), at the initiative of SS-Standartenführer Wilhelm Fuchs, commander of Einsatzgruppe "Belgrad" who, with an order dated April 16, imposed the registration of all Jews living in Belgrade to be completed by April 19, under threat of execution for all those who would not show up[21]. 9,145 Jews still in town, of the about 12,000 present in Belgrade before the invasion, obeyed the order and were registered by the Gestapo section of Einsatzgruppe "Belgrad" (SS-Ustuf. Fritz Stracke). Then, in accordance with Belgrade's Feldkommandant, Oberst von Kaisenberg, further provisions about forced labor standards and the imposition of the compulsory Star of David were enacted. The same provisions, implemented by additional measures concerning the *definition of a Jew* and the recording and *aryanization* of public offices and businesses resulting in expropriations, were extended on May 30 throughout all occupied Serbia, on the orders of general plenipotentiary Ludwig von Schröder[22]. Thus, as noted by historian Walter Manoschek, all the usual steps of anti-Jewish policy, marginalization and discrimination in preparation for the next phase of annihilation were made in Serbia in a single day[23].

There are traces of these early vexations – still mild, in relation to those that followed – in an interesting photographic documentation dated April 1941, produced by Kriegsberichter Neubauer of Propagandakompanie 691. The images – 36 frames of high quality currently stored at Bundesarchiv Berlin[24] – portray exclusively Jewish men of all ages, huddled at the foot of the Kalemegdan fortress in Belgrade, partly isolated by metal fences and already *marked* by the star of David, probably about to be registered for forced labor. Just as had happened in Mogilev with Kriegsberichter Kessler's reportage, again – albeit with a more neutral approach, at least apparently – some of the images linger on those who, according to the canons propagated by the propaganda of the regime, were to be seen as *typical Jews*. And again, as events would show, very few, if any, of the subjects in the photos, would survive that autumn 1941.

The point of no return for the fate of the Jews of Serbia was reached soon after June 22, 1941, when, with the start of Operation *Barbarossa,* communist guerrillas began to spread in Serbia, which sparked a sort of Pavlovian reflex about the natural affinity between communists and Jews, seen as irreconcilable enemies of the state and disturbers of public order, among the military establishment and in particular the army establishment. Thus, they started to apply measures of policing that were increasingly rigid, but unrealistic, like kidnapping and shooting of hostages. The previously mentioned Turner's order of June 22, to proceed with the deportation in the Topovske camp of all the Communist *leaders* of Serbia and a contingent of Jews to be used as a "hostage tank (*Geiselreservoir*)" was followed by the first shootings of prisoners taken directly from the same camp; there is evidence of the execution of 13 Jews and communists that took place on July 5[25] which was followed by further reprisals in the following days: July 8, 18, 22 and 25, with a total of 275 victims, almost half of which being Jewish [26].

The daily routine of executions was admitted without hesitation in the letters of German soldiers to their families. On July 26, Lieutenant Peter G., a member of 714.ID, refers how "almost every day whole hordes of communists are being shots", while in the following letter of July 29, he announces the *record* of 122 Jews and communists killed that morning in Belgrade[27]. In total, between July and August, at least a thousand Jews and communists were hanged or shot, but even so, the expansion of the insurgence could not be slowed down[28]. In contrast, the stiffening of repressive measures – that by July 27 had begun to affect also the Serbian population not included in these categories[29] – proved to be counterproductive and a harbinger of massive defections of civilians in favor of guerrilla units, regardless if they were communists or Chetniks.

At that point, facing the prospect of losing control of the situation and concerned about the damage to the prestige and morale that resulted from the frequent setbacks that even the most isolated garrisons suffered at the hands of enterprising partisan groups[30], the army commands began to outline two different strategies to address the problem of communist insurgency, of which Jews, presumptively and simplistically, were considered a key component.

While within the German administration in Belgrade there was a *political* component represented by Turner and Benzler which considered the expulsion to Romania of all the 8,000 Serbian Jewish men still detained in camps[31] as a quick solution the problem of insurgency, the *military* component of Bader and Böhme, on the contrary, judged as inappropriate the prospect of doing without such a large number of *cheap* hostages, and pressed for a further intensification of the repression. Around the same time they also began to ponder the problem of thousands of Jewish women and children[32]; their internment in a new camp in Sremska Mitrovica, in view of their subsequent deportation *to the east*, by spring 1942[33] was one of the suggestions made.

The debate between these two opposing visions lasted from late August to late October. In the meantime, however, the pendulum began to swing inexorably toward the most radical solution.

11.4 AUTUMN TIME

On September 13, 1941 Benzler received from Berlin the negative opinion of RSHA about the proposed deportation to Romania of the male Jews of Serbia: as suggested by Eichmann, it was more convenient to simply shoot them as hostages[34]. On September 16, on orders given by OKW commander Wilhelm Keitel, the shooting of hostages at a ratio of 100 to 1 (for every German killed, 100 hostages would die – editors note) was authorized in Serbia. Two days later Franz Böhme, the newly appointed general plenipotentiary arrived in Belgrade: he was the man that the army considered most suitable to remedy the problem of insurgency. From then on, things started happening very quickly. On October 2, in the village of Topola, south of Belgrade, not far from Kragujevac, 21 German soldiers fell victim to an ambush, which was followed by the October 10 retaliation ordered by Böhme in the proportions set: 2,100 hostages, mostly Jews and a few gypsies, were taken from the camps of Belgrade and Šabac and shot between October 9 and 13. A few days later in Kraljevo, between October 15 and 16, after a guerrilla attack on a unit of 717.ID, 1,755 Serbs were rounded up from house to house and shot, and finally in Kragujevac, where 10 German soldiers were killed in an ambush and another 15 were injured, 2,300 civilians seized at random without any selection were killed in retaliation on October 21.

It was clear that beyond the terror spread by the executions, this level of brutality had counterproductive effects in terms of control over the population, so that even those who had unleashed such terror, i.e. Böhme and Bader, were forced to a partial reverse, at least with regard to the Serbs. Thus, while on one hand all the mass killings of Serbs were suspended by an order dated October 22 and directed to the departments of Army Corps 45th[35], on the other the *new course* had opposite effects on the remaining Jewish males that were still alive and on the gypsies, who saw confirmed their position as *hostages tout-court*. Turner also shared this opinion at this time, as he expressed in his memo sent to Feldkommandanturen on October 26, 1941[36]. This change of idea with respect to his previous hypothesis of deportation to Romania, can be explained by the inexorable extinction of the *Jews' reserve*, which by October 18 had fallen to no more than 1,500 people, and by the enforcement of the will to proceed with the executions of all survivors expressed by Fuchs and the two representatives of the Ministry of Foreign Affairs and the RSHA, Rademacher and Suhr, sent from Berlin to investigate the situation. At that point, outvoted, Turner gave up all remaining objections, so that on October 25, Rademacher was able to communicate to Berlin the decision to proceed with the execution of all Jewish men of Serbia within the same week[37].

Then, *the problem of men being solved*, they were left to deal with the seemingly more difficult problem: women and children.

11.5 THE FIVE KINGS

According to Christopher Browning's definition, there were five kings that in the fall of 1941 ruled the simulacrum of Serbia: Böhme, Turner, Fuchs, Benzler and Neuhausen[38]. Usually committed to pursue their individual interests, they all agreed to resolve the *problem* represented by Jewish women and children that the army refused to use as hostages through deportation[39]. Prior to that there had been a proposal, later abandoned, to transfer them into a ghetto to be established for that purpose in the town of Majdanpek[40]. The deportation, to be performed as soon as possible, would have been preparatory – apparently at least – to a subsequent transfer of inmates *somewhere to the east*. In fact, as written by Rademacher in his report of October 25, it was decided to keep the Jews locked in a Belgrade ghetto until technical conditions would make it possible to transfer them to a concentration camp to the east. Not only was this project refuted by the events of spring 1942, but also by a subsequent statement by Turner – controversial as it was – that after the opening of the Semlin camp, he himself obtained the dispatch from Berlin, via the SD, of a *Delousing* truck, thanks to which it would have been possible to clear the camp over four weeks[41]. If we are to believe Turner, this statement would shift the decision to proceed with the genocide in Serbia a few weeks back, up to that stage of gray area between 1941 and 1942, between the end of the *reign* of Fuchs and the takeover by Schäfer.

In any case, whether or not it was Turner who pressed for the new invention in genocidal technique to be sent to Belgrade, or the RSHA that sent it directly to Schaefer as he maintains, the fact remains that only a few weeks after it passed from the hands of the army to those of Sicherheitspolizei, the *Jewish question* in Serbia was finally solved: starting from the chosen place of detention.

On October 28, 1941, when the idea of building a new internment camp in Jarak first and then in Zasavica, near Sremska Mitrovica was deemed logistically impractical, the decision was taken to use the big spaces of the International Fair of Belgrade on the river island at the confluence of the Danube and the Sava, within the boundaries of Croatia, a reason for which it was necessary to reach an agreement with the government in Zagreb[42].

Then, according to an order issued by Turner to the Feldkommandanturen, the deportation to Sajmiste was supposed to happen once the necessary works were complete – including a barbed wire fence around the perimeter of the camp. In any case, not before November 15, beginning with Jewish women and children in Belgrade, and then extending it in the following weeks to those living in other parts of Serbia.

In fact, the deportation order was issued on December 8, directed to all Jews still living in Belgrade, who began to reach the camp with their household goods and stocks of food for a few days through a pontoon bridge across the Sava. By December 15, the transfer of 5,291 Jews of Belgrade, mostly women and children, could be considered completed[43].

With their deportation to Semlin, the jurisdiction of the Jews of Serbia finally passed from the Wehrmacht to Sicherheitspolizei, whose command of Belgrade remained in Fuchs' hands until January 5, the day he was replaced by SS-Obersturmbannführer Emanuel Schaefer, in his new role as BdS "Belgrad".

With regard to the field command, this was initially assigned to SS-Scharführer Edgar Enge and then, towards the end of January 1942, to SS-Untersturmführer Herbert Andorfer, an Austrian from Linz who, in November / December 1941, had gained some experience in the concentration camp of Šabac as a political investigator and recruiter of Chetnik prisoners[44]. As for the men on watch, in compliance with the agreements with the government in Zagreb, which prevented the use of auxiliary Serbs in Croatian territory, it was decided to employ the personnel of Polizei-Bataillon 64, with shifts of about 25 men on patrol around the outer perimeter[45].

In late December 1941, everything was ready to stage the local version of the Final Solution in Belgrade. Victims, perpetrators and the stage: it was all there. But despite the wishes of the *five kings* to begin the genocide there was something missing: technical equipment.

That too would arrive, very soon.

11.6 LETTERS FROM SAJMISTE

In December 1941, the arrival of women and children into the camp marked the opening of the second phase of the Jewish genocide in Serbia: not only the most dramatic, considering the nature of the victims, but also the most technologically *innovative*. It is at this point that there is a passage from *ordinary* executions by firing squad – the only means of extermination used up to that moment, in Serbia as elsewhere – to the systematic genocide by gas poisoning – in this case carbon monoxide – almost as in a preparatory escalation to the imminent launch of the *death factories* in Poland.

As a matter of fact, the use of gas vehicles in the execution of Jews was not something completely new, because this method had been used, albeit limitedly, in Poltava and Kharkov in late fall 1941. However, tragic as they were, these first two experiments were not comparable in magnitude to the events in Belgrade, where the real general tests of chemical genocide went on stage, through the total obliteration of the most vulnerable segments of an entire community: women and children. In this respect, it can be said that Belgrade had the primogeniture of this new form of extermination. Perhaps it was by chance, or by choice, but it appears as a tragic symbolism the fact that it was precisely the mothers, generators of power, with their children, future progeny, to have been the first victims of this new form of *definitive genocide*, whose ultimate goal was the eradication of a race.

After the gate closed behind them, the women and children of Sajmiste entered another dimension. In short, they probably suspected what they would face in the months ahead, and it is likely that, despite the harsh conditions of internment, most of them looked at their imprisonment in the camp only as a temporary measure. At least, this is what can be guessed by reading the first three letters of Hilda Dajč, a twenty-year old university student, daughter of the vice-chairman of Belgrade's *Judenrat* who, despite being exempt from deportation owing to her father's role, volunteered as a nurse in the makeshift hospital organized in one of the halls in the camp.

From her letters, four in all, written between December 1941 and February 1942, many details of what survival in the field was like can be deduced. Also, from a certain point onwards, there appears a feeling of suspended humanity, the unsustainable perception of a totally empty and unknown horizon and the awareness of the moral slope along which the inmates of the camp, and Dajč herself by her open admission, were gradually slipping. It was the tyranny of the camps imposing itself after only nine weeks of internment, not so much through the presence of the guards – who Dajč barely mentions – but for the deaf struggle for survival that pervaded every moment, or for the presence of those "hideous tangles" of defeated humanity that were impossible to help, thus to rise above them became necessary in order to keep on surviving. It was the loss of the ideal vision of a positive humanity; it was the end – especially in the fourth letter – of the ideal of *humanitas*, overwhelmed by a slow passive and hopeless individualism, vile but compassionate. It was the triumph of the camp, a subverted microcosm, which eventually became almost an abst ract entity, but precisely because of this it was even better internalized by each of the inmates.

After the fourth letter, undated, but written after nine weeks of detention, roughly around early February 1942, there was no other. Hilda Dajč was killed in the gas van that reached Sajmiste in early March 1942. Her first three letters are preserved at the Jewish Museum in Belgrade. The fourth, the most dramatic, at the Historical Archives of Belgrade.

11.7 BEHIND BARBED WIRE

According to a document drawn up by the camp administration, on February 16, 1942 there were 332 men, 3,933 women and 1,238 children in Sajmiste[46]: a total substantially confirmed in Dajč's third letter dated December 9, 1941, in which – after the first two major waves of arrivals during the days around December 7 – she describes the deplorable conditions reserved to about 5,000 people, with essentially no means to get by and massed in one single pavilion, on long planks with decks covered only by a little straw. Deplorable conditions marked by food shortages, cold seeping in from fissures in the roof, the light constantly on, the everlasting murmur of thousands of voices forced within a single space that made it impossible to rest and where hygienic conditions were unsustainable. These are all indications that hint at how the arrangement of the Jews of Sajmiste, obviously *parked* in the wait for a permanent solution, was considered temporary by the German administration. There is no doubt that the camp – whose command structure was limited to the essentials – was a real logistical hassle of no economic value, constantly at a loss and that committed men and means. From this point of view it was nothing but bankruptcy which could not be sustained for long.

It was at that point, presumably, that someone thought of the *Saurer*.

Whether the input started from Belgrade, or came directly from Berlin, the decision to proceed with the slaughter of women and children is framed within a destructive mechanism that met two different needs: on one hand the need for the German administration of Belgrade to get rid of what was an economically unproductive burden, and on the other hand the will of RSHA to frame the genocidal project within more *systematic* ways, abandoning that somehow handicraft improvisation that until then had characterized the massacres perpetrated in Soviet territory, and that precisely from that spring onward was gradually set aside and replaced by gassing.

Therefore, as Browning correctly points out, what we witness here is not Berlin merely tagging along with a local situation[47], but a convergence of purposes, between center and periphery, synergistic to a project which, even if dealt with starting from different perspectives and interests, was mutual. In other words, the extermination of the Jews of Serbia represents an example of that *genocidal decentralization* that, through the use of local resources and specific situations, allowed the implementation of the general destructive project that had long been cherished, but that would hardly be possible to plan in detail at central level without the intervention, support and convergent interests of the local realities.

In that respect, questioning at what decisional level the extermination of women and children in the Sajmiste camp was decided upon (Turner, Schäfer or RSHA), appears as an essentially academic exercise, since that decision, once taken, was functional to the needs of the various subjects involved in each case.

Except, of course, for the victims.

11.8 SAJMISTE-AVALA: ONE-WAY ONLY

Excerpt from the indictment of the Dortmund public prosecutor, against Herbert Andorfer[48]:

> *Since the killing of Jewish women and children could not be perpetrated under the guise of a shooting of hostages, the Nazi leaders matured a different plan for their destruction. Between early to mid-March 1942, after a written notice to Befehlshaber der Sicherheitspolizei "Belgrad", the RSHA sent a genocidal kommando formed by SS sergeants Götz and Meier to Belgrade with a special truck. This truck was a Saurer model, its size and appearance approximately those of a removal van. The vehicle had a loading compartment of seven-eight yards in length, two yards in height and two yards in width. At its rear end was a solid hinged lockable door. The compartment could contain at least 50 people. The vehicle was equipped with a special device (levers, connecting hoses and tubes), with which it was possible to divert the carbon monoxide contained in the exhaust fumes of the engine into the compartment, so that the people inside, stricken with panic, nausea and headache, were quickly killed by carbon monoxide poisoning, or suffocated from lack of oxygen. The device was not visible from the outside and was operated by drivers Götz and Meier.*
>
> *The witness Schaefer entrusted Sturmbannführer Sattler, the skilled Director of Department IV, to kill the Jews in the Semlin camp using the gas van that arrived in Belgrade. One day before the killings started Sattler called the defendant [SS-Obersturmführer Andorfer Herbert, A/N], telling him to initiate a so-called "resettlement" of the Jews, who were "dealt with" in five minutes, thanks to the special truck arrived from Berlin. He then gave the order to ensure the secrecy of the operations during the journeys of the special truck while traveling from Semlin's camp to the shooting range of Mount Avala, about 10 miles away, chosen as the burial site. Finally, the defendant also received the order to ensure the secrecy of the exhaust of the gas van, near the above mentioned burial site. For this purpose, four members of Polizei-Bataillon 64, including witnesses Karl W[etter] and Leo L. were detached from the headquarters of Befehlshaber der Sicherheispolizei.*
>
> *Early in the morning the special vehicle with his drivers Götz and Meier reached Semlin's camp. The Jews in the camp were informed that, little by little, they would all be transferred to another camp. In order to make this operation more credible, an open truck was also sent together with the gas van. Then, 50 people were invited to climb into the gas van, while their luggage was loaded onto the open truck. Then the gas van moved towards the bridge over the Sava, followed by the truck with the luggage [...].*

The luggage was then taken to an NSV [Nationalsozialistische Volkswohlfahrt, A/N] collection center, while the gas van crossed the whole of Belgrade to the outskirts of the city, bound to Avala's shooting range which was located along the main road to Niš. During this trip the defendant followed the gas van with his car, because he did not know the way very well.

The first day of the action, the two witnesses Karl W. and Leo L., together with two other policemen and a kommando of Serb prisoners, were already at Avala. Previously, at least one pit had been dug for the burial of the Jews killed.

The defendant, who was the most senior police officer on the scene, gave the witness gave Karl W. the order to ensure the security of the burial site [...]. Then, the gas van approached in reverse one of the pre-prepared pits. Götz and Meier, the drivers, opened the rear doors. Immediately, the first bodies fell outside the gas van. The members of the kommando of Serb prisoners then received orders to unload the gas van, pushing the bodies of the killed Jews into the pit. While this was occurring, the defendant was about 10 yards away together with the witness, Karl W. The faces had the typical pinkish color that revealed poisoning by carbon monoxide. The compartment of the gas van was visibly contaminated by fluids released by the victims during their agony, to the point that it was brought back to the BdS headquarters to be cleaned off. After the burial of corpses, the defendant and the police kommando with the prisoners withdrew from the burial site. This process continued the same way until early June, until the complete gassing of all Jewish prisoners in the camp [...]. The journeys were made every day except Sunday. At least twice a week, a second journey was made in the afternoon.

While the decision-making dynamics behind the genocide in Serbia were rather tortuous and incomplete, the manner in which it was perpetrated was extraordinarily simple and linear, as well as quick and efficient.

Many of the details that allowed the public prosecutor in Dortmund to outline the framework of this *timed massacre* which lasted from the first ten days of March to May 10, 1942, was carried out once or twice a day, six days a week, excluding Sundays[49] and cost the lives of about 7,500 Jews, come from Andorfer's statements.

His statements also allow us to understand to what extent the division of *labor* had been meticulously organized and divided, so as to minimize the risks of self-accountability by the direct perpetrators (very few, actually), who took part in the death trips to Mount Avala[50]. Despite this precaution, deemed necessary, there would still be discontent both among policemen in charge of guarding the victims, for the misuse that they were destined to, and by Andorfer himself, who had taken the time to familiarize himself with many of the women prisoners, to the point of even allowing himself cups of coffee and card games with some of them[51].

The exact date when was the first Saurer trip took place is unknown, but the methods remained the same until the last, without any incident, in a repetitive, monotonous *routine*.

According to Andorfer's statement[52] he received the order to begin the death trips directly from the top of BdS (from Schaefer or SS-Sturmbannführer Bruno Sattler, commander of Gestapo's section IV B4) in early March, disguising the operations in the form of a transfer of victims to another camp in Serbia. He, Andorfer, would have to accompany each trip, equipped with a special pass in order to avoid detection by any checkpoints along the way. The gas van – a large Saurer truck able to contain between fifty and one hundred people at a time – had to take on the victims in front of the buildings in which they were detained while, as a further disguising measure, all baggage was loaded on a second vehicle travelling along. The unsuspecting victims, many of whom volunteers, had been told that they would find great living conditions in the hypothetical camp they were being transferred to, while sweets were distributed among children before departure. After that, crammed to the limit, the Saurer crossed the bridge over the Sava that linked the Sajmiste island with Belgrade and then stopped just across the river. At that point one of the two drivers got out of the cockpit and through a fitting extension connected the exhaust pipe to an air intake practiced in the compartment which contained the victims, so as to convey the exhaust gas produced by the motor inside it. After that, the Saurer drove off without stopping until Mount Avala, a hill on the southern outskirts of Belgrade, about ten miles away, where the victims killed during the journey would be unloaded and buried in mass graves dug in the shooting range fields. A small detachment of four men of 2/Polizei-Bataillon 64 who took orders from Polizeimeister Karl Wetter, ensured security in the area and surveillance of a group of seven Serb prisoners, previously taken from a prison and charged with unloading and burying the victims: admissions to that effect were given by Wetter and his colleague Leo L., during the Dortmund trial against Andorfer, the Stuttgart trial against Enge and the Hanover trial against Pradel and Wentritt[53]. Further evidence also emanated from testimonies given by other members of 2/64.

Opening the rear doors of the Saurer was probably the most gruesome stage of the whole operation. From the loading of the victims, the journey and the unloading of the bodies, the operation was likely to be finished in two hours or perhaps a little longer. We can only remotely imagine the drama that took place inside the compartment, once the first waves of gas penetrated inside began to produce their poisonous effect: the panic that certainly seized the victims plunged into darkness, the screams, the crowding towards the tightly barred door, the smallest children ending up trampled or suffocated in the tangle of bodies, the inevitable onset of vomit caused by gas and the spreading of other body fluids as a result of poor muscle control that precedes the approaching death, the clumping together of dozens and dozens of dead bodies contorting in agony. All this was what the team of Serb prisoners, always the same, had to face for nine weeks and for a total of 70 - 72 journeys[54].

Hilda Dajč, the twenty-year old student and volunteer nurse died during one of these trips, we do not know which one.

11.9 THE LAST SHOUT

We reproduce Hilda Dajč's last letter, written to her friend Mirjana Petrović in early February 1942. Unlike the first three letters, the tone of the latter is depressed and desperate, and with the looming dire portent of a tragic end, which had replaced the trust, hitherto placed, for a possible positive outcome of her imprisonment[55].

My dear,

I could never have imagined that our meeting, even though I was expecting it, would arouse in me such a flurry of emotion and create even more unrest in my already frenzied soul which simply won't calm down. All philosophizing ends at the barbed-wire fence, and reality, which, far away on the other side you can't even imagine or else you would howl with pain, faces one in its totality. That reality is unsurpassable, our immense misery; every phrase describing the strength of the soul is dispersed by tears of hunger and cold; all hope of leaving here soon disappears before the monotonous perspective of passive existence which, whatever you compare it with, bears no resemblance to life. It is not even life's irony. It is its profoundest tragedy. We are able to keep going, not because we're strong, but because we are simply not conscious all the time of the eternal misery that surrounds us – everything that makes up our life.

We have been here for almost nine weeks and I am still quite literate – I can still think a little. Every evening, without exception, I read your and Nada's letters and this is the only moment when I am something else, not just a Lagerinsasse [German for female camp intern]. Hard labor is golden compared with this – we don't know why, on what charge – we've been convicted, nor how long we'll be here. Everything in the world is wonderful, even the most miserable existence outside the camp, while this is the incarnation of every evil that exists. We are all becoming evil because we're starving – we're all becoming cynical and count everyone else's mouthfuls, everyone is desperate – but in spite of this, no one kills anyone because we're all just a bunch of animals that I despise. I hate every single one of us because we've all fallen as low as we can go.

We are so near the outside world, yet so far from everyone. We have no contact with anyone; the life of every individual out there carries on as usual, as if half a mile away a slaughterhouse containing six thousand innocent people doesn't exist. Both you and we are equal in our cowardice. Enough of everything!

Even so, I'm not the anti-hero you might think I am from what I'm saying. I put up with everything that's happening to me calmly and painlessly. But the people around me. That's what upsets me. It's the people that get on my nerves. Not the hunger that makes you weep, not the cold that freezes the water in your glass and the blood in your veins, nor the stench of the latrines, nor the Kosheva wind – nothing is so repulsive as the crowd of people who deserve to be pitied, but who you are unable to help and can do nothing else than put yourself above them and despise them. Why do all these people talk about nothing else other than what is offending their bellies and all the other organs of their so highly esteemed cadavers. By the way, a couple of days ago we were laying out the dead bodies – there were 27 of them – in the Turkish pavilion, right at the front. I don't find anything repulsive anymore, not even my filthy work. Everything would be possible if only we could know what can never be known – when the gates of compassion will be opened. What do they intend to do with us? We are in a continual state of tension: are they going to shoot us, blow us up, transport us to Poland...? All that is of secondary importance! We just have to get through the present, which is not pleasant in the least – not in the least.

It's now half-past two, I've been on duty in the surgery all night (every fourth night), in the pavilion they're coughing in unison and you can hear the patter of rain on the roof. Here in the surgery the stove is smoking like hell, but, as the saying goes: who doesn't inhale the smoke, isn't warmed by the fire.

This is my most exciting day in the camp. To want something so much and then to get it is more than happiness [this is a reference to the meeting with Mirjana at the inn across the river from the camp]. Perhaps one day we'll get out of here alive into a happier life, because that's what we all desperately, but by now rather anemically, want. Mirjana, my dear, we are imprisoned slaves, in fact even lower than that, we're not so much wretched as a despised and starving horde, and when from this position one sees a little of life – meaning you – then one senses so many of life's juices that flow through it. Only – yes that eternal only – to wrench oneself away from that life afterwards is so painful and bitter that not even the sea of tears that one sheds can express it. I cry and they all start laughing: How can you, who conduct yourself like a man, allow yourself to cry like a sentimental teenager?!

But what can I do when in the depths of my heart everything is so horrible. That's the refrain I repeat to myself all night. I know there's no hope of our getting out soon, and outside are you and Nada, all that binds me to Belgrade which, by some incomprehensible contradiction, I deeply hate and deeply love at the same time. You don't know, just as I didn't know, what it's like to be here. I hope you will never find out. Way back when I was a child I was afraid they would bury me alive. And now this is some sort of vision of death. Will there be some sort of resurrection? I've never thought so much about the two of you as I do now. I continually talk with you and yearn to see you, because to me you are that 'paradise lost'. You are the only people that exist for me, I hold contempt for those who are here and hatred for those who are outside. Many times, when I think I won't make it, I think of you, you are all that's worth living for. The thought of you and the desire to meet you again keeps me alive. I was not aware of the greatness of our friendship. Do not worry in any way for me, my body and my soul have pursued a path that is more than fair, and I am calm and happy, except in a few days, like today, when I reopen the wounds.

I must resist – I do not say that with much belief – and yet I must. Love from your camp inmate

11.10 FUMUS COMMISSI DELICTI

In spite of the obvious historical significance, besides the obvious human and legal implications arising from the massacre of thousands of Jewish women and children locked up in the concentration camp of Sajmiste, the consequences that would be paid by the perpetrators after the war amounted to essentially zero, at least in the West, and this is despite the various proceedings against members of Polizei-Bataillon 64 and of the other structures involved.

In fact, except for Harald Turner and Bruno Sattler, convicted *beyond the Iron Curtain* respectively to death by hanging by the military court in Belgrade in 1947 and to life imprisonment by the Eastern German court in Rostock in 1953[56], for one reason or another, in the West all other subjects directly involved in the massacre suffered only minor consequences, or none at all. So, while Schaefer and Andorfer were sentenced to respectively six years and six months and two years and six months in prison by the courts in Cologne and Dortmund[57], Andorfer's deputy, Edgar Enge, drivers Götz and Meier and all the police officers of Polizei-Bataillon 64 – both the four participants to the gassing and those, far more numerous, who were used for the monitoring of the field and got involved in several individual shootings – were not sanctioned in any way for their criminal deeds[58].

ZStL had opened a file regarding Polizei-Bataillon 64 in the late fifties and forwarded it to the public prosecutor in Dortmund who, after verifying the participation of staff belonging to all three companies of the battalion in the massacre of the Jews of Sajmiste, by shooting or gas poisoning, decided to initiate preliminary investigations and split the file – originally registered as StAwDo 45 Js 50/61 – in four separate processes:

As for the main suspect, Herbert Andorfer, the request for trial StAwDo 45 Js 41/64 was put forward by the public prosecutor in Dortmund. In this process the four members of 2/64 who had taken part in the gassing operations on Mount Avala together with him, namely former police officers Wetter and Karl Leo L. and their two colleagues were tried as well as Andorfer. One of the latter, however, killed himself in Koln on November 25, 1964, shortly before the date set for his interrogation, while the other found his death in combat in Belgrade, in autumn 1944[59]. Then, as requested by the same prosecutor, the positions of the remaining two policemen, Wetter and Leo L., were deleted, the benefit of *Befehlsnotstand* being applied to them. The role of Andorfer also was likewise diminished, as he was found guilty of only "complicity in murder (*Beihilfe zum Mord*)"[60].

As for 1/64, investigated in the file StAwDo 45 Js 14/64 especially for the executions of Serbs and Gypsies perpetrated in the Šabac lager, it would be involved also in several shootings of Jews that took place during guard duty around the perimeter of Sajmiste camp, as reported by some testimonies of former policemen. The latter, however, were largely omitted from the application to the court to drop the proceedings, advanced on December 7, 1964 by the public prosecutor in Dortmund who, stressing the military reasons that were behind the reprisals against Serbs and Gypsies, conducted each episode within the terms of exemption from punishment or, alternatively, of murder for criminal causes, thus liable to be closed[61].

As for 2/64, the file StAwDo 45 Js 15/64 was opened with regard to several massacres perpetrated around Skela, Belgrade, Mount Avala (executions of partisans) and other locations around the Serbian capital. Furthermore, the participation of company staff to the surveillance of Sajmiste and of four policemen to the operations of gassing was ascertained: however, since the position of the latter four was severed from this file and matched to that of Andorfer (StAwDo 45 Js 41/64), the slaughter of Sajmiste women and children was not a subject of investigation in this trial, nor were any of the crimes committed by the company staff during guard duties around the camp uncovered or detailed[62]. In this respect, the request for dismissal of the case was sent by the prosecutor to the Court of Dortmund on December 8, 1964.

Regarding 3/64, held in the file StAwDo 45 Js 50/61, the investigation had been opened in relation to the numerous executions perpetrated by the company staff in the concentration camp at Šabac and in other locations, both in Greece and in Serbia, including Pancevo, Dedinje, Skela and Mount Avala (relative to the shootings of 25 partisans). From the outset, however, these actions were conducted by the prosecutor in the sphere of anti-partisan war and thus reduced to the level of manslaughter, with complicity in murder as the only charge that, in any case, was later prescribed. All this in spite of the interpretation of ZStL, which framed the killing of Jews and Gypsies as a racial crime. In any case, the possibility that crimes of a racial nature were or were not committed by staff of 3/64 on call around the camp of Sajmiste, was not even explored, despite the presence of evidence in this direction. On these grounds, on December 1, 1964, the request to dismiss the proceeding against 3/64 was forwarded by the prosecutor at the Court of Dortmund[63].

The only tangible result after at least five years of preliminary investigations was the indictment of two perpetrators, sentenced to a total of nine years in prison compared to about 7,500 murders: that is to say a sentence of about ten hours (!) in prison for each victim, to be split between both defendants. Clearly, something had gone wrong. Or rather, it had worked upside down: instead of trying to frame the events within a criminal paradigm likely to bring to a trial and hopefully a conviction, the prosecutor himself resorted to any possible interpretation that could lead the events within terms of non-criminality, almost as in a paradoxical research for the groundlessness of the *fumus commissi delicti*[64].

11.11 CONSIDERATIONS

The conclusion of the above mentioned legal procedures shows a major imbalance between the events in Sajmiste and the effects that these events (did not) have from the legal point of view.

From this point of view, it was pointed out that the legal procedures related to the prosecution of crimes place themselves in a dimension that does not necessarily reflect the historical interpretation and, to that extent, as stated by Lutz Klinkhammer, "the management of legal problems [says] a lot more about postwar and how it relates to the past rather than to the massacres and the war"[65]. Then, beyond the more or less specious legal interpretations, or the different approach to the facts by one attorney over another[66], there seems to be no doubt, from the historical point of view, about the fate suffered by the Jewish women and children of Serbia, despite the recurring resurgence of rants by Holocaust deniers committed to assert the contrary. In truth there is no doubt that:

- In fall 1941, when the contraindications of the reprisal ratio of 100:1 and its inapplicability towards the Serbs became clear and more care in the selection of the hostages was thus required, this *moderation* was not extended to Jewish men[67], who were indiscriminately slaughtered in a few weeks. Beyond the alleged military needs linked to the reprisals, such racial discrimination appears to be a mindset bent on elimination, in which the Jews had the role of targets to hit, regardless of any other consideration. What we witness is, in essence, the implementation a sort of Lombrosian pattern with regard to the occupation policies, and the fact that it was the Wehrmacht that put it into practice, is not a mitigating factor, but rather an aggravating one.
- The lack of a precise plan, prepared in advance, relative to the annihilation of women and children is in no way related to an alleged desire to solve the *Jewish question* in Serbia with methods other than mass murder. Nor, consequently, the decision to proceed with the extermination seems to be related to an alleged *lack of viable alternatives*, such as the establishment of a ghetto or the deportation outside of Serbia. This is because, even admitting that there were alternatives, they would be impromptu and temporary *hypothesis of forced labor*, advanced by certain sectors of the Nazi establishment for reasons of mere opportunity. In contrast,

for the most ideological sectors of Sicherheitspolizei (central or peripheral), or those more directly involved in the *Jewish question* (Eichmann), from a certain point onwards the genocidal solution was probably the only one to be really taken into consideration.

- Also, it is to be proved how really *alternative* to extermination, solutions such as the deportation to the delta of the Danube [sic], in Romania, actually were, taking into account the genocidal frenzy that had swept the entourage of Antonescu in the summer and autumn of 1941, culminating in the expulsion and massacre of tens of thousands of Moldovan and Romanian Jews. Thus, to think of deporting Serb Jews to Romania meant, in practice, to carry out a murder scheme through an *intermediary regime*, or to trace the outline of a real *induction of Genocide*[68].

- The possibility that women and children locked in Sajmiste could be used as a valuable reservoir of workforce, thus making their elimination non-convenient, is entirely abstract, if not sheer fantasy. Apart from the conditions of near-exhaustion of the inmates, subject to a high mortality rate, as confirmed by Dajč, no economically productive activity was ever established in the camp (a former trade fair), and neither were work brigades for outdoor activities, to be held in Belgrade or elsewhere. From the first arrivals at the camp in December 1941 and the last gassing of May 1942, about five months passed – a time lapse sufficient to organize some sort of useful activity, if they had wanted. The fact that this did not happen, but instead the camp was considered an intolerable burden by the German authorities in Belgrade, proves that the Germans never had any will to turn Sajmiste into something economically productive, or that they ever considered the inmates as anything other than *dead women walking.*

- The possibility that the decrease of the inhabitants of the camp could be explained in terms of *deportations to the east* instead of extermination is flimsy and laughable: a hypothetical transfer of the entire population of Sajmiste would take seven to eight trains, each of which identified by a train code, travel plans, stockpiles, loading operations at the station in Belgrade and the crossing of the city center by columns of trucks loaded with women and children. Not to mention the real possibility that the rumors of a possible transfer could have leaked outside the camp, as shown by Dajč's letters which were easily smuggled beyond the fences. None of this ever took place, and there are no tracks or documents or testimonies or letters that may suggest an operation of this type.

- The presence of confirmatory documents of the gassing of women and children seems to be unquestionable and certainly not limited to alleged distortions of the terminology, particularly in relation to the "special vehicle (*Spezialwagen*)" or "disinfestation (*Entlausungswagen*)" sent from Berlin: indisputable documents, of course, unless one wants to consider as counterfeit, or as merely the result of coercion, the admissions and statements of the various participants to the gassings such as Andorfer, Engels, Karl Wetter and Leo L., not to mention the statements made by the additional police officers and members of other structures, about the general knowledge and awareness in the ranks of the various departments and facilities, of what was happening on Mount Avala[69]. We refer to admissions and testimonies like that of policeman Georg., who said that: "those gassed in the Semlin camp were buried in Avala"[70]. Testimonies entered and accepted in legal proceedings and impossible to become invalidated by the findings, debatable to say the least, of those proceedings.

According to reports by Andorfer himself, the gassings went on every day, six days a week, except Sundays. We do not know what Andorfer did on Sunday, and perhaps he was not even asked. He did not reside permanently in the camp, but in a lodging in Belgrade, and was in Sajmiste only during his working hours. He would spend his spare time elsewhere.

Andorfer, perhaps, spent the Sundays with his fellow soldiers, perhaps in a movie house with the troops, or drinking and joking along with the comrades of his department, trying to ease the tension after a long week of bloodsheds. On the seventh day Andorfer rested, as God before him, and after having usurped God's right over death.

ENDNOTES

1 «Restore order with the most drastic measures». Führerweisung Nr. 31A, 16.9.1941. See Manoscheck Vernichtung, p. 217.

2 Manoscheck Vernichtung, p. 209.

3 The number of Serbian Jews victims of the genocide is not known with precision. At the moment of the occupation (April 1942), in Serbia as we know it there were about 12,500 Jews, and 4,200 more in the Banato. Another thousand refugees coming from other countries should be added to the figure (the so-called *Kladovo-Transport*) Manoscheck Vernichtung, p. 209, Manoschek Shoot, p. 39. For them, probably, the percentage of survival did not exceed 30 %, with an estimate of at least 12.000 victims. Other estimates report slightly different figures, with the percentage of victims of at least 90 % of a population of 16,000 persons.

4 Hilberg, p. 712.

5 Manoschek Vernichtung, p. 219.

6 *«Mit den schärfsten Mittlen die Ordnung wiederherzustellen».* Führerweisung Nr. 31A, 16.9.1941. Manoscheck Vernichtung, p. 217.

7 Browning Origini, p. 345.

8 Manoschek Vernichtung, p. 213, Manoschek Shoot, p. 39.

9 Manoschek Judenfrei, p. 29, Klemp Kommunisten, p. 209, Klemp Ermittelt, pp. 154-155.

10 Klemp Kommunisten, p. 209, Klemp Ermittelt, p. 155.

11 Manoschek Vernichtung, p. 215, Manoschek Judenfrei, p. 43, Manoschek Shoot, p. 40. See also Browning Origini, pp. 345-346.

12 Browning Orgini, p. 355, Manoschek Shoot, p. 44.

13 List's opinion with regard to Dankelmann, military commander in Belgrade, is summarized in one of his reports to OKW in which, after judging Serbia's command chain "intolerable", he explicitly described Dankelmann as "vain", "superficial" and "seduced by Turner's and Benzler's political ruminations". Browning Origini, p. 348.

14 Browning Semlin, p. 56, Manoschek Judenfrei, pp. 41-42, Shimzu, p. 162: *«Bekämpfung von reichs- oder staatsfeindlichen Organisationen, Kommunisten, Juden, Terroristen und Saboteuren».*

15 Browning Semlin, p. 56.

16 After having been EGII commander in Poland in September 1939, Schäfer had become director of Koln's Gestapo: he kept this position until late January 1942, when he was transferred to Belgrade. Shimzu, pp. 163-164.

17 *Ibid.*, pp. 154, 158.

18 *Vojnoistoriski glasnik, 1941 godina,* p. 84.

19 Klemp Kommunisten, p. 213. Investigation of the public prosecutor of Dortmund against 3/64 – StAwDo 45 Js 50/61.

20 *Ibid.*, p. 215. Šabac's concentration camp had been opened around the end of summer of 1941, initially to confine a group of about 1,200 German, Austrian, Dutch and Czechoslovak Jews who were trying to flee to Istanbul and Palestine through the Danube. Considered hostages for reprisals, after the shooting of the 400 men of the group, between October 9 and 11, the about 750/800 survivors, women and children, were transferred to the Sajmiste camp, near Belgrade, in January 1942. Hilberg, p. 938.

21 Manoschek Judenfrei, p. 35.

22 Manoschek Vernichtung, p. 213, Browning Semlin, p. 58.

23 Manoschek Vernichtung, p. 213.

24 Bild 101I-185-0112-03/38

25 Manoschek Judenfrei, pp. 43-44, Hilberg, pp. 705-706. The order, issued by Schröder on June 28 and carried out on July 5, followed the discovery of a certain quantity of explosives in a house in Belgrade.

26 Manoschek Judenfrei, p. 44. Browning Origini, pp. 346 and 516, Hilberg, p. 706. On July 5, 13 Jews and communists were shot; on July 8, ten communists and three Jews; on July 18, 16 communists and Jews, on July 22, 111 communists and Jews and on July 25, 22 communists and 100 Jews were hanged.

27 Manoschek Vernichtung, p. 215.

28 *Ibid.*, p. 216.

29 Browning Origini, p. 347. Following an ambush on a German vehicle, 81 peasants from a village nearby were shot. The execution was carried out by a group of Serbian police officers who were being held at gunpoint by the soldiers of a German department.

30 Only during the early days of September for example, 175 Germans had been killed or taken prisoner during hit and run actions. Browning Origini, p. 349.

31 As Turner explained to Rademacher on October 18, the number of 8,000 Jews detained in the camps was the result

of an inexplicable misunderstanding and was then corrected to about 4,000. See Rademacher's report to the Ministry of Foreign Affairs of October 25, 1941. Hilberg, pp. 711, 939.

32 The number of 20,000 women, elderly and children quoted in several sources was overestimated by Rademacher in his October 25 report to the Ministry of Foreign Affairs. Following evaluations this figure decreased to 15,000 but it still was excessive in comparison to the Jewish population of Serbia before the invasion (about 17/18,000). The estimate of 10,000 women and children quoted by Turner on October 20, 1941, of which about 7,000 were surely enclosed in the camp of Sajmiste. Manoschek Vernichtung, p. 228, Hilberg, pp. 711, 939.

33 Browning Semlin, p. 58.

34 Hilberg, p. 707, Browning Origini, p. 352.

35 Browning Origini, p. 354.

36 *Ibid.*

37 *Ibid.* Rademacher's report to the Ministry of Foreign Affairs of October 25, 1941.

38 Browning Semlin, p. 59.

39 According to Turner, taking women as hostage "was against the ideas of the German soldier". See Hilberg, pp. 771, 939. Turner's memorandum to Feldkommandanturen, dated October 26, 1941. Also Manoschek Vernichtung, p. 217.

40 Manoscheck Vernichtung, p. 213. Majdanpek is a small village in western Serbia, not far from the borders with Bulgaria and Romania.

41 *Ibid.,* p. 229, Manoschek Judenfrei, p. 170, Browning Semlin, p. 73. Turner's letter to Wolff dated April 11, 1942. With regard to what Turner maintains, there are two different interpretations by Manoschek and Browning. For details, refer to their books.

42 Hilberg, p. 711, Browning Semlin, p. 59.

43 Browning Semlin, p. 60. Report of the general Plenipotentiary in Serbia, dated December 20, 1941. The about 500 men considered necessary, who avoided the autumn shootings, were also transferred to Sajmiste.

44 Manoschek Vernichtung, p. 176. After serving in SD Abteilung III (Inland) in Innsbruck and Salzburg, in April 1941 Andorfer (3/11/1911) was detached at Fuchs' Einsatzgruppe E, being assigned anti-partisan tasks in the area of Maribor. Transferred to Belgrade on October 29, he was assigned to the Šabac camp, were he stayed until it was dismantled, in early December. Back in Belgrade, he was appointed commander of Sajmiste camp in late January 1942.

45 Manoschek Vernichtung, p. 177.

46 Browning Semlin, p. 62.

47 *Ibid.*, p. 89.

48 StAwDo 45 Js 41/64, 45 Ks 2/68,. Klemp Kommunisten, pp. 200-201.

49 Browning Semlin, p. 82, Hilberg, p. 712. Overall, 6,280 of the about 7,500 Jews who lost their lives in the Sajmiste camp were killed through gas vans. The rest of the victims would have died by starvation and diseases and a certain number of executions. Klemp Kommunisten, p. 201, Klemp Ermittelt, p. 151.

50 The death trip to Mount Avala generally involved a *kommando* of seven men: Andorfer or, alternatively, Enge, the Saurer drivers, Götz and Meier and four members of Polizei-Bataillon 64 taking orders from Wetter. Seven Serbian prisoners (later killed) in charge of unloading and burying the victims must be added. Those who, in one way or the other, became aware of the matter, were many more. Manoschek Vernichtung, p. 231.

51 Hilberg, p. 712, Browning Semlin, pp. 78-79, 81. Soon after the start of executions Andorfer asked to be transferred to active service with the Waffen-SS; his request was rejected, even if he was allowed to switch with Enge the task of travelling in the gas van during the death trips. Only after the end of operations was Andorfer assigned to anti-partisan activities at the Sipo-SD detachment of Novi Pazar.

52 Prior to his indictment before the Court of Dortmund, Andorfer had been investigated by ZStL, in the dossier 503 AR 2656/65 later transmitted, on account of his Austrian citizenship, to the Court of Vienna – LG Wien 27e Vr 2260/67. The reconstruction of the gassing of Sajmiste's Jews is partly based on his declarations given before such judicial offices. Manoschek Vernichtung, pp. 229-230, Browning Semlin, p. 78.

53 Friedrich Pradel was responsible for the vehicle section of Berlin's RSHA and Harry Wentritt was his chief mechanic, in charge of preparing the gas vans. They were convicted to detention for seven and three years respectively at the Hanover trial, 2 Ks 2/65 of June 7, 1966. Browning Origini, p. 366.

54 On May 10, the day of the last trip, the seven Serbian prisoners were shot with a burst of automatic weapon, maybe by Enge, who was accompanying the van instead of Andorfer, maybe by Wetter, or by both. See Leo L.'s testimony, given before the public prosecutor in Hanover, who heard the shots from his watchtower. Browning Semlin, p. 82.

55 The English version of Hilda Dajč's letters are published on the following website: *www.open.ac.uk/socialsciences/semlin.*

56 Belgrade, Military Court of the Yugoslav Third Army, Feb-

ruary 27 – March 5, 1947; LG/BG Rostock December 3, 1953 Az, SS 2/52.

57 LG Köln, 24 Ks 1/52 (crimes Serbia) and 2/53 of June 20, 1955 (deportations to Lodz and Riga); LG Dortmund 45 Ks 2/68 of January 16, 1969, Browning Semlin, p. 66.

58 Edgar Enge was indicted and then tried by the Court of Stuttgart, LG Stuttgart, Ks 21/67, but was acquitted with sentence of June 11, 1968. Wilhelm Götz and Erwin Meier, however, managed to disappear after the war without trace. Browning Semlin, p. 79.

59 Klemp Kommunisten, pp. 212, 216-217.

60 *Ibid.,* pp. 221. Soon after the war Andorfer managed to disappear without trace and expatriate to Sweden first and Venezuela later with the help of the ODESSA organization. Back in Germany during the fifties with a false name, he obtained a visa to Austria in 1964; back again in Germany, in 1966 he was arrested in Munich and delivered to the Austrian authorities that, however, sent him back to Germany as a defendant at the Dortmund trial. Manoschek Vernichtung p. 183.

61 Klemp Kommunisten, pp. 202, 215-216.

62 *Ibid.,* p. 216.

63 *Ibid.,* pp. 213-214.

64 With regard to Polizei-Bataillon 64, the Yugoslav courts were harsher than western German ones, however, their focus was on the crimes committed against the Serb population and not, specifically, against the Jews. In any case, apart from battalion commander Adolf Josten, who was hanged in Belgrade on April 10, 1947 together with another police officer, about 25 battalion members were convicted with imprisonment and progressively released during the fifties. Klemp Ermittelt, pp. 155-165.

65 Lutz Kinkhammer, Susanne Meyer: *Stragi naziste in Italia. La guerra contro i civili (1943-1944),* p. X.

66 In March 1964, when preliminary investigations relating to two of the cases (against companies 1/64 and 2/64) could be said to be essentially completed and able to withstand the scrutiny of the court where the indictment of the defendant was expected, both the prosecutor in charge of the investigations since 1961 and his immediate superior were promoted and assigned to other duties. After the arrival of their replacements, the whole lot of accusations was drastically reworked to the point that, in December 1964, no request for judgment (except for Andorfer) was made, but requests were made for the deletion of the charges on the basis of the previously mentioned reasons. Although there was no talk of a successful cover-up, it is evident that a more virtuous approach to the facts collected in the investigation, and less tied to questionable legal interpretations, could produce different results. See Klemp Kommunisten, pp. 218-219.

67 Manoschek Vernichtung, p. 226. Order by Turner to Feldkommandanturen, dated October 26, 1941.

68 The words of Conductor Ion Antonescu in a letter dated September 6, 1941 addressed to the Deputy Prime Minister Mihai Antonescu, are explicit in that respect: "war in general and fighting for Odessa have shown that the Jews are Satan" [sic!]. See Radu Ioanid's article: *The deportation of the Jews to Transnistria,* p. 70.

69 Manoschek Vernichtung, p. 231, Browning Semlin, p. 84.

70 *«In Avalar wurden die Vergasten des Lagers Semlin beerdigt».* Klemp Ermittelt, p. 152, Klemp Kommunisten, p. 204. Georg B. was a weapons technician at 2/64 and admitted before the public prosecutor in Dortmund that he was aware of the mistreatment and gassings that his comrades were perpetrating in the Sajmiste camp and on Mount Avala. StAwDo, 45 Js 50/61. Other colleagues denied even *the existence* [sic] of the camp.

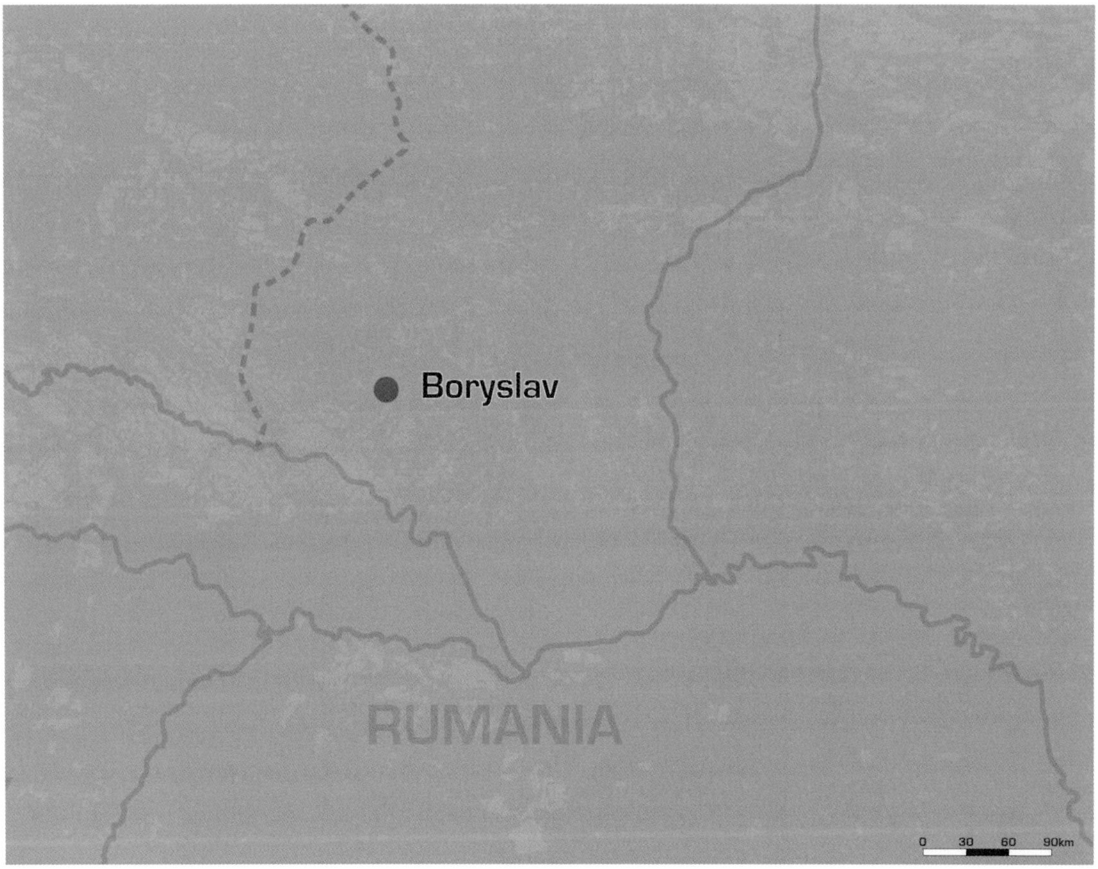
Boryslav
RUMANIA
0 30 60 90km

CHAPTER TWELVE

"OIL FOR BLOOD"

DEATH AND SALVATION IN THE JEWISH COMMUNITY OF BORYSLAV AUGUST 6 - 8, 1942

«Völkl, was machst Du; schieß doch anständig!
Ein guter Schuß ist das beste,
was man den Leuten mitgeben kann!»

Hauptmann Gustav Wüpper
Boryslaw, February / March 1944[1]

12.1 INTRODUCTION

Boryslav train station, August 7, 1942

> *One day, in Boryslav's train station, I saw several hundred Jews who had been waiting in the cold to be loaded on the train to Belzec. Among them were many children in a lamentable state. One woman was clutching a little girl to her. The child was coughing in a disquieting way. I said to the SS officer who was guarding the group that he ought to find a doctor as quickly as possible. "Where they are all going, they won't need a doctor!" he replied, guffawing*[2].

They were taken early in the morning from the Jewish orphanage, along with the adults who took care of them: 173 children now awaiting the arrival of the train with destination Belzec[3]. A little further, along the same track, several hundred men and women, many of whom elderly and in poor health, also found themselves waiting for a journey with no return herded on cattle wagons. Around them, Sicherheitspolizei armed policemen of the SchPDA "Boryslaw", German railway workers and Ukrainian auxiliaries in black uniforms. A little further from that mass of waiting humanity, a young German couple dressed in civilian clothes of good quality watched the scene unfold in front of them in astonishment: although they had already witnessed many episodes of violence against Jews since they had moved from Essen to Boryslav about a year before, that, for them, was a *first time*. It was the first time they faced the forced *resettlement* of such a large number of Jews in miserable conditions, owning only the few things they carried with them. But beyond the scene, dramatic in itself as it was, it was especially the eyes that struck the two young Germans: the eyes of those children that looked even bigger in the low light of early morning[4].

Then, somewhere in the crowd, the man's attention was attracted to a little girl of only a few years who coughed incessantly while a young woman next to her, perhaps her mother, tried to console her by holding her tightly. That child, the man thought, needed a doctor urgently.

The man looked for a moment his wife Else close to him and he felt that she was holding back tears. He approached an SS officer a few yards away from them: he was not sure it would be of any good, but in any case something needed trying. He, Berthold Beitz, would try to convince that officer.

12.2 ONCE UPON A TIME, A SHTETL

It was a country of thirty thousand, more than a third of whom were Jews. It stood along the river Tys'mienica, on a plain pocked by oil wells where, in their midst, incessantly, *black gold workers* toiled, torn and bent under the weight of their loads and covered by an omnipresent oily film. They were called *Lebaks* and were almost all Jews. For decades they had specialized in separating the oil from the water and mud that filtered out of the wells and that ended up flowing in the Tys'mienica in many small streams. Although they were Jews, the oil workers were the last in the genocide machine to disappear in Boryslav. First came the others, those considered *harmful* – the elderly, the sick and the family members of suspected communists and people linked to the Soviet regime – who were rounded up in late November 1941 and shot in mass graves dug in a wooded area between Truskawiec and

Tustanowice. Then came the *useless*: women, children and those unable to work, who ended up deported to Belzec between August 6 and November 20, 1942. Eventually, their turn came, the *indispensable* and their families, namely skilled artisans and oil workers – including those serving the Karpahten-Öl firm – who were temporarily saved for the needs of the German war economy, but who were gradually reduced in number so they almost disappeared. In fact, the Jews of Boryslav who survived the genocide were only a few hundred, many of which were allowed to step down from the train headed to Belzec at the last minute, thanks to the intervention of the German director of the Karpahten Öl, who claimed them to work in his refinery thus saving them from the fate awaiting them at the death camp.

Nothing remained of the old *shtetl* with piled-up izbas in the summer of 1944, after the return of the Red Army: the genocide had run over it with the power of a hurricane and had destroyed forever a vital community, which was not one of the oldest in the centuries-old Eastern European Ashkenazi world, but, on the contrary, had developed in the wake of nineteenth century modernism, its economy prospering thanks to the discovery of oil fields, its culture identifying with Zionism. Thus, rather than a traditional and mystical community destined to decline, it was a reality in full development, in which Judaism remained in the background as a spiritual and cultural heritage, not ideologically antithetical to the late nineteenth century liberalism, but as a reinforcement of their identities.

Thus, what the genocide destroyed with its brutal coarseness, was not the faded postcard of a decadent and alien Judaism – like those depicted in anti-Semitic feature films screened in the cinemas of the Reich, or like the images published in newspapers of the regime – but something more similar to the filthy but vital Ruhr industrial suburbs of the late nineteenth century, so perpetually covered with coal dust, and so vivid with political and social turmoil.

The genocide made a desert out of all this and after the desert was the neglect from communism, which also destroyed the traces of memory.

> *When at long last, on August 8, 1944, the Nazi army withdrew, no more than two hundred Jewish survivors sprung from forests and hideouts. Here, the extermination was almost complete: it was a world to forget. The generations I come from have disappeared up there, among conifers and oaks, covered with a carpet of flowers and raspberries. Or incinerated in the crematoria of Belzec. As for the tombstones of the ancient Jewish cemetery, in 1959 the Soviets built a bus station above them*[5].

Of the perhaps 14,000 Jews of Boryslav and the surrounding area present on the eve of the invasion, nothing now remains. After the war the survivors, a few hundred, spread around the world. Vague memories still exist only in the faded memory of the elderly: the Petryshin, the Bassarab, the Cimejko...[6]. Glimpses destined to disappear, surviving in the vacuum as wreckage after the storm. Once upon a time... a *shtetl.*

12.3 AT THE GATES OF THE ABYSS

Berthold Beitz saw the abyss for the first time on July 3, 1941, soon after his arrival in Boryslav.

The city had fallen into German hands only a couple of days earlier and was in chaos and crossed by groups of Ukrainian nationalists who had imposed their law on the population: both on the majority of the people who gladly supported the collapse of the Soviet yoke and on the Jewish minority, which immediately became the subject of collective and indiscriminate punishment by the most extremist Ukrainian elements.

The discovery of several dozen young Ukrainians and Poles brutally tortured and murdered by Soviet prison guards in the NKVD prison[7] provided the occasion for an anti-Jewish pogrom, partly run by Terleckyj, local OUN representative, and partly encouraged by the attitude of the German military command that gave the Ukrainians a *free hand* against the *Judeo-Bolsheviks* for 24 hours[8]. As a consequence, about 300

Jews were taken from their homes or work-places and forced to march to the NKVD prison amid beatings and violence by the crowd armed with sticks, axes and iron bars. Once here, they had to take out of the cell the bodies of the murdered Ukrainians, who were then aligned in the courtyard and washed with water and disinfectants. Among the crowd in the courtyard there were many Germans who were watching curiously, without intervening, but taking pictures.

This is how a Polish witness remembers the arrival of 300 Jews at the prison, beaten and half-naked, in the midst of the furious crowd[9]:

> *They formed a guard of honor along the road, from the northern entrance. Among the crowd on both sides there were also women and children younger than me [the witness was 17 at the time, A/N]. Each of them was holding a long object: a club, a walking stick, an axe, an iron pipe. Half-naked men were brought from the city center amid blows. The swaying mass of people engulfed its victims and pushed them into the yard, hitting them wildly.*

While the Jews were preparing the bodies of the mutilated victims extracted from the prison for burial, groups of frenzied Ukrainian peasants coming from nearby villages and armed with pitchforks, axes and knives, began to wander through the city breaking into the homes of the Jews, pillaging and killing many of the inhabitants. Several women and girls were forced to go to the prison courtyard to take part in the arranging of the corpses. Dead and wounded lay strewn on the streets[10]. The pogrom spread without control to all the districts inhabited by Jews and was interrupted only by the curfew. The next morning it resumed with unabated violence, and was finally stopped by the Germans only on the afternoon of July 4, 194[11].

At that point, when the outbreak finally ended, the Wehrmacht's motorized patrols, until then totally passive before the events, intervened to *restore order*, covering the city and giving the death blow to the wounded Jews who still lay abandoned in the streets. In total, 183 Jews were victims of the pogrom in Boryslav[12].

Talking with a former Israelite classmate about why all that had happened, a Ukrainian militiaman who claimed to personally have nothing against the Jews, said that it was *a necessary political measure, to involve the Ukrainian peasantry in the dynamics of events...*[13].

Berthold Beitz witnessed the pogrom and was disgusted by it. It was especially the passivity of the German soldiers who were watching from the sidelines in amusement that struck him. A passivity that was quite different from the events that would see him as an active protagonist in the three years to come.

12.4 KRIEGSSCHAUPLATZ OSTGALIZIEN

Occupied by the Wehrmacht in the early days of *Barbarossa*, Galicia formally became the fifth district of the General Government on August 1, 1941, with the transition from the military administration of Befehlshaber des rückwärtigen Heeresgebietes Süd, Karl von Roques to the civil authority of the district governor Karl Lasch, directly subordinate to the general governor Hans Frank[14]. Regarding the August 1942 deportations from Boryslav, a variety of facilities and departments were involved to varying degrees and in relation to their operational roles.

12.4.1 – SSPF "Lemberg"

As with the civil administration offices and as had happened in other districts of the General Government, the usual structures of SS and police were formed in Galicia, at whose summit the role of SS-und Polizeiführer (SSPF) was activated. This position was vacant until October 13, 1941, when after a long dispute between Himmler (via HSSPF Krüger) and Frank (via governor Lasch), SS Brigadeführer Friedrich Katzmann was eventually appointed[15]. Regarding the so-called *Jewish question*, it was permanently absorbed – through the offices in charge (Referat IIIB) of KDS "Lemberg" – in the sphere of competence of Katzmann, who had already had the opportunity to gain experience in this regard during his previous service as SSPF "Radom" (from November 1939 to June 1941), during the many deportations of Jews to labor camps in the Lublin area. Thus, following his arrival in Lviv, Katzmann took control of *Judenverfolgung*, and regarding the deportations from Boryslav, these were done through two of his employees who were present during the actions, namely SS-Obersturmführer Rudolf Gschwendtner and SS-Untersturmführer Richard Rokita: the first was Katzmann's personal advisor and inspector of Jewish labor camps in the district of Galicia, the second was vice-commander of the Janowska labor camp on the outskirts of Lviv. Overall, Katzmann could count on a staff of about 70 elements.

12.4.2 – KdS "Lemberg"

On September 1, 1941, the position of KDS "Lemberg", represented by SS-Sturmbannführer Helmut Tanzmann[16] was activated in Lviv, mainly due to the restructuring of the dissolved Einsatzgruppe zbV. This command was directly subordinate to Eberhard Schöngarth's BdS "Krakau" and was structured like the RSHA in Berlin, with the command of Abteilung III (then IV) Gestapo handed over to Kurt Stawizki (who was also Tanzmann's deputy). Within the command, Referat IIIB (then IVB) directed by Erich Engels was in charge of Jewish issues. Both Stawizki and Engels were radical anti-Semites. Between five and eight officials operated in Referat IIIB; they could be integrated, if necessary, with elements from other departments, in particular from Volkstums-Referat of Abteilung-II (then III) SD, led by Hauptsturmführer Alfred Kolf[17]. On October 13, 1941, after the creation of the SSPF role, Referat IIIB in particular and KDS "Lemberg" in general passed under Katzmann's operational authority.

As usual, after the activation of its central command in Lviv, some local branches (KDS-Außenstellen) were formed from KDS Tanzmann including that of Drohobycz[18]. Structurally weak and chronically short of staff, KDS-Außenstellen relied on local auxiliaries in the role of *Hilfspolizisten*, recruited especially among Hungarian and Romanian *volksdeutschen*. Polish elements, instead, were co-opted in Abteilung IV (later V), Kriminalpolizei[19] of KDS "Lemberg". Overall, in April 1942, KDS "Lemberg" could count on approximately 400 German officials (approximately 600 if we take into account the personnel assigned to local offices), over half of them from the Gestapo, reinforced by an unknown number of Ukrainian and Polish auxiliaries[20].

12.4.3 – KdS-Außenstelle "Drohobycz"

This detachment of KDS "Lemberg" was activated in October 1941 with jurisdiction over the areas of Boryslav, Sambor and Stryj where, in August 1941, about 130,000 Jews lived, about 10 % of which in Boryslav[21]. Since June 1942 and during the deportations, the direction of the department was held by SS-Sturmbannführer Hans Block, whose orders were also taken by, among others, the Jewish office (IVB) led by Sturmscharführer Josef Gabriel, and a nucleus of SD commanded by Hauptsturmführer Benno Paulischkies[22]. Overall, the department could count on approximately thirty men: slightly above average compared to other Außenstellen that barely reached 25 elements. Furthermore, five Lithuanian *volksdeutschen* were employed as drivers. This office was the main operational element of KDS "Lemberg", involved in the deportations from Boryslaw in August 1942.

12.4.4 – KdO "Lemberg"

Formed in late August 1941 as a regional office of BDO "Krakau" Herbert Becker, the position of KDO "Lemberg" was held from June 5, 1942, by Oberstleutnant Walter von Soosten who, however, did not have the necessary authority to undertake anti-Jewish initiatives on his own. In this sense, his role in the deportations of 1942 was mainly focused on his [considerable] readiness to have his departments, both mobile and resident, take part in *Judenaktionen*, based on requests received from the offices of SSPF Katzmann and KDS Tanzmann[23]: a constant participation, because of the relatively numerous departments of the Ordnungspolizei relocated in Galicia, which equilibrated the shortage of staff available for services of the security police. In particular, within KDO, the allocation of departments available to the various actions against the Jews was the responsibility of officer Ia, Oberstleutnant Franz Heitzinger[24].

In addition to mobile units (*truppenpolizisten*) represented in the summer of 1942 by Polizei-Regiment 24 – that, however, would not be involved in the deportations of August 6-8, from Boryslawv – a leading role in the annihilation of Jewish communities throughout Galicia was carried out by territorial departments of Schutzpolizei at whose top, in the role of KdSchupo at KDO "Lemberg" was an officer named Müller: in particular, in the main towns of the district so-called Schutzpolizei-Dienstabteilungen had been activated, including Boryslav, which was fully involved in the deportations during August[25].

However, the role that the police had during the deportations of August 6-8 from Boryslav is not very clear. Beyond the presence of the commander of Drohobycz's "Captaincy (*Hauptmannschaft*)" Hauptmann Junge at the train station during the selection of victims, there is no confirmation about the involvement in the roundups of other staff from the German police. In any case the police network in the district of Galicia – which depended on KdGend, Oberstleutnant Alois Schertler, at the KDO "Lemberg" – played a leading role in many anti-Jewish actions committed in rural areas.

Overall, between mobile units, Schupo policemen and police staff, in January 1943 KDO von Soosten could count on about 2,000 men (1,093 *truppenpolizisten*, 706 policemen and 210 Schupo) in Galicia[26]. In addition, a number of Volksdeutsche were recruited as police auxiliaries (*Hilfspolizisten*), while the Ukrainian militia (*Ukrainische Hilfspolizei*) provided additional reinforcements, thanks to its staff divided between police stations and Schutzpolizei garrisons[27].

12.4.5 – Schutzpolizei-Dienstabteilung "Boryslaw"

The core of Boryslav's Schutzpolizei was established on November 18, 1941, around a small group of Austrian policemen commanded by an officer from Hamburg: Revierleutnant Gustav Wupper, a veteran of WWI of past socialist leanings, recalled from Luftschutz in September 1941 to take command of Boryslav's Schutzpolizei-Dienstabteilung and to secure the oil fields and the airport. On October 7, 1941, eighteen more policemen were rounded up among the various departments of KdSchupo "Wien"[28] and embarked with him at the station Wiener-Nordbahnhof, bound for Galicia. These men, ordinary neighborhood policemen, would not have to wait for the first impact of genocide: according to the testimony of one of them, Hauptwachtmeister Leopold Mitas, during a long stop in Zalishchyky, along the Dniester north of Chernovci , just beyond Romania's occupation zone, the department was mobilized on November 14, 1941 for the round-up of the local Jewish community. This was about 600 people who were then shot by a detachment of Sicherheitspolizei coming from Czortków and led by Willi Müller. During this action, Schupo would also take part in different executions, as confirmed by Mitas himself, while Wüpper would assist Müller in finding a suitable execution site[29]. The following participation in the roundups of Boryslav, starting from the *Invalidenaktion* of November 27-29, 1941, was not something completely new for Wüpper's Schupo, who, in 1942, received a second supporting officer in Oberleutnant Wittmann. Within the department, the operational functions were divided into internal and external services, the latter managed by Hauptwachtmeistern Josef Pöll and Leopold Mitas: these external services included investigation and contrast on the black market as well as, of course, the activities related to the so-called *Jewish question*. A detachment of Ukrainian auxiliaries made operational in the spring of 1942 and commanded by Hauptwachtmeister Heinrich Nemec, also depended on Schutzpolizei-Dienstabteilung "Boryslav". These *Ukrainische Hilfspolizisten*, housed in the same building as the German policemen, were widely used in anti-Jewish activities[30]. The commander of these auxiliaries was a Ukrainian named Bojcu[31]. Mitas, Pöll and Nemec were among the members of SchPDA "Boryslav" who distinguished themselves for acts of brutality against the Jews, spurred on by the *good example* set by their commander Wüpper.

12.4.6 – *Nebenstelle "Boryslaw"/ Arbeitsamt "Drohobycz"*

This office, included in the civil administrative structure of Boryslav's Stadtkommissar, SA-Hauptsturmführer Bornemann, depended on the district office of Drohobycz which was run by Hellmut Bräunlich and at whose dependencies Adolf Güldner worked in the role of adviser for Jewish affairs (*Judeneinsaz-Referent*). Güldner had responsibility for the management of Jewish forced labor through a section called *Jüdisches Arbeitsamt* which was in charge, among other things, of providing lists of Jews unable to work (*Unfähige, arbeitslosen...*), to be sent to be shot[32]. As for Bornemann, who was in charge of the administration of the Jews of Boryslav, on March 11, 1942, he proposed the division into three categories: skilled workers (A), apt to work (B) and disabled (C). Only the first, of course, could enjoy their (relative) protection, and were used in refineries or other essential industries, while all the others eventually became the main target of the first deportations. According to lists provided by the *Judenrat* to KDS-Außenstelle "Drohobycz" 3,037 Jews were actually used in essential activities in June 1942, with an increase of 70 % compared to the previous January[33].

Bornemann also had the task of establishing a Jewish ghetto in Boryslav, but this was delayed until March 1942 because of a typhus outbreak which in practice prevented the transfer of approximately 10,700 Jews still present in the city[34], in the areas assigned to them in Potok Gorny (A), Wolanka (B) and Mickiewicza (C)[35]. In fact, there is no confirmation about the involvement of personnel of the civil administration – whose direction had passed to Wilhelm Möllers in July 1942 – in the deportations of August 1942: however, these were made easier by the cooperation provided by the bureaucrats of Stadtkommissariat and the local employment office. In any case, within a few weeks of his appointment Stadtkommissar Möllers tried to meddle in the deportations perpetrated between fall 1942 and 1943, also informing KDS-Außenstelle "Drohobycz" of reports he received from his local collaborators about hiding or fleeing Jews[36].

12.5 WHEN YOU MEET THE EYES OF A CHILD

On August 3-4, 1942, with the roundup of the Sambor ghetto, about 20 miles north of Boryslav, the *Jewish problem* in the district of Drohobycz began to be solved[37]. From that moment on until November, one *action* after the other, trains to Belzec methodically took up and transported thousands of Jews of various communities: Drohobycz, Sambor, Stary Sambor, Turka, and of course Boryslav, whose ghetto was *emptied* during several round-ups: on August 6-8, during October, November, on February 17, 1943 and finally late in the following May[38].

The *strategic* management of the operation was taken by SSPF Katzmann, who, towards the beginning of August had instructed his subordinates, Gschwendtner, Rokita and Janowska's ZAL commander Gustav Willhaus, to proceed with the *reduction* of the ghettos of the Drohobycz district, through the selection of useful Jews towards the needs of war economy: they had to be temporarily saved and imprisoned in labor camps, in particular Janowska's. In order to achieve this goal a *kommando* of about 150 men of SSPF "Lemberg" led by Gschwendtner had been mobilized. This *kommando* was reinforced by personnel of KDS-Außenstelle "Drohobycz", which, two days after hitting the Sambor ghetto, on August 3, was moved to that of Turka[39]. Boryslav came next, as planned.

Actually, the action against the Boryslaw-Wolanka ghetto, scheduled for August 6, began with a hitch: alerted by the raids that had occurred a few days before in Sambor and Turka, hundreds of Jews to be *resettled in the Pinsk area* whose names were on a list that the Gestapo had given to Herz, chairman of the *Judenrat*, in late July 1942, fled into the woods in the imminence of the action, taking advantage of the absence of a fence around the ghetto. So, having managed to get their hands upon only a few hundred Jews, who were then locked up in the cinema Graszyna, the leaders of the raid decided to leave the city, to trick the *Judenrat* into believing that the operation had been completed. Incredibly, the trick proved successful, so much so that in the course of the day, after the Germans had withdrawn, most of the fugitives returned to the ghetto, only to be inevitably trapped when the staff of SchPDA "Boryslaw", Ukrainian auxiliaries and the kommando of KDS-Außenstelle "Drohobycz" suddenly returned to town late in the evening, blocked all escape routes and (re)started an indiscriminate and brutal raid[40].

No longer taking account of any list, the *Räumungskommandos* began to break into every house, forcing the Jews to go out with nothing but what they were wearing. All those who were unable to move – elderly, sick and children – were killed on the spot, while abandoned houses were looted, particularly by some members of SchPDA "Boryslaw", including Mitas, Pöll, Guldan, Neumayer and Nemec, who took possession of money and valuables[41]. In the midst of a confusion of cries, gunshots and bursts of automatic weapons[42], every Jew met outside his home was arrested or killed, and soon the streets were littered with abandoned corpses. During the raid no exception was made: all were arrested, family members of the Jewish Council also and all the refinery workers, hitherto considered essential, including those of Karpathen-Öl. A kommando of SchPDA raided the Jewish orphanage, crowded with children even of tender age, who were literally torn from their beds and forcibly loaded "in a barbaric way (*auf barbarische Weise*)" on a truck by Hauptwachtmeister Heinrich Nemec and his Ukrainians[43]. Younger or sick children, or those unable to walk fast enough were killed[44]. Some were lifted and thrown in the street through the windows. According to one witness, Hauptwachtmeister Leopold Mitas, of the SchPDA "Boryslaw", grabbed by feet a three year old child who had survived a flight through the window and killed him by violently slamming his head against a telegraph pole[45]. Overall, 173 children, barefoot and in pajamas, were torn from their orphanage beds that night.

The raided victims were massed in the Graszyna cinema and in the premises on Zielinkastrasse which once housed the banned Polish Socialist Party (PPS), as well as in a warehouse near the train station, where they remained under surveillance until dawn of August 8 when, partly walking in column, partly driven by trucks, they were transferred to the station and lined up on the platform and along the tracks, waiting for the train to Belzec. During the transfer, apart from the ill-treatment inflicted by the security staff, several executions were also carried out[46].

The train's arrival marked the beginning of the last phase. At that point, under the direction of Rudolf Gschwendtner and Junge, commander of Drohobycz's German gendarmerie, about 5,000 people began to be crowded into the cattle trucks. Willhaus and Rokita, probably, were there too, committed to selecting *useful* Jews, to be transferred to the ZAL of Janowska.

Then Berthold Beitz arrived.

The previous day, August 7, concerned about the course of events, he found himself at Boryslav station, where many of the Jews rounded up during the night had been taken and where others would keep arriving during that chaotic day. Since the late evening of August 6, shortly after the beginning of the raids, Beitz was told the alarming news about what was happening in the city by his colleagues: this news was later confirmed by a phone call from the commander of SchPDA Wüpper, who made him aware of the transfer to Lviv of the 5,000 Jews of Wolanka. Among these were also included all the workers and employees of Karpathen-Öl Beitz, arrested at the refinery in spite of the work permit that was supposed to protect them from deportations[47].

Puzzled and worried, but determined to take advantage of the wide powers conferred on him as director of a strategic refinery, Beitz decided to intervene to save at least part of *his* Jews, moving within KDS-Außenstelle "Drohobycz", through his contact with SS-Untersturmführer Friedrich Dengg.

Finally, at about dawn of August 8, when the victims were already being loaded on the train to Belzec, Drohobycz's Gestapo gave the pending authorization to Beitz to proceed to the extraction of *his* Jews from the crowd of about 5,000 deported, already piled into the cars, or waiting on the platform of the train station.

It was the dawn of August 8, 1942, when, in the light of the street lamps that lit up the mass of those desperate people, Beitz found himself judge of the fate of hundreds of unarmed people. Such arbitrary was so absolutely overwhelming as to induce him to focus not only on *his useful* Jews, but also on others, those considered *superfluous*, those whose fate had been sealed precisely because of their apparent uselessness.

During an interview given many years later, on February 28, 1989[48] Beitz described that August morning:

> *And then I saw the children, in their striped pajamas, lit by streetlights. And then came the others, pushed forward on all sides and then loaded onto the cattle cars. Each of them had to carry a baby. There was a doctor among them, he said quite casually: "Oh, also in heaven there is a need for doctors...". The atmosphere that was there cannot be imagined. The way they dragged all their possessions, and the street lamps that cast such a strange light [...]. And all those people [...] they really were nothing, numbers, objects, things. The police treated those people with indifference and cruelty.*

Berthold Beitz walked along the platform throughout its length, calling the names of those who had worked for him and even those who had *not* worked for him. Some were let off the cattle trucks, many made themselves recognizable in the crowd. Some were rejected and forced to climb back on the train by the Gestapo officers who accompanied Beitz – Gschwendtner being one of them –, others gave up being saved so as not to leave their families.

That day, before the train moved, Berthold Beitz managed to save about 200 Jews[49]. Among them, in addition to the refinery workers, there were also women and children whose eyes he could not avoid:

> *When you meet the eyes of a child, you realize how... in the streets, in the station... he is rejected everywhere, by everyone, except death – and in that first light of dawn that child looks at you with eyes so big, so huge: what else could I do? I just did it. For those children and their mothers, whom I helped get off the train thanks to my special permits and then hired as secretaries: off those trains ready to leave for the camps, torture and mass murder*[50].

12.6 POLIZEIKAMERADEN

As Berthold Beitz committed to save Jews within the limit of his possibilities, his fellow countrymen did their best to send as many they could to the gas chambers of Belzec. Apart from the about 200 rescued by Beitz and 400 more selected by Gschwendtner and Rokita to be sent to Janowska's labor camp, all the remaining Jews rounded up between August 6 and 7 in Boryslav – at least 4,000 – were taken to Belzec, together with a further group of 2,000, taken from the surrounding communities[51].

Several perpetrators began to be investigated for this crime in the early postwar, both by Austrian and West German authorities.

The Austrian investigators were placed in charge of dealing with former members of SchPDA "Boryslaw" against whom, since 1946, the so-called *Volksgerichtshof* had been applied. Established by the Ministry of Justice, the *Volksgerichtshof* was the application of *Verbotgesetzes*, i.e. the Law on Prohibition of the reconstitution of the NSDAP, and the punishment of Nazi crimes. This Act, passed unanimously by the three parties that made up the democratic coalition, had come into force on May 8, 1945 and was soon followed by the institution of popular Chambers, the first of which, Vienna's, became operational within the summer at the headquarters of the Court of Appeals.

The collection of testimonies of survivors and witnesses to the massacre was one of the main activities of Vienna's *Volksgerichtshof* that, with regard to the facts of Boryslav and the nearby village of Drohobycz, succeeded in assembling extensive documentation and in carrying out numerous arrests as early as February 1946. This was also due to the fortunate discovery in the archives of Vienna's Polizeidirektion, of a list containing the names of some 7,000 former Austrian members of Schutzpolizei, many of whom had served in the Occupied Territories[52]. However, the work of *Volksgerichtshof* was blocked in 1947 by the intervention of the authorities of Soviet military occupation, which imposed their jurisdiction over those who were guilty of crimes within the borders of the Soviet Union. This was the context in which, between 1948 and

camouflaged bandits who murdered, plundered and robbed [...]. With courage, determination and constant attention, he avoided any loss [...]. In the course of his activity he neutralized about 500 bandits and criminals". This figure probably included 173 orphanage children who were torn from their beds the night of August 6, 1942[66]. In 1948 he was convicted by a Soviet military court to 25 years' hard labor, but committed suicide in his prison cell on February 3, 1948, before being deported to Russia.

NEUMAYER, Ferdinand: born November 21, 1909. Reservist. A professional waiter, in 1941 he was recalled to police service. A member of SchPDA "Boryslaw" from late November 1941, he was assigned to external services as a subordinate to Pöll and Mitas. In February / March 1944 he participated in the shooting of at least 20 Jews hidden in an underground shelter, captured through a tip-off given by a Polish peasant who was later rewarded with 5,000 zloty and a bottle of vodka. Owner of a dog named *Harass* [sic], he would often pit it against the Jews arrested [67]. On April 29, 1948 he was sentenced by a Soviet military court to 25 years' hard labor for *brutality against citizens of the Soviet Union during the war*, and was then deported to Russia. He was granted freedom between 1955 and 1956 and returned to Austria. Processed by the Court of Vienna, he was acquitted on July 26, 1956.

NIEHOFF, Erich: a driver for SchPDA "Boryslaw", he participated in the massacre of February 15-17, 1943, becoming responsible for the killing of many Jews. After the action, during which they were distributed extra rations of liquor, Niehoff had an altercation with Mitas, as to who had killed more Jews [sic][68]. He died in combat during the retreat from Boryslav in the summer of 1944.

PÖLL, Josef: born July 24, 1907 in Terfens, Tyrol. Hauptwachtmeister. In service at Bundesheer from 1927 to 1934, in the same year he served with the Vienna police (*Wiener Sicherheitwache*) at Rudolfsheim's police station. After the Anschluss he was automatically reinstated into Schutzpolizei and transferred to Krakow and Lodz after the war began. Back in Vienna in 1941, he was then sent to Galicia sometime in October, at SchPDA "Boryslaw" and served as paymaster: a post he held until July 1942, when he was assigned to external services as a team leader, with tasks concerning price control and black market. There is no evidence that he ever joined the NSDAP[69]. Between February 15 and 17, 1943 he took part in the execution of several hundred Jews, including many children; he would personally kill some by smashing their skulls with blows of a rod[70]. In February / March 1944 he participated in the shooting of at least 20 Jews hidden in an underground shelter, captured through a tip-off given by a Polish farmer. On September 23, 1949 he was convicted by the Soviet military tribunal of Baden (Niederösterreich) to 25 years' hard labor and was deported to Russia. His freedom restored between 1955 and 1956, he returned to Austria. Processed by the Court of Vienna, he was sentenced to 20 years in prison on July 26, 1956, but he would be released on July 31, 1957.

SCHUCH, Jakob: a member of SchPDA "Boryslaw", where he arrived in October 1941 after having volunteered for service in the east. Deputy Commander of the guard corps, he played simultaneously the role of Karl Weigl's deputy in the air-raid protection auxiliary service, of which he would then become solely responsible in the spring of 1943, after Weigl's transfer elsewhere. On November 21, 1942, on Wüpper's orders, he would take part, with his air-raid protection core, in the technical preparation of the site chosen for the massacre of several hundred Jews living in the vicinity of Boryslav, who were executed with shots to the neck by personnel of KDS-Außenstelle "Drohobycz" and SchPDA "Boryslaw"[71]. In 1948/49 he was convicted to 25 years' hard labor by a Soviet military court and was then deported to Russia. His freedom restored between 1955 and 1956, he returned to Austria. Processed by the Court of Vienna, he was acquitted on July 26, 1956.

VÖLKL, Friedrich: a member of SchPDA "Boryslaw", where he arrived in October 1941 after having volunteered for service in the east. Quartermaster in charge of the economic department, he replaced Pöll in that role, after the latter was transferred to external services. In February / March 1944 he participated in the shooting of at least 20 Jews hidden in an underground shelter, captured through a tip-off given by a Polish farmer. On this occasion, however, in the grip of a nervous breakdown, he would not be able to carry out the execution of a Jewish woman who was then killed by Wüpper, who would scald him, saying: "Völkl, what are you doing? Shoot decently! A good shot is the best thing you can do for these people!"[72]. Recognized as *alte Kämpfer*, in 1949 he was sentenced by a Soviet military court to 25 years' hard labor and during April of that year he was deported to Russia. He died during his imprisonment in Siberia.

VEIGL, Karl: born September 3, 1894 in Vienna. A railway worker until 1915, he fought on the Russian and Italian fronts during The Great War. A member of *Volkswehr* from 1918 to 1919, he joined the Vienna police. Of socialist tendencies at first, he affiliated with the Christian Socialists until 1938, the year he joined the NSDAP. After the Anschluss he tried to move on to the rank of reserve officer, but his request was rejected in 1941 for unfitness. On October 7, 1941 he was transferred to SchPDA "Boryslaw" as head of *Luftschutzhilfsdienst*, the anti-aircraft protection auxiliary service. He remained in Galicia until the spring of 1943. Recognized as *alte Kämpfer*, he was regarded by his superiors as a staunch Nazi. In 1948/49 he was sentenced to 25 years' hard labor by a military court and was then deported to Russia. His freedom restored between 1955 and 1956, he returned to Austria. Processed by the Court of Vienna, he was acquitted July 26, 1956.

In addition to those mentioned above, the following officers were part of SchPDA "Boryslaw" between November 1941 and autumn 1942: Anton Beschliessmayer, Karl Beutelberger, Friedrich Brandstatter, Hofer, Johann Lackner, Peter Mayer, Nikolaus Spatzenegger, Heinrich Springer, Maximilian Steindl, Wittman[73].

12.7 CHOOSING A WAY

This is a story of horror and honor. This is a story of despair and hope. This is a story of life and death.

This is a story that has two guiding threads. This story was built around these threads: not by the author of these pages, but by the people who lived through it, for better or for worse. Two threads as two opposing interpretations that can mark the dividing line between what some of the characters did and what someone else did not do but especially between what *could* be done and what *could not* be done. These things did not happen because of conformity, misplaced sense of duty, obedience, fear of consequences, ideological belief, inertia against the situations, for all those variables that overlap each time one is in a position of having to make a choice.

Berthold Beitz chose. He chose to save lives taking risks for himself and his family, taking advantage of the good cards that his privileged position had put in his hands. He could have continued to live in peace in his little five-bedroom house on the hill on the outskirts of Boryslav that the company had made available for him, running the refinery the way he preferred without a care for those who were working there as slaves. He could have chosen the orderly monotony of the respected and distant leader, just like many others would have done in his stead, without having to feel responsible for something, nor for anyone, and taking into account only the welfare of his family and the functionality of his company. Instead, he decided to follow the harder way, a way that, in the days when he was living, was likely to lead him to the *unknown land*. He, Berthold Beitz, saw the July pogrom and was disgusted by it. Then he saw the children at Boryslav's train station and then he saw a mother with her child in her arms being killed before his very eyes[74]. He was not responsible for any of this, Berthold Beitz, but still he decided to take responsibility and do something: to react to those who really were responsible but instead, paradoxically, did not feel that burden at all. Berthold Beitz had a moral reaction, toward the victims but also toward himself, that is, toward the Man who refused to cease to be such.

The 200 Jews at Boryslav's station in August 1942 were only the first to be saved: many more came in the following months and years. Not only skilled workers and workers needed for his firm, but tailors, shoemakers, women with children, Talmudic students, elderly... people who would have had less chances to survive than others. Eventually, they were about a thousand, and it is now that the first thread becomes interwoven with the second, with the choices of those who did nothing even though they had the chance.

As a matter of fact, many, the great majority *did not choose*: they followed the easy way, the way of immediate self-interest, prudence or indifference, they did not accept the risk to bear a moral responsibility. They looked only to themselves for fear of discovering what was around them.

Yet, for many of those who *did not*, the choice was not dictated by a lack of alternatives or the imminent danger of reprisals for themselves or their families, or perhaps by the more prosaic risk of jeopardizing their own property or career, but from a genuine moral atrophy, which not only hindered the visualization of alternative ways, but probably prevented taking them even if they conceived their existence. Indeed, for that Polish peasant rewarded with a liter of vodka, *giving up* the idea of spying on the presence of Jews in hiding would not have been an act of courage. It would not have taken so much courage for Pöll and Neumayer to save the lives of the two Jewish women found hidden in an izba[75]; for that German (maybe Junge or maybe Gschwendtner) who forced an old woman, already called by Beitz, to get back on the train to Belzec, thus condemning to death her daughter who chose not to

A view of Boryslav's oil wells, around the end of the Thirties.

be saved so as not to abandon her mother[76]; for Mitas, to ignore that child who survived the flight through the orphanage window, or for that *volksdeutsche* auxiliary named Rolow, who could have avoided notifying Wüpper immediately after the farmer's tip-off about the 30 Jews hiding in an underground shelter... None of this would have required special bravery or meant the danger of exposing themselves and they would not have been heroic gestures, but a simple human act. There was no need for anything that was not within reach, but only a different choice to what was done instead: a choice dictated by moral impulse, not aesthetic heroism, a choice dictated by ideal virtues, not by physical boldness.

It did not take to be heroes to make that choice. Remembering to be human would have been enough. To regain a scrap of honor was what it took, to believe in hope a little more was what it took. To choose in favor of life was what it took. Sometimes it was done, more often it was not, but the memory remains of those few who did.

And that is why on the hill of the Yad Vashem two trees now bear the names of two of those few: Berthold Beitz and Else Beitz.

ENDNOTES

1 «Völkl, what are you doing? Shoot decently! A good shot is the best thing you can give to these people!» Geldmacher, p. 132, Sandkühler, p. 389.

2 Halter, p. 73.

3 LG Wien 20 Vr 3333/56 Bd. 1. Testimony by Moritz Grossmann. Geldmacher, p. 104, Sandkühler, p. 338.

4 Halter, p. 74.

5 Gad Lerner: *Una cartolina dallo shtetl.* In *La Repubblica,* August 21, 2008.

6 *Ibid.*

7 On the massacre perpetrated by NKVD in Boryslaw, see Musial Konterrevolutionäre, pp. 163-165, Sandkühler, pp. 303-304.

8 Musial Konterrevolutionäre, p. 186, Sandkühler, p. 304.

9 Musial Konterrevolutionäre, p. 187.

10 Sandkühler, pp. 303-304.

11 Musial Konterrevolutionäre, p. 189.

12 Pohl Ostgalizien, p. 60, Sandkühler, p. 304. However, there are no accurate figures with regard to the number of Jews killed during the pogrom of Boryslav who, according to a testimony, would have been about 250. Musial Konterrevolutionäre, p. 189.

13 Sandkühler, p. 304. ,

14 Pohl Ostgalizien, pp. 75-76. Lasch was informed of his new position on July 26 by Frank and took possession of his new office in Lviv during the following days.

15 *Ibid.*, p. 84, Sandkühler, p. 84.

16 Pohl Ostgalizien, pp. 86-87. Tanzmann had been sent to Galicia by Schöngarth himself in late June 1941, as a member of a *kommando of* Einsatzgruppe zbV. After the dissolution of this EG, his staff was used to form KdS "Lemberg".

17 Pohl, p. 88.

18 Beside Drohobycz's, also KdS-Außenstellen "Czortków", "Kolomea", "Stanislau", "Tarnopol" and "Sokal" were activated. Pohl Ostgalizien, p. 88.

19 *Ibid.*, p. 89.

20 The Polish were basically drafted into the Kriminalpolizei, subdivided in small commands in all main Galician towns: their number swelled from the about 260 of 1941 to about 600 a year later. *Ibid.*, pp. 87, 90.

21 Sandkühler, pp. 309, 526. The figures of Boryslav refer to September 1939: after this date the number of Jews in town increased because of the arrival of refugees from central Poland. All this in spite of the Soviet deportations perpetrated in 1940.

22 *Ibid.*, pp. 310, 440, Pohl, pp. 89, 411. Block had replaced SS-Hauptsturmführer Franz Wenzel.

23 On this issue Walter von Soosten, a staunch Nazi, distinguished himself from his predecessor Joachim Stach who, on the contrary, had tried, to the extent possible, to keep Ordnungspolizei out of the executions of Jews, and was replaced precisely because of that. Pohl Ostgalizien, pp. 206-207.

24 *Ibid.*, p. 91.

25 *Ibid.*, p. 91. Apart from Boryslav's, at the same time the SchPDA of Drohobycz, Kolomyia, Stanislaviv, Stryj and Tarnopol were activated. Except for the latter – constituted in Heidelberg – they were all formed with Austrian personnel led by Germans.

26 *Ibid.*, p. 91.

27 The Ukrainian police in Galicia held the same role that the Polish Blaupolizei performed in the General Government and originated from local militias which formed spontaneously after June 22, 1941, in the days of the Soviet retreat. These militias were dissolved and reorganized as Ukrainische-Hilfspolizei with KDO orders of August 10 and 13. In April 1942, the Ukrainian police counted on 3,400 men

in service in addition to a considerable reserve and was heavily involved in the *Jewish question* in Galicia. On this theme see Dieter Pohl, *Ukrainische Hilfskräfte beim Mord am den Juden*. In particular, pp. 217-218.

28 Geldmacher, p. 76, Pohl Ostgalizien, p. 149, Sandkühler, p. 311.

29 Sandkühler, pp. 154-155, 311, 498, Geldmacher, p. 76, Pohl Ostgalizien, p. 149. StAw Hamburg 14a Js 429/53 against Wüpper. The department of Sicherheitspolizei that had the leadership during the action was KdS-Außenstelle"Czortków", led by SS-Untersturmführer Willi Müller.

30 Geldmacher, pp. 78-80.

31 Sandkühler, p. 311.

32 *Ibid.*, p. 318. Güldner, for instance, delivered the list of 350-400 unemployed Drohobycz Jews, 250 of which were then shot in Bronica's wood on November 22, 1941. Moreover, he supervised the deportation of at least 1,500 Drohobycz Jews, perpetrated on March 25, 1942, with destination Belzec. Apparently, he was not aware of the victims' final destination.

33 Pohl Ostgalizien, p. 199.

34 *Ibid.*, pp. 121, 161. Of the about 14,000 Jews in Boryslav on the eve of the German invasion, about a thousand had been killed during the August 2-3, 1941 pogrom and during the so-called *Invalidenaktion* of November 27-29. 1,500 more had starved to death or had been killed by disease and about 500 had been transferred to labor camps outside of town – data from *Jüdische Soziale Selbsthilfe.* Sandkühler, pp. 321, 528.

35 Sandkühler, p. 323.

36 Pohl Ostgalizien, p. 286.

37 Sandkühler, p. 334.

38 Arad, p. 385, In the action of October 21, 1,020 Jews were deported to Belzec, upon intervention of 1/Polizei-Bataillon 133 (Hptm. Ernst Lederer), part of Polizei-Wachtbataillon "Breslau", of Boryslav's Schutzpolizei and of the Ukrainian militia. Pohl Ostgalizien, p. 240, Curilla, p. 776, Geldmacher, pp. 109-111. For the action of November 20-21 See Chapter 1, note 52. In the action of February 15-17, 1943, ordered by Hildebrand, ZAL-Referent at Stab SSPF "Lemberg", a few hundred Jews were shot, mainly women and children, by Boryslav's Schutzpolizei, the Ukrainian militia and Polizei-Reiterzug "Boryslaw" led by Oltn. Gotzen. Once the selection of the victims detained in the "Coliseum" cinema was completed, the carnage was perpetrated in a common grave dug near the old slaughterhouse. Curilla, pp. 785-786, Geldmacher, pp. 117-118, Sandkühler, pp. 370-371, Pohl Ostgalizien, p. 250. In the action of late May 1943, about 1,000 Jews, mainly elderly, women and children were brought to the old slaughterhouse and killed with gunshots to the neck: Wüpper and Mitas, affected by alcohol, would carry out many executions. I/Polizei-Regiment 23 (already Polizei-Bataillon 307) took part in this slaughter. Geldmacher, p. 124, Sandkühler, p. 377, Curilla, pp. 786, 923. Polizei-Reiterzug "Boryslaw" was a sub-unit of Polizei-Reiterschwadron "Galizien", which had several platoons detached respectively in Lviv, Tarnopol and Boryslav.

39 Geldmacher, p. 102. During the two actions against Sambor and Turka, about 4,000 Jews were rounded up and deported to Belzec.

40 Sandkühler, pp. 336-337.

41 Geldmacher,pp. 104-105. Testimony by Filip Oberländer. LG Wien 20 Vr 3333/56 Bd. 1.

42 Sandkühler, p. 336.

43 Geldmacher, p. 104. Testimony by Moritz Grossmann, given on February 28, 1946. LG Wien 20 Vr 3333/56 Bd. 1.

44 Sandkühler, p. 338.

45 Geldmacher, p. 104. Testimony by Markus Backenroth, given on February 28, 1946. LG Wien 20 Vr 3333/56 Bd. 1.

46 Sandkühler, p. 338.

47 *Ibid.*

48 Sandkühler, p. 339.

49 According to Sandkühler, p. 341, the Jews saved by Beitz were *at least* 150; according to Pöhl Ostgalizien, p. 224, they were 250: a figure confirmed by the Court of Bremen in the conviction to life imprisonment of May 12, 1966, against Friedrich Hildebrand, ZAL-Referent at Stab SSPF "Lemberg". LG Bremen 29 Ks 1/66.

50 Halter, p. 73, interview with Berthold Beitz.

51 Pöhl Ostgalizien, p. 224.

52 Kuretsidis-Haider, s.p. Also Pohl Ostgalizien, p. 394 who talks of about 200 Ordnungspolizei Austrian members arrested and, in part, extradited.

53 Geldmacher, pp. 161-162.

54 Kuretsidis-Haider, s.p.

55 *Ibid.*

56 Geldmacher, p. 162.

57 Sandkühler, p. 445, Sandkühler Judenfrage, p. 121.

58 Geldmacher, pp. 73-74, Sandkühler, pp. 444-445.

59 Geldmacher, pp. 130-131, Sandkühler, p. 389.

60 Geldmacher, pp. 78, 93.

61 *Ibid.*, pp. 153. Testimony by Josef Viehtauer. LG Wien 20 Vr 3333/56 Bd. 1.

62 *Ibid.*, pp. 118-119. Testimonies by Marceli Horowitz and

Bernhard Haberman. LG Wien 20 Vr 1077/57 Band 2.

63 Geldmacher, pp. 73, 76, 79.

64 *Ibid.*, p. 153. Testimony by Friedrich Völkl of February 12, 1946. LG Wien 20 Vr 3333/56 Bd. 1.

65 *Ibid.*, pp. 129-131.

66 Sandkühler, pp. 444-445, Geldmacher, pp. 77, 80, 104.

67 *Harass* = Tormentor. Sandkühler, p. 389.

68 Geldmacher, pp. 118-119. Testimonies by Marceli Horowitz and Dzimmek Erlbaum given before the Court at Wien. LG Wien 20 Vr 1077/57 Band 2.

69 *Ibid.*, pp. 73, 78-79, 131-132, Sandkühler, p. 389.

70 Geldmacher, p. 118. Testimony by Bernhard Haberman. LG Wien 20 Vr 1077/57 Bd. 1.

71 Geldmacher, pp. 112, 118, Sandkühler, p. 359, Curilla, p. 785. The slaughter of about 500 victims was ordered by the commander of KdS-Außenstelle "Drohobycz", Hans Block, through his representative for Jewish affairs Josef Gabriel. Ukrainian auxiliaries and personnel of Polizei-Reiterzug "Boryslaw" were among the perpetrators.

72 *«Völkl, was machst Du; schieß doch anständig! Ein guter Schuß ist das beste, was man den Leuten mitgeben kann!»*. Geldmacher, p. 132, Sandkühler, p. 389.

73 Anton Beschliessmayer: there is no evidence of his enrollment in the NSDAP; Karl Beutelberger: assigned to external services; Friedrich Brandstatter: assigned to external services; Hofer: Meister der Schupo. Assigned to the guard corps he died in Vienna during an air-raid in early 1945; Johann Lackner: assigned to external services; Peter Mayer: driver for SchPDA "Boryslaw" he died in Vienna during an air-raid in early 1945. Nikolaus Spatzenegger: assigned to external services. He stayed in Boryslaw until spring 1943; Heinrich Springer: Meister der Schupo. Assigned to the guard corps, he disappeared at the end of the war; Maximilian Steindl: a member of SchPDA "Boryslaw", assigned to internal services. He died in combat during the withdrawal from Boryslav in the summer of 1944; Wittman: Oberleutnant. He was assigned to SchPDA "Boryslaw" in early 1942 as deputy commander. He died in Vienna during an air-raid in early 1945.

74 The woman was killed by Pöll or Mitas before Beitz's eyes on February 15, 1943. Sandkühler, p. 371.

75 The two women, hidden in the izba of a Polish family near Horodysche in the summer of 1943, were casually discovered by two policemen who killed them on the spot. After the murder they went to eat their ration as if nothing had happened. Geldmacher, p. 130. Testimony by Raoul Harmelin, LG Wien 20 Vr 3333/56 Bd. 1.

76 The incident occurred on August 8, 1942 at Boryslav's train station: the young Jewish woman was a secretary of Beitz, who decided to follow her mother as soon as the German officer forced her to board the train. Halter, pp. 74-75, Sandkuhler, pp. 339-340.

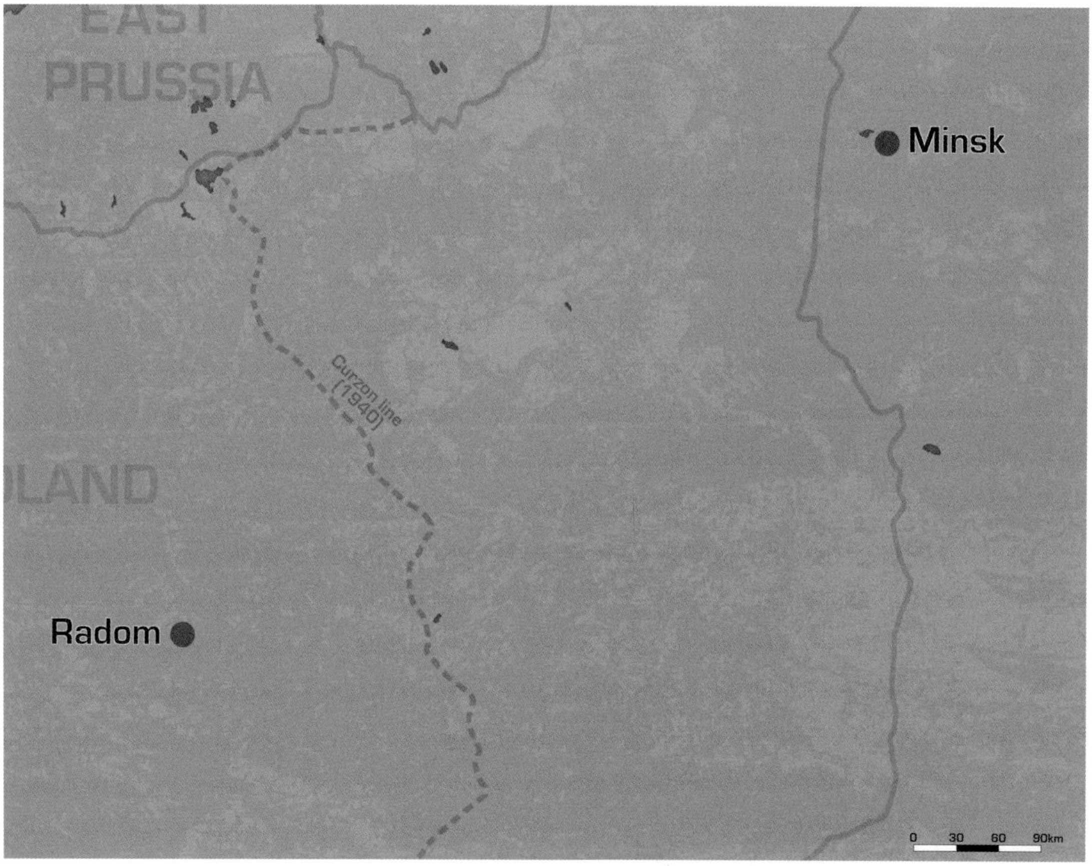
EAST
PRUSSIA
Minsk
Curzon line
(1940)
OLAND
Radom
0 30 60 90km

CHAPTER THIRTEEN
"RÄUMUNG IN RADOM"
AUGUST 1942

Diese Aussiedlung der Juden hänge jetzt nur noch vom dem Transportprobleme ab...

Alfons Oswald, June 18, 1942[1]

13.1 INTRODUCTION

According to figures provided by the public prosecutor in Hamburg during the trial against Hermann Weinrich and Paul Fuchs, in the summer of 1942 about 32,000 Jews survived in Radom, divided between a main ghetto in the city (about 27,000) and a smaller ghetto in the suburb of Glinice (5,000)[2]. Within five days during August 1942, all these people were *evacuated* by force and deported to Treblinka by a diverse contingent of the Waffen-SS, German and Polish police officers and Ukrainian and Baltic auxiliaries, whose number was probably less than 500 men, with a ratio between resources used and results obtained corresponding to at least 65 Jews deported for each perpetrator mobilized. Such effort shows the extent to which the operational dynamics were already oiled and the level of technical and synchronic perfection that the procedures of annihilation had reached. These procedures were now applied in a pattern that Henry L. Feingold – referring to Auschwitz, but the same idea can be extended to the dynamics related – defined as "an extension of the modern factory system", and as "a reflection of the modern scientific spirit deflected from its path"[3]. In short, these were the results obtained at the end of the operations. But what were the dynamics that allowed this undeniable *success*?

In his masterly work on Polizei-Bataillon 101, Christopher Browning placed for the first time in the spotlight of History and in particular of a non-specialist audience, the involvement of police battalions in the Jewish genocide[4], a crime that in 1942 Poland – the period in which the narration of Ordinary Men begins – was hatched under the code name *Aktion Reinhardt*, that served as a prelude, or took place simultaneously, to similar operations in other parts of Eastern Europe, including northern Belarus, western Ukraine (*Sonderaktion Ukraine judenfrei*[5]), and the district of Bialystok.

Now then, to complete this criminally great project – which, in Poland alone, was supposed to annihilate about two million Jews by means of the extermination camps of Belzec, Sòbibor and Treblinka – only extremely limited resources were made available to Himmler's proconsuls. Everything else – materials, transport, genocidal workforce – was to be found *on site*, maximizing the available assets and putting a strain on the *imagination* of those who were called upon to perform this huge task [6]: a task that the general governor Hans Frank, on December 16, 1941, defined as "a unique and gigantic event (*gigantische und einmalige Ereignis*)"[7].

With regard to Ordnungspolizei, apart from the police battalions garrisoned in Warsaw and the exception represented by Polizei-Bataillone 67 and 101 which were sent as reinforcements to the Lublin district in summer 1942 as a sort of *encouragement gift* from Himmler to his trusted SSPF Globocnik, there was little else in the other districts of the General Government. In Radom, in particular, after the departure of Polizei-Bataillon 307 for Belarus, which took place on August 18, 1942, SSPF Herbert Böttcher could still count on three autonomous companies of German police officers – 450/500 men in all – divided between the main towns in the district: Radom, Czestochowa and Kielce, in whose ghettos there were still tens of thousands of Jews[8]. Nevertheless, within a few weeks, between August 4 and September 22, these vast populations were systematically uprooted and forcibly loaded onto the trains to Treblinka, without any incident worthy of note and with outstanding results when it came to organizational efficiency, especially in light of the workforce used, which hardly could be described as *ideologically specialized*, but *generic*. In fact Böttcher's Räumungskommandos drew most of their staff from three independent police companies, that is to say from departments that it would not be too daring to label as random, in that they were formed from what remained, in terms of *human material*, in the police administrations (of Munich, Frankfurt and Koln), after the exodus of the best elements to the battalions. Also, in the case of Kielce, in order to meet the staff deficiencies a training company coming from Leipzig was mobilized, Polizei-Ausbildungs-Kompanie "Leipzig"[9].

There is no doubt then that the three deportations from the main towns in the district of Radom in September / October 1942, as well as the countless *minor* actions performed in the same period in the surrounding rural areas, mainly by the gendarmerie, have been perpetrated by a majority of *normal* Germans and in the presence of three conditions essential to overcoming moral inhibitions, as identified by Herbert C. Kelman, namely: authorizing, routinizing and dehumanizing[10]. A scheme that had become a real trademark in the procedures of annihilation and that made those peaks of ideological enthusiasm that in some cases, limited as they were, had accompanied the *experimental* phase of genocide in Poland in 1939 and in the Soviet Union in summer 1941[11], completely obsolete and in some ways counterproductive.

In other words, in the summer of 1942, the *factory of residential genocide* that had been unveiled in Belzec a few months earlier, could already count on strategic plans, professional echelons, a trained workforce and, of course, an almost inexhaustible reserve of *raw material* to assimilate and transform into victims.

13.2 ECHELONS

In the same way as the Ordunungspolizei in its various specialties provided that genocidal manpower which Klaus-Michael Mallmann aptly defined as *fußvolk der Endlösung*, in the district of Radom the professional echelons able to plan and manage the process of annihilation of approximately 340,000 Jews in the period from August to November 1942 were drawn from the various subdivisions of Sicherheitspolizei[12].

As in any social structure organized hierarchically, these cadres, who took on specialist operational roles, represented a minority of the total workforce involved. In the district of Radom though, this physiological minority was particularly weakened by a chronic shortage of staff, which left vacant no less than 50 % of the jobs requested. This problem, however, did not stop or even slow down the *work* performance of the officials present, but on the contrary it enhanced their skills and professional dedication.

13.2.1 – SSPF "Radom"

The position of SSPF "Radom" – created in November 1939 – during the period when the main deportations to Treblinka were perpetrated, was held by SS-Oberführer Herbert Böttcher, a *volksdeutsche* of Proküls (Priekulė), near Memel, who occupied that post on April 28, 1942. In August, his staff, reduced in numbers, could count on perhaps a dozen officers and as many noncommissioned officers and secretaries, and this was after it had been strengthened in previous weeks. Despite this lack of numerical strength, the role of Böttcher and his command proved central in the Jewish genocide, and remained so until the end of the conflict, to the point that in August 1944 it was able to arrange the transportation to Auschwitz of the last surviving Jewish forced laborers in the district of Radom. Among Böttcher's officials who were more involved in the genocide we should remember: SS-Hauptsturmführer Hermann Weinrich, Böttcher's Personalreferent, SS-Sturmbannführer Wilhelm Josef Blum, chief of staff, whose role – although not entirely clear – would be one of liaison between Globocnik and Böttcher, in order to coordinate the operations of deportation from Radom, according to the annihilation plan established by Globocnik himself[13]; Oberleutnant der Schutzpolizei Walter Subklewe, Böttcher's aide and advisor to the relationship between the SSPF office and that of KDO, SS-Untersturmführers Erich Kapke and Paul Nell, both officers / employees of Jewish issues (*Referent / Sachbearbeiter für Jüdische Ang-*

elegenheiten[14]), the first also in command of the auxiliary SSPF company available for *special tasks*. It should also be remembered, among the main police officers involved in the so-called *Jewish question* in Radom, SS-Untersturmführer Hans Schippers, who formally held the function of Böttcher's Spotreferent[15].

13.2.2 – KdS "Radom"

While the jurisdiction of strategic planning in relation to the so-called *Jewish question*, as well as the coordination between the various security forces, fell on SSPF, the direct management of police operations, persecution and intelligence (*polizeiliche Maßnahmen*) remained the main activity of KdS, through its various departments (Gestapo, SD and Kripo)[16]. This position, activated in November 1939, was held by SS-Obersturmbannführer Fritz Liphardt, whose staff was formed by 350 - 400 people depending on the period, against a planned force of 600. In the summer of 1942 in particular, the *Jewish question* was addressed by Abteilung III (later IV) Gestapo[17], led by SS-Sturmbannführer Lothar Wandel, who held the chairmanship of SS-Standgericht[18]. Its role, however, was weakened in part – something that its shadowy past was also responsible for. Indeed, within this department there were two officers operating who, after giving ample proof of their genocidal skills during the deportations of September 1942, would rise to the role of section leaders following the restructuring of the service carried out in late October, to the extent that they became the two real *deus ex machina* of Department IV: SS-Hauptsturmführers Adolf Feucht for Referat IVB and Paul Fuchs[19] for Referat IVN. The former also held the role of commander of the so-called Sonderkommando "Feucht", that is to say that special unit of KdS "Radom" specifically mobilized during the evacuation of the ghettos in August / September 1942. Feucht's deputy and director of IVB 4 (Jews), was SS-Untersturmführer Richard Schöggl. In addition to

Radom's Jewish neighborhood, March 1941. This sign, placed at the entrance to a house reserved for Jews reads: "Risk of disease (sic). All Germans are forbidden from entering this house". The note is signed by "The head of the district of Radom". Source: Bundesarchiv. The photograph was taken by Kreigsberichter Nrenner, Propagandakompanie 666.

the central command of Radom, KdS Liphardt also oversaw a number of branch offices in the major cities of the district known as KdS-Aussendienststellen; the five branches in the summer of 1942 (Czestochowa, Kielce, Piotrkow, Trybunalski and Tomaszow Mazowiecki) rose up to 11 in 1944. These commands had a central role in the deportations from the localities where they were stationed at.

13.2.3 – KdO "Radom"

From late July, the meager forces of Ordnungspolizei present in Radom in the summer of 1942 were subordinate to Oberst der Schupo Paul Baehren who, however, did not have the necessary autonomy in decision-making with regard to the *Jewish question*: as subordinate to Böttcher, his role in this area was to ensure the availability of the Ordnungspolizei departments in case of special needs. The central command of KdO, based in Radom, was formed of 174 men and from August 1, 1942, it formally took the name of Polizei-Regiment 23. At the same time his only units – after the departure for Belarus of Polizei-Battalion 307 – were Polizei-Kompanien "München" (Hptm. Friedrich Auerhammer), "Koln" and "Frankfurt am Main" relocated respectively to Radom, Czestochowa and Kielce. In addition to these mobile units, Baehren could count on weak Schutzpolizei nuclei present in some major cities. In Radom in particular, a Schutzpolizeikommando (KdSchupo) of forty elements had been activated, while other similar departments were also present in Czestochowa, Kielce and a few other places. Overall, at the moment of their greatest expansion, the detachments of Schutzpolizei probably did not amount to 300 people throughout the whole district, taking orders from KdSchupo, Maj. Ernst Möller, who in turn was directly subordinate to Baehren. Whatever the number, however, the staff of Schutzpolizei was regularly involved in the actions of 1942, including those of Radom on August 4 and 16. Otherwise, the departments of the gendarmerie, which played an important role in the deportations from rural areas, were not involved in the deportation from the town of Radom and are therefore not discussed here[20].

13.3 WORKFORCE

Beyond the strategic plans and the cadres called to mastermind them, even the Jewish genocide, as well as any other complex social initiative, needed a large number of more or less *specialized* workers, but still sufficiently prepared to perform the operational guidelines. It was not, however, an ideological specialization – almost entirely superfluous or even, as already said, counterproductive at times – but the full *availability to act* on the part of those called to perform, independently or regardless of any possible moral relapse. In this sense, the workforce were not required to have any particular commitment to the ideological cause – in this case, the resolution of the *Jewish question* – but simply some basic executive skills which would suffice in beginning, carefully and rationally, the required bureaucratic processes, according to the classic Weberian scheme. From here, were the almost endless possibilities to find, easily, a sufficient number of reliable performers, within strongly hierarchical systems such as military and militarized communities. The case of Radom, under this aspect, seems paradigmatic.

13.3.1 – SS-Sonderkommando "Feucht"

This *kommando* was formed in August 1942 within KdS "Radom", with the express purpose of proceeding to the resettlement of Jews from cities and rural areas of the Radom district. Given the task, it was essentially the Gestapo personnel of Abteilung III KdS "Radom" to be mobilized: in total, a dozen men commanded by SS-Hauptsturmführer Adolf Feucht who, according to the conclusions of ZStL, were the most qualified for this position, by virtue of their role[21]. It is worth emphasizing that doing service in the General Government was considered by many members of Sicherheitspolizei as a punishment, as a rehabilitation for further assignments elsewhere and that such vision certainly favored zeal and personal application, in order to shorten its duration as much as possible[22]. In other words, the General Government became a kind of receptacle of shady characters, eager only to do well in order to be transferred elsewhere. Thus, it does not come as a surprise that those who, perhaps, had been accused of corruption or misappropriation in their own country, would prove to be the most eager to action[23]. In any case, Feucht's group took part in all major roundups in the ghettos of the Radom district: in this sense, the role of this *kommando* in the *evacuations,* and specifically Feucht's role, would be essential, especially in the phase of preparation and tactical coordination between the different structures and departments engaged in the various actions, including the organization of the trains to Treblinka. In several cases – like the round-up of Czestochowa – Feucht and his men would supervise the operations of selection of the few Jews regarded as indispensable, which were spared the deportation to Treblinka. At a later date, as reconstructed by ZStL, the *kommando* would be attached to one of the police companies used to form II / Polizei-Regiment 23[24].

13.3.2 – Polizei-Kompanie "München"

After the activation in Munich of Polizei-Bataillone 71 and 72 in September / October 1939, and Polizei-Bataillon 73 a few weeks later, another independent company was established in November 1939, probably around a third group of policemen recovered from *Reviere* service. This company, named Polizei-Kompanie "München", was transferred to the Protectorate, probably during 1940, where it remained until the spring of 1941. In this period it was sent to Munich, substantially reduced after the transfer of much of its staff to another department mobilized for Yugoslavia in March 1941 (presumably Polizei-Bataillon 72) and then complemented with a share of reservists. Then, in late September, it was transferred to Krakow. Commanded by Hptm. Friedrich Auerhammer, in late October 1941 the company was moved to Kielce and then Radom in March 1942. Directly subordinate to KdO "Radom" Paul Baehren, after the activation of Polizei-Regiment 23 in the summer of 1942, it was renumbered 9/III/23. In August 1944 it was mobilized for the suppression of the Warsaw uprising. During its period of service in Radom it took part in the mopping up of both the small and the large ghettos. According to the testimonies of Auerhammer and other members of the company, given before ZStL during the investigation that led to the trial against Fuchs and Weinrich, although not always followed there was the explicit order to shoot to kill all the Jews on the run from the ghetto. Staff of the company would also provide the escort for the trains to Treblinka[25].

13.3.3 – Wachtkompanie/SSPF "Radom"

As reconstructed by ZStL, an auxiliary company identified as Wachtkompanie was made available to SSPF "Radom", apparently for the performance of generic services, such as surveillance of the building where

Signs like this ("Warning! The road access is forbidden to all Germans") delimited the perimeter of the ghetto in Radom.March 1941. Fotoreportage Kriegsberichter Brenner. Source: Bundesarchiv.

the SSPF was located. Formed with staff of Baltic and Ukrainian origin, this company was widely used in ghetto raids made in the district during the fall of 1942. Commanded by SS-Untersturmführer Erich Kapke, with a strength of 80-100 former prisoners of war recruited in the camps, this company was probably formed at the Trawniki training camp, in south-eastern Poland, and took part in the roundups of other district ghettos as well as in the Radom actions of August 4 and 16, 1942[26]. Frequently, especially from the beginning of 1943, its staff was involved in numerous executions during the surveillance or the transfer of groups of Jewish workers, or even directly inside the labor camps. In some cases, elements of the company would form the firing squads in the series of mass shootings perpetrated throughout the course of 1943. As well as being co-responsible for roughly tens of thousands of deportations to Treblinka, the staff of the company appears to have been the direct perpetrator of at least 350 executions[27].

13.3.4 – SS-Veterinär-Ersatz-Kompanie "Radom"

A small contingent of reinforcements to the units engaged in the mopping-up of the ghetto in Radom was also provided by a reservist veterinary company of the Waffen-SS stationed in the city: this particular was ascertained by the public prosecutor in Hamburg during the preliminary investigation against Weinrich and others[28]. We know only scant details concerning this company, founded in Radom on October 28, 1941 as a veterinarian department linked to SS-Kavallerie-Division and then transformed, on June 28, 1942, into SS-Veterinär-Ersatz-Abteilung. From the following August 1, thus during the period of the roundups in the ghetto, the department was commanded by SS-Hauptsturmführer Dr. Heinrich Held[29]. According to one witness, two other structures of the Waffen-SS present in Radom, in addition to this veterinary company, provided some small contingents during the roundups of August 5 and 14, namely SS-Standortverwaltung commanded by Obersturmführer Grabau and SS-Bauleitung commanded by Oberscharführer Seiler. Both these officers, it seems, were present during the action[30].

13.3.5 – Polnische "Blaupolizei"

The presence of personnel from the Polish police, the so-called *Blaupolizei*, would be a fixed constant in the raids of the fall of 1942. During the *action* in the Radom ghetto – but also in most other cases – the role of these policemen, who were dependent on local control of the German Schutzpolizei (KdSchupo), was essentially limited to the surveillance of sections of the outer perimeter of the ghetto, road blocks and road patrols[31]. There are no reports of their use in the ghetto during the raid itself. However, beyond the tactical involvement of a few dozen policemen in the actions of August 4 and 16, the role of the Polish police in the *Jewish question*, especially in the surveillance of the ghettos, in the suppression of smuggling and black market between the ghettos and the outside and in the search and tracking of fugitive or hidden Jews – from who bribes were often extorted in order for them to be allowed to flee – was not secondary but suited to the German provisions, enough to elicit positive comments from the major German police authorities[3].

Everything said so far makes it clear that the annihilation of the Radom ghetto was perpetrated by a haphazard collection of units and structures whose ideological fervor, for various reasons, may be doubted. In this respect we witness: the operating diligence of Sicherheitspolizei officials anxious to do well in the eyes of their superiors; the mercenariness of Trawniki auxiliaries; the ransom-prone opportunism of Polish *blaupolizisten*; the bureaucratic efficiency of the German policemen; not to mention the use – as a further reinforcement for *Räumungskommandos* engaged in house to house raids – of the so-called Jewish order service, to which everything can be blamed except an ideological propensity to collaborate with their tormentors. In other words, we are faced with a set of rather coarse motivations which, at least with regard to the workforce, were but poorly linked to abstract ideological theorems. An ideology which, as already said, was no longer an essential requirement before the enormity of the task, but at most a motivational reinforcement or perhaps, for some, a moral screen. In summary, while for the middle cadres the Jewish genocide was essentially reduced to a managerial problem which could be solved by technical solutions associated with good planning, for the workforce it was nothing more than an optimization of the execution modalities. Eventually, it could turn into a good opportunity for them all to exploit for their own ends.

In conclusion, in autumn 1942 the mechanisms of destruction were already in full swing and had reached the point where, in order for them to work properly, concepts such as *concreteness, objectivity* and *efficiency* were needed rather than slogans. The "winged words", to quote Eichmann, the Nazi *weltanschauungs* and the transcendent pseudo-millennial visions, seemed ever more like esoteric ruminations, pieces of coarse propaganda that only "poor fools" the likes of Julius Streicher and some "Teutonic-Germanic party bigwigs" who "behaved as goats" could still give some emotional significance to[33].

13.4 LIGHTS IN THE NIGHT

> *Two closed Jewish quarters have been established, with immediate effect, for the Jews residing in the city of Radom. Their boundaries are shown on the adjacent sketch. (Mit sofortiger Wirkung werde für die in der Stadt Radom ansässigen Juden, zwei geschlossenen jüdische Wohnbezirke gebildet. Ihre Abgrenzung ist aus nebenstehenden Skizzen ersichtlich).*

With this bilingual (German and Polish) announcement, issued on April 3, 1941 by Stadthauptmann Hans Kujath, the Jewish ghetto in Radom was established, with immediate effect and procedures to be completed by April 12[34]. The Jews that resettled in their new *residential areas* [sic] were *generously* allowed 55 pounds of luggage per person, with fines and imprisonment for offenders. All this was addressed to a community of about 33,000 people, many of whom were the subject of photographic reportage on two separate occasions by war correspondents Wisniewsi and Brenner, engaged in propaganda activities[35]. Just as in Mogilev and Belgrade, in fact, in this case too, the photographs taken of the Jews in Radom – apparently shot in moments of everyday life – are part of a work of systematic deconstruction of the image of the *Jew, the eternal enemy*, as well as one of remodeling of the same image around the most typical and coarse stereotypes that were to be crept into the social consciousness of the Arian citizen, through the words and images of the newsreels.

A typical example of this stereotyping is a photographic sequence produced by SS-Kriegsberichter Bruno Wisniewski, in which through the script of a group of three Jews intent on haggling among themselves, their eyes crooked and holding banknotes in their hands, the crudest anti-Semitic clichés, namely that of the greedy and treacherous *Jew*, took form in concrete *reality*. In other images, in particular through close-ups, grim and elusive facial expressions of the Jews are obtained through sidelong glances, a slight overexposure and the direct illumination with strong contrasts. In others, the emphasis is on those that had to be interpreted as specificities of *Ostjuden*, so as to demarcate the border between *us* and *them*, between the *Arians* and the *Jews* by the common German citizen: the particularly thick beards, their typical hats, a setting of decay, patched and dirty clothes were certainly unusual and repulsive images in the eyes of the orderly audience that these images were intended to reach [see Photo Section II, Photo n. 4].

Even in Radom then, after Mogilev and Belgrade, one can witness the use of propaganda as a means of *social education*, through the induction of stereotypes in order to facilitate the dehumanization, estrangement and marginalization of the Jews by the common feeling of the Arian citizen: in other words, the focus was to erase the Jews from collective consciousness, and then proceed smoothly to their physical elimination. Moreover, the fact that Wisniewski had produced his reportage with these stylistic features as early as 1940, confirms the *farsightedness* of the genocide planners in taking all the time needed to settle stereotypes into the public opinion, in order to take advantage of its effect at the appropriate time. Until then it was all about taking the necessary steps to make the Jews a foreign body within the rest of the population. In March 1941, when Kriegsberichter Brenner of Propagandakompanie 666 went to Radom to do his job, the ghetto had not yet been formally established, but already there were plaques and signs indicating the exact areas of the city that were off-limits to the *Arians*: in this sense, seen from a social perspective, the marginalization had already been implemented successfully and the physical barriers, and guarded entrances – that would come to Radom shortly thereafter – would simply reveal its existence. From this point of view we can therefore say that the ghetto in Radom was a reality internalized in the consciousness of both victims and perpetrators long before April 3, 1941. On that date, Kujath's order only served to mark the entrance onto the stage of bureaucracy, of specialized echelons capable of giving substance to the social dynamics and to plan the tasks of the arriving workforce.

The specialists took care of their work according to the dogmas of efficiency. The 33,000 Jews of Radom were divided into two separate ghettos: the main one enclosed within the old town center, designed to accommodate 25,000 inhabitants, and the smaller one in the suburb of Glinice, for the remaining 8,000 or so. Both ghettos were placed under the command of the Polish police, who presided over the entrances at all times, facing from the outside the nuclei of the so-called Ordnungsdienst posted inside. After being activated, on April 1941[36], the Jewish police was divided into two departments, one for each of the two ghettos, with about 80 men in the main one and about 40 in that of Glinice. Called *Jüdische Ordnungsdienst*, this service was dependent on the *Judenrat* which, like all other Jewish institutions, was located in the main ghetto. Both departments made sure that the transfer of the Jews in the ghetto would be completed by April 12, as per Kujath's provisions.

Then, once the route had been planned and the car started, all it took was to drive the last stretch of the way.

The last mile was reached around mid-February 1942. In this period, after a long phase of stabilization, nuclei of Sicherheitspolizei and Orpo departments – perhaps belonging to KdSchupo – started the roundup of suspected communists and *intellectuals*: in particular, a first action performed on February 19 – during which 40 Jews were shot and as many were deported to Auschwitz – was followed by a second on April 27, with at least 70 deaths and dozens of deportations, including several members of the *Judenrat* and of Ordnungsdienst[37]. Executed on the orders of Paul Fuchs of KdS "Radom", these actions – formally made in order to disrupt the communist apparatus – were meant to decapitate the leadership of the ghetto and its Ordnungsdienst, so as to leave the population more disorientated than ever and without reference points, precisely in its most critical moment. A moment that, however, did not seem imminent: in fact, once the echo of the raid in April extinguished, a precarious calm returned again to hover above the ghetto. For some weeks nothing happened. Then, suddenly, on the night between August 4 and 5, 1942, spotlights were mounted in the ghetto streets.

13.5 GLINICE

As reconstructed by the public prosecutor of Hamburg during the investigation against Weinrich and others, the *liquidation* of the ghettos in Radom started with the easier target: the small ghetto of Glinice, that, on the evening of August 4, 1942 was surrounded by a double cordon of German Schutzpolizisten, Polish Blaupolizisten and 50 members of Polizei-Kompanie "München" with machine guns positioned at the main entrances. At the same time, the approximately 80 men of the Ordnungsdienst assigned to the large ghetto were put on alert and called, at about 11 pm, before the SD command, where Richard Schöggl, Feucht's deputy, informed them on the outline of an operation described as a simple *transfer* of the population to a labor camp. According to orders, it was necessary that the Jewish policemen went from house to house in order to induce the inhabitants to go out with all their baggage, holding work permits in hand so they could be inspected and sorted as appropriate. At that point, the Jewish policemen were brought to Glinice, where they joined with about 40 colleagues who, in turn, had been mobilized in the small ghetto[38].

These words were spoken by Schöggl, according to Chaim Sytner's testimony, a Jew and former policeman who survived:

> *We have orders to resettle the men of the Glinice ghetto into labor camps. You of the Jewish police must help us carry out this action peacefully by seeing to it that all Jews obey our orders. You are responsible for the maintenance of discipline among Jews*[39].

The spotlights placed in the streets were lit at midnight sharp, illuminating the last night of the Glinice ghetto. As instructed, the Jewish policemen, in groups of three, went from house to house, whose occupants were given half an hour to prepare personal items and a limited amount of food. In the streets of the ghetto, meanwhile, in the midst of the chaos that immediately spread and among the roar of trucks equipped with loudspeakers which blasted orders at full volume, SSPF officials and members of the SS-Sonderkommando "Feucht" positioned themselves and began to sort the Jews as they left their homes, directing them to two different collection points: the holders of work permits to Kuszno Strasse and all others to Graniczna Strasse.

Let's keep reading Styner's testimony:

> *The streets were brightly lit by searchlights. Germans with the insignia of the lightning on their black uniforms filled the streets. They were bestially drunk. I saw them smashing windows with empty vodka bottles. Terrifying orders thundered from loudspeakers placed on top of trucks that roamed up and down the Ghetto streets. We were ordered to go in groups of three from house to house*[40].

However, obviously the timing of this type of raid must have seemed excessive to the officers of the Sicherheitspolizei, including Blum, Fuchs, Feucht, Schippers and Kapke, so at some point, around half midnight, they ordered their men to break into the houses to speed up operations. At that point, all those who could not move fast enough – the elderly, sick, women with children – were killed on the spot, while all the others, many of which still half-naked, were forced to run on roads towards the collection points, amid gunshots and bursts of automatic weapons. In between the screaming and confusion, many families drifted apart on the way up to the collection points [41].

The final selection began at about two o'clock at night in the square in front of the Bata shoe factory, after all the houses had already been emptied and hundreds of murdered Jews were lying everywhere. According to the testimony of a survivor, holder of a work permit, a number of Jews, between 500 and 1,000, chosen from among the younger and healthier among those gathered in Kuszno Strasse, were separated from the others and then brought to the main ghetto under the escort of policemen. All the others, mainly women, children and those who appeared weaker, or whose work permit was not convincing for those who were selecting, were pushed to the collection point of Graniczna Strasse[42].

Chaim Styner's words describe what happened later:

> *The stream of thousands of people was funneled into Graniczna Street, which led to the railroad sidings. Along the route, on the sidewalks, the SS had taken up the battle position, kneeling behind machine guns. Others practiced sharpshooting at individual targets in the crowd, mostly children who were crying or who could not keep up with the pace. The crackling machine gun fire mingled with the horrible screams of the wounded. Hysterical and panic-stricken, the crowd stepped over the dead and wounded, who lay in pools of blood. At the railroad siding, Germans with drawn pistols forced the helpless people onto the waiting freight cars. Before entering, each person had to leave his or her belongings in neat piles upon the ground […]. One hundred and fifty people were thus crammed into each cattle-car*[43].

Then, when the raid seemed to be coming to an end, one of the Security Police officers responsible for the action realized that not all the wagons of one of the trains about to leave for Treblinka had been properly packed with the deported. Evidently, in obedience to some impulse of *efficiency* and *optimization of resources*, it was therefore decided to proceed with another raid, this time in some areas of the main ghetto, from which another 2,000 Jews were taken through a *kommando* of policemen led by Weinrich, Feucht, Schippers and Schöggl. Once these new victims were loaded, the train could finally leave with a proper load [44].

Overall, at least 5,000 Jews were deported to Treblinka on August 5, 1942; another 600/700 were killed during the raid, while between 500 and 1,000 were temporarily saved and transferred to the main ghetto. Many of these, the next day, were arranged into work brigades and sent to remove the bodies of the victims from the streets and houses of Glinice. They were later buried in a mass grave on land near the Lentz factory. A testimony given to the public prosecutor in Hamburg confirms this last phase of Glinice:

> *The guards escorted us to the Lentz property, in Ulica Biala, where hundreds of Jews were digging graves under the watchful eyes of the SS. A great number of bodies were lying face down. The Jews were forced to remove the clothing from the dead, search the pockets, remove rings and watches and sort out all items in separate piles. Böttcher and his staff, including officers Blum and Schippers, were everywhere, giving out detailed instructions as to how to lay the corpses in the ditches and other things like that. They repeatedly went close to the piles of valuables, selected the best jewelry items and loaded their pockets with them*[45].

The minor of two *problems* solved, it was now high time to deal with the main one.

13.6 SHEMA YISRAEL

As with Glinice, the end of the large ghetto also came with the light.

The powerful spotlights that had already lit the last night of the Jews of Glinice began to be installed in the streets of the large ghetto in the afternoon of Sunday, August 16, 1942. For the terrified survivors of Glinice, who had already experienced the traumatic experience, and for all the others who had seen them from afar, it was a clear sign of the impending inevitable[46].

Given the vastness of the ghetto and the number of inhabitants to mop up – about 25,000 – the action was divided in two phases: initially, the night between August 16 and 17, the western part would be hit, while the action in the eastern sector was postponed to the following night.

All police units were mobilized: Sonderkommando "Feucht", Polizei-Kompanie "München", the Ukrainians of Erich Kapke (Wachtkompanie / SSPF), the staff of SS-Veterinär-Ersatz-Kompanie "Radom" and SSPF, the Polish *Blaupolizisten* and the Schupo of Radom's command. Herbert Böttcher took control of the entire operation, along with KdS Fritz Liphardt and several members of his command[47]. Again, Feucht instructed the Jewish policemen to cooperate, threatening a bloodbath if they did not[48]. The *evacuation* plan implied that the Jews – who would be allowed to carry a single piece of luggage, food supplies for three days and all their valuables – would be initially concentrated in the large square Stare Miasto, to be later divided according to whether they possessed a work permit or not.

Promptly, at midnight, the raid began.

Alfred Lipson, head of the Jewish workers of a German factory located outside the ghetto who after the war became a researcher at the *Holocaust Resource Center and Archives in New York* describes that night, that he spent hiding in the factory together with his colleagues, after the spotlights had begun to illuminate the deserted streets of the ghetto with blades of light:

> *I had never before witnessed a pogrom or a battlefield, but the sounds reaching us from the Ghetto indicated a combination of both. The firing of machine guns, rifles, pistols, shouted commands, heartbreaking cries of children, panic-stricken shouts of mothers, all mixed into one terrible tragedy [...]. At about dawn we were not sure anymore whether that was reality or a horrible nightmare. It just could not*

be real, in the heart of civilized Europe, in plain view for the world.

Completely surrounded by a cordon of Polish and German policemen – both of Schupo and Friedrich Auerhammer's Polizei-Kompanie "München" – the ghetto was systematically rounded up over two consecutive days by 80-100 Ukrainians led by Kapke, by staff of SSPF including Weinrich, by the Sipo led by Fuchs and Feucht and by Heinrich Held's SS, accompanied by teams of the Ordnungsdienst. Every possible hiding place was raided, and all those who were caught or captured while trying to escape were taken to a nearby public park and shot in mass graves, together with the sick and the ill, who had remained in their homes as they were unable to follow their family members to the trains. Overall, during the raids and searches 1,000 to 1,500 Jews were killed[50]. Among the people shot at Pentz park there were also 59 patients from the Jewish Hospital[51]. According to a source, several children were slain by SS-Hauptscharführer Erich Schildt, a member of Sonderkommando "Feucht", with hand grenades[52].

This is how survivor Joseph Freeman describes the scene of the raid:

The SS chased us with dogs, constantly hitting and shoving us toward the marketplace. Their shots resounded through the streets. The sick, the elderly, the slow ones were killed […]. I saw old men in prayer shawls knelt, saying their final prayers as the SS stood behind them and shot them dead with their revolvers.

While some of us were chased, others were pushed into a large group […]. There we saw the SS throwing small children out of second and third storey windows. Some of them who had survived lay crying on the ground […]. The women who tried to protect their children were shot. In the horror we watched the crying, the bursts of machine guns, the bodies falling to the ground. We heard the Shema Yisrael prayer being murmured on the lips of the dying[53].

From various parts of the ghetto all the Jews rounded up reached the collection point of Stare Miasto, pushed with blows of a whip and under the threat of weapons. Here they were subjected to a rapid selection, depending on whether or not they possessed a work permit: the first were then driven to the Jewish hospital, while the latter were left near the headquarters of the Jewish police. At that point, the final selection of the Jews gathered around the hospital began, on the basis of their working *usefulness* and their physical condition, but very often also based on the free will of the selectors: in this way about 3,000 Jews were saved, temporarily retained in the courtyard of the Gelka tannery in Szwarlikowskastrasse, destined to be locked in a *restghetto* later. As ascertained by the public prosecutor in Hamburg, the selection was controlled directly by Weinrich[54].

Let's keep on reading Freeman:

The selecting and killing went on for hours. Meanwhile, the SS took approximately one hundred young men from our group and put them to work collecting the dead strewn everywhere in pools of blood, dragging them onto horse wagons, piling them on top of each other. The wagons full of corpses were driven from the ghetto and the bodies were buried in a large ditch at Pentz Garden […].

We stood for hours in the middle of the marketplace […]. Some of us passed away from hunger and exhaustion. The rest of us prayed, looking to the sky […]. We wondered if we would be next. At 5:30 in the evening, the SS told those of us who remained to go back home[55].

While the selection proceeded, some 20,000 victims began to be piled on the trains with destination Treblinka[56], on one of which, among the last to leave on August 18, the Jewish orphanage children with their nurses and the staff that took care of them were also loaded. On the same day nearly all the surviving members of the *Judenrat* and the Ordnungsdienst were also deported[57].

As confirmed by several witnesses, the surveillance of victims during the boarding on trains as well as the escort of the same trains up to Treblinka, was entrusted to the staff of Polizei-Kompanie "München"[58]. Some years later, on December 29, 1972, at the request of the public prosecutor in Hamburg, the case against Friedrich Auerhammer and other members of the company was suspended and then permanently filed.

We report the reconstruction of the events of August 16, 1942 in Radom, extracted from the final judgment of the Court of Hamburg against Weinrich and others:

> *Sunday, August 16, 1942, the evening approaching, the large ghetto was sealed off by some departments, including those of German Schutzpolizei. At around midnight, members of the SS and men of the Ordnungsdienst began to order the Jewish population, shouting out loud, to leave their homes. Amid screams and beatings the SS brought the Jews to the Stare Miasto square. All those who could not run fast enough or fell to the ground were brutally killed. In the Stare Miasto square a selection took place whose purpose was to separate those fit for work, who would remain in Radom, from those who were unable to work and were destined for deportation to an extermination camp. The selection was made by SS members. Those who were in possession of work permits were generally deemed fit and then brought into the yard of the Gelka tannery, located on the Stare Miasto. All other Jews were transferred under guard to the train station and in part along the stretch of a track inside the area of a factory in Mary-Wilska-Straße, where they were loaded on board some waiting freight cars. In the early morning at least 100 Jews capable of work, among those gathered in the Gelka tannery were brought to the Pentz gardens, where they were forced to dig large pits in which the Jews killed during the action, who had meanwhile been brought up there, were buried in layers after being stripped of their clothes. During the morning, groups of elderly and sick Jews were brought to the graves and then killed by SS members. Their bodies were also buried in mass graves*[59].

13.7 REVENUES AND COSTS: THE BALANCE

On June 18, 1942, during a meeting in Krakow chaired by Hans Frank between the governors of the district and the main commanders of the SS and of the police in the General Government, the progress of Aktion Reinhardt, now in full swing, were examined and appreciated. In fact, with regard to the district of Radom, there was some discontent because, at that date, none of the numerous deportations, whose completion would finally represent the removal of the Hebrew *burden* almost everywhere in the General Government, had been carried out. This drawback, that the district vice-governor Alfons Oswald had rushed to attribute to a mere "transport problem"[60], was soon overcome with the arrival in Radom of Wilhelm Josef Blum, *the solver* sent by Globocnik to coordinate with Böttcher during the planning phase of the roundups in ghettos and subsequent deportation to Treblinka. With the arrival of Blum, therefore, the small team of genocide specialists, efficient, professional and utterly determined to obtain the best results, compatibly with the resources available, was complete. Like skilled managers, these men fixed the target, set the timetable, planned the procedures, and finally allocated the assets. The operation, in the end, was a success proved by the results: the *revenues* were at least 25,000 Jews deported to Treblinka, about another 2,000 *liquidated* on the spot and perhaps 3,000 kept alive as a useful resource to be reused in the war economy, in addition, of course, to portions of urban areas *liberated* to be later converted if necessary into more profitable uses than those guaranteed by a Jewish ghetto; the *costs* amounted to five days of work, perhaps 500 men mobilized and half a dozen trains in motion. The balance was a substantial *net profit* for *SSPF Böttcher Aktiengesellschaft*.

Except that, some years after the closure of the *genocidal accounting year 1942*, what in retrospect turned out to be real *deferred costs,* began to emerge.

In fact, unlike many major perpetrators who after the war were not called to pay the bill for their crimes, or paid it with a discount mainly because of the legal mechanisms adopted by the courts and the Federal Republic public prosecutors, in the case of Radom, and by extension in the case of the many deportations perpetrated throughout the district in autumn 1942, several major leaders faced heavy sentences, imposed mainly by courts of Poland, where they were extradited immediately after the war. The following are details regarding some of those who were tried in Poland after the war and who played a leading role in the two deportations from the ghetto in Radom[61]:

BÖTTCHER, Herbert, born April 24, 1907 in Proküls (Priekulė), south of Memel. A member of NSDAP from 1933 and an SS member from 1939. SS-Obersturmbannführer from August 1, 1940 and SS-Standartenführer from October 9, 1941. Polizeipräsident of Kassel from October 1940 to May 1942. SSPF "Radom" from May 12, 1942 to January 16, 1945. Decorated with KVK I and KVK II. Main organizer of the deportations of Jews to Treblinka in the district of Radom, he managed to reach Essen immediately after the war, but subjected to investigation by British military police, he was recognized by witnesses and arrested in 1946. Extradited to Poland, Radom was placed on trial and sentenced to death on June 18, 1949, a judgment executed by hanging on June 12, 1950.

BLUM, Wilhelm Josef: born April 30, 1890 in Dellwig, a suburb of Essen. NSDAP member from 1930 and SS member from 1931. SS-Sturmbannführer from 1942 and SS-Obersturmbannführer from 1943. An official in the Stab of Odilo Globocnik's SSPF "Lublin" from November 27, 1941 and Chief of Staff at SSPF "Radom" Böttcher from August 1, 1942. At the end of the war he was extradited to Poland by the British zone of occupation on August 28, 1946. Tried by a Polish court, he was sentenced to death on August 19, 1947, a judgment executed by hanging in Radom on April 10, 1948.

LIPHARDT, Fritz: born May 3, 1905 in Szczecin. NSDAP member from May 1, 1933 and SS member from November 15, 1936. SS-Obersturmbannführer. Commander of 2/III Einsatzkommando in Poland from September 2, 1939 (area of Lodz). KdS in Radom from November 1939 to September 18, 1943, the date when he was moved to Szczecin as a result of conflicts of competence with SSPF Böttcher,[62]. Captured in Poland after the war, he was held in Szczecin and committed suicide in his cell in autumn 1947[63].

In addition to the Polish one, the West German Justice system also became interested in the events of Radom and all the districts in general, on the initiative of ZStL, which as early as 1959, through its Referat 206, began to investigate the crimes perpetrated in various parts of the district by different departments and facilities, including Sicherheitspolizei, Ordnungspolizei, civil administration, etc. Consequently, a voluminous dossier was opened, filed as ZStL 206 AR-Z 15/65, containing the names of hundreds of suspects. This dossier, then transmitted from Ludwigsburg to different competent prosecutors on a territorial basis, served as the core for subsequent preliminary investigations, initiated in the mid-sixties.

With regard to the two deportations from the ghetto in Radom on August 4 and 16, 1942, the prosecution involved was mainly that of Hamburg, through the dossier StAw Hamburg 147 Js 38/65, which made reference to all the main culprits identified, several of whom, however, were later withdrawn from the investigation – because of disease, suicide or other causes – so they never came to receive the final judgment in 1973 by the Hamburg court.

The following are details of some of those who were included in the dossier of the public prosecutor in Hamburg:

WEINRICH, Hermann: born May 20, 1902 in Gelsenkirchen. NSDAP member from January 1, 1929 and SS member from April 20, 1929. SS-Hauptsturmführer from July 28, 1942. Personalreferent at the Stab SSPF "Radom" commanded by Böttcher. Investigated after the war by ZStL with dossier 206 AR-Z 15/65, he was subjected to preliminary investigations by the public prosecutor in Hamburg with dossier

StAw Hamburg 147 Js 38/65, in connection with three murder cases[64]. Trialed by the Court of Hamburg, on February 5, 1973 he was sentenced to seven years in prison (LG Hamburg 50 - 13/72).

KAPKE, Erich: born May 29, 1898 in Belgard, Pomerania. NSDAP and SS member. SS Untersturmführer. Officer at Stab SSPF "Radom" in the role of "responsible for Jewish affairs (*Referent für Jüdische Angelegenheiten*)", as well as commander of the auxiliary company (*Wachtkompanie*) available to SSPF. Heavily involved in all the deportations that took place in the district from autumn 1942 and through all of 1943, he was investigated after the war by ZStL with dossier 206 AR-Z 15/65 and then subjected to preliminary investigations by the public prosecutor of Hamburg with dossier StAw Hamburg 147 js 38/65, in connection with three murder cases[65]. Placed on trial by the Court of Hamburg, he was declared unfit to stand trial because of failing health. For this reason, after a temporary suspension of the trial, the case against him was finally filed with Court judgment of February 5, 1973 in Hamburg (LG Hamburg 50-13 / 72).

NELL, Paul: Born August 29, 1899 in Cammin, Pomerania. SS member with the rank of SS-Untersturmführer. Officer at the Stab SSPF "Radom" with the role of "officer for Jewish issues (*Sachbearbeiter für Jüdische Angelegenheiten*)", in the summer of 1942 he was ordered by Böttcher to organize the ZAL of Szkolnastrasse in Radom, of which he was commander until March 1943. On that date he was given the task of organizing a second labor camp, ZAL Bliżyn, which he commanded until early 1944. By virtue of his role he was heavily involved in the deportations of autumn 1942, particularly as regards the transfer of Jews to the Szkolnastrasse camp selected as *fit for work*. In 1948, during the denazification phase, he was sentenced two years in prison by Recklinghausen's Spruchkammer, only one of which he actually served. Investigated after the war by ZStL with dossier 206 AR-Z 15/65, he was subjected to preliminary investigations by the prosecutor in Hamburg with dossier, in relation to ten murder cases[66]. Placed on trial by the Court of Hamburg, he was sentenced to life imprisonment on July 12, 1973. This judgment was quashed on January 28, 1975 by the Bundesgerichtshof with a subsequent revision of the process taking place, again before the Court of Hamburg. Accused of the murder of at least 12 people in the camp of Bliżyn, he was finally sentenced to life imprisonment on October 3, 1977[67].

FUCHS, Paul: Born June 19, 1908 in Höchst bei Frankfurt. He joined the NSDAP in 1941. SS member ranking SS-Hauptsturmführer. Gestapo official in Munich and then Darmstadt, he held the command of Gestapo's Außenstelle in Mainz from 1938 until September 1939, when he was assigned to EK 2/II during the invasion of Poland. Member of KdS "Radom", as director of Referat IVA (*Gegner, Sabotage, Schutzdienst*), in October 1942 he also received the direction of Referat IVN (*Nachrichtendienst*)[68]. Heavily involved in the roundups of Jews during the spring of 1942, as well as the repression of clandestine movements, he succeeded in organizing a vast network of agents and informers at the service of the Gestapo, who put him in contact with elements of Polish ultranationalists among whom, in early 1945, he managed to recruit several saboteurs who parachuted behind Soviet lines (SS-Jagdeinsatz "Polen")[69]. According to one version, endorsed by some of his former colleagues in Radom, in the final phase of the conflict he managed to retreat to Czechoslovakia and then Salzburg from where he eventually reached the area of Munich. Included on the wanted list of the *Counter Intelligence Corp* (CIC), he knew important people and had relations with the G-2 Section of the U.S. Army and, perhaps, with the Gehlen organization: such contacts, it seems, would guarantee his impunity against the CIC investigators[70]. This version was later refuted by Fuchs himself, who admitted only to having been in Germany under a false name until he was tracked down by ZStL investigators who inserted his name into a first dossier called 206 AR-Z 15/65 that was forwarded to the public prosecutor in Hamburg, as well as in the following two dossiers sent to the competent prosecutor of Augsburg (206 AR-Z 40/65) and Darmstadt (206 AR-Z 15/67). None of these practices, however, ended with a conviction: in the case of Hamburg, after the indictment of Fuchs with dossier StAw Hamburg 147 Js 38/65, the subsequent trial ended on February 5, 1973 with a judgment of acquittal. In the case of Augsburg, after 12 years of investigation, the dossier StAw Augsburg 7 Js 85/65 was filed by the prosecutor due to lack of evidence on March 19, 1976. Finally, for the same reasons and without even being trialed, Darmstadt's dossier was filed on January 3, 1978[71].

AUERHAMMER, Friedrich, commander of Polizei-Kompanie "München", was heavily involved with his company in the August 1942 deportations from Radom, as well as those in the ghettos of Szydlowiec and Satachowice in September / October 1942. The same company, reorganized in January 1943 as 9/III/Polizei-Regiment 23, also took part in the suppression of the Warsaw uprising. Based on evidence collected in the dossier ZStL 206 AR-Z 15/65 against Auerhammer and other members of Polizei-Kompanie "München" the StAw Hamburg 147 Js 7/69 dossier was opened on the initiative of the public prosecutor in Hamburg which, however, ended up being filed with the decision of December 29, 1972. For his part, during the trial against Fuchs and Weinrich, Auerhammer was called to testify as a person informed of the facts[72].

Besides those who were investigated and eventually convicted, some other key leaders of the deportations from Radom in August 1942 who for various reasons could not be called into question should be mentioned:

WANDEL, Lothar: born January 10, 1902 in Löetzen, East Prussia. SS member ranking SS-Sturmbannführer. Investigated by the SD of Dresden, Wandel was subjected to two disciplinary proceedings that substantially cost him the punitive transfer to Poland. Assigned to KdS "Radom" with the role of director of Abteilung III (later IV) by the Gestapo from March 1941 to April 1944, he came into conflict with both his supervisor Liphardt and his subordinate Fuchs[73]. SS-Standgericht President, during his service in Radom he issued several hundred death sentences. Transferred to the Dresden Gestapo in December 1944, after the war he remained for a short period in Dittersdorf, Saxony, from where he passed to the West and reached Berlin in July 1945. Arrested by Berlin's police in July 12, 1945, he was handed over to British authorities who locked him up in the Eselheide *Civil Internment Camp* until June 1947. There is no evidence that he was ever subjected to investigations, but before his death – which was sometime after 1964 – he had time to testify as a person informed of the facts, during the trial against Weinrich and others.

FEUCHT, Adolf: born May 7, 1909 in Malmsheim, near Stuttgart. NSDAP and SS member. SS-Hauptsturmführer from April 20, 1942. Transferred to Poland in September 1939 as a member of Einsatzkommando V/2, he was sent to Czestochowa the following October as director of Stapo-Aussendienststelle "Tschenstochau"; in this position he had a crucial role in the persecution of the so-called Jewish and Polish *intelligentsia*. Then, in mid-1942 he was moved to KdS "Radom" as a member of Referat III (later IV) Gestapo, as well as commander of Sonderkommando "Feucht"[74]. By virtue of his genocidal *merits*, from October 1, 1942 he became commander of Referat IVB (formerly IIIb). In late October he also received the direction of Referaten C, D and W[75]. In his position he was heavily involved in the deportations from the ghetto in Radom and from all the other ghettos in the district: his role, in particular, would be one of coordination between the various agencies taking part in the deportations, including private economic enterprises that were encouraged to employ Jewish workers in order to keep them busy and then catch them in the imminence of the *action* [76]. Transferred towards the end of 1944 to KdS "Reichenberg" – Hauptaussenstelle "Karlsbad" – he was killed on May 8, 1945 near Glatz, Silesia[77].

SCHÖGGL, Richard: born January 16, 1899 in Neu-Erlaa bei Wien. NSDAP member from July 1, 1931, SS member ranking SS-Untersturmführer. Director of IVB Referat 4 (Jews), he was Feucht's deputy to Referat IVB[78]. There is no further information about him.

SCHIPPERS, Hans: born September 23, 1914 in Rheydt. NSDAP member from March 1, 1935 and SS member from November 1, 1933. SS-Untersturmführer. Officer at Stab SSPF "Radom", apparently as Böttcher's Sportreferent, he took part with Böttcher and Blum in the organization of the ghetto in June 1942. Heavily involved in the deportations to Treblinka, as well as in the selection of Jews unable to work and locked up in the ghetto of Skarzisko Kamiena, in the autumn of 1942 he was appointed commander of the *restghetto* of Radom and in March 1943 of the ZAL in Szkolnastrasse[79]. After the war he managed to disappear without a trace. He was pronounced dead by a judgment of the District Court of Rheydt on April 21, 1954, with acknowledgment by the public prosecutor in Hamburg on December 14, 1971[80].

13.8 THE MIDAS TOUCH

> *I hereby order that the resettlement of the entire Jewish population of the General Government be implemented and completed by December 31, 1942. As of December 31, there must not be any more elements of Jewish origin in the General Government, unless they are already in the collection camps of Warsaw, Krakow, Czestochowa, Radom and Lublin*[81].

With this order, sent by Himmler to HSSPF Krüger on July 19, 1942, after his visit to SSPF Globocnik in Lublin, the resident genocide was formally launched in the General Government: a real official license issued to cover the numerous massacres and especially the massive deportations to death camps perpetrated ever since the previous spring, especially in the district of Lublin and in Galicia. A stroke of pen and a few bureaucratic lines – which would find complete fulfillment only within the autumn of 1943 – sealed the fate of hundreds of thousands of Jews, at least 350,000 of whom in the district of Radom, in August 1942, before the deportations to Treblinka began: of these, only a small minority – in the region of a few thousand – escaped the genocide and the causes of death related to it. The Jews of Radom who survived the war were very few, maybe 300 out of about 32,000[82].

The structures that bear greatest responsibilities for this catastrophe were those belonging to district SSPF – Böttcher in the case of Radom – which, on Himmler's orders, imposed their authority over other forces of occupation: KdS and KdO. At the same time, however, without the presence of the latter structures, the resolution of the *Jewish question* in the district and more generally throughout the whole General Government would have been virtually impossible. The role of Ordnungspolizei in particular, through its various subdivisions – mobile companies and battalions, Schutzpolizei, gendarmerie, etc. – was essential, especially in those operations in which there was no need for any special *technical* skill or intelligence, but instead required an adequate number of faithful and conscientious workers. In this sense, after the arrival of Böttcher in Radom in May 1942, all departments belonging to KdO were included in the extermination machine, without this measure arousing any apparent anxiety among authorities and Ordnungspolizei staff[83]. In fact, as a mechanism that was perfectly integrated into the bureaucratic machine – in this case focused on Project Genocide – the Ordnungspolizei was considered one of the tools available and nothing but the disciplined and punctual performance of any task assigned from time to time was expected from it. As Hilberg astutely pointed out as early as 1985, "any member of Ordnungspolizei could be assigned as a guard in a ghetto or a train [...]. In other words, all necessary operations were performed using the staff at its disposal, [from which], no obstacle was placed that could immobilize the German gear of destruction, [for which], no moral problem proved insurmountable"[84].

So, basically, it was not a problem of men, projects or resources, nor one of moral affliction to affect the implementation of the Jewish genocide, it was rather a matter of timing in the execution of what was one of the strategic objectives of the Nazi regime: the ultimate resolution of the *Jewish question*, which for a variety of reasons – from ideological postulates to operational decisions going through the peripheral dynamics – was implemented by means of physical extermination. A *solution* that in a fundamentally immoral regime, served by an inherently amoral bureaucracy, inevitably, at some point, was bound to appear as wholly rational and feasible.

Thus, since autumn 1941 in Russia and then officially since July 19 in the General Government, absolute violence was institutionalized and praised as the best solution: rapid, radical and, especially, irreversible. A violence that would be applied with rational methods, which involved, on the side of the perpetrators, a large number of individuals willing to fulfill any task assigned to them: individuals who were part of structures in no way abnormal or pathological, individuals who indeed were quite ordinary and proved willing to commit brutal atrocities, beyond any moral inhibition. Through a process of rapid exponential growth, in that spring / summer 1942 one witnessed the emergence of absolute violence as a dogma, freed from what still remained of social defenses. Dramatically, however, the violence that emerged was not a direct consequence of the barbarization of the conflict, the result of a lack of alternatives or a pathological deviation, but rather an extreme consequence in the evolutionary process of a civil society confronted with its darkest side, which dictated choices that were cruel but well thought over, applied at the time that was considered most appropriate and feasible. In this context, apart from some special cases, the perpetrators were not sadistic psychopaths, but an integrated part of society. Many of them, especially middle echelons within the hierarchy, were precise bureaucrats who performed their work aseptically, applying Weber's patterns on the efficiency of bureaucracy. It can be said, in this sense, that the Jewish genocide was a product of its time: the time of primacy of factory and production. Quoting Bauman, the Jewish genocide was a result of modernity, ethically immoral but coldly rational. In this sense, just like factories assembled objects, extermination camps produced death: death as the final and extreme product of modernity. Man as a gear to be replaced in case of failure or for a strategic decision.

Yet, another ingredient was necessary for this architecture to hold on and function. This ingredient, as Hilberg noted, was the "interaction between performers of the crimes and their victims"[85]. Reiterating what happened in Radom, in both August 1942 raids the members of the Ordnungsdienst followed their *Herrmenschen* into their victims' homes, forcing them to obey, to line up the streets and get on the trains. After that, their usefulness extinguished, even *Ordnungsmännern* were largely selected and deported or killed in mass graves, as well as members of the Jewish Councils. Again, beyond the dispute regarding the alleged collaborationism of these victims with their tormentors, one cannot help but notice the extent reached by the Nazis in their titanic effort of rationalization of resources and execution of tasks. It seems very appropriate to use Bauman's words: "If the Midas touch turned everything into gold, the SS administration turned everything that was falling into its orbit – including victims – into an integral part of the chain of command, in an area subject to strict disciplinary rules and released from moral judgment [...]. This reveals the technical superiority of a mass murder deliberately planned and rationally organized"[86].

But while the result of Midas' touch was gold, the product of the *genocide Lords* was death.

ENDNOTES

1 «This Jews' expulsion now only depends on transportation problems». Seidel, p. 298.

2 Seidel, p. 311. StAw Hamburg 147 Js 38/65.

3 Henry L. Feingold. *How Unique is the Holocaust?* In *Genocide: Critical Issue of the Holocaust,* p. 399.

4 Christopher Browning: *Ordinary Men: Reserve Police Battalion 101 and the Final Solution in Poland.* 1992.

5 See Chap. 14.

6 Browning, p. 50.

7 Musial, p. 215.

8 Apart from the 32,000 Jews of the Radom ghetto, there were

18-20,000 in the ghetto of Kielce and 50,000 more in that of Czestochowa. Seidel, pp. 313, 315.

9 Seidel. p. 313.

10 Herbert C. Kelman: *Violence without moral restraint: Reflections on the dehumanization of victims and victimizers.* In *Journal of Social Issues, 29(4),* pp. 38 ff., pp. 46 ff., pp. 48 ff.

11 Limiting to Ordnungspolizei, see for example the genocidal zeal of von Woyrsch's police departments in the Krakow area, in September 1939 and the ideological inebriation boasted by Polizei-Bataillon 309 in Bialystok, in June 1941. On von Woyrsch see Alexander B. Rossino: *Nazi Anti-Jewish Policy During the Polish Campaign. The Case of the Einsatzgruppe von Woyrsch,* in *German Studies Review, XXIV/1,* pp. 35-53. On the Bialystok massacre, see Chap. 1.

12 See Seidel, pp. 329-330, who reports a minimum of about 338,000 victims and a maximum of about 341,000, the vast majority of which (97 %) were deported to the extermination camps (essentially Treblinka) and the rest were *liquidated* on site. For the same period, Arad (pp. 39 ff.) quotes a total of about 380,000 victims.

13 Blum had officially been in Globocnik's commando until July 1942; after that, on August 1 he was transferred from Lublin to Radom, where he was appointed CSM in Böttcher's staff. See Seidel, p. 304. It is very plausible then, that Blum's task was to coordinate the start of deportations from Radom according to Globocnik's programs and Treblinka's *disposal* capacity.

14 The difference between *Referent* and *Sachbearbeiter* was basically hierarchical, the first being superior in rank to the second, but the former role had the main responsibility for the tasks assigned. In the event of equal rank, as with Kapke and Nell, the years in service made the difference.

15 Seidel, pp. 63-66. According to Karay, p. 35, Schippers' role was communication official.

16 Seidel, pp. 67 ff.

17 In late October 1942, Abteilung III Gestapo became Abteilung IV Gestapo. Seidel, p. 69, Borodziej, p. 57.

18 Seidel, p. 67. Wandel stayed in charge of Abteilung III (later IV) Gestapo, from March 1, 1941 to summer 1944. Borodziej, p. 65.

19 According to Borodziej, p. 49, there was a strong rivalry between Fuchs and Wandel, to the point that the first regularly bypassed the second, referring directly to KdS Liphardt.

20 Seidel, pp. 75 ff.

21 Testimony by Hermann Altmann, former commander of Stapo-Aussendienststelle "Petrikau", given before ZStL. Seidel, p. 303.

22 Seidel, pp. 67-68.

23 As Borodzjei points out, p. 50, an example of such a *redeemed* figure is represented by SSPF Odilo Globocnik himself who, after being accused of corruption and relocated to Vienna as punishment, gained great *genocidal credits* during his service in Lublin.

24 Seidel, p. 303. Conclusions of ZStL 206 AR-Z 15/65 dated April 13, 1965.

25 *Ibid.*, p. 312-313. ZStL 206 AR-Z 15/65. Testimonies by Friedrich Auerhammer, Johann Drexler, Markus Beer and Johann Reichl.

26 *Ibid.*, p. 303. ZStL 206 AR-Z 15/65. StAw Hamburg, 147 Js 38/65, Anklageschrift December 14, 1971.

27 Seidel, pp. 66, 303, 338, 341-343, 347, 357.

28 Seidel, p. 312.

29 Cüppers, pp. 285, 423. Testimony by Mojzesz Goldberg before Nuremberg's NMT, Vol. XX, Session 196, p. 314.

30 Testimony by Mojzesz Goldberg before Nuremberg's NMT, vol. XX, Session 196, p. 314.

31 Seidel, p. 312.

32 Borodziej, p. 37, Seidel, p. 83.

33 Arendt, pp. 77, 113, quoting Eichmann's words during the Jerusalem trial.

34 The guidelines for the institution of the ghettos in the Radom district had been established by district governor Karl Lasch on March 19, 1941 and complied with by Kujath, in the case of Radom, the following April 3. See Seidel, pp. 238-239. Lipson, p. 42.

35 They are Kriegsberichter Bruno Wisniewski, member of an SS-Propagandakompanie which travelled around Poland in 1940, and Kriegsberichter Brenner of Propagandakompanie 666, who followed him to Radom in March 1941, that is a few weeks before the official establishment of the ghetto. BAB Bild 146-1994-071-08>; Bild 146-1994-072-12>; Bild 101I-030-0794-01A>; Bild 101I-030-0795-03A>; Bild 101I-030-0797-28>.

36 Seidel, p. 238. The Ordnungsdienst was established on April 4, 1941 on SSPF orders, on a basis of three men every 1,000 inhabitants, equipped with truncheon, a cap with the star of David and an armband bearing the *Jüdische Ordnungsdienst* Inscription. Essentially, young Radom Jews aged at least 21, who had already served in the Polish Army before September 1939 were selected. Then, in order to make up for the vacancies left because of the frequent arrests, elements of nearby localities were "drafted", some of whom were considered to be Gestapo informers. Lipson, pp. 42-43.

37 Seidel, pp. 301-302, Lipson, pp. 49, 52. Among the so-called *intellectuals* there were members of religious institutions, those who worked in ritual butchering and preparation of *kosher* food [!].

38 Indictment of the public prosecutor in Hamburg, Seidel, p. 310.

39 Lipson, p. 52.

40 Lipson, pp. 52-53.

41 Testimony by M. Friedman, Lipson, p. 53. Seidel, p. 310.

42 Testimony by J. Manela, Lipson, p. 53. Seidel, pp. 310-311.

43 Lipson, p. 53.

44 Seidel, p. 311, Wein/Freundlich/Orbach, p. 541, Lipson, p. 54.

45 Testimony by Israel Zaidenweber, Lipson, p. 53.

46 Lipson, p. 54.

47 Seidel, p. 312.

48 Lipson, p. 55.

49 *Ibid.*, p. 55.

50 StAw Hamburg, 147 Js 38/65, Anklageschrift December 14, 1971. Act of suspension of the proceedings of the public prosecutor of Hamburg in the investigations against Auerhammer and others, StAw Hamburg, 147 Js 7/69 dated December 29, 1972. Sentence of the Court of Hamburg against Weinrich and others. Seidel, p. 312.

51 Seidel, p. 311, Lipson, p. 57.

52 Radom Ghetto, in ARC.

53 Freeman, p. 23.

54 StAw Hamburg, 147 Js 38/65, Anklageschrift December 14, 1971.

55 Freeman, p. 26.

56 StAw Hamburg, 147 Js 38/65, Anklageschrift December 14, 1971.

57 Lipson, p. 57.

58 Testimonies by Johann Drexler, Markus Beer and Johann Reichl collected by ZstL, in particular during the preliminary investigations against Weinrich and others. Seidel, p. 313.

59 LG Hamburg (50) 13/72, of February 5, 1973.

60 Seidel, p. 298.

61 For the complete list of those extradited to Poland who were involved in the deportations from the entire Radom district see Seidel, p. 373-374.

62 The rivalry in the district of Radom between KdS and SSPF, and within KdS was such that it could be solved only through and inspection on site by Heinrich Müller, supreme Gestapo commander, at Berlin's RSHA. Borodziej, p. 49.

63 MacLean, pp. 25, 85, Seidel, p. 67.

64 StAw Hamburg, 147 Js 38/65, Anklageschrift December 14, 1971.

65 *Ibid.*

66 *Ibid.*

67 Seidel, pp. 66, 356-358, 375, 378.

68 Borodziej, pp. 65-70.

69 *Ibid.*, p. 258, Morgan, pp. 251, 253.

70 Morgan, pp. 253-255.

71 Borodziej, pp. 266-267.

72 Seidel, p. 312.

73 Borodziej, p. 65, Seidel, p. 71.

74 Seidel, pp. 72, 74.

75 Borodziej, pp. 67-68, Seidel, p. 72.

76 Seidel, p. 304. Ricostruction by ZStL 206 AR-Z 15/65.

77 Seidel, p. 373. StAw Augsburg, 7 Js 85/65, Anklageschrift.

78 *Ibid.*, p. 72.

79 In autumn 1942 the Radom *restghetto* was basically formed by the survivors of the two August *actions,* gathered in a camp in Szwarlikowskastrasse and used as forced labor. The camp was *liquidated* on January 13, 1943 and some of the survivors were transferred to the ZAL of Szkolnastrasse, a labor camp adjacent to an arms factory of the Steyr-Daimler-Puch group, subordinated to SSPF and commanded by Paul Nell.

80 Seidel, pp. 66, 304, 321, 338, 341, 356, 372.

81 *Ibid.*, p. 296, Musial, p. 284.«*Ich ordne an, dass die Umsiedlung der gesamten jüdischen Bevölkerung des Generalgouvernements bis 31 Dezember 1942 durchgeführt und beendet ist. Mit dem 31. Dezember dürfen sich keinerlei Personen jüdischer Herkunft mehr im Generalgouvernement aufhalten. Es sei denn, dass sie sich in den Sammellagern Warschau, Krakau, Tschenstochau, Radom, Lublin aufhalten.*

82 Seidel, p. 370.

83 *Ibid.*, p. 393.

84 Hilberg, pp. 1141-1142.

85 *Ibid.*, p. 1161.

86 Bauman, p. 43.

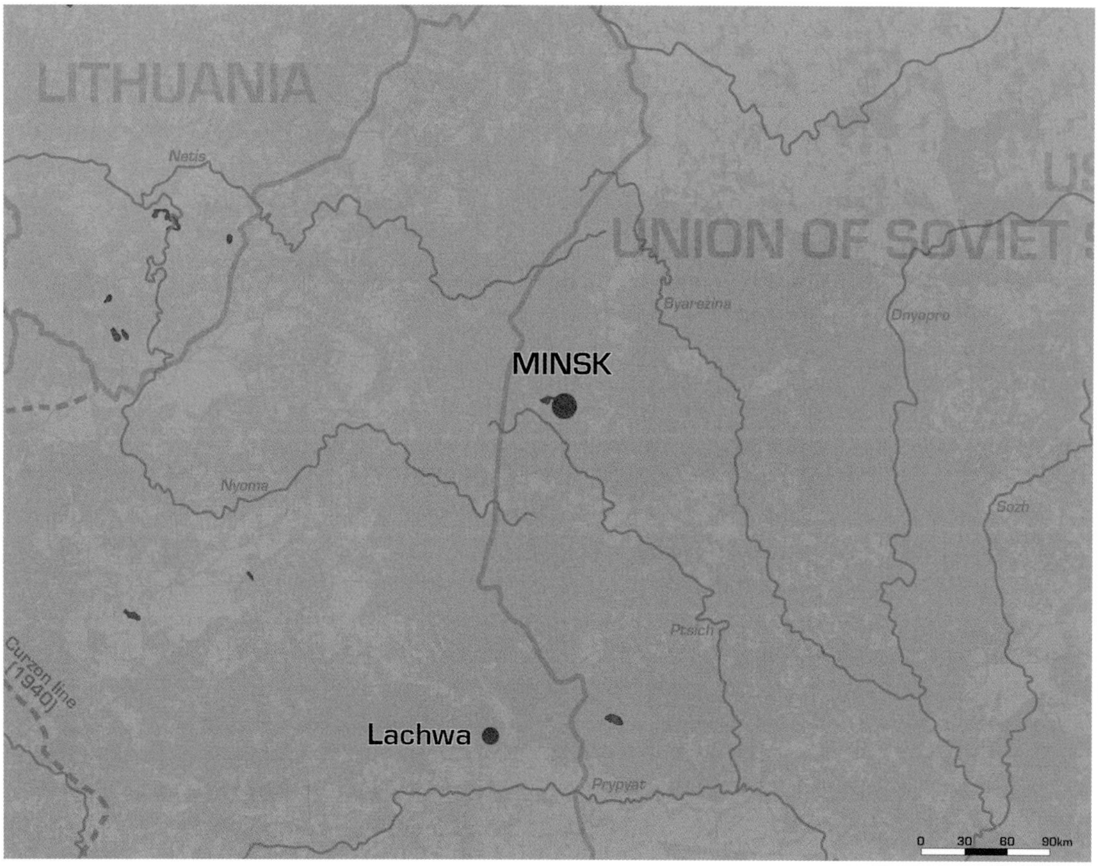
LITHUANIA
UNION OF SOVIET S
Natis
Byarezina
Dnyapro
MINSK
Nyoma
Sozh
Ptsich
Curzon line (1940)
Lachwa
Prypyat
0 30 60 90km

CHAPTER FOURTEEN

"THAT VILLAGE IN THE SWAMP"

LACHWA, SEPTEMBER 3, 1942

Then one night in desperation
A young man breaks away
He buys a gun, steals a car,
Tries to run, but he dont get far

M. Mac Davis/E. Presley
– In the Ghetto, 1969

14.1 TRACING A LINE. FEBRUARY 6, 1973

Gerhard Ott was 13 years of age when the crime was committed, on September 3, 1942. He was probably a young member of the Hitlerjugend who could never have imagined that 31 years later he would be called to give evidence against a group of men who, at the time of his compulsory militancy among the Führer's youth, he would address with the deference of a young boy towards officers in uniform.

Three decades later, outside of a classroom of the Court of Frankfurt am Main, the chief prosecutor Gerhard Ott awaited the decision of the court, presided over by Judge Adalbert Schaefer. The decision pending was in regard to the indictment against some members of Polizei-Bataillon 306, Polizei-Reiter-Abteilung II and SD-Außenstelle "Pinsk", charged with killing about 20,000 Jews at different sites in southern Belarus, and about 5,000 Soviet prisoners of war in Huisinka, Poland. Around him, gathered in clusters along the dimly lit hallway, a half-dozen spectators commented on the events of that hectic day that would mark the conclusion of a proceeding that had lasted over 10 years, including pre-trial investigations and trial proper. In their indictment, the prosecutor Ott and his collaborator, Roth, had insisted on charges of "joint complicity in murder (*gemeinschaftlichen Beihilfe zum Mord*)", excluding any hypothesis of *Befehlsnotstand* and granting the defendants, as the sole extenuating circumstance, the acknowledgment of the subjugation of the police structure to criminal orders coming from the Nazi government. For this reason, Ott did not sue simple policemen of the battalion because they were recognized as mere executors of orders, and instead focused his attention only on those few who had command responsibilities. During an interview given after the indictment, Ott declared "to have drawn a line between those who received the orders and those who gave them". Otherwise, he added, "there would be 300 to 400 defendants before the Court" [1] resulting in the high probability that none of them would be convicted. Thus, having concentrated merely on those mostly responsible for the killings, the two attorneys, with their stringent but admissible requests for conviction, believed their indictments had good *chances* before the judge. Of the eighteen defendants originally brought to trial twelve were exempted or could not be judged upon due to their death or other reasons. Only six defendants were left: Heinrich Plantius, Johann Josef Kuhr, Rudolf Karl Eckert, Heinrich Groß, Hans-Dieter Teltz and Adolf Petsch. According to the indictment of the prosecutor Ott, during the hearings none of them had demonstrated any sign of remorse or compassion towards the victims and instead had continued to assert their innocence, describing themselves as scapegoats. All this in spite of the accumulation of evidence against them by former comrades and by many Soviet citizens during the investigations related to the court trial that had started on November 25, 1971. The evidence given by Soviet citizens was collected in Kobryn, Belarus, during a long visit to the crime scene, performed by the entire Court (nine judges and jurors, the two prosecutors and twelve defense lawyers), in agreement with the General Prosecution of the Soviet Union[2].

It had been a long and complicated process, made difficult by the replacement – at some point – of the Court President, Judge Wolf Schwalbe, with Adalbert Schaefer[3]. Almost the same age as Ott, Schaefer had also served for the Reich, 31 years earlier, as an auxiliary in an anti-aircraft battery[4]. And, like Ott, he too was now called upon to judge men who, at that time, he probably regarded with respect.

14.2 INTO THE WILDE

The destruction of the Jewish community of Lachwa, as well as several other locations in the Pinsk area, perpetrated in autumn 1942, involved a diverse set of structures, united into what can be considered as a real genocidal synergy. In particular, the local detachment of Sicherheitspolizei, some departments of Ordnungspolizei and auxiliary contingents of Ukrainian and Polish nationalities employed by SS-und Polizeigebietführer, Ltn. Leo Tessmann, took part in the operations of mopping-up, transportation and execution of the victims. The offices and the civilian personnel of Gebietkommissar Paul Gerhard Klein also had a role in the running of the ghetto.

14.2.1 – SD-Außenstelle "Pinsk"

In September 1941, while most of the territories of Eastern Poland already annexed by the Soviet Union in September 1939 had become part of GK "Weissruthenien", that portion south of Belarus between the course of the Pripjet and the border with Ukraine had instead been assigned to RK "Ukraine". In particular, the western districts of Brest Litovsk, Pinsk, Kobryn and Stolin were assigned to GK "Wohlynien und Podolien", while those further east passed under the authority of GK "Zhitomir"[5].

This reorganization was justified by the need to keep under one operational control the vast and difficult area of the Pripyat marshes, which fell entirely within the remit of KdS "Rowno", SS-Sturmbannführer Karl Pütz, who, in turn, took orders from BdS Max Thomas, based in Kiev.

Pütz's position in Rovno began in December 1941 with a detachment of EK5 / EGC[6], and in addition to its core office in the city of Pripyat, it also included several peripheral commands (*Außenstellen*) dispersed in the Prupyat district, including that of Pinsk, formed in late May 1942 under the command of SS-Sturmscharführer Wilhelm Rasp[7]. Rasp's main task, assigned directly by Pütz, was *to combat gangs* and to perform activities of criminal police leading a group of 6 members of SD, Kripo and Gestapo, including the previously mentioned Adolph Petsch. Rasp's deputy was Josef Geigenscheder. In late August 1942, with the arrival of a large detachment from France under the command of SS-Sturmbannführer Walter Gäde, it was possible to create a further branch of Außenstelle "Pinsk" from which the *Zweigstellen* of Janov, Luninec, David Gorodek, Stolin and Wysok emanated. Finally, in November 1942, Gäde replaced Rasp at the command of Außenstelle "Pinsk"[8]. From an operational standpoint, the *kommando* of Pinsk's SD would enjoy large autonomy with respect to other authorities in the area, such as Gebietkommissar Klein and SS-und Polizeigebietführer Tessmann: this at least according to Gäde's testimony, given to the public prosecutor of Frankfurt and not completely confirmed[9]. However, judging from the tasks that the department had been intended to perform, Gäde's version appears plausible. In any case, there are no doubts about the role of SD-Außenstelle "Pinsk" in the massacres of autumn 1942, as confirmed by the public prosecutor in Frankfurt, according to whom the department was "*the central operating structure for the extermination of Jews in the Pinsk and Stolin districts*"[10].

14.2.2 – Polizei-Bataillon 306

Constituted in Frankfurt am Main on October 3, 1940, Polizei-Bataillon 306 was transferred to Polessia on August 28, 1942, after working for several months on the Leningrad front with front-line duties. Formally, at the time of its arrival in Polessia the battalion was renamed II/Polizei-Regiment 15 but its original structure did not change[11]. The battalion commander at the time of the massacres was Maj. Paul Landwehr, who held the position from February 20 to December 3, 1942 and who was hated and feared by his own officers and company commanders[12]. These were Heinrich Plantius of 1/306; Johann Josef Kuhr of 2/306; Rudolf Karl Eckert of 3/306. The main task of the battalion was patrolling Pripyat's wetland area which had become a haven for partisan groups and Jews who had fled from the ghettos of the district. For this reason, this area was divided between the companies along a stretch of a hundred kilometers, with the command and 1/306 in Pinsk, 2/306 in Luninec and 3/306 in Drahichyn[13]. According to the public prosecutor in Frankfurt, the murder of people found guilty, even in large numbers, was on the agenda[14]. From a structural standpoint, the battalion was probably commanded by KdO "Wolhynien-Podolien" (Oberstleutnant Hänschmann): in fact, operationally, it acted more as a support department to SD-Außenstelle "Pinsk".

14.2.3 – 4/Polizei-Bataillon 69

Traces of the involvement of 4/Polizei-Bataillon 69 in the action at Lachwa are found in the annals of the Court of Bochum, in relation to the proceedings against the company commander, Hptm. August Huft, accused of involvement in the massacre of Luninec perpetrated on September 4, 1942, the day after the massacre at Lachwa[15]. The same annals show that the 4/69, coming from Vitebsk, had been transferred to Polessia during April 1942, the company command deployed in Luninec and the four platoons divided between the nearby towns of Staruski, Zhitkovichi and Mikashevichi. The task of the company was to provide safety to the construction sites of the Todt which were scattered along the Brest-Litovsk-Gomel railway tracks, on the stretch around Luninec[16]. Then, within the sphere of the *resolution of the Jewish problem* in Polesia, 4/69 was involved in the massacres of autumn 1942, particularly those of Luninec and Lachwa, essentially with tasks of surveillance and cordoning off of the ghettos. A confirmation of the presence of 4/69 in Lachwa, the day of the massacre, is given by some photographs depicting the company staff in the village streets, amid the smoke of fires and among the lifeless bodies of numerous civilians[17].

14.2.4 – Schutzmannschaft Einzeldienst

The presence of local staff, in auxiliary service at different German departments and facilities on the Eastern Front, was a well-established reality since the first weeks after *Barbarossa*. Apart from Schuma battalions, more or less regular and organized, there were a large number of heterogeneous local militias that helped to strengthen the low number of policemen and to form the garrisons of more remote rural areas. These auxiliaries were recruited on the basis of the main nationality in the area in which they were called to perform, but also between different local minorities, providing equilibrium and balance in the most ethnically diverse areas. Generally, these militias were dependent on the local police stations, that is, Schutzpolizei command in urban areas. With regard to the region of Pinsk, five or six district commands (*Rayon-Posten*) were established, each formed by 10 to 20 German policemen and 80 to 100 Ukrainian auxiliaries divided into numerous control points in the various villages and main localities. This network depended upon SS-und Polizeigebietführer Leo Tessmann[18] who had to report to Gebietkommissar Klein and his deputy Alfred Ebner. The relations between these two authorities are not clear and were only partially clarified by Rosenberg's decree of August 27, 1942, which attributed the administration and supply of the ghettos to the civil commissioners and the surveillance, control and other similar tasks to the SS and police departments[19]. Sources differ with regard to nationalities as well: the auxiliaries, in fact, were Ukrainian and/or Polish. Stefan Klemp, for example, describes them as "*polnischer Milizionär*" and "*polnischer Hilfswilliger*"[20], while Torsten Schäfer talks of Ukrainian militia in some areas and Poles (in Pinsk and Janov) and also Latvians (Drahichyn) in others. In any case, they were all equally engaged in actions against the Jewish ghettos[21]. Furthermore, the presence of Polish *Volksdeutschen* cannot be ruled out, one of whom may appear in a picture in Lachwa already mentioned in paragraph 14.2.3 and annexed to the indictment of the public prosecutor in Dortmund against Paul Jordan[22].

14.3 INTENT ON GENOCIDE

Albeit concentrated in a time-span of about two months, between September and November 1942, the destruction of the Jewish communities in the Pripyat area was not a sudden or improvised phenomenon. On the contrary, it was the last step of a process that had been initiated in the previous spring and would see its peak in the annihilation of the Pinsk ghetto, which took place between October 29 and November 1. In this sense, we can probably talk about an *announced destruction*, pursued through a long-term plan which commenced in the spring with the segregation of the Jewish communities. This plan continued with the activation of the network of Sicherheitspolizei headed by SD-Außenstelle "Pinsk" and was finally completed with the arrival of the Ordnungspolizei departments – in particular Polizei-Regiment 15 – in the role of *fußvolk der Endlösung*. The construction, in May / June 1942, of the extermination camp in Bronnaya Gora, northeast of Brest Litovsk, on the grounds of an old train station, must be added to the figure[23]. In this respect this site may have represented the hub in Western Ukraine of a network of temporary and *regional* centers of extermination, which became effective in rapid succession from the end of 1941 and took place on the three fields of the so-called *Aktion Reinhardt* (for the General Government and Galicia): those of Maly Trostenez (for Western Belarus), of Chelmno (for Warthegau), and – if it had been established –of Mogilev (for Eastern Belarus)[24]. A project in which there seems to be a glimpse of common direction and that demonstrates the will to prepare the second phase of the Jewish genocide as early as fall 1941, through policies of destruction that were more systematic and well-organized with respect to the method of "wandering genocidal cohorts (*Völkermordkohorten*)"[25] used so far.

So, once again – as stressed on other occasions – the propulsive forces *from above*, in terms of general guidelines, ideological assumptions, implicit approval, legal and authoritative alchemies and technical-operational support were completed by forces coming *from below*, related to contingent problems, alleged local needs, political and power struggles of little importance, and a wide range of situational dynamics, including the well-established habit of using the reassuring tool of genocide as a simple, quick and effective method to drastically solve the *Jewish problem* on a local base.

We have already had occasion to portray the Jewish genocide through an onion-like pattern of concentric rings, whose outer edge – which increased enormously during the eastward *expansionary phase* of the summer of 1941 – at first involved those Jewish communities which were the furthest (geographically and in the sense of their social, cultural and even ethnic distance), and then gradually went back inward to the heart of the problem: German and Western Jews. Well, from the spring of 1942, the expansion phase is substantially followed by one of *reflux*, during which a large number of communities were involved. There could be differences between these communities, but they all shared something: they had survived – despite serious losses – the first wave of massacres. This was possible because they somehow managed to produce some economic and social counter-measures which allowed them to promote some sort of coexistence – albeit fleeting and precarious – with the occupation authorities.

In fact, the opportunity to use a willing and cost-free workforce which was often specialized in all skills of craftsmanship; the production structures, at times of some significance, that were opened within the ghettos; the possibility to exploit the *Judenräte* as tools to impose control on the people while waiting for the genocide hour to be ripe, were all important factors, albeit not decisive. These factors did, however, contribute to *slow down,* in some areas rather than others, the implementation of the Final Solution because they absorbed the thrust *from below*, which is where issues of different nature related to the demise or survival of the ghettos and communities were mostly felt.

Obviously though, this unstable balance, based on such blatant disproportion of forces could not last long. The destructive dynamics coming *from above*, which began to spread from autumn 1941 onwards (the experiments with gas, the construction of the first extermination camps, the beginning of the transfer of Germans Jews to the East that made the local extermination camps more *superfluous* than ever, etc..), gradually became more and more unbearable and forced these communities and ghettos to the most painful compromises in order to prolong a simulacrum of survival. At different times but with similar dynamics, starting from spring 1942, the Final Solution began inexorably to overflow from the outer ring toward the intermediate rings. In this sense, the fires of *systemic genocide* began to flare up even among those communities that had been affected only marginally by the massacres of the first phase and that somehow had experienced an illusory period of stability. Between the spring and summer of 1942, the annihilating wave hit the ghettos of northern Belarus (districts of Glebokye and Vileika); between summer and autumn the hurricane moved to the General Government, then spread to Galicia. Between September and November 1942, the destruction finally extended to the communities of Pripyat.

At that point, while the annihilation of the last regional community that was still (almost) intact, namely that of the district of Bialystok, was launched in November, the end of 1942 saw the *wandering* genocide, with its *systemic* variant, substantially completed: curiously, as the summer of 1941 saw the opening of the first phase in the Pripyat region, with the extravagant and impromptu order to *push* (drown) Jewish women and children in the wetlands[26], the same phase also ended in Pripyat in the fall of 1942, with the methodical eradication of entire communities living there.

From that moment on, in the second and final phase, the *resident* phase, the Jewish genocide would assume continental proportions and the fumes of Birkenau would become its most dramatic symbol.

14.4 SONDERAKTION: UKRAINE JUDENFREI

Lachwa is located along the river Smierc, now in Belarus. Apparently, the first Jewish settlement in Lachwa can be traced back to the late half of the seventeenth century. In the late thirties Lachwa had a population of about 3,800 inhabitants, of whom approximately 2,300 were Jews, present in the city on the eve of World War II.

On 17 September 1939 the Red Army entered Lachwa, passing through the city on its westward march. During Soviet rule the Jewish cultural and religious life suffered limitations, so that the Jews were forced to work also during the Sabbath, and the religious functions were limited by the authorities.

On July 5, 1941 after the German attack on the Soviet Union, the Soviet authorities abandoned Lachwa, leaving the city without administration for three days. During this interregnum local residents robbed Jews of their properties. The first German troops reached Lachwa between July 7 and 8. A Jewish Council (Judenrat) was formed under the direction of Dov Lopatin, who, before the war, had been the president of the Zionist organization in Lachwa[27].

Unlike other Jewish communities in western Ukraine, which suffered heavy losses during the summer of 1941, that of Lachwa remained essentially intact, in part thanks to its geographical isolation, in the heart of the marshes of Pripyat along the line that linked the southern margin of the Army Group “Mitte” and the northern margin of Army Group “Sud”. In this sense we can say that several other Jewish communities around the region of Pinsk, in addition to Lachwa, managed to go almost *unnoticed*. This may be because in their advance towards the east the various Sonder and Einsatzkommando of groups B and C roamed around the marshes in July / August 1941, respectively from the north and from the south. A similar situation occurred with the SS cavalry brigade, detached in the region as part of the second wave of genocide and after having ravaged the area between Kobryn and Luninec until late August,[28], was moved more to the east, between Mozyr and Bobruisk, *ignoring* many smaller communities[29].

In spite of that, at least one hundred Jews were rounded up by a squad of SS-Kavallerie-Regiment 2 that was passing through Lachwa between August 9 and 14, 1941. Their shooting, though, was not carried out only by accident, to allow the sudden departure of the squadron following an alarm, and, possibly, thanks to the payment of a ransom[30].

Then, with Jeckeln's attention focused on the main targets (Rovno, Kamenec Podolski, etc..) and with the front moving rapidly eastward, the northern Volhynia ended up being almost forgotten, partly because of the chronic shortage of SS and police units. Except for a quick *passage* of a few small detachments of EG zbV in July 1941[31], later withdrawn, the area saw the settling of Sicherheitspolizei garrisons only from spring 1942, after the dissolution of much of EG C.

The period of relative stability for the Jews of Lachwa ended on April 4, 1942, when the *Judenrat* – established since July 1941 under the chairmanship of Dov Lopatin[32] – was reached by the order of transfer of the entire community to a fenced area of a few hundred square yards, constituted around a group of 45 houses divided into two areas: overall, after the arrival in April of the small communities of David Gorodek and Sienkiewicze, about 2,350 Jews were forced to clump together in the living space of about one square yard per person[33].

However, the German maneuvers were not entirely unexpected. In fact, since January 1942, a clandestine resistance movement had gathered around the young Zionists active in the city since before the Soviet invasion. This movement was led by Yitzhak Rochczyn and backed by the afore-mentioned Lopatin who, on more than one occasion, had attempted, with little results, to make contact with the groups of Soviet partisans operating in the forests of the area. Also, some of the Red Army drifters, on the run from prison camps, were welcomed, in great secret, by the community; all attempts to smuggle firearms though would prove rather fruitless. In this sense, the operating weight of such a movement was extremely limited and unrealistic and only served as a palliative for the morale of the community.

Although the reasons why the establishment of ghettos was ordered in some places and not in others[34] – something that was probably linked to local issues, such as the availability of housing, surveillance staff, etc. – the fact that the sporadic contacts between Jewish youth groups and partisans in the forest could provide the occupation authorities a pretext to adopt this interim solution – which, in any case, was functional to the final annihilation – cannot be ruled out. Then, the real extent of this potential danger coming from sparse and isolated groups of hungry and unarmed Jews is a matter that reasonably falls within the sphere of *perceived threat* rather than the *real* one, and, more likely, under the sphere of ideological automatisms.

Whatever the reasons, what is certain is that the creation of ghettos for the Jewish communities of Volhynia was meant, from the outset, only as a temporary measure. In fact, according to the testimony that Rasp gave before the public prosecutor in Frankfurt, as early as June 1942 SD-Außenstelle "Pinsk" received an RSHA order signed by Eichmann in which the *liquidation* of the ghettos was arranged[35]. Consistently, during a meeting held in Lutsk from August 29 to 31, 1942 with the participation of Generalkommissar "Wolhynien-Podolien" Heinrich Schoene and the district commissioners, KdS Karl Pütz urged those responsible – after the successful transfer of Jews in ghettos – *to speed up the actions, so that they would be over within 5 weeks*[36]. It was also clarified that Reichkommissar Koch would welcome a *one hundred per cent solution*, with partial exceptions only where the war production could have been affected[37]. During the meeting, in relation to the need to resolve the so-called *Jewish question* in Volhynia, famine and difficulties in the supply that plagued much of the Ukrainian population were mentioned – almost as a form of *prior justification.*

In fact, since the beginning of 1942, as a result of the dramatic winter famine that was gripping Ukraine, Koch had obtained the intervention of police units to be deployed along the northern border of its domain, in order to prevent the infiltration of "hungry looters (*hungernden Plündern*)" from Belarus through the swamps of Pripyat. Among the units mobilized there was Polizei-Bataillon 315, one of whose company commanders, Hptm. H.W, had confided in a private letter, as early as autumn 1941, the risk of starvation for at least half the population of Ukraine during the coming winter[38]. Given this dynamic, however, something did not seem to work: in fact, the food problem in Ukraine could be effectively alleviated, if not solved, through the extermination of the local Jewish population – but then it is hard to understand why this *solution* was not adopted as early as the end of 1941, coinciding with the first winter of famine, instead of waiting until the autumn of 1942. Alternatively, the reasons given at the meeting of Lutsk are to be considered essentially specious and self-absolving, especially in view of the level and quality of the rations granted to the Jews, which could scarcely have had a more than minimal impact on the overall food budget[39].

Whatever the reason, the usual local *motivations* received impulses coming from the outside. According to the testimony of Wilhelm Rasp, given before ZStL on December 18, 1961 during the preliminary investigation that led to the Frankfurt trial, the order to proceed with the *liquidation* of the ghettos would have been received directly from Berlin through BdS Thomas and KdS Pütz and the whole operation was carried out with the support of the staff led by Gebietkommissar Klein and his deputy Ebner[40].

In late summer 1942, therefore, the dynamics that would lead to the destruction of the Jewish communities of northern Volhynia were lined up like pieces of a puzzle: there were excuses, there were perpetrators and there were victims. And, above all, there was a favorable political environment in which to replicate in Volhynia what elsewhere (Belarus and northern General Government) had already been completed with undeniable success; indeed the environment was so favorable that even the stringent procedures of secrecy that normally enveloped the preparation and execution of the killings could be neglected. Large mass graves were dug in advance and in broad sunlight by Jewish workers near the *shtetl* that would be the target of the actions, and uncontrolled rumors spread from village to village, as the wave of genocide began to sweep one community after the other. Obviously, there was no need to disguise anything: in just a few weeks, without any subterfuge, the whole of Ukraine would have been *cleansed* of Jews, as the former commander of 2/306 would explain about a year later in Holland, in November 1943, to students of a course on anti-partisan warfare. The title of the lesson was: "*Bataillon-Sonderaktion zur Lösung der Judenfrage. Ukraine Judenfrei*"[41].

14.5 THE FIRES OF RAGE

They stormed out running through the gap that they had opened in the fence, heading to the river, and over the river towards the forest, wet with mist. They would have to run through a stretch of sandy shore of sixty yards completely in the open, out of the suffocating, but protective, embrace of smoke from the fires that burned behind them: only sixty yards, before diving in the shallow waters of the Smierc, but enough to mark the difference between life and death. And as they ran they could hear the executioners behind them, scattered everywhere among the alleys of the ghetto, hampered by the fire but enraged by the surprise, and determined to stop them before they reached the river and advanced into the forest, where escape became possible and their capture would become more difficult. Just a few yards before the shoreline, just a few moments before the shooting. Then he heard them, the shots. Angry bursts of automatic weapon and single gunshots... Another few yards, and with a little luck he would have managed to avoid them...

The alarm began to spread in the Lachwa ghetto from late July 1942, in the wake of rumors coming from neighboring localities that had already been reached by the genocidal wave: Mikaschevichi, Mokrovo, Malorita..., where hundreds of Jews, men and women, had been shot[42]; these rumors found substantial confirmation on September 2, when the news reached Lopatin, president of the Jewish Council and Rochczyn, leader of the resistance movement, of large pits of thirty yards in length, two and a half yards in width and three yards in depth, dug in the forest a short distance away from the ghetto. Then, evening approaching, police departments armed with machine guns and auxiliary groups were seen placing themselves outside the fence. At that point, beyond any reasonable hope, it was clear to the members of the Council and to the inhabitants of the ghetto, what the real intentions of the Germans were, and what alternatives they had before the inevitable getting so close.

Meanwhile, panic began to spread in the ghetto as the perpetrators completed their deployment all around the outside perimeter. The *evacuation* order had been sent to the departments directly by Wilhelm Rasp, who could count for the occasion on a platoon of Polizei-Bataillon 69, part of Johann Josef Kuhr's 2/Polizei-Bataillon 306 and staff of SD-Außenstelle "Pinsk", for a total of about 150 men, reinforced by a contingent of about 200 Ukrainian and / or Belarusian auxiliaries[43].

The Jewish resistance group moved against them, equipped with only axes, knives, iron bars and pitchforks. Bottles of kerosene were distributed in some houses, to be lit at the appropriate time. From inside the enclosure they found what looked like a weak point in the German camp: a stretch of sixty yards of open ground, guarded by a dozen policemen, through which in theory it was possible to try and reach the river, and then the forest, on the opposite bank.

The last night of the Lachwa ghetto was spent in a crescendo of tension, arguing about which was the best time to go for broke and groped in the concern for those – the elderly and sick – who in any case would not have been able to follow the young over the fence. Finally, despite the doubts of Rochczyn who preferred immediate action, the prevailing opinion was that of Lopatin to wait until dawn, and take best advantage of the river fog mixed with smoke from the fire, which would have helped the fugitives in their desperate attempt to escape. According to the story of a survivor, called to testify during the Frankfurt trial: "we decided that in any case, if they wanted to liquidate us, we would resist, sell our lives as dear as possible and die hard"[44]. A second survivor confirms his words: "anxiety for those who were left behind and the desire to delay their fate pushed the Jews of Lachwa to wait... The truth is, it was decided that if all the entreaties and bribes proved fruitless, we would never go to the graves prepared for us, but we would get killed in the territory of the ghetto, in battle"[45].

The dawn of September 3, 1942 came in the form of five trucks loaded with policemen standing outside the entrance to the ghetto, willing to impose the order transmitted to the *Judenrat* to select 30 particularly skilled craftsmen: the only ones, besides some members of the Council, who would have been allowed to survive. Then, after Lopatin gave them a negative response, the policemen stormed the ghetto amid screams, gunshots and the first columns of smoke which began to rise from the burning houses. Groups of young Jews, with improvised weapons, rushed into the streets, in the mist and darkness which were beginning to thin, succeeding in some cases to snatch the weapons from the hands of some policemen caught by surprise. Some Germans or auxiliary policemen were killed in the first minutes of complete confusion, while storming from house to house in order to mop up the residents[46]. Yitzhak Rochczyn struck violently on the head of a German with an axe, opening his way to the river, and others would do the same. They also engaged in firefights with the policemen who were forced to take a defensive posture, especially around the Market Square and in homes not reached by the flames, so much so in fact that at one point – especially because of the fire – the core of those making the raid had to be withdrawn beyond the fence, firing on all those Jews who in turn tried to push it down or climb over it. Blocked by the barrier and intoxicated by the smoke many Jews fell exhausted to the ground and ended up being reached and charred by the flames: the day after all these victims were loaded onto agricultural wagons and buried in mass graves along with those who had been shot[47].

Amid flames, smoke and utter confusion, each prearranged plan vanished. Mere survival was the only goal and the only goal was beyond the fence. This is how a survivor describes the scene:

> *We had only one goal: not to go like sheep to the slaughter, but to break through the fence and the*

gates of the ghetto and flee beyond the radius of the killing bullets. Instinctively we tried to take refuge in the houses as yet untouched by the fire and we moved through the courtyards of the houses... We moved towards the gates, which meanwhile had already been torn down, we passed and reached the market and then we left the city. The Nazis were firing incessantly, without taking aim. They were shooting while standing and killed many of us. Those who managed to avoid the bullets, running desperately, were mostly children and young people, aged from five to twenty. None of them went to the pits[48].

Dozens of Jews managed to break through the opening in the fence, throwing themselves headlong into the river, braving gunfire and the anger of the followers who tried to stop them. Despite wounded hands after hitting a German, Dov Lopatin succeeded in crossing the river to reach the forest still enshrouded in darkness.

The shots whizzed around him, sticking in the ground at his feet. They had not reached him yet, owing also to the smoke, shadows and fog that rose from the waters. A few more steps and perhaps he would make it. He heard his comrades fall behind him, stopped by the bullets, and, without looking, he had seen them die. There were flashes of fire behind him, and before him were the lights of a cold, gray September dawn. His hands were bloody, but it was not his blood, it was the blood of a Gestapo officer whose head he had smashed with an axe-blow properly delivered a few minutes earlier, when he had tried to raid his home. That was the blood that his hands were smeared with and only for that reason, perhaps, that would be a good day for him to die. But the truth was, he knew, that no day was ever a good day to die. With a final leap he reached the river and entered the water, just as he felt something sharp hit his back. Surprised, he stopped, trying to understand.

After the escape of the younger Jews, the German policemen took control of what remained of the ghetto: a stretch of burned-down homes and a column of several hundred prisoners – at least 500/600 according to conservative estimates by the Court of Frankfurt, more likely 1,200, according to other sources[49] – mostly women, children and old people, rounded up one by one and now amassed under surveillance in the market square, past the doors of the demolished fence. At least 800 Jews had already died that morning, killed by fire, while trying to escape, or during the raids because they were unable to move. Everyone else, maybe 500 or 600, managed to flee into the forest, towards Hryczyn[50].

Then, as the public prosecutor in Frankfurt reconstructed, the victims were brought to the common graves, dug about a mile away from the village, where, after being forced to take off their clothes, they were killed with shots to the head by SD members who took turns in groups of three at a time. In some cases the victims were made to lie face down on the bodies of those who preceded them, and were then killed at a distance of about 20 inches, in other cases they had to be thrown forcibly into the pit, after their refusal to do so voluntarily. Amid the shots of the executions, which followed uninterruptedly, the cries of the victims waiting for their turn, especially children, could be heard. Every now and then, small amounts of alcohol were distributed to the SD members committed to shoot[51].

While the execution was in progress, a cordon of policemen of Polizei-Bataillon 306 provided the security of the slaughter site. For the staff of this battalion it was the first mass execution of defenseless people, including women and children; despite that, there are no traces, evidence or anything which may suggest their hesitation or doubt "while opening fire mercilessly, with rifles and automatic weapons, on a large number of defenseless human beings, who only wanted to save their lives"[52].

It took him an instant to realize that he would not be lucky. Around him many Jews had fallen, some on the shoreline and some in the water; but many others, he now realized, were reaching the forest across the river. They were the youngest, those who had fled with him, the most eager to live; because of this, maybe there was still hope. Not for him though. Perhaps, indeed, that was a good day to die: not because he had killed an enemy, but because something had been done to oppose the fate that otherwise would have swept them all. He was smiling, and by the time he realized that he did not even notice that second bullet that reached him a few seconds after the first, hitting him in the head and killing him instantly.

He fell into the water, while some of his companions reached the forest. No, the death of Yitzhak Rochczyn was not a useless death: it was the death of a free man.

14.6 VICTIMS OF INHUMAN TIMES

According to Christian Gerlach, the number of Jews who died on September 3, 1942 in Lachwa were 1,946 – of which 698 women and 724 children. Some died in the flames, and most were killed by the bullets of the units brought to annihilate them[53]. Motorcycled commandos, along with policemen of SS-Reiter-Polizei-Abteilung II on horseback, hurtled through the forest chasing the fugitives. The latter was a department that had not taken part in the massacre directly, but that would be soon called upon to do its part, as during the annihilation of the Pinsk ghetto. Shortly, during the manhunt these *jagdkommandos* managed to capture and kill on sight – often helped by the farmers who had been promised a reward of one pound of salt for every Jew caught[54] – at least 350 fugitives. With these additional killings then, the number of survivors of the Lachwa ghetto fell to about 120, several of whom – including Dov Lopatin – were accepted into partisan units. Many of them, including Lopatin himself, were later killed in combat in the months and years that followed, until July 1944 when, after having forced the German front line to fall back to the Carpathian line, the Red Army re-entered the territory, now almost entirely Jew-free.

Lachwa, in fact, was only a stage in the great genocidal wave that swept the Jewish communities of Western Pripyat during the fall of 1942. Then came Kozan Gorodek, Luninec, Vysokoie, David Gorodek, Stolin, Ivanava, Drogichin and Pinsk[55], in addition to other *smaller* massacres, for a grand total – including the liquidation of the ghettos of Bereza Kartuska (September / October) and Brest Litovsk (October 15) – of at least 50,000 victims in two months, at the hands of the same reduced group of departments: SD-Außenstelle "Pinsk", Polizei-Bataillone 306 and 320, part of Polizei-Bataillone 69 and 310 and Polizei-Reiter-Abteilung II, in addition to the ubiquitous Ukrainian and / or Belarusian auxiliaries and staff of the civil administration.

A limited selection of perpetrators was implicated in cases initiated by various courts of postwar Western Germany. The massacre of Lachwa, in particular, was included in the whole accusation complex initiated by ZStL investigators with dossier 204 AR-Z 393/59 centered on Pinsk, during which various branches of investigation were identified and then sent to the attorney responsible for preliminary investigations . In particular, on July 31, 1962 the public prosecutor in Frankfurt took on the full dossier on Polizei-Bataillon 306 and SD-Außenstelle "Pinsk" (StAw 4 Js 901/62)[56], while the public prosecutor in Stuttgart received the dossier against vice-Gebietkommissar of Pinsk, Alfred Ebner, and seven other suspects (StAw 13 Js 22/62).

Then, on January 3, 1966, the three suspects who had remained in Stuttgart, including Ebner, were also sent to the prosecution in Frankfurt which, after merging the two cases became the sole body responsible for the investigation, its dossier now listed as StAw 4 Ks 1/71.

The work of the public prosecutor in Frankfurt lasted from the beginning of 1966 to September 1971, including the deletion, for various reasons, of the position of many suspects (36 initially, only seven of whom were then actually tried) and the listening to of testimonies, some of which had been given in Israel. Other testimonies had been collected in Kobryn, Soviet Union, by a section of the Court who went there with permission of the attorney general of Moscow. Overall, out of the over 200 pieces of evidence, 67 criminal cases were obtained which allowed, in November 1971, the indictment of eight defendants, of whom only six were then actually sentenced to prison terms[57]:

PETSCH, Adolph: born January 31, 1905, a Sudeten German, he moved to Rovno, Ukraine, in autumn 1941. In May 1942 he was admitted to the *kommando* in charge of setting up SD-Außenstelle "Pinsk". Involved in the main massacres perpetrated by this department in autumn 1942, from August 10, 1962 he was remanded in custody by order of the Court of Frankfurt during the preliminary investigation. Based on his previous testimonies – in which he had admitted his participation in the killing of at least 6-7,000 Jews – he was accused of complicity in 12,700 murders. Despite the conviction for life imprisonment requested by the prosecutor, who said he was the perpetrator (*Täter*), he was only sentenced to 15 years in prison. In addition to ordinary complicity in murder he was also charged with the aggravating circumstance of excessive cruelty during the executions (*Exzeßtäter*). This is what he declared before the investigators of ZstL[58]: "I had to participate in executions, so I usually did as an executioner. When children were among the victims, then women were required to place these children close to themselves, so that their heads would be clear. Women and men had to lie face down in the pits. With submachine guns selected on single shot they were killed with blows to the neck. The number of people killed is estimated between 6 and 7,000".

PLANTIUS, Heinrich: born 25 October 1914 in Duisburg. Commander of 1/306 and aide in the Stab of Polizei-Bataillon 306 from March 30, 1942. Decorated with KvK II. Prisoner of war in Italy from March 1945 to April 28, 1948 he was readmitted to police service in Frankfurt ranking Polizeikommissar from February 1, 1952 to 1961. Remanded in custody during the preliminary investigations from August 10, 1962, by order of the Court of Frankfurt, he was released on bail pending trial, after which he was sentenced to four years in prison for complicity in the massacre of 16,200 Jews in Pinsk, in October / November 1942.

KUHR, Johann Joseph, born February 18, 1916 in Mannheim. Commander of 2/306. NSDAP member from 1940. Back in Frankfurt police service with the rank of Polizeikommissar, from August 10, 1962 during the preliminary investigation, he was remanded in custody by order of the Court of Frankfurt. Released on bail pending trial, he was sentenced to two and a half years in prison for complicity in the massacre of 16,200 Jews in Pinsk, in October / November 1942.

ECKERT, Karl Rudolf: born February 27, 1914 in Neisse. In police service since January 1938 at Kd-Schupo "Hamburg" ranking platoon commander, he later assumed command of 3/306. Wounded in combat on the Don in January 1943, he was convalescent until the following July. Sent to Italy in the summer of 1944, he was taken prisoner of war and held until 1946. Back in police service in Hamburg in the summer of 1948 ranking Polizeikommissar, from August 10, 1962 he was remanded in custody by order of the Court of Frankfurt during the preliminary investigation, only to be released almost immediately while awaiting trial, on bail of 25,000 DM. He was sentenced to three and a half years in prison for complicity in the massacre of 16,200 Jews in Pinsk, in October / November 1942.

GROß, Heinrich: born May 8, 1911 in Frankfurt. Platoon commander in 3/306. Sentenced to four years in prison for aiding and abetting in the murder of a Jewish woman.

HOFMANN, Wilhelm: born October 12, 1890 in Eschbach. In voluntary military service in a dragoon regiment, after WWI he joined a Mecklenburg *freikorp*. He joined the police in Hamburg and was appointed captain, and from June 1933 to September 1939 he held the command of the infantry detachment of KdSchupo "Hamburg". Sent to Poland with Polizei- Reiter-Abteilung I up to May 1940, he was admitted to the SS on December 1, 1941. Commander of Polizei-Reiter-Abteilung II from March 1,

1942 to January 1944, he then went on to command Polizei-Reiter-Abteilung III from August 2, 1944 to February 1945. Discharged at the end of the conflict with a war retirement pension from April 1, 1951 he was investigated for the massacre of Pinsk on November 10, 1971 but was not indicted owing to his failing health.

TELTZ, Heinz-Dieter: Born June 4, 1916 in Wiesbaden, he served the police with KdSchupo "Berlin" and was then admitted to a graduate course at the police academy in Berlin-Köpenick. Assigned from September 1939 to March 1940 to Polizei-Bataillon 4 in Poland, in August 1941 he was appointed commander of the first platoon of Polizei-Reiter-Abteilung II. Involved with his department in the Pinsk and Janov massacres, he was wounded by the explosion of a mine in September 1943. A liaison officer for a Cossack department from June 1944, he took part in the suppression of the Warsaw uprising. Transferred to Italy he was taken prisoner, being released in June 1945. Back in police service in Düsseldorf since 1946, he reached the rank of Polizeihauptkommissar. Remanded in custody from August 23, 1963 by order of the Court of Frankfurt during the preliminary investigation, he was released on bail pending trial. Sentenced to three and a half years in prison on February 6, 1973, he died a few months later, on October 11, 1973.

EBNER, Alfred: born 1913, he became a NSDAP member in 1931 and was admitted to the Ordensburg schools in 1936. Drafted by the Wehrmacht at the beginning of the war, in the summer of 1941 he was transferred to the civil administration of the occupied eastern territories as "District Deputy Commissioner (*stellvertretender Gebietskommissar*)" in the city of Pinsk, where he arrived in September 1941 in the role of "agent for Jewish issues (*Sachbearbeiter für jüdische Angelegenheiten*)". Directly subordinate to Gebietkommissar Paul Gerhard Klein and responsible for the establishment of the ghettos of May 1942, he became involved in the massacres of 1942 and personally took part in numerous executions. Subjected to preliminary investigation by the public prosecutor in Stuttgart, he was remanded in custody on January 1, 1962 only to be released on bail of 200,000 DM. Indicted before the Court of Stuttgart on November 30, 1964 his case was moved to the public prosecutor in Frankfurt on January 3, 1966 from which he was indicted before the Court of Frankfurt on March 28, 1968. In December 1971, the trial barely started, he was declared affected by pseudo-senile dementia, which was followed by the temporary removal of his position in the case. On August 25, 1978 the Ebner dossier was finally closed. When he died, in 1987, he had never been convicted[59].

In addition to the eight defendants tried in Frankfurt, several other characters in positions of responsibility involved in the massacres in Polesia during the fall of 1942 were not even brought to trial for one reason or another, or had the case against them dropped during the preliminary investigations, or at least before the trial (November 1971). Among them:

PÜTZ, Karl, commander of KdS "Rowno" from February 3, 1942. Born February 7, 1911 in Aachen. Wilhelm Rasp's direct superior. Appointed KdS "Lublin" in October 1943 and then KdS "Posen" from July 1944. He committed suicide in the internment camp of St. Märgen im Schwarzwald on May 6, 1945.

RASP, Wilhelm, commander of SD-Außenstelle "Pinsk", directly subordinate to Pütz. Born December 7, 1887. Involved in the preliminary investigation, he had time to give his testimony before the public prosecutor in Frankfurt before dying from a serious illness in 1963[60].

LANDWEHR, Paul: commander of Polizei-Bataillon 306. Born November 21, 1906 in Schale (Tecklemburg). SS-Sturmbannführer. Killed in combat in Taubendorf, Gruben district, on February 28, 1945. Posthumously decorated with the Iron Cross on March 17, 1945.

HUFT, August: commander of 4/Polizei-Bataillon 69. Born May 22, 1904 in Strasbourg, Alsace. Decorated with EK II on May 6, 1943. In addition to the massacre of Lachwa, he was involved with his company also in the massacre of Luninec, for which he was tried and acquitted by the Court of Bochum on October 20, 1970 (LG Bochum, 16 Ks 1/70).

TESSMANN, Leo: SS-Polizeigebietfürer, referring to the Ukrainian militia, in connection with deputy-Gebietkommissat Ebner. Having succeeded in disappearing after the war, Tessmann was eventually traced and placed under investigation by the public prosecutor in Frankfurt, but the case against him was dropped immediately after his death in Brunswick on April 19, 1964[61].

KLEIN, Paul Gerhard: Gebietkommissar "Pinsk". Born June 4, 1906 in Quernheim-Kirchlengern, Nordrhein / Westfalen, he was appointed District Commissioner in October 1941 in Pinsk replacing the deceased Roempler. Ebner's direct superior, he died in Gdańsk in 1945, probably committing suicide.

Let's read what the author Katharina von Kellenbach writes in a passage of her article focused on the figure of her uncle, district deputy commissioner Alfred Ebner, published in 2003 in the journal *Holocaust and Genocide Studies*:

> *According to a statistic published in 1986 by the West German Ministry of Justice, German prosecutors opened 90,921 investigations against National Socialist perpetrators between 1945 and 1986. However, only a fraction of these reached the courts.*
>
> *Of those suspects brought to trial only 6,479 were convicted. This disturbingly low number is further reduced when one excludes defendants who were prosecuted for robbery or assault charges. According to Dick de Mildt, "between May 1945 and January 1992, only 1,793 cases related to Nazi capital crimes as committed during the period of the Second World War appeared before West German courts. Of these, 974 led to convictions, while 819 ended with either the acquittal of the defendants, or the termination of the proceedings for other reasons"*[62].

The case of the Frankfurt trial was paradigmatic of this situation, only apparently distorted. Specifically to the killings in Polesia during the fall of 1942, the *biological solution* killed several prominent leaders during the investigations and subsequent trials, who, thus, were never held accountable for their responsibilities. Apart from these (many) cases, the factor that, in general, marked the substantial failure of a forty-year cycle of investigations by the courts of West Germany, was the essentially *pro-offender* legal approach which the majority of the judges of the courts – most of whom were serving during the Third Reich and were quickly *denazified* in the post-war – felt obliged to take with regard to the perpetrators, in principle considered as mere tools in the hands of an immoral regime. This *solution* was originated by the paradox that the judges were called to re-evaluate as objectively criminal acts that only a few years earlier, during the regime, had been perpetrated in the context of [aberrant] legal lawfulness, with obvious unmanageable repercussions in terms of retroactivity of the law (*ex-post facto*).

On the basis of these assumptions, and the sole leadership of the regime (*Haupttäter*) identified as guilty of murder (*Mord*) under Section 211 of the German Penal Code, the charge of simple complicity in murder (*Beihilfe zum Mord*) to all other perpetrators, under Section 212, came automatically. Consequently, all those convictions for murder that could be liable for life imprisonment, were reduced to the short-term sentences liable for complicity alone, with excess of cruelty as the only aggravating factor.

Basically, almost all the war crimes trials held in West Germany were afflicted with this real legal quagmire in which, to a degree, the arguments from the defense prevailed before the judges whose difficulties were more often than not of a *structural* nature. Therefore, the favorable attitude of the judges towards the defendants was only and not necessarily due to a possible ideological proximity but also, conceivably, to the discomfort they certainly felt whenever they were called to resolve situations which, legally speaking, were paradoxical. In an interview given at the end of the Frankfurt trial, Judge Adalbert Schaefer described the six defendants that he had just condemned, as "victims of inhuman times" and had no trouble admitting that "many people want an end to these processes – and we are not enthusiastic about them either. We are going along with them only because lawmakers have commissioned us to do so"[63].

14.7 CONSIDERATIONS

Beyond the legal environment and the objective difficulties to prosecute it by legal terms, it is quite clear that the massacre of Lachwa of September 3 was a crime unjustifiable for two types of reasons. Firstly, and obviously, from a moral point of view, having caused about 75 % of deaths among women and children – with the addition, in the next few days, of several hundreds of young people, mostly males, who had fled into the forest and were killed *in dribs and drabs*.

Secondly, Lachwa was only one of the stages of annihilation, planned and methodical, of the Jewish communities living in the Pripyat area: for this reason it cannot be read as an episode in itself, but it must be included in a wider context and as an element of that great work of criminal social engineering that *systematic genocide* represented.

That said, what it is worth noting about this criminal event is what makes it the rare exception of a uniform sequence: the willingness on the part of certain sectors of the Jewish community of Lachwa, not to meekly accept the fate that had been chosen for them, but to put up – perhaps for the first time in the history of the Jewish genocide – a reaction which was objectively desperate, but that could be defined as animated by the *Spirit of Masada*. In the words of one of the survivors of the revolt, it was all about rejecting the idea *of going like sheep to the slaughter*, not only and not so much in order to try to save their own lives – which of course all the rioters wished – but also in order to redeem their existence, with a gesture that was not one of dazzling and sterile heroism, but the rebellion to the perversion in which their souls had been forced by the humiliation endured daily and the extreme choices that were imposed upon them: first of all, the chilling prospect inflicted to the *Judenrat* to choose 30 (sic!) *necessary* Jews to be saved from the slaughter, implicitly condemning to death the remaining 2,000[64]. Such order eschewed any humanly tolerable ethical limit. Its eventual acceptance would have outlined – in this case more than in any other – the contours of the open complicity of the *Judenrat* with its tormentors, with the resulting share of the same moral disgrace. Thus, it was no longer about the horrendous choice to sacrifice a minority in order to allow the majority another day's survival – an alternative that was shameful in itself, but often used in the name of pragmatic utilitarianism – but the horror of having to surrender to the perversion imposed by their persecutors, selling off the last value that could be left to the victims: the respect of their own morality. In this sense, the dilemma imposed upon the *Judenrat* of Lachwa was not having to decide according to the principle of the *lesser evil* – that Hannah Arendt despises so much – but the alternative between saving their own souls or losing them forever. And in the end, rightly so, the dilemma was not such and was solved by what was the only possible choice: the choice towards the *greater good*.

Certainly, the Jewish revolt of Lachwa was a desperate attempt that could not succeed and that in fact did not really change the substance of things. However, those few young people who proved lucky and talented enough to survive the uprising, the police hunt and the peasants' tip-offs, were able to obtain *greater goods* which otherwise would have been lost forever: the freedom to take control of their own destiny, the opportunity to reaffirm their value as human beings and the privilege of being able to impose their own will upon an enemy accustomed to regard them as nothing but a dehumanized and faceless mass (*stücke*).

By accepting to lose their lives out of their own will, the young Jews of Lachwa claimed back the ownership of their lives. Not only did they escape the pernicious spiral of the lesser evil, but they also managed to resolve the stalemate of *doing-nothing*, although, in some cases, the latter was still preferable to passive acceptance of the will of others. Eyal Weizman comments[65]:

> *When nothing else is possible, doing-nothing is actually the ultimate form of resistance, and the practical consequences of the refusal, and thus of chaos, are almost always the best possible, if enough people refuse.*

Through their gesture, which was not a heroic act but a claim on their morality, the young Jews of Lachwa refused passive acceptance and went beyond the doing-nothing form of resistance. Instead, they chose to choose, regaining possession of their lives and, ultimately, of their deaths as well.

> *As a crowd gathers 'round an angry young man*
> *face down on the street with a gun in his hand*
>
> M. Mac Davis/E. Presley – In the ghetto, 1969

ENDNOTES

1 *St. Petersburg Times,* June 17, 1973.

2 *Der Spiegel,* 45/1972, p. 100.

3 On the *Schwalbe case* see Schäfer, pp. 421 ff.

4 *St. Petersburg Times,* June 17, 1973.

5 Gerlach, pp. 164-165.

6 *Ibid.*, p. 188, Curilla, p. 863. Pütz, who held this position until November 1943, was the main person responsible for the massacre of about 300,000 Jews of his district, perpetrated mainly during 1942. He committed suicide on May 6, 1945 in St. Märgen im Schwarzwald. Schäfer, p. 144.

7 Rasp, a Kriminalpolizei official at the RSHA was transferred to Ukraine on May 8, 1942 together with other colleagues of Munich and assigned to SD office, with the role of commander of the Pinsk detachment. Testimony given by Rasp before the public prosecutor of Frankfurt am Main, 4 Ks 1/71 of January 4, 1962. Schäfer, p. 144.

8 The detachment coming from France was the so-called *Ernteschutzkommando Metz,* formed in July / August 1942 by BdS "Lothringen-Saarpfalz", Anton Dunckern, on orders by RSHA, with 30-35 elements of the Sipo detachments of Saarbrücken, Ludwigshafen, Kaiserslautern, Neustadt / Weinstrasse and other localities of Rhineland. The *kommando* arrived in Brest Litovsk between August 20 and 24, 1942 and was later posted to several Zweigstellen. Schäfer, pp. 144-146, Gerlach, p. 710.

9 Having to drive away from him the suspicion of having organized the slaughters of the fall of 1942, it seems that Rasp tried to put all the blame on deputy-Gebietkommissar Alfred Ebner who, obviously, rejected the accusations and blamed Rasp. When Gäde was questioned, he confirmed Ebner's version.

10 *«Zentrale Einsatzstelle der Judervernichtungsaktionen in den Bezirken Pinsk und Stolin».* StAw Frankfurt am Main 4 Ks 1/71. Schäfer, p. 142.

11 In this chapter the original denomination of both battalion and companies will be kept.

12 Schäfer, pp. 61-62.

13 In August 1942 another battalion of the same regiment, namely Polizei-Bataillon 310 (III/5), was deployed between Brest Litovsk and Korbyn, while III/Polizei-Regiment 11 (earlier Polizei-Bataillon 320) was in Kobryn. Gerlach, p. 710.

14 Curilla, p. 630.

15 LG Bochum of 20.10.1970, 16 Ks 1/70 against August Huft, p. 671.

16 Klemp Ermittelt, p. 188, Curilla, p. 615, LG Bochum 16 Ks 1/70, pp. 699-700.

17 The photos are attached to the indictment of the public prosecutor in Dortmund against Paul Jordan, platoon commander of 3/69, accused and acquitted for the executions of Dowsk and Peklana, Belarus. StAwDo 45 Js 11/64, LG Wuppertal 11 Ks 1/69 of April 30, 1970. Klemp Ermittelt, pp. 195-196, 503.

18 Schäfer, p. 150.

19 *Ibid.*, pp. 150-151. Also, von Kellenbach, p. 312.

20 Klemp Ermittelt, p. 196.

21 Schäfer, pp. 312 ff.

22 Klemp Ermittelt, p. 196, describing the four auxiliaries in the photo distinguishes betwenn "militians *(polnischer Milizionär)", "*auxiliaries *(polnischer Hilfswilliger)"* and "local firemen *(einheimische Feuerwehrleute)",* in addition to a fifth member of Polizei-Bataillon 69. What is certain is that the uniforms are completely different: that of the *militian,* of a dark color, probably black, reminds us of the uniform of Sonderdienst recruited among the *volksdeutschen* of the General Government, while that of the *auxiliary* is similar to the combinations worn by Schuma units.

23 Gerlach, p. 710. More than a real extermination camp, Bronnaja Gora reminded more of a *killing field,* with huge mass graves scattered here and there for the victims' executions.

24 On the Mogilev camp see Christian Gerlach's article: *Fail-*

ure of plans for an SS Extermination Camp in Mogilev, Belorussia. Holocaust and Genocide Studies, vol. 11 nr. 3.

25 Goldhagen, p. 216.

26 «*Judenweiber in die Sümpfe treiben*». Order by SS-Kavallerie-Regiment 2 dated August 1, 1941. Gerlach, p. 560, Browning Origini, pp. 293, 501. Maybe, who knows, this was exactly what EM 52 of August 14, 1941 hinted to when he suggested that the Jewish masses be used *in excess* to crop [sic!] the swamps of Pripyat.

27 USHMM. *Encyclopedia of Camps and Ghettos. 1939-1945.*

28 Hilberg, pp. 316-317. The SS cavalry brigade entered Soviet territory on July 21, 1941.

29 Of the main massacres perpetrated by 1. SS-Kavallerie-Brigade in the western area of Pripyat, those of Telechany (August 6-7, 2,000 victims), Gantsevichi (August 11, 2,500), Pinsk (August 5, 1,950; August 7, 2,450) should be mentioned. Curilla, pp. 902 ff.

30 *Ibid.*, p. 904. According to Cholawsky, p. 193, the mop up was executed between August 16 and 18, and the victims were released after the payment of a ransom in gold and valuables.

31 A Teilkommando of Schöngarth's EG zbV, commanded by SS-Hauptsturmführer Hess (17 men of KdS "Lublin"), remained deployed in Pinsk from early June to early October. Curilla, p. 860, Gerlach, p. 541.

32 Dov Lopatin, already president of one of the clandestine Zionist movements of Lachwa during the Soviet occupation, managed to run away from the ghetto the day of the slaughter. He joined the partisan group "Stalinsky" and was killed by a mine explosion on February 1, 1944. Cholawsky, pp. 193, 198.

33 Gerlach, p. 676.

34 *Ibid.*, p. 532. In addition to Lachwa's, the ghettos of Janov and Serniki (April 1942), Pinsk (May 1, 1942) and Lenin (May 10) were established in the region of Pripyat.

35 Schäfer, p. 100.

36 Gerlach, p. 714. Considering that the transfer of the Jews to the ghettos had been completed much earlier (May 1942), it is obvious that the *speeding* requested by Pütz referred to the extermination project. Then, considering that the last great massacre of the Pripyat region, namely that of Pinsk, was perpetrated at the end of October, we understand that the *five-week* goal desired by Pütz in the meeting of late August had only just been missed.

37 Dean, pp. 93, 195, Gerlach, p. 714. The exceptions would have been in favor of workers considered essential, for a period of two months not exceeding 500 people. Koch's will was well-known to the top levels of the Wehrmacht: see the communiqué of Wbfh. "Ukraine" Gen. Karl Kitzinger, of September 12, 1942.

38 Curilla, p. 650, Gerlach, p. 56.

39 Curilla, p. 650, Gerlach, p. 56. The desperate search for food was a matter of survival for the ghetto residents, who often defied the punishments imposed by the occupiers. In one case seven women intent on finding food in the nearby locality of Prinovo were shot. Schäfer, p. 101, Cholawsky, p. 195. This episode confirms the obvious inadequacy of the supplies granted to the ghetto, and the minimum impact that they could have had if they had been diverted in favor of the Ukrainians.

40 Dean, pp. 93, 195. On the possible controversies concerning Rasps's testimony, see previous note n. 9/14.

41 Gerlach, pp. 715-716.

42 *Ibid.*, p. 716, Curilla, p. 864: Mikaschevichi, August 6, 420 victims; Mokrovo, August, 280÷300 victims; Malorita, 1,000 victims, mid August.

43 Schäfer, p. 101, Cholawsky, p. 195, Curilla, p. 630.

44 Schäfer, p. 101, testimony given before L.S., StAw Frankfurt am Main, 4 Ks 1/71, dated November 26, 1965.

45 Cholawsky, p. 196.

46 Overall, six Germans and eight Belarusian policemen would have been killed, and several others were wounded. Cholawsky, p. 197, Schäfer, p. 101.

47 Lichtenstein, p. 183.

48 Cholawsky, p. 197.

49 Lichtenstein, p. 183.

50 Cholawsky, p. 197, Schäfer, pp. 102-103, Curilla, pp. 630-631, Lichtenstein, p. 183.

51 Curilla, p. 631. StAw Frankfurt am Main, 4 Ks 1/71.

52 Schäfer, p. 103.

53 Gerlach, p. 718, who quotes testimonies of survivors and resident civilians, given in 1992, and data from the museum of the Great Patriotic War in Minsk.

54 Curilla, p. 631, Cholawsky, p. 198.

55 Kozan Gorodek, September 3,500 victims; Luninec, 2,800 victims, September 4; Vysokoie, September 9, 1,400 victims; David Gorodek, September 10, 1,100 victims; Stolin 6,500÷7,000 victims, September 11; Janov, September 24-25, 3,000 victims; Drahichyn, October 14, 2,000 victims; Pinsk, October 29, 18,000 victims. Curilla, p. 864-865, Gerlach, pp. 718-719.

56 Schäfer, p. 374.

57 Lichtenstein, pp. 177-178, Schäfer, pp. 61 ff.

58 ZStL 204 AR-Z 393/59. Mallmann/Riess/Pyta, pp. 45-46, 177.

59 For the reconstruction of the vicissitudes of the procedure against Ebner, see the article written by his niece Katharina von Kellenbach: *Vanishing acts: Perpetrators in post-war Germany.* In Holocaust and Genocide Studies, vol. 17 nr. 2, pp. 305-329.

60 Schäfer, p. 156.

61 *Ibid.*, p. 417.

62 Von Kellenbach, p. 310.

63 *St. Petersburg Times,* June 17, 1973.

64 The fact that the Germans tried to induce the *Judenrat* to betray their own community, offering the reward of thirty Jews to be rescued, thirty like the coins Judas was offered to betray Christ, appears viciously symbolic. In this sense, although it was likely the result of a numerical coincidence, the possibility that the perpetrators wanted to make fun of their victims, disgracing them on the charge of deciding and insisting on the stereotype of the false and treacherous *Jew* is plausible. A wickedness completely consistent with the established Nazi of *celebrating* the Jewish anniversaries through mass executions. However, the *Judenrat* should be remembered for honorably not accepting the disgraceful trade.

65 Eyal Weizman: *Il male minore.* Rome, 2009.

Warsaw: German police escorting a group of Polish civilians.

PHOTO SECTION 2

"Propaganda is an art: it has nothing to do with the truth."
(Joseph Goebbles).

Examples of Jewish physiognomy, as per Nazi propaganda (see paragraphs 6.2 and 11.3)

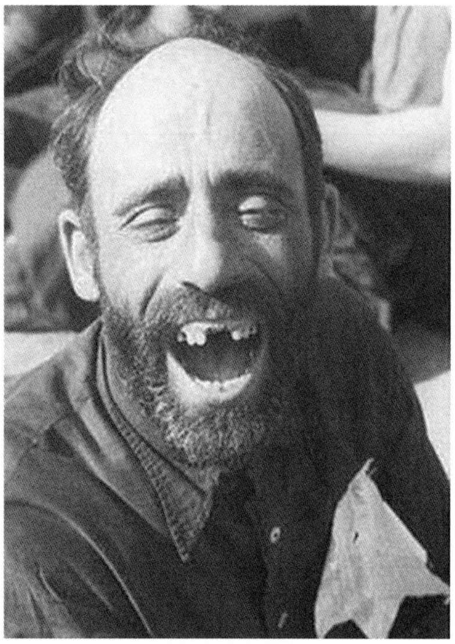

Mogilev, July 1941
(Kriegsberichter Kessler)

Kielce, January 1940.

Belgrade, April 1941
(Kriegsberichter Neubauer).

Belgrade, April 1941
(Kriegsberichter Neubauer).

Examples of Jewish physiognomy, as per Nazi propaganda (see paragraphs 6.2 and 11.3)

Belgrade, April 1941 (Kriegsberichter Neubauer).

Thessaloniki, July 1942 (Kriegsberichter Dick).

Thessaloniki, July 1942 (Kriegsberichter Dick).

Thessaloniki, July 1942 (Kriegsberichter Dick).

A dying old Jew on a street of the Warsaw ghetto, summer 1941. Death by starvation, especially among the poorest, was a tragic rule in Eastern ghettos. Source: Bundesarchiv.

The primitive makeshift shelters reserved for the Jews of the Kutno ghetto. September 1940. Note the "hairdresser" (Friseur) sign, as if to symbolize the search for a grotesque normality of life. Source: Bundesarchiv.

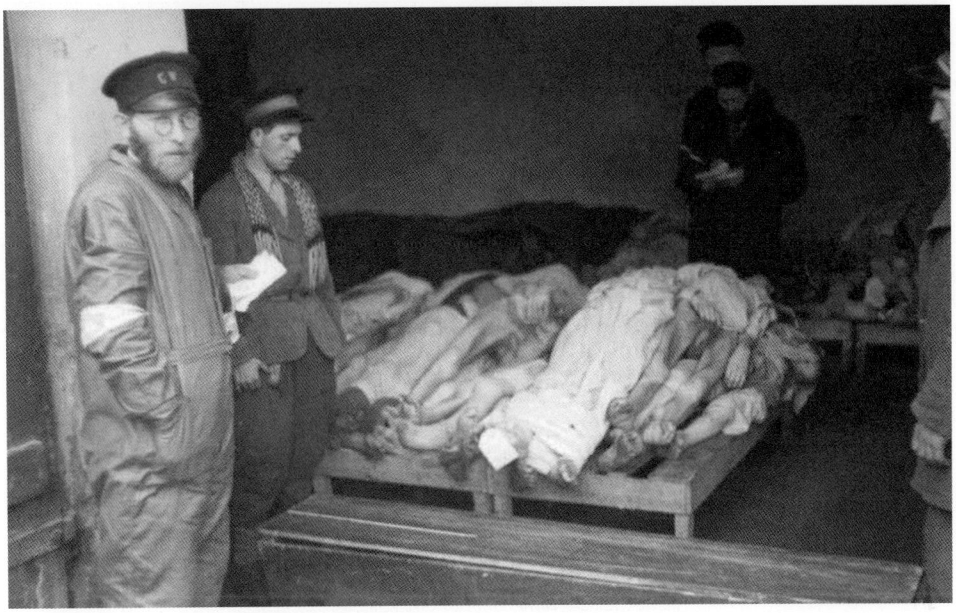

Warsaw Jewish ghetto, May 25, 1941: men of the Jewish police in service at the ghetto's morgue. Source: Bundesarchiv.

July 1941: a group of Jews arrested by men of an auxiliary Lithuanian unit in an unspecified location. Source: Bundesarchiv.

Jewish ghetto in Lodz, 1941. Film shots by Propagandakompanie 689. Source: Bundesarchiv.

Lodz, 1941: the bridge that linked the two parts of the Jewish ghetto overlooking the road reserved for "Aryan" traffic. German police guarded the entrances so that no Jew might trespass. Note the cameraman of Propagandakompanie 689 intent on filming to the right of the road along the fence. Source: Bundesarchiv.

Krakow, December 1939. Jews waiting to be deported, probably to forced labor in Germany. Source: Bundesarchiv.

Radom ghetto, 1940: a propaganda photo by Kriegsberichter Bruno Wisniewski, playing around the most typical racial stereotypes of the time, portraying three Jews made to pose bargaining. See paragraph 13.4. Source: Bundesarchiv..

Lodz, 1940. A group of Jews carries their pitiful belongings during the resettlement within the perimeter of the ghetto. Source: Bundesarchiv.

A famous image of the liquidation of the Krakow ghetto in March 1943. Note the sign for the police station, heavily involved in the raid, on the left.

Lithuanian activists in front of a burning synagogue in an unspecified location. Note the armbands typical of the first days after Barbarossa, with crude hand-drawn swastikas. Source: Bundesarchiv.

A chaotic moment of the resettlement of a group of Jews in the Grodno ghetto in November 1941, under the watchful eyes of the German policemen.

A glimpse of the dilapidated Chişinău ghetto in August 1941, just days after the massacres perpetrated by SK 11a and a platoon of Polizei-Bataillon 9. See paragraph 9.3.2. Source: Bundesarchiv.

Warsaw, around 1940: the miserable conditions in which many dwellers of the Jewish ghetto were forced to survive.

One of the entrances to the Vilnius ghetto, watched by a uniformed Lithuanian policeman. In front of him, first from the left in plain clothes, a member of the Jewish Ordnungsdienst, his armband on the left arm barely visible in the picture.

EPILOGUE

DAYS AFTER JUNE

Hier werden sämtliche Juden erschossen.
Überall sind solche Aktionen im Gange.
Gestern nach sind aus diesem Ort 150 Juden erschossen.
Männer, Frauen, Kinder, alles umgelegt.
Juden werden gänzlich ausgerottet.

Hermann Gieschen, Polizei-Bataillon 105, August 7, 1941[1]

1 REACHING THE NIGHT[2]

Eastern Belarus, somewhere along the flow of Dnieper River. September 1, 1941.

It slid southwards, slow and silent, wrapped in brief turbulences only where the line of the current broke around the small muddy banks which the summer drought had caused to emerge. It flowed indifferently, dragging small branches in the muddy waters and sometimes stranded in meanders of dead waters suffocated by the great swamp that stretched along both banks. It advanced between reeds, almost losing itself in a single horizon, and then exited after finding itself again. The river. As the Zambezi in Livingston's chronicles, or the Nile in Gordon's visions, or the Congo in Conrad's words. The river: like a flow towards the end, torpid unraveling of Atropos' thread of life; or like upstream way back towards the origin, a slow rewind of a tape on the spool. Estuary mouth and source, origin and end, binary math suspended midway between metaphysics and reality. The river as a metaphor for the path, place of arrival or departure point for a journey that could begin, and, in fact, had already begun a few weeks before but, in reality, an eternal time before, beyond the meander, along the flow, until the night was reached.

The night enveloped the river in currents of darkness which, as the path went on, became thicker and thicker; they had found themselves "landing in a swamp, marching through the woods, and feeling that, someplace inland, cruelty and sheer barbarism were waiting and had already locked up" around them[3]. They were descending into maelstrom, supported by their will of omnipotence, yet imbued with death at every step.

They had already used sword, torch and voice, as in the solstice rites of the sacred Externsteine site, but that time the flames had lit the night but had not illuminated it, the blade had spread terror but had not demonstrated power and the word had not vibrated for mercy but to cry out screams of pain. There was no honor in anything they had done, but then again: how could there be honor in barbarism, or light in the darkness, or even only understanding for the incomprehensible? How could there be moral when human civilization was yet to come?

After all, it was not up to them to seek honor: their mission was to bring the light. And if in order to bring the light they would have to use the torch, then, by God, they would not pull back, and the glow of the flames would predict the dawn of a new era. It would take time, perseverance and determination, so that the destiny might be fulfilled, and it was necessary to first destroy and then rebuild on the ruins, in the same way as soil has to be ploughed, deeply ploughed, for new seeds to be planted. There would be many casualties, even among themselves, but that blood would be as necessary as water in the concrete for the foundations of the future, ideal symbol of a new *Blutfahne* to celebrate the sacrifice. And then, perhaps, there would be compassion, but only after the end, once the horror of darkness was removed, and the immoral horde was finally conquered: only then could there be mercy for the defeated, a few of whom, perhaps, but only a few, could be converted and claim a place into the new society. All the others, most of the others, *had to be uprooted so that they*, Arminius' warriors, *could keep on living*[4].

2 LONG AFTER MIDNIGHT

Minsk, September 2, 1941, about 02:25 hours

He would have wanted to forget that day by simply deleting it, like a diary page botched and rewritten, but he feared it would not be possible. Not that he had not tried, actually, he was trying at that very moment as well; however, while the rational half of his brain struggled to reassure the other half, a malignant instinctive voice whispered that he would not be able to get away with it cheaply by pretending that nothing had happened. Perhaps, with the passing of days, images would become muffled and sounds confused, replaced by new, fresher impressions. After all, they were at war and every day brought something new, and different experiences that they had never had before, that one day would eventually be reduced to a single frame of a much longer film, before which it would have been enough to just shut his eyes for a moment, to let it pass. Like that time many years before – it was the summer of 1933 and he had just turned 18 – when he had attended the screening of a horrible feature movie of a German expressionist director, whose name he did not even remember anymore, a homosexual degenerate, as it was whispered back then, in which there were disgusting images of a monster that fed on human blood, before which he had closed his eyes waiting for them to finish.

So, perhaps that's what will happen again. In time. Because meanwhile, laying on his bed in the darkness of his lodging, every time he tried to close his eyes to try and sleep, he saw those frames appear again before him, and again he heard the sounds and even felt the smells of that day, the stench of sweat, fear, that obscene mixture of blood and body fluids released without restraint, which smeared the clothes of the victims and that even lime could not absorb completely...

Gerhard Riebel opened his eyes for the umpteenth time during that night of lost sleep, irritated at the more than two hours that were still to pass before the alarm clock beeped and that he – it was clear by now – would not be able to take advantage of. It had not been like that right from the beginning, but only since he took leave of the other officers, shortly after consuming the evening meal. During the afternoon, he had been too busy with his work, to stop and *see* what they were doing.

They had been busy since dawn, when, with a group of trucks, they had entered the Minsk prison to collect the victims that would end up in the mass graves. In truth, except at the beginning, he had been almost always with the battalion command officers and had left the heavy work to his lieutenants; the platoon leaders. Like Rasche: that fanatic who seemed to enjoy himself doing what he did. He had seen him repeatedly beat the victims with a club, while they descended off the trucks and he shoved them, in columns, along the ramp of earth that from the edge of the trench led to the bottom of the ditch, where the firing squad was waiting. He had also thought of rebuking him, especially after seeing him savagely beat up an elderly man who had failed to get off the truck fast enough. But then he let go, distracting himself with the battalion commander Nagel, who swore nervously against that dirty *work* they were carrying out and about to finish.

There were orders and they had to obey, that was clear, as it was clear that those who were shot were Jewish, i.e. those who were the main culprits for all that filth. At the same time, however, no one could explain why the choice fell precisely on them, ordinary policemen, when there were others in the field, SS and Gestapo people who were certainly more suitable and willing to do that sort of thing. Its commander, Nagel, thought so, and even his old friend Uhl, the battalion adjutant, a rather pale Swabian who looked disgusted and seemed perpetually on the verge of being sick. And, certainly, many other colleagues felt the same way. Many, except Rasche of course, who always plunged into the pit to give orders to the firing squad, one group of victims after the other, asking for a replacement only for the time needed to smoke a cigarette or drink a sip of brandy, generously made available by an Inspectorate van.

In a sense, he envied Rasche because Rasche hated

the Jews and everything was easier for him. He gave the firing orders with satisfaction and did not hesitate to get his hands dirty himself, inflicting death blows to those injured: not always, however, only when the wound was minor and there was no risk of wasting a bullet only to accelerate a death that would be accomplished nonetheless. Yes, it was easier to work that way. He had seen him, after the execution, gather his platoon as if nothing had happened to give a *reprimand* to two men who had showed up untidy, just as would happen after an exercise with some negligent freshmen. He had seen Rasche volunteer where others pulled back and had heard him threaten punishment for his men who were more hesitant when killing or reluctant to join the firing squad. Rasche believed in what he did and he did it well. But for them it was different. They killed without hate, with a sense of duty, but without enthusiasm. They knew that it was necessary because there was no doubt that things worked that way. There was always someone who gave orders and someone else who had to act upon them and they were among the latter, because that was the way things went and no one could do a thing about it.

The truth is that once, only once, he, Riebel, had tried to raise an objection, actually before the commander in chief of German police himself, who had visited Bialystok a few weeks before. Daluege had stared into his eyes for a moment, perhaps surprised by such impudence and coldly rebuked him, reminding him of his oath and his duty as a soldier. He, Riebel, had felt stupid before those severe words, and realized that it was not his job to judge what others above him had deemed adequate. That very moment he had decided to remain silent, keeping his doubts and continuing to do his duty normally and as he knew he could do well. In the end it was not difficult, all it took was to follow the instructions that he received; orders were neither good nor bad, they were orders and that was it, and if sometimes any doubt arose, well, that did not depend on the order in itself, but on his weakness of man. It was his problem alone, and he would have to work on this in the future, on how to strengthen his own sense of duty, and not on how to weaken it, in order to make everything easier.

Yes, he did envy Rasche, indeed, because that night, Rasche, would manage to sleep.

A partaker in the killings at Bialystok, Bialowieza, Minsk and Mogilev, Gerhard Riebel was tried and acquitted together with his colleagues Uhl and Hülsemann by the Court of Freiburg which, in its judgment of July 12, 1963, rejected the request for conviction to five years' imprisonment advanced by the public prosecutor of the same city.

Described by all his colleagues as "Judenhasser", Erich Rasche, platoon leader and deputy commander of 3/322, was killed in action near Mogilev on December 2, 1942.

3 BEFEHLSEMPFÄNGER

Schutzpolizeikommando Memel, around mid-September 1941

Quite unexpectedly it seemed that his name, in those last weeks, had been forgotten, as an object that too much use has deteriorated. If it were so he would not take offense nor lose his wits over it; on the contrary, he would be pleased by it, so much so in fact that he wished it would stay that way forever. However, rationally, he knew that amnesia could not be the reason explaining his estrangement, there were far more valid reasons to it: first and foremost the fact that now other *wood-heads* were available to take care of the most unpleasant work, sparing him and his men this burden. Indeed, ever since July, numerous Lithuanians policemen had been recruited who seemed not to despise having to get their hands dirty and that on several occasions, as far as he knew, had diligently *committed themselves* to complying with the orders of this or that SD or Grenzpolizei department [5]: as a few days earlier, in late August, when just outside Garsden a hundred Jewish women, with their children, were shot. Actually, that time there had been some problems due to the fact that at a certain moment, the Lithuanians had finally had too much to drink and had become almost uncontrollable, but it was the price to pay for using that mob in their stead. After all, they had resolved a trouble and in any case there was not that much difference, for a Jew, to be killed by a disciplined German policeman, or some auxiliary drunk; so to hell with everything and may the Lithuanians or anybody else continue to manage it all by themselves. After all, were they, the Germans, or were they not the *Herrenrasse?*[6]

Werner Schmidt Hammer finished checking out his department's roster: everything was in order, except for the usual two or three drifters who, like almost every day, reported sick and prevented his squad being at full strength. He vowed to make himself heard, but he knew that would have been a complete flop: those he had to refer to were not warriors, just a bunch of lazy and overweight cops, and the best individuals among them were often detached and transferred to some battalions to the front. He could talk again with Maj. Günther, but he knew that as always, the answer would be to fix things as best as he could with what he had. So he could not but resign himself: that morning also his *Alarmzug* would face the *desantniki* short of three men. However, thank heaven!, there was no sign of any *desantniki*, actually, to tell the truth, there never had been.

Schmidt-Hammer checked the watch around his wrist: his men were having breakfast so that meant almost another twenty minutes before the inspection, the time needed to smoke a cigarette in peace. He relaxed leaning on the back of his chair. It was a strange war he was fighting, so strange in fact that if someone had talked about it to him only a few months earlier, he would have taken that person for a madman. Yet that was what had happened. He had not yet seen an enemy face in uniform, but in compensation he had already shot and killed many times, though with much reluctance, especially that first time, in Garsden, a few weeks before.

That day, June 24, it had been very hard.

He remembered that day well. He had been told that there were several terrorists to be shot; guilty of the murder of some German soldiers in an ambulance, and that was what they had prepared for, in the courtyard of their barracks. But then, in front of the barrel of their rifles, lined up along the edge of the pit, what they found before themselves were Jewish civilians, many of them older than 70 or very young, like a twelve-year old child, who did not have the appearance of guerrilla fighters at all. Some, indeed, came from Memel, they had known them personally, like Feinstein, the soap maker, who, before being killed, called out by his name one of the platoon policemen, Oberwachtmeister Gustav Knopens, and asked him to aim straight[7].

Yes, that had been a difficult experience, and one that had lasted a long time. The Jews had been brought before them amid blows of sticks, in groups of ten, and they had to repeat the same procedure at least twenty times, with the level of the victims in the pit rising more and more, the firing by the exhausted policemen becoming less and less accurate, to the point that he himself, Werner, had been forced to intervene frequently to inflict the final blow to the head of the wounded ones[8].

Eventually, the job done, some SD member had pulled out bottles of liquor and some, perhaps to commemorate the event, had even taken photos. But there had been no goliardery or relief among his men at the end of the execution; the mood was very somber and several of his men went up to him asking why they had been forced to do those things. They had asked him once back in Memel, and he, who could not do anything about it, who knew not more than them, had had to answer awkwardly, almost apologetically, that he was only "a small receiver of orders"[9].

That's how things had gone, actually, but despite considering himself rationally justified in his actions, long after the action he had continued to remember the words of Sergeant Kersten to his comrades, uttered in the truck during the return trip from Gardsen, after they had managed to escape, almost miraculously, the sudden incursion of a Russian aircraft: "See? Our punishment is following us"[10].

Schmidt-Hammer stubbed out the cigarette in the ashtray and left his office in the building that functioned as the headquarters of 1. *Polizeirevier* which was in front of the yard where he had already gathered his small department. It looked like it was going to be a quiet *routine* day, an absolutely perfect day, and he was happy with such perfection.

He was glad that after the massacre at Garsden, then at Krottingen, and then at Polangen, which came soon after, someone had decided to finally give his men and himself a little break, replacing them with the Lithuanians. He was pleased that after having given so much, someone had finally forgotten about them, turning elsewhere.

Indeed, the Lithuanians were more suitable for that type of *work*: he was sure about that. Just as he was certain that he, *a small receiver of orders*, preferred to devote himself to perfect *routine* days such as that day.

A partaker in the massacres at Gargždai, Kretinga and Palanga, for a total of 526 victims, Oltn. Walter Schmidt-Hammer was sentenced on November 3, 1960 by the Court of Ulm to three years' imprisonment for complicity in murder.

Previously, on August 29, 1958 the same court of Ulm had sentenced SA-Oberfüher Bernard Fischer-Schweder to 10 years in prison.

4 CRIME AND PUNISHMENT[11]

Kirovograd, Ukraine, September 30, 1941

What zbV meant was now clear to everyone.

They had learned that day after day, moving along a road that someone had already dubbed the *Durchgangstrasse IV* which was being built for military traffic that led from Western Ukraine to the east, towards the Black Sea, through villages that none of them had ever heard of: villages of small izbas spread along a single street, or gathered in small isolated groups around the clay courts. Old Ukrainian peasants had offered them bread and salt and some *starosts* as old as time had uttered words of welcome. And when they had asked for eggs and potatoes they also received some milk; they had ordered and had been obeyed.

They did not stay long in the villages, just enough for the men to stop and have some refreshment and top up the water of the vehicles' radiators and then they resumed the march, no one knew whither, but everyone knew that it was very far away.

Sometimes, however, they stopped for longer, and these stops could last for one or two days, in some cases even more: it depended on the number of Jews to be shot. In those cases, they could take things easy, take time to organize themselves and wait for *the boss* to arrive.

The boss traveled accompanied by his personal guards, the *Stabskompanie*, SS and Security Police men with automatic weapons, who traveled aboard large passenger cars and big trucks and that, it was said, had left bloody traces in their wake: like in Kamenec Podolski, in August, and Berdychiv, only a few days earlier, where their colleagues of Polizei-Bataillon 45 had killed many Jews. It worked that way, and no one was surprised about that by now. The boss arrived, conferred with the battalion commander, at times witnessed the execution and then left again towards the next village. By now they had learned to remember his name: Jeckeln, before which it seemed that no one would dare argue. Even their commander, Maj. Kurt Deckert, who tolerated with satisfaction the *Judenhasser* nickname that he was known by among the men of his battalion[12], appeared to be intimidated in front of that Jeckeln, easily angered and arrogant when approaching his subordinates. In fact, each time he appeared around the battalion or even every time he sent an order through some liaison officer of his staff; it meant trouble, or, quite simply, some new group of Jews to be killed. That is how it had been since they had entered Ukraine, in early August and so it was that day, near Kirovograd, while his company was preparing to give death to four thousand Jews.

Yes, what zbV meant was now clear to all. They had left some men to guard the entrances, while another platoon was placed on the edge of a mass grave of 30 or 35 yards in length and at least five-yards deep, already partially filled with bodies. At one end, at regular intervals, the platoon leader gave the firing order on the victims forced to lie down in the trench, while at the other end, at the beginning of a slide of land that led directly into the pit, the following group of victims that had just been pushed off the trucks was assembled[13].

This had been going on for several hours already, including periodic replacement of the platoon involved in killing with those assigned to other duties. Now it was now their turn.

By now Manfred Pohlig did not even remember any more how many times they had already shot the Jews. They had passed through many villages and also quite large towns, and every time there had been some new group of Jews to be eliminated. He had discussed it with his battalion colleagues, like Melzer and Schumann, who, in addition, had been among the ones who had attended the *special course* in Krakow and thus understood about it and concluded that, indeed, there *must have been* a reason why they were ordered to do those things so often: civilians, after all, should not have been killed without a reason even in war, and if every time they found themselves having to deal with those Jews, then obviously it was because the Jews had done something wrong. Everybody in the battalion, even among command officers, said that the Jews were insolent and treacherous, something that was also repeated by Jeckeln's envoys, who inquired about everything, took notes and wrote their reports. It did not take much imagination to understand that those rumors about the Jews were true, it was enough to see what happened when the Department entered a new village: the Ukrainians would get close and so would the Russians, sometimes. They would bring bread, salt and milk, the kids would ask soldiers for candies, the most brazen ones would even ask for cigarettes. The Jews would not, on the contrary, they hid, they stayed away, many would even try to pass themselves off as Russians or Ukrainians by altering their names or by cutting their curls to camouflage themselves, as if they had something to hide, indeed, perhaps, *precisely because they had* something to hide. As had happened in those days in Kirovograd, where, upon exhibiting false documents, many Jews had managed to hide their origin, thus obtaining new identity cards that reclassified them as non-Jews, and in some cases, at the height of their impudence, even as *volksdeutsche*[14].

It was obvious, thus, that finally someone had decided to punish such arrogance, and take more stringent measures to block the spread of frauds. It might have seemed unpleasant, but it was only the just punishment following crime. After all, these Russian Jews should have known how things went around there; they should have known that punishment would inevitably follow a crime committed: they should have accepted that instead of hiding, they should have confessed instead of lying. On closer inspection, it was actually famous men of Russia, their homeland, who had said and written so much about crime and punishment. But, obviously, they were not real Russians, they were not *Rodja Raskol'nikov*, nor did they consume in guilt in order to redeem in punishment: they were only lying and treacherous Jews, who in the end could not redeem themselves, but only pay for their wrongdoings. And, who knows, beyond the criminal acts that they could have committed from time to time, perhaps it was because of their being Jews that they were punished: because of their false religious messianism, which eventually would now have to come to terms with the new messianism embodied by the Führer, as if for a divine revenge[15].

Yes, it *had to be* so. Those people who were shot by the hundreds in mass graves, who staggered on seemingly helpless in front of the barrels of their guns, did actually carry within themselves the stigma of a collective guilt; perhaps individually some of them had not committed any crime but this basically meant nothing, because, if punishment had to be dispensed, the blame rested *on the whole lot*, and it could not have been otherwise. Furthermore, obviously, it was all about punishment, because if it had not been so, then all of them would not have happened to be there at that time: those who fired and those who were killed, both instruments of God's will.

So, that was the reason why all this was happening, and that was why there could not be a rebellion by those who were killed and there could be no doubt from those who were called to shoot. The Jews, resigned and mournful, seemed to have understood that, therefore he, Manfred Pohlig, should have understood it too, while leading them to their deaths along the earth slide, without looking at them, one victim after another.

Moreover, after all, who on earth was he to think he could question God's will?

A partaker in the killings at Vinnitsa, Gaisin and Kirovograd, Manfred Pohlig was convicted and sentenced to life imprisonment by the Court of Halle on July 11, 1988. His request for reinstatement was rejected by the Court of Magdeburg on June 3, 1992. The same penalty was imposed by the Court of Halle on his colleagues Kurt Melzer and Arno Ernst Schumann on October 26, 1978.

5 I'VE SEEN THINGS…

Kempolovo Lager, south of Krasnoje Selo, Leningrad area, April 30, 1942

Hans knew that eventually, he would get into trouble, but did not really care that much.

When he was younger, someone had taught him that things had to be done if you felt like doing them, and, at that time, he had felt like doing that in spite of everything. He was not a hypocrite, Hans Hespe, and did not like hiding behind words of convenience or circumstance, nor did he like hiding behind the mask of obedience, as almost all his colleagues did. From the beginning he had decided to respond only to his own conscience, despite the sorrow that this attitude would have procured him. And so he did, and so, punctually, sorrow came to him. However, at the moment he did not worry about it, because the prospect of having to deal with his conscience, in case he had resigned and repressed himself, would have destabilized him a lot more.

Thus, he had not repressed himself, and the furious dispute that a few weeks earlier, on February 24, 1942, he had had in Lyuban with his company commander, Hptm. Theodor Westphal, had set in motion a mechanism that he did not know where exactly would lead him. For the moment he had been arrested and had to answer before an SS military tribunal, he was completely aware that it would lash out a severe punishment against him.

He had taken all that into consideration and still it was not enough to dissuade him, immediately after the altercation, to present his own heavy countermemorial – signed and motivated, accusing nearly all his officers, including the battalion commander, Maj. Hans Helwes – to the command of the 254th Infantry Division, upon which his battalion depended.

That is how sour things had gone. He had thrown the stone into the pond despite the risk of soaking himself with water, and he was not sorry. On the other hand, there were many reasons that had led him to that act; reasons that had accumulated since the battalion had entered Soviet territory, in late June 1941.

He, Hans Hespe, had seen the corruption of his officers, ready to satisfy their low instincts of thieves, entering the homes of the people to plunder them, despite the condemnation of the same population of Latvia who initially had welcomed them with a smile. Food, fabrics, cameras, watches, silverware… all was packaged and shipped to Germany, to the wives at home, especially by his immediate superior Westphal, or by Hptm. Ernst Petersen, First Company's commander[16]: acts of surreal insult to the orders of the *Stadtkommandantur* of Riga itself which, through wall posters put up everywhere, bluntly threatened with shooting – *Wer wird plündert erschossen!* – looters caught red-handed.

He, Hans Hespe, had seen the cowardice and ineptitude of his officers, always ready to beg medals and decorations from their superiors even before having faced a single Russian soldier, but not as zealous in defending the positions when they finally found themselves having to fight in the front line: as in Nowaja Derewnja, in January 1942, where what was to be only a retreat turned into a stampede, evidently considered the best solution in that moment[17].

He, Hans Hespe, had seen the felony of his officers when they covered-up incidents, such as death in battle by a sniper, the killing of Hamburg policeman Robert Baar by one of his fellow soldiers and at whose funeral, held with full honors in Raseiniai, Latvia, he himself had to attend in the guard of honor for *the Führer, the People and the Fatherland*[18].

He, Hans Hespe, had seen the amorality and vice of his officers, some of whom were so addicted to alcohol to the point of being unable to continue to lead their departments. That had happened with Theodor Westphal, found drunk and away from his leadership positions, entirely forgetful of his own duties during the Russians' attacks; vice and amorality that he, Hespe, had not hesitated to denounce in his letters home, describing his officers as drunkards, sadists, whoremongers, thieves, arsonists and clowns...[19].

He, Hans Hespe, had seen the brutality of his officers, ready to kill for a simple suspicion, or even for the physical characteristics, such as Hptm. Fritz Dittmar, commander of 3/105, which fired on sight any civilian with a shaved head, considering him to be a partisan or a prisoner escaped from a concentration camp, or like many others who suggested to kill point blank all those who they met in forest. He had witnessed the destruction of entire villages, in order to deprive the partisans of possible shelters during the winter nights, with the result of condemning women, children and the elderly to a freezing death[20]. He had been witness to many executions of alleged prisoners of war, men and women, behind a simple order of Maj. Helwes, and he was had also been placed in a firing squad in Kempolovo, from which, however, he had managed to escape after convincing his sergeant to replace him with other volunteers[21].

He, Hans Hespe, had seen all those things, so he had decided not to remain silent, even if he knew that he would have to pay in person for what he had said and especially for what he had *not* done: adapt to the situation.

So, he was now imprisoned, on Helwes' orders, in the Kempolovo concentration camp, guarded by his own comrades and soon to appear before the military tribunal of the SS in Riga. He had accepted the inevitable, whatever the price. And then, in so doing, he had even found great satisfaction: most of all the satisfaction of saying politely to his commander Maj. Helwes' face exactly what he thought of him: "Major, in this battalion, the first coward is you" [2].

After his imprisonment in Kempolovo, Hans Hespe was tried by SS-und Polizeigericht of Riga in September 1942, which sentenced him to five years in prison for insubordination. Transferred to Dachau in January 1943, he remained there until February 1945 when he was sent to the front in the SS Division "Dirlewanger". Taken prisoner by the Russians, he was released the following September. Again arrested by the Soviets in Berlin on May 15, 1946 on false charges of spying for the United States, Hespe was imprisoned in Sachsenhausen in Speziallager no. 7, run by the NKVD and destined primarily for political prisoners and former-SS. Released on January 18, 1950, he moved to West Berlin. Picked on by the Stasi for alleged activities against the GDR government, Hespe was kidnapped in October 1954 and moved to East Berlin, where he received a new sentence of six years in prison. Finally released in May 1961, he ended his days in West Germany, where he died of illness on December 1, 1968.

With regard to the officers attacked by Hespe, while company commanders Ernst Petersen and Fritz Dittmar were killed in combat, battalion commander Helwes and Hptm. Westphal survived and after the war continued in the police service. Helwes, in fact, retired with the rank of Lieutenant Colonel[23].

ENDNOTES

1 «All the Jews are being killed. Similar actions are taking place everywhere. Here, where we are, 150 Jews were shot yesterday. Men, women, children, all eliminated. The Jews are being completely exterminated». Curilla, p. 201.

2 See Introduction, note 6.

3 From Joseph Conrad, *Cuore di tenebra (Heart of Darkness),* p. 7.

4 Sentence pronounced by an official of Polizei-Bataillon 320 during the slaughter of Kamenec Podolski. Testimony given by Wilhelm W. in Mallmann/Riess/Pyta, p. 87. See Chap. 3.

5 In July/Spetember 1941, Lithuanian auxiliaries participated in slaughters of Jews in different localities in the area between Memel and Tilsit: Taurage, Smalininkai, Jurbarkas, Palanga, Batakiai, Kretinga, Veivirzenai and Gargždai, with a total of at least 1,300 victims. See Curilla, pp. 841-842.

6 About the massacre of Gargždai (Garsden) of late August / early September 1941, see Joachim Tauber: *Garsden, 24 Juni 1941*. In *Annaberger Annalen 5/1997*, pp. 129-130. Also Curilla, p. 842.

7 Feinstein's words to Knopens, already his friend and neighbor, were: «*Gustav, schieß gut!*». After that episode, Knopens asked and obtained to be replaced. See Tauber Gardsen, p. 128, Curilla, p. 142, Browning Origini, p. 266.

8 In addition to Schmidt-Hammer, SA-Oberführer Bernhard Fischer-Schweder, Polizeidirektor "Memel", under whose authority the entire operation took place, sometimes inflicted the death blow to the wounded ones. Curilla, p. 142.

9 The words that Schmidt-Hammer pronounced to his men were: «*Ich weiß ich bin ja auch ein kleiner Befehlsempfänger*».

10 The words that Kersten pronounced to his comrades were: «*Siehst Du, die Strafe folgt auf dem Fuß*». Curilla, p. 142, Tauber Gardsen, p. 128.

11 Taking as a starting point the massacre of about 4,000 Jews in Kirovograd, Ukraine, on September 30, 1941 perpetrated by Polizei-Bataillon 304 in probable collaboration with staff of Sonderkommando 4b, we have tried to suggest an *ideal* motivational context that went beyond the objective contributing factors indicated in EM 94 dated September 25, 1941. Thus we have borrowed the figure of the deputy platoon Manfred Pohlig – recognized by the Court of Halle as one of the physical perpetrators of the massacre – imbuing to him, of our will, a religious-mystical vision, useful to provide *one of the many* points of view that motivated the genocidal choices of the perpetrators. As mentioned in the introduction, alongside the historical, philosophical, social and psychological dynamics that helped to fuel the magma of the Jewish genocide, there were undoubtedly also mystical-religious anti-Semitic visions of the traditional type, which we wanted to mention briefly in this paragraph. Obviously, not being able to know the mystical conception of Pohlig, our reconstruction should not be understood as referring specifically to himself, but as representative of a form of religious anti-Semitism, which was probably a minor one but still present in Nazi Germany.

12 Klemp Ermittelt, p. 236.

13 The description of the common grave was given and illustrated with drawings by Walter Hofmann, leader of a platoon of Polizei-Bataillon 304. See Klemp Ermittelt, pp. 238-239.

14 See EM 94 dated September 25, 1941, in IMT Green Series, vol. X, p. 1223 – Doc. NO-3416, Exibit 943. Also Arad Holocaust, p. 178.

15 On Nazi political messianism see Gabriele Guerra: *L'Avvento del Führer. Il Reich dello Spirito ed il messianismo politico nazista*, in B@beleonline/print, n. IV, 2008, pp. 169-178.

16 Memorial Hespe, transmitted to *Entschaedigungskammer* of the Court of Bremen in 1964, as well as a letter from the battalion's photographer Hermann Gieschen to his wife on October 8, 1941. Schneider, pp. 32-33, Curilla, p. 202.

17 Schneider, pp. 35-36. Testimonies of former policemen Joachim V. and Gerhard H. of 2/105, counter-memorial of Hespe against Maj. Wagner, Chief of Staff of 254.ID.

18 Memorial Hespe, transmitted to *Entschaedigungskammer* of the Court of Bremen in 1964. Baar's death by one of his fellow soldiers was confirmed by the testimony of another policeman, Gerhard F., given on January 17, 2002. Schneider, p. 30.

19 Schneider, pp. 34, 38. Testimonies given by former 2/105 policemen Joachim V. and Gerhard H. Hespe's views on his officers spread around the battalion and his correspondence was intercepted, both when sent from Kempolovo, and upon arrival in Bremen.

20 Memorial Hespe, transmitted to *Entschaedigungskammer* of the Court of Bremen in 1951 and 1964, Hermann Gieschen's letters to his wife dated September 7 and 28, 1941. Schneider, pp. 34-35.

21 Memorial Hespe, transmitted to *Entschaedigungskammer* of the Court of Bremen in 1964. Schneider, pp. 36-37.

22 Hespe's words to Helwes, also quoted in a letter to his wife, were: «*als Feigling Nr. 1 des Bataillons gelten Sie, Herr Major; Feigling Nr. 1 der 2. Kompanie ist Hauptmann Westphal*». The letter was intercepted and ended up in the acts of the SS Court in Riga. Schneider, pp. 42, 219.

23 Schneider, p. 121.

BIBLIOGRAPHY

Chapter one

BENDER, Sarah *The Jews of Bialystok during WWII and the Holocaust.* 2008. Lebanon, NH, 2008.

BENDER, Sarah *The "Reinhard Aktion" in the "Bialystok District".* **Bielefeld, 2003. Quoted as: Bender Bialystok.**

BROWNING, Christopher *Uomini comuni. Polizia tedesca e "soluzione finale" in Polonia*, Turin, 1995.

CURILLA, Wolfgang *Die Deutsche Ordnungspolizei und der Holocaust im Baltikum und in Weissrussland, 1941-1944.* Paderborn, 2006.

GERLACH, Christian *Kalkulierte Morde. Die Deutsche Wirtschaft- und Vernichtungspolitik in Weissrussland 1941 bis 1944.* Amburgo, 1999.

GOLDHAGEN, Daniel Jonah *I volenterosi carnefici di Hitler*, Milano, 1998.

HIS – Hamburger Institut für Sozialforschung Verbrechen der Wehrmacht. Dimensionen des Vernichtungskrieges 1941-1944. Amburgo, 2002. Quoted as: HIS.

KLEMP, Stefan *"Nicht Ermittelt". Polizeibataillone und die Nachkriegsjustiz. Ein Handbuch.* Essen, 2005. Quoted as: Klemp Ermittelt.

KLEMP, Stefan *Kölner Polizeibataillone in Osteuropa: die Polizeibataillone 69, 309, 319 und die Polizeireservekompanie Köln.* Quorted as: Klemp Osteuropa.

LICHTENSTEIN, Heiner *Himmlers grüne Helfer. Die Schutz- und Ordnungspolizei im «Dritten Reich».* Colonia, 1990.

LICHTENSTEIN, Heiner *Ein Lügengewirr – Der Wuppertaler Prozeβ gegen Angehörige des Polizeibataillons 309.* Quoted as: Lichtenstein Wuppertaler.

MALLMANN, Klaus Michael/ RIESS, Volker/PYTA Wolfram *Deutscher Osten 1939-1945. Der Weltanschauungskrieg in Photos und Texten.* Darmstadt, 2003.

OKROY, Michael *"Man will unserem Batl. Was tun…". Der Wuppertaler Bialystok-Proze⊠ 1967/68 un die Ermittlungen gegen Angehörige des Polizeibataillons 309.* Essen, 2001.

WESTERMANN, Edward B. *Hitler's Police Bataillons. Einforcing Racial War in the East.* Lawrence, 2005.

Chapter two

ANGRICK, Andrej/VOIGT Martina/AMMER-SCHUBERT, Silke/KLEIN, Peter *"Da hätte man schon ein Tagebuch führen müssen". Das Polizeibataillon 322 und die Judenmorde im Bereich der Heeresgruppe Mitte während des Sommers und Herbst 1941.* Berlino, 1994.

BROWNING, Christopher *Uomini comuni. Polizia tedesca e "soluzione finale" in Polonia*, Turin, 1995.

BROWNING, Christopher *Nazi Policy, Jewish Workers, German Killers. Cambridge, 2003.* Quoted as: Browning Policy.

BROWNING, Christopher *Le Origini della Soluzione finale. L'evoluzione della politica antiebraica del nazismo. Settembre 1939-marzo 1942.* Milano, 2008. Quoted as: Browning Origini.

CURILLA, Wolfgang *Die Deutsche Ordnungspolizei und der Holocaust im Baltikum und in Weissrussland, 1941-1944.* Paderborn, 2006

GERLACH, Christian *Kalkulierte Morde. Die Deutsche Wirtschaft- und Vernichtungspolitik in Weissrussland 1941 bis 1944.* Hamburg, 1999.

GITELMAN, Zvi *Bitter Legacy. Confronting the Holocaust in the USSR.* Bloomington, 1997.

HIS – Hamburger Institut für Sozialforschung *Verbrechen der Wehrmacht. Dimensionen des Vernichtungskrieges 1941-1944.* Amburgo, 2002. Quoted as: HIS.

HÜTTMAN, Heiko *Das Polizeibataillon 307 (Lübeck) "im Osteinsatz" 1940-1945.* Ein Ausstellung der Landespolizei Schleswig-Holstein. Lubeck.

KLEMP, Stefan *"Nicht Ermittelt". Polizeibataillone und die Nachkriegsjustiz. Ein Handbuch.* Essen, 2005.

KOHL, Paul *Der Krieg der Deutschen Wehrmacht und der Polizei 1941-1944. Sowjetische Ueberlebende berichten...* Frankfurt am Main, 1995.

KOPITZSCH, Wolfgang *Bandenbekämpfung, Geiselerschiessungen, Umsiedlung, Endlösung. Hamburger Polizeibataillone im Zweiten Weltkrieg.* Kiel, 2001.

LICHTENSTEIN, Heiner *Himmlers grüne Helfer. Die Schutz- und Ordnungspolizei im «Dritten Reich».* Koln, 1990.

LONGERICH, Peter *Politik der Vernichtung. Eine Gesamtdarstellung der nationalsozialistischen Judenverfolgung.* Munich, 1998

MALLMANN, Klaus-Michael *Der Einstieg in den Genozid. Das Lübecker Polizeibataillon 307 und das Massaker in Brest-Litowsk Anfang July 1941.* In Archiv für Polizeigeschichte nr. 29, 3/1999, pp. 82-88, Lubeck, 1999.

WESTERMANN, Edward B. *Hitler's Police Bataillons. Einforcing Racial War in the East.* Lawrence, 2005.

WESTERMANN, Edward B. *"Ordinary Men" or "Ideological Soldiers"? Police Bataillon 310 in Russia, 1942.* In German Studies Review XXI, pp. 41-68, Arizona State University, 1998. Quoted as: Westermann Soldiers.

Chapter three

ANGRICK, Andrej/

KLEIN, Peter *The final solution in Riga. Exploitation and annihilation 1941-1944.* New York, 2009.

BIRN, Ruth Bettina *Kollaboration und Mittäterschaft. Die Inkorporierung von einheimischen Personal in dier Sicheretispolizei in den besetzten Ostgebiete.* Hamburg, 2003.

BUBNYS, Arūnas *The Holocaust in Lithuania: an Outline of the Major Stages and their Results.* Amsterdam, 2004.

BROWNING, Christopher *Le Origini della Soluzione finale. L'evoluzione della politica antiebraica del nazismo. settembre 1939-marzo 1942.* Milano, 2008. Quoted as: Browning Origini.

CURILLA, Wolfgang *Die Deutsche Ordnungspolizei und der Holocaust im Baltikum und in Weissrussland 1941-1944.* Paderborn, 2006.

EIBER, Ludwig *"... ein bißchen die Wahrheit" – Briefe eines Bremer Kaufmanns von seinem Einsatz beim Ers.Polizei-Bataillon 105 in der Sowjetunion.* In: 1999, Zeitschrfit für Sozialgeschichte des 20.und 21.Jahrhunderts, I / 91. Hamburg, 1991.

EKSTEINS, Modris *"Walking since daybreak". A Story of Eastern Europe, World War II and the Heart of our Century.* New York, 1999.

EZERGAILIS, Andrew *The Holocaust in Latvia 1941 –1944.* Riga, 1996.

EZERGAILIS, Andrew *Pašaizsardzības komandantūru loma holokaustā.* Riga, 2000.

EZERGAILIS, Andrew *Six versions of the Holocaust in Latvia.* Riga, 2004. Quoted as: Ezergailis Versions.

GRÄFE, Marlis/POST Bernhard/

SCHNEIDER, Andreas *Die Geheime Staatspolizei im NS-Gau Thüringen 1933 – 1945.* Erfurt, 2004

KLEMP, Stefan *"Nicht Ermittelt". Polizeibataillone und die Nachkriegsjustiz – Ein Handbuch.* Essen, 2005. Quoted as: Klemp Ermittelt.

KLEMP, Stefan *"Ab nach Sibirien?" – Zur Sanktionerungspraxis gegenüber Polizeibeamten des Dritten Reichs: Der Fall des Polizeibataillons 9.* Essen, 2001.

KRAUSNICK, Helmut/

WILHELM, Hans-Heinrich *Die Truppe des Weltanschauungskrieges. Die Einsatzgruppen der Sicherheitspolizei und der SD 1938-1942.* Stuttgart 1981.

KAUFMANN, Max *Churbn Lettland. The destruction of the Jews of Latvia.* Munich, 1947.

LASMANIS, Uldis *Holokausts Jēkabpils pilsētā.* Riga, 2008.

LASMANIS, Uldis *Nairi pilsētas ebreju kopienas gals (holokausts Jaunjelgavā).* Riga 2003. Quoted as: Lasmanis 2003.

LONGERICH, Peter *Politik der Vernichtung. Eine Gesamtdarstellung der nationalsozialistischen Judenverfolgung.* Munich, 1998.

MUSIAL, Bogdan *I persecutori non tedeschi nell'Europa centrale e orientale.* Turin, 2005

PAVLOVIČS, Juris *Okupācijas varu maiņa Zemgalē 1941. gada vasarā: Jelgavas apriņķis 1941. gada jūnija beigās – jūlija sākumā.* Riga, 2007.

PAVLOVIČS, Juris *Okupācijas varu maiņas īpatnības Liepājā un tās tuvākajā apkārtnē: aktīvās karadarbības faktoru analīze.* Riga, 2003. Quoted as: Pavlovičs 2003

STRANGA, Aivars *Holokausts vācu okupētajā Latvijā: 1941–1945.* Riga, 2008.

STRANGA, Aivars *Holokausts Latvijā: 1941–1945.* Riga, 2003. Ed. inglese: *The Holocaust in Occupied Latvia: 1941-1941.* Riga, 2005. Quoted as: Stranga Holocaust.

TOMAŠUNS, Andris *Jelgavā nogalinātie ebreji: padomju un nacistu dati.* Riga, 2006.

ZELLIS, Kaspar *Nacionālsociālistiskās Vācijas propaganda okupētajā Latvijā (1941. gada jūnijs–decembris).* Riga, 2004.

Chapter four

ANGRICK, Andrej *Besatzungspolitik und Massenmord: Die Einsatzgruppe D in der südliche Sowjetunion 1941-1943.* Hamburg, 2003.

ANGRICK, Andrej *The Escalation of German-Rumanian Anti-Jewish Policy after the Attack on the Soviet Union, June 22, 1941.* In Shoah Resource Center, The International School for Holocaust Studies, pp. 1-33. Quoted as: Angrick Escalation.

ANGRICK, Andrej/

KLEIN, Peter *The final solution in Riga. Exploitation and annihilation 1941-1944.* New York, 2009.

ARAD, Yitzhak *The Holocaust in the Soviet Union.* Lincoln, 2009. QQuoted as: Arad Holocaust.

BANKIER, David *La conoscenza dell'Olocausto e le relazioni in Europa, negli Stati Uniti e nelle comunutà ebraiche.* Turin, 2005.

BAUMAN, Zygmunt *Modernità e Olocausto.* Bologna, 1992.

BRAHAM, Randolph *The Politics of Genocide: the Holocaust in Hungary.* Detroit, 2000.

BREITMAN, Richard *Official Secrets. What the Nazis planned, what the British and American knew.* New York, 1998.

BROWNING, Christopher *Ordinary Germans or Ordinary Men? Another Look at the Perpetrators.* Evanston, Ill., 1998.

CURILLA, Wolfgang *Die Deutsche Ordnungspolizei und der Holocaust im Baltikum und in Weissrussland, 1941-1944.* Paderborn, 2006.

EZERGAILIS, Andrew *The Holocaust in Latvia 1941-1944.* Riga, 1996.

GERLACH, Christian/

GÖTZ, Aly *Das letzte Kapitel. Der Mord an den ungarischen Juden 1944-1945.* Francoforte sul Meno., 2004.

HEADLAND, Ronald *"Messages of Murder". A Study of the Reports of the Einsatzgruppen of the Security Police and the Security Service, 1941-1943.* Cranbury, 1992.

HILBERG, Raul *The destruction of the European Jews, Yale, 1961.*

HIS – Hamburger Institut für Sozialforschung *Verbrechen der Wehrmacht. Dimensionen des Vernichtungskrieges 1941-1944.* Amburgo, 2002. Quoted as: HIS.

KLEMP, Stefan *"Nicht Ermittelt". Polizeibataillone und die Nachkriegsjustiz. Ein Handbuch.* Essen, 2005. Quoted as: Klemp Ermittelt.

KRAUSNICK, Helmut/

WILHELM, Hans-Heinrich *Die Truppe des Weltanschauungskrieges. Die Einsatzgruppen der Sicherheitspolizei und des SD 1939-1942.* Stuttgart, 1981.

LONGERICH, Peter *Politik der Vernichtung. Eine Gesamtdarstellung der nationalsozialistischen Judenverfolgung.* Munich, 1998.

LOWER, Wendy *The Holocaust and Colonialism in Ukraine: a Case Study of the Generalbezirk Zhytomyr, Ukraine, 1941-1944.* In: The Holocaust in the Soviet Union: symposium presentations. Washington: US Holocaust Memorial Museum, 2005.

LOWER, Wendy *Facilitating Genocide. Nazi Ghettoization Pratices in Occupied Ukraine, 1941-1942.* Syracuse, NY, 2005. Quoted as: Lower Ghettoization.

MALLMANN, Klaus-Michael/

RIESS, Volker/PYTA, Wolfram *Der Weltanschauungskrieg in Photos und Texten*, Darmstadt, 2003.

MERMALL, Gabriel/

YASHAROFF, Norbert *By The Grace of Strangers: two Boys' Rescue during the Holocaust.* Jerusalem, 2006.

POHL, Dieter *Nationalsozialistische Judenverfolgung in Ostgalizien 1941-1944. Organisation und Durchführung eines staatlischen Massenverbrechens.* Munich, 1996. Quoted as: Pohl Ostgalizien.

POHL, Dieter *Hans Krüger and the Morder of the Jews in the Stanislawow Region (Galicia).* Yad Vashem Studies, vol. 26, 1998, pp. 239-265. Quoted as: Pohl Krüger.

POHL, Dieter *Die Täter der Shoah. Fanatische Nationalsozialisten oder Ganz Normalen Deutschen?* Göttingen, 2003. Quoted as: Pohl Täter.

POHL, Dieter *The Murder of Ukraine's Jews under German Military Administration and in the Reichkommissariat Ukraine.* Bloomington, 2008. Quoted as: Pohl Ukraine.

POHL, Dieter *Die Herrschaft der Wehrmacht: Deutsche Militärbesatzung und einhemische Bevölkerung in der Sowjetunion 1941-1944.* Oldenburg, 2008. Citato Pohl Herrschaft.

UNGVÁRY, Krisztián *Magyarország és a második világháború.* Budapest, 2005.

ISRAEL State Archives *The Trial of Adolf Eichmann*, Session 51-04, 05, Volume III.

Chapter five

AEDTNER, Alfred *An Ort und Stelle eschossen. Der Kriminalist Alfred Aedtner über die Massenmorde des Polizeibataillons 322.* In Der Spiegel, 44/1986.

ANGRICK, Andrej/

VOIGT, Martina/AMMERSCHUBERT, Silke/KLEIN, Peter *"Da hätte man schon ein Tagebuch führen müssen". Das Polizeibataillon 322 und die Judenmorde im Bereich der Heeresgruppe Mitte während des Sommers und Herbst 1941.* Berlin, 1994. Quoted as: AVAK.

BREITMAN, Richard *Official Secrets. What the Nazis planned, what the British and Americans knew.* New York, 1998.

BROWNING, Christopher *Le Origini della Soluzione finale. L'evoluzione della politica antiebraica del nazismo. settembre 1939-marzo 1942.* Milan, 2008. Quoted as: Browning Origini.

CURILLA, Wolfgang *Die Deutsche Ordnungspolizei und der Holocaust im Baltikum und in Weissrussland, 1941-1944.* Paderborn, 2006.

DEAN, Martin C. *Collaboration in the Holocaust. Crimes of the local Police in Belorussia and Ukraine, 1941-1944.* New York, 2000.

EPSTEIN, Barbara *The Minsk Ghetto 1941- 1943. Jewish resistance and Soviet internationalism.* Berkeley, 2008.

GERLACH, Christian *Kalkulierte Morde: die deutsche Wirtschafts- und Vernichtungspolitik in Weissrussland 1941-1944.* Hamburg, 1999.

KLEE, Ernst/DRESSEN, Willi/

RIESS, Volker *"Schöne Zeiten". Judenmord aus der Sicht der Täter ung Gaffer.* Frankfurt am Main, 1988.

KLEMP, Stefan - *"Nicht Ermittelt". Polizeibataillone und die Nachkriegsjustiz. Ein Handbuch.* Essen, 2005. Quoted as: Klemp Ermittelt.

KWIET, Konrad *From the Diary of a Killing Unit.* Providence, 1993.

LANGERBEIN, Helmut *Hitler's death squads. The Logic of Mass Murder.* College Station, 2003.

LICHTENSTEIN, Heiner *Himmlers grüne Helfer. Die Schutz- und Ordnungspolizei im «Dritten Reich».* Koln, 1990.

LONGERICH, Peter *Politik der Vernichtung. Eine Gesamtdarstellung der nationalsozialistischen Judenverfolgung.* Munich, 1998.

MALLMANN, Klaus-Michael/ RIESS, Volker/PYTA, Wolfram *Deutscher Osten 1939–1945. Der Weltanschauungskrieg in Photo und Texten.* Stuttgart, 2003.

POHL, Kohl *Der Krieg der deutschen Wehrmacht und der Polizei 1941-1944. Sowjetische Überlebende berichten.* Frankfurt am Main, 1995.

TEC, Nechama *La resistenza ebraica: definizione e interpretazioni storiche.* Turin, 2005.

WESTBERG, Lennart *Zwei Polizistenschicksale im Zweiten Weltkrieg – Befehlsverweigerung und Widerstand.* In Archiv für Polizeigeschichte 3/1991.

WESTERMANN, Edward B. *Hitler's Police Bataillons. Einforcing Racial War in the East.* Lawrence, 2005.

Chapter six

ANGRICK, Andrej/VOIGT, Martina/AMMERSCHUBERT, Silke/KLEIN, Peter *"Da hätte man schon ein Tagebuch führen müssen". Das Polizeibataillon 322 und die Judenmorde im Bereich der Heeresgruppe Mitte während des Sommers und Herbst 1941.* Berlin, 1994. Quoted as: AVAK.

BREITMAN, Richard *Official Secrets. What the Nazis planned, what the British and Americans knew.* New York, 1998.

BROWNING, Christoper *Le Origini della Soluzione finale. L'evoluzione della politica antiebraica del nazismo. settembre 1939-marzo 1942.* Milan, 2008. Quoted as: Browning Origini.

CURILLA, Wolfgang *Die Deutsche Ordnungspolizei und der Holocaust im Baltikum und in Weissrussland, 1941-1944.* Paderborn, 2006.

FRIEDLANDER, Saul *Gli Anni Dello Sterminio. La Germania nazista e gli ebrei (1939-1945).* Milan, 2009.

GERLACH, Christian *Kalkulierte Morde: die deutsche Wirtschafts- und Vernichtungspolitik in Weissrussland 1941-1944.* Hamburg, 1999.

GERLACH, Christian *Failure of Plan for an SS Extermination Camp in Mogilev, Belorussia.* In Holocaust and Genocide Studies, Spring 1997. Quoted as: Gerlach Extermination.

HIS – Hamburger Institut für Sozialforschung *Verbrechen der Wehrmacht. Dimensionen des Vernichtungskrieges 1941-1944.* Amburgo, 2002. Quoted as: HIS.

HOCHSTETTER, Dorothee *Motorisierung und "Volksgemeinschaft". Das Nationalsozialistische Kraftfahrkorps (NSKK) 1931-1945.* Munich, 2004.

HÖLZL, Martin *Buer und Belzec. Die Polizeibataillone 65 und 316 und der Mord an den Juden während des Zweiten Weltkrieg.* Essen, 2005

KLEMP, Stefan *"Nicht Ermittelt". Polizeibataillone und die Nachkriegsjustiz. Ein Handbuch.* Essen, 2005. Quoted as: Klemp Ermittelt.

KOHL, Paul *Der Krieg der deutschen Wehrmacht und der Polizei 1941-1944. Sowjetische Überlebende berichten.* Frankfurt am Main, 1995.

KRAUSNICK, Helmut/

WILHELM, Hans-Heinrich *Die Truppe des Weltanschauungskrieges. Die Einsatzgruppen der Sicherheitspolizei und des SD 1939-1942.* Stuttgart, 1981.

LANGERBEIN, Helmut *Hitler's death squads. The Logic of Mass Murder.* College Station, 2003.

MALLMANN, Klaus-Michael/

RIESS, Volker/PYTA, Wolfram *Der Weltanschauungskrieg in Photos und Texten*, Darmstadt, 2003.

Chapter seven

BARTUSEVIČIUS, Vincas/

TAUBER, Joachim/

WETTE, Wolfram *Holocaust in Litauen. Krieg Judenmorde und Kollaboration im Jahre 1941.* Koln, 2003.

BENZ, Wolfgang/KWIET, Konrad/ MATTHÄUS, Jurgen *Einsatz im Reichkommissariat Ostland. Dokumente zum Völkermord im Baltikum und in Weissrussland 1941- 1944.* Berlin, 1998.

BREITMAN, Richard *Official Secrets. What the Nazis planned, what the British and Americans knew.* New York, 1998.

BUBNYS, Arūnas *The Holocaust in Lithuania: an Outline of the Major Stages and their Results.* Amsterdam, 2004. Quoted as: Bubnys Outline.

BUBNYS, Arūnas *Holocaust in Lithuanian Province in 1941.* PDF Doc. Quoted as: Bubnys Holocaust.

BUBNYS, Arūnas *Die Litauische Hilfspolizeibataillone und der Holocaust.* Koln, 2003. Quoted as: Bubnys Hilfspolizeibataillone.

CURILLA, Wolfgang *Die Deutsche Ordnungspolizei und der Holocaust im Baltikum und in Weissrussland, 1941-1944.* Paderborn, 2006.

DIECKMANN, Christoph/ SUŽIEDĖLIS, Saulius *The persecution and mass murder of Lithuanian Jews during Summer and Fall 1941: sources and analysis.* www.komisija.lt.

DIECKMANN, Christoph *Das Ghetto und das Konzentrationslager in Kaunas 1941-1944.* Gottingen, 1998.

DEAN, Martin C. *Die Suche nach litauischen Kriegsverbrechen in Australien den Vereinigten Staaten von Amerika und Großbritannien 1979-2001.* Koln, 2003.

FAITELSON, Alex *The Truth and nothing but the truth: Jewish resistance in Lithuania.* Jerusalem, 2006.

GANOR, Solly *Light one Candle. A Survivor's Tale from Lithuania to Jerusalem.* New York, 2003.

INČIURIENĖ, Joheved *Rettung und Widerstand in Kaunas.* Koln, 2003.

LONGERICH, Peter *Politik der Vernichtung. Eine Gesamtdarstellung der nationalsozialistischen Judenverfolgung.* Munich, 1998.

MARGOLIAN, Howard *Unauthorized Entry: The Truth About Nazi War Criminals in Canada 1946-1956.* Toronto, 2000.

NEUMANN, Alexander *Leben und Sterben im Ghetto Kaunas, 1941.* Koln, 2003.

NIKŽENTAITIS, Alvydas/

SCHREINER, Stefan/

STALIŪNAS, Darius *The Vanished World of the Lituanian Jews.* 2004.

SINGER, David/

GROSSMANN, Lawrence *American Jewish Yearbook, 2002.* American-Jewish Committee, 2002.

STANG, Knut *Kollaboration und Massenmorde. Die litauische Hilfspolizei, das Rollkommando Hamann und die Ermordung der litauischen Juden.* Frankfurt am Main, 1996.

TORY, Avraham *Surviving the Holocaust. The Kovno Ghetto Diary.* Cambridge, (Mass.), 1990.

US COURT OF APPEALS, Eleventh Circuit *United States of America, v. Kazys Palčiauskas, A/k/a Kazimieras Palčiauskas, Nr. 734 F.2d 625.* Quoted as: Palčiauskas Sentence.

Chapter eight

ALLEN, Charles R. Jr *Nazi War Criminals in America. Facts, Action. The Basic Handbook.* New York, 1985.

AA.VV.: *Bericht der Kommission zur Überprüfung der Ausstellung "Vernichtungskrieg. Verbrechen der Wehrmacht, 1941 bis 1944".* 2000.

ARENDT, Hannah *La banalità del Male. Eichmann a Gerusalemme.* Milan, 2009 (XVI).

ARENDT, Hannah *Le origini del totalitarismo.* Ed.It., Torino, 2004. Quoted as: Arendt Origini.

BARTUSEVIČIUS, Vincas/

TAUBER, Joachim/

WETTE, Wolfram *Holocaust in Litauen. Krieg Judenmorde und Kollaboration im Jahre 1941.* Koln, 2003.

BETTELHEIM, Bruno *La Vienna di Freud.* Milan, 1990.

BREITMAN, Richard *Official Secrets. What the Nazis planned, what the British and Americans knew.* New York, 1998.

BREITMAN, Richard *Himmler's Police Auxiliaries in the Occupied Soviet Territories.* Simon Wiesenthal Center, Annual 7, Chapter 2. Quoted as: Breitman Auxiliaries.

BUBNYS, Arūnas *Lithuanian Police Battalions and the Holocaust (1941-1943).* www.komisija.lt. Quoted as: Bubnys Holocaust.

BUBNYS, Arūnas *Die Litauische Hilfspolizeibataillone und der Holocaust.* Koln, 2003. Quoted as: Bubnys Hilfspolizeibataillone

CHOLAWSKY, Shalom *The Jews of Belorussia during World War II.* Amsterdam, 1998.

CURILLA, Wolfgang *Die Deutsche Ordnungspolizei und der Holocaust im Baltikum und in Weissrussland, 1941-1944.* Paderborn, 2006.

DEAN, Martin C. *Collaboration in the Holocaust. Crimes of the local Police in Belorussia and Ukraine, 1941-1944.* New York, 2000.

DEAN, Martin C. *Lithuanian Participation in the Mass Murder of Jews in Belarus and Ukraine, 1941-1944.* Amsterdam, 2004. Quoted as: Dean Participation

DIECKMANN, Christoph *Lihuania in Summer 1941 – The German invasion and the Kaunas Pogrom.* Leipzig, 2007.

DIECKMANN, Christoph/

SUŽDIELIS, Saulius *The Persecution and Mass Murder of Lithuanian Jews during Summer and Fall 1941: Sources and Analysis.* www.komisija.lt.

GERLACH, Christian *Kalkulierte Morde: die deutsche Wirtschafts- und Vernichtungspolitik in Weissrussland 1941-1944.* Hamburg, 1999.

HEER, Hannes/

NAUMANN, Klaus *Vernichtungskrieg. Verbrechen der Wehrmacht 1941 bis 1944.* Hamburg, 1995.

HEER, Hannes/

NAUMANN, Klaus *War of Extermination. The German Military in World War II 1941-1944.* New York, 2000. Quoted as: Hern/Naumann Extermination.

HIS – Hamburger Istitut

für Sozialforschung *Verbrechen der Wehrmacht. Dimensionen des Vernichtungskrieges 1941-1945.* Amburgo, 2002. Quoted as: HIS.

HILBERG, Raul *La distruzione degli ebrei d'Europa.* Turin, 1995.

IMT – International

Military Tribunal *Trial of the Major War Criminal before the International Military Tribunal.* Norimberga, 1949. Quoted as: IMT Blue Series.

KLEMP, Stefan *"Nicht Ermittelt". Polizeibataillone und die Nachkriegsjustiz. Ein Handbuch.* **Essen, 2005.** Quoted as: **Klemp Ermittelt.**

KNEZYS, Stasys *Kauno karo komendantūros Tautinio darbo batalionas 1941 m.* Genocidas ir rezistencijia, 2000 nr. 1

REINMANN, Christina L. *Fencing the Fifth Amendment in Our Own Backyard.* Pace International Law Review, 7-1, 1995.

RYAN, Allan A. Jr. *Quiet Neighbours. Prosecuting Nazi War Criminals in America.* San Diego, 1984.

STANG, Knut *Kollaboration und Massenmorde. Die litauische Hilfspolizei, das Rollkommando Hamann und die Ermordung der litauischen Juden.* Frankfurt am Main, 1996.

US DISTRICT COURT,

N.D. Indiana *United States of America v. Kazys Ciurinskas. Nr. 2-93 CV 97JM – 18/06/1997.* Quoted as: Ciurinskas Sentence.

WYMAN, Davis S./

ROSENZWEIG, Charles H. *The World reacts to the Holocaust.* West Bloomfield, 1996.

ZUROFF, Efraim *Beruf Nazijäger: die Suche mit dem langen Antem. Die Jagd nach dem Tätern des Völkermordes.* Friburg, 1996.

Chapter nine

ANGRICK, Andrej *Besatzungspolitik und Massenmord. Die Einsatzgruppe D in der Südliche Sowjetunion 1941-1943.* Hamburg, 2003.

ANGRICK, Andrej *The Escalation of German-Rumanian Anti-Jewish Policy after the Attack on the Soviet Union, June 22, 1941.* In Shoah Resource Center, The International School for Holocaust Studies, pp. 1-33. Quoted as: Angrick Escalation.

CURILLA, Wolfgang *Die Deutsche Ordnungspolizei und der Holocaust im Baltikum und in Weissrussland, 1941-1944.* Paderborn, 2006.

GREEN, Warren *The Fate of the Crimean Jewish Communities: Ashkenazim, Krimchaks and Karaites.* In Jewish Social Studies, vol. 46 nr. 2 (Spring 1984).

HIS – Hamburger Institut

für Sozialforschung *Verbrechen der Wehrmacht. Dimensionen des Vernichtungskrieges 1941-1945.* Amburgo, 2002. Quoted as: HIS.

KLEMP, Stefan *Nicht Ermittelt". Polizeibataillone und die Nachkriegsjustiz. Ein Handbuch.* Essen, 2005. Quoted as: **Klemp Ermittelt.**

KLEMP, Stefan *"Ab nach Sibirien?" – Zur Sanktionerungspraxis gegenüber Polizeibeamten des Dritten Reichs: Der Fall des Polizeibataillons 9.* Essen, 2001. Quoted as: Klemp Sibirien.

KRAUSNICK, Helmut/

WILHELM, Hans-Heinrich *Die Truppe des Weltanschauungskrieges. Die Einsatzgruppen der Sicherheitspolizei und ds SD 1938-1942.* Stuttgart, 1981.

KUNZ, Norbert *Die Feld- und Ortskommandanturen auf der Krim und der Judenmrd 1941/42.* Berlin, 2002.

MACLEAN, French *The Field Men. The SS Officers Who Led the Einsatzkommandos – the Nazi Mobile Killing Units.* **Atglen 1999.**

MALLMANN, Klaus-Michael/

RIESS, Volker/PYTA, Wolfram *Deutscher Osten 1939-1945. Der Weltanschauungskrieg in Photos und Texten.* Darmstadt, 2003.

OLDENBURG, Manfred *Ideologie und Militärisches Kalkül. Die Besatzungspolitik der Wehrmacht in der Sowjetunion 1942.* Koln, 2004.

NMT – Nuremberg Military Tribunal *Trial of War Criminals before the Nuremberg Military Tribunals.* vol. IV. Nuremberg, October 1946 - April 1949.

STEIN, Marcel *Field Marschal von Manstein. The Janus Head. A portrait.* Solihull, 2007.

STREIM, Alfred *Saubere Wehrmacht? Die Verfolgung von Kriegs- und NS-Verbrechen in der Bundesrepublik und der DDR.* Hamburg, 1995.

Chapter ten

ARENDT, Hannah *La banalità del Male. Eichmann a Gerusalemme.* Milan, 2009 (XVI).

ANGRICK, Andrej *Das Beispiel Charkow: Massenmord under deutscher Besatzung.* Monaco, 2005. Quoted as: Angrick Charkov.

ARAD, Yitzhak *The Holocaust in the Soviet Union.* Lincoln, 2009. Quoted as: Arad Holocaust.

CURILLA, Wolfgang *Die Deutsche Ordnungspolizei und der Holocaust im Baltikum und in Weissrussland, 1941-1944.* Paderborn, 2006.

DER SPIEGEL *Schuss im Hof.* Vol. n. 49/1967.

FRIEDRICH, Gunther *Kollaboration in der Ukraine im Zweiten Weltkrieg. Die Rolle der einheimischen Stadtverwaltung während der deutschen Besetzung Charkows 1941 bis 1943.* Dissertation, Bochum, 2008.

HIS – Hamburger Institut

für Sozialforschung *Verbrechen der Wehrmacht. Dimensionen des Vernichtungskrieges 1941-1945.* Amburgo, 2002. Quoted as: HIS.

DE MILDT, Dick/

RÜTER, Christiaan F. –

Justiz und NS-Verbrechen *Sammlung deutscher Strafurteile wegen NS Tötungsverbrechen.* Amsterdam University Press: Band XXVII, pp. 134-174, *Gericht der BRD, LG Wiesbaden, 2 Ks 1/67 von 23/02/1968*, against Oskar J. Christ

KLEMP, Stefan *"Nicht Ermittelt". Polizeibataillone und die Nachkriegsjustiz. Ein Handbuch.* Essen, 2005. Quoted as: Klemp Ermittelt.

KRAUSNICK, Helmut/

WILHELM, Hans-Heinrich *Die Truppe des Weltanschauungskrieges. Die Einsatzgruppen der Sicherheitspolizei und des SD 1939-1942.* Stuttgart, 1981.

LONGERICH, Peter *Politik der Vernichtung. Eine Gesamtdarstellung der nationalsozialistischen Judenverfolgung.* Munich, 1998.

RUBINSTEIN, Josua/

ALTMAN, **Ilya** *The Unknown Black Book: The Holocaust in the German-Occupied Soviet Territories.* Bloomington, 2007

WESTERMANN, **Edward B.** *Hitler's Police Battalions. Enforcing Racial War in the East.* Lawrence, 2005.

Chapter eleven

BROWNING, **Christopher** *Le origini della Soluzione finale. L'evoluzione della politica antiebraica del nazismo. settembre 1939 – marzo 1942.* Milan, 2008. Quoted as: Browning Origini

BROWNING, **Christopher** *The Final Solution in Serbia. The Semlin Judenlager – A Case Study.* In Yad Vashem Studies 15 (1993). Quoted as: Browning Semlin.

HILBERG, **Raul** *La distruzione degli ebrei d'Europa.* Turin, 1995

KLEMP, **Stefan** *"50 Kommunisten aufgehängt, 350 Häuser niedergebrannt". Der Einsatz des Reserve-Polizei-Bataillons 64 auf dem Balkan 1941-1943.* Essen, 2001. Quoted as: Klemp Kommunisten.

KLEMP, **Stefan** *"Nicht Ermittelt". Polizeibataillone und die Nachkriegsjustiz – Ein handbuch.* Essen, 2005. Quoted as: Klemp Ermittelt.

MANOSCHEK, **Walter** *Die vernichtung der Juden in Serbien.* Frankfurt am Main, 1998. Quoted as: Manoschek Vernichtung

MANOSCHEK, **Walter** *"Gehst mit Juder erschiessen?" Die Vernichtung der Juder in Serbien.* Hamburg, 1995. Quoted as: Manoschek Shoot.

MANOSCHEK, **Walter** *Serbien ist Judenfrei. Militärische Besatzungspolitik und Judenvernichtung in Serbien, 1941/1942.* München, 1995. Quoted as: Manoschek Judenfrei.

SHIMZU, **Akiko** *Die deusche Okkupation des serbischen Banat 1941-1944. Unter besonderer Berücksichtigung der deutschen Volksgruppe in Jugoslawien.* Münster, 2003.

Chapter twelve

ARAD, **Yitzhak** *Belzec, Sobibor, Treblinka. The Operation Reinhard Death Camps.* Bloomington, 1987.

CURILLA, **Wolfgang** *Die Deutsche Ordnungspolizei und der Holocaust im Baltikum und in Weissrussland, 1941-1944.* Paderborn, 2006.

GELDMACHER, **Thomas** *"Wir als Wiener waren ja bei der Bevölkerung bebliebt". Österreische Schutzpolizisten und die Judenvernichtung in Ostgalizien 1941-1944.* Wien, 2002.

HALTER, **Marek** *Stories of Deliverance. Speaking with Men and Women who Rescued Jews from the Holocaust.* New York, 1997.

KURETSIDIS-HAIDER, **Claudia** *Die KPÖ und die Ahndung von NS-Verbrechen in Österreich.* Referat am Symposium der Alfred Klahr Gesellschaft "Befreiung und Wiederaufbau – Die KPÖ als Regierungspartei". Wien, 2005.

MUSIAL, **Bogdan** *Konterrevolutionäre Elemente sind zu erschießen. Die Brutalisierung des deutsch-sowjetischen Krieges im Sommer 1941.* Berlin, 2000.

POHL, **Dieter** *Nationalsozialistische Judenverfolgung in Ostgalizien 1941-1944. Organisation und Durchführung eines staatliche Massenverbrechens.* Munich, 1996. Quoted as: Pohl Ostgalizien.

SANDKÜHLER, **Thomas** *"Endlösung" in Galizien. Der Judenmorde in Ostpolen und die Rettungsinitiativen von Berthold Beitz 1941-1944.* Bonn, 1996.

SANDKÜHLER, **Thomas** *Berthold Beitz und die "Endlösung der Judenfrage im Distrikt Galizien 1941-1944".* Francoforte sul Meno., 2004. Quoted as: Sandkühler Judenfrage.

Chapter thirteen

ARENDT, **Hannah** *La banalità del male. Eichmann a Gerusalemme.* Milan, 2009.

BAUMAN, **Zygmunt** *Modernità e Olocausto.* Bologna, 1992.

BORODZIEJ, Wlodzimierz *Terror und Politik. Die Deutsche Polizei und die Polnische Wiederstandbewegung im Generalgouvernement 1939-1944.* Mainz, 1999.

CÜPPERS, Martin *Wegbereiter der Shoah: Die Waffen-SS, der Kommandostab Reichführer-SS und die Judenvernichtung 1939-1945.* Darmstadt, 2005.

FREEMAN, Joseph *Job. The Story of a Holocaust Survivor.* Santa Barbara, 1996.

HILBERG, Raul *La Distruzione degli ebrei d'Europa.* Turin, 1995.

KARAY, Felicia *Death comes in Yellow. Skarzysko-Kamienna Slave Labor Camp.* Abingdon, 2004.

KELMAN, Herbert C. *Violence without moral restraint: Reflections on the dehumanization of victims and victimizers.* In *Journal of Social Issues, 29(4).* Harward, 1973.

LIPSON, Alfred *The book of Radom. The Story of a Jewish Community in Poland Destroyed by the Nazis.* New York, 1963.

MACLEAN, French L. *The Field Men. The SS Officers Who Led the Einsatzkommandos – the Nazi Mobile Killing Units.* Atglen, 1999.

MORGAN, David & Todd *The Anabasis of the Holy Cross Brigade. Reflected in the document of the US Government 1945-1950.* In Glaukopis 5/6 – 2006, pp. 242-274.

MUSIAL, Bogdan *Deutsche Zivilverwaltung und Judenverfolgung im Generalgouvernement.* Wiesbaden, 1999.

SEIDEL, Robert *Deutsche Besatzungspolitik in Polen. Der Distrikt Radom, 1939-1945.* Paderborn, 2006.

WEIN, Abraham/

FREUNDLICH, Bracha/

ORBACH, Wila *Pinkas hakehillot Polin: entsiklopedyah shel ha-yishuvim ha-Yehudiyim le-min hivasdam ve-ad le-ahar Sho'at Milhemet ha-`olam ha-sheniyah.* Jerusalem, 1999.

Chapter fourteen

BROWNING, Christopher *Le Origini della Soluzione finale. L'evoluzione della politica antiebraica del nazismo. settembre 1939-marzo 1942.* Milan, 2008. Quoted as: Browning Origini.

DEAN, Martin C. *Collaboration in the Holocaust. Crimes of the local Police in Belorussia and Ukraine, 1941-1944.* New York, 2000.

CHOLAWSKY, Shalom *The Jews of Bielorussia During World War II.* Amsterdam, 1998.

CURILLA, Wolfgang *Die Deutsche Ordnungspolizei und der Holocaust im Baltikum und in Weissrussland, 1941-1944.* Paderborn, 2006.

GERLACH, Christian *Kalkulierte Morde: die deutsche Wirtschafts- und Vernichtungspolitik in Weissrussland 1941-1944.* Hamburg, 1999.

HILBERG, Raul *La distruzione degli ebrei d'Europa.* Turin, 1995.

KLEMP, Stefan *"Nicht Ermittelt". Polizeibataillone und die Nachkriegsjustiz. Ein Handbuch.* Essen, 2005.

LICHTENSTEIN, Heiner *Himmlers grüne Helfer. Die Schutz- und Ordnungspolizei im «Dritten Reich».* Koln, 1990.

MALLMANN, Klaus-Michael/

RIESS, Volker/PYTA, Wolfram *Deutscher Osten 1939-1945. Der Weltanschauungskrieg in Photos und Texten.* Darmstadt, 2003.

SCHÄFER, Torsten *"Jedenfalls habe ich auch mitgeschossen".* Hamburg, 2007.

VON KELLENBACH, Katharina *Vanishing acts: Perpetrators in post-war Germany.* In Holocaust and Genocide Studies, Vol. 17 nr. 2.

DOCUMENTS

DOCUMENT 1:
Radiomessage HSSPF Jeckeln dated August 27, 1941

<table>
<tr><td>Transmitting position
Kommando Stab RF SS
Transmission Company
Telegraph nucleus</td><td colspan="2" rowspan="2"></td></tr>
<tr><td>Received or transmitted
Berlin 27.8, 18:40, Pahlmann</td></tr>
<tr><td>Transmitted:
27.08
08:30</td><td>To: RF SS
Chef Orpo
Chef Sipo
Kommando Stab RF SS</td><td>Retransmitting position
Pol. Funk s q m
Nr. 6</td></tr>
<tr><td colspan="3">1. Locations unchanged
2. Activities: 1 SS-Brigade: cleanup action north of the highway KOROSTEN-BIALOKUROVICZE; general direction MICHAILOVKA-RUDNIAVYZRANKA-STEPANOWKA-ZORO. Sector east of BIALOKUROVICZE: destroyed bridges were restored. Polizei-Regiment "Süd": rail safety, unchanged. Battalion deployed 303 [PB 303 NdA], no contact with the enemy. Polizei-Bataillon 320: special action with Einsatzgruppe of Stabskompanie in KAMENEZ-PODOLSKJ.
3. Outcome: 1 SS-Brigade: 99 prisoners taken and 16 Jews and partisans shot. [Pol] Rgt. Süd: 22 former-prisoners held and 914 Jews shot. Special action with Polizei-Bataillon 320: 4,200 Jews shot.
4. Losses: none

HSSPF Russland Süd</td></tr>
</table>

DOCUMENT 2:
Radiomessage HSSPF Jeckeln dated August 28, 1941

<table>
<tr><td>Transmitting position
Kommando Stab RF SS
Radio station of police 200 W dso</td><td colspan="2" rowspan="2"></td></tr>
<tr><td>Received or transmitted
dqh 28.8, 16:45, Heimann</td></tr>
<tr><td>Transmitted:
28.08, 18:30</td><td>To: RF SS, Chef Orpo, Chef Sich.Pol.,
Kdo.-Stab RF SS</td><td>Retransmitting position
HSSUPF "Süd"</td></tr>
</table>

Locations unchanged. Activities: 1 SS-Brigade: during the clean up action north of the Korosten-Bialokurovicze line, established daily targets were achieved; persisting floods will make cleanup action harder to implement.

Pol. Rgt. "Süd": deployed for the purpose of rail safety, unchanged; meticulous searching in the wooded areas north of Jwatki. Pol Batl. 304: search for two paratroopers on the run; Polizei-Bataillon [unnamed A/N]: continuation of special action in Kamenetz-Podolskij.

Outcome: 1 SS-Brig.: 42 prisoners taken; 16 Jews and one partisan shot. Two guns, 200 crossed pieces and 30 cross-cutter pliers seized.

Pol. Rgt. "Süd": 4 prisoners made; 369 Jews shot; Polizei-Bataillon 304: the two parachutists were made prisoners, in addition to three Bolsheviks and one Jew who supplied the paratroopers. They were all shot on 28.8. Leaflets, dynamite and hand grenades seized.

Pol. Batl. 320: during the special action in Kamenez-Podolskij, about 5,000 Jews were shot.

Losses: commander of I.R. 8, SS-Staf. Sacks, died in Zwiahel field hospital on 27.8 because of the injuries suffered on 19.8

DOCUMENT 3:
Radiomessage HSSPF Jeckeln dated August 29, 1941

<table>
<tr><td>Transmitting Position
Kommando Stab RF SS
Police radio station</td><td colspan="2" rowspan="2"></td></tr>
<tr><td>Received of transmitted
29.8, 17:15, Eibensteiner</td></tr>
<tr><td>Transmitted:
29.08, 10:20</td><td>To: RF SS, Chef Orpo, Chef Sipo,
Kdo.-Stab RF SS</td><td>Retransmitting position</td></tr>
<tr><td colspan="3">1. Locations unchanged.

2. Activities: 1 SS-Brigade: further clean up north of the Korosten-Bialokurovicze line. Ignatpol-Malachowka-Uschwo line reached in the evening. The destroyed bridges were partly restored by recce platoons. Polizei-Regiment "Süd": used in activities of railway security, without variations. Nothing else to be reported. Stabskp. HSSuPF "Russland Süd" has completed the action in Kamenec Podolski, guided by SS-Obergruppenführer Jeckeln.

3. Results: 1 SS-Brigade has captured 18 prisoners and has shot 77 Jews. Stabskompanie has shot 7,000 more Jews, so the total number of Jews liquidated in the Kamenec Podolski action is about 20,000. Change from tactical reports of 26 and 27.8.41; Stabskompanie to be used instead of Polizei-Bataillon 320; message of 27.8: 11,000 instead of 5,000. Polizei-Bataillon 320 used only for cordoning.

4. Losses: none.

HSSuPF Russland Süd</td></tr>
</table>

DOCUMENT 4:
Riebel's Report of October 3, 1941

9./III Polizei-Regiment "Mitte" No fixed location, October
3, 1941

Report

On the Jewish action of October 2-3, 1941

On October 2, 1941, at 13:30 hours, 9./III Polizei-Regiment "Mitte" has received the order to go to HSSPF "Russland Mitte", in order to carry out a Jewish action.

At around 14:15 hours I arrived at the location with the officials, the platoon commanders and the team leaders, for the briefing regarding how to perform the action. The briefing took place through Oltn. der Schupo Horn. The action was carried out in the area of the new Mogilev ghetto and has resulted in the arrest of 2,208 Jews of both sexes who were driven in trucks to a detention center.

During the action we often had to proceed to search the Jews who, moved by cowardly and subtle fear, tried to hide in any possible corner, to the point that it was often necessary to drive out those filthy elements from their hideouts. This circumstance has led to the shooting on site of 65 Jews by 9./III Polizei-Regiment "Mitte".

Supporting 9./III Polizei-Regiment "Mitte" 23 officials and men of the Ukrainian police intervened, as well as officials and men of HSSPF "Russland Mitte" high command.

The action took place on October 2, 1941, and finished at around 19:30 hours.

The execution of those who were arrested on 2.10.1941 was carried out during the morning of 3.10.1941.

Overall, 9./III/Polizei-Regiment "Mitte" carried out the shooting of 555 Jews of both sexes.

The action was completed at 12:30 hours.

Riebel

Oberleutnant der Schutzpolizei

and company commander

DOCUMENT 5:
Evaluation of Maj. Gottlieb Nagl

Schutzpolizei commander

Recklinghausen, June 11, 1941

Global evaluation of

Schutzpolizei Major Nagl

I hold as correct my evaluation of 13.2.1940.

Maj. Nagl is a police official with competences superior to average in all fields of Schutzpolizei. He can operate as a Reviere and as a medium level police commander, as a government official and as battalion commander.

During the war he proved to be diligent, energetic and mentally apt, with a remarkable ability to act on his own initiative. His anti-aircraft sector, that in the summer of 1940 has borne the main bulk of aircraft attacks in the Recklinghausen area, proved to be fit to the task.

During the aircraft attacks, Schutzpolizei Major Nagl often engaged himself personally and for this reason he will be awarded KvK II Class with swords.

With regards to personal relationships, both in service and out of service in his liaising with the party and other structures, Maj. Nagl is respected and trusted in his official role even if, at times, his corporative stance has not been fully understood.

The official must renounce his excessive consumption of alcohol, even if occasional, because such flaw could undermine his very favorable picture. He has always willingly accepted the advice of his old comrades, thus I hope that Maj. Nagl will be able to preserve his new position in Luxembourg also outside working hours.

He did well in his position as sector commander.

Signed

Schutzpolizei colonel

and Schutzpolizei commander

DOCUMENT 6:
Leslie Gordon's testimony

The present testimony by Leslie Gordon, a surviving Hungarian Jew, relative to the deportations of the summer of 1941 to Kamenec Podolski, was given on June 1, 1961 at the Jerusalem trial against Eichmann, Session 62. President of the Court, Judge Benjamin Halevi. Public Prosecutor, Dr. Ya'kov Robinson.

Attorney General: I call Mr. Leslie Gordon. He was deported from Budapest to Poland. He was one of the 1941 deportees to Kamenets-Podolski, of whom we have heard; subsequently, he returned to Budapest and saw the Accused. The witness at present resides in Canada [...]

[The witness is sworn.]

Presiding Judge: What is your full name?

Witness: Leslie Gordon.

Attorney General: Mr. Gordon, do you now live in Canada?

Witness Gordon: I live in Canada, in Montreal.

Q. You were born in Budapest?

A. Yes.

Q. Your parents had come from Poland?

A. My father was born in Poland.

Q. Hence you were regarded as Polish citizens?

A. According to the Hungarian laws, we were Polish citizens.

Q. What happened to you in June 1941?

A. In June 1941, when the Nazi hordes overran Poland, we heard rumors that the Polish citizens will be taken out of Hungary.

Q. When you say the Germans occupied Poland, which part of Poland do you mean?

A. That was the east part of Poland.

Q. If I may lead you with a few questions, Mr. Gordon. You were interned by the Hungarian authorities?

A. Yes, we were interned by the Hungarian authorities.

Q. You were brought to the then Polish border?

A. Yes, we were taken first to the Budapest synagogue. There we were told that orders came from the Germans, since the Hungarians had no authority over the German occupied territory, and these orders came strictly from Germany.

Q. What happened then?

A. We were taken from the synagogue next morning, to the Hungarian rail station, where we were placed in passenger cars, and we have been taken to the border of Koeroesmezoe.

Q. And to whom were you handed over at the border?

A. At Koeroesmezoe, we were handed over to the Hungarian gendarmerie until overnight. But next morning, we were loaded up on German trucks - clearly visible German licence plates on them.

Q. Who drove these trucks, and who were the guards?

A. We could not see the drivers until we arrived to the place where we have been taken, but then they turned out to be Germans.

Q. What Germans?

A. SS.

Q. How did you recognize them as being SS men?

A. From the skeleton (skull) on their caps - 'Totenkopf'.

Q. Where did the Germans take you to?

A. We were passing close by several small villages, and then we were passing through Kolomea until we came to about two or three miles - or kilometres - outside of Kolomea, where we had been told: "Schweine-Juden, herunter!" (Jewish Pigs, get down).

Q. So you got off?

A. Yes.

[...]

Q. So where did you go?

A. Once we got down from the trucks, they put up two machine-guns either side of the road and told us: "Go eastwards. Don't come back or don't even look back." Some of the people had to do their hygienic doings on the side, and they were shot right on the spot.

Q. By whom?

A. By the SS.

Q. What did you do? Tell us just what you yourself did.

A. Well, we were together. My father was 58, my mother - she was 43. My brother was 22, I was 21, my sister was 19, my brother was 16, another brother was 14, a sister was eight, and my little brother was five. We were trying to keep together and go along on the road - as has been told by the "brave" SS.

Q. Who, of all those members of your family, remained alive?

A. Only myself. One of my sisters, she got exempted from the deportation because she was married to a Hungarian citizen, and she is in Canada with me.

Q. But of those who were sent on their way there, you are the only survivor?

A. As far as I know, yes.

Judge Halevi: Are you referring to the members of your family or to the whole transport?

Attorney General: We shall still come to the whole transport. How many people were there in that transport, together with you yourself?

Witness Gordon: In this group, we were about three to four hundred, approximately. I cannot say the exact figures, but it was three to four hundred. I remember we occupied about eight trains, eight cars, and on each from forty to sixty people were in, most of them children. Like our family - we were seven children. Other families had eight or nine children; it consisted of two-thirds children under fourteen years of age.

Q. How many people, of those who were with you in the group, survived?

A. As far as I know, all by myself.

Q. So I understand, you went northwards from Kolomea to a town called Tluste?

A. That's right.

After crossing the Dniester and reaching the town of Tluste [Tovste], *Gordon's family and many other refugees reached Buchach. Here, together with other young Jews, Leslie Gordon was recruited by an SD department to dig mass graves thus losing contact with his family, which was probably massacred in one of the slaughters that were perpetrated in Buchach for several days in a row. After 10/12 days of forced labor, Leslie Gordon managed to flee and reached Kamenec Podolski soon before the great carnage of August 28-29. Keeping in hiding in an abandoned house outside of town, about a week after the slaughter he managed to cross the Dniester and return to Budapest, where he arrived in early November 1941.*

DOCUMENT 7:
Excerpt from Stahlecker's Report dated January 31, 1942

Excerpt of Stahlecker's Report of January 31, 1942, in particular of *§ II.B.1 – "Triggering self-cleansing actions" – presented to Nuremberg's IMT as Document 180-L – Blue Series*

DOCUMENT 180-L

REPORT BY SS-BRIGADEFÜHRER STAHLECKER, COMMANDER OF EINSATZGRUPPE A, CONCERNING THE GROUP'S ACTIVITIES ON THE NORTHERN RUSSIAN FRONT AND IN THE OCCUPIED TERRITORIES OF THE BALTIC STATES UNTIL OCTOBER 1941: COOPERATION WITH THE WEHRMACHT; INCITATION OF THE PEOPLE TO CARRY OUT POGROM AGAINST THE JEWS; MASS EXECUTIONS OF JEWS AND COMMUNISTS (NUMBERS PROVIDED); SYSTEMATIC SLAUGHTER OF DISABLED PEOPLE; BRUTAL MEASURES TO BE TAKEN AS DETERRENTS IN THE WAR AGAINST PARTISANS AND OTHER TOPICS (EXHIBIT USA-276)

Persönliches Stück des SS-Obergruppenführers. ::-::Wv. 31.1.1942 ::-::

Top-secret!

40 Copies Copy n. 23

Einsatzgruppe A
Overall Report until October 15, 1941

I. SUMMARY

II. POLICE ACTIVITIES

A. Organizational measures

B. Cleansing and security of the operating area

C. Counterintelligence

D. Monitoring and recording of population

E. Criminal Police activities

III. REPORT ON THE SITUATION

A. Situation before the arrival of German troops

B. Situation in the area until 15.10.1941

C. Jewish influence in the Ostland terrritories

IV. COMPLAINTS AND SUGGESTIONS FOR THEIR REMOVAL

[...]

- Page 21 -

II.B. Cleansing and Security of the Operating Area

1) Triggering self-cleansing actions

Considering how much the population of the Baltic countries had to suffer because of the domain of Bolshevism and Judaism in the time of their annexation to the Soviet Union, it is hard to believe how it kept so passive in front of their opponents, after the liberation from this foreign rule and after the Red Army retreated from the country. The task of Sicherheitspolizei was to put in motion self-cleansing actions and head them in the right direction, so as to obtain the intended cleansing in the shortest possible time.

No less important, at a later stage, was to give prominence to certain and tested circumstances, to the fact that the population had taken, of its own initiative, the most severe measures against the Jew and Bolshevik enemy, without any apparent intervention by German authorities.

In Lithuania we accomplished that for the first time in Kauen, through the use of partisans. It was surprisingly difficult, at first, to organize a large-scale massacre of Jews. Thanks to the instructions given to small advanced detachments of Kauen, Klimatis, commander of the aforementioned group of partisans that was used here, managed to organize a pogrom,

- Page 22 -

without any clear German order or incitement. During the first pogrom, in the night between June 25 and 26, over 1,500 Jews were rounded up by Lithuanian partisans, several synagogues were burned down or destroyed and a Jewish residential neighborhood with about 60 homes was burned down. Likewise, the following night, 2,300 more Jews were rendered harmless. Following the example of Kauen but on a smaller scale, similar actions have taken place, also extended to the communists, in other parts of Lithuania.

Through information to the army authorities, who showed sympathy for these operations, self-cleansing actions proceeded without a hitch. It was clear from the outset that only the first few days after the occupation would bring along the opportunity to carry out pogroms. After the disarmament of the partisans, self-cleansing actions inevitably ceased.

In Latvia it was much harder to perform similar self-cleansing actions and pogroms. Essentially, this was due to the fact that the entire national leadership, especially in Riga, has been murdered or kidnapped by the Soviets. However, through an intervention of the Latvian auxiliary police, it was possible to organize a massacre of Jews in Riga, during which all synagogues were destroyed and about 400 Jews were killed.

- Page 23 -

Since then calm was restored among Riga's population, and further pogroms were no longer viable.

Where possible, both in Kauen and Riga, through films and photographs it has been documented that the first actions against Jews and communists were made spontaneously by the Lithuanians and Latvians.

In Estonia there was no chance to start a pogrom, also due to the relatively low number of Jews in that country. Only in individual cases Estonian self-defense units have rendered harmless particularly hated communists, but in general they limited themselves to imprisoning actions.

- Pag. 24 -

DOCUMENT 8:
Testimony given by Hermann Friedrich Graebe

The following testimony by Hermann Friedrich Graebe was given on November 10, 1945 before the investigator, Maj. Homer B. Crawford, and was presented to Nuremberg's IMT as Document 2992-PS – Blue Series, vol. V, pp. 696-699.

Before me, Homer B. Crawford, being authorized to administer oaths, personally appeared Hermann Friedrich Graebe, who, being by me duly sworn through the interpreter Elisabeth Radzie-Jewska, made and subscribed the following statement:

I, Hermann Friedrich Graebe, declare under oath:

From September 1941 – January 1944, I was manager and engineer-in-charge of a branch office in Sdolbunow, Ukraine, of the Solingen building firm of Josef Jung. In this capacity it was my job to visit the building sites of the firm. Under contract to an Army Construction Office, the firm had orders to erect grain storage buildings at the former airport of Dubno, Ukraine.

On October 5,1942, when I visited the building office at Dubno, my foreman Hubert Moennikes of 21 Aussenmuehlenweg, Hamburg-Haarburg, told me that in the vicinity of the site, Jews from Dubno had been shot in three large pits, each about 30 meters long and 3 meters deep. About 1,500 persons had been killed daily. All of the 5,000 Jews who had still been living in Dubno before the pogrom were to be liquidated. As the shootings had taken place in his presence he was still very upset.

Thereupon I drove to the site, accompanied by Moennikes and saw near it great mounds of earth, about 30 meters long and 2 meters high. Several trucks stood in front of the mounds. Armed Ukrainian militia forced the people off the trucks under the supervision of an SS-man. The militia men acted as guards on the trucks and drove them to and from the pit. All these people had the regulation yellow patches on the front and back of their clothes, and thus could be recognized as Jews.

Moennikes and I went directly to the pits. Nobody bothered us. Now I heard rifle shots in quick succession, from behind one of the earth mounds. The people who had got off the trucks -- men, women, and children of all ages -- had to undress upon the order of an SS-man, who carried a riding or dog whip. They had to put down their clothes in fixed places, sorted according to shoes, top clothing and underclothing. I saw a heap of shoes of about 800 to 1000 pairs, great piles of under-linen and clothing. Without screaming or weeping these people undressed, stood around in family groups, kissed each other, said farewells and waited for a sign from another SS-man, who stood near the pit, also with a whip in his hand. During the 15 minutes that I stood near the pit I heard no complaint or plea for mercy. I watched a family of about 8 persons, a man and woman, both about 50 with their children of about 1, 8 and 10, and two grownup daughters of about 20 to 24. An old woman with snow-white hair was holding the one-year old child in her arms and singing to it, and tickling it. The child was cooing with delight. The couple were looking on with tears in their eyes. The father was holding the hand of a boy about 10 years old and speaking to him softly; the boy was fighting his tears. The father pointed toward the sky, stroked his head, and seemed to explain something to him. At that moment the SS-man at the pit shouted something to his comrade. The latter counted off about 20 persons and instructed them to go behind the earth mound. Among them was the family, which I have mentioned. I well remember a girl, slim and with black hair, who, as she passed close to me, pointed to herself and said, "23". I walked around the mound, and found myself confronted by a tremendous grave. People were closely wedged together and lying on top of each other so that only their heads were visible. Nearly all had blood running over their shoulders from their heads. Some of the people shot were still moving. Some were lifting their arms and turning their heads to show that they were still alive. The pit was already 2/3 full. I estimated that it already contained about 1,000 people. I looked for the man who did the shooting. He was an SS-man, who sat at the edge of the narrow end of the pit, his feet dangling into the pit. He had a tommy gun on his knees and was smoking a cigarette. The people, completely naked, went down some steps which were cut in the clay wall of the pit and clambered over the heads of the people lying there, to the place to which the SS-man directed them. They lay down in front of the dead or injured people; some caressed those who were still alive and spoke to them in a low voice. Then I heard a series of shots. I looked into the pit and saw that the bodies were twitching or the heads lying already motionless on top of the bodies that lay before them. Blood was running from their necks. I was surprised that I was not ordered away, but I saw that there were two or three postmen in uniform nearby. The next batch was approaching already. They went down into the pit, lined themselves up against the previous victims and were shot. When I walked back, round the mound I noticed another truckload of people which had just arrived. This time it included sick and infirm people. An old, very thin woman with terribly thin legs was undressed by others who were already naked, while two people held her up. The woman appeared to be paralyzed. The naked people carried the woman around the mound. I left with Moennikes and drove in my car back to Dubno.

On the morning of the next day, when I again visited the site, I saw about 30 naked people lying near the pit -- about 30 to 50 meters away from it. Some of them were still alive; they looked straight in front of them with a fixed stare and seemed to notice neither the chilliness of the morning nor the workers of my firm who stood around. A girl of about 20 spoke to me and asked me to give her clothes, and help her escape. At that moment we heard a fast car approach and I noticed that it was an SS-detail. I moved away to my site. 10 minutes later we hear shots from the vicinity of the pit. The Jews still alive had been ordered to throw the corpses into the pit -- then they had themselves to lie down in this to be shot in the neck.

I make the above statement at Wiesbaden, Germany, on 10 November 1945. I swear before God that this is the absolute truth.

Hermann Friedrich Graebe

Subscribed and sworn to before me at Wiesbaden, Germany, 10 November 1945.

Homer B. Crawford Major, AC Investigator Examiner, War Crimes Branch

I, Elisabeth Radziejewska, being first duly sworn, state: That I truly translated the oath administered by Major Homer B. Crawford to Hermann Friedrich Graebe and that thereupon he made and subscribed the foregoing statement in my presence.

Elisabeth Radziejewska Interpreter
Subscribed and sworn to before me at Wiesbaden, Germany, 10 November 1945.

Homer B. Crawford,
Major, AC Investigator Examiner,
War Crimes Branch

DOCUMENT 9:
Excerpt from EM 94 dated September 25, 1941

Excerpt from EM 94 of September 25, 1941, specifically § II.4.II "Adopted measures and Sicherheitspolizei considerations", presented to Nuremberg's IMT as Document No-3146 Exhibit 943 – Green Series, vol. X., pp. 1222-1224

PARTIAL TRANSLATION OF DOCUMENT NO-3146 PROSECUTION EXHIBIT 943

EXTRACTS FROM OPERATIONAL SITUATION REPORT U.S.S.R. NO. 94, 25 SEPTEMBER 1941, CONCERNING ACTIVITIES OF THE EINSATZGRUPPEN

The Chief of the Security Police and Security Service (SD) IVA 1/Journal No. 1/B41, Top Secret

Berlin, 25 September 1941

48 copies-36th copy

Operational Situation Report U.S.S.R., No. 94

Top Secret

II

Reports from the Einsatzgruppen and Einsatzkommandos

II.IV

Situation in occupied area of Old Soviet Russia

II.IV.II.

Measures taken and observations made by the Security Police

During the preparation period for the military offensive now under way, the operations of the Einsatzkommandos could be continued intensively and on a broad basis.

In the southern region of the operational area, because of the sparseness of the Jewish population, the main effort had to be directed toward individual investigations and search actions, while particularly in the region of Zhitomir and Berdichev there was an opportunity for actions on a larger scale.

This also explains the difference in the number of executions reported by the individual Kommandos.

Sonderkommando 4a has now surpassed the number of 15,000 executions. Einsatzkommando 5, for the period between August 31, and September 6, reports the liquidation of 90 political officials, 72 saboteurs and looters, and 161 Jews. Sonderkommando 4b, in the period between 6 - 12 September 1941, shot 13 political officials and 290 Jews, primarily of the intelligentsia, whereas Einsatzkommando 6, in the period between 1 - 13 September 1941, executed 60 persons. Group staff was able to liquidate during the last days, four political officials and informers of the NKVD, six asocial elements (gypsies) and 55 Jews. The units of the Higher SS and Police Leader during the month of August shot a total of 44,125 persons, mostly Jews.

As already mentioned, the procedure against the Jews is necessarily different in the individual sectors, according to the density of their settlement. Especially in the northern sector of Einsatzgruppe C, a great many Jewish refugees have returned to the villages and, present now a heavy burden in regard to the food situation. The population neither houses nor feeds them. They live partly in caverns, partly in overcrowded old huts. The danger of epidemics has thus increased considerably, so that for that reason alone a thorough cleanup of the respective places became necessary.

The insolence of the Jews has not yet diminished even now. Apart from the fact that, on the occasion of raids, they like to pass themselves off for Russians, Ukrainians, even ethnic Germans, they often are in the possession of passports which, though showing their names correctly, give a false nationality. Concealment of their Jewish descent has been made easier for them by the Russification of the names which has taken place to an ever-increasing degree during the last years.

At Kirovograd it became known that Jews tried to obtain all the register's office identity papers with a false nationality. Several Jews, on the basis of forged papers, even succeeded in obtaining various posts with the administration where they performed such acts of "re-baptism" in a system of patronage as practiced already previously. The Ukrainian population, for fear of revenge by the Jews, often does not dare to report this situation to the authorities. The most severe measures are taken here in dealing with such cases.

Difficulties have arisen insofar as Jews are often the only skilled workers in certain trades. Thus, the only harness-makers and the only good tailors at Novo-Ukrainia are Jews. At other places also only Jews can be employed for carpentry and locksmith work. The cause of this shortage of skilled workers is to a large extent to be found in the unlimited compulsory evacuation of skilled Ukrainians by the Soviets. In order not to endanger reconstruction and the repair work also for the benefit of transient troop units, it has become necessary to provisionally specifically exclude the older Jewish skilled workers from the executions.

DOCUMENT 10:
Excerpt from EM 40 dated August 1, 1941

Excerpt from EM 40 of August 1, 1941, specifically § B "Considerations regarding the population": The Commander from Security Police and Security Service (SD)

Berlin, August 3, 1941
44 copies – copy n. 34

Report on the Operative Situation U.S.S.R N. 40
Top secret

Einsatzgruppe A:
Detachment: Novoselye

B.
Considerations regarding the population

[...]

The Latvian national consciousness remained intact and was powered by the extra-slow political situation. If there is interference, organizations such as Perkonkrust, with its nationalist political purposes outlined, will have no difficulty in their plan to awaken a strong national pride among the Latvian population. While in Latvia a part of the local intelligentsia has completely disappeared, the obvious outward Nordic semblance of the population both in Riga and in small towns continues to strike us. On the contrary, the population of Latgale, which differs greatly in its way of life from the rest of the country, reveals a terrible racial framework. The high level of crime and alcoholism may be due to the racial mix between Russians, Polish and Latvians.

Self-cleansing operations in Latvia have started late. Although Jews have been completely removed from public life, they can still be seen on the streets of Latvian towns. The impertinence of the Jews helped increase self-cleansing actions. Thus, in all Latvian cities there were pogroms, destruction of synagogues and liquidation of Jews and Communists. The 1,550 Jews who still remained in Jelgava (Mitau) and its environs, were removed from the population, without exception. Self-cleansing activities in Latvia are still continuing.

DOCUMENT 11:
Excerpt from an undated report by Stahlecker

Excerpt from an undated report, in particular § III.3, compiled by Stahlecker and sent to RSHA, regarding the massacres perpetrated by Einsatzgruppe A "Juden, Latvia"– presented to Nuremberg's IMT as Document 2273-PS – Blue Series.

DOCUMENT 2273-PS

UNDATED SECRET REPORT ON MASS SLAUGHTERS OF JEWS, SYSTEMATICALLY CARRIED OUT BY EINSATZGRUPPE A IN WESTERN RUSSIA, IN BELARUS AND IN THE BALTIC STATES, WITH DATA REPORTING THE NUMBER OF SLAIN JEWS (EXHIBIT USA-487).

Top secret

Einsatzgruppe A

III.

Jews

The systematic mopping up of the Eastern Territories embraced, in accordance with the basic orders, the complete removal if possible, of Jewry. This goal has been substantially attained-with the exception of Belarus - as a result of the execution up to the present time of 229,052 Jews (see Appendix). The remainder still left in the Baltic Provinces is urgently required as labor and housed in Ghettos.

To attain this object various kinds of measures were necessary in the different areas of the [Ostland].

In the three Baltic States of Estonia, Latvia and Lithuania, Jewry did not make itself decisively felt until the Bolsheviks had come into power there. But even before that the Jewish influence on the one hand and the anti-Jewish feeling of the population on the other hand, were very strong.

In the following, the various areas of the Eastern Territories will be dealt with separately:

3. Latvia

The total number of Jews in Latvia in June 1935 amounted to 93,479 or 4.79 % of the total population.

When the Bolsheviks came into power in Latvia in June 1940, their Soviet-Russian racial comrades succeeded in obtaining authoritative influence for the Latvian Jews, who previously had been predominantly Zionist. Before 1940 there were no Jews as State officials in Latvia, in fact were no Jews in the State Administration at all; in the Soviet Russian Republic all the influential State positions were quickly in the hands of the Jews. Half of all the Judges were Jewish. The number was up to 80 % in the Higher Courts and in particular in the Tribunal. Equally strong was the influence of the Jews on the economy as well as cultural life.

When the German troops marched in there were still 70,000 Jews in Latvia. The remainder had fled with the Bolsheviks. The Jews left behind were actively engaged in sabotage and setting fire to places. In Duenaburg so many fires of this kind were started by the Jews that a large part of the town was destroyed.

After the terror of the Jewish-Bolshevik rule-altogether 33,038 Letts were transported, imprisoned or murdered-an extensive pogrom carried out by the population might have been expected. In fact, however, only a few thousand Jews were eliminated by local forces on their own initiative. In Latvia it was necessary to carry out extensive mopping-up operations by means of Sonderkommandos with the help of forces picked from the Latvian Auxiliary Police (mostly relations of the Letts who had been carried off or murdered).

Up to October 1941, approximately 30,000 Jews had been executed by these Sonderkommandos. The remaining Jews who were still considered useful from an economic point of view were collected in Ghettos, which were established in Riga, Duenaburg and Libau.

As a result of punishments imposed for not wearing the Jewish star; black market activities; thieving; fraud, but also to prevent the danger of epidemics in the Ghettos, further executions were subsequently carried out. In this way 11,034 Jews were executed in Duenaburg on 9.11.41, and, as the result of an action ordered and carried out by high authorities and Police chiefs, 27,800 were executed in Riga at the beginning of December 1941, and, in the middle of December 1941, 2,350 were executed in Libau. At the moment there are in the Ghettos (other than Jews from the Reich) Latvian Jews in

Riga: approximately 2,500

Duenaburg: approximately 950

Libau: approximately 300

ABBREVIATIONS

Abt.	Abteilung
Adj.	Adjutant
AOK	Armeeoberkommando
AK	Armee-Korps
BA	Bundesarchiv
Bd.	Band *(volume)*
BdO	Befehlshaber der Ordnungspolizei
BdS	Befehlshaber der Sicherheitspolizei
Berück	Befehlshaber des rückwärtigen Heeresgebietes
BGH	Bungesgerichtshof
BIA	Board of Immigration Appeal
Bl.	Blatt *(page)*
Chap.	Chapter
CIC	Civil Internment Camp
CIC	Counter Intelligence Corps
DDR	Deutsche Demokratische Republik
D.P.	Displaced Person
Dulag	Durchgangslager
EG	Einsatzgruppe
EK	Eiserne Kreuz
EK	Einsatzkommando
EM	Ereignismeldung
FGA	Feldgendarmerie-Abteilung
FK	Feldkommandantur

Fl.	Florida
GFP	Geheime Feldpolizei
GK	Generalkommissariat
GKWR	Generalkommissariat Weissruthenien
Gen.Ltn.	Generalleutnant
HA-Orpo	Hauptamt-Ordnungspolizei
HHStAW	Hessisches Hauptstaatsarchiv Wiesbaden
Hptm.	Hauptmann
HSSPF	Höherer SS- und Polizeiführer
ID.	Infanterie-Division
Ill.	Illinois
IMT	International Military Tribunal
IR	Infanterie-Regiment
KEOKH	Külföldieket Ellenőrző Országos Központi Hatóság
KdO	Kommandeur der Ordnungpolizei
KdGend	Kommandeur der Gendarmerie
KdS	Befehlshaber der Sicherheitspolizei
KdSchupo	Kommandeur der Schutzpolizei
KfZSt/K-Staffel	Kraftfahrzeugstaffel
KL	Konzentrazionlager
Korück	Kommandeur des rückwärtigen Heeresgebietes
KS-RFSS	Kommandostab Reichsführer-SS

KTB	Kriegstagebuch
KVK	Kriegsverdienstkreuz
LG	Landgericht
LkW	Lastkraftwagen
LKA	Landeskriminalamt
LPKDA	Latviešu Pretestības Kustības Dalībnieku Apvienība
Ltn.	Leutnant
MA	Militärarchiv
Maj.	Major
Mass.	Massachussets
NKVD	Narodnyj komissariat vnutrennich del
NMT	Nuremberg Military Tribunal
NRW	Nordrhein-Westfalen
NSDAP	Nationalsozialistische Deutsche Arbeitspartei
NSKK	Nationalsozialistische Kraftfahr-Korps
NSV	Nationalsozialistische Volkswohlfahrt
Ogruf.	Obergruppenführer
OSI	Office of Special Investigations
OKH	Oberkommando des Heeres
OK	Ortskommandantur
OKW	Oberkommando der Wehrmacht
Oltn.	Oberleutnant
OUN	Orhanizatsiya Ukrayins'kykh Natsionalistiv
PAI	Police of Italian Africa
PB	Polizei-Bataillon
PPT	Pagalbinės Policijos Tarnibos
RCMP	Royal Canadian Mounted Police
RFSS	Reichsführer-SS
RK	Reichkommissariat
RoKo	Rollkommando
SFSR	Soviet Federative Socialist Republic
RSHA	Reichssicherheitshauptamt
SA	Sturmabteilung
SchPDA	Schutzpolizei-Dienstabteilung
Sich.Div.	Sicherungs-Division
SD	Sicherheitsdienst
SIU	Special Investigation Unit
SK	Sonderkommando
SS	Schutzstaffel
SSPF	SS- und Polizeiführer
SS-VT	SS-Verfügungstruppen
StAwBo	Staatsanwaltschaft Bochum
StAwDo	Staatsanwaltschaft Dortmund
TDA	Tautines Darbo Apsaugos
TK	Teilkommando
u.a.	und anderen
v.	versus
VK	Vorkommando
VPS	Verstärkte-Polizeischutz
VU	Voruntersuchung
Whbf	Wehrmachtbefehlshaber
ZAL	Zwangsarbeitlager
zbV	zur besonderen Verwendung
zV	zur Verfügung
ZStL	Zentrale Stelle der Landesjustizverwaltungen in Ludwigsburg